Marketing research
TEXT AND CASES

Marketing Research
TEXT AND CASES

HARPER W. BOYD, JR., Ph.D.
Robert O. and Vivian Young Distinguished Professor
of Business Administration
University of Arkansas, Fayetteville

RALPH WESTFALL, Ph.D.
Associate Dean for Academic Affairs
Northwestern University

THIRD EDITION · 1972

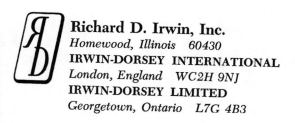

Richard D. Irwin, Inc.
Homewood, Illinois   60430
IRWIN-DORSEY INTERNATIONAL
London, England   WC2H 9NJ
IRWIN-DORSEY LIMITED
Georgetown, Ontario   L7G 4B3

Third Edition

First Printing, February, 1972
Second Printing, September, 1972
Third Printing, March, 1973
Fourth Printing, July, 1973
Fifth Printing, February, 1974

Library of Congress Catalog Card No. 70–172964
Printed in the United States of America

To
L. B. B.
and
C. E. W.

Preface

W HEN the revised edition of this book was published eight years ago, the authors commented in the preface that the period since the first edition had seen an unusual growth in marketing research and a great increase in the sophistication of the techniques used. The same comment is appropriate at this time, but the areas in which the major new thrusts have come have been somewhat different. While applications of behavioral science to marketing research continue to be of a major magnitude, the growth of this area has leveled off. Currently, the most exciting developments are taking place in decision theory, advanced statistical analytical procedures, and in the application of experimentation to marketing problems. Sixteen years ago the authors called for greater imagination in designing marketing experiments as the best way to develop a science of marketing. The number of authentic experiments in marketing is now at last burgeoning.

The format and general organization of this edition are still essentially the same as those of the first edition. The rationale for this is that the research process, as a way of implementing a research project, has not changed. The research process was and will continue to be a logical series of interrelated steps, each of which anticipates those which follow.

Substantial changes have occurred within the various research steps, and we have attempted to incorporate those appropriate to a beginning research book. Many of the changes have been of a technical type in the quantitative area. In this area we have attempted to exercise restraint so as not to bury the reader under mathematical formulas. We have added one new chapter on the statistical design of experiments to balance the survey sampling material and in recognition of the growth in experimentation. Some decision theory has been added to the chapter on project design. In all of this we have concentrated on developing an understanding of the theory and its applications rather than on the mathematics. All chapters have been revised to bring in the latest material and examples.

The case material has been revised to incorporate the new and to provide fresh teaching materials. We have not altered our strong belief that cases furnish concrete, real-life problems in the application of research procedures and also furnish a means by which the student can become involved in the material he is studying. This revision includes many new cases, all of which are taken from actual research projects, although most have been disguised to protect the companies involved.

In our revision work we have received help from many associates in both the business and academic fields. Many of these we must leave unmentioned. William D. Barclay of the Quaker Oats Company, who developed the sampling material in the first edition, has prepared the revision of those chapters and the chapter on the statistical design of experiments. We continue to owe a debt to Richard W. Tully (formerly of Foote, Cone & Belding) and to Professor Ira D. Anderson of Northwestern University for their major contributions to the first edition. Dr. David Allen, ICAME Librarian, Stanford Graduate School of Business, has provided important assistance in the current revision. To those companies that have released case material to us, we can but say "thanks," since most wish to remain anonymous. We are grateful to Mrs. Patricia T. Gilchrest, Mrs. Lenore Strauss, and Mrs. Hilda Hebden for their skill and patience in helping to prepare the manuscript.

Despite all this good and well-qualified help, it is quite possible that some errors have occurred. It goes without saying that these are the responsibility of the authors.

Palo Alto, California   HARPER W. BOYD, JR.
Evanston, Illinois   RALPH WESTFALL
February, 1972

Contents

questionnaire studies. Observational method: *Advantages and disadvantages of observation. Methods of observation*. Summary.

Part II   MARKETING RESEARCH PROCEDURE

variance. Explaining why differences exist: *Cross tabulations. Correlation analysis*. Making recommendations: *Facts must support recommendations*. Summary.

Part III   SELECTED APPLICATIONS OF MARKETING RESEARCH

List of Cases

List of Figures

Introduction to marketing research

This book is divided into three parts. Part I introduces the student to marketing research. It is divided into four chapters. The first chapter discusses what constitutes marketing research, why business uses it, how business uses it, and its limitations. The following three chapters deal with research in marketing as compared to research in the physical sciences, various types of research designs, and the basic methods of collecting data in marketing research.

1

Nature and scope of marketing research

THE COMPLEXITY of management decision making has increased greatly during recent years—not only in the United States but throughout the world. This is especially true with respect to the marketing activity of most business firms because this activity is located at the interface between the firm and the ever changing external environment. Dynamic factors such as the rapidly changing character of most markets (e.g., population growth, rising incomes, and shifts in the age composition); the increase in competition from a variety of sources (not only other brands of the same product, but substitute products); and rapidly changing technology give rise to the growing difficulty of making efficient marketing decisions.

Most management groups are far removed from their customers—the individuals who in the final analysis determine success or failure. A complicated system of branch offices, wholesalers, and retailers intervenes between the manager and his widely scattered customers. Consequently, the executive who must make decisions based on the market has almost no direct contact with his actual, or prospective, customers. Yet he must know who his customers are, what they want, and what his competitors are doing, if he is to make sound decisions. Often the executive relies on his salesmen and dealers for information, but more and more the final link in the communication channel through which consumers communicate with the company is marketing research.

The magnitude of many marketing problems is on the increase. Today, for example, the launching of a new product may cost several millions of dollars. If the cost of research and development and the cost of a new plant are included, the total may run into the tens of millions of dollars. It is small wonder that management is turning more and more to rigorous marketing information as a way of reducing the uncertainties inherent in its decision making.

Definition of marketing research

The purposes of marketing research are to obtain information which helps in the identification of a marketing opportunity or problem; to determine the issue's dimensions and magnitude; to enumerate and evaluate the alternative "solutions"; to select the "right" course of action; and to follow through. The American Marketing Association defines marketing research as: "The systematic gathering, recording, and analyzing of data about problems relating to the marketing of goods and services."[1] This is a broad definition stating, in effect, that marketing research includes investigations of market segments, product differentiation, channel relationships, effectiveness of salesmen and advertisements, pricing practices, and so forth. The point is that marketing research is not restricted to research on any given type of marketing problem but applies to any phase of marketing. *The essential purpose of any marketing research is to provide data which will facilitate the identification and solution of a marketing problem.*

But a definition of marketing research must also stress *how* the data are obtained and evaluated. Thus, objectivity and accuracy are essential and require the use of special techniques. At first thought it might not seem too difficult to obtain marketing information—it might seem that special and often sophisticated techniques would not be necessary. Why shouldn't a marketing manager, for example, base a decision on a number of "informal" talks with consumers? Unfortunately, the consumers he selected might not be typical of *all* consumers. Even if he selected a group of typical consumers, he would still face the problem of getting accurate information from them and interpreting it correctly. This usually involves a questioning process, but experience has shown that great care must be used in such questioning or the data obtained will be misleading. How much do consumers remember of their past actions? How much do they understand of their buying motives? If they don't know the answer to a question, will they say so, or will they make up an answer which is socially acceptable? These questions suggest some of the problems encountered in collecting data, and indicate why marketing research has increasingly become a specialized activity.

---

[1] *Report of the Definitions Committee of the American Marketing Association* (Chicago: American Marketing Association, 1961).

Research versus intuition

Most marketing decisions are made without the use of formal marketing research. In many cases the time required to do marketing research is not available; the decision maker simply cannot wait that long! In other cases the cost of obtaining the required data is in excess of the worth of the information. In still other cases the desired data cannot be obtained in reliable form. As a consequence, intuition which comes from experience is often substituted for systematically obtained facts. No one should deprecate the use of intuition to solve problems.

But it is important to recognize that intuition is rarely subject to formal testing. It tends toward specific solutions in contrast to the development of general hypotheses that will be helpful over a range of related problems. Moreover intuition derives from past experience which may not be pertinent to the future.[2] Research tends to overcome the first two of these shortcomings. Sometimes research is helpful in recognizing the trend towards the future. Hence research should not be deprecated, either. Successful marketing executives make decisions on the basis of a blend of facts and intuition.

USES OF MARKETING RESEARCH BY BUSINESS MANAGEMENT

One way of identifying the various ways in which marketing research can be used is via the steps in the administrative process.[3] No complete listing of uses is practical, since any such attempt would approach a list of all activities included in the term "marketing." Still, some listing is valuable in giving the reader insights into the many ways in which marketing research is used by various companies.

The remainder of this section is, therefore, devoted to a discussion of the more common types of uses under the headings of the major steps contained in the administrative process—setting objectives, developing a plan of action, organization, control, and reappraisal. In reading this material it is important to keep in mind that individual marketing research studies may cost anywhere from a few hundred dollars to as much as several hundred thousand. The latter amount is unusual, but studies costing between twenty-five and fifty thousand dollars are relatively common.

---

[2] For more discussion on this subject see Harry V. Roberts, "The Role of Research in Marketing Management," *Journal of Marketing* (July, 1957), p. 22.

[3] For a discussion on this subject see Harper W. Boyd, Jr. and Steuart Henderson Britt, "Making Marketing Research More Effective by Using the Administration Process," *Journal of Marketing Research* (February, 1965), pp. 13–19.

Setting objectives

The objectives of any firm must be rooted in the marketplace. Unless the firm can satisfy the basic wants and needs of a certain part of the market and do so at a profit, the firm cannot survive. Marketing researchers can play an important role in helping management to think of the firm's objectives in terms of consumer satisfactions in contrast to the more traditional view of products being produced. Management finds it advantageous to think in terms of the *functions* which the product performs instead of in terms of the product *per se*.

The setting of objectives includes understanding wants and needs and the consumption systems employed by consumers to satisfy these wants. A consumption system is a series of steps frequently involving several products, labor, and one or more machines, the end result of which is the achievement of a certain goal—the satisfaction of some want or need. The advantage of thinking in terms of the entire consumption system is illustrated by the development of a new bleach which diminished the possibility of damaging clothes through putting too much bleach in the washing machine. This product seemed to meet a consumer need, but further study of the consumption cycle showed that it was often used in conjunction with detergents, some of which reacted with it in such a way as to reduce its effectiveness substantially.

Ideally, markets are divided into segments, some of which can be exploited more effectively than others. The process by which segmentation is accomplished provides another significant opportunity for the use of marketing research.[4] Demographic data, attitudes, and usage information are often used as bases for segmentation. For example, one west coast brewer found that by obtaining the attitudes of male consumers on salient product characteristics with reference to his brand and with reference to his major competitors, he could segment the market usefully. He found that there was a wide difference in attitudes toward his brand and one major competitor, while this was not true with regard to two other competitors. He chose, as a result of this study, to define his target segment to include consumers who had similar attitudes toward his and the two other brands and to concentrate his advertising effort on the individuals so included.

A substantial amount of research is conducted to determine who consumes various amounts of the product. A typical market profile is shown in Figure 1–1, which shows the percent of families buying a household paper product and the rate of purchase within different population groups. Families in the top economic class buy more than

---

[4] For an excellent discussion of alternative ways of classifying consumers see Ronald E. Frank and Paul E. Green, "Numerical Taxonomy in Marketing Analyses: A Review Article," *Journal of Marketing Research* (February, 1968), pp. 83–93.

FIGURE 1–1. Market comparisons and consumer characteristics for a paper product

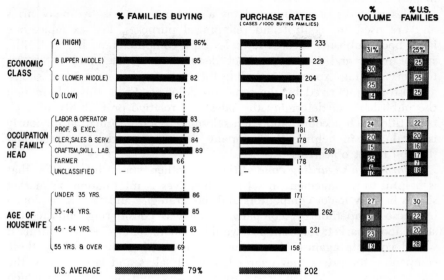

SOURCE: Market Research Corporation of America.

twice the amount of the product than do the lowest economic class families, yet the two groups contain exactly the same number of families. Families with housewives between thirty-five and forty-four years of age have higher purchase rates than do those in any other age group. Such information tells the paper manufacturer the population groups on which he will want to concentrate his selling effort.

As part of finding out who uses the product, the researcher can estimate the worth of the market segments, both as of the present and the future. If several product types lie within the overall product category (for example, frozen orange concentrate, fresh squeezed orange juice sold in cartons, orange concentrate powder, and canned orange juice), it is important to obtain the user profile for each type as well as the relative importance of each. Trends in such a situation and information as to what kinds of people are "switching" brands help a firm change its marketing objectives as markets shift. Other data such as seasonal use, quantities purchased at one time, and the amount of the product in inventory within the home, help management understand the consumption process for the product.

Sales analysis research.   Sales analysis involves the measurement of sales, sales possibilities, and sales expenses for product lines by different market segments—such as frozen orange juice sales to large families in different areas. It is termed sales analysis because typically it involves, in part, an analysis of sales records.

Sales analyses are conducted on a continuous basis by many firms and are used for control and reappraisal purposes. For example, one large book publisher records his sales on a computer tape by book title, school name and location, school denomination, salesman, and sales territory. Selling expenses, including the cost of samples and workshops, are also computerized by the same breakdowns. From this information the publisher can determine the sales and relative profitability of each book title, each account, and each salesman. Such information obviously is invaluable in helping the company determine market potential and thereby to set objectives.

Information regarding competition.   Another type of information that is helpful to management in setting objectives is information on market shares held by major competitors and the strategies and tactics employed by these competitors. A company which was considering entering the snack food market, for example, would want to determine what firms it would compete against, the amount of advertising employed by these companies, the prices they charged to wholesalers and large chains, the use of company salesmen versus food brokers, and the extent to which the snack food industry relied on "deals" to promote its products.

A number of large consumer goods companies that sell their products through food stores, drug stores, and variety stores spend many thousands of dollars annually subscribing to the services of A. C. Nielsen and the Market Research Corporation of America. These research houses provide continuous information on the purchases of items sold in these various retail outlets. Using different methods both services provide market share data for all major companies selling a product, plus other data such as price, which help a firm understand the dynamics of the competitive world in which it lives.

Developing a plan of action

Once the firm has determined its market objectives, it must develop a plan of action to achieve these objectives. Such a plan has to consider the resources of the firm and the strategies and tactics used by competitors. Any plan will, of necessity, deal with strategies related to product and product line, price, channels of distribution, personal selling, and advertising. Marketing research can help management develop the most effective strategies in each of these areas and decide how these tactical elements should be combined into the optimum marketing mix.

Product research.   During the last decade many thousands of new products have been introduced into the American market. American industry has been spending for research and development in excess of

$16 billion annually.[5] Many additional dollars have been spent in marketing the new products developed. The fact that a substantial number of these new products fail indicates that very large sums have been "wasted." While the rate of new product failures varies from industry to industry, Booz, Allen & Hamilton's study of 366 new product introductions found that one third failed.[6] Other studies have placed the failure rate as high as 80 to 90 percent.[7] These failures have led to increased use of marketing research to increase the probabilities of success.

While the role of marketing research relative to product planning varies by company, it is clear that many, if not most, firms make extensive use of marketing research in their product work. As a minimum, marketing research is needed to define the market in terms of types and kinds of customers, the needs that such customers have regarding the product, what products are now satisfying these needs, what product attributes are important, and what standards consumers use to evaluate the efficiency of the product. Since consumer preferences are dynamic, such research is needed on a continuous basis.

Product research at the customer level is essential to the successful operation of the research and development function which provides the technical skills needed to build the "right" product. But even after the new product is designed, marketing research is used to determine whether the product meets the needs of the market.

Marketing research also makes a contribution to the development of industrial products. A manufacturer of miniature walkie-talkie machines used in simultaneous translation work needed marketing research to determine to what shocks the instrument would be subjected when in use, i.e., what objects it would strike, with what frequency, and with what impact. This information was critical in developing the best design and in specifying how the unit should be packaged to prevent damage to its delicate contents.

Product line and quality research. What products constitute the optimum line? Producers of red grapefruit, in attempting to determine whether to add a line of canned juice, encountered difficulties with the appearance of the new juice when processed in the usual manner. A way to eliminate the discoloration was developed (through fortification with pulp) and marketing research was then undertaken to learn whether consumers would like the "new" juice. The study showed that consumers found the red fortified juice reasonably acceptable, but that a sweetened juice might be more popular. Other kinds of information

---

[5] Dr. Victor J. Danitov, "R & D Expenditures," *Industrial Research* (January, 1968), p. 60.

[6] *Management of New Products* (New York: Booz, Allen & Hamilton, 1965).

[7] "How Many New Products Die?" *Printers' Ink* (August 26, 1966), p. 19.

were needed to determine the market potential, but first it had to be determined whether a satisfactory product had been found.

A manufacturer of power lawn mowers recently conducted an inquiry into the sales, expenses, and profits of each item in its product line. As a result of this investigation it decided to drop its low cost riding mower, not because the item was not profitable, but because dealers reported an increasing number of complaints about the product's durability and a lack of safety features which had resulted in a number of serious accidents.

Other types of product research. Research on package, brand name, and price may be considered types of product research. The rapid growth of self-service and the impact of the package at the point of sale have greatly increased the use of package research. The package must be of the right size, shape, and color if it is to be an effective salesman for the product and, overall, the package must reflect the desired image of the product. A leading manufacturer of kitchenware initiated a quality improvement program. As part of this program the company had specialists undertake an analysis of the company's packages versus those of its competitors. The research found that "the old package looked 'cheap'; not only was it poor from an aesthetic viewpoint, but its lack of style, haphazard arrangement of elements, and failure to stress any strong visual motif, all combined to indicate to the consumer that the product was not a quality item."[8]

During the past several years American business has paid increasing attention to selecting brand names only after researching their impact among consumers. No doubt one reason for this is the increased number of new products coming on the market. Another reason is that many companies, either because of acquisitions or the development of new products unrelated to the "old" line, have decided to change their corporate names to identify themselves better to the consumer.

Pricing strategies may also be tested by research, although relatively little is actually being done. Retail chains and mail order houses have done some work in measuring the effects of special offers such as 1-cent sales and special low prices.

Jewel Food Stores inaugurated a pricing program in 1970 to show prices per unit, per ounce for instance, on each package to facilitate comparison of different brands and different package sizes. It then established experimental studies to measure the effect on consumer purchasing habits. Of particular importance is the pricing of new products, since they are less likely to have close substitutes. A manufacturer can either attempt to skim the market by charging a relatively

---

[8] Gordon Lippincott and Walter P. Margulies, "Packaging in Top-Level Planning," *Harvard Business Review* (September–October, 1956), pp. 47–48.

high price, or he can try to penetrate a larger market with a low price. Research can help in making this decision by providing data on the degree of market segmentation, the size of the various segments, and the prices of substitute products.

Channels of distribution. Since many consumer items are sold by more than one type of retail outlet and since the relative importance of these outlets changes, it is important to know sales trends by outlet types. An illustration of this is seen in a study of health and beauty aid products. In the middle sixties sales of 20 large volume health and beauty aid product groups through mass merchandisers increased 10 to 20 percent a year, while grocery and drug store sales either suffered a decrease, or at best experienced a slight gain.[9] These statistics are shown in Figure 1–2. Implications for channels strategy are clear.

FIGURE 1–2. Recent sales trends in major health and beauty aid outlets (20 product groups)

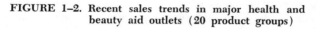

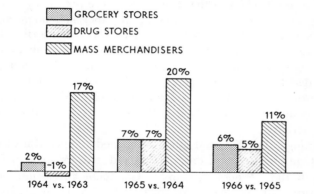

SOURCE: *33rd Annual Nielsen Review* (Chicago: A. C. Nielsen Co., 1967) p. 31.

Middleman cooperation. Many companies conduct periodic dealer attitude studies to find out what dealers think of the company, its selling methods, and its policies. Such information is important in determining what action, if any, should be taken to improve relations with the channels. A manufacturer of electric clocks found that its retail dealers were upset by a company decision to sell through discount catalogs. The situation was so serious that nearly 25 percent of the retailers, representing 39 percent of total dollar sales, were thinking of discontinuing the company's line. On the basis of such information, the company decided to manufacture a different line of electric clocks which would be sold

[9] *33rd Annual Nielsen Review* (Chicago: A. C. Nielsen Co., 1967), p. 31.

exclusively to discounters. This decision enabled the firm to maintain good relations with almost all of its dealers.

Many companies, particularly those selling high-value products, obtain regular reports from their channels as to the amount of inventory in dealer stocks. Such data are highly useful from a production scheduling standpoint and may indicate the need for more or less aggressive sales campaigns. The A. C. Nielsen Company collects data of this type on a wide variety of food and drug products. Interested manufacturers can purchase the information on a subscription basis.

Middleman efficiency. A large part of the cost of distribution involves middlemen and the efficiency with which they operate. Studies of middleman efficiency are particularly important to manufacturers who have the choice of several different channel systems. One channels research study was done by a package materials company which, although its sales were increasing, believed that greater sales and profits would result if its own salesmen were used in lieu of manufacturer's agents. The results showed that the agents were not always willing to do missionary sales work and that frequently other noncompeting items in the agent's line which were easier to sell received priority. The agents were not following up promptly the leads they received as a result of the company's national advertising. As a result of this study, the company decided to replace its agents with its own salesmen.

Sales promotion. More marketing research is done in sales promotion than in any other area. Within this category, advertising research is the main activity.

Advertising. In 1967 total advertising media expenditures were $17.3 billion.[10] One hundred and one national advertisers spent over $10 million each in 1967; Procter & Gamble Co. spent $210.6 million; General Motors Corp., $168.4; Bristol-Myers Co., $115.3; General Foods Corp., $111.9; and the Ford Motor Co., $94.2.[11] It is not difficult to understand from such figures why manufacturers, advertising agencies, and media are interested in doing advertising research.

One of the most difficult problems facing any marketing manager is to decide how much to spend in selling his product and, of this amount, how much to spend on advertising. This decision can be made more accurately if the executive knows who his customers are, where they are located, how many of them there are, and how much and how frequently each buys. Such information can be obtained from market and product studies. The same information is useful in determining what markets to concentrate on, the type of advertising media (maga-

---

[10] Seymour Banks, John B. Kovas, and Charles Y. Yang, "Ad Volume Rises 3.1% to $17.3 Billion in '67," *Advertising Age* (April 8, 1968), p. 55.

[11] "The Top 125 National Advertisers of 1967," *Advertising Age* (June 24, 1968), pp. 44–45.

zine, newspaper, billboards, radio, or television) to use, and the basic advertising objectives to establish.

Advertising objectives.   In attempting to set operationally useful goals, the advertiser must concern himself with the attitudes of the relevant audiences toward the product generally, his brand, and competing brands. If such attitudinal knowledge is available, the goals of advertising can be stated in terms of shifting the attitudes of a given group of consumers with respect to the relevant brand.

It is difficult to effect attitudinal change, since not all consumers hold the same ideal profile, and there are variations in attitudes toward competing brands. Research on dentifrices showed that people had different ideas on what was important in a dentifrice and that they rated alternative brands differently with respect to effectiveness in "solving" their problems; for example, the person who felt that tooth appearance and mouth odor were salient would choose that brand which rated higher than the others in "getting teeth white" and "makes mouth fresher."[12] Definite advertising objectives could be set with regard to the number of consumers who thought a given brand had these qualities. This research also established a copy platform—guidelines for the contents of messages.

Copy testing.   Once the advertising objectives have been set there is the job of developing a message which will obtain the desired results— that is, reinforce or shift certain attitudes. To determine whether this job has been completed successfully, most advertising agencies engage in copy testing. Several different pieces of advertising copy may be developed and research used to select the best alternative. Since the effect of a message on attitudes typically can only be measured over time, copy tests which attempt to measure attention, readability, understandability, and believability are used. Sometimes several alternative "ads" are run to see which is "best" based on relative drawing power of coupons or inquiries. Many different techniques of copy testing have been developed; a number of them are discussed in the chapter on advertising research.

Media research.   Once the copy is determined, it is still necessary to select the most efficient media to carry the advertising. The fact that there are thousands of radio and television stations, newspapers, magazines, billboards, and car cards, and that these vehicles can be combined in an almost infinite number of ways, indicates the magnitude of the job of media selection. The media buyer needs to know many facts about the market to be reached before selecting the individual radio or television show or the specific newspaper or magazine in which the ad should appear. Ideally, he would like to know who uses or buys his

---

[12] Niels Vinding, "Awareness, Belief, and Choice as Effects on Tooth Paste Advertising," *Journal of Advertising Research* (March, 1964), pp. 19–21.

product and which media can do the best job of selling this group. He requires from marketing research quantitative information concerning the number and kind of people a particular medium reaches and knowledge about the effect of the medium on its audience.

Advertising effectiveness.   Once an advertising campaign has been completed, most advertisers attempt to check the effectiveness of the campaign in terms of the specified objectives. Analysis of the results obtained can be used to improve future campaigns. Since sales are the usual objective of advertising, measures of effectiveness should measure the effect on sales. But it is extremely difficult, if not impossible, to separate the effect of current advertising on sales from such other factors as past advertising efforts, changes in competitive advertising, salesmanship, general economic conditions, product characteristics, and price. Consequently, most tests of advertising effectiveness are indirect and attempt to measure changes in attitudes relative to the company and its product, changes in the amount and kind of information known about the product, and/or changes in the number of consumers who have learned the advertising message or slogan.

Personal selling.   Marketing research studies dealing with the wants and needs of the various market segments, the product and product line, channels of distribution, pricing, and advertising help determine the role of the sales force. In addition, such studies can provide salesmen with information that they can use in their sales calls. If they know in advance what their prospects want to learn about the product, they can do a more effective job of presenting the "facts." If the product has been tested in the laboratory and in the marketplace, they will have greater confidence in it and can better answer any questions raised by the prospective buyer. In short, research can provide salesmen with better selling tools. Many companies insist that their salesmen use the results of marketing research in their sales presentations.

Most companies of any size undertake a continuous evaluation of their salesmen and their activities. Such analyses are often the responsibility of the marketing research division. In addition, many researchers have the task of helping in the setting of territorial sales goals (quotas) which are based on research to determine the territorial potential.

Organization.   Personal selling research as described above has an obvious effect on the sales organization with respect to the number and size of sales territories, the number of calls by account type and size, and the kind of support required by field salesmen. Research has also been used effectively to define the nature of the selling job, to specify its more meaningful components (e.g., traveling, waiting, selling, writing reports), and to identify the personality characteristics desirable for different sales jobs.

Fortune magazine.[17] While this company cannot be called typical, its growth suggests the growth of marketing research.

In 1947 it was estimated that some $50 million a year was being spent in marketing research.[18] It seems safe to conclude that present expenditures on this activity by American business are in excess of $300 million, and may well be over $400 million. Even so, marketing research budgets are insignificant in proportion to company sales—a fraction of 1 percent. Consumer goods manufacturers outspend industrial producers, but advertising agencies and media spend more proportionate to sales than do consumer goods manufacturers.[19]

A study of 248 companies (including representatives from manufacturing, insurance, banking, utility, and transportation) released in 1969 by the Conference Board reports that over 90 percent of the sample firms have one or more research departments. Some respondents were multidivisional companies with departments in each division. Even so, considerable marketing research was also accomplished by other company departments such as sales, advertising, research and development, merchandising, and corporate planning. Marketing research expenditures were less than 1 percent of annual sales in nine out of ten companies.

A number of companies in the Conference Board study had recently relocated their research units. The changes most mentioned included merging the unit into a new marketing services department; making it a part of corporate planning; splitting it into two parts, e.g., sales analysis and market and product research; and restructuring it to provide more direct support to product managers. In addition, there was greater emphasis on having the research operation do more problem solving research versus survey work.[20]

It is clear that marketing research has matured greatly during recent years—that it has gained acceptance from able business executives who increasingly view it as an important activity in their operations. It is equally true that marketing research has not yet reached its full potential. Certainly the growing acceptance of the marketing concept will cause many companies to place greater emphasis on marketing research

---

[17] *Annual Report, 1967* (Chicago: A. C. Nielsen Co., 1967). It must be recognized that not all sales are derived from marketing research activities. Since the company does not report its sales by type of business engaged in, the amount attributable to the sale of its marketing research data cannot be obtained even though it is thought to represent a substantial majority.

[18] Donald M. Hobart, ed., *Marketing Research Practice* (New York: Ronald Press, 1950), p. 9.

[19] Dik Warren Twedt, *A Survey of Marketing Research* (Chicago: American Marketing Association, 1963).

[20] *The Role and Organization of Marketing Research* (New York: The Conference Board, 1969), pp. 6–23.

since the concept stresses planning on the basis of market needs. The continuing stream of new products which must be marketed will also further the use of marketing research.

In a way, marketing research has pioneered the move toward the broader view of marketing. Marketing research serves as a coordinating factor between marketing and the other functions of the business such as engineering, manufacturing, accounting, and finance. This integrative role has the long-run effect of enhancing the importance of marketing research to the corporation as a whole.

AGENCIES DOING MARKETING RESEARCH

Many types of business use marketing research, and most of these firms that use it do some of the research work internally. Some organizations, however, specialize in research for others, and use little or none themselves. The organizations that use or perform marketing research can be classified under nine different headings.

1. *Manufacturers* are the major users of marketing research and are also among the major groups conducting research. Almost all large manufacturers use some research, and most of them have a department of one or more persons specializing in research.

2. *Advertising agencies* have been leading practitioners and users of marketing research from its earliest days. Almost all large and medium-size agencies have research departments. While these departments specialize in advertising research, they often do other types of marketing research for their clients.

3. *Advertising media* rely heavily on research for data that will help them sell their space or time to advertisers. Such research usually describes the market covered by a magazine, newspaper, or TV station and the audience reached. In the past, much of this "research" has been done for promotional purposes and has been criticized for lack of objectivity. To an increasing extent, however, media are providing technically sound market studies.

4. *Retailers and wholesalers* are beginning to use marketing research, but to date have done little. A few of the large retail chains and department stores have research departments. These departments concentrate primarily on advertising and display effectiveness and store location studies. Research departments are almost unknown among wholesalers.

5. *Independent marketing research firms* are a vital and dynamic part of the marketing research field. Some of these agencies operate as specialized consulting firms and are usually brought in to define and "solve" individual marketing problems. Most of these firms are relatively small. Other research firms conduct market research on a continuing basis and sell the results to subscribers. These firms tend to specialize

in certain research techniques such as store audits, consumer panels, or advertising recall.

6. *Government agencies* carry on research which is indispensable to the marketing field. The federal government is easily the biggest producer of marketing facts. The Bureau of the Census, the Small Business Administration, and the Bureau of Labor Statistics—to mention a few—annually spend millions of dollars collecting information about a wide variety of marketing subjects.

7. *Trade and professional associations* have become increasingly important in the development of certain types of marketing information. They are especially important to small firms, since these firms often can afford research only through cooperative effort. Much trade association work centers around the collection and dissemination of operating statistics obtained from their members. Professional associations (e.g., the American Medical Association) often do research pertaining to their members.

8. *Universities and foundations* have always been known for their research work. It is only in recent years, however, that universities have done large amounts of applied research. Much of the marketing research done by universities is carried on through bureaus of business research. Almost all such work is for the "public" and is released in published form. Some foundations have been active in providing market information. They tend to deal with broad economic and business problems more often than with problems of specific application to individual firms.

9. *Other agencies* such as banks, financial institutions, and financial reporting services such as Dun & Bradstreet and Poor's provide information of considerable value to the marketing man. Also included here are those organizations which specialize in providing continuous statistical information regarding advertising media; examples are Standard Rate and Data Service and *Advertising Age*.

ORGANIZATION OF THE MARKETING RESEARCH DEPARTMENT

The organization structure and staffing of marketing research departments varies greatly. The majority of departments have only a few full-time employees including clerks and secretaries. According to a 1963 study made by the American Marketing Association the median number of full-time marketing research employees in consumer products companies with annual sales of between $5 and $25 million was two, with only 25 percent having more than three. Very large consumer companies (those having annual sales of $500 million and more) had a median number of 12 full-time employees, with 25 percent having more than 36.

Industrial goods companies had smaller departments—those with annual sales of $5 to $25 million had about the same number of full-time employees, but the companies with $500 million and over in annual sales had a median number of full-time research employees of only 10, with 25 percent having more than 22. Advertising agencies with annual billings of $50 to $100 million had 22 marketing research employees, with 25 percent having more than 32.[21]

Many of the companies that use substantial amounts of marketing research do not have large research staffs because they buy much of the work from outside agencies. These companies use their own staffs mainly to design and guide the work and to interpret the findings. Marketing research is a technical activity and requires skills developed in a variety of disciplines. Most firms, regardless of size, do not conduct enough research to use full-time specialists in each of the various disciplines. Data collection frequently requires a large field force and high speed computers. Such activities can frequently be performed better and more economically by independent firms specializing in such work.[22]

Factors affecting organization

Variations in the organization and staffing of different research departments are the result of many factors including the assignment of research activities to other departments (for example, the accounting department often prepares sales analyses); the type of products and markets involved (for example, consumer goods companies do more survey work than industrial firms); the relationship between the company and its advertising agency regarding who does what research; the extent of new product development; the personalities and attitudes of top operating executives; the extent to which the firm embraces the marketing concept; the maintenance of a research library; and the availability of clerical typing pools and tabulating equipment within the firm. Thus, it is impossible to state categorically how the ideal research department should be staffed. What may suit the needs of one company may be unsuited to the needs of another.

Organization of particular research departments

The organization of the marketing research department of the Chicago office of Foote, Cone and Belding, one of the largest advertising agencies in the United States, is given in Figure 1–3. As is true with most adver-

---

21 Twedt, *op. cit.*, pp. 18–19.

22 For a detailed discussion of this subject see *Using Marketing Consultants and Research Agencies*, Studies in Business Policy Number 120 (New York: The Conference Board, 1966).

FIGURE 1-3. Research department organization (Chicago office—Foote, Cone and Belding Advertising Agency)

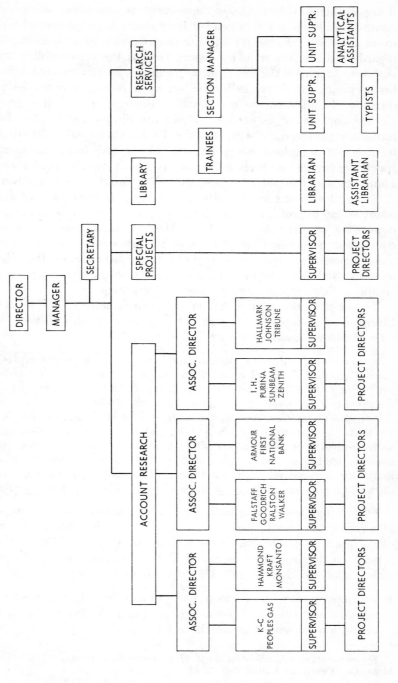

tising agencies, this research department is organized along account group lines. Each group is headed by a research supervisor who reports to an associate director. This supervisor operates as a research director regarding the accounts in his group. He has the responsibility and the authority to undertake any kind of research activity needed by any of his accounts. He is typically assisted by a limited number of project directors. In addition, he can draw on the research services group for clerical and typing assistance and on the library for help in locating secondary source data. Although the Foote, Cone and Belding department is not organized along "specialty" lines, individual members have special expertise in such fields as sociology, psychology, economics, sampling, and computer science, as well as marketing and advertising.

Except for pilot surveys, all interviewing is bought from professional interviewing organizations. Coding and tabulating may be subcontracted depending on the office workload. Machine tabulation is always subcontracted. Sometimes entire surveys are farmed out, but then departmental personnel work closely with the contractor in the planning, analysis, and interpretation phases. A total of 23 full-time employees comprise this organization; 9 hold masters degrees.

The organization of the marketing research office of the Ford Motor Company is presented in Figure 1–4. This office reports to the company vice president—marketing and the director is

. . . responsible for directing and/or coordinating a comprehensive program of marketing research in all areas of the Company, including organizing and interpreting marketing research data as it applies to broad Company problems; developing a program of marketing research studies for North American Automotive Operations, the Central Staffs, and for those areas of the Company not having a marketing research activity; and maintaining a continuing review with North American Automotive Operations management to ensure that their research needs are met; providing staff guidance and assistance in developing marketing research programs for Overseas Automotive Operations; and conducting special research studies as directed by the Vice President—Marketing.[23]

Of the four research department heads, two have Ph.D.'s and a third is working on his doctorate. The director of the marketing research office has a doctorate. An illustration of the responsibilities assigned to a research department is provided in the following listing of functions which apply to the Advanced Product Research Department.[24]

1. In cooperation with divisional and product development management, identify and prioritize product development problems requiring the utilization of market research techniques.

---

[23] *Organization Manual—Statement of Functions* (Dearborn, Mich.: The Ford Motor Co., December 1, 1967), p. 10-D.

[24] In letter received from Ford Motor Company, October 15, 1968.

FIGURE 1–4. Marketing research office (marketing staff, Ford Motor Company)

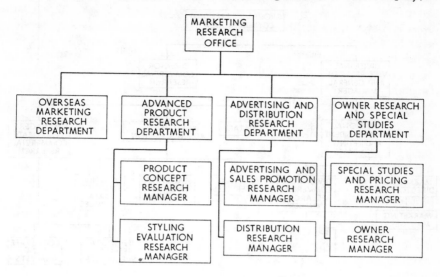

2. Develop means for utilizing marketing research studies as an aid to determining forward product requirements, developing new products, or improving existing product lines.
3. Plan and direct styling and advanced vehicle research studies for the purpose of projecting demand and special trends affecting the transportation industry.
4. Review and approve forward product study designs, survey questionnaires, selection of outside marketing research firms to execute studies, and marketing research reports prior to publication.
5. Interpret marketing research findings obtained from outside research agencies, formulate recommendations for product actions based on research findings, and present reports of the findings and recommendations to management and affected activities.
6. Consult with divisional and product development management in establishing research program budgets consistent with their needs for forward product research studies.
7. Maintain a continuing review of all marketing research activity in overseas manufacturing, sales, and assembly locations. Assist in the development of research programs; administer the project notification system; and summarize research findings from surveys conducted for overseas areas.

The organization of the Marketing Research Department of the Pillsbury Company is shown in Figure 1–5. From this exhibit it can be noted that the director has the responsibility for managing certain central

FIGURE 1–5. Pillsbury commercial research organizational relationships

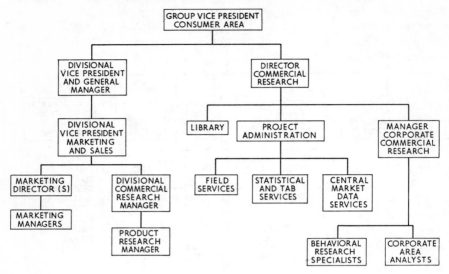

facilities including the field force, library, statistics, an analysis group which handles data received from such services as A. C. Nielsen and Market Research Corporation of America, and a behavioral science research unit comprised of specialists who are concerned with the development and use by Pillsbury of advanced research methodology; and for providing research services to divisions which do not have research departments.

The other part of the organization chart (Figure 1–5) shows the general nature of the reporting arrangements of the divisional research groups. All three of the consumer divisions have their own divisional research groups and each is headed by a manager which reports to the top marketing man in the division. The type and amount of research work done within each division is determined by the needs of the divisional marketing management group.

WHAT MANAGEMENT SHOULD NOT EXPECT FROM MARKETING RESEARCH

Despite the versatility and proven value of marketing research, many executives tend to expect too much from it. Research should *never* be thought of as the complete answer to any marketing problem, if only because there are so many intervening factors between the findings of a research study and the response of the marketplace. Much marketing research consists of collecting data about products purchased, TV program audiences, and advertisements read—all in the past. Data of this type are of course helpful in predicting the future, but they cannot predict with certainty. No one yet has found a sure way of determining how much of a product will be sold before it is put on the market. Today it is generally agreed that our research techniques have outdistanced our ability to use the results of research effectively in making business decisions. Thus, management must center, first, on the decision-making process and, second, on what help marketing research can provide in making this process more efficient.

Too frequently research deals with fragments of the problem. The cause of this too-narrow approach is a tendency on the part of both management and research personnel to view the decision-making process as past or present history rather than a continuous process including the future. Research is a vital "arm" of management, but it can be no better than the environment in which it lives. It cannot "solve" management's problems unless it looks toward future opportunities. If research looks *back* instead of *forward* this is, in large part, the fault of management. While the marketing research administrator can and should be creative in designing studies, general management must also be creative in the formulation of the goals and strategies of the enterprise if research is to fulfill its potential. Too often the researcher himself is not sufficiently management-oriented to participate actively in the problem formulation, or is not a fully respected member of the management group and, therefore, is not fully aware of the problems facing the group.[25]

The major reason why managers fail to get the most value from marketing research is because they do not understand the nature of the decision process including the role of information in it. Other reasons follow.[26]

1. Resistance on the part of business executives to use research because they see it as a threat to their personal status. Such individuals fear that research may evaluate them unkindly.
2. Absence of clearly articulated corporate objectives, with the result that executives develop their own objectives which often are in conflict with each other. In such situations, individuals inevitably want research to support their views.

---

[25] As to what the researcher should do to "sell" management on the value of research see Howard L. Gordon, "What Is the Next Breakthrough in Research?", *Journal of Marketing* (January, 1965), pp. 25–27.

[26] Joseph W. Newman, "Put Research into Marketing Decisions," *Harvard Business Review* (March–April, 1962), pp. 107–10.

3. Inability to use specialists—indeed, to understand them. Marketing research now draws on a variety of specialists from such disciplines as mathematics, statistics, economics, psychology, sociology, general semantics, and anthropology. Since each science uses its own vocabulary, the problem of finding a common language is difficult.

4. Isolation of the marketing research department from key executives.

As a consequence of the above impediments, management sometimes expects too little from marketing research and at other times expects far too much. Without a reasonably defined decision-making process aimed at achieving definite objectives, it is impossible for management to define the role to be played by the marketing research unit or for the unit to execute its role with efficiency.

In summary, it is clear that marketing research cannot and should not make decisions for the executive. It can provide him with information that will help him solve problems, but this information will never be complete. Thus, the executive must still operate in an area of uncertainty. Research can only decrease the size of the area.

SUMMARY

Marketing research is a management tool of great importance, and one which has wide acceptance among business executives. It has grown substantially in use since the end of World War II and will, no doubt, grow even more in the years ahead.

Research can be applied to problems in almost every aspect of marketing. At the present time, most marketing research studies fall into one or more of the following groups: product, market, sales organization, channels of distribution, and advertising. One way of looking at the potential usefulness of marketing research is by relating it to the administrative process which consists of the four interrelated steps of objectives, plan of action, organization, and control and reappraisal. If top management looks at research in this light—essentially as an important aid to decision making at various steps in the process—research can be used more profitably. It must be kept in mind, however, that while research can do much to substitute facts for hunches, it cannot give an absolute answer to most questions. It can, of course, narrow the area in which judgment must operate.

At present the use of marketing research is concentrated among the larger firms in the manufacturing, advertising agency, and advertising media fields. Some large retailers, but only a few wholesalers, do research. Much marketing research is done by other organizations such as independent marketing research firms, trade associations, universities, foundations, and governmental agencies.

Case 1—1.　MacFADDEN FEED COMPANY

The MacFadden Feed Company, with headquarters in a small town in Iowa, was a relatively small producer of concentrate feeds for livestock and poultry. Its marketing area included the states of Indiana, Illinois, Wisconsin, Minnesota, North and South Dakota, Iowa, Nebraska, Missouri, and Colorado. Sales of the company's line, which included prestarter (weaning), starter, feeder, and rounding out feeds for dairy cattle, beef cattle, horses, hogs, and poultry totaled over $12 million.

After several generations of continued growth, sales had turned downward, and the firm experienced its first losses. This led to a reorganization, and a new group of executives assumed control. The new president was concerned about the decline in sales which had been experienced over the past five years, but was uncertain as to what might be done to check the decline.

The company had been founded in 1898 by Mr. John MacFadden, the owner of a feed mill and a farm supply store. He had been one of the first to recognize the importance of adding small quantities of minerals to livestock feeds. Through the years, and largely because of the dynamic leadership provided by Mr. MacFadden, the company prospered and became a highly regarded producer of quality concentrates. His death in 1948 marked, in retrospect, the beginning of the company's difficulties which culminated in the reorganization.

Company sales and profits had reached their high points ten years before, and then had declined each year until sales were less than half their peak level and losses were incurred. Despite these developments, the firm was in excellent financial condition. Working capital exceeded $3 million, there was no long-term debt, and the company's plant and equipment were completely modern.

MacFadden had always placed great emphasis on quality. The company's products not only contained such minerals as zinc, copper, cobalt, iodine, and iron, but vitamins and antibiotics as well. A modern laboratory was maintained, as well as a research farm which conducted experiments to determine the weight gains and health of animals fed on MacFadden products versus those fed on other products. The competitive nature of the animal and poultry feed industry was such that a number of other companies sold similar products.

MacFadden products were more concentrated than their competitors' and, therefore, sold to farmers at somewhat higher prices, typically about 10 percent higher than the average of prices charged by competitors. Thus, for example, the price to farmers for the company's dairy and beef cattle line, which accounted for 60 percent of total sales, was $115 a ton versus competitive products which sold for about $100 per ton. Dealers worked on a gross margin of about 20 percent of the selling price.

Management had always felt that this price differential was justified by the fact that less of the company's concentrate was required in the mixing with other products to achieve the same results as those obtained with competing products. Typically, the product was mixed (by grinding) either by the dealer or the farmer according to specifications which varied greatly depending on such variables as farmer preferences, time of the year, number of animals involved, and the general health of the animals.

Company executives estimated that while there were approximately 6,000 feed manufacturers, better than 80 percent of the total business was accounted for by less than 20 percent of the manufacturers. Some 30 percent of the total business was thought to be accounted for by the leading ten manufacturers such as Ralston Purina and Allied. In recent years the company had become increasingly concerned about the changes that had taken place in the industry's structure and the channels of distribution. Traditionally the company had relied almost exclusively on the small independent feed store to sell its products. But the tonnage moved by such outlets had been declining each year. It was thought that feed tonnage consisted of about 70 percent complete feeds and 30 percent concentrates. The latter went to the custom mixer, the grain bank operator, or the large commercial feeder to be mixed with local grains or other products. Thus, the country grain elevator assumed great importance and was thought to market better than two thirds of all feeds. Farm co-ops represented an important channel, although the percent of feeds flowing through this outlet was not known.

A study made in MacFadden's marketing area revealed that 76 percent of the farmers interviewed purchased their feed from one source; that the average feed purchase was made about once a week; that nearly 60 percent were buying their feed at the source nearest to their farm, but that the larger the buyer the more willing he was to travel farther from his farm; and that most had been visited by fieldmen and salesmen from feed manufacturers.

Company executives were watching with interest the increase in the amount of bulk feeding, that is, the purchase of "loose" products in preference to obtaining it in bags. The development of large commercial feeding operations (for example, the average size of commercial bulk feedlots was estimated to be in excess of 8,500 head) had made possible this trend since savings of about $5.00 per ton were possible. To date the larger commercial feeders were located for the most part outside of the company's marketing area, but it was thought that it was only a matter of time until this trend developed in the area served by the company.

More and more chemical and pharmaceutical companies interested in the animal health market were marketing to the animal feed market through a variety of channels. Some sold to the larger feed companies for resale. Others by-passed the major feed manufacturers by going directly to distributors and country grain elevators. These specialized products were then added by either the dealer or the farmer to the feed mix. It was difficult for MacFadden executives to estimate the impact of these new well-advertised products on the sales of company products.

Another trend of importance was the growing tendency toward integration in the animal production industry. This was especially true in the case of poultry; for example, the Quaker Oats Company operated a huge poultry farm in Georgia.

MacFadden executives did not know who purchased their products, but were reasonably sure that their sales were concentrated among the smaller farms. The company distributed its products on a tonnage basis as follows:

	Percent of tonnage
Poultry	6.0
Dairy	29.9
Beef	30.4
Swine	32.6
Horse	1.1
Total	100.0

Company advertising expenditures in recent years had been running about $500,000 including fees paid to the company's advertising agency for publicity and marketing research services. Advertising was concentrated primarily in farm magazines and in those publications specializing in a given animal type (for example, *Hoard's Dairyman*). Little use was made of radio, and the company had never used TV. Over $100,000 was spent in outdoor advertising including dealer signs. A recent study made by the company's advertising agency revealed that most farmers knew and respected the MacFadden feed line; that they did not, however, feel that the company's research efforts were more extensive than other companies; and that they were concerned about new feed additives.

Sales were made through 1,246 dealers, most of which were small independent operators. In some counties as many as ten dealers might be franchised, while in others the company was unable to obtain dealers and had given some thought to buying into one or more dealers. Over half the company dealers sold less than 50 tons of the company's product annually. Few carried only the company feed line, and only the larger dealers did any local promotion of the line. The company did not make available any co-op advertising funds.

The company products were sold direct to dealers through a sales force of 53 salesmen and 12 district sales managers. The total cost of the sales force exceeded $900,000 annually. The company had records showing sales by product by dealer for each county. In addition, the company had developed from the latest Census of Agriculture an estimate of the total dollar worth of each county relating to its products. This potential figure had been calculated by taking the animal population of each county by types and annual turnover, estimating the total amount (in tons) of feed consumed, and converting this tonnage figure into dollars by using company prices. Management felt that such data could be used to undertake a sales analysis which would help the company rethink its marketing program.

How could MacFadden use marketing research to improve its sales and profit situation?

Case 1—2. THE BURKE COMPANY

The Burke Company of Cleveland, Ohio acquired rights to manufacture and sell on a royalty basis an electric ice crusher for home use. A year after introducing the product the management faced the problem of developing plans for the next year.

Burke, with sales of less than $1 million, was one of the leading producers and marketers of office, photographic, dairy, and portion control scales. The latter were designed for use in the food service industry to assure servings of uniform weights. The plant work force, which averaged about 20 employees, assembled parts supplied on a contract basis by job shops using dies and tools supplied by Burke. The company did little fabrication of parts. The sales organization consisted of 24 manufacturers' agents, who also sold noncompeting products for other manufacturers. Fourteen served the stationery and office equipment market, 10 served the restaurant market, and 3 served both of these markets. In addition to supervising the agents, both the president and sales manager did some selling. The president called upon dealers and wholesalers in New York and supervised the activities of representatives in 11 western and 4 southwestern states. The sales manager covered the rest of the United States and Canada.

A preliminary investigation by Burke's management revealed that three types of ice crushers were being sold. Besides electric ice crushers such as Burke's, there were manually operated ice crushers, as well as special ice-crushing attachments for electric blenders. These last two types, however, were not regarded as competitive with the electric crusher. Although manually operated ice crushers were inexpensive, sometimes retailing for as little as $5.00, they were slow and awkward to use. On the other hand, the ice-crushing attachments for blenders were more efficient than the manual models. In addition to the crusher attachment, which generally sold for $16.95 or $17.95, a blender (list price from

$42.95 to $59.95) was required. Moreover, the attachments did not seem to appeal to customers because of their storage and adjustment requirements.

Recognizing that its chief competition would come from other electric ice crushers, Burke's management studied this segment of the market closely. It found that the only significant competitive product of the electric type was the Crush-o-matic, which had been on the market for several years. The Burke ice crusher, however, had several advantages over the Crush-o-matic. These were as follows:

1. It was much faster.
2. It would not stall or jam.
3. It could be loaded and then started.

The manufacturer's suggested retail price for the Crush-o-matic was $29.95. It was sold through appliance stores, discount houses, department stores, and prestige specialty stores such as Von Lengerke & Antoine in Chicago and Abercrombie & Fitch in New York. Initially, it had been sold by a large mail-order house with retail outlets throughout the country. Subsequently another model, known as the Magic Server, replaced the Crush-o-matic in the mail-order house's catalog. It was listed at $21.88, was similar in appearance to the Crush-o-matic, and was made by the same manufacturer.

Burke did not know its competitor's annual sales volume, and no reliable information on the size of the consumer market for electric ice crushers was available from published sources. Based upon an informal investigation, it was estimated that the volume of electric ice crushers sold to the consumer market by retail stores and mail-order outlets would be from 50,000 to 100,000 units a year for the next three years. The comments of some of the retailers interviewed are given in Exhibit 1.

After several months of investigation and planning the company had been able to put the ice crusher into production, get the product in the hands of the 10 manufacturers' representatives already selling its scales to the restaurant market, sign up 16 manufacturer's representatives to solicit appliance distributors throughout the United States with the understanding that only one such distributor would be appointed in each territory, and make an agreement with a large national mail-order house to buy the item at $12.95 and sell it as a private label product at $19.95. The retail list price of the same crusher bearing the Burke name and sold in all other outlets was $27.95.

During the first year following its introduction 4,200 units were sold, 3,700 of them to the mail-order house. After the first few months, orders from appliance distributors and the restaurant market commenced to decline.

A limited amount of direct mail advertising was sent to dealers and distributors, but no consumer advertising had been undertaken and none was planned. The cooperative advertising plan for dealers provided dealers with an amount equal to 3.5 percent of their purchases from distributors, provided tear sheets or other proof of advertising performance was submitted to the manufacturer. The plan did not apply to the private label sales by the mail-order house.

EXHIBIT 1. Results of informal investigation

A survey of several stores in the area where Burke was located revealed the following concerning the size of the market for electric ice crushers and consumer buying habits:

A *prestige specialty store.* The buyer for this store indicated that they had carried the Crush-o-matic electric ice crusher for approximately one year and that sales were greatest during the Christmas and summer seasons. In response to the question, "To whom does the electric ice crusher appeal?" the buyer stated that it appealed most to home owners who did entertaining, and to people who served drinks in their homes often. It was emphasized that the electric ice crusher was only infrequently used in the preparation of salads and desserts.

It was also learned that after the introduction of the electric ice crusher, sales of hand crushers dropped off markedly, mostly because of their slow speed. The number of Crush-o-matic electric ice crushers sold by this store last year was between 300 and 350.

A *large prestige department store.* The buyer here revealed that even though the electric ice crusher had been featured recently as one of the items of the month, the store had sold only about a gross and a half all year. However, the buyer felt that within a few years they would be able to sell two to three gross annually. It was described as a "luxury" item with a limited demand, and commonly was bought to be given as a gift.

A *large mail-order and retail store organization.* The buyer in charge of the department handling electric ice crushers felt that they appealed primarily to those people who liked to serve drinks often, and who wanted to impress their neighbors. The item proved marketable to this company's customers in the $6,000 to $15,000 income bracket, and was considered a "fringe" or "luxury" item. The buyer pointed out that if the electric ice crusher were promoted enough by the manufacturer and retailer, sales might be boosted above present levels. This company sold about 5,000 through their mail catalogs and retail stores during the past year.

A *large hotel supply company.* The buyer said they did not stock the Crush-o-matic ice crusher, but would order it if requested. He added that there was virtually no demand for this item from small bars, fountains, or hotels because of its high price and newness. He believed that the "home" represented the best market for the electric ice crusher. He mentioned that, when an institution needed a more efficient machine than the hand crusher, it usually bought a larger and more expensive electric type. But this was not a common move. The company sold 6 to 12 dozen hand crushers a year.

A *suburban discount store.* The manager of this three-store appliance discount store stated that they sold between 35 and 40 electric ice crushers a year. Their price was $20.90. The employee interviewed felt that middle-class people who were electrically minded, such as those who had electric kitchens, were the most likely buyers.

A *central city discount store.* This appliance and auto accessory discount house sold electric ice crushers for $19.97. Sales volume or other comments could not be obtained.

In an effort to sell the department store market, demonstrators were placed in two department stores selling to middle-income consumers, one in Cleveland and one in New York City. Each demonstrator worked for two weeks in August. During this period 25 crushers were sold in Cleveland and 32 in New York at a total expense of $700. Both the stores bought an additional 12 units, but neither reordered after that.

Besides the consumer market, Burke's management also thought that the gift and premium markets were worth considering in the future. One survey of business gifts indicated that a widely known blender was the fourth most popular gift in the $35–$50 class. Electric ice crushers were not mentioned in this report.

The premium market was made up of several segments. A trade source estimated that trading stamp companies distributed $700 million worth of merchandise in exchange for stamps. The ice crusher was well within the price range of items included in these plans, of which there were many. Most such companies purchased their merchandise directly from the manufacturer, bargaining for rock-bottom prices.

Premiums were also used by manufacturers to stimulate the sale of their own products. Such premiums were usually sold at cost or slightly above to customers who mailed in a stated number of labels or other proof of purchase of the sponsor's product. Specialized companies were frequently used by manufacturers to plan and operate premium plans, thus relieving the manufacturer of the many detailed problems created by periodic premium offers. Here again, buyers of merchandise to be used as premiums were price conscious. Moreover, it was difficult to determine in advance the response to an offer. Thus the supplier had to be able to adjust his delivery rate on short notice.

In attempting to arrive at a basis for determining the profitability of the product and the availability of promotional funds, management made some estimates. Variable manufacturing costs per unit were as follows: $8.95 in lots of 1,000; $8.75 in lots of 5,000; and $8.50 in lots of 10,000. Annual fixed costs were estimated to be $6,475 up to 10,000 units and an additional $1,500 for the second 10,000. Start-up costs, covering such items as Underwriters' Laboratory certification, amounted to $3,287. In addition, $2,743 was spent on direct mail and cooperative advertising, a trade show exhibit, and miscellaneous promotional efforts.

The usual discounts for items similar to the electric ice crusher were 40 percent to retailers and 50 and 5 percent to wholsalers; commissions of 5 to 7.5 percent were paid to manufacturers' representatives when they were used in connection with wholesalers and retailers. Burke, in an effort to get better trade cooperation, paid a 10 percent commission to representatives.

In discussing the disappointing performance of the appliance distributors, the sales vice president was told by several representatives that the distributors thought that the retail list price ought to be below $25, a consumer advertising campaign undertaken, and the cooperative advertising plan made more attractive. Specifically, the dealers wanted cooperative advertising funds advanced against future purchases in sufficient amounts to allow them to advertise, and also wanted Burke to drop its proof of advertising performance requirement.

When questioned about their sales performance, the representatives serving the restaurant market reported that they were getting complaints that the ice crusher did not stand up under heavy usage requirements in a commercial application and were reluctant to push the product. Further, they asked about the company's repair service plan.

At the end of the first year, the sales vice president, who was able to give only about 10 percent of his time to the ice crusher, was asked to prepare a marketing plan for the next year, keeping in mind that the company was able and willing to invest a reasonable amount of money in the ice crusher program, including consumer advertising, if it could be justified.

How should the vice president use marketing research in developing the marketing plan?

Case 1—3.   FOREST PRODUCTS, INC.

Forest Products, Inc., a large integrated producer of all types of materials made from wood, faced a problem in connection with the distribution of its building products to the retail trade and small builders in a major southern city. The competitive and financial position of its independent distributor, Johnson Plywood Company, had become so serious that Forest Products acquired the firm to assure continued representation in that area. It then faced the problem of how to make this branch profitable. Johnson Plywood's problems were in part the result of post-World War II developments which led to more intense competition and changes in distribution in the building materials industry.

Forest Products was among the ten leading producers in the forest products industry. Its sales were in excess of $250 million annually, of which about $100 million came from the sale of lumber, plywood, hardboard, and other wood products through over 100 wholesale distribution outlets, some of which were company owned and operated, in all sections of the United States. The balance of the total sales volume came from nonbuilding products and paper.

A typical company wholesale branch had annual sales of about $1 million, an investment of about $450,000 in inventories, accounts receivable, and plant equipment, and from 400 to 600 accounts. Branch managers were judged on the basis of percent of earnings on the investment in the branch. It was generally felt that the total dollar volume of wholesale lumber, building materials, and hardware sales in a market area should be at least $100 million annually before it would pay Forest

Products to open a branch, provided that such a branch could get at least 1 percent of the market. The company's branches sold to building supply dealers and industrial buyers who bought materials for use in making products, packaging, and in maintenance activities. Every effort was made to avoid selling to builders and others who might be considered customers of dealers on the retail level.

The city in which the Johnson Plywood Company was located and the region it served embraced excellent shipping and transportation facilities, had substantial defense installations, and was considered one of the leading southern markets. Moreover, its urban renewal efforts and the continued influx of industry suggested it would become even more important as a market. Residential and nonresidential construction were continuing to grow at a rate above the national average.

When acquired by Forest Products the Johnson Plywood Company was unprofitable. While it had obtained as much as 10 percent of the local business when materials were in short supply, its market share had steadily deteriorated. Lacking a strong sales forces and merchandising ability, the firm resorted to selling to builders, homeowners, and anyone else willing to buy, which made it unpopular with its retail dealers. Moreover, it sold on a price basis, which further irritated retailers and wholesalers. Even worse, Johnson was accused by competitors of changing the grade of various plywood panels so that they might be sold at a higher price, and was slow to settle claims made by customers. In time, local building materials dealers stopped buying from Johnson except when its prices on commodity items were significantly lower than major firms.

The condition of the Johnson Company was in some measure a result of changes in the market and the organization of distribution in the industry. At the close of World War II building materials were sold to small builders through retail lumber yards or building supply dealers, who were supplied by wholesalers, known in the trade as distributors, who bought directly from producers. Some of the distributors were owned by producers, but until the 1950's the wholesale sales branches of any one producer tended to be restricted to a limited part of the country. Gradually producers acquired more outlets on the wholesale level.

By the late 1960's competition for the builders' business had become quite intense. Small independent wholesalers were in some cases well entrenched in local markets. The weaker ones were among the first to sell out to producers. On the retail level multi-unit operations known as line-yards had become increasingly important. Some were owned by producers but others were independent. On the basis of service, line-yards along with other building material retailers could be classified as (1) full-service, (2) cash-and-carry, or (3) combination service and cash-

and-carry. The cash-and-carry type had made considerable progress in the area served by Johnson Plywood.

Some major producers with nationwide wholesale warehouse facilities sold direct to builders, creating ill will among the retailers to whom they also sold. Direct sale by independent wholesalers was becoming more common, but every effort was made to avoid offending retailers.

Among the developments in the last 20 years leading to more intense competition were the following:

1. Growth of large-scale builders.
2. Increase in business-minded builders.
3. Increase in cash-and-carry type of retail operation.
4. More emphasis on merchandising activities.
5. Increase in multiple-outlet ownership and operation.
6. Forward integration by producers to include the wholesale level.
7. Increased movement toward nationwide wholesale operations by producers.
8. Increase in the number of producers' warehousing points to improve delivery service.
9. Increase in production capacity and more idle capacity.

The management of Forest Products was uncertain concerning what could be done to improve the Johnson operation. There was some question as to whether the Forest name, as well as those of its products, might have been damaged by the actions of its distributor. The district manager summarized the Johnson situation as follows: "The firm's reputation is very poor, its customers are price-buyers with no sense of loyalty, and it sells only commodities. There are no high-margin specialty items to offset the losses incurred by price cuts on the commodities."

The competitive situation in Johnson's area had become quite intense, and price-cutting common on commodity items. Many dealers were using price leaders and, in turn, expecting wholesalers to share a part of the price reduction. While many distributors followed any announced price cut, they revised prices upward only when the large multi-unit distributors led the move upward. The market had become so competitive that there was a question of whether a large company could profitably operate a branch in the area. A branch manager from another area was asked to take charge of the Johnson operation.

How could the new manager of the Johnson operation use marketing research effectively?

2

Scientific method and research design

$\mathbf{M}$ARKETING is more of an art than a science. The successful practice of marketing depends on the skill and judgment of the individuals involved and cannot be reduced to an organized body of principles. The typical marketing executive makes many decisions every day. In most cases these decisions must be made quickly and are based on experience and judgment. In other cases the executive may be able to collect a considerable amount of information on which to base his decisions. In either circumstance he must choose one alternative from among those open to him, with something less than certainty that he is right. It is the function of marketing research to reduce the degree of uncertainty. But what is marketing research? Is it the same as research in other fields? What is research in general?

SCIENTIFIC METHOD

"No method known to man can entirely eliminate uncertainty. But scientific method, more than any other procedure, can minimize those elements of uncertainty which result from lack of information. By so doing, it reduces the danger of making a wrong choice between alternative courses of action."[1] "Research" could be substituted for "scientific method" in this quotation without changing the meaning; i.e., the terms "research" and "scientific method" are synonymous in practical usage.

---

[1] Marie Jahoda, Morton Deutsch, and Stuart W. Cook, *Research Methods in Social Relations,* Part I (New York: Dryden Press, 1951), p. 28.

Businessmen use the two terms interchangeably. Research in marketing, then, like research in other fields, is the application of scientific method.

Probably all marketing research men would agree that their work is devoted to bringing some scientific discipline to a field that is otherwise not scientific. They would not apply the term research to studies that they considered unscientific. But it is inappropriate to apply many of the common definitions of scientific method to the work done in marketing research. Certainly, if the definitions of scientific method used in the physical sciences are considered, it is difficult to classify much marketing research as scientific.

Scientific method in the physical sciences

In most physical sciences the reproducible experiment is the accepted scientific method. In chemistry, for example, an experiment is conducted under controlled conditions. Such variables as temperature, atmospheric pressure, and quantities of chemicals are carefully measured and all but one held constant during the experiment. These conditions are reported in detail along with the results of the experiment so that others may reproduce the same conditions and validate the results. In marketing it is difficult, if not impossible, to control all the conditions of an experiment. As a result, experiments which can be reproduced exactly are not common. Until recently relatively few marketing research projects could be called experiments, much less reproducible experiments. The same is true, however, for the social sciences and for some of the natural sciences, astronomy for example.

Scientific method in marketing

Many scholars have refused to limit their definition of scientific method to a procedure the application of which is confined primarily to the physical sciences. The following is an example of this point of view:

The field of science is unlimited; its material is endless, every group of natural phenomena, every phase of social life, every stage of past or present development is material for science. The unity of all science consists alone in its method, not in its material. . . .

The scientific method is marked by the following features: (a) careful and accurate classification of facts and observation of their correlation and sequence; (b) the discovery of scientific laws by aid of creative imagination; (c) self-criticism and . . . equal validity for all normally constituted minds.[2]

---

[2] Karl Pearson, *The Grammar of Science,* Part I (London: A. C. Black, 1911), pp. 6 and 12.

This view of the scientific method coincides, in a general way, with the definition of marketing research given in Chapter 1—the gathering, recording, and analyzing of facts about marketing problems. In addition to the gathering, recording, and analyzing of facts, however, scientific method emphasizes that these must be done with care and accuracy, that imagination must be exerted to find relationships among the facts, and that the conclusions reached must be the same as the conclusions which other qualified individuals would reach from analyzing the same data. The simple gathering and tabulation of facts is not scientific method, nor is it research.

Distinction between scientific and nonscientific method

It is useful to think of scientific method as a very general method which can be adapted to many widely varying situations according to the subject matter and specific problem involved. Since subject matter and problems vary across the whole range of human interest, it is obvious that the specifics of the methods applied will vary. Certain criteria, however, distinguish those methods that may be called scientific from other methods. Three major differences between scientific and non-scientific method are in: (1) the objectivity of the investigator; (2) the accuracy of measurement; and (3) the degree to which the investigation is continuing and exhaustive.

Objectivity of the investigator. The methods commonly used to eliminate uncertainty can be classified into four categories: (1) the method of tenacity, (2) the method of authority, (3) the method of intuition, and (4) the method of science.[3] The method of tenacity involves the continued holding of an opinion regardless of any new evidence which may conflict with that opnion. The method of authority involves appeal to one who is presumed to be an authority and whose opinion is taken as fact. The third method, intuition, consists of the conclusion that some proposition is "obviously true." Anyone who "understands it" can see that it is true even though he can't prove the point. None of these methods is independent of the desires and wills of the individuals involved. Each investigator may begin with different ideas, may appeal to different authorities, or may have different intuitive insights. The fourth method of removing uncertainty is the scientific method, which attempts to eliminate the preconceptions or desires of the investigator from the results. The scientist must base his judgments on facts, not preconceived notions, authoritative statements, or intuition.

---

[3] Morris R. Cohen and Ernest Nagel, *An Introduction to Logic and Scientific Method* (New York: Harcourt, Brace & Co., 1939), pp. 193–96.

If the investigator is not completely objective in his thinking, if he is not just as anxious to find facts supporting one outcome of his study as another, it is difficult, if not impossible, to keep bias out of his work. The history of the drug krebiozen, which was claimed by some to be a cancer cure, is an example. Men with outstanding reputations as scientists took positions on both sides of the argument as to the effectiveness of the drug. The sponsors of the product claimed to have research evidence of its effectiveness, but refused to disclose complete details of their materials and methods. Other scientists lacked faith in the reported results because they suspected the sponsors of bias. The sponsors refused to disclose detail because they claimed others were biased against krebiozen. The scientific approach would call for the original investigator to disclose all details of his work; others who attempted to duplicate tests would do likewise, and the scientific world in general would draw conclusions.

Accuracy of measurement.   Scientific method attempts to obtain the most accurate measurements possible. Since the factors to be measured and the measuring devices available differ from one field of study to another, the accuracy of measurements differs widely. In the physical sciences, electronic measuring devices of great accuracy are available for some measurements. In marketing and in the social sciences, a relatively crude measuring device, the questionnaire, is often used. Both may be scientific if they are the best measuring devices which are available for the purpose at hand.

Continuing and exhaustive nature of investigation.   A scientific investigation considers all the facts that are pertinent to the problem at hand. No bit of evidence is passed over because it fails to fit a previously established pattern. But the mark of the scientific method is more than just refusal to overlook conflicting data; it is the aggressive searching for additional evidence to support, or confound, the existing conclusion. The scientist is never sure that he has found the ultimate truth. He knows that many well-established conclusions have been found to be erroneous (for example, throughout the 19th century scientists accepted the "fact" that the atom was the smallest unit into which matter could be divided). It is this constantly challenging attitude which leads to continual progress in science.

During most of the 1950's, motivation research was much in vogue among marketers. Following the introduction of this type of research, many large corporations conducted one or more such studies. One of the fundamental concepts on which this type of research is based is the idea that products have images or personalities in the minds of consumers. The latter are assumed to purchase products which are extensions of their own personalities. When a study appeared which purported to show that no personality differences existed between the owners of two different automobiles (Fords and Chevrolets) which motivation research had earlier shown to have different images, it raised a question as to the soundness of the theory on which much motivation research is based.[4] This should have led to immediate attempts to reproduce the image research results or to disprove them. Unfortunately, many of the motivation research proponents leaped to the defense of their positions instead of seeking the "truth."

In summary, scientific method can be distinguished from other methods of investigation by the degree to which it subordinates all other considerations to the pursuit of objectivity, exactness, and certainty.

Difficulty of applying scientific method in marketing

In the previous discussion, the difficulties of defining scientific method and the differences of opinion as to what constitutes scientific method have been touched upon. To a large extent these differences of opinion arise from the desire of each man to appropriate the term "scientific," with its favorable connotations, to his field, but to keep as many other fields as possible on a lower, "unscientific" level. By so doing the individual hopes to raise himself and his special field of study in public esteem. Arguments on the point are useless since each participant can define "scientific" to fit the current practice in his own field.

Despite the sterility of arguing over definitions, it is worthwhile to note the reasons why some think marketing research cannot be scientific. Study of these reasons serves to emphasize the basic problems encountered in marketing research. Some of these reasons have been touched on above but will be stated more explicitly here.

Great complexity of subject. Marketing is concerned with the movement of goods from producers to consumers. The most important determinant of marketing activity is the reaction of people to given stimuli (e.g., advertisements) or, more exactly, the anticipated reaction of people to stimuli. Thus, marketing research is concerned with humans who in themselves and in their activities are more complex than the subjects of the physical scientist.

Perhaps this seems an overstatement to the physicist working on the project to land men on Mars or to the pathologist trying to solve the mysteries of cancer. But man himself is different from these subjects; he has a mind and the ability to reason and, therefore, he is able to alter his environment or his adjustment to it. A copper sulfate solution placed

---

[4] Franklin B. Evans, "Psychological and Objective Factors in the Prediction of Brand Choice: Ford versus Chevrolet," *The Journal of Business,* Vol. 32 (October, 1959), pp. 340–69.

in a test tube by a chemist will be there tomorrow, but a man placed in a given environment may change his location by his own will. The copper sulfate will be the same whether studied in Chicago or Bombay, whether studied today or next year. The same is not true of humans. Reactions of people to a given sales appeal would undoubtedly be different in Bombay than in Chicago. The style that is the fad this year may be discarded by next, and the advertising appeal that is most effective during the hot, humid days of July will likely have little influence next January. This complexity of man and his activities makes the development of an exact science explaining these activities difficult.

Additional obstacles encountered in adapting scientific methods to marketing relate to this complexity of the human being as a subject of study—particularly his ability to reason and to act on his own will. Although this central factor influences the other basic difficulties, the difficulties themselves differ to a degree sufficient to warrant further discussion.

Difficulty in obtaining accurate measurements. One of the characteristics which distinguishes scientific method from nonscientific activities is the emphasis put on accuracy of measurement. Since marketing is concerned with people, much of the information collected in marketing research is obtained by interview—a subjective procedure which rarely leads to accurate measurements. Furthermore, much of the information desired relates to opinions and attitudes which, at best, can be reduced to quantitative terms in only rough approximations. For example, the strength of a man's liking for cigarettes can be measured, but only in a relatively crude way. The measuring devices available to the marketing research man are, in general, not as accurate as those available to the natural scientists.

Contrast, for example, the accuracy obtained in measuring a teenager's attitude towards oatmeal with that obtained in the experiment to measure the effect of gravity on light rays. In the latter experiment, changes as small as one part in ten thousand million million were measured under the best of laboratory conditions.[5] In the measurement of attitude towards oatmeal, data were obtained by questioning teenagers; there was no way of determining the accuracy of the measurement, but if the results were accurate within one part in ten they would be considered excellent. A number of interviewers were used; each differed from the rest in ability, experience, and training. Some interviews may have been conducted with one foot in the door or while the respondent had one eye on her housework. However, examples of very accurate measurements in marketing research do exist, exceptional as

---

[5] Guy Suits and Miles J. Martin, *World Science and Technology in 1960* (Schenectady, N.Y.: General Electric, 1960), p. 3.

they may be. For example, the A. C. Nielsen Company, in obtaining radio and TV audience data, uses an electronic "audimeter" which records when the radio or TV set is turned on and to what station it is tuned.

Most of the measurements used in marketing are of the type obtained in interviews. Some question exists, therefore, about whether marketing research can be called scientific. As previously noted, however, this difference in accuracy of measurement is one of degree only. No measurement in any field is exact. The distinction, then, should be made on the basis of the care which is taken to obtain the most accurate measurements possible with the methods of measurement available in a field of study.

Process of measurement may influence results. When a chemist weighs the precipitate resulting from the combination of two chemicals or when a physicist measures the speed of sound, neither is concerned with the effect his measurement process has on the results. He can repeat the measurement another day and get essentially the same answer. Such is not always the case in marketing research. When humans recognize that they are being measured, they frequently change. For example, the family which has an audimeter put on its TV set may modify its TV viewing habits because it knows all the viewing is recorded. Similarly, individuals who are questioned about specific opinions may find their opinions changing as a result of the questioning. This is particularly important in studies which include interviews of the same people a second time at a later date to determine what changes have taken place in their opinions. People previously questioned frequently change their opinions in a different way than they would have done had they not been questioned. The interview may call their attention to the subject, say a brand of soap. Thereafter, they are more apt to note advertisements for this soap, the slogans used, and changes in the product than are other individuals whose attention has not been called to it.

Difficulty in using experiments to test hypotheses. Some think of experimental research as the only type of scientific study. Certainly the experiment has important advantages in testing tentative ideas on cause and effect relationships.[6] Unfortunately, in many instances in marketing research, the use of experimental research is impractical or even impossible. In marketing it is impossible to control all the factors affecting sales of a product. Human attitudes, the weather, and competing sales effort change. Therefore, it is impossible to reproduce the same experiment time after time. Thus, this powerful scientific tool is not completely available to marketing research; it is, however, partially available. Even

---

[6] For a more complete discussion of experiments in marketing research, see Chapter 3.

though complete control of the environment of a marketing experiment cannot be obtained, methods of statistical control have been developed. These permit many useful experiments in marketing.

Accurate prediction is difficult. The objective of scientific method is to predict. The scientist attempts to discover cause and effect relationships so that, given a set of conditions, he can predict what will happen. Certainly, in marketing research the objective is to determine cause and effect relationships so that the best of the available alternatives can be selected. For example, one may experiment to find which of several package designs is purchased most frequently. The prediction is then made that greatest sales will be obtained if that package design is used.

Unfortunately, accurate prediction is limited to the natural sciences. Astronomers can predict the appearance of comets to the second, years or even centuries in advance. Social relationships are more ephemeral. Who would care to predict the style of women's clothing which will be popular ten years hence? Not only do human whims and desires change, but the very act of predicting may influence the factor being predicted. Suppose a firm predicts that the use of TV advertising will produce greater sales than the use of any other medium. But suppose competitors make the same prediction and increase their TV advertising at the same time. Would the first firm still have a sales increase?

In marketing, then, exact prediction is rarely possible. But this does not mean that marketing predictions of reasonable accuracy cannot be made and are not made every day. The types and quantities of products shipped to each of thousands of markets are based on forecasts of demand. Prices of farm crops are based on predictions of consumer acceptance. Predictions in marketing may not be as exact as predictions in the natural sciences, but again the difference is one of degree. In fact, one may question whether many marketing predictions are not as accurate as the predictions of the "weatherman"—a natural scientist.

Objectivity of investigator. "The physical scientist sets himself, as an impartial observer, outside of nature, inquires into nature's processes, and tries to reduce them to simple general relations. He does not hope to be able to change nature, or even in any literal sense to gain 'increased power over nature.' The social scientist cannot, in any comparable way, put himself, as an impartial observer, outside of society, so as to get a view of social processes as a connected whole. His interests, his values, his ends, lie *within* that connected whole."[7]

The implication of this statement is that marketing researchers cannot be objective. While it is true that the marketing researcher is more a part of his subject of study than the natural scientist, it is easy to over-

---

[7] Allyn A. Young, "Economics," in Wilson Gee, ed., *Research in the Social Sciences* (New York: Macmillan Co., 1929), pp. 53–54.

emphasize the effect this may have on his impartiality. Since all research workers are human, none is without personal prejudices. Each has hopes of finding something new. Part of the measure of the researcher as a scientist is his ability to subordinate his personal desire to the facts at hand. The main distinction in this respect between marketing and the natural sciences is in the objectivity of the measuring devices available. Those used in marketing, e.g., the interview, are more subjective than those in, say, physics. Hence, in marketing the researcher has more opportunity to project himself into his findings. It is likely, therefore, that results in marketing research are not as objective as those in the more exact sciences. It does not mean that objectivity is impossible in marketing research, but that the researcher must make a greater effort to be objective.

Summary of scientific method

Marketing research is sometimes defined as the application of scientific method to marketing. Scientific method is difficult to define, but it is characterized by objectivity on the part of the investigator, emphasis on accuracy in measurement, and exhaustive investigation.

Unfortunately, a number of difficulties are encountered in applying scientific method to marketing problems: (1) The subject of investigation is usually the human being—a very complex subject. (2) This complexity of the subject, combined with the use of relatively crude measuring devices, makes it difficult to get accurate measurement. (3) The process of measuring humans may cause them to change. (4) It is difficult to use experiments in many marketing problems. (5) Since people's attitudes change frequently, it is difficult to make accurate marketing predictions. (6) Since the measuring devices available are relatively subjective, it is difficult to keep marketing research completely objective.

RESEARCH DESIGN

Every research project conducted scientifically has a specified framework for controlling the collection of data. This framework is called the research design. Its function is to insure that the required data are collected and that they are collected accurately and economically.

Despite the difficulty of establishing an entirely satisfactory classification system, it is helpful for this discussion to classify marketing research designs on the basis of the fundamental objective of the research. Consideration of these different types of designs, their applicability, their strengths, and their weaknesses will help the student in selecting the design best suited to a specific problem. Two general types of research design are established: (1) exploratory, and (2) conclusive. Each of these is further subdivided as follows:

Exploratory research	Conclusive research
a) Search of secondary data	a) Descriptive research
b) Survey of knowledgeable per-	(1) Case study
sons	(2) Statistical study
c) Case study	b) Experimentation
	c) Simulation

The terms are suggestive of the nature of each class. Exploratory research seeks to discover new relationships, while conclusive research is designed to help the executive choose among various possible courses of action.

Exploratory research

In well-established fields of study, hypotheses are usually drawn from ideas developed or glimpsed in previous research studies or are derived from theory.[8] Until recent years marketing has been seriously handicapped by a lack of significant theory and by a lack of thoroughly developed research programs to provide a background in depth for specific situations. By now, however, many companies have developed "data banks," i.e., stores of information, on their standard products which include the results of scores of studies made over a period of many years. Each study adds a little more to the total knowledge about the product and the marketing forces influencing it. General Electric reports that one study it made to identify community leaders in the adoption of new products led to a hypothesis for the next study that young people influenced their parents in this process. This led to further studies of the process of social learning in relation to age and family structure, each study providing hypotheses for the next.[9]

Marketing theory has developed rapidly in recent years and now provides the source for many research hypotheses. As recently as 1964, one author was stating, "Marketing has no theory that is defensible on the grounds of logical consistency, philosophic adequacy, or experimental

---

[8] At this point, the student should become familiar with the term *hypothesis*. It is used frequently in research work and will be used frequently in this book. When a researcher has a tentative answer to a question, he calls it a hypothesis. For example, a candy manufacturer, on the basis of his experience, might establish the hypothesis that consumers will prefer crushed peanuts over whole peanuts in a particular candy bar. Once the hypothesis is stated, the researcher attempts to design a research project to prove or disprove it.

[9] Nelson N. Foote, "Asking the Right Questions," *New Directions in Research Design,* Proceedings: American Marketing Association, 2d National Conference on Research Design (1965), p. 9.

foundation."[10] Since that time a torrent of tentative theories has rushed into the literature. A large influx of behavioral scientists into marketing has spurred the development of theories of consumer attitude, motivation, and behavior. It now seems safe to say that in another ten years a significant body of marketing theory will exist.[11]

Despite these developments, too little is known about consumer reaction to marketing stimuli to permit the drawing of sound hypotheses in many specific situations. As a result, much marketing research is of an exploratory nature; emphasis is placed on finding practices and policies that need changing and on developing possible alternatives.

Use of exploratory research. Exploratory research usually results when a research firm is called in by a client who says, "We're not getting the sales volume we think we should. What's wrong?" The researcher might guess at a number of factors—the product might be inferior in quality or style, the wrong channels of distribution might be used, the number of salesmen in the field might be too few, the advertising appeals might not be the best, and so on.

Since the number of possible difficulties is almost infinite, it is impractical to test them all. Exploratory research is required to find the most likely explanations. Such research may also be involved when the perceived problem is much less general, e.g., the research department may be requested to find why one group of salesmen is particularly unproductive or why certain market segments are buying less than others. Exploratory research is needed in each case to develop likely alternatives.

Exploratory research may be considered the step which defines the problem, while conclusive research "solves" the problem. It is useful, however, to think of the research process as a circular system. Exploratory research is the first step. As it develops likely hypotheses, conclusive research projects are designed to test these hypotheses. Many conclusive projects provide new hypotheses as byproducts and, in so doing, provide the exploratory work which leads to further conclusive studies.

Design of exploratory studies. Since the object of an exploratory study is to find new ideas of relationships, no formal design can be established. Flexibility and ingenuity characterize the investigation. As he goes along, the researcher must be on the alert to recognize new ideas.

---

[10] Michael H. Halbert, "The Requirements for Theory in Marketing," in Reavis Cox, Wroe Alderson, and Stanley J. Shapiro, eds., *Theory in Marketing* (Homewood, Ill.: Richard D. Irwin, Inc., 1964), pp. 17–36.

[11] For an interesting discussion of the use of theory in the development of research, see William F. O'Dell, "Theory or Research for the Marketing Decision-Maker?" *Journal of Marketing*, 30 (April, 1966), pp. 52–55. For an example of the use of marketing theory to develop a hypothesis for testing see A. S. C. Ehrenberg and G. J. Goodhardt, "A Comparison of American and British Repeat-Buying Habits," *Journal of Marketing Research*, 5 (February, 1968), pp. 29–33.

He then swings his search in the new direction until he has exhausted the possibilities in the idea or has found a better idea toward which to turn his investigation. Thus, he may be constantly changing his focus of investigation as new possibilities come to his attention.

Formal design is conspicuous by its absence in exploratory studies. The imagination of the researcher is the key factor. However, three lines of attack may aid in finding hypotheses of value: (1) study of secondary sources of information; (2) survey of individuals who are apt to have ideas on the general subject; and (3) analysis of selected cases.

Study of secondary data. Probably the quickest and most economical way for the researcher to find possible hypotheses is to take advantage of the work of others. In a relatively short time, he can scan a large volume of published and unpublished ideas and data. The most useful sources of such information are books, newspapers, government documents, trade journals, and professional journals which are available in libraries; company records such as those kept for accounting and sales analysis purposes; reports of previous research projects conducted for the company, including reports from research organizations furnishing continuing data of interest (e.g., Nielsen reports on sales of branded products and Starch reports on advertising readership); and data collected by trade associations related to the area of interest.

A large food manufacturer's experience furnishes an example of such research. To get a particular network radio show that it wanted, this manufacturer had to take stations in markets in which it was already advertising as much as apparent potential warranted. In studying Nielsen data on sales in all markets, the marketing research director of this firm noted that sales had shown significant gains in those markets in which the new radio show caused an "overspending" on advertising. From this he hypothesized that larger advertising expenditures generally would be profitable in all markets. Conclusive research of an experimental type substantiated the hypothesis and advertising was increased from 5.6 percent to 9.3 percent of sales. Within three years, the firm's market share rose from 20 percent to 50 percent.[12]

A survey of previous work of this type can be expedited if it is organized. The fact that the exploratory study has no formal design and that investigators exercise their individual initiative in spotting and following leads does not mean that such a study is done in an aimless manner. Enough is known about marketing so that major areas which frequently are worth investigating can be identified. Also available are many guides and indexes which the investigator can use to help locate published and some unpublished materials. Some of these are discussed in Chapter 6.

[12] A. C. Nielsen, Jr., *Key Factors in Building and Maintaining a Strong Consumer Franchise* (undated monograph).

Current developments are changing the character of secondary data searches, and this problem may soon be simplified. Electronic data processing systems now make it possible to store large quantities of data and to retrieve such data rapidly with automated search techniques. At the same time the quantity of secondary data of the types both internal and external to the company is multiplying at a tremendous rate. The result will be to make a much larger volume of secondary data operationally available to the future researcher. The impact is just beginning to be felt.

Survey of individuals with ideas. Individuals with ideas on the general subject of interest may be found in widely diversified groups. All persons who have any association with the efforts to market the product in question are potential sources of information in a marketing research project. Such individuals may include the top executives and sales managers of the company in question and of companies making similar or related products; salesmen, wholesalers, and retailers who handle the product or related products; and consumers who have used a product of the type in question or have had occasion to need such a product.

While people with ideas of this type may be found in the groups mentioned above, it does not follow that everybody in these groups will have such ideas. Unfortunately, because of limited experience with the problem at hand, lack of ability as observers, inability to express their ideas, or other reasons, most individuals are unable to give any new insights into a marketing problem. Therefore, if time and effort are to be used economically, it is necessary to single out those individuals who are the most imaginative. Among salesmen and dealers this can partially be accomplished by getting suggestions from sales managers and salesmen, respectively; among consumers it is difficult. In some instances, however, research departments have been able to locate consumers of special ability along these lines. General Motors, for example, at one time built up a list of consumers who had a special interest in automobile engineering and design and who were imaginative about future developments in these fields.

Despite the desire to find those individuals who have ideas, it is important not to concentrate the investigation only among the better educated, more articulate persons. Individuals in this group are apt to have similar ideas, whereas reactions to product characteristics or sales appeals may be quite different in other more important population groups. As a result of this desire to reach heterogeneous groups and because of the difficulty of finding those particular consumers with ideas, the typical exploratory survey is made by interviewing individuals known to be cooperative and to have ideas on the subject, plus some others selected somewhat haphazardly from among various population groups thought to be important. This is as good a practical solution as is available.

Since the objective of exploratory research is to find new ideas, it is important to give respondents the greatest possible freedom of response. Within the context of the problem at hand, it is often important to permit respondents to determine the actual factors to discuss. At the same time, most respondents need stimuli to bring out their attitudes and ideas. Various techniques have been developed to aid in this process; the following two are suggestive—role rehearsal and concept sorting.

In a study for the U.S. Department of Agriculture to determine the limits of possible consumption of poultry products, the researcher developed the "role rehearsal" technique. The interviewer asked respondents: "Suppose you were asked to serve chicken three times a week for a year to your family; in return for doing so you would be paid $15.00 a week; you could not tell anyone in your family that you were experimenting on them or that you were being paid. Will you do it?" The following responses were typical of those received:

"I'd get out my cookbook again."

"There are so many ways to make chicken. It doesn't have a lot of flavor itself."

"I think that what would happen is that there would be more variety, and you'd be inventive and branch out."

From the ideas obtained from these "role rehearsals," the researchers developed hypotheses that were later tested in a structured questionnaire.[13]

Concept sorting is a method of determining how individuals conceptualize a group of items without requiring the respondents to put their concepts in words. In one example, the respondent was given forty slips of paper with names of different cereals on them and asked to sort them into as many different groups as was appropriate on any basis he chose. When the task was completed, the respondent explained the basis for his groupings and was then asked to repeat the process on some other conceptual basis. The first sorts were on such bases as manufacturer and grain from which the cereal was produced. After these obvious conceptual bases were exhausted, however, other concepts developed such as sex of likely user, serious or amusing cereal, and everyday versus change-of-pace cereal.

Analysis of selected cases.   In some instances, detailed case analysis of a few selected individuals or organizations may be particularly helpful in gaining ideas about possible relationships. Case studies are

---

[13] Herbert I. Abelson, "A 'Role Rehearsal' Technique for Exploratory Interviewing," *Public Opinion Quarterly,* 30 (Summer, 1966), pp. 302–5.

characterized by intensive study. Emphasis is placed on understanding the subject of investigation as a whole. All aspects of the case are investigated. This intensive study of a case is apt to turn up relationships which might not otherwise be found. In one study to improve the productivity of the sales force of a particular company, the investigator studied intensively two or three of the best salesmen and two or three of the worst. He collected data on the background and experience of each man and then spent several days making sales calls with them. As a result, he came up with the hypothesis that checking the stock of retailers and suggesting items on which they were low were the most important differences between the successful and the poor salesmen.

Since case analyses are also used in the descriptive type of conclusive study, the case method will be discussed further under that heading.

Conclusive research

When a marketing executive makes a decision, he normally is selecting one course of action from among a number available to him. The alternatives may be as few as two, or virtually infinite; they may be well defined or only vaguely glimpsed. Conclusive research provides information which helps the executive make a rational decision. In some instances, particularly if an experiment is run, the research may come close to specifying the precise alternative to choose; in other cases, especially with descriptive studies, the research will only partially clarify the situation and much will be left to the executive's judgment.

Descriptive research. Descriptive studies, as their name implies, are designed to describe something, for example, the characteristics of users of a given product; the degree to which use of the product varies with income, age, sex, or other charactertistics; or the number who saw a specific TV commercial. A majority of marketing research studies are of this type.

It should not be concluded because the emphasis is on description that such studies should be simply fact-gathering expeditions. Unfortunately, it is relatively easy to start a descriptive study with the vague thought that the data collected will be interesting. As a result many descriptive studies are made with only hazy objectives and with inadequate planning. Much of the data collected in such studies turns out to be useless. Descriptive studies of this type, in which there is no clear hypothesis, are actually more exploratory in character than they are conclusive. If such studies are conceived and conducted as exploratory projects, equal or better information can usually be obtained at smaller cost.

To be of value, a descriptive study must collect data for a definite purpose. Nevertheless, descriptive studies vary in the degree to which a specific hypothesis is the guide. In a market definition study, frequently no specific statement of a hypothesis is made. The idea that selling effort should be concentrated on the market most likely to buy is, however, implicit. The descriptive study is designed to find that market, with the assumption that selling effort will then be concentrated where it will do the most good. In other instances, descriptive studies may be guided by much more explicit hypotheses. A cereal company may find its sales slipping. On the basis of market contacts (or perhaps exploratory research), the company may hypothesize that teenage children do not eat its cereal for breakfast. A descriptive study can then be designed to test this hypothesis.

Importance of design in descriptive studies. Descriptive studies differ from exploratory studies in the rigor with which they are designed. Exploratory studies are characterized by flexibility, while descriptive studies attempt to obtain a complete and accurate description of a situation. Formal design is required to insure that the description covers all phases desired. Precise statement of the problem indicates what information is required. The study must then be designed to provide for the collection of this information. Unless the study design provides specified methods for selecting sources of information (sample design) and for collecting data from those sources, the information obtained may well be incorrect.

Formal design is also required to forestall collection of unnecessary data. Since descriptive studies often cost many thousands of dollars, the unnecessary expenditures could be large.

Descriptive data are commonly used as direct bases for marketing decisions. After analyzing the data, the investigator attempts to predict the result of certain actions, e.g., he may predict that concentration of advertising on upper-income people will increase sales volume. Descriptive data, however, do not show direct cause and effect relationships. Purchases of a product and income may vary together, but this does not prove high income is the cause of the purchases. Experimental data are needed to establish cause and effect. Frequently in marketing, however, the investigator finds that he has neither the funds nor the means of controlling a situation necessary to establish an experiment; thus, he must rely on descriptive data. If descriptive data are to be used as a basis for prediction, their collection must be designed so that the ambiguous nature of cause and effect relationships will be reduced as much as possible.

Careful design of descriptive studies is necessary, therefore, to insure complete description of the situation, to insure minimum bias in the collection of data, to hold costs to a minimum, and to reduce the error to which the interpretation is subject.

Types of descriptive study designs. To facilitate the discussion on the design of descriptive studies, two types, or methods, of study are considered separately—the case method and the statistical method. The separation is required because analysis of results is approached differently in the two instances.

Case studies are not unknown in marketing research, but they are used only to a limited degree. However, they are worth some discussion and perhaps more use than they have been given in the past. The term statistical method is unfortunate, since it suggests other studies are not statistical, which is not true. However, the term is used widely, and no other term adequately describes the method involved.[14]

1. *Case method.*   The case method involves intensive study of a relatively small number of situations. For example, an investigator might make a detailed investigation of a few consumers, a few retail stores, a few sales control systems, or a few small town markets. In some instances, the number of cases studied is reduced to one.[15] The emphasis is on obtaining a complete description and understanding of the relationships of factors in each instance, regardless of the number involved.

There is some question as to whether the case method is a type of descriptive research, or should be considered only as a method of exploratory research or as a step in the research process. One view considers the case method applicable only to exploratory studies and considers exploratory studies as the first step in the research process. Thus, the case method would be used to discover new ideas about relationships which could then be tested by conclusive research.

The case method is often used in the above manner—as a first step in the research process. Without doubt, this is the best application of the case method. In many situations, however, case studies are the end procedure as far as formal research is concerned. Testing of the conclusions reached occurs only as they are put into practice. The distinction between the case method in exploratory research and the case method in descriptive research, then, is largely a distinction based on the finality of the results. If further testing is planned, the work is exploratory. The procedure, in either instance, is much the same except that more flexibility obtains in exploratory work. In descriptive research, the procedure may be more formalized, so that the points investigated

---

14 The term "survey" is frequently used to describe the method covered by the term "statistical study." However, "survey" is also used, and perhaps more frequently, to denote any study in which data are gathered by interviewing. This is a more limited connotation than covered by the present use of "statistical study."

15 Whether one or more cases is investigated, each individual case is commonly referred to as a case study and the procedure, regardless of the number of cases, is termed the case method. See, for example, Paul E. Nelson and Lee E. Preston, *Price Merchandising in Food Retailing: A Case Study* (Berkeley: Graduate School of Business Administration, University of California, 1966) in which one case is studied and the case is an entire market area.

are definitely known, and analysis can approach the quantitative analysis used with the statistical method.

USE OF CASE METHOD.   Case studies are of particular value in marketing when one is seeking help on a problem in which interrelationships of a number of factors are involved, and in which it is difficult to understand the individual factors without considering their relationships with each other. For example, independent wholesalers are constantly trying to improve their operations so as to enable their retail store customers to compete with chain stores. The case method might be applied to this problem. One researcher who has made such a study comments:

> [This] study is the first of a series of case studies designed to fill the gap on delivery cost data at the wholesale level. Subsequent discussions with other firms indicate that a number of the findings in [this] study have general application throughout the industry.[16]

Probably more than anything else, the marketing man would like to know why people buy or don't buy his product. The case method, using what are known as depth interviews, is one of the ways of studying this problem. A trained psychologist interviews a small, selected group of consumers in a manner roughly similar to that used by the psychiatrist. The objective is to get at subsurface, even subconscious, motivations. The advocates of this system believe that this intensive study of a few consumers will turn up more "true" motives than a study of the more casually expressed motives of a much larger group.

Most motivation research studies are case studies. A relatively small number of consumers are studied in depth and hypotheses are developed from the results. Unfortunately, a tendency has developed to draw statistical conclusions rather than hypotheses from the data collected. Since such studies are seldom designed as statistical studies, such conclusions are not warranted. This has been one of the major criticisms of motivation research.

CASE METHOD DESIGN.   Analogy is the method of analysis most applicable in the case method.[17] Cases collected are typically studies to find three factors: (1) features which are common to all cases in the general group; (2) features which are not common to all cases, but are common to certain subgroups; and (3) features which are unique to a specific case.

Conclusions are formulated from comparisons of these similarities and differences. In some instances, the investigator is most interested in

---

[16] James R. Snitzler, "How Wholesalers Can Cut Delivery Costs," *Journal of Marketing*, Vol. 23 (July, 1958), p. 25.

[17] In fact, analogy is the only method of analysis which can be used in the real case method. If a number of cases are collected, there is a tendency to determine such measures as averages and frequency distributions. When these procedures are used, however, the method becomes "statistical" rather than "case."

the first two groups of factors—those that are common to all in the class or those that are common to all in a subclass. For example, in a study of consumer motivations the investigator would be interested in those motives which were common to all consumers or to all in certain sub-groups such as those living on farms, those over fifty years of age, or those of German extraction. In other instances, the latter two groups of factors are most important, i.e., those factors which are common to a subgroup and those factors unique to the individual case. If grocery stores are being studied, the investigator may seek the characteristics which are common only to the profitable stores and the characteristics which are common to the unprofitable stores.[18] When a department store had difficulty with the alteration room of its men's clothing depart-ment, the store management made case studies of several alteration rooms. In studying one particularly successful alteration room, the ob-jective was to find the features which were unique as well as those which were common to other alteration rooms.

Design of case studies, then, will be based on the specific objectives of the study, and is primarily a question of sampling. If factors common to all items of a group are sought (e.g., motivations of consumers buy-ing sports cars), then a "representative" group of cases from the universe of sports car buyers might be selected. If it were desired to find what made some salesmen more successful than others, the design might in-clude cases from two abnormal subgroups—successful salesmen and un-successful salesmen.

ADVANTAGES AND DISADVANTAGES OF THE CASE METHOD. "To work it (the case method) well requires a rare combination of judgment in selecting cases, and of insight and sympathy in interpreting them. At its best, it is the best of all; but in ordinary hands it is likely to suggest more untrustworthy general conclusions than those obtained by the extensive method of collecting more rapidly very numerous observa-tions, reducing them as far as possible to statistical form, and obtaining broad averages in which inaccuracies and idiosyncrasies may be twisted to counteract one another to some extent."[19] This statement summarizes well the situation relative to case studies. In general, they are less used than the more formal statistical and experimental studies. The chief advantages of the case method are: (1) inferences are obtained from study of an entire situation, an entity, rather than from study of one or several selected aspects alone; (2) a case study is a description of a real

---

[18] Hauser reports such a study. Good housekeeping was found common to virtually all stores, but good stock control procedures were found common only to the subclass of profitable stores. J. David Hauser, "Measurement of the Vital Products of Business," *Journal of Marketing*, Vol. II (January, 1938), pp. 186–87.

[19] Alfred Marshall, *Principles of Economics*, 8th ed. (New York: Macmillan Co., 1930), p. 116.

event or situation, whereas a statistical study involves abstraction from real situations (e.g., an average may be typical of a large group but not be descriptive of a single unit in the group); and (3) more accurate data are obtained, probably as a result of the longer, more intimate association of the researcher and respondent, the greater rapport that is normally developed between the two, and the reduced reliance on formalized questions and answers.[20]

Disadvantages of the case method center around the lack of objectivity, which is inherent, and the sampling methods used. (1) Since case studies involve detailed description of complete situations, it is difficult to develop formal methods of observation and recording. Informal methods tend to become subjective rather than objective, and involve the danger that the investigator will see what he hopes or expects to see. (2) This lack of objectivity carries over into the analysis of case data. Since, by definition, formal statistical procedures are not used, the analysis is based on the intuition of the investigator. As pointed out above, this may lead to unwarranted conclusions. (3) In analzying cases, the investigator is inclined to generalize, although the case method does not lend itself to generalization. Because the sample is usually very small, because cases are selected subjectively, and because a tendency exists to select unusual cases, any generalization is dangerous.

A good example of the problems encountered when the case method is inappropriately used occurred in a case study of promotion methods.[21] A review of this project concluded:

Instead of selecting cases from as widely varying backgrounds as possible to obtain as many ideas as possible, they studied only firms purposely selected to be as homogeneous as possible. Then instead of studying each case as an integrated unit, the cases were lumped into composites, thus losing the valuable interrelated aspects. At the same time, statistical analyses were attempted with a total sample of 12 and subsamples of 6 each. Conclusions as to the differences between consumer and industrial firms from samples of this sort can only be meaningless.[22]

In summary, it may be said that, when data from a case study are classified and summarized, the study becomes statistical rather than case in nature. When this is so, statistical methods should be used. The

---

[20] For a strong statement of the advantages of the case method, see Thomas R. Williams, "A Critique of Some Assumptions of Social Survey Research," *The Public Opinion Quarterly,* Vol. 23 (Spring, 1959), pp. 55–62.

[21] Patrick J. Robinson and David J. Luck, *Promotional Decision Making: Practice and Theory* (New York: McGraw-Hill Book Co., Inc., 1964).

[22] Ralph Westfall, book review of *ibid., Journal of Marketing Research,* 2 (November, 1965), p. 421.

case method has its greatest value in exploratory research where the objective is to find hypotheses to be tested by more formal research methods.

2. *Statistical method.* The statistical method differs from the case method in the number of cases studied and in the comprehensiveness of the study of each case. While the case method involves complete study of a few cases, the statistical method involves the study of a few factors in a larger number of cases. Since more cases are involved, the statistical method must use different methods of analysis—methods designed for mass data. Instead of comparing individual cases by analogy, the statistical method ceases to identify individual cases and focuses instead on classes, averages, percentages, measures of dispersion, and more sophisticated statistical procedures. It is from the use of these statistical tools for analyzing quantities of data that the term "statistical method" is derived.[23]

USE OF STATISTICAL METHOD. Because it is difficult to apply the experimental method to many marketing situations, the statistical method has been substituted. The latter is the method most used in marketing research and is the method most used in the collection and study of data of many types. Data which the accounting department compiles showing sales by type of customer, by geographical area, or by product are analyzed by the statistical method to find the most profitable allocation of selling effort. Standard surveys to find whether a product is used more by young or old people, whether a given advertisement was seen or not, the quantity of soft drinks consumed in the past week, or the attitude towards permanent-press clothes are also examples of the statistical method.

Concrete illustration will clarify the nature of these statistical studies. A milling company wishes to find out who eats its breakfast cereal and how much each consumer eats. Accordingly, the company makes a statistical study. A sample of approximately one thousand consumers is chosen. From each of these consumers, the company obtains information as to whether or not he has ever eaten the company brand of cereal, and how many times, if any, he has eaten the cereal in the last week. In addition, information is obtained on the age, sex, income, occupation, and size of family of the consumer. The company can then compute such things as the percentage who have eaten the cereal in the last week; the average number of times that each consumer ate the cereal in a

---

[23] As noted previously, the term "statistical method" is unfortunate and is used here only because of wide usage in the field. Its use in the sense discussed here applies the term to this type of descriptive study only. No definition of statistics can apply to descriptive studies more than to experimental studies in which many of the same statistical procedures are used.

week; the percentage of "eaters" in each of several income, age, sex, occupation, and family-size groups; and the proportion of "heavy eaters" and "light eaters" of the cereal.

STATISTICAL METHOD DESIGN. If a statistical study were to be purely descriptive, i.e., if the objective were to present the situation existing at a particular time, the design of the study sample would tend to be a cross section of the universe under study. A cross section of the charge account customers of a department store might be obtained by selecting every hundredth such customer from the charge account files maintained by the store. The objective of such a design would be to select a relatively small group which would be similar to the entire group of charge account customers. A description of this small group would then be obtained and used as if it were a description of the entire list of charge account customers.[24]

Marketing research studies which are purely descriptive, however, are unusual. Most descriptive studies are designed to indicate something about cause and effect. Since the statistical study does not lend itself to proof of cause and effect relationships, the researcher must design his study to give as much evidence as possible on such relationships. This is usually done by designing a system of classification and cross classification. The objective is to establish categories such that classification in one category implies classification in one or more other categories; for example, if older people consume product X heavily, classification in the older age group will imply classification in the heavy consumption group. Detailed analysis of an example may make this more clear. A study of 1,036 families found that 35 percent bought a household durable good (refrigerator, stove, etc.) during a given year.[25] If more could be learned about why those who bought did so, it would be helpful in planning selling effort for the next season. At an earlier date, these families had been questioned as to their plans for such a purchase. A cross classification of the two sets of data gave the results shown in Table 2–1.

The table indicates that those who plan to purchase durables during a year are more apt to do so than those who do not, 54 percent to 30 percent, but it is clear that planning to purchase is not an accurate predictor of actual purchasing. Perhaps another factor is also related to the buying action. The number of such possible factors is limitless; the researcher must use his judgment and general knowledge of the field to select the most likely factors. In the example at hand, the researcher

---

[24] The degree to which a description of a small group or sample coincides with a description of the total group or universe is discussed in the chapters on sampling.

[25] The following example is drawn from Jean Namias, "Intentions to Purchase Related to Consumer Characteristics," *Journal of Marketing*, Vol. 25 (July, 1960), pp. 32–36.

TABLE 2–1. Proportion of families planning to purchase durables at start of year that actually purchased

Action	Planned to buy		Did not plan to buy		Total	
	Number	Percent	Number	Percent	Number	Percent
Did buy	128	54	236	30	364	35
Did not buy ...	108	46	564	70	672	65
Total	236	100	800	100	1036	100

obtained information as to the consumers' expectations of an increase in prices (see Table 2–2).

Actual purchases differed little among those who thought prices would drop, stay the same, or rise. But the greatest value in cross classification does not come from analysis of one factor and then another; it comes from the analysis of several variables at the same time. Table 2–3 shows the cross classification of actual purchases with plans to buy and with expectation of price changes.

When one considers only those who planned to buy, the percentage actually buying increases from 46 percent among those expecting a price drop, to 50 percent among those expecting stable prices, to 59 percent for those expecting price rises. Among those not planning purchases, the proportions actually buying are lower and do not follow the same pattern on the basis of price expectations. These data suggest that both price expectations and purchase plans influence actual purchases, but they do not prove it. Income, for example, may be closely related to buying plans and might explain more of the actual purchases. To separate this factor, different income classes could be established within each price expectation class within each purchase plan class.

Many more factors could be considered in the analysis, but it can readily be seen from Table 2–3 that more factors make the analysis complex and make presentation of results awkward. No matter how many factors are considered, one can never be sure there are not others that are more basic influences on the action under study. Cross classification is useful in indicating possible relationships, but it cannot prove cause and effect relationships.

Statistical study designs, then, must be such as to permit the cross classifications which are important to the analysis. The cross classifications which are desired must be determined in advance, and the study sample designed to give enough respondents in each cell for analysis. In some cases a representative cross section may be satisfactory. In many instances, however, such a design would require an extremely large sample if each cross classification were to be represented adequately. In Table 2–3, for example, data from a fairly large cross section sample of

TABLE 2-2. Expectation of price increases and purchase of household durables

| | Expect price to: | | | | | | | |
| | Drop | | Stay same | | Rise | | Total | |
Action	Number	Percent	Number	Percent	Number	Percent	Number	Percent
Did buy	28	37	134	32	202	37	364	35
Did not buy	48	63	284	68	340	63	672	65
Total	76	100	418	100	542	100	1036	100

TABLE 2-3. Fulfillment of plans to purchase durable goods classified by expectation of price change

| | Planned to purchase Expect price to: | | | | | | Did not plan to purchase Expect price to: | | | | | |
| | Drop | | Stay same | | Rise | | Drop | | Stay same | | Rise | |
Action	No.	Percent	No.	Percent	No.	Percent	No.	Percent	No.	Percent	No.	Percent
Did buy	6	46	52	50	70	59	22	35	82	26	132	31
Did not buy	7	54	52	50	49	41	41	65	232	74	291	69
Total	13	100	104	100	119	100	63	100	314	100	423	100

1,036 are itemized, but this sample produced only 13 respondents who planned to purchase and also expected the price to drop. To increase this subsample to only 52 respondents would require a total sample of 4,144 if a cross section were used.

To overcome this problem designs are frequently used in which unusual cross classifications are weighted more heavily than they actually occur in the universe under study. If it were possible to select separately respondents who planned to purchase and expected the price to drop, a sub-sample of 52 such respondents could be obtained by adding only 39 to the sample in Table 2–3 instead of 3,108 which a cross section selection would require. Selection of such a subsample might be difficult in this case, but in others is simple. For example, the researcher may wish to contrast the purchase rate for dried milk among rural residents with the rate among city dwellers. Two samples, one of city residents and one of rural residents, could be selected easily to give the size needed in each category.

In some studies, more sophisticated methods of analysis will be used, such as correlation analysis, factor analysis, and discriminant analysis. Some of these methods require skills in statistical technique beyond the scope of this book; others will be discussed in the sampling and analysis chapters.[26] In any case, the designs of such studies should be planned with the problems of analysis in mind.

ADVANTAGES AND DISADVANTAGES OF STATISTICAL METHOD. Compared with case studies, statistical studies involve a relatively large number of observations. As a result the analysis uses techniques adapted to mass data. Each individual item tends to lose its identity. This is both an advantage and a disadvantage. The advantage lies in the objectivity with which the analysis can be made. Averages and percentages are computed. Two competent researchers, working with the same information, will get the same average or percentage. Such is not true with the case study. In the latter, the analysis is based largely on intuition and judgment and, hence, two researchers might easily differ in their analyses of the same data. A second advantage of the statistical method relative to the case method is that it permits the researcher to make more accurate generalizations. The tendency in case studies is to jump to general conclusions from a few sample cases which may or may not be typical of the universe under investigation. A properly selected sample for a statistical study, since it involves more cases, is apt to be typical of the universe. Furthermore, if the research is properly designed, the

---

[26] For examples and discussion of some of these methods see: Thomas Robertson and James H. Myers, "Personality Correlates of Opinion Leadership and Innovative Buying Behavior," *Journal of Marketing Research,* 6 (May, 1969), pp. 164–68, and Donald G. Morrison, "On the Interpretation of Discriminant Analysis," *Journal of Marketing Research,* 6 (May, 1969), pp. 156–63.

reliability of generalizations drawn from statistical data can be measured.[27]

Another disadvantage of the statistical method is its inability to prove cause and effect relationships. This is a disadvantage relative only to the experimental method, for the case method has the same inadequacy. As was discussed previously, the statistical method can imply cause and effect only by cross classification. When several cross classifications are used, the analysis becomes complex. Furthermore, no matter how many factors he included in his cross classifications, the researcher never knows that he has all that are of importance. Thus, the statistical method may suggest cause and effect relationships, but it cannot be used to prove them in the way the experimental method can be used.

An additional problem is that the direction of the causal effect is not always clear in statistical studies. Where advertising and sales are found to vary together, for example, it is not clear whether advertising causes sales or sales cause the expenditure of more advertising effort because of greater apparent potential sales results.

Experimentation is discussed in the following chapter.

Case 2—1.   CARDIN COMPANY

On the recommendation of its advertising agency, the Cardin Company, a leading detergent manufacturer, purchased a five-day-a-week, fifteen-minute national network radio program at an annual cost of over $800,000. After the program had been on the air for about six months, the Cardin advertising manager requested an investigation in some depth to determine to what extent the program was helping sell his company's products. The company's advertising agency had provided him with audience figures that showed the program had received good ratings—especially when compared to similar daytime network programs. The advertising manager, however, was not satisfied with this evidence of the program's worth and requested the company's research department to design a research project for determining its effectiveness. In his memo to the research director he noted that it would not be possible to compare the trend of sales of the company's products in the territory served by the network in contrast to that in the territories not served by the network, since the Cardin brand of detergents was sold through wholesalers, thereby making it impossible to determine the location of the final sale to the consumer.

About two weeks after receiving the request from the advertising manager, the research department forwarded the following research proposal to him for consideration:

---

[27] Reliability of estimates made from samples can be measured where probability sampling methods are used. These are discussed in the chapters on sampling.

Research Proposal to Measure Effectiveness of Cardin Radio Program in Selling Detergents

Introduction

The Cardin Manufacturing Company has been sponsoring a daytime radio program for seven months. The question now arises as to how effective this program has been in selling our brand of detergents. A study to provide sufficient data to measure accurately the sales effectiveness of our radio program would ideally require the following kinds of information:

1. A determination of the basic characteristics of the audience correlated with data on detergent usage.
2. A determination of the basic characteristics of nonlisteners correlated with data on detergent usage.
3. A comparison of detergent usage between listeners and nonlisteners in terms of brand regularly used, type used, size and frequency of purchase, and past usage.

These are the basic types of information that are needed. In addition, the same information on other or alternative radio daytime network programs should be obtained in order that our program might be judged not only by itself but also in relation to the type of selling job being done by other network daytime radio programs.

Alternatives

There are a number of alternative ways of getting this ideal set of information. Each of these alternatives is discussed briefly below. It should be noted here that A. C. Nielsen no longer provides Pantry Audit data which can be correlated with their radio listenership sample.

1. *Market Research Corp. of America.* This organization maintains a National Consumer Panel of 5,800 families. It maintains present and past usage data for each family on many household products, including brand(s) purchased, size purchased, and amount and frequency of each purchase. They have data on detergent consumption among their families but, of course, would need to obtain radio listenership data. This they would do by mail. Assuming a 95 percent return on their mail survey, we would expect about 275 families to have listened to our program within one past month. This number is based on a cumulative monthly audience of 5 percent. Were we to employ the service of MRCA this project, as outlined above, would cost us approximately $3,100. They would not, however, provide us with usage data on products sponsoring any alternate radio programs.

2. *National Family Opinion, Inc.* This is another consumer panel operation. They maintain a basic panel of 20,000 families, but do not have any past usage data regarding household products. They could not, for example, provide usage data on detergents as to brand, size, amount, and frequency of purchase for a three-month period prior to the start of our program, nor for any later time period. Any measurement of past usage among the panel would have to be obtained via a mail questionnaire. Since this would rely on the memory of the respondents stretching back over a period of seven months or more, it is of doubtful reliability. Due to the mechanics of this particular panel, it would be necessary to make an initial mailing to locate the listener and nonlistener groups. Operating on the basis of the estimated cumulative audience figure of 5 percent, if NFO were to send 10,000 questionnaires to locate listeners and expected a 90 percent return, we could expect to have a "panel" of about 450 listeners. A second questionnaire would then be mailed to these 450 listeners, plus another 450 mailed to nonlisteners to obtain information on their usage habits for detergents. Again, assuming a return rate of 90 percent, we would end up with two groups of about 400 respondents upon which to make our final analysis. A sample of this size is statistically reliable as to the information it would yield. NFO has submitted an estimate on the project, as outlined herein, totaling $2,650, but excluding tabulation.

3. *Contest entry matched panels.* Our company ran a contest recently from which we have the names and addresses of all contestants. Presumably these individuals were detergent users. In addition, we would need to sample—by mail for cost reasons—a general cross section from the total universe of all households. If the project were to be conducted using this approach, it would be conducted by our research department. This approach differs from those previously described in that the sample would be broken into detergent users and detergent non-users; the other methods were concerned with measuring listeners and nonlisteners. Serious objections arise at this point:

  a. Using contest entries for one-half of our sample gives us a biased group of respondents. They are not likely to be typical, since many are "professional contestants," i.e., people who habitually enter contests. This, we feel, builds a bias of unknown magnitude into the survey and, in our opinion, is sufficiently damaging to warrant abandonment of this approach.

  b. We feel it more important to measure listeners and nonlisteners rather than buyers of our brand as opposed to nonbuyers. The buyer versus nonbuyer approach assumes that if there is a higher listenership to our program among the buyer group, then their being buyers is due to the fact that they are listeners. This is not necessarily so.

c. In comparison with the other methods previously described, this method leaves much to be desired from a research methodology point of view. The rate of response from our mailing would be relatively small in comparison to that of the other methods, even if we were to use a premium to induce a higher rate of return.

The out-of-pocket cost of such an approach would be approximately $2,400, not including tabulation and analysis. This is based on the need for a final sample of 600, broken into 300 detergent users and 300 non-users. The total mailing needed to provide this sample would be 6,000, based on an anticipated completion rate of 30 percent for the detergent users (contestants) and a liberal 20 percent for the nonuser group (noncontestants). In the case of this latter group of 5,000 mailings, we would need to assume that a certain percent—say 30 percent—would be detergent nonusers. Thus, for every 100 replies, only 30 could be used to build up our final quota of 300 detergent nonusers. The estimated cost-per-contact, including the cost of a premium to induce a higher completion rate, would be 40 cents. Cost of coding, tabulating, analysis, and report would be about $600, giving a total final cost of approximately $3,000.

Recommendations

A project of this nature is essentially quantitative. For this reason, it is recommended that we use the method which would give us the most statistical reliability and yet remain within reasonable cost boundaries. This would mean retaining the services of the National Family Opinion panel.

The main difficulty here, as previously stated, is the lack of any continuous purchase data on detergents among the listener and nonlistener group. This would have to be obtained by direct questioning or a mail questionnaire. While MRCA could provide us with continuous information, they will not provide us with information on the brand and product usage for other selected daytime network radio programs, since they prefer to sell these data to their clients only on a continuing basis in order to prevent "one-shot" jobs such as this. NFO will give us a mail questionnaire measurement on "brand, amount, and frequency" for all products that we wish to include. This will allow us to make a comparative analysis. Specifically, here is what we propose should be done:

I. Locate listeners to our program through an initial mailing of 10,000 "locater" questionnaires.
  A. Establish listenership for the following daytime radio network programs:
    1. Our program
    2. Arthur Godfrey Time (CBS)

    3. Art Linkletter's Houseparty
    4. Backstage Wife
    5. Helen Trent
    6. One Man's Family
    7. Don McNeill's Breakfast Club

II. Establish usage of the sponsoring products of the above programs, covering the following areas of inquiry:
  A. Whether sponsoring product type is used at all, and if yes,
    1. The brand used most regularly.
    2. The frequency of purchase.
    3. The size (amount) of purchase.
    4. The date respondents started using "regularly."
  B. Regular brand used prior to present regular brand.

III. Establish daytime network radio program listened to most frequently.

IV. Obtain basic characteristics of listeners and nonlisteners, detergent users versus detergent nonusers, and our brand users versus users of competing brands as to:
  A. Age
  B. Size of family
  C. Geographic location
  D. Education level
  E. Economic status
  F. Occupation of head of family
  G. Automatic washer versus wringer-washer and non-washer ownership

By comparing the foregoing information, through means of cross tabulation, we can determine whether or not this program appeals basically to the types of people who are the users of detergents. Furthermore, we can focus our attention on the characteristics of the users of our brand as opposed to the characteristics of the listeners to our program.

Thus, a schematic presentation of the final analysis would look something like the following:

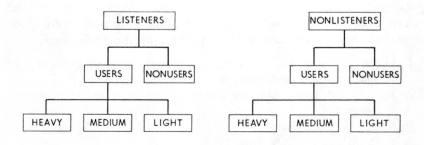

The same analysis can be made of the products sponsoring the other radio programs under observation, thereby allowing us to determine the efficiency of each program in selling its sponsor's brand.

Should the advertising manager accept the recommendation of the research department?

Case 2—2. CHEMAGRO COMPANY

The Chemagro Company was a well-known and well-respected producer of chemicals for agriculture. Because of its excellent technical staff, it had been uniquely successful in bringing to the market in a relatively short period of time a number of specialized products which were highly successful. The company was currently considering how best to sell its first consumer product—a plant insecticide named Syston.

Chemagro sold its products through its own sales force to distributors, who in turn sold to dealers, who then sold to the final user. Company salesmen were well trained and possessed considerable knowledge about the chemical properties of each of the products they sold and the effect of these properties, under varying conditions, on crops and livestock. The efforts of the sales force were supplemented by an aggressive promotion program which cost the company over $1 million annually.

The Syston product was an insecticide which, unlike most other insecticides, worked systematically, that is, granules of the product were distributed on the ground surrounding the base of the plant and were absorbed into the ground where, having dissolved, the chemical compound was picked up in liquid form by the roots of the plant and from there circulated throughout the plant. It was especially effective against sucking insects, and one treatment of one-half pound would immunize a common bush for perhaps as long as three months. The toxicity level was not dangerous although, like other insecticides, it could be dangerous to both humans and animals if large amounts were taken internally. It was thought to be an especially effective product with rose bushes.

The company planned to sell Syston through a variety of retail outlets including nurseries, hardware stores, department stores, garden supply stores, filling stations, and supermarkets. Company executives had not decided upon either package sizes or package design. While the firm knew it would have to do consumer advertising, it had made no decision on the extent and type of such advertising. No decision had been made on price, although the company knew its own costs at various production levels and the margin required by the various types of distributors and retailers who would handle the product. Before making these and related marketing decisions, the product manager felt that he needed to know more about how potential consumers viewed gardening and the use of insecticides. He therefore requested that pilot research be undertaken to determine ". . . as much as possible about consumer attitudes towards our product versus those they are now using."

The proposed research project was discussed with the marketing research director, who suggested that several small group interviews be conducted with men to learn more about their gardening habits, including the use of insecticides. These interviews would be nondirective and the entire discussion would be taped. It was thought that perhaps one such interview should be conducted and analyzed to determine the value of this particular approach. After analyzing the results a decision would be made as to whether to undertake additional group interviews using a more structured approach among both men and women in various parts of the country. The initial interview would not include any discussion of Syston because the product as yet was not available in a package with any use instructions.

The test interview was conducted among six men all of whom owned their own homes and did gardening work. All of the participants lived close to one another. The interview was done in the home of one of the men and was moderated by a member of the research staff. The participants were not given advance notice of what subject would be discussed.

The discussion moderator introduced the subject by making a brief statement of the purpose of the meeting. He asked the group to begin their discusion by talking about their use of garden insecticides, herbicides, and fungicides in relation to their own gardening. He pointed out that he would enter the discussion only to obtain clarification of a point or to ask questions which would carry the discussion further into a subject. The interview lasted over an hour, and the summary report is presented below.

Group Tape Summary

The knowledge and use of garden insecticides, herbicides, and fungicides varied widely among the individuals within the group. While all the respondents had gardens as well as lawns to care for, partiality for particular areas evolved as the discussion developed. Some were more concerned with their lawns, while others expressed ardent interest in special plants and flowers.

The garden problems confronting the members of this group varied considerably. Each respondent currently had one particular problem, but most of the problems mentioned at one time or another had also been experienced by the others. As the problems varied, so did the cures or preventives. Each problem solicited the interest of the group. They would offer advice and suggestions based on their own experiences.

Examples of some of the existing problems were: cutworms, tent worms, crab grass, dandelions, and birds and rabbits. There was no formal usage pattern of insecticides or herbicides among members of the group. In a few instances, insecticides were used as a preventive, as in the case of fruit trees or rose bushes, but for the most part they were not resorted to until it was necessary. As one man put it "I used an insecticide when I didn't have an insect problem, and when I stopped using them I still didn't have any insects, so I just stopped using them."

Later on another man said, "One time I bought this DDT, a liquid, and made up a gallon of it—that's the only directions they gave . . . for a gallon—and I was spraying for *free*, I mean didn't see anything on the plants, but I had all of this sitting in the basement so. . . . "

Definition of terms

Knowledge about the differences between herbicides, fungicides, weed killers, and in some instances fertilizers, was almost nonexistent. The term insecticide in some instances was used correctly; however, most of the time they used the word in reference to problems dealing with plant diseases and weeds. One man commented, after being asked what kind of spray he used on his roses, "Plant diseases get on them (rose bushes) . . . you know, you get some of this *insect spray* and spray it on."

Brand awareness

While specific brand names were mentioned, like *Ortho, Blackleaf Antro, Scotts,* and *Vaughan's* they usually came as an afterthought. In most instances, the respondents would describe the products' physical characteristics first, and then attempt to identify them with a particular brand name or manufacturer. A typical remark which exemplifies this was: "I used . . . actually three types of fertilizers, can't think of the name of it, but you buy an outfit of green glass and you get these like little biscuits, one is for fertilizing, one is like an insecticide, and another is for worms and what not. . . . " Another man interjected, "What was the name of that?" The answer was, "I don't remember the name of it but it's quite popular."

This pattern of describing the product first before naming the brand was prevalent throughout the discussion. Another example was when one man was asked what specific product he used on his rose bushes—"We buy a spray from Amlings (local nursery) and spray the whole bush with it."

Monitor: "Do you remember what brand that was?"

"Some type of rose spray . . . was a tube like this (hands describing) . . . I can't think of the name of it. It was a powder."

Another man acknowledged this product by further describing, "It had a picture of a rose on the can." But neither could remember what the brand name was, or its manufacturer.

Forms used

On the subject of the various forms of insecticides used, reference was made almost exclusively to liquid spray, dust, or powders. The granular form was mentioned very infrequently, and when it was, it was usually in reference to lawn fertilizers or plant foods. There was no general consensus of opinions in regard to which form was preferred. The fact that some concentrated liquid insecticides required mixing was not thought to be ojectionable. The immediacy of the problem or the amount one plans to apply seem to be the basic criteria used in determining what form or type is bought.

Liquid sprays were felt to be advantageous when a big area had to be covered—easier if one had to reach tops of trees or a whole bed or area of plants. Specific reference was made by one man to the type which could be attached to the hose or sprinkler. He felt this was most convenient. Another leaned toward the dust or powder because it was easy to apply and ready to use. The general consensus of opinion on the types or forms of insecticides used, however, was summed up by the comment "It depends on the size of the job."

Ways in which the various forms of insecticides were applied to the plants ran the gamut from application by hand to the elaborate tank sprays. In the main, the form used, in most instances, dictated the method of application; hence, as in the case of form, the way it was applied varied among the group, with no one method being mentioned with any strong degree of frequency.

Sources for information

The availability of information on garden insecticides and herbicides was thought to be abundant. One highly considered source was the U.S. Department of Agriculture. Another good source was thought to be friends and relations whose opinions were respected with regard to gardening. One man mentioned that he belonged to a garden club, and this was his main source of information.

While retailers, greenhouses, and nurseries were mentioned, their relative position in terms of who the respondents would contact first for information was not as high as the aforementioned sources. The apparent unwillingness to turn to the local retailer first can be illustrated by one man's comment, "I would go to the guy at the hardware store—in the meantime. I mean I would try to find out what this thing (problem) is, what it's called, then I would contact the Department of Agriculture and find out what they use."

The buying of insecticides

No one type of retailer was mentioned as being the place where insecticides were bought most often. Equal mentions were given to such outlets as hardware stores, nurseries, greenhouses, and department stores. It was generally felt price and convenience would be the main determinants of where to buy. The one experienced gardener in the group brought up the point that almost all garden stores will carry a known brand line like *Ortho*, and it was just a matter of making sure the prices were the same in each store.

While the other men in the group showed no brand awareness or loyalty, this one individual did continue to say he would be inclined to repurchase *Ortho* products because he has heard of them, and because he is familiar with them.

Toxicity and insecticides

A certain degree of fear was expressed when the subject of poison and insecticides was broached. While this apprehensive feeling was in fact prevalent, it was not enough to prevent their usage of such products. The group's attitude towards perceptions of insecticides was one of respect, rather than actual fear. Whatever degree of fear that did exist was manifested more in regard to vegetable plants or fruit trees than weeds or flowers. One man remarked, "Frankly, I'm a little afraid of using something like that on my plants . . . you read different materials about the possibility of it affecting other foods or vegetables, that's one of the reasons I'm a little leery about stuff like that. Perhaps I should study up on it more, but . . . I don't know."

Another added, "Any sprays for fruits—instructions always say wash (the fruit) before using."

The general feeling was one of extreme caution when it came to using insecticides on plants that are later consumed. They were thought of as being something a professional or truck farmer would use and know all about, but for the home gardener, insecticides weren't that important.

1. Should additional group interviews be conducted? Should they be more structured? If so, in what ways?

2. What hypotheses can be derived from this research which should be checked out using more quantitative techniques?

Case 2—3. GRIMM CANDY COMPANY

The Grimm Candy Company, one of the largest manufacturers of bar and packaged candies in the United States, was a heavy TV advertiser in promoting its products to children. Annual advertising expenditures were in excess of $3 million, of which nearly $2 million was in television. TV commercials were built around an animated cartoon character called Doctor Orbit. The company used spot commercials, mostly thirty seconds, during the late afternoon and early evening hours when children would be most apt to be watching TV.

The Doctor Orbit commercials had been developed after marketing research showed that Grimm's advertising slogans and jingles had less recognition and memorability among children under twelve years of age than did those of competing candy manufacturers. Because of the interest of children in outer space and science fiction in general, the firm's advertising agency, with the help of a cartoon consultant, developed the character known as Doctor Orbit. Research, prior to the final decision to accept Doctor Orbit, showed that he was a unique character with wide appeal. What could not be tested was how well the character would "hold up" after relatively long and intensive exposure. After a year of continued use of Doctor Orbit, therefore, it was decided to study his acceptance. An independent research firm, the Phillips Marketing Research Company, was given the assignment, and recommended the following study design.

SAMPLE

The study will employ a sample of approximately eight hundred children between the ages of six and twelve in the eight metropolitan areas of New York, Boston, Philadelphia, Atlanta, Chicago, Los Angeles, Dallas, and Denver. A sample of fifty boys and fifty girls will be interviewed along with their mothers in each of the metropolitan areas. All interviewing will take place in the home of the child, and mother and child will be interviewed separately (the mother will be interviewed first to demonstrate that the questionnaire is a satisfactory one to use with children).

The sample will be randomized down to the block level. Within the specified blocks, interviewers will be allowed to select respondents. No more than two households within a given block will be permitted in the sample. Interviews will be made with only one child within a family group. Both the mother and the child will be interviewed separately. Interviewers will be instructed to make appointments with mothers where desirable. As an incentive to cooperate, each mother will be told she will receive at the end of the interview with the child a gift certificate which can be redeemed for either $1.00 in cash or for $1.50 in merchandise. The merchandise will be a pound box containing an assortment of Grimm's candies. All interviewing will be completed within a two-week period of time.

EXHIBIT 1. Proposed questionnaire to be used with mothers

Date _____
Job #62–40 _____
Code number _____

1. Have you ever seen or heard this commercial before? (STORY BOARD)   Yes ☐
   No ☐
2. About how many times do you think you have seen or heard this commercial?
   _____
3. In your own words tell us what you think of this commercial. (PROBE AS OFTEN
   AS NECESSARY)
   _____
   _____
   _____
   _____

4. Do you think it is suitable for children?   Yes ☐   No ☐ (IF No) Why not?
   (PROBE)
   _____
   _____
   _____

5. Is there anything about this commercial that you think is especially good? Yes ☐
   No ☐ (IF YES) What is that? (PROBE)
   _____
   _____
   _____

6. Is there anything about this commercial that you think is especially bad? Yes ☐
   No ☐ (IF YES) What is that? (PROBE)
   _____
   _____
   _____

A. What is your husband's occupation? _____
B. What business or industry is that in? _____
C. How many years of schooling did your husband complete?
   Grade school ☐   Some high school ☐   High school graduate ☐
   Some college ☐   College graduate ☐   Graduate or professional degree ☐
D. How many children do you have? _____
E. Into which of the following groups does your yearly family income fall?
   Less than $4,000 ☐ $4,000–$8,000 ☐ $8,001–$12,000 ☐ $12,001–$16,000 ☐
   Over $16,000 ☐
F. What is your age? _____
G. When was the child that is to be interviewed born?
   _____ Day _____ Month _____ Year

NAME OF RESPONDENT _____
ADDRESS _____

INTERVIEWER _____

EXHIBIT 2. Proposed child's questionnaire

CITY _____   Code number _____
DATE _____   Boy—Girl
                                                (Circle one)

1.   Do you watch television?   Yes ☐   No ☐
1a.   What is your favorite program? _____
1b.   I'd like you to tell me what programs you watched yesterday. (TAKE OUT LIST OF PROGRAMS FOR YOUR CITY. FOR EACH PROGRAM ON THE LIST ASK IF HE OR SHE SAW THAT PROGRAM YESTERDAY. RECORD BELOW IN THE SPACE PROVIDED. ON THE BLANK LINES LIST ANY OTHER PROGRAMS THAT SUBJECT SAYS WERE SEEN.)

	Check if viewed	Other programs viewed
Program #1	☐	_____
Program #2	☐	_____
Program #3	☐	_____
Program #4	☐	_____
Program #5	☐	_____
Program #6	☐	_____
Program #7	☐	_____
Program #8	☐	_____
Program #9	☐	_____
Program #10	☐	_____
Program #11	☐	_____
Program #12	☐	_____
Program #13	☐	_____
Program #14	☐	_____
Program #15	☐	_____
Program #16	☐	_____
Program #17	☐	_____
Program #18	☐	_____
Program #19	☐	_____
Program #20	☐	_____
Program #21	☐	_____
Program #22	☐	_____
Program #23	☐	_____
Program #24	☐	_____
Program #25	☐	_____

2.   (CHILD'S NAME) If you had ten cents to spend, what would you buy? _____
_____
2a.   (IF CHILD GIVES PRODUCT ASK) What kind of (PRODUCT IN Q. 2) _____ would you buy? _____
2b.   (CHILD'S NAME) If you had ten cents to spend on some candy, what kind would you buy? _____ (IF CHILD GIVES PRODUCT TYPE ANSWER SUCH AS CHOCOLATE OR NUT, ETC., ASK) What kind of _____ candy would you buy?
2c.   And if you had ten cents to spend on chewing gum, what kind would you buy? _____ (AS ABOVE, IF CHILD GIVES PRODUCT TYPE ASK) What kind of _____ gum would you buy? _____
2d.   If you had some money to spend on ice cream, what kind would you buy? _____

3.   Do you remember seeing anything about candy on television?   Yes ☐   No ☐ (IF NO GO TO 3b.)
3a.   (IF YES) What do you remember seeing? (PROBE, BUT DO NOT GIVE CLUES. IF SUBJECT MENTIONS DOCTOR ORBIT, ASK WHAT HE WAS DOING OR SAYING, AND WHAT

EXHIBIT 2. (*Continued*)

IS THE BRAND NAME OF THE CANDY MENTIONED. IF SUBJECT MENTIONS ANY OTHER ASPECT OF THE COMMERCIAL, ASK WHAT WAS HAPPENING.)

_____

What did it mean?

_____

3b. (SHOW SUBJECT STORY BOARD AND ASK) Do you remember seeing something like this on television? (IF NO SKIP TO 4a.)   Yes ☐   No ☐

_____

3c. (IF YES) What do you remember about it? (AGAIN, PROBE, BUT DO NOT GIVE SPECIFIC CLUES.)

_____

What did it mean?

_____

4a. Do you think what Doctor Orbit said was true?   Yes ☐   No ☐
4b. Why do you say that?

_____

Anything else? _____

_____

5. How old are you? _____
6. When is your birthday? _____
7. Do you go to school?   Yes ☐   No ☐
7a. (IF YES) What grade will you be in next September? _____

CHILD'S NAME _____
ADDRESS _____

INTERVIEWER'S NAME _____

INFORMATION SOUGHT

The general areas of inquiry for the mother's interview are:

1. Recall of Grimm's TV commercials.
2. Reaction as a parent to Grimm's commercials.
3. Family socioeconomic data.

The proposed questionnaire appears as Exhibit 1 of this proposal, and requires the use of a story board (a series of cartoon frames or pictures in black and white). This series of frames will show, in a simulated sense, a recent Doctor Orbit commercial.

The general areas of inquiry for the child's interview are:

1. Brand and product preferences for candy, chewing gum, and ice cream.
2. Television viewing habits.
3. Recall of Grimm's commercials.
4. Believability of Grimm's commercials.

The proposed child's questionnaire appears as Exhibit 2 of this proposal. Please note that it requires the use of the same story board as that used on the interview with the mother.

What changes, if any, should be made in the proposed research design?

Case 2—4. REGAN BREWING COMPANY

The Regan Brewing Company was an old and well-established brewery selling both packaged and draft beer in an area extending about fifty miles from the plant which was located in central Wisconsin. Since the termination of World War II, the company had faced increasing competition from such well-known national brands as Schlitz, Budweiser, Hamm's, and Pabst. Despite this fact, Regan had been able to maintain its brand share. Other local beers, as well as several regional beers, had borne the brunt of the attack and had lost considerable volume in the Regan marketing area. In its continuing fight to maintain its position, the management of the Regan Company was considering the introduction of a new beer, which would be sold at a premium price.

In discussing the reasons why the company had not lost brand share, the president cited three major factors. First was the type of beer produced. He maintained that it had a heavier body, was browner in color, and a bit stronger in taste than any of the competing products. Second was the company's price, which was always just under the price of the nationals and equal to the price charged by the other local beers. Third was the strength of the company in its distribution through the village taverns and liquor stores. Regan always followed closely and quickly any packaging moves made by competitors. Advertising expenditures, as a percent of the total sales, had increased only slightly since 1950.

For the past several years, the company had followed with keen interest the growing importance of the supermarket as an outlet for beer. The president was convinced that, as more and more beer was sold through such outlets in his marketing area, company sales would inevitably decline because of the heavy advertising push by the national brands and the fact that housewives would be exercising greater say in what brand of beer would be purchased.

As part of a plan to cope with such changes Regan developed a new lighter beer which it hoped eventually to sell under the same price charged for the existing brand. This product was developed by the company's own laboratory after more than three years of experimentation. Despite the fact that employees who taste-tested the product thought it superior to the national brands, the president decided to hire an outside marketing research firm to conduct a taste test among men and women residing within the company's present market. If the results showed high acceptance, the president then planned to market test it in a nearby city.

The plan proposed by the research firm consisted of sampling about two hundred men and two hundred women. Respondents were to be selected from the four cities located in the company's marketing area. These four cities accounted for about 55 percent of all packaged beer sales in the area. Fifty men and fifty women were to be interviewed in each city. While no plan had been worked out as to how to select and gain the cooperation of the respondents, the marketing research firm stated that on the basis of past experience they felt certain that this posed no real problem because of their contacts with various clubs and fraternal organizations in each of the cities involved. By "donating" $10 to $20 to the club or a charity designated by the club, cooperation of members following a meeting could usually be obtained.

Each respondent would be interviewed under carefully controlled conditions. All taste testing would be done with only the respondent and the interviewer present. No one else would be allowed in the room while a taste test was in progress. Procedures would be established which would prevent respondents from communicating with other respondents upon the completion of the test.

Each respondent would be requested to taste three samples of beer. All samples would be made available in regular size beer glasses. All would be on the table ready to be tasted when the respondent entered the room. All glasses would be filled to exactly the same level and the respondent would be asked to take a normal swallow of each. The beers would be chilled to exactly the same degree and the bottles used for the test would be kept iced during the test. All beer glasses used would be dark colored so that any color differences between the different brands used in the research would not be noticed by the respondents. There would be no identification of any kind on the glasses used. All samples were to be poured before the respondents entered the interviewing room. Every other respondent was to taste the Regan Company's new beer and two other brands (A and B), which were leading national beers. The remaining half of the sample would test Regan versus another two national brands (C and D). Thus, the final sample would consist of one hundred men and one hundred women who tested Regan and national brands A and B, and one hundred men and one hundred women who tested Regan and national brands C and D. The order in which the samples were presented to the respondents would be rotated to prevent any order of presentation bias.

Each respondent would rate each sample on two ten-point rating scales as follows:

Flavor

Poor flavor	1	2	3	4	5	6	7	8	9	10	Good flavor
Too weak	1	2	3	4	5	6	7	8	9	10	Too strong

A separate sheet of paper would be used for scaling each sample.

After taste-testing all three samples, respondents were to be asked which of the three they liked best on flavor and on taste and which they liked least. They would then be asked to fill out a questionnaire on what brand of beer they bought last, the occupation of the male head of the household, age, education, and their approximate total family income.

Should the proposed research design be accepted?

3

Research design: Experimentation

$\mathbf{C}$ONCLUSIVE RESEARCH PROJECTS may be either descriptive or experimental in design. If the former design is used, cross classification is relied on to identify the effect of the causal factor. But as pointed out before, measurements of cause and effect by cross classification are never completely satisfactory. One is always able to think of other hypotheses that would explain the observed relationship, but which cannot be disproved by the available data.

Experiments are much more effective in measuring cause and effect relationships; the collection of data in an experiment is organized in such a way as to permit relatively unambiguous interpretation. One measure of the development of science in marketing is the rapid growth of marketing experiments in recent years. Only by the use of experiments can one develop the understanding of cause and effect relationships that are the basis of a science.

Because of this importance of experimentation in the development of science in marketing, experimentation is given more extensive treatment here than are the other basic types of research design. A second reason for this emphasis is that the design of experiments lends itself more readily to rational analysis.

The following discussion does not deal with experimental design in the strict statistical sense in which the objective is to obtain optimum statistical efficiency. This aspect of the subject is developed in Chapter 10. The objective of the present chapter is to point out the factors which obscure the conclusions which can be drawn from most marketing research projects and to show how various experimental designs reduce or eliminate specific factors which contribute to this confusion.[1]

Definition of experiment

Experimentation is not easy to define. As used here, it will refer to that research process in which one or more variables are manipulated under conditions which permit the collection of data which show the effects, if any, of such variables in unconfused fashion. Such a definition indicates that the distinction between experimental and non-experimental research may sometimes be a matter of degree rather than of kind.

Under most circumstances, the experimenter must create an "artificial" situation so that he can obtain the particular data he needs and can measure them accurately. Experiments are artificial in the sense that situations are usually created for testing purposes. This artificiality is the essence of the experimental method, since it gives the researcher more control over the factor he is studying. If he can control the factors which are present in a given situation, he can obtain more conclusive evidence of cause and effect relationships between any two of them. Thus, the ability to set up a situation for the express purpose of observing and recording accurately the effect on one factor when another is deliberately changed permits the researcher to prove or disprove hypotheses that he could otherwise only partially test. It is for this reason that experiments have been the basis for the advancement of knowledge in most scientific fields.

Experimental studies can be used in marketing when the researcher has established a hypothesis (e.g., that advertisement A will produce more sales than B) and when he can control conditions pertinent to testing the hypothesis. It must be emphasized that both of these requirements must be met before an experiment can be conducted, i.e., a hypothesis must be formulated and conditions pertinent to the problem must lend themselves to the necessary control.

Uses of experimental research

Although experiments are still used to only a limited degree in marketing, the variety of problems on which experiments have been conducted covers virtually the entire range of marketing activity. In each of the four major policy areas of marketing, researchers have conducted many

---

[1] For more extended treatment of experimentation in marketing see Seymour Banks, *Experimentation in Marketing* (New York: McGraw-Hill Book Co., 1965) and M. Venkatesan and R. J. Holloway, *An Introduction to Marketing Experimentation* (New York: The Macmillan Co., 1970).

different types of experiments. All aspects of product design from the basic character of the product to the smallest detail of color, shape, and size are frequently studied by experiments. For example, consumer willingness to buy soft drinks in returnable bottles instead of "one way" containers is best studied by experiment. Similarly, whether the tooth cleanser will, in fact, be most acceptable in the form of a paste, a powder, or a liquid can be further tested by experiment, as can the flavor, color, and texture of the product. Package design also lends itself to experimentation. The colors that can be most easily seen on the store shelf, the shape that the housewife finds most convenient in her refrigerator, the material (metal, glass, paper, plastic) that will be the most convenient for handling and dispensing the product and will best lend itself to disposal are typical package questions studied effectively by experiment. The United States Department of Agriculture has conducted numerous experiments to determine the variations for agricultural products that will be most in demand by consumers and the size and type of container that they prefer for various products. One early experiment of this type attempted to determine the effect that the use of cartons with varying amounts of open space in the top (called windows) had on sales of eggs. It was found a carton with 50 percent of the top open, which permitted inspection of the eggs, produced an increase in sales per customer of 26 percent over the ordinary carton.[2]

Pricing experiments, particularly tests to determine the price elasticity of demand, are frequent. Magazines, for example, frequently experiment by offering subscriptions at varying prices to different mailing lists. Retailers test the effect on sales of odd prices, "one-cent sales," and multiple unit discounts.

One carefully designed experiment to measure the price elasticity of demand is of particular interest because the researcher also conducted two other studies of the problem—one a laboratory experiment and one that was more a descriptive study. Four different products were used. In the "real" experiment the products were placed in 16 different stores and the prices varied according to a carefully controlled plan. Sales at each price level were recorded. In the laboratory experiment, an artificial "store" was set up and housewives were asked to go through the "store" and select products as if on a regular shopping trip. Prices were varied in a manner similar to that used in the "real" in-store experiment. Actual selections (comparable to sales in the in-store experiment) were recorded. In the descriptive study, housewives were shown pictures of the different products at the different prices and asked what purchases they would make if they saw the same items while on an actual shop-

---

[2] L. B. Darrah and K. S. Carpenter, "Windows Are Important," *Marketing Activities,* Vol. 17 (June–August, 1954), pp. 9–12.

ping trip. The conclusions from the three different studies are shown in Table 3–1.[3]

TABLE 3–1. Estimated percentage change in sales volume for a one percent change in price for four products based on three methods of data generation

Product	In-Store experiment	Laboratory experiment	Personal interview
A	−1.57	−1.25	−0.33
B	−1.27	−0.64	0.71
C	−1.58	−0.76	−1.86
D	−1.74	1.13	0.35

The researcher concluded that only the in-store "real" experiment generated results that were significant and consistent. Why this was so will be clarified in the following discussion.

Experimentation is probably more widespread in the area of promotion than in any other marketing activity. More and more companies are seeking methods of testing the effectiveness of their advertising expenditures, the types of media used, various appeals, the size of individual ads, frequency of repetition, the effect of color, and so on. Other experiments attempt to determine the optimum frequency of call by a salesman.

All of these problems can be studied by nonexperimental methods, but the results are not apt to be as clear as the results from experiments. The percentage of persons who say they prefer package A to package B does not tell the researcher as much as do the sales which result from using each.

EXPERIMENTAL DESIGNS[4]

As a start, it is useful to visualize an experiment in an oversimplified form. The experiment consists of exposing an experimental unit (e.g., a group of consumers, a store, some salesmen) to an experimental variable (e.g., advertising, displays, training) and measuring the effect on the dependent variable (e.g., memory of the brand name, units sold, calls made). The problems encountered are of two general types, internal to the experiment and external. The *internal problems* are those encountered in seeking to obtain data which show the effect on the dependent

[3] Roy G. Stout, "Developing Data to Estimate Price-Quantity Relationships," *The Journal of Marketing*, 33 (April, 1969), pp. 34–36.

[4] The following discussion draws heavily on Donald T. Campbell and Julian C. Stanley, "Experimental and Quasi-Experimental Designs for Research on Teaching," in N. L. Gage, ed., *Handbook of Research on Teaching* (Chicago: Rand McNally & Company, 1963), pp. 171–246.

variable from exposure to the experimental variable. *External problems* are those encountered in collecting data in such a way that one can conclude that the effect of the experimental variable on the dependent variable in the experimental situation is the same as the change that would take place in the entire universe of experimental subjects if they were all exposed to the experimental variable. In the following discussion of experimental designs, problems of internal validity are emphasized. Some attention is given to external problems, but more detailed discussion of these is postponed to the chapters on sampling and Chapter 10 on statistical design of experiments.

"After only" design

This is the simplest of all experimental designs; in fact, it should not be called an experiment, but by starting with this design, it will be easier to see the need for the more complex designs. As the "after only" name suggests, this design consists of measuring the dependent variable after, and only after, the experimental subjects have been exposed to the experimental variable. In the notation that will be used hereafter, this can be shown as follows:

	Experimental group
Experimental variable introduced	Yes
"After" measurement	Yes (x_1)

Effect of experimental variable $= x_1$

An example will illustrate. Roe herring is a traditional breakfast dish in Virginia, but in modern times is not widely eaten. In an attempt to widen the market, the firm owning Tidewater brand ran an advertisement in the Sunday morning Richmond newspaper and in both the morning and evening newspapers during the following six days. This ad carried a coupon which could be exchanged at a grocery store for one free can of Tidewater roe herring. A total of 46,486 free cans were so claimed. The conclusion drawn from this study was that no other advertising medium could produce such immediate action at such low cost. [5]

Presumably, the conclusion from the roe herring experiment is arrived at in the following manner. The 46,486 coupons redeemed is a large number—undoubtedly much larger than the number of cans that would have been consumed during the same period without the advertising. If the advertising had been run in other media, it is unlikely that the

---

[5] Alan S. Donnahoe, *The Great Roe Herring Experiment* (Richmond: *Richmond Times-Dispatch,* undated).

results obtained would have been so large as those obtained with newspaper advertising.

Problems of internal validity are so apparent in the above interpretation that one is not inclined to take the experiment seriously. Yet there is just enough logic on the surface to make the conclusion believable. This superficial believability leads to many studies of this type and to wide circulation of the results. Such studies are a dubious basis for current business decisions, and no basis at all for long-run scientific development of marketing.

In the roe herring example, the conclusion that the number of cans of Tidewater roe herring obtained by consumers through coupon redemption was much larger than the number that would otherwise have been purchased is based on an implicit comparison of the 46,486 figure with some idea of the number of cans that consumers otherwise would have obtained. Executives of the company have, on the basis of experience, a general idea of what sales of Tidewater roe herring would normally be during a period similar to that in which the advertising ran. It would be more scientific, however, to make an explicit measurement of this "normal" sales volume rather than to rely on a vague implicit estimate. A further question is entirely ignored in the interpretation presented; viz., did the large number of free cans go to consumers who would otherwise have bought these cans, although perhaps over a much longer period of time? A comparison of actual sales following the advertising period with "normal" sales for the same period would help to answer this question.

The "after only" design is even weaker with respect to the conclusion that newspaper advertising brought larger results than a similar amount of advertising in other media would have achieved. This conclusion is based on a comparison of the results obtained from newspaper advertising with an implicit estimate of what would have been obtained from advertising in other media. The latter estimate is based on past experience with other media in other places and with other products, and perhaps on general advertising philosophy. How much more scientific it would have been to divide the newspaper advertising money among several media in such a way as to permit measurement of the results actually achieved with each.

External validity problems are also involved in the roe herring experiment. To what universe can the results be generalized? In fact, the results can be said to apply only to the newspaper circulation area in Richmond, Virginia, at the particular time the campaign was run. In this particular case, this universe may be the only one with which the company was concerned. Methods of broadening the base to which results can be generalized will be discussed under some of the more complex experimental designs, particularly the section on test markets, and in the chapters on sampling.

Perhaps a more glaring example of the danger of drawing conclusions from an "after only" experiment was contained in the many analyses of the behavior of Americans taken as prisoners of war during the Korean conflict. Much was made of the growing "softness" of American men as shown by their inability to withstand the stresses of prisoner-of-war life and by the many soldiers who defected to the enemy. All of these analyses were based on simple counts of the number of prisoners who did various things considered to be less than patriotic. A later study, however, attempted to compare the actions of American prisoners in the Korean situation with the actions of Americans who were prisoners in previous wars. The conclusion was that there was no significant difference.[6]

The "after only" experimental design is better considered an exploratory case study than a real experiment. If the results are looked at as suggestive and used to establish a hypothesis for testing with a properly designed experiment, they will serve a better purpose than if used as true experimental results.

"Before-after" design

In this design, the experimenter measures the dependent variable before exposing the subjects to the experimental variable and again after exposure to the experimental variable. The difference between the two is considered to be a measurement of the effect of the experimental variable. This is summarized in the following notation:

	Experimental group
"Before" measurement	Yes (x_1)
Experimental variable introduced	Yes
"After" measurement	Yes (x_2)

Effect of experimental variable $= x_2 - x_1$

This design differs from the previous "after only" design in that an explicit measurement is made before the experimental variable is introduced, whereas in the "after only" design the before measurement is implicitly estimated on the basis of vague past experience. Therefore, the "before-after" design is definitely superior to the "after only" design, but it is still subject to many shortcomings.

---

[6] Albert D. Biderman, "Dangers of Negative Patriotism," *Harvard Business Review,* Vol. 40 (November–December, 1962), pp. 93–99.

Schwerin Research Corporation uses the "before-after" design in its testing of TV commercials. A group of consumers in a theater is told that a drawing is to be held; the winner will receive, for example, $10 worth of hair spray. Each consumer is to check on a card which of a list of major hair spray brands she would like if she should win. The drawing is held. Next, the consumers are shown a thirty minute movie in which three different commercials are interspersed. One commercial is for a given brand of hair spray. After the movie, another drawing is held. Each consumer indicates the brand of hair spray she wants if she should win this second drawing. Schwerin counts the number requesting the brand promoted by the hair spray commercial. The difference between the percentage of consumers wanting the brand in the second drawing and in the first drawing is a measure of the effectiveness of the commercial.[7] The following data are reported by the company from such a test:

	Experimental group (*205 women*)
"Before" measurement (percentage preferring Brand X in first drawing)	4.2% (x_1)
Experimental variable introduced (Brand X commercial) ...	Yes
"After" measurement (percentage preferring Brand X in second drawing)	12.4% (x_2)

Effect of experimental variable (Brand X commercial) = $x_2 - x_1 = 12.4\% - 4.2\% = 8.2\%$ increase in brand preference

This design seems clear-cut: the dependent variable is measured, the experimental subjects (consumers) are exposed to the experimental variable (hair spray commercial), and the experimental variable is measured again. The difference between the two measures is the result of exposure to the advertising. More thorough study, however, will show that a number of other factors might have caused some, or all, of the variation found; at the least, they create doubt as to the internal validity of the measured effect of the experimental variable. The most important of these factors are discussed here in some detail because they are common to all research projects and should be considered in designing all projects.

History is one factor that could cause the "before" and "after" measurements to differ. The amount of history in the Schwerin example above, in which only thirty minutes separated the two measurements, is

---

[7] Schwerin Research Corporation urges the users of its service to compare the results on any one commercial with the results from other such tests. To the extent that this is done, the design becomes more like a "before-after with control group" design. The latter will be discussed later.

so small as to be an unlikely factor of importance. If, however, the two measurements were several days, or even months, apart, the effect of history might become a major factor. For example, if a period of several months were involved, advertising activities of other brands or changes in hair styles, such as a shift from bouffant to straight and sleek, could make major changes in the "after" measurement. Thus, the longer the time period between the two measurements, the greater the danger that history will confound the results. All happenings outside the sphere of the experiment may be considered part of history.

In the Schwerin example, it is possible that the entire situation would become boring to some of the subjects. By the time of the "after" measurement they would react differently than at the "before" measurement, regardless of what took place in the interim. Such changes of a biological or psychological type taking place with the passage of time will be called *maturation*. Experiments which require elaborate contrivances of an artificial nature and which require the willing cooperation of test subjects over a significant period of time are the most subject to maturation effect.

Pretest effect is a third factor which may endanger the internal validity of the "before-after" design. In the Schwerin example, when the women were asked at the start to indicate the brand of hair spray they would prefer, they immediately knew, even if they didn't particularly think about it, that the researcher was interested in hair spray. This could easily influence their responses to the "after" measurement. For example, some women might be stimulated to think about hair sprays, to notice the hair of other women on which spray had been used, or to discuss sprays with other nearby women. All of these might influence their response at the second request for brand preference. Simply remembering the brand she had reported as her preference at the first drawing, a woman might automatically report the same brand or, just to be different, report a different one to "change her luck." Pretesting can influence later measures in many ways. It is difficult, if not impossible, to know what the net effect of these influences might be, or even their direction.[8] The more artificial and the more obvious the measurement process, the more effect it may be expected to have on later results. On the other hand, if the measurement process is not apparent to the experimental subjects (for example, if the measurement is the adding up of sales at the end of a day), then it will probably not influence results.[9]

---

[8] *Pretesting* may have more complex interaction effects. These will be discussed with the "before-after with control group" design.

[9] For an interesting analysis of pretest bias in one particular study see D. T. Kollat and R. P. Willett, "Customer Impulse Purchasing Behavior," *Journal of Marketing Research,* 4 (February, 1967), pp. 21–31; R. W. Pollay, "Customer Impulse Purchasing Behavior: A Reexamination," *Journal of Marketing Research,* 5 (August, 1968),

Measurement variation is another factor which may cause variations in the "before" and "after" measurements that may be confused with the effect of the experimental variable. It does not seem likely that this effect occurred in the Schwerin example, but in other experiments where interviewers are more active in determining the measurements, their techniques may vary between the two measurements. In testing two different formulations of breakfast cereals, for example, one cereal formula might be left with a sample of housewives. At a later date, the interviewer would bring the second formula and interview the housewife about the first. On a third call, the housewife would report on the second formula. By the time of this third call, it is likely that the interviewer would have become more experienced or blasé about the project, and would have become better acquainted with the test subject. Thus, the last interview would be apt to elicit somewhat different information than it would have if it had been made on the first call.

The four factors which raise doubt as to the internal validity of conclusions from a "before-after" design are: *history, maturation, pretesting,* and *measurement variation.* These factors suggest the need of a control group against which to compare the results in the experimental group.

"Before-after with control group" design

This classical experimental design, developed to permit measurement of the effect of the experimental variable alone, may be depicted as follows:

	Experimental group	Control group
"Before" measurement	Yes (x_1)	Yes (y_1)
Experimental variable	Yes	No
"After" measurement	Yes (x_2)	Yes (y_2)

$$\text{Effect of experimental variable} = (x_2 - x_1) - (y_2 - y_1)$$

The experimental group and the control group are selected in such a way that they are similar, i.e., they are interchangeable for purposes of the test. The control group is measured at the same times as the experimental group, but no experimental variable is introduced. Thus, the difference between the "after" and "before" measurements of the control group $(y_2 - y_1)$ is the result of uncontrolled variables. The difference between the "after" and "before" measurements in the ex-

pp. 323–25; and R. P. Willett and D. T. Kollat, "Customer Impulse Purchasing Behavior: Some Research Notes and a Reply," *Journal of Marketing Research,* 5 (August, 1968), pp. 326–30.

perimental group $(x_2 - x_1)$ is the result of the experimental variable plus the same uncontrolled events affecting the control group.[10] The effect of the experimental variable alone can be determined by substracting the difference in the two measurements of the control group from the difference in the two measurements of the experimental group $(x_2 - x_1) - (y_2 - y_1)$.

An experiment run by the National Broadcasting Company illustrates this design.[11] A carefully selected sample of 2,441 male and female household heads in a medium-sized midwestern market was interviewed at two different times three months apart. Purchases during the preceding four-week period of twenty-two different brands in eleven different household product categories varying from beer to toothpaste were determined in each of the two interviews. In the first interview, the percentage buying one or more of the brands was determined for the entire sample and used as the "before" measure. In the second interview, the sample was separated into two subsamples—those exposed to TV and magazine advertising of the products and those not exposed to the advertising. The results were as follows:

	Experimental group (exposed to advertising)	*Control group (not exposed to advertising)*
"Before" measurement (percentage purchasing in past 4 weeks)	19.4% (x_1)	19.4% (y_1)
Experimental variable (exposed to advertising of products)	Yes	No
"After" measurement (percentage purchasing in past 4 weeks at time of second interview)	20.5% (x_2)	16.9% (y_2)

$$\text{Effect of experimental variable} = (20.5\% - 19.4\%) - (16.9\% - 19.4\%)$$
$$= (1.1\%) - (-2.5\%) = 3.6\%$$

Purchases by those exposed to advertising during the three-month period increased slightly, while purchases by those not exposed to the advertising decreased. The net effect of the experimental variable was an increase of 3.6 percent of the total sample, or an 18.6 percent increase over the rate of purchase in the starting period.

In this example, the control group is a group of consumers, presum-

---

[10] This assumes the effects of the various factors, experimental and uncontrolled variables, are additive. This is a common assumption which has not been proved. It is quite possible, for example, that the total effect is more nearly equal to the product of the factors than to the sum, or the relationship may be more complex. See Richard L. Solomon, "An Extension of Control Group Design," *Psychological Bulletin,* Vol. 44 (March, 1949), p. 140.

[11] Thomas E. Coffin, *Beyond Audience: The Measurement of Advertising Effectiveness* (mimeographed report, undated).

ably similar to the experimental group except for not being exposed to the experimental variable. Another type of control could have been purchases of similar, but unadvertised, products by the same consumers, or conceivably another market where the products were not advertised. When the experiment is limited to one medium-sized midwestern market, it is clear that the degree of external validity, i.e., the degree to which the results can be generalized, is limited to the one market studied, although strong suggestions may be drawn relative to other medium-sized midwestern cities and even beyond.

This design has definite advantages over the simple "before-after" design. The effects of *history, maturation, pretesting,* and *measurement variability* should be the same for the control group as for the experimental group. In this case, these factors appear to have had a negative effect on purchases of 2.5 percent. If it had not been for the experimental variable, presumably the experimental group would have shown a similar drop in purchases during the period. The fact that the experimental group showed an increase in purchases indicates that the advertising overcame the negative effect of the four factors mentioned above and added a plus factor of 1.1 percent in addition.

Selection of test subjects is a further confounding factor that may occur in this design. The selection of people for the experimental and control groups was on the basis of whether or not they were exposed to advertising of the products in question. If the 2,441 subjects had been divided into two groups on a random basis and one group exposed to advertising while the other was not, no selection problem would exist. In the example given, however, the subjects were separated on the basis of their own verbal reports of whether or not they had been exposed to the advertising in question.[12] Thus, the respondents in each group were self-selected, almost automatically guaranteeing that those putting themselves in the experimental group would show a larger purchase rate for the products in question than those in the control group. Individuals who have purchased a product are more apt to be aware of the advertising than those who have not. The cause and effect relationship might be in reverse order to that inferred from the experiment. More generally, however, self-selection is almost sure not to give two groups that are comparable. The "after" measurement for two such groups is apt to differ even if neither is exposed to the experimental variable.

If the selection of test subjects for both the experimental and control groups is controlled by the experimenter and if the assignment to each group is on a random basis, the degree to which the two groups differ can be measured statistically. Such measurements will be discussed in

---

[12] Coffin was aware of this limitation and pointed it out specifically in his report.

the chapters on sampling. A tendency in early experiments was to "match" experimental and control groups by making them similar on various characteristics such as age, sex, income, nationality of origin, etc. Since it is impossible ever to match two individuals—let alone two groups—on all possible characteristics, the "matching" of the two groups is only a little better than self-selection.

Even though *history* seems to be adequately controlled in the "before-after with control group" design, it is possible to have biases of this type if the two groups are handled differently, e.g., are handled by different observers or at different times. Instructions by the experimenter or offhand comments by some of the participants may influence the result.

Mortality is a factor which becomes a particularly noticeable source of bias in the "before-after with control group" design. This is the loss of some test subjects between the "before" and "after" measurements. Such a loss can occur in the simple "before-after" design, but is usually ignored for the sake of convenience. It is more serious to ignore losses when the mortality rate is different between the experimental and control groups. Even in the latter case, those who drop out are often disregarded, but the danger of bias as a result is more apt to be noted. If the rate of mortality is significantly different between the two groups or if the type of subject dropping out of one group is different from that dropping out of the other, the possibility that the results will be affected is clear. In experiments where the experimental group has to perform certain tasks during a period of time, mortality may become relatively heavy among the experimental group. For example, if the experimental group has to keep a diary of certain activities, many may become disinterested and fail to keep the diary or do so only in part.

While the "before-after with control group" experimental design is the classic for laboratory experiments, it has a serious weakness when applied to the study of opinions, attitudes, and ideas—these factors may change in the process of being studied. Since many marketing studies, including the example cited earlier of the effect of advertising, are of the type that can be influenced by the process of measurement, this design cannot be considered the ideal for marketing experiments.

When people are questioned about their attitudes, opinions, or ideas before the introduction of an experimental variable (e.g., advertising), they may become more aware of the product or service and, thus, be more influenced by the advertisements than those individuals not questioned in advance. On the other hand, the "before" test may tend to crystallize the opinions of people interviewed and to reduce the influence of the advertisements on them. Or, of course, the pretesting may have no effect. All three of these types of effects have been found.[13] While the number of studies measuring this effect has been limited, the results to date suggest that the interaction effect between pretesting and the experimental variable may not be an important factor in many cases. Nevertheless, *interaction* of this type must be considered a weakness of this design.

When considered in connection with the simple "before-after" design, the effects of the "before" measurement and the interaction between this measurement and the experimental variable reduce internal validity, i.e., they bias the measurement of the effect of the experimental variable. When these effects are considered in connection with the "before-after with control group" design, they become more matters of external validity. Since both experimental and control groups are pretested, the direct effect of the pretest is measured and can be accounted for. The *interaction* effect, however, occurs only within the experimental group. If the experiment is considered to be for the purpose of measuring the effect of the experimental variable on pretested subjects, internal validity is not damaged. It is inaccurate, however, to generalize from the effect of the experimental variable on a pretested population to the effect on an unpretested population, and it is the unpretested population, of course, which is almost always of interest.

A United Nations' education campaign in Cincinnati provides an unusually dramatic example of the interaction between pretest and experimental variable.[14] Two equivalent samples of one thousand each were selected. The members of one of these samples were interviewed to determine their information and attitudes on the United Nations. After this a publicity campaign was conducted in the city for several months and the second sample was then interviewed to determine the effects of the campaign. Practically no results were discovered—the members of the second sample were not better informed and had no different attitudes than the members of the first sample had had prior to the publicity campaign. The second sample was generally not even aware that a publicity campaign had been going on. The first sample was then reinterviewed. It was found that the members of this group

---

[13] S. A. Star and H. M. Hughes, "Report on an Educational Campaign: The Cincinnati Plan for the United Nations," *American Journal of Sociology*, Vol. LV (1949–50), p. 389, illustrates the first effect; the dampening effect is illustrated in Carl I. Hovland, Arthur A. Lumsdaine, and Fred D. Sheffield, *Experiments in Mass Communication: Studies in Social Psychology in World War II* (Princeton, N.J.: Princeton University Press, 1949), Vol. III, pp. 310 ff; the lack of any effect is reported by R. E. Land, "Pretest-treatment Interaction Effects in Attitudinal Studies," *Psychological Bulletin*, Vol. 56 (July, 1959), pp. 293–300, and R. E. Land and D. J. King, "Learning Factors as Determiners of Pretest Sensitization," *Journal of Applied Psychology*, Vol. 44 (June, 1960), pp. 189–91. For a summary of pretest-effect studies and an interesting new study see T. A. Nosanchuk and M. P. Marchak, "Pretest Sensitization and Attitude Change," *Public Opinion Quarterly*, 33 (Spring, 1969), pp. 107–11.

[14] Star and Hughes, *op. cit.*

had undergone definite changes in attitude and information about the United Nations and were well aware of the publicity campaign. The "before" measurement had a definite effect on the influence of the publicity on the respondents.

"Four-group—six study" design

As shown above, when the investigator is obtaining information in an undisguised manner directly from persons, the "before-after with control group" design is inadequate. Both the experimental and control groups are apt to be influenced, and in different ways, by the "before" measurement. To overcome these difficulties, a "four-group—six study" design is established as the ideal where there is interaction between the respondent and the questioning process.[15] It can be depicted as follows:

	Experimental group I	Experimental group II	Control group I	Control group II
"Before" measurement ..	Yes (x_1)	No	Yes (y_1)	No
Experimental variable ...	Yes	Yes	No	No
"After" measurement ...	Yes (x_2)	Yes (x_3)	Yes (y_2)	Yes (y_3)

Experimental group I and control group I form the "before-after with control group" design. An additional two groups, one experimental and one control, are added. Neither is measured before the experimental variable is introduced. The variable is introduced into the two experimental groups only, and all four groups are measured "after." All four groups are preselected in such a way that they are equivalent (i.e., subjects are assigned to the four groups on a random basis). This means that the "before" measurement should be the same in all four groups except for random variations. It is presumed, therefore, that the two "before" measurements will be approximately equal ($x_1 = y_1$). It is then inferred that the other two groups would have shown similar measurements if they had been measured. The average of x_1 and y_1 is, therefore, taken to be the "before" measure of experimental group II and control group II.[16] If the "before" measurements had no effect on the variable being studied (e.g., purchases of dietetic colas), the two experimental groups should give the same "after" measurements and the two control

---

[15] Solomon, *op. cit.*, p. 140.

[16] It is necessary to have a control group for which no premeasurement is made because the "before" study may influence the "after" results for a control group as well as for an experimental group. This was shown dramatically in the experiments on worker productivity reported in F. J. Roethlisberger and U. J. Dickson, *Management and the Worker* (Cambridge: Harvard University Press, 1939). In the instance of the control group, however, no interaction of the experimental variable with the "before" measurement occurs, because no experimental variable is introduced.

groups should give the same "after" measurements. If the experimental variable had any influence, the results in the two experimental groups will differ significantly from the results of the two control groups.

If the "before" measurement does influence the test subjects directly and also interacts with the experimental variable, as is probable, each of the four groups will give a different "after" measurement, and the differences between the "before" and "after" measurements in the four cases will be the result of various factors as shown in the accompanying table.[17]

Group measured	Factors making up the difference between "before" and "after" measurements
Experimental group I $(x_2 - x_1)$	Experimental variable + "before" measurement + interaction of "before" measurement with experimental variable + miscellaneous uncontrolled variables[18]
Experimental group II $[x_3 - \frac{1}{2}(x_1 + y_1)]$	Experimental variable + miscellaneous uncontrolled variables
Control group I $(y_2 - y_1)$	"Before" measurement + miscellaneous uncontrolled variables
Control group II $[y_3 - \frac{1}{2}(x_1 + y_1)]$	Miscellaneous uncontrolled variables

These results can be presented, as shown above, as four simultaneous equations with four unknowns. They can then be solved to obtain a value for each of the four unknown factors affecting the difference between the "before" and "after" measurements.

This "four-group—six study" design may be taken as a model for marketing experiments in which data are collected from individuals in such a way that they realize it is being done. The design, however, has little practical value. The expense of selecting four groups in such a way as to insure they are equivalent and the added expense of making six studies among these four groups makes this design impractical for most marketing studies. The use of inferred "before" measurements also creates statistical difficulties in testing the significance of results.

Despite these practical and theoretical weaknesses, the "four-group—six study" design is a useful "ideal" against which to compare proposed designs. Such comparisons emphasize the assumptions on which the

---

[17] This presentation assumes that the effect of the factors presented is additive. Whether or not this is a sound assumption has not been proved. The relationship could easily be multiplicative or more complex. The presentation here is that normally used.

[18] "Miscellaneous uncontrolled variables" includes all the confounding factors previously discussed (history, maturation, etc.) plus any other possible influences. No specific account is taken of possible interaction between these variables and the experimental variable or interaction among these variables themselves.

more simple designs are based and, thus, emphasize the limitations of the data collected in the more simple designs. Fortunately, marketing experiments often permit the collection of data without the knowledge of the consumers involved (e.g., sales data) and, hence, the more simple "before-after with control group" design can be used. Even more fortunately, many marketing experiments lend themselves to the more simple "after only with control group" design.

"After only with control group" design

In the "four-group—six study" design, it is possible to determine the effect of the experimental variable from only two groups—experimental group II and control group II. Referring to the summary table of the factors affecting the results in that design, one can see that the difference between the "before" and "after" measurements of experimental group II is made up of the effects of the experimental variable and miscellaneous uncontrolled variables; the difference between the "before" and "after" measurements of control group II is the result of miscellaneous uncontrolled variables. Since the "before" measurement in both these cases was inferred, it would be the same in both instances. Therefore, the effect of the experimental variable can be determined simply by computing the difference between the "after" measurements for the two groups $(x_3 - y_3)$.

This raises the question: Why include the other two groups in the experimental design? The answer for the scholar is that the four groups and six studies enable him to study the experimental variable under different conditions, to study the individual cases of change, and to develop better methodology. To the average businessman, these may not be compelling enough reasons to sustain the added expense. Therefore, the "after only with control group" design becomes a logical modification. This would appear as shown:

	Experimental group	*Control group*
"Before" measurement	No	No
Experimental variable	Yes	No
"After" measurement	Yes (x_1)	Yes (y_1)

Effect of experimental variable = $x_1 - y_1$

The experimental and control groups are selected in such a way as to be equivalent. No "before" measurement is made in either group. The effect of the experimental variable is determined by computing the difference between the two "after" measurements $(x_1 - y_1)$. Notice that this design escapes the problems of pretest effect and interaction. Compared to the "four-group—six study" design, this "two-group—two study" design is much simpler to administer and much less expensive. It is not surprising that it is by far the most widely used design in marketing.

In a recent "after only with control group" study to determine the image of the housewife who uses instant coffee, the following design was used. Two comparable groups of housewives were shown similar shopping lists and asked to describe the housewife who prepared the list. On the list shown the control group, one of the items was "Maxwell House Coffee (drip grind)." On the list shown the experimental group, this item was replaced by "Nescafe Instant Coffee." The results measured were the percentages of the respondents who described the shopping list author as having various characteristics. The effect of the experimental variable (Nescafe Instant Coffee user) was the difference in the percentage ascribing each characteristic to the "instant coffee woman" from the percentage ascribing the same characteristics to the "drip grind woman." The results are summarized below.[19]

	Experimental group		Control group[20]	
"Before" measurement	No		No	
Experimental variable—(shopping list)	Instant coffee		Drip grind coffee	
"After" measurement—(consumer description of shopper)	Lazy	18%	Lazy	10%
	Thrifty	36	Thrifty	55
	Spendthrift	23	Spendthrift	5
	Bad wife	18	Bad wife	5

$$\text{Effect of experimental variable} = \text{Lazy } (18\% - 10\%) = 8\%$$
$$= \text{Thrifty } (36\% - 55\%) = -19\%$$
$$= \text{Spendthrift } (23\% - 5\%) = 18\%$$
$$= \text{Bad wife } (18\% - 5\%) = 13\%$$

No problems of "before" measurement effect were encountered because no premeasurements were made. Uncontrolled variables such as history and maturation influenced both the experimental and control groups to the same degree. On one basis, the "after only" design is at a disadvantage relative to the "before-after" design. The "before-after" design permits an analysis of the process of change, whereas the "after only" design does not. Thus, individual respondents can be identified and their reactions noted in a "before-after" study. For example, in an

---

[19] F. E. Webster and F. von Pechmann, "A Replication of the 'Shopping List' Study," *Journal of Marketing*, 34 (April, 1970), pp. 61–63. Only part of the results are shown.

[20] Either group could be considered the control group and the other the experimental group. In this case, the purpose was to measure the image of the shopper who buys instant coffee. Therefore, that group is considered the experimental group.

attitude and opinion study one can measure the effect of the experimental variable on those people who had favorable attitudes as contrasted with those who had unfavorable attitudes in the "before" measurement.

The "after only with control group" design fits many marketing problems and is easy to use. Many promotional devices can be tested this way. A dry milk company believed its biggest problem was to get consumers acquainted with its product. Therefore, it put most of its promotional money into sampling campaigns, but it had no real knowledge of their effect. An "after only" experiment was devised whereby the experimental group was given samples of dry milk. Then the experimental group and the control group were both sent coupons for purchase of the dry milk at a discount at grocery stores. The coupons were coded to indicate whether they were sent to the experimental group or control group, and the number of coupons redeemed by each group was counted.

Product tests are also frequently of the "after only with control group" design. General Motors ran such an experiment to determine the desirability of nylon cord tires as compared to the traditional rayon cord tires.[21] Nylon cord tires were more expensive than rayon cord tires and were alleged to whine and thump, but there was little evidence as to the importance of these defects if, in fact, they existed at all. Accordingly, General Motors equipped 40,000 Chevrolets with nylon cord tires and kept track of the serial numbers of the cars. Later they interviewed owners of cars with both types of tires to get their appraisals of their tires.

Ex post facto design

One variation of the "after only" design is called the *ex post facto* design. This differs from the "after only" design because the experimental and control groups are selected *after* the experimental variable is introduced instead of *before*. One advantage is that the test subjects cannot be influenced, pro or con, toward the subject by their knowing they are being tested, since they are exposed to the experimental variable before being selected for the sample.

Another advantage of this method is that it permits the experimenter to let the experimental variable be introduced at will and to control only his observations. This is useful in advertising tests which use commercial media. A large grocery product manufacturer ran an advertising campaign in one midwestern city. Then, it selected an experimental group of consumers who reported they had seen the advertisements and a control group of consumers who said they had not seen the ads. The

---

[21] "Are Nylon Cord Tires Too Noisy? GM Seeks Answer in Secret Test," *Wall Street Journal* (circa 1958).

two groups were asked questions about the tendency of the manufacturer's product to cause people to gain weight. Since the advertising campaign had emphasized that the product was not fattening, it was hypothesized that those who had seen the advertisements would report the product as being nonfattening to a greater degree than would those who had not seen the campaign.

The results supported this hypothesis: the product was reported not fattening by 63 percent of those seeing the advertisements, but by only 56 percent of the control group. But the conclusion that the advertisements were successful might be premature. The members of the experimental and control groups were actually self-selected. Those who said they had seen the ads were very likely the ones on whom the ads made some impression. It is also quite likely that some of those who said they had not seen the ads actually had, but did not remember having seen them.[22]

If the experimental variable is such that exposure to it can be determined objectively on an *ex post facto* basis, this bias of self-selection can be eliminated and the design becomes essentially the same as the "after only with control group" design. In this latter case, the *ex post facto* design may have a definite advantage over the other design, as the experimental variable will have exerted its influence in an entirely natural setting. Whether this is an advantage or not depends on whether or not the experimenter wants to study the effect of the variable on a representative segment of the population or on those who by choice expose themselves to the variable. An example would be a study to determine the effect of ownership of color television on the TV station watched. Ownership, or at least possession, of a color television set can be determined objectively. It should be noted that the *ex post facto* design is the same as the statistical, cross-classification type of study discussed in the previous chapter. For example, families under study might be classified into two classes—those with color TV sets and those without. The number of hours each group viewed each of the available TV stations could then be recorded and comparisons made. Because the *ex post facto* design is essentially cross classification, some students prefer not to consider it an experimental design.

The term *ex post facto* is also used to describe designs in which an attempt is made to create equivalent experimental and control groups after the experimental group has been exposed to the variable under

---

[22] These results were found in the classic study of the effect of orientation films on soldiers during World War II. Samuel A. Stouffer, "Some Observations on Study Design," *American Journal of Sociology*, Vol. LV (January, 1950), p. 356. Stouffer reports it was much easier to "sell" the results of the *ex post facto* experiments, no matter how biased they may have been, because they tended to show the desired results. This has a familiar ring for most market researchers.

study. This equalizing is attempted through matching of individual subjects on a number of characteristics for which information is available. The hopelessness of such matching, either on an *ex post facto* basis or before exposure to the experimental variable, is illustrated in one such study.[23] Starting with a universe of 2,127, the experimenter ended with experimental and control groups of only 23 each and, of course, these were matched on only a few variables.

Panel design

In most marketing research experiments, the subjects (individuals, dealers, etc.) from whom information is to be obtained are selected by some sampling procedure. After the information required by the project is obtained, these subjects are not "used" again. In some instances, however, a sample is recruited, and information is obtained from the members continuously or at intervals over a period of time. A permanent or fixed sample of this type is called a panel. Panels are used for both exploratory and conclusive studies. The procedure in using them is basically the same in each case; however, when used in an experiment the panel must be viewed as having a design which can be depicted in the manner shown in the accompanying table.

	Experimental group
First measurement	Yes (x_1)
Second measurement	Yes (x_2)
First experimental variable	Yes
Third measurement	Yes (x_3)
Second experimental variable	Yes
Fourth measurement	Yes (x_4)
Fifth measurement	Yes (x_5)
Third experimental variable	Yes
Etc.	

Measurements are taken at intervals (e.g., weekly reports by consumers on food products purchased), and experimental variables (e.g., a new package size) are introduced when desired. The result is a design similar to a series of "before-after" experiments.

Any of the measurements can be considered "before" measurements for the introduction of experimental variables thereafter. Similarly, any measurement can be used as an "after" measurement for preceding variables. When used in this simple manner (e.g., using the second and third measurements in the above table as the "before" and "after" measurements around the first experimental variable), panel data become

---

[23] F. S. Chapin, *Experimental Designs in Sociological Research,* rev. ed. (New York: Harper and Brothers, 1955), pp. 99–124.

essentially the same as the "before-after" design. As such, panel data are subject to criticism with respect to the lack of control of *history.* Such use of panel data is weak at best.

Better experimental design is achieved with panel data if the data are looked at as a time series—numerous measurements are made both before and after the introduction of the experimental variable. Trends can then be established as a base from which to measure the effect of the experimental variable. From the following hypothetical examples, however, it can be seen how difficult this may be.

FIGURE 3–1

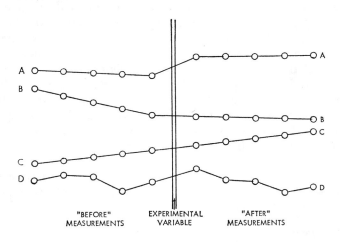

In the graph, the small circles to the left of the line labeled "experimental variable" are meant to indicate on a vertical scale the relative size of a series of measurements of some particular factor under study, for example, consumer purchases of a product; the circles to the right of the "experimental variable" line are a series of measurements after the introduction of the experimental variable. Assume that the experimental variable is a shift in channel of distribution. In examples A and B in the graph, one would be inclined to infer that the experimental variable (change in channels) had a favorable effect on sales. In C and D, it seems unlikely that the change in channels had any effect. The latter example, D, probably suggests the type of data that are most frequently obtained from panels, i.e., no clear change of purchase pattern occurs immediately after the experimental variable.

To use panel data as an effective experiment, it is important that the experimenter predict in advance the trend that he would expect if the experimental variable were not introduced. This prediction becomes, in effect, a control group measurement against which the measurement obtained after the introduction of the experimental variable is compared. Even so, it is clear that any of innumerable factors of *history* could influence the subject under study (consumer purchases in the example) and, thus, confuse the interpretation of the effect of the change in channels. Intimate knowledge and observation of the subject under study will enable the experimenter and executives using his results to make judgments as to the probability of outside factors (*history*) affecting the outcome.

The practice of hunting through past panel data to find a time when sales (or another factor) changed and then attempting to find some causal factor that changed at the same time cannot be considered experimentation. Such practice may be good exploratory research, but hypotheses drawn in this manner must be subjected to more controlled study.

Panels are used widely in marketing research. For this reason, they are given a more extended discussion at this point.[24]

Use of panels. In marketing research practice, the term panel is applied to two different types of operation. The most common usage of the word in the past has been with respect to a fixed sample from which the same type of information was collected continuously or at regular intervals; panels which reported all food products purchased or all television shows viewed were typical. The preceding discussion of the flow of data from a panel viewed as an experimental design is based on this concept of a panel.

In recent years, another type of panel operation has become common. A panel of respondents is maintained for use on any appropriate research project which may come up. The panel operator records various characteristics of each respondent on the panel so that, when a particular project materializes, he can select the proper number of participants with the desired characteristics. Respondents in such panels may be asked to participate in a number of different projects, each an entirely separate research study, unrelated to any of the others. The use of a panel in this latter manner is of the "after only" design and not a *bona fide* experiment. Nevertheless, the discussion of panel advantages and limitations which appears below is pertinent to both types of panel unless otherwise noted.

Continuous panels of consumers are maintained to furnish data on consumer purchases of various products by types of consumers; to test new products or modifications of old ones; and to measure the number and types of individuals viewing specific TV programs, listening to

---

[24] For a more detailed discussion of panels see Harper W. Boyd, Jr. and Ralph Westfall, *An Evaluation of Continuous Consumer Panels as a Source of Marketing Information* (Chicago: American Marketing Association, 1960).

radios, and reading magazines and newspapers. Retail store panels furnish continuous data on sales of individual products in total, by package types, by store types, at various prices, and with different markups for the retailer. Panels of business executives are used to obtain "expert" forecasts of sales and general business conditions.

In recent years effective use has been made of panels in developing early forecasts of long-run sales for new products. A consumer panel is established in one or more test markets and the new product then introduced to those test markets. The percentage of consumers buying the product and the percentage making repeat purchases are obtained from continuing reports furnished by the panel. For example, the hypothetical results shown in Figures 3–2 and 3–3 might be obtained for a new cold breakfast cereal.

FIGURE 3–2. Cumulative percentage of all cold cereal buyers buying Brand A the first time

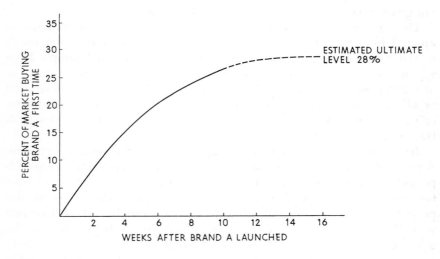

The data in Figures 3–2 and 3–3 suggest that 28 percent of all cold cereal buyers could ultimately be persuaded to buy Brand A at least once (market penetration), and that these buyers would continue to buy Brand A at a rate that would stabilize at about 12 percent of their cold cereal purchases (repeat purchase rate). The dotted lines at the outer ends of the curves are intended to suggest that the leveling-off points can be predicted from the rates of change in the curves before they actually do level off. From the above hypothetical data the predicted long-term market share for Brand A would be:

market penetration × repeat purchase rate = market share
28% × 12% = 3.36% of market

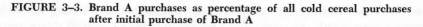

FIGURE 3–3. Brand A purchases as percentage of all cold cereal purchases after initial purchase of Brand A

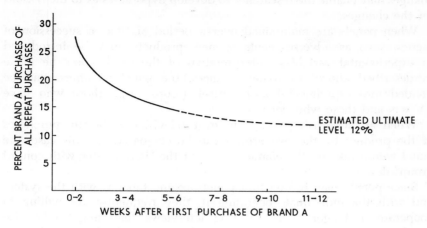

This percentage applied to estimated total sales of cold cereal gives a forecast of sales of Brand A. The above is the basic model for forecasting new product sales from early panel data. A number of refinements have been developed by various researchers and current work is expected to provide further improvements.[25]

While the above examples suggest the most common uses of continuous panels, there are many others.[26]

Advantages in using panels. The various methods used in collecting data from panel members have both advantages and disadvantages; however, these apply to any type of sample, and will be discussed in the chapter on data collection. Other advantages and disadvantages, however, are unique to the panel design.

Probably the most important single advantage of the panel design is analytical. Since data are collected from the same individuals over time, the specific individuals who change or who do not change (e.g., those who switch to different brands and those who are loyal to a specific brand) can be studied. This enables the researcher to determine the kind of person who changes brands and who does not change, thus suggesting the segment of the population on which promotional effort

---

[25] The interested reader is referred to J. Baum and K. E. R. Dennis, "The Estimation of the Expected Brand Share of a New Product" (ESOMAR Congress, 1961); J. H. Parfitt and B. J. K. Collins, "Use of Consumer Panels for Brand-Share Prediction," *Journal of Marketing Research*, 5 (May, 1968), pp. 131–45; and D. H. Ahl, "New Product Forecasting Using Consumer Panels," *Journal of Marketing Research*, 7 (May, 1970), pp. 160–67.

[26] Panels are maintained by various types of organizations. Some companies make a business of conducting such panels and selling the results on a subscription or fee basis. Other panels are maintained by manufacturers, large retailers, publishers, and radio and TV organizations for their own use and/or for sale to subscribers.

can most successfully be concentrated. Analysis of the timing of such changes may enable the researcher to develop hypotheses as to the reasons for the changes.

When panels are maintained over a period of time, a succession of tactics, such as advertisements or new products, may be introduced as experimental variables. Interpretation of the results may be made as described above. In some instances, the panel members may be divided into experimental and control groups (e.g., those who have TV sets and those who don't).

When an advertising campaign over television is begun, purchases of the product by the two groups can be compared. In this case, the panel would take on the characteristics of the "before-after with control group" design.

Since people who belong to a panel become familiar with the system and with the individuals operating it, they frequently are willing to cooperate in longer, more exacting interviews than might otherwise be the case. When data are collected from a sample on only one occasion, only a limited amount of classification information (income, age, occupation, etc.) can be obtained, because long interviews become difficult to manage. When the same individuals are included in a panel, a larger volume of classification data can be collected, because the research organization can afford to spend more time and effort in securing information that will be used in a number of projects. With the wider variety of classification data, more detailed analyses can be made.

Since the same individuals are involved in all the "before" and "after" measurements, small changes can be identified more easily than if separate studies were made using two independent, but comparable, samples. In the latter case, small changes can be caused by sampling fluctuations and cannot definitely be attributed to the experimental variable.

When data are collected from panels on a continuous basis with a "diary," another advantage is alleged. Since consumers presumably record their purchases when they arrive home with them, or record the programs they listen to while the TV set is on, the memory problem tends to be eliminated and the information tends to be more accurate than would be the case if an interviewer inquired about the purchases or programs a day, a week, or a month later. To the extent that panel members do not make entries currently, this advantage is, of course, lost.

A growing body of evidence indicates that well-run consumer panels using continuous reporting diaries can yield fairly accurate projections of total retail sales of a variety of consumer products. Comparison of such data with data obtained from surveys in which consumers are asked to recall purchases of various products during a previous period indicates that recall methods greatly overstate sales of some products, overstate the sales of most products to some degree, but understate the sales of other products. Compared to sales estimates based on panel diaries, recall methods overstate market shares 50 percent for leading, nationally advertised brands and 10 percent for other nationally advertised brands, but understate sales of leading chain store private brands by 62 percent according to one study. Similarly, recall methods tend to overstate sales of perishable foods by 83 percent, staple foods by 54 percent and nonfoods by only 5 percent.[27]

In another study, the results obtained by a combination of a diary and mechanical recorder as a method of measuring TV viewing were compared to the results from questioning over the telephone during the progress of the programs in question.[28] No significant differences were found between the results obtained by the two methods.

In regard to the cost factor, the panel may be at an advantage in some cases and a disadvantage in others. If data are desired at frequent intervals, it is undoubtedly cheaper to maintain a continuous panel from which to obtain the information than to select a new sample at each interval. If data are needed less frequently, this advantage may turn into a disadvantage. In the use of a panel for a number of independent "one shot" studies as compared to collecting the same information by a series of individual studies, the cost question becomes one of fixed versus variable costs. Fixed costs of the panel are the costs of recruiting and maintaining a proper assortment of panel members. For a national research firm, such a panel might include 15,000 members. Fixed costs of handling individual studies are sunk in the recruitment, training, and maintenance of perhaps 150 supervisors and 1,000 interviewers. The fixed cost for the panel is, thus, much larger than for the field force.[29]

Since the panel members have agreed to cooperate on projects as they come along, data can frequently be obtained from them by mail with close to 100 percent response. This is much cheaper than collecting information by personal interview, in which case interviewer costs (variable costs) become the major single item of expense. In all but a few instances of short questionnaires and flexible sampling methods, these variable interviewer costs will more than offset the higher fixed costs

[27] Seymour Sudman, "On the Accuracy of Recording of Consumer Panels: II," *Journal of Marketing Research,* 1 (August, 1964), pp. 69–83. See also J. H. Parfitt, "A Comparison of Purchase Recall with Diary Panel Records," *Journal of Advertising Research,* 7, pp. 16–31.

[28] Warren N. Cordell and Henry A. Rahmel, "Are Nielsen Ratings Affected by Non-Cooperation, Conditioning or Response Error?" *Journal of Advertising Research,* Vol. 2 (September, 1962), pp. 45–49.

[29] William F. O'Dell, "Personal Interviews or Mail Panels?" *Journal of Marketing,* Vol. 26 (October, 1962), p. 38.

of the panel.[30] This cost advantage is largely the advantage of collecting data by mail instead of by personal interview, although it is the membership in the panel that insures a high percentage return. Problems are encountered, however, in collecting data by mail; these will be discussed in some detail in the chapter on data collection methods.

Disadvantages of using panels. Basic panel disadvantages can be grouped into two categories: (1) those relating to the nonrepresentativeness of the members of a panel; and (2) those relating to bias in responses from panel members.

Since cooperating with a research organization continuously or at regular intervals involves some effort on the part of panel members, many individuals will decline to serve on panels. This raises the question of whether the sample can be truly representative of the universe being studied, regardless of the fact that the sample may correspond with the universe on certain selected characteristics. To hold refusals of this type to a minimum, many panels pay the members in money or merchandise; but this raises the further question of whether or not premiums attract a special type of panel members. It is often assumed that both the highest and lowest social classes are underrepresented in panels. The former are not interested in the small payments and the latter lack the ability to perform the reporting tasks. No measure of the effect of this probable bias is available.

The best continuing panels use an objective sample design to designate the individuals or homes to be included in the original panel. Refusal to participate immediately eliminates a significant percentage of those so designated, up to as much as 50 percent, or perhaps more, depending on the type of cooperation requested.[31] These losses are replaced by substitutes with similar characteristics, such as geographical area and city size in which they live, income level, and age of housewife.

It is usually assumed that a panel is made up of the same individuals at each time information is collected. To keep the same individuals active in the panel, most researchers offer inducements such as payments that increase as continued cooperation is obtained. Nevertheless, every panel has a certain mortality—often as much as 20 percent per year for those operating over that long a period. Some people die, others move away, and others just quit. These losses are replaced by new members with similar characteristics as far as these characteristics are known, but the probability that the replacements differ from the original

[30] *Ibid.* O'Dell suggests as a rule of thumb that any study in which interviewer time per completed interview exceeds thirty minutes can be done more cheaply by mail panel.

[31] See Cordell and Rahmel, *op. cit.*, pp. 45–49; and Marion G. Sobol, "Panel Mortality and Panel Bias," *Journal of the American Statistical Association*, Vol. 54 (March, 1959), pp. 52–68.

group in some significant, but unknown, ways is always present. Panels from which a continuous record of television viewing are obtained tend to stabilize at about 45 percent of the homes originally designated for the panel.[32] A panel which was interviewed only once every six months had shrunk to 52 percent of the designated sample by the fifth interview.[33]

Despite these alarming rates of original noncooperation and mortality thereafter, the few studies that have attempted to measure the effect of such losses on the makeup of the panel have tended to conclude that those remaining are quite similar on known characteristics to those who drop out and that purchasing, television, and radio habits are similar.[34] There is some evidence, however, that those who have the least interest in the subject under study are most apt to drop out. A consumer panel studying certain products found that nonusers of the products were more apt to drop out after the first interview than were users. The results shown in the accompanying table were encountered.[35]

	Percentage dropping out after fir t interview		
	Coffee	*Cosmetics*	*Tobacco*
Users	46	40	41
Nonusers	54	59	49

Most panels maintained for use on "one shot" studies are kept in proportion to the total population with respect to such characteristics as those mentioned above. It is probable that such panels are less representative than those originally based on an objective sampling design. Evidence indicates that at least one such panel included a considerably larger percentage of home and car owners than the total population, and that consumption of products not related to the characteristics on which the panel was "balanced" was considerably different from consumption by the total population.[36]

Response errors by members of panels are generally thought to result from change of habits, from self-consciousness, development of "expertise," attempts by the panel members to "look good," the bias of boredom or annoyance from repeated interviews or continuous reporting, failure to keep diaries on a current basis, and fatigue from completing overly

[32] Cordell and Rahmel, *op. cit.*, p. 46.

[33] Sobol, *op. cit.*, p. 55.

[34] *Ibid.*, and Cordell and Rahmel, *op. cit.*, p. 46.

[35] Reported in Morris Rosenberg, Wagner Thielens, and Paul F. Lazarsfeld, "The Panel Study," *Research Methods in Social Relations*, Part II (edited by Marie Jahoda, Morton Deutsch, and Stuart W. Cook) (New York: Dryden Press, 1951), p. 599; Sobol, *op. cit.*, found the same result, but to a smaller degree.

[36] O'Dell, *op. cit.*, p. 35.

long questionnaires or diaries. The latter is no different from that which occurs with single surveys, unless panel questionnaires and diaries tend to be made longer than others because of the established rapport with the panel members. Some consumer purchase diaries, are, in fact, quite lengthy.

Most operators of commercial "continuous" panels concede that the actions of new members of their panels are not typical, but they provide little data as to the extent of this bias or the length of time that it persists. The tendency appears to be for new panel members to increase the activity that is being recorded, e.g., television viewing or food purchasing.[37] One study found new panel members shopped more on weekends and concentrated their purchases in particular shopping trips more than did older panel members, while the latter tended to buy fewer brands.[38] To eliminate the effects of this bias, panel operators exclude the data from new members from final results. When members have belonged to the panel for a period of four to six weeks, they are included in the tabulation of the entire panel.

After participating in a panel for some time, some individuals may begin to think of themselves as "experts" and to try to act as they think experts would act, rather than as they themselves would normally act.[39] Others may attempt to "look good" by buying higher priced items than they might otherwise, or by trading at more fashionable stores. Plausible as these arguments seem, the limited data available indicate that these effects do not occur, or occur in such a manner as to offset each other. Even membership over periods of ten years or more apparently has little effect.[40] One exception may be in the case of repeated studies in which learning can take place. Individuals who are used on repeated product tests involving the same product may learn to spot particular brands even though the names are disguised.[41]

As the novelty of panel membership wears off, interest will decline and cooperation will tend to become mechanical. Diaries may be filled out just before they are sent in rather than as the events recorded take place. Panel operators try to overcome such tendencies by encouragement,

---

[37] A. S. C. Ehrenberg, "A Study of Some Potential Biases in the Operation of a Consumer Panel," *Applied Statistics: A Journal of the Royal Statistical Society,* Vol. 9 (March, 1960), pp. 20–27.

[38] D. G. Morrison, R. E. Frank, and W. F. Massy, "A Note on Panel Bias," *Journal of Marketing Research,* 3 (February, 1966), pp. 85–88.

[39] At least one research organization thinks the development of "expertise" may be an advantage rather than a disadvantage. (Unpublished report on the panel operated by Market Facts, Inc. [Chicago: no date], p. 7.)

[40] Cordell and Rahmel, *op. cit.,* p. 47; Ehrenberg, *op. cit.,* p. 22; and C. H. Sandage, "Do Research Panels Wear Out?" *Journal of Marketing,* Vol. 20 (April, 1956), pp. 397–401.

[41] John Ortengren, "When Don't Research Panels Wear Out?" *Journal of Marketing,* Vol. 21 (April, 1957), p. 442.

emphasis on the importance of the data, remuneration, and "inspirational" communications. An experiment with a special shopping trip record that was designed to get the housewife to open the diary after each shopping trip proved to increase measurably the purchases recorded.[42]

In the same study purchases were found to be more completely recorded in a ledger diary, which listed the items to be recorded, than in a journal diary, in which purchases were recorded in time sequence. Rather large increases in the work load assigned panels was found to have little effect on reporting. Compensation was found to be necessary to keep households reporting, but the level of compensation had little, if any, effect on the accuracy of reporting.[43]

Factorial designs

In the experimental designs that have been discussed, a single experimental variable, with usually only one "level," was considered. In the "after only with control group" design, the possibility of testing several versions of the variable was pointed out; e.g., several different ads could be tested, each with a separate group. All but one group alternately could be considered as control groups against which to compare the experimental group, or an additional control group not exposed to any advertising could be used to protect against possible negative effects of all ads.

Factorial designs permit the experimenter to test two or more variables at the same time and to determine not only the main effects of each of the variables, but also to measure the interaction effects of the variables. Consider the problem of determining the proper concentration of sugar and flavor in a soft drink. A simple approach would be to make up a batch of the optimum mixture as judged by the producer and to have a sample of consumers taste it and competing products and indicate an order of preference. The consumers might even be asked to comment on the degree of sugar and flavor. Another approach would be to have several different degrees of sugar content with the flavor held constant. Consumers could then taste a sample of each and indicate a preference. Sugar could then be held constant and flavor varied.

The latter approach might indicate that heavy sugar and heavy flavor were both preferred, but a product with such a mixture might turn out to be unpalatable. When the flavor is strong, sugar may become less desirable. Such considerations make it important to test various levels of sugar content combined with various levels of flavor. Suppose four different degrees of sugar content and four of flavor were selected as

---

[42] Seymour Sudman, "On the Accuracy of Recording of Consumer Panels: II," *Journal of Marketing Research,* 1 (August, 1964), pp. 69–83.

[43] *Ibid.*

possible characteristics of the final product.[44] Sixteen different combinations can be made from these variations, as shown in the following table.

Flavor intensity	Sugar content			
	1	2	3	4
1)	a	b	c	d
2)	e	f	g	h
3)	i	j	k	l
4)	m	n	o	p

Each of the sixteen formula variations (a to p) can be given to a sample of consumers and their reactions measured on various bases—for example, a preference scale from one to ten. The following hypothetical data illustrate results that might be obtained.

Flavor intensity	Sugar content			
	1	2	3	4
1)	4.9	6.0	5.0	3.6
2)	6.1	7.3	5.1	3.8
3)	8.1	9.2	8.3	4.6
4)	6.2	6.4	6.2	3.2

The second degree of sugar content and third degree of flavor intensity are each preferred over all levels of their own variable, no matter what the level of the other variable. The combination of these two is the preferred product formula, i.e., it has the highest preference rating of 9.2. The combination of the fourth level of each of the variables is the least preferred product formula; its preference rating is 3.2.

In the above example, each of the two variables was tested at four different levels. Actually, the number of levels for each variable is determined by the thoroughness with which the experimenter wishes to study the problem, the range over which he considers it useful to study the variable, the degree of change necessary to make a discernible difference to the consumer, and cost.[45]

While two variables were considered in the factorial design given above, it is possible to test three or more variables. Assume that color was a third factor that might influence consumer preference for a drink.

---

[44] The example given is drawn from *Product Evaluation* (Chicago: Market Facts, Inc., 1962), p. 30 ff.

[45] For an interesting 2 × 2 factorial design in a pricing experiment with findings analysis see W. D. Barclay, "Factorial Design in a Pricing Experiment," *Journal of Marketing Research,* 6 (November, 1969), pp. 427–29.

Four different colors could be tested, but to include each color variation with each possible combination of sugar and flavor would require sixty-four different cells and would make the experiment an expensive one. To economize in situations of this sort a variation of the factorial design has been developed—the Latin Square.

If a meat packer wanted to test the effect of price differentials on the sale of prepackaged chickens, he might design a Latin Square experiment as follows:[46]

Date of test	Stores			
	1	*2*	*3*	*4*
April 13–15	X	W	Z	Y
April 16–18	Y	Z	W	X
April 20–22	W	X	Y	Z
April 23–25	Z	Y	X	W

Four different prices are represented by the letters W, X, Y, and Z. Note that each price is tested once, and only once, with each of the stores and with each of the test periods, i.e., each appears once in each column and once in each row. Each price is not tested with all possible combinations of store and time period.

In one sense, this can be viewed as sixteen "after only" designs, but results for each price (each letter in the design) can serve as a control group for the others. The sum of values for all four of any one letter should show the sales achieved with that price with the effect of differences in the stores and time periods averaged out. If, however, interaction effects occurred between stores and time periods (e.g., one store might have had a special promotion during one time period), the results obtained from this design might be misleading for generalization to other stores and other times. Thus, the saving in expense (sixteen cells instead of sixty-four) might result in confusing the main effect of price with an interaction effect of store and time period. Careful observation of the stores during the experimental period would help the experimenter judge whether such interaction effect was likely or not, but, of course, this judgment cannot be considered proof.

Each price appears at the first time period in one store, the second time period in another, the third in another, and fourth in the other. This tends to balance out the effects of order, but it does not really control them because all possible sequences are not represented. In the example, price Y follows price X twice, but it never follows price

[46] Ronald Gatty and Alan Meredith, *Consumer Response to Quality Broilers Sold at Various Premium Prices* (New Brunswick, N.J.: Rutgers—The State University, October, 1961), p. 10.

Z. If sequences of this sort have any effect, the design does not control them.

PROBLEMS IN MARKETING EXPERIMENTATION

Experimental studies were rare in marketing before 1960. During the following decade there was a significant increase in experimentation, but the number of experiments is still small as a percentage of all marketing research projects. The advantages of experimentation in determining cause and effect relationships are strong enough to warrant the prediction that there will be continued expansion in its use. Some of the factors which limit the use of experiments have been brought out in the above discussion; however, there are additional practical problems which deserve comment.

Lack of theoretical base

True experimentation cannot take place without hypotheses to test. Such hypotheses are usually developed from underlying theory which in turn develops from extensive observation and description. Marketing research of the past has been primarily descriptive; as a result, extensive information on markets and marketing methods is now available. Little theory is yet available, but conditions are ripe for more extensive development in the future. This situation suggests that the researcher in the future will be able to develop more useful hypotheses and, thus, will be able to conduct more experiments.

Time factors

Individual markets vary from one time to another, and the same is true, of course, with people. Preferences and motivations change from year to year or even day to day. This dynamic nature of the consumer is particularly important because of the time factor involved in many marketing experiments. Sales tests must be given a considerable period of time if complete results are to be obtained. How long after an advertisement is run is its impact on sales felt? No one knows for sure, but it is likely that some effect may carry over a period of several weeks or even months. If various tests are to be rotated among the same markets as in Latin Square designs, the time required for the entire experiment may run into many months, or even years. By the time such a test is finished, consumer opinions may have changed. As experiments are continued over longer periods, mortality becomes a greater threat to validity.

Brief experiments measure only short-term effects. Most experiments assume that the immediate results (e.g., sales) measure the effect of the experimental variable. But what are the cumulative effects of advertising which may build good will and consumer acceptance over a long period of time? Innovations in product design may be immediate successes but lose popularity in the long run. Other products may meet initial resistance only to go on at a later date to become successes. Experiments should cover long enough periods to enable the "after" measurement to include most, or all, of the effect of the variable. This is simply not feasible with many business problems, since decisions are usually made at an early date.[47]

Cost of experimentation

Experimental research is often expensive. In most cases, at least one control group will be required in addition to the experimental group. In some instances, these groups will have to be measured twice or data will have to be collected continuously over a period. Thus, the cost of an experiment tends to be greater than the cost of a descriptive study.

In some experiments, control of the experimental variable is relatively simple (e.g., the number of shelf "facings" in display of the product in the store), but in other instances control of the variable can be extremely expensive. Preliminary investigation of a possible experiment involving the substitution of local variables in a nationally televised commercial indicated that the cost of controlling the experimental variable in this manner would be $180,000.

Test marketing of a new product is another form of experimentation that may become very expensive. Since the costs of introducing a new product into even a relatively small market may be quite high, the tendency is to test new products in only one or a few markets. This may keep cost within feasible limits, but it raises serious questions as to the external validity of the results. Variation among markets is probably greater in many cases than variation in preference among different test products. In general, the effect of the experimental variable is often relatively small as compared to the effects of miscellaneous variables. While the latter can be prevented from biasing the results through randomization, very large samples (which mean very large costs) are necessary if the experimental effects are to be measured accurately.

---

[47] The need for speed is probably overstressed in many cases. Every marketing research man is familiar with the company which has sold the same product in the same way for fifty years; then a vice president has an idea for a change in some marketing procedure and wants it tested by the research department prior to the executive committee meeting the following week.

Administrative problems of experimentation

Many administrative problems are encountered in conducting experiments. Frequently, cooperation must be obtained, and maintained, from individuals who find this interferes with their normal work, or who are at least aware that "something different" is going on. In order to see that the conditions of the experiment are maintained as prescribed, the experimenter may have to maintain very close (and expensive) supervision. An experiment to determine the effect of a sampling campaign may measure the number of consumers redeeming a coupon for a second package. If the grocer exchanges cash or other products for the coupon instead of insisting that the consumer take the brand in question, the results may be misleading.

Competitive circumstances may create difficult experimental conditions. Experiments are more open to observation by competitors than "one shot" surveys. If a new product is tested in the market, competitors are apt to become aware of the test and are thus alerted to new developments. If the results of the test are measured in sales, the competitor may be able to learn as much from the test as the experimenter, and at considerably less expense. Some firms maintain an emergency special promotion plan which they can throw into any competitor's test market and confuse the results. The longer the term of an experiment, the more possible these competitive reactions become.

CONCLUSIONS ON EXPERIMENTAL RESEARCH

While the number of marketing experiments has been growing in recent years, experiments still constitute a small percentage of all marketing research. Most of the reasons for this, as indicated, are inherent in the experimental method when applied to human beings. Yet in the fields of psychology and sociology, experimentation is more widely used than it is in marketing, even though marketing has a fundamental characteristic that makes experiments more practical than they are ever apt to be in the behavioral sciences. One of the major problems encountered in social science experiments is that of conducting an experiment without the experimental subjects being aware of the fact. Human attitudes and actions change when the individuals involved are aware that they are being studied. In marketing, innovations appear constantly. It is often easy, therefore, to introduce one on an experimental basis without the experimental subjects being aware that it is not a normal activity. This "naturalness" is further available in many marketing experiments, because the effect to be measured is the effect on sales. Sales results can be measured without interfering with consumer behavior. Thus, it is often easier to obtain measures of normal reactions to a stimulus in marketing than it is in the social sciences.

Experiments have a basic advantage over descriptive type studies —they are less apt to be useless. By their very nature, experiments are conducted to determine cause and effect. Before an experiment can be made, the researcher must develop a hypothesis. This forces the researcher to state specifically what cause and effect he expects to find. He is, thus, likely to face in advance the question of "what will I do with the results." Experimental results, therefore, are more likely to relate to a specific decision that must be made than are descriptive data.

As marketing becomes more scientific, it seems inevitable that experimental research will be more widely used. When new products are developed, they are tested and retested in many technical experiments before the final models are determined. Months, or even years, are spent in experimental work of this type. Marketing programs, however, are designed in more limited time periods. The marketing department has no equivalent to a "tooling-up" time. Yet the cost of an erroneous marketing decision may be as staggering as a mistake in technical development. In many marketing situations, the alternatives from which a choice must be made can be tested at a relatively small cost. Experiments are particularly useful for this purpose.

Case 3—1. HARDON AND WALES, INC.

Hardon and Wales, Inc., numbered among its advertising clients the McLaughlin Small Appliance Company. The latter produced a limited line of small kitchen appliances such as mixers, coffee makers, electric fry pans, and toasters. Annual sales of the McLaughlin Company were about $8.5 million, and approximately $450,000 was allocated for advertising. Hardon and Wales used national consumer magazines, trade publications, and newspapers to advertise the McLaughlin line. Television was not used because it was considered to be too expensive and to place the client in a poor competitive position, since the top two sellers of small appliances (General Electric and Sunbeam) used the medium extensively. Spot radio was also considered, but the client did not believe this medium suitable for promotion of its products.

At the suggestion of the McLaughlin Company's advertising manager, the medium of outdoor advertising was given consideration; however, before launching into any extensive use of billboards, the client wanted the agency to test this medium for sales effectiveness. The McLaughlin advertising manager thought that billboard advertising of his company's appliances would have several advantages. First, this type of medium permitted a "king-size" view of the products and gave a fast sales message. Second, other appliances did not use outdoor advertising, and this could give the McLaughlin campaign the advantage of being a first in the industry.

After some discussions along these lines, the marketing research director of Hardon and Wales received the following memo from the agency account supervisor on the McLaughlin account:

TO: ERNEST PACKARD, Research Director
FROM: FRANK W. DARR, Account Supervisor

I have just finished a lengthy phone conversation with Randell, advertising manager of McLaughlin, as to how we might "prove" or "disprove" the effectiveness of outdoor advertising as a medium for their products.

We finally agreed that the best way would be to select one of their weaker metropolitan areas in which to try a "before and after" brand awareness test, plus measuring the sales "before and after" some adequate outdoor advertising. Randell didn't want to go into more than one market because he says we really don't know very much about the effectiveness of this medium yet.

The objective would be to test this weak market in ample time to be able to determine by spring whether we would recommend outdoor advertising in the more important markets.

Randell assures me that we can find some market where distributors sell exclusively to retailers located within the area. He also assures me that their sales department will cooperate by taking a beginning inventory at the distributor's level and, of course, there's no problem in keeping track of shipments from the factory to these distributors. At the end of the test period salesmen will take a closing inventory of the items involved in the study.

I told Randell we could probably do a brand awareness study among consumers by phone—and that we'd pick up the tab on this part of the job. As I see this, we'd do a "before and after" measurement among, say, a couple of hundred housewives. We'd find out what brands of small appliances they could recall (without any reminding)) and also how they would rank these brands on quality. We'd repeat the job among a different group at the end of the test period.

Randell said his company would leave the test market alone except for normal or routine activity.

Can we proceed along the lines outlined above? Let me know your reactions as soon as possible. Thanks!

How should Mr. Packard reply to this letter? Should he accept the procedure outlined in the memo above? What changes, if any, should he recommend?

Case 3—2. THORSTAD PIPE COMPANY

The Thorstad Pipe Company of Pennsylvania produced a line of pipe fittings and flanges. Founded in 1910, the company was one of the leaders in the industry and had annual sales of about $35 million. The company sold its products through distributors to a variety of users, including chemical plants, oil pumping stations, and companies using steam for power and heat. The Thorstad sales manager proposed that the company increase its sales force in order to make more calls on plant engineers and top executives.

The Thorstad Company's line of pipe fittings consisted of such items as welded elbows, tees, reducers, returns, crosses, and laterals in a wide variety of sizes and pressures and in various metals and alloys. These products were welded to a piece of pipe in lieu of threading or bending. The welding process was a well-accepted method in many industries. The company also produced a line of flanges[1] which were bolted to a pressure kettle. Almost all products in the company's line were produced in accordance with specifications set forth by various engineering societies, such as the American Society of Testing Materials. Prices tended to be identical to those of competitors.

Thorstad had four major competitors, all of whom had about the same sales volume as Thorstad. All produced similar items. Competition also came from a number of smaller firms that tended to concentrate on producing and selling only a few of the items sold by the industry leaders.

The company maintained eight sales offices scattered throughout the country, and employed 14 salesmen who operated out of these offices. These men sold to 38 distributors and were paid a salary plus expenses. The distributors were pipe and pipe supply houses which maintained stocks. The nature of their product line tended to vary, depending upon the nature of the industries to which they sold. For example, in the southwest the Thorstad distributor specialized in selling to the oil industries. The distributors were exclusive company distributors, that is, the company sold to only one distributor in an area, and the distributor carried no products competitive to the Thorstad line.

The buying procedure of final customers was as follows:

1. The purchasing agent of a plant received a set of specifications from the plant engineers that indicated the number and type of pipe fittings and flanges needed for a particular job. The products were identified by an engineering code number; the purchasing agent could get in touch with any of a number of suppliers.
2. The purchasing agent took bids on the job from various distributors. Since in many cases the competing distributors quoted identical prices, the purchasing agent had to determine to whom to give the order. In some cases he split it between two or more companies.

---

[1] A flange is a rim or rib made as a part of the product or attached to it later. Its purpose is to provide strength or, as in this case, to provide a fastening edge or "lip."

Distributors received a 15 percent discount off list price. While manufacturers of pipe fittings priced their products to distributors at almost identical prices, there was much bargaining by distributors to obtain a particular job.

Thorstad salesmen performed a variety of functions. Their primary job was to work with distributors to obtain business. They were frequently used as consultants by distributors on difficult jobs. All Thorstad salesmen were trained mechanical engineers, and many of the older and more experienced salesmen earned between $15 and $20 thousand a year. Because of their training and experience they were frequently able to go over installation or maintenance specifications and suggest a different and better way of handling the pipe arrangements. Even where this was done, however, there was no assurance that the Thorstad distributor would receive the order.

Thorstad salesmen also visited distributors frequently to make certain that the latter's salesmen were devoting enough of their time to selling the Thorstad line. Since the distributors carried many other items, none of which supposedly was competitive to Thorstad products, it was always a problem to get the distributors' salesmen to devote enough time to Thorstad fittings. Thorstad salesmen attempted to overcome this by spending time in the field with the salesmen whenever possible.

Company salesmen also were charged with keeping in close contact with the purchasing agents of the larger companies that bought pipe fittings and flanges. Usually, but not always, these calls were made with a distributor's salesman. As a result of this effort, the salesmen knew many purchasing agents. The company thought that these personal contacts were responsible for an important part of its sales.

In the previous year the company sales manager decided to enlarge the activities of the sales force. He increased the number of salesmen who attended various professional meetings such as those of the American Petroleum Institute. Salesmen who did this were given a liberal expense account and instructed to take a hotel suite in which to entertain plant engineers and executives.

In addition, the older salesmen were instructed to join business clubs. The company agreed to pay all club costs. They were to use the clubs to entertain purchasing agents, plant engineers, and executives. Over the years most of the older salesmen had gotten to know some of the plant engineers and corporate executives through professional meetings and from inspecting and bidding on various jobs. Entertainment of these men, therefore, was not always a matter of making contacts, but rather of cultivating them. Because more sales time was spent at meetings and in cultivating contacts, the company hired three new salesmen.

The company increased its annual advertising expenditures by $35,000, an increase of nearly 30 percent over the preceding year. The increase resulted largely from adding a number of "executive" magazines to the list, such as *Business Week.* All company advertising stressed (1) heavy name identification, (2) the company's long experience in the industry, (3) the company's engineerings skills, and (4) the company's full line of fittings and flanges. The sales manager asked the executive committee for funds to hire two more salesmen, which would increase the sales budget by over $20,000 for the remainder of the year.

How could the hiring of two additional salesmen be organized as an experiment that would provide the maximum information relative to the value of the additions?

Case 3—3. RELIABLE CLOCK MANUFACTURING COMPANY

The Reliable Clock Company produced a line of quality household clocks which was sold nationally under the company's name through such outlets as jewelry stores, hardware stores, drug stores, electrical appliance stores, department stores, and stamp redemption stores. Reliable had produced a line of quality clocks for over a century, and enjoyed an excellent reputation with both consumers and the trade. Many of its first clocks were known still to be operating. When the firm introduced a new line of electric clocks, it decided to promote the line heavily with local spot radio commercials and to attempt to measure the effectiveness of the advertising in at least one major market.

The clock industry was highly competitive. Most of the firms were small- or medium-sized compared to General Electric, which sold its products under the Telechron name. Sales of the Reliable Company varied around $10.5 million. To support these sales, which were made through some 14,000 stores, the company typically budgeted about $250,000 annually for advertising, of which two thirds was spent on consumers and one third on the trade. To introduce the new line, Reliable budgeted $350,000, with the added $100,000 to be spent on consumer advertising.

Reliable's marketing research director singled out Cleveland, Ohio as the locale for a test to determine the effect of the company's radio advertising. The objective of this research was "to determine the consumer brand awareness of Reliable before and after radio advertising in the Cleveland market." The research methodology consisted of two parts as follows:

1. Two hundred housewives were selected at random from the Cleveland telephone directory. Through the use of a Cleveland research firm these housewives were contacted and interviewed by phone using a questionnaire consisting of three questions (see Exhibit 1). Interviewing took place during the second week in February.

2. Two hundred different housewives in Cleveland, Ohio were selected and interviewed using the same methods as in phase one (including the identical questionnaire) after a six-week radio advertising schedule consisting of twenty-eight 30-second radio commercials weekly (four per day). The only difference (aside from random errors in the sample) between phase one and phase two was the introduction of the radio schedule.

The results of the evaluation study are shown in Tables 1–4. In commenting on these findings, the company's research director stated: "It seems clear that our radio schedule in Cleveland had no traceable effect. There is no escaping the conclusion that such advertising is ineffective and, therefore, it is recommended that we consider seriously dropping our radio schedules for the remainder of the year and investing our advertising monies in other media."

Are the research director's conclusions sound? Why, or why not?

EXHIBIT 1. Consumer clock awareness telephone survey

Cleveland

Name _____ Respondent # _____

A.M.
Telephone no. _____ Date _____ Time _____P.M.

1. Would you be good enough to tell me all the brands or makes of electric or wind clocks that you can think of? Any others?

   _____   _____
   _____   _____
   _____   _____

2. Have you seen or heard any clock advertising lately?   Yes ☐   No ☐   (IF YES, THEN ASK)
   A. Which brands were advertised and how? (radio, television, etc.)

   Brands   *Medium used*

   _____   _____
   _____   _____
   _____   _____

   B. Can you recall anything about the clock advertisements you have heard or seen; i.e., what was the message, what did it say?

                                          Product features
   Brands   *or ideas conveyed*

   _____   _____
   _____   _____
   _____   _____
   _____   _____

TABLE 1. Brand of clock advertised and medium used in response to question 2A (percentages based on responses from only those who replied "yes" in answer to question 2)

	Phase I					Phase II				
	TV	Radio	Magazine	Newspaper	Other	TV	Radio	Magazine	Newspaper	Other
General Electric	3.0%	1.0%	—	1.5%	2.0%	3.0%	—	2.0%	2.5%	—
Seth Thomas	1.0	1.0	—	—	1.0	2.5	—	—	—	—
Big Ben	—	—	1.0%	1.5	1.0	1.5	—	—	—	—
Westclox	0.5	0.5	0.5	—	—	1.5	—	1.0	—	—
Reliable	1.5	—	0.5	—	—	1.0	1.0%	—	—	0.5%
Telechron	2.5	0.5	1.5	—	1.0	3.0	2.0	—	—	1.5
Westinghouse	1.5	0.5	0.5	—	0.5	2.0	1.5	—	1.0	0.5
All other	5.5	1.5	4.5	1.0	4.0	6.5	2.5	4.0	1.5	5.5
Don't know	1.5	1.0	2.0	1.0	3.0	2.0	1.5	2.0	1.5	3.5

NOTE: Several respondents gave more than one answer.

TABLE 2. Brand or make of electric or wind clock mentioned in response to question 1 (percentages based on 200 completed questionnaires in both phases)

Brand	First phase percent	Second phase percent	Brand	First phase percent	Second phase percent
West Bend	0.5	2.5	Benrus	1.0	—
Seth Thomas	5.5	6.5	Anniversary	1.0	—
Sessions	3.0	4.0	Universal	1.0	—
Frigidaire	—	1.0	Wesson	1.0	—
Swiss	0.5	1.0	Westclox	39.5	38.0
Hammond	1.0	1.0	Westinghouse ...	13.0	11.5
Sunbeam	0.5	0.5	Ingraham	2.0	0.5
G.E.	38.5	37.5	Telechron	13.5	11.5
Baby Ben	9.0	8.0	Gruen	2.0	—
Reliable	3.0	2.0	Big Ben	26.0	23.0
Hamilton	2.5	1.5	Bulova	3.5	0.5
Timex	2.0	1.0	Other°	8.0	8.0
R.C.A.	1.5	0.5	D.K. or none	22.0	30.5
Waterbury	1.0	—			

° Brands mentioned only once in either phase.

NOTE: The number of mentions total more than the base of 200 for each phase, because in many cases respondents mentioned more than one brand.

TABLE 3. Response to clock advertising seen or heard lately in response to question 2 (percentages based on responses from 200 respondents in each phase)

Answer	First phase percent	Second phase percent
Yes	12.0	16.0
No	88.0	84.0
Total	100.0	100.0

TABLE 4. Advertising message recall in response to question 2B

No tabulations were thought desirable for this question because of the small number of "vague" replies. Only two respondents recalled with any degree of accuracy the Reliable clock advertising, and one of these volunteered the information that she had only recently purchased a Reliable clock for a wedding gift. For the most part, the same vagueness was true with those responses having to do with the advertising of other clocks. No effort was made, however, to determine the precision of recall since the overall recall in response to question 2B was so poor.

Case 3—4.   LAWSON & WORTHINGHAM, INC.

Lawson & Worthingham, Inc., was an old and well-known producer of sauces used in flavoring meats and in other household cooking. The company's products were of high quality and were widely imitated by other firms, many of whom sold their brands at substantially lower prices than those charged by Lawson & Worthingham. To offset this competition, the company supported its excellent reputation by a modest expenditure for advertising in national magazines, and by a series of cooking school promotions. These demonstrations were held in a leading department store in each of several cities.

It was the impression of executives that this type of promotion was successful in increasing sales, but they believed that more objective evidence should be gathered regarding the plan's effectiveness before funds were appropriated for the expansion of the program. The problem was presented to A. J. Nichols, a sales consultant with whom one of the executives was acquainted. He agreed to conduct a sales test of the demonstration plan. The sales test he planned was to be a store audit procedure in which sales information on meat sauces would be obtained by checking the inventories and purchases of a sample of food stores.

The city of Fort Worth, Texas was selected as the locale for the experiment, principally because the company's demonstration school "team" was next scheduled to appear there, but also because this city was sufficiently large to be fairly representative of most cities.

Mr. Nichols went to Fort Worth and obtained the cooperation of the national advertising manager of the *Star-Telegram,* who introduced him to division managers of chain stores represented in the city and to many of the larger independent grocers. A sample of 37 stores was selected as an adequate cross section of the grocery retailers serving middle- and upper-class consumers. The cooperation of these store owners was obtained and a practice inventory count was taken in each store by an experienced investigator. Care was taken to make certain that the investigater knew the location of reserve stocks as well as those on the shelf, and that she was acquainted with the invoice records of each store so that she could compute receipts of merchandise.

The test began officially on February 10, the week before the opening of the cooking school promotion in a Fort Worth department store. Inventories of the test stores were taken on that day and at the end of each of the four succeeding weeks. From these data and information on purchases each week, Mr. Nichols computed weekly sales of Lawson & Worthingham sauces (see Exhibit 1) and prepared the following summary:

Sales of Lawson & Worthingham sauces before, during, and after the cooking school promotion

Test week	Bottles sold in 35 stores*	Index of sales relative to base week
Feb. 10–Feb. 17 before school	240	100.0 (base)
Feb. 17–Feb. 24 week of school	275	114.7
Feb. 24–Mar. 3 week after school	292	121.7
Mar. 3–Mar. 10 2nd week after school	301	125.4

* Questions about the accuracy of the invoice and purchase records of two stores caused Mr. Nichols to omit them from the test.

On March 24, Mr. Nichols submitted a report to the executives of Lawson & Worthingham in which he presented the above table along with certain comments and conclusions, among them the following:

"The evidence indicates clearly that the cooking school promotion stimulated a sales increase of approximately 25 percent for each of the two weeks following the promotion.

"It seems likely that this increase in sales can be attributed almost entirely to the stimulation from the cooking school. This conclusion is based on the fact that improvement in display, as observed in the stores checked, would appear to be of little influence.

"Some idea of the competitive situation in Fort Worth . . . can be gained from the following description of the stock and display of sauce

EXHIBIT 1. Complete tabulation of sales of Lawson & Worthingham sauces in 35 Fort Worth stores—February 10 to March 10*

Store no.	Week ending February 17	Week ending February 24	Week ending March 3	Week ending March 10
1	5	0	9	0
2	3	15	3	13
3	4	12	6	4
4	44	42	18	20
5	55	28	48	77
6	1	0	2	2
7	6	8	14	7
8	5	16	8	13
9	5	5	8	6
10	4	3	3	1
11	3	18	4	12
12	20	21	5	8
13	4	1	3	3
14	1	3	1	2
15	7	7	22	18
16	1	1	13	1
17	2	5	4	2
18	2	4	2	2
19	1	1	3	1
20	2	1	2	1
21	2	16	16	10
22	1	3	3	3
23	3	10	6	6
24	3	2	4	2
25	3	2	9	9
26	12	14	27	27
27	0	2	1	1
28	6	6	12	4
29	2	4	5	9
30	5	5	9	7
31	8	6	8	6
32	1	0	1	2
33	5	4	5	9
34	4	2	3	3
35	10	8	5	10
Total	240	275	292	301

* Two stores were eliminated from the total because of doubtful accuracy of the data.

in . . . store during the test. . . . On a large six-shelf self-help display case, only seven bottles of Lawson & Worthingham sauces were displayed. These bottles, marked 25¢, were placed so that the customer saw only two of them. . . . Other sauces, three of which were displayed in two-dozen lots, included:

> Brand A at 14¢
> Brand B at 10¢
> Brand C at 22¢
> Brand D at 10¢
> Brand E in two sizes at 10¢ and 19¢

The obvious conclusion is that less expensive sauces were being given dominant display in this store. In other stores checked, Lawson & Worthingham was given a better break on display, but in few stores was it given dominant display."

1. Were Mr. Nichols' conclusions justified?
2. Could the test be designed more effectively?

Case 3—5. MAGEE CHEMICAL COMPANY

The Magee Chemical Company, with headquarters in St. Louis, Missouri, produced a line of chemicals mainly for use on the farm. The company was a relatively small one, with annual sales of just under $12 million. It was known primarily for its insecticides and fungicides, which it sold through its own sales force to various distributors who, in turn, sold to a variety of different types of retailers. One of its products was a broad spectrum, systemic insecticide that had been sold successfully to large commercial nurseries. This product was produced in crystal form and was particularly effective against sucking insects which attacked flowering shrubs. It was easy to apply since the crystals were "scratched" into the ground surrounding the base of the shrub. The crystals "melted" and merged with moisture and as such were absorbed by the plant's roots. From here the chemical circulated throughout the plant. One such treatment would immunize the plant for several months. A pound of crystals would treat four to six plants. The product was nontoxic and left no dangerous residue. No similar products of equal effectiveness were available. Competitive products were typically of the dust or spray type, and were effective for only a matter of a few days. Such products were particularly ineffective during rainy periods since they were "washed off." Because of the success of this product with commercial nurseries the company had decided to sell it to the consumer market. The marketing director was asked to approve the preliminary plans for test marketing it.

The brand manager for this product decided that before launching this product nationwide it was necessary to test it first in several different markets. Since this was the company's first attempt to sell a consumer product and since this product would be the building block in a line of home and garden products, the brand manager thought it extremely important to gain some idea of how to market it on a test market basis.

Because of the company's limited sales force (two salesmen plus the brand manager) and the lack of any established outlets, the test markets were limited to greater St. Louis and the Philadelphia metropolitan area. The St. Louis area was serviced by two distributors calling on or contacting by mail about 2,500 dealers. Only about 800 of these were thought to put much effort behind selling lawn and garden chemical products. These dealers were made up of nurseries, hardware stores, discount houses, supermarket garden centers, drug stores, service stations, and national chains such as Montgomery Ward and Sears.

The Philadelphia area was chosen because of its proximity to a large-volume sales area, and although nothing yet had been settled on distribution, the brand manager had two wholesale hardware distributors in mind.

In addition, the brand manager was planning to sell the product to a large home and garden distributor located in Texas. This company would sell the product under its own label to about 500 dealers located in Texas and Louisiana.

The product would be in one-pound packaged lots in a translucent plastic container in order to incorporate a measured application feature. A colorful label design and display carton had been developed by the company's advertising agency. In commenting on the use of the translucent plastic container the brand manager said: "We realize that plastic will not contain all of the product odor and it is likely we will have to change to something else within a year or two."

The product was to have a suggested retail price of $2.95, with a 50 percent markup for the retailer and a 25 percent markup for the distributor. The product cost the company 52 cents a pound to manufacture. This figure included all direct costs and an allocation of factory overhead. It did not include general overhead, marketing costs, or a profit.

Finished packages of the product would be ready to ship by April 1. One of the St. Louis companies planned to have dealer meetings on April 5 and 6 to "kick off" the sale of this product. This would be followed by an unspecified number (but at least three) of TV messages by the distributor and continued promotion at the weekly dealer meetings. The company planned to participate in these dealer meetings and to share in the cost of all cooperative advertising up to $2,000.

The other St. Louis distributor would hold a special sales meeting on March 23 to introduce the new product to salesmen. This meeting would feature Magee Company personnel. This distributor held very few dealer meetings, but did use mail campaigns. The company estimated that its cost regarding its part of the dealer mailings would be about $1,000. All dealers in the St. Louis area would be offered a guaranteed sales plan, that is, all unsold merchandise would be taken back by the distributor at the end of the season. The company would then take back any stock from the distributors.

The Texas and Louisiana distributor planned to launch the product with a barbecue in San Antonio. This would be followed by dealer clinics in major cities. The Magee Company was to allow the distributor $2,500 for promotional expenses with the understanding that it would be matched. The distributor agreed to purchase 17,500 pounds under their label.

The company's advertising program for St. Louis was scheduled as follows:

1. Half-page announcement ad to appear in Sunday newspaper (supplement section) on March 17.
2. On April 1 the same newspaper to carry another ad with a coupon worth 25 cents. The coupon provides for recording of name, address, phone, and name of dealer where product purchased.
3. One-minute radio spots on leading radio station 12 times a week during month of April.
4. Twenty-second TV commercial to appear five times during first week in April.
5. Local paper advertising in five suburban weeklies. One ad per paper weekly for April, May, and June.
6. Point-of-purchase streamers and placards.
7. Mailers and descriptive literature available as giveaways to distributors and dealers.
8. Meetings by company personnel with local garden clubs to discuss the merits of the new product.
9. Mailings to garden club memberships of a 25-cent coupon good on the purchase of a one-pound unit.

A similar program was planned for Philadelphia. While the details of the promotional programs for these two cities had yet to be worked out, it was estimated that the total costs of such programs, excluding the program worked out with the Texas distributor, would approximate $20,000. This amount excluded the salaries of all company personnel engaged in the project, but did include their expenses. Of the $20,000, about $2,000 was allocated to a survey to be made the following fall among known users of the product to determine their experience with the product. Names would be obtained from the coupons.

How should the research to accompany this test market program be designed?

4

Basic methods
of collecting data

Gigo—Garbage In, Garbage Out—has become a common phrase among people who work with computers. It refers to the fact that computers only process what is given them and can turn out results only as good as the data put in. The phrase has equal application to all aspects of marketing research—if poor data are collected, poor conclusions will be forthcoming. No matter what the basic design of the research, it is necessary to collect accurate data to achieve useful results. For this reason, it is helpful to consider methods of collecting data and the quality of information they may be expected to produce.

Questioning and observation are the two basic methods of collecting data in marketing research. Questioning, as the name suggests, is distinguished by the fact that data are collected by asking questions of people who are thought to have the desired information. Questions may be asked in person or in writing. A formal list of such questions is called a questionnaire.

When data are collected by observation, the researcher asks no questions. Instead he keeps track of the objects or actions in which he is interested. Sometimes individuals make the observations; on other occasions, mechanical devices note and record the desired information. Observations may be made of information such as census reports, of objects such as the number of signs for a given company, or of people and their activities. No matter what research design is used, the necessary data are collected by one or both of these two methods.

ACCURACY OF DATA COLLECTED

Surveys have become so commonplace in today's world that the average person seldom questions the idea that useful information can be obtained in this manner. The fact that findings of one type or another are developed and usually seem plausible furthers this acceptance. When formal efforts are made to check the accuracy of survey data, however, the results are often disquieting.

In one of the earliest attempts to verify the accuracy of survey data, a researcher traveled with a Chinese couple noting the hotels, motels, and restaurants where they stayed and ate. Later he queried the managers of these same places of business, asking if they would accept Chinese as guests. Over 90 percent said they would not.[1]

Since the date of the above study, many advances have been made in survey methods, yet inconsistent data continue to be found when tests are made. The Bureau of the Census made an intensive study of selected areas after the 1960 census and concluded that 3.0 to 3.5 million persons were not counted in the official census.[2] Although this is a large error in absolute numbers, it is less than 2 percent of the total— small enough to make little difference in many marketing studies.

Perhaps the best study of the accuracy of responses to questionnaires was one in which a carefully selected sample of 920 individuals was asked a variety of questions for which correct answers were available from official records.[3] Table 4–1 shows some of the results of this survey. Ninety-eight percent of the respondents reported accurately on telephone ownership, but as few as 56 percent reported correctly on whether or not they contributed to the Community Chest.

Errors of the above size on factual data are upsetting enough, but of even more concern to the marketing researcher are data obtained by questionnaire, presumably accurately, but which report incorrectly what the situation actually is. For example, a food manufacturer, who was testing three possible designs (three colors, five colors, and six colors) of a new package, asked consumers to pick the one they preferred. Sixty-two percent reported they liked the six-color package best. When the three packages were put on the shelf and sales observed, only 11 percent

---

[1] R. T. LaPiere, "Attitudes vs. Actions," *Social Forces,* Vol. 14 (1934) pp. 230–37.

[2] "Little Nuggets from Big Books," *Journal of Advertising Research,* Vol. 3 (March, 1963), pp. 59–60.

[3] Don Cahalan, "Correlates of Respondent Accuracy in Denver Validity Survey," *Public Opinion Quarterly,* 32 (Winter, 1968–69) pp. 607–21. For a good summary of references to tests of survey accuracy see Eugene C. Hagburg, "Validity of Questionnaire Data: Reported and Observed Attendance in an Adult Education Program," *Public Opinion Quarterly,* 32 (Fall, 1968) p. 453.

TABLE 4-1. Accuracy of data obtained by survey when compared to official records

| | *Percentage of respondent reports* | | | |
	Correct	*Exagger-ated*	*Under-stated*	*Other**
Telephone in house	98	1	1	0
Home ownership	96	3	1	0
Automobile ownership	94	3	0	3
Age	92	4	4	0
Possession of driver's license	88	10	2	0
Valid library card	87	9	2	2
Registered to vote	82	16	2	0
Voting in congressional election	69	19	2	10
Contributed to Community Chest	56	34	0	10

* Such as "no answer."
Source: Don Cahalan, "Correlates of Respondent Accuracy in the Denver Validity Study," *Public Opinion Quarterly,* 32 (Winter, 1968–69) p. 610.

bought the six-color package; 16 percent bought the five-color package; and 72 percent bought the three-color package.[4]

Such results have led to the substitution of observation for questioning where at all feasible. In general, observation data are undoubtedly more accurate than questionnaire data, especially when observation of an action can be obtained in place of a verbal report of what action the respondent would take (as in the above example).

Many survey data are accurate, as shown in Table 4-1, and some information can be obtained on most problems by asking questions. There are some data, however, that can only be obtained by observation. Human perception of space and its use, tone of voice, and stress and pitch in language are examples of topics on which direct questioning will yield little information. People develop habits in these areas which are not consciously recognized and which they cannot describe.[5]

On the other hand, observation does not automatically produce accurate data. Physical difficulties in the observation situation or on the part of the observer may result in errors. Even more important, however, is the influence on observations of the observer's training, philosophy, opinions, and expectations. Significant variations in observation of the same phenomena have been reported for such diverse projects as the state of repair for telephone poles, the transit of stars in a telescope, and the reading of chest X-ray films.[6] Perhaps Bertrand Russell's comment on the study of animal behavior summarizes the situation as well as any:

---

[4] Louis Cheskin, *Why Is She Buying Package 2?* (undated brochure).

[5] Edward T. Hall, "Proxemics," *Current Anthropology,* 9 (April–June, 1968) p. 83.

[6] Herbert Hyman, *Interviewing in Social Research* (Chicago: The University of Chicago Press, 1954), p. 13.

One may say broadly that all the animals that have been carefully observed have behaved so as to confirm the philosophy in which the observer believed before his observation began. Nay, more, they have all displayed the national characteristics of the observer. Animals studied by Americans rush about frantically, with an incredible display of hustle and pep, and at last achieve the desired result by chance. Animals observed by the Germans sit still and think, and at last evolve the solution out of their inner consciousness.[7]

From the above it is obvious that data collected by any method are subject to considerable error and can be used only with caution. Questionnaire and observation are the only methods available, however, for collecting data. More detailed discussion of the two methods will help in understanding how each can be used most effectively.

QUESTIONNAIRE METHOD

If one wants to know what type of dentifrice people use, what they think of television commercials, or why they buy particular brands of cars, the natural procedure is to ask them. Thus, the questionnaire method has come to be the more widely used of the two data collection methods. Many housewives are now familiar with the doorstep interviewer who greets them with, "We are making a survey," and then proceeds to ask a series of questions. Businessmen also frequently receive written or oral requests for information. The common factor in all varieties of the questionnaire method is this reliance on verbal responses to questions, written or oral.

Interviews vary widely. Most are conducted on an individual basis, but some are made with groups. A formal list of questions—a questionnaire—is commonly used, but the method is sometimes employed without a formal questionnaire. In this case, the interviewer adapts his questioning to each interview as it develops. Some interviews are conducted in person, others by telephone, and still others by mail. Each of these procedures has its special advantages and limitations. Each will be discussed later in this chapter. The questionnaire method in general, however, has a number of pervasive advantages and disadvantages. Discussion of particular variations will be more meaningful if these characteristics of the general method are brought out first.

Advantages of questionnaire method

Versatility. Probably the greatest advantage of the questionnaire method is its versatility. Almost every problem of marketing research can be approached from the questionnaire standpoint. Every marketing

---

[7] Bertrand Russell, *Philosophy* (New York: Norton, 1927), p. 30.

problem involves people. Therefore, ideas relative to the problem and its solution can be obtained by asking these people about the problem. Many problems can be studied only by questioning. Knowledge, opinions, motivations, and intentions are usually not open to observation. Except where records have been maintained, past events can be studied only through the questionnaire method. Similarly, it is not normally feasible to observe personal activities such as brushing teeth. All this does not mean that the questionnaire method can be used satisfactorily to solve all marketing problems. It can be used, however, to get some data relative to most problems.

Speed and cost. Questioning is usually faster and cheaper than observing. Interviewers have more control over their data-gathering activities than do observers. As a result, less time is typically wasted in a questionnaire study. For example, in a research study to find whether consumers prefer beer in bottles or cans, one could either ask people their preference or wait in package liquor stores to observe which containers customers asked for when they came in to buy beer. The latter method would require observers to wait until customers came into the store to buy beer. Interviewers, however, could proceed from one interview to another with no wait in between. Thus, the lost time would be less with the questionnaire method. Some events that take place over a period of time, such as the number of trips to the supermarket in a week, would require lengthy observation, but a question on this behavior can be answered in a few seconds. In many cases, however, this advantage of the questionnaire may be negligible.

Disadvantages of questionnaire method

Despite the fact that the questionnaire method is widely used in marketing research, it has several important limitations.

Unwillingness of respondent to provide information. Most interviews are obtained at the sufferance of the respondent. The respondent answers the doorbell to find the interviewer waiting with a list of questions. The interviewer is unknown to the respondent, and the subject of the proposed interview may be of little or no interest. The interviewer counts on the natural politeness and good nature of most people to gain their cooperation. But in some cases potential respondents will refuse to take the time to be interviewed or will refuse to answer some specific questions. Questions about income or about very personal subjects frequently meet refusals. The number of such refusals varies with individual interviewers and with the subject of the interview, but in some cases refusals have run as high as 55 percent of the attempted calls.[8] A

---

[8] Warren Cordell and Henry A. Rahmel, "Are Nielsen Ratings Affected by Non-Cooperation, Conditioning or Response Error?," *Journal of Advertising Research,* Vol. 2 (September, 1962), p. 46.

more typical figure for the usual household survey is probably 5 to 10 percent. When questionnaires are sent through the mails, the percentage which is not returned may exceed 90 percent,[9] although 50 percent is more typical among skilled researchers.

Various methods of reducing unwillingness on the part of respondents have been developed. The most important of these is salesmanship on the part of the interviewer or a covering letter with mail questionnaires. Rewards in the form of premiums or cash often help to gain cooperation. Assurance that the information will be held in confidence and in no way will be related to the individual may reduce refusals when data are particularly personal or of value to competitors.

Inability of respondent to provide information.   Despite a willingness to cooperate, many persons are unable to give accurate information on questions which the marketing man would like to ask. Many motivations, for example, are largely subconscious. How many consumers analyze their reasons for buying a particular bar of soap or suit of clothes and then formulate those reasons so that they can be expressed quickly and clearly when an interviewer unexpectedly asks about them? Most products are bought without any conscious array of reasons for and against. Questions on such motivations are, therefore, apt to be useless. Current work on motivation is attempting to obtain the information indirectly by asking questions which can be answered and which, by their pattern, indicate motivation. This is discussed more extensively in the chapter on motivation research.

In other cases, respondents cannot furnish information because they are unable to remember the facts desired or because they have never known the facts. One can ask: How many times did you eat corn flakes for breakfast last month? Few could answer such a question accurately because most people do not attempt to note or remember such information.

Many times the only way to overcome this problem is to make the survey at a time when the events of interest are fresh in the respondent's mind. Memory, however, is related to other factors besides recency. One experiment found that respondents could report correctly only 31 percent of the programs to which their radios were tuned the previous day.[10] When Market Research Corporation of America changed its reporting period from monthly to weekly, the reported volume of purchases of convenience goods increased 20 percent.[11] Most people, however, could probably remember for many days, or even years, the

---

[9] In a survey among subscribers to a do-it-yourself magazine, for example, only 3.7 percent of the questionnaires *mailed* were returned.

[10] John L. Karol, "Analyzing the Radio Market," *Public Opinion Quarterly*, Vol. I (1937), pp. 92–96.

[11] James D. Shaffer, "The Reporting Period for a Consumer Purchase Panel," *Journal of Marketing*, Vol. 19 (January, 1955), p. 252.

place at which they bought their present car. *Look* magazine found that the recall of ads in its pages averaged 25.1 percent twenty-four hours after respondents read the magazine but dropped to 20.1 percent forty-eight hours after reading. When the ads were separated into two groups, however, those best remembered and those least remembered, a distinct difference in recall was discovered between the two groups. After twenty-four hours, 34 percent had recalled the most memorable ads; this had dropped to 31 percent after forty-eight hours. The least remembered ads dropped from 21 percent recall to only 14 percent in the same period.[12] Thus, the impression made by the event at the time of its occurrence, the associations surrounding the event, and the importance of the event to the respondent all influence his ability to remember it at a later date. All of these must be considered in deciding whether or not to ask certain questions.

In some situations, it is possible to help the respondent's memory. Aided-recall techniques are used for this purpose. If a consumer is asked what advertisements he saw in a given magazine, he can remember very few. If, on the other hand, he goes through a copy of the magazine and looks at individual ads, he will remember having seen more of them, i.e., he will recognize them.

Aided-recall is often used in advertising research. Each respondent is shown copies of ads or a list of the programs which were on the air. He is then asked which of the ads or programs he saw or heard. One study of recall of ads by doctors obtained the results shown in Table 4–2.

TABLE 4–2. Recall of twenty selected ads by 317 doctors

Number of ads recalled	Unaided recall	Aided recall
0	39.4%	5.7%
1–2	30.8	11.1
3–4	20.1	13.6
5–6	7.6	15.1
7–8	1.8	15.1
9–10	.3	15.1
11–12	—	12.0
13–14	—	6.3
15 or more	—	6.0
Average number recalled per doctor	1.7	7.2

SOURCE: Robert Ferber and Hugh Wales, "Advertising Recall in Relation to Type of Recall," *The Public Opinion Quarterly*, Vol. 22 (Winter, 1958–59), p. 531.

Doctors were asked to recall ads and then were shown twenty specific ads to which they had probably been exposed. The average number of

[12] *Consumer Interest and Advertising Retention* (Cowles Magazines and Broadcasting, Inc., 1963), pp. 3–4.

ads recalled with aid was over four times as large as the number recalled without aid. Similarly, aided-recall of TV viewing has been shown to obtain data for recall periods of up to seven days that are comparable with data for twenty-four hour unaided recall periods.[13]

Using aids to recall involves dangers which must be considered when the technique is used. Such aids may cause respondents to think they have seen or heard the item in question even when they haven't. One experiment to measure the extent of such erroneous reporting found that just as many individuals reported having seen certain elements of an ad they were shown when the elements had not been in the ad as when they had been.[14]

If consumers are asked any question which they cannot answer correctly because they do not know and have never known the information requested, they may still answer. Such answers are sometimes honest mistakes and at other times are made to impress the interviewer. In any case, these answers appear as valid responses and so give erroneous results. It is important, then, to ask people *only* those questions they are qualified to answer. Where alternate respondents are available, the one most apt to have the information should be used. Because housewives are at home more than other members of the family, they are frequently asked questions about activities and opinions of the other members. In many cases this may be satisfactory, but in some cases this undoubtedly leads to incorrect responses when the housewife has only incomplete knowledge of the facts. Many housewives, for example, do not know how much money their husbands earn, how much insurance they carry, or what investments they have made.

Influence of questioning process. A third major limitation of the questionnaire method is the effect of the questioning process on the results obtained. The situation in which a person is questioned about routine actions is an artifical one at best. As a result, respondents may furnish reports quite different from the facts.

If the true answer to a question would be embarrassing or damaging to the ego, some respondents will manufacture an answer. Whereas respondents may answer accurately questions such as whether or not they smoke cigarettes or what brand of washing machine they have, they may tend to modify answers to questions on their income or the magazines to which they subscribe. One study found that beer consumption as reported by consumers was considerably less than sales by brewers. When the approach to the problem was changed to obtain beer purchases, such purchases reported by consumers exceeded reported beer

---

[13] A. S. C. Ehrenberg, "How Reliable Is Aided Recall of TV Viewing?" *Journal of Advertising Research,* Vol. 1 (June, 1961), pp. 29–31.

[14] Eric Mander and Mort David, "Recognition of Ad Elements: Recall or Projection," *Journal of Advertising Research,* Vol. 1 (December, 1961), pp. 23–25.

drinking by 37.6 percent.[15] Consumers reporting purchases of food and drug items by brand reported 45 percent more purchases of the best known national brands than was known to be the case, but 62 percent less purchasing of leading chain store brands.[16]

Other respondents attempt to give answers that they think will please the interviewer. For example, if respondents know the product for which a particular survey is being made, the percentage reporting use of that product tends to be higher than otherwise. Some respondents use the interview as an occasion to amuse or astonish the interviewer or reader of the questionnaire.

Semantic difficulties also arise with questionnaires. It is difficult, if not impossible, to state a given question in such a way that it will mean exactly the same thing to every respondent. Similarly, two different wordings of the same question will frequently produce quite different results. Problems of this type will be discussed in detail in the chapter dealing with questionnaire construction.

Types of questionnaire studies

As noted previously, it is possible to classify questionnaire studies on a variety of bases. Three such bases which are of importance are: (1) the degree to which the questionnaire is formalized or structured; (2) the disguise or lack of disguise of the objectives of the questionnaire; and (3) the method of communication used. The first two of these bases are considered together.

Questionnaire studies classified by structure and disguise. Questionnaire studies can be conducted either with or without formal lists of questions. When no formal questionnaire is used, the interviewer adapts his questioning to each interview as it progresses or perhaps elicits responses by indirect methods such as showing pictures on which the respondent comments. Following a prescribed sequence of questions is referred to as structured study while the other is nonstructured. Questionnaires can be constructed so that the objective is clear to the respondent (nondisguised), or they can be constructed so as to disguise the objective. Using these two bases of classification, four types of studies can be distinguished:[17]

---

15 Elmo Roper organization house organ (September, 1960).

16 Seymour Sudman, "On the Accuracy of Recording of Consumer Panels: II," *Journal of Marketing Research,* 1 (August, 1964) p. 77.

17 This cross classification was first suggested by Donald T. Campbell, "The Indirect Assessment of Social Attitudes," *Psychological Bulletin,* Vol. 47 (January, 1950), p. 15.

1. Structured—nondisguised.
2. Nonstructured—nondisguised.
3. Nonstructural—disguised.
4. Structured—disguised.

Structured—nondisguised questioning. Most questionnaire studies made in marketing research are of the first type—they are structured and are not disguised. If the sales manager for a musical instrument company wants to find out how many and what type of people play various types of instruments, he may set up a formal list of questions which ask directly about the ownership and playing of various instruments. Each of a selected group of persons is then asked this set of questions in the given sequence. Answers are frequently limited to a list of alternatives which is stated or implied. Several questions taken from an actual survey of this type are given below:

Does your family own a piano?
  Yes ——— No ———
(If Yes ask)
What type of piano do you have?
  Upright ——— Spinet ——— Grand ——— Other ———
Did you buy it or was it a gift?
Which members of your family, if any, can now play the piano?

Collection of data in a structured interview of this type has definite advantages in marketing research. By reducing the chance for interviewers to influence results through different phrasings of questions and even different questions, and through different judgments of answers and what to record, the structured questionnaire produces more reliable results—i.e., if the research project is repeated in the same manner, similar results will be obtained. Perhaps the ultimate in structuring was accomplished in one study in which respondents were seated in a chair which was fastened to the floor a given distance from the chair in which the interviewer sat. The interviewer asked questions by handing the respondent cards on which the questions were printed.[18]

The greater reliability which comes with structuring may be obtained at the loss of some validity. By restricting interviewers to an established procedure, the researcher prevents them from using their skill and judgment to obtain more information when it appears the respondent has more to give, or to explore points when the respondent's answer appears misleading, evasive, or otherwise inaccurate. To do this effectively, how-

---

[18] G. V. Hamilton, *A Research in Marriage* (New York: Boni, 1929).

ever, interviewers must be skilled in the art and well trained for the specific project.

Most marketing research projects seek to collect data from a fairly large number of respondents in a short period of time, often over a large area such as the entire United States. Such projects require the use of large numbers of interviewers. Since they are often dispersed geographically, it is economically disadvantageous to gather them for intensive training. The result is that most interviewing in marketing research is not highly skillful. Under these circumstances, structured questionnaires are highly desirable. Some attempt is usually made to offset the restrictions on interviewer freedom by instructing her to probe, i.e., to encourage the respondent to comment further, at various points in the interview. In some projects, interviewers are also asked to appraise the quality of each interview after it is completed.

Data obtained in structured-nondisguised studies are easier to tabulate and interpret than data gathered in other ways. This does not necessarily mean that they are more useful or valid in solving the question at hand, as will be shown below. But answers to formal questions of clear purpose can be counted and their apparent meaning determined in a more objective fashion than is true for data obtained by other methods.

Structured-nondisguised studies can be handled by telephone, mail, or personal interview. Unfortunately, such studies tend to be limited to the collection of factual information or opinions. They are subject to the three limitations of the questionnaire method—respondents may be unable to furnish the information desired, they may be unwilling to furnish it, or the questioning process may tend to stimulate incorrect or misleading answers.

Nonstructured—nondisguised questioning. More than anything else, marketing men want to know why people buy or don't buy their products. Direct questions dealing with motives rarely elicit useful answers. As pointed out above, most people do not have a clear idea as to why they make specific marketing decisions. Direct questions do not measure the relative importance of the various types of reasons, and many individuals will not report motives which might be considered base or socially unacceptable. The family which bought a new Cadillac to make the neighbors envious, would be unlikely to report such a motivation. Instead it might mention that Cadillacs are really economical in the long run.

To overcome these difficulties, research men have copied the technique of the psychoanalyst. Instead of approaching the respondent with a fixed list of questions, the interviewer attempts to get the respondent to talk freely about the subject of interest. By so doing, the interviewer hopes to put the respondent at ease and to encourage him to express any ideas which he has on the subject. If some idea of interest is passed over too quickly, the interviewer may seek more information by "probing." For example, he may comment, "That's interesting. Why do you feel that way?" This encourages further discussion of the point. Various probes can be used as needed to get the respondent to expand on any particular ideas. Although no formal questionnaire is used in interviewing of this type, the interviewer has an outline in mind. If the respondent does not get into areas of special interest, the interviewer will insert questions opening up these topics. The objective of these interviews is to get below the respondent's surface reasons for particular marketing decisions, and to find the underlying, or basic motives. For this reason the procedure is often called "depth interviewing."[19] Depth interviews do not involve the use of formal questionnaires, yet the discussion is directed to the specific problem at hand. They are non-structured, nondisguised questioning.

The advantages of depth interviews are obvious. They secure more information from the respondent. He is not kept in the straitjacket of a set list of questions. Ideas which would not normally be expressed are brought out. The significance of individual points, their relationships, and the background in which each is set are obtained. The interviewer is free to adjust each interview to the situation and to the personality of the respondent. This flexibility on the part of the interviewer is a major advantage of the method, but it is also a major weakness. Since each interviewer handles each interview differently, it is difficult to compare results. Averages and percentages cannot be computed with validity. Thus, depth interviews are best used in exploratory research where the objective is to find ideas for specific hypotheses which may be tested with other methods.

This reliance on the judgment of the individual interviewer also creates other problems. Since so much depends on his ability, highly skilled interviewers must be used. One study suggests that such interviewers should have training and experience comparable to an academic background in social psychology and field experience of five hundred or more interviews.[20] Frequently, individuals with postgraduate work in psychology are employed. Such interviewers are both hard to find and expensive. Furthermore, the freedom of the interviewer makes it possible (or

---

[19] A complete depth interview is published in George H. Smith, *Motivation Research in Advertising and Marketing* (New York: McGraw-Hill Book Co., Inc., 1954), pp. 214–20. An extensive social work interview with commentary on the procedure is published in Robert Kahn and Charles Cannell, *The Dynamics of Interviewing* (New York: John Wiley and Sons, Inc., 1957), pp. 328–51. See also Raymond L. Gordon, *Interviewing* (Homewood, Ill.: The Dorsey Press, 1969), pp. 272 ff.

[20] Natalie Harris and Gordon M. Connelly, "A Symposium of Interviewing Problems," *International Journal of Opinion and Attitude Research,* Vol. II (Spring, 1948), p. 75.

even necessary) for him to influence the results. The probes he inserts and his interpretation of responses will be influenced by his own feelings. The problem of recording these long interviews often increases the opportunity for such bias. Word-for-word recording is usually too laborious, so most depth interviews are sifted by the interviewer, who records what he thinks is pertinent. An interviewer who has a strong preference for one brand of car will be apt to find different attitudes toward that car than one who dislikes the car. In some cases, depth interviews are taken verbatim by recording machines. This reduces interviewer bias, but may put respondents ill at ease and so damage the interview.

Depth interviews take longer than the typical structured interviews. Many of them last for an hour or more. This creates two problems. One is cost again. High-priced interviewers spending a long time on each interview lead to high total costs. As a result, most studies using depth interviews are limited to very small samples. The length of the interview also creates difficulties in securing the cooperation of respondents and, hence, may lead to biased samples.

A final and major disadvantage of the depth interview is the difficulty and cost of interpretation. Skilled psychologists must be used to interpret the results. Even then interpretations are subjective and may vary from one analyst to another. Interpretation is further complicated by the difficulty encountered in recording answers. As previously noted, interviewers usually digest the responses they get to save time in recording. Interpretation of this extracted record is more difficult than interpretation of a complete record which includes everything said by both respondent and interviewer.[21]

Nonstructured—disguised questioning. Many people are either unwilling or unable to give accurate reports as to their own attitudes and motivations. Thus, even depth interviews (nonstructured-nondisguised questioning) probably give biased results. To overcome this difficulty, clinical psychologists have developed disguised methods of gathering such data. Disguised methods are designed so that the respondent does not know what the objective of the study is. Such disguised methods may also be nonstructured. Projective techniques are an example of this type.

The theory of projective techniques is that every individual, in describing a situation, interprets that situation to a degree. The description given reflects a certain amount of the individual giving it. Thus, if an individual describes a situation, what he reveals is his interpretation of the situation.

---

[21] For an interesting discussion of new efforts to use the computer to improve the analysis of such studies see Seymour Sudman, *Reducing the Cost of Surveys* (Chicago: Aldine Publishing Co., 1967), pp. 154–83.

Various projective techniques are used, but the most common are word association, sentence completion, and story telling. In word association, a series of words is read one at a time to the respondent. After each word the respondent says the first thing that comes into his mind. Sentence completion requires the respondent to complete partial sentences. In story telling, the respondent is shown a picture or given a description and asked to tell a story about it.[22]

A classic study of instant coffee illustrates the general approach.[23] When asked why they didn't like instant coffee, most consumers said they didn't like the flavor. Since this seemed to be a stereotyped answer, one researcher decided to use a disguised method to test it. He constructed two grocery shopping lists which were identical except the coffee on one was Nescafé Instant Coffee and on the other it was one pound Maxwell House Coffee (drip grind). He then selected two matched samples of housewives. One grocery list was shown to one sample and the other list was shown to the other sample. Each house wife was asked to describe the woman who made up the shopping list.

Some of the differences in the women described as making up the lists are revealing of attitudes towards instant coffee.

Nescafé woman	*Maxwell House woman*
48% said lazy	4% said lazy
48% said failed to plan household purchases	12% said failed to plan household purchases
4% said thrifty	16% said thrifty
12% said spendthrift	0% said spendthrift
4% said good wife	16% said good wife

Since projective techniques are unstructured, they have much the same limitations as depth interviews. Interpretation is very subjective, and, hence, is subject to the criticism that it reflects the interpreter as much as the respondent. Cost, time, and difficulty in securing competent field workers are problems which plague projective techniques in a manner similar to depth interviews.

The big advantage of projective techniques lies in their ability to uncover subconscious and socially unacceptable attitudes and motives. When women were asked why they didn't use instant coffee, they said they didn't like the taste. When they were asked to describe the woman who had instant coffee on her shopping list, they described a lazy, un-

---

[22] For a summary of the principal techniques and a discussion of their relative merits see L. C. Lockley, *Use of Motivation Research in Marketing* (Studies in Business Policy #97) (New York: National Industrial Conference Board, 1960).

[23] Mason Haire, "Projective Techniques in Marketing Research," *Journal of Marketing,* Vol. 14 (April, 1950), pp. 649–52, and F. E. Webster, Jr. and F. von Pechmann, "A Replication of the 'Shopping List' Study," *Journal of Marketing,* 34 (April, 1970), pp. 61–63.

skilled housekeeper. When housewives who were low users of milk as a beverage were asked why, they gave no significant reasons, whether the questions were of a direct or indirect type. When a projective technique was used based on pictures of women of different weights, concern for the fattening effect of milk came out clearly.[24]

A further advantage of projective techniques over depth interviews lies in the greater standardization of the stimulus given to the respondent. Stimuli are not standardized in depth interviews, and hence comparisons of results are not valid. But all respondents can be given exactly the same stimulus in projective tests, e.g., word associations. Results are, therefore, more comparable and less subject to bias. Direct comparison of projective results, however, is still not as easy as with most structured studies, because each answer is given in the respondent's own words rather than in terms of one of several established answers.

Despite the obvious merits of projective techniques for obtaining data on motives and attitudes, some evidence indicates that imaginative use of structured questionnaires can obtain similar results with the accompanying advantages of economy. One study with the express purpose of testing this hypothesis found close correlation between the results.[25]

Structured—disguised questioning. Questioning of the structured-disguised type has the advantages of disguise which were pointed out above—primarily that the respondent does not know what is being measured and, hence, is not biased in his answers. The advantages of the structured aspect lie in the reduction of bias on the part of the interviewer and on the part of the interpreter.

Some structured-disguised tests of attitudes are based on the theory that an individual's knowledge, perception, and memory are conditioned by his attitudes. For example, Democrats listen to more speeches by other Democrats than by Republicans; therefore, Democrats have more information about Democratic candidates than about Republican candidates. A simple test of information about candidates would then serve to separate Democrats from Republicans. A straightforward question— Are you a Democrat or a Republican?—might get a biased answer.

Similarly, it is theorized that if respondents are asked questions to which they do not know the answers, they will tend to guess in the direction of their own attitudes. For example, when asked whether various types of people ate hot cereal for breakfast, most respondents reported doctors ate a lot of it but movie actors ate very little hot cereal. This

---

[24] Howard L. Steele, "On the Validity of Projective Questions," *Journal of Marketing Research,* 1 (August, 1964) pp. 46–49.

[25] B. A. Maher, Norman Watt, and Donald T. Campbell, "Comparative Validity of Two Projective and Two Structured Attitude Tests in a Prison Population," *Journal of Applied Psychology,* Vol. 44 (August, 1960), pp. 284–88.

suggests that those respondents thought hot cereal was healthful but "unglamorous."

Data collected by structured-disguised techniques on attitudes towards instant coffee were compared with the similar data collected by nonstructured-disguised techniques as described above. Although the samples in the two studies were not directly comparable, the results obtained with the simple structured-disguised questionnaire were similar in nature to those obtained by the nonstructured approach. The former study, however, benefitted from having the prior data as a guide to the study design.[26]

Another imaginative study of this type used a set of pictures as stimuli, but instead of asking respondents to tell a story, they were asked to select one of a given list of alternatives.[27]

These studies suggest that it is possible to obtain the advantages of disguise and structure in the same study with the attendant ease of handling in doorstep interviews, ease of comprehension by respondent, ease of administration and tabulating, objectively measurable reliability, and economy.

Questionnaire studies classified by methods of communication. In the preceding discussion, questionnaires were classified on the basis of a combination of structure and disguise. Another classification, which overlaps the preceding one but which is useful for illustrating other types of opportunities and problems, is classification on the basis of the method of communication used. Three different methods of communication with questionnaires are available: (1) personal interview, (2) telephone, and (3) mail. Personal interviews are those in which an interviewer obtains information from respondents in face-to-face meetings. Telephone interviews are similar except that communication between interviewer and respondent is via telephone instead of direct personal contact. In most mail surveys, questionnaires are mailed to respondents who also return them by mail. Sometimes, however, mail questionnaires are placed in respondent hands by other means, such as by attaching them to consumer products, putting them in magazines or newspapers, or having field workers leave them with respondents. In each case, respondents complete the questionnaires by themselves and return the completed forms through the mail.

While each of these means has the advantages and disadvantages of the questionnaire in general, each also has its own relative strengths and

---

[26] Ralph Westfall, Harper Boyd, Jr., and Donald T. Campbell, "The Use of Structured Techniques in Motivation Research," *Journal of Marketing*, Vol. 22 (October, 1957), pp. 134–39.

[27] Herbert Kay, "A New Approach to Projective Testing in Survey Research," *The Public Opinion Quarterly*, Vol. 23 (Summer, 1959), pp. 267–78.

weaknesses. Since a strong point of one of these methods is a relative weakness of another, a discussion of each method in turn would involve considerable repetition. Therefore, the discussion is organized around the points of interest rather than the methods of communication.

Flexibility. In considering the method to use in a particular study, the personal interview is almost always the starting point. While telephone interviews are limited to those with telephones, and for mail questionnaires an address list is needed, personal interviews are a possible method in almost any study.

The content of both personal and telephone interviews is more flexible than that in mail questionnaires. Some questions can be asked only of certain respondents, e.g., those who give a specified answer to a preceding question. Interviewers can probe for more information when answers seem not clear or incomplete. Completely unstructured interviews (depth interviews) can be handled in person. Presumably, such studies could also be done by telephone, but it is difficult to gain enough of the respondent's interest and confidence to carry out such projects in the latter method. Both telephone and personal interviews provide an opportunity to catch contradictory statements by respondents, and perhaps to try to reconcile them by further questioning.

These comments, however, may suggest more flexibility than is commonly used in personal interviews. Relatively little advantage is taken of most of these flexibility features with one exception. Most personal interviews vary the questioning from respondent to respondent—some questions are asked only if certain answers are obtained to previous questions. Mail questionnaires can instruct respondents to answer certain questions only if they have answered a previous question in a specified manner. The conditional question, however, cannot be concealed from the respondent.

While the above discussion indicates the flexibility of personal and telephone interviews is an advantage, it may also lead to bias in the results obtained. The researcher must be sure to take advantage of the flexibility only when the possible bias which results can be controlled or is not relevant.

A further advantage to projects using personal and telephone interviews is that such projects can be stopped or altered at any point during the study.[28] Such is not possible with a mail study. Once the questionnaires are mailed, such a study is committed, and the sample or the questionnaire cannot be changed.

Amount of information to be obtained. Questionnaires can usually be longer and more complex with personal interviews than with tele-

---

[28] See, for example, E. M. Birt and R. H. Brogren, "Minimizing Number of Interviews through Sequential Sampling," *Journal of Marketing Research*, 1 (February, 1964), pp. 65–67.

phone or mail. The latter two have to be more brief to gain the cooperation of respondents since they can both be terminated easily. Most
respondents do not find it as easy to stop an interview when they are
face-to-face with an interviewer. A long, complex mail questionnaire is
apt to "scare off" respondents since they can see the length and difficulty
before they ever start filling it out. Using a personal interview does not
solve completely the length and complexity problems, but it does soften
them. Since the interviewer can observe the difficulties and irritations
being experienced by the respondent, he can adjust the pace of the interview to ease these difficulties.

Most commercial research organizations operate on the basis indicated above—that long questionnaires can be handled best by personal
interview, next best by mail, and least well by telephone.

Much has been learned about mail questionnaires in recent years that
has helped to increase the proportion of all questionnaire types which is
returned (as is discussed below). This appears to have reduced greatly
the problem of length, as such, in mail questionnaires. Most recent
studies show just as many people will return a long mail questionnaire
as a short one. In one experiment, for example, equivalent samples were
sent a long questionnaire or one of two short questionnaires which,
when added together, made up the long questionnaire; the long version
obtained responses from 89.6 percent of the recipients, while the two
short versions averaged 90.5 percent.[29]

Little experimental evidence exists as to the effect of length on the
success of telephone interviews. Probably such interviews do have to be
shorter than those conducted in person or by mail.[30] This problem may
also be exaggerated; the authors have conducted a number of telephone
studies of shopping habits in which the average interview with housewives was over twenty minutes in duration. Less than 5 percent of those
initially reached have refused to cooperate or to finish the interview.
The University of Michigan Survey Research Center, however, limits its
telephone interviews to about eleven minutes in length, although its
personal interviews run sixty to seventy-five minutes.[31]

Certain kinds of questionnaires use such devices as pictures and
actual products. It is obvious that only videophone can be used under
such conditions, and that the personal interview may present advantages
over the mail questionnaire when extensive explanation is needed, or

---

[29] C. Scott, "Research on Mail Surveys," *The Journal of the Royal Statistical Society,* Series A, 124 (1961), p. 167. Scott also reviews a number of other experiments
with similar results, including one which found little difference in return with questionnaires up to 35 pages in length.

[30] See Glen H. Mitchell, *Telephone Interviewing* (Wooster, Ohio: Ohio Agricultural Experiment Station, undated), p. 8.

[31] Jay W. Schmiedeskamp, "Reinterviews by Telephone," *Journal of Marketing,*
Vol. 26 (January, 1962), p. 30.

when products must be shown or demonstrated. Personal interviews have another advantage over mail and telephone surveys in that interviewers can observe while asking questions. Interviewers can observe such things as age and evidence of income and, thereby, verify answers given by respondents. In some cases, it is desirable to combine questioning and observation in collecting the basic data. For example, if one wished to find out whether or not housewives know the brand of coffee they use, he might use such a combination of methods. First the interviewer could inquire as to what brand was being used. Then he could seek permission to observe the brand in the pantry. Interviewer observation of the quality of the interview, i.e., the respondent's apparent knowledge of the subject and his willingness to cooperate, are sometimes helpful in interpretation of results. Such observation is possible to a very limited degree in telephone surveys, and in mail studies only to the extent that the questionnaire appears to have been completed carefully or carelessly.

Accuracy of information obtained. Much of the question of the accuracy of data obtained by the three methods of communication relates to the differences in the groups which are actually reached by the different methods. This problem will be considered under the question of sampling below. At this point, the discussion is focused on the effect of the method of communication on the accuracy of the information obtained.

In general, well-conducted studies have been found to obtain similar data from the same respondents whatever method of communication was used.[32] In a study of newspaper readership in New York City, data were collected by telephone and the same respondents were interviewed personally the same night; 93 to 98 percent of the respondents reported the same readership of each of the seven papers studied as they had reported over the telephone.[33] Another telephone survey found the same distribution of drug product sales by brand as did a mail survey, and both were comparable with actual sales as audiited in stores.[34]

Interviews by telephone produce more noncommittal answers than definite choices as compared to personal interviews.[35] People are usually found to be reluctant to report over the telephone personal items such

---

[32] See, for example, Joseph R. Hochstim, "Alternatives to Personal Interviewing," *Public Opinion Quarterly,* Vol. 27 (Winter, 1963), pp. 629–30; and M. A. Baeza, "Sampling and Response Differences for Three Methods of Enumeration" (Ph.D. thesis, Michigan State University, 1950), p. 72.

[33] Don Cahalan, "Measuring Newspaper Readership by Telephone: Two Comparisons with Face-to-Face Interviews," *Journal of Advertising Research,* Vol. 1 (December, 1960), p. 1–6.

[34] Henry Assael, "Comparison of Brand Share Data by Three Reporting Systems," *Journal of Marketing Research,* 4 (November, 1967) pp. 400–01.

[35] Schmiedeskamp, *op. cit.,* pp. 33–34.

as family incomes, plans to buy a car, and use of installment credit, yet some studies have obtained such data successfully by telephone.[36]

Mail questionnaires have been shown to be generally superior to either telephone or personal interviews in collecting data on topics that might be embarrassing.[37] Data from one of the best studies of this problem are shown in Table 4–3. Even though the questions asked appear to be only mildly embarrassing at most, the differences in answers obtained by mail and by personal interview are large.

TABLE 4–3. Responses to the same questions by mail and personal interview

Subject	Personal interview	Mail
Have used hair rinse	37%	51%
Have used eye shadow	46	59
Have purchased margarine	75	82
Have borrowed money at regular bank	17	42
Have borrowed money at credit union	16	22
Have borrowed money at small loan company	11	13
Sample size	200	100

SOURCE: William F. O'Dell, "Personal Interviews or Mail Panels," *Journal of Marketing*, Vol. 26 (October, 1962), pp. 34–39.

Sequence bias is also a threat in mail surveys—respondents can change their answers after seeing later questions. This bias may not be as great as it is usually thought to be. In an experiment to determine the extent of sequence bias, a questionnaire was loaded with references to a particular brand of gasoline before a question as to the brand of gasoline used. Only a 6 percent increase in the proportion reporting use of the specified brand occurred with the mail questionnaire.[38]

In answering open end questions, i.e., questions which the respondent must answer in his own words, respondents tend to be more brief and more general in mail surveys than in personal or telephone interviews.[39] Complex questions with rating scales or other procedures that can be confusing tend to draw more "no answers" in mail surveys.[40]

Without doubt ingenious question design and sound procedure will improve the accuracy of the data collected by any method. Even well-handled studies, however, may show conflicting results as to the accuracy of the data collecting methods. In two such studies, readership

---

[36] John Colombotos, "The Effects of Personal vs. Telephone Interviews on Socially Acceptable Responses," *Public Opinion Quarterly*, 29 (Fall, 1965) pp. 457–58.

[37] D. D. Knudsen, H. Pope, and D. P. Irish, "Response Differences to Questions on Sexual Standards," *Public Opinion Quarterly*, 31 (Summer, 1967) pp. 290–97.

[38] O'Dell, "Personal Interviews or Mail Panels?," p. 36.

[39] O'Dell, *op. cit.*, pp. 36–37; and Schmiedeskamp, *op. cit.*, p. 34.

[40] O'Dell, *op. cit.*, p. 37.

of selected groups of business publications was measured through the use of different types of mail questionnaires and then the same respondents were interviewed personally. Both studies concluded that the mail responses were extremely inaccurate in all but one case. When cover pictures of recent issues were used in an aided-recall mail questionnaire, one study found results that checked closely with personal interview results,[41] while the other study found the same technique greatly inflated the reading figures for some publications and penalized others.[42]

In most comparisons of results such as the above, it is assumed that the results from the personal interview are the most accurate. However, it is not always certain that this assumption is valid. An experiment on the reporting of hospitalization experiences gave an opportunity to test data obtained by mail and personal interview against actual hospital records. Little difference was found, but if anything, the mail results were more accurate.[43] Nevertheless, interview data are generally accepted as the most accurate.

The opportunity for interviews in both personal and telephone studies to adapt to each situation is an advantage, but also can be a distinct threat to accuracy of the data collected. It is generally believed that the greatest error in most surveys comes from this interaction of interviewers and respondents. Each interviewer is different and adapts to each respondent in a different way. Interviewers typically receive little training and work with little or no supervision. A new technology is now making it feasible to improve this element in telephone interviews.[44]

Wide Area Telephone Service (WATS) as offered by the Bell System provides unlimited telephone calls to a given zone of the United States for a fixed charge. Monthly charges from Chicago range from $700 for a nearby zone to over $2,000 for the most distant zone in the country. Using WATS, a small number of interviewers can make a sizable survey quickly from one central location. The fixed line rental charge makes this feasible. Because the interviewing crew is small and concentrated at one place, better training can be provided the interviewers and very close supervision can be maintained throughout the survey. The major

[41] *A Comparative Study of Mail Questionnaire Techniques for Measuring Reading of Business Publications* (Chicago: Putnam Publishing Co., 1960).

[42] *Techniques and Standards for Mailed Readership Questionnaires* (Princeton: Industrial Advertising Research Institute, 1963).

[43] Charles Cannell and Floyd Fowler, "Comparison of a Self-Enumerative Procedure and a Personal Interview," *Public Opinion Quarterly*, Vol. 27 (Summer, 1963), pp. 250–64.

[44] The following discussion on WATS is based on Malcolm A. McNiven, "Why duPont Uses WATS for Surveys," *Marketing Forum*, 1 (November, 1965) pp. 24–25; R. K. McMillan, "The Advantages of WATS in Research," *op. cit.*, pp. 26–27; and J. O. Eastlack, Jr. and Henry Assael, "Better Telephone Surveys through Centralized Interviewing," *Journal of Advertising Research*, 6 (March, 1966), pp. 2–7.

benefits from using WATS appear to be: (1) accurate control of persons interviewed (the sample); (2) control over what the interviewer asks and how she asks it; and (3) control of the quality of the interviewing as measured in such things as number of refusals, interviews per hour, number of incomplete interviews, and amount of editing required on completed interviews.

Careful planning of questionnaires and interviewing procedures and detailed scheduling of interviews to use the WATS lines to capacity are necessary if costs are to be held to levels obtained in normal decentralized telephone surveys. When such planning is well done, the cost of surveys using WATS is about the same as for normal procedures. Data obtained in WATS studies are different from data obtained via standard methods and are believed to be more accurate.

The use of WATS provides close, centralized supervision of the actual process of data collection. No such supervision is feasible with personal interviews. With mail questionnaires, the wording of questions is held constant, but other aspects of the data collection are completely unknown to the researcher. The possibility is always present that the respondent got aid from others in answering the questions. Another possibility is that the respondent read over the questions, but then put them aside to answer at a later date. In the meantime, the respondent would be more sensitive to factors related to the questions. For example, if a respondent is asked to list all the brands of canned beans with which he is familiar, he might be able to name five or six immediately. If he is permitted to think about it for a while, however, he may remember more, particularly if he visits a store during this time.

This disadvantage of the mail questionnaire may be an advantage under certain conditions. In some studies it may be desirable for the respondent to think over his answers carefully, to discuss the question with others, or to consult records. Studies which seek such things as sales or expenses from business firms may be of this type. Personal interviews, and especially telephone interviews, are weak in this respect.

Telephone and personal interviews have one important advantage in getting accurate data—they can be used to collect information on events at the same time they are happening, thus reducing the errors resulting from failure of memory. Radio and television listening are often checked in this manner. Telephone interviews are particularly good in this respect as the speed with which they can be conducted permits a relatively large number of interviews during a short period, e.g., the period during which a particular TV program is on.

Sampling. The largest difference among the three methods of communication is in the amount of control they permit over the sample from which information is collected. A method of data collection is weak if it does not permit close control of the respondents. The discussion here is organized around two aspects of the sampling problem: (1) selecting the sample, and (2) collecting data from the sample selected.

1. Selecting the sample.   Theoretically it is easy to select a representative sample for use with either the personal interview or mail survey since both can reach all members of the population. But the execution may be difficult. To select a representative sample, it is usually necessary to have a list of all members of the universe under study. This may be unavailable. With personal interviews it is often possible to substitute lists of areas, such as city blocks. These lists are more readily available than are lists of people, but the process of planning and selecting a national or large area sample in this way is arduous, time consuming, and expensive.[45]

In mail surveys it is necessary to work with mailing lists, but such lists which purport to cover the general population are not likely to be representative. Approximately 10 percent of the adult population is illiterate for the purpose of completing even a simple questionnaire.[46] However, for many special universes, such as the charge account customers of a department store, complete lists are available. A number of firms now provide established mail panels—lists of families that have agreed to answer mail questionnaires on almost any topic. These panels are set up to be representative of the population on various characteristics, but there is always the fact that only about one family in five will join such a panel, which suggests that those that won't join may differ in some respects from the others.

Historically, telephone surveys have been thought to be especially weak in sampling for general population studies because many people did not have telephones. Even those who did were not all listed in the telephone directories. When new directories are issued, about 9 percent of the actual telephones are unlisted; and by the time the next directory comes out, about one year later, 18 percent of the telephones are unlisted.[47]

By 1965, there were telephones in 81 percent of U.S. households and the percentage was growing. There was considerable variation among population groups—56 percent of the households with annual income below $10,000 had telephones as compared to 96 percent for those with incomes over $15,000; 86 percent of the households in the northeast and north central regions had telephones, but only 70 percent in the south; and in urban areas the percentage was 85 as compared to 73 in rural areas.[48]

---

[45] This procedure is discussed in some detail in Chapter 9.

[46] Claire Selltiz, Marie Jahoda, Morton Deutsch, and Stuart W. Cook, *Research Methods in Social Relations* (New York: Henry Holt and Co., 1959), p. 241.

[47] S. L. Cooper, "Random Sampling by Telephone: An Improved Method," *Journal of Marketing Research*, 1 (November, 1964), pp. 45–58.

[48] "Characteristics of Households with Telephones: March, 1965," *Current Population Reports* (Bureau of the Census, 1965), Series P–20, No. 146, pp. 5–6.

While one should still hesitate to use telephone homes as the sampling base for studies in which income distribution, size of city, region, education, race, or similar characteristics were major factors, the wide ownership of telephones now makes it feasible to use telephone homes as the sampling population for many studies. New methods of sampling telephone listings by generating random numbers make it possible to include all telephones whether they are listed or not.[49] When these possibilities are coupled with the efficiencies of Wide Area Telephone Service, they result in an increase in the use of the telephone method of communication. The telephone interview is particularly useful from a sampling standpoint in studies involving individuals who are almost sure to have telephones, e.g., doctors, layers, and druggists.

2. Collecting data from a representative sample.   While it is difficult to select a representative sample, it is even more difficult to collect data from all the people or organizations selected. Unfortunately, this factor is often overlooked and results are compiled as though they represented data from every individual in the selected sample.

There are two elements to the problem, making contact with the party selected in the sample and obtaining the proper information from the respondent after contact is made. Information is not obtained from all individuals selected for the sample in personal interviews because some of them are not at home when the interviewer calls and others refuse to be interviewed. The percentage of not-at-homes varies with the time of year, time of day, and day of the week, but frequently it runs as much as 40 to 60 percent on the first call by the interviewer. After two or three callbacks, personal interview studies usually achieve response rates between 75 and 90 percent. Up to 14 percent of respondents selected for a sample are not reached even after repeated callbacks. Not-at-homes are the greatest problem in cities, particularly in the upper-class apartment sections of cities. The growing number of high-rise apartments with doormen to keep out strangers is making it increasingly difficult to reach upper-middle and upper-class population groups. The percentage of refusals varies considerably according to the nature of the study and the type of respondent involved; percentages range from 0.5 to 13 percent, with 10 percent fairly typical. Refusals tend to be concentrated among lower-class respondents as measured by education, occupation, and ethnic identification. Failure to include data from the not-at-homes and refusals may cause considerable bias in results. Families who were not at home on the first call, but who were later interviewed, have been found to differ materially from those at home on the first call in ownership of homes, washing machines, and sewing machines.

After a telephone survey of TV viewing habits, respondents were in-

---

[49] S. L. Cooper, *op. cit.*, and J. O. Eastlack, Jr. and Henry Assael, "Better Telephone Surveys through Centralized Interviewing," *Journal of Advertising Research*, 6 (March, 1966), pp. 2–7.

vited by post card to attend a group meeting to discuss TV programming. Of the top 5 percent on a social class scale, 38 percent attended, whereas only 24 percent attended from the lowest 75 percent on the social class scale.[50] Telephone interviews encounter not-at-home and refusal problems similar to those found in personal interviews. Not-at-homes probably average somewhat less in telephone surveys than in personal interviews because people who will not answer the door to a stranger will answer the telephone. Most investigators report refusals are lower in telephone surveys, 4 percent or less,[51] but some report refusal rates twice as large on the telephone, particularly on intimate or controversial topics.[52]

Callbacks are relatively easy to make by telephone, and several such calls will usually reach a large proportion of those called. Using up to seven callbacks, one researcher obtained telephone interviews with 98.4 percent of his selected sample of over ten thousand.[53] In another study of 5,711 households in 187 different places throughout the United States, only 86.7 percent of the calls were completed despite "repeated calls." Language difficulties, refusals, and not-at-homes accounted for the balance.[54]

Telephone calls will often reach individuals who are difficult to reach by personal interview—wealthy individuals, doctors, and businessmen, for example, who are protected from interviewers by "gatekeepers" of various types.

Mail surveys presumably are not bothered by the not-at-home problem, but the number of individuals who fail to return completed questionnaires is usually large. Whereas the percentage of not-at-homes and refusals is usually not as large as 50 percent in personal interview or telephone studies, the number who do not return mail questionaires may run far above this unless great care and ingenuity are shown. As recently as ten years ago, returns from questionnaires mailed to the general pulic tended to run between 3 percent and 10 percent.

Current mail surveys are tending to achieve higher proportions of returns. Five different studies among general population groups in England achieved usable returns of 85 to 94 percent and failed to

---

[50] William Belson, "Volunteer Bias in Test-Room Groups," *Public Opinion Quarterly,* Vol. 24 (Spring, 1960), pp. 115–26.

[51] S. S. Kegeles, C. F. Fink, and J. P. Kirscht, "Interviewing a National Sample by Long-Distance Telephone," *Public Opinion Quarterly,* 33 (Fall, 1969), p. 416.

[52] "Current Status of Telephone Surveys," *Public Opinion Quarterly,* 33 (Fall, 1969), p. 506. But see L. Coombs and R. Freedman, "Use of Telephone Interviews in a Longitudinal Fertility Study," *Public Opinion Quarterly,* 28 (Spring, 1964), p. 114 for very low refusal rate on a highly personal subject.

[53] Mitchell, Glen H., *op. cit.,* p. 7.

[54] *The Characteristics of the Reading Audience* (New York: Newsweek, 1959).

obtain returns of any kind from only 4 to 10 percent.[55] Studies among selected groups of relatively small size have achieved 100 percent returns.[56] Several companies now claim to average over 70 percent returns on consumer mail questionnaires and over 50 percent returns on industrial mail surveys.[57] Returns of less than 50 percent usually should not be accepted today.

The degree of interest in the subject of the survey is a major factor in determining whether or not a respondent will return a mail questionnaire. Table 4–4 illustrates how widely returns will vary among seg-

TABLE 4–4. Returns of mail questionnaires on value of audit committees by various population segments

Population group	Questionnaires mailed	Questionnaires returned	Percentage returned
Chief executive officers	1,732	420	24%
Nonofficer directors	1,950	245	13
Independent CPA's	186	140	75
Internal auditors	51	37	65
Total	3,919	842	21%

SOURCE: R. F. Mautz and F. L. Neumann, "The Effective Corporate Audit Committee," *Harvard Business Review,* 48 (November–December, 1970), p. 58.

ments of the survey population when their interest in the subject varies. Obviously, if some of the segments differed significantly in their opinions on the subject under investigation, such large differences in rate of response would bias the general results.

Many commercial marketing research firms now maintain panels of consumers that can be used for mail surveys. Since these panels are recruited for the express purpose of participating in such studies, the response rate should be high and does, in fact, tend to average 80 to 90 percent.[58] This high return reduces the likelihood of serious bias from nonresponse. Panels are selected to correspond to the general population in geographic and city-size location, age of housewife, and family income. If the subject under study is related to other factors such as family composition or nationality of origin, data obtained may be misleading. One mail survey within such a panel found 65 percent had

---

[55] Scott, *op. cit.,* p. 146. See also Stanley C. Plog, "Explanations for a High Return Rate on Mail Questionnaire," *Public Opinion Quarterly,* Vol. 27 (Summer, 1963), pp. 297–98.

[56] J. Fred Weston, ed., "Handbook on Defense-Space Market Research" (unpublished manuscript, 1963), p. V–1.

[57] See, for example, E. G. Francel, "Mail-Administered Questionnaires: A Success Story," *Journal of Marketing Research,* 3 (February, 1966), pp. 89–91, and J. J. Watson, "Improving the Response Rate in Mail Research," *Journal of Advertising Research,* 5 (June, 1965), pp. 48–50.

[58] O'Dell, *op. cit.,* p. 35.

drunk milk within the last twenty-four hours, but only 31 percent had drunk tea. A controlled sample interviewed in person showed the proportions for the two were essentially the same, 42 and 41 percent, respectively.[59]

Undoubtedly, there are other, less obvious, factors that influence the return of mail questionnaires. The more of these that can be identified, the more able the researcher is to interpret their influence on the results. Subtle personality characteristics may be very important. One researcher asked county agricultural agents to identify farmers who were "innovators." One hundred fifty who were so designated were mailed a questionnaire and 146, or 97 percent, responded.[60] Further studies to investigate factors of this type are needed.

The most important consideration to insure that a mail questionnaire obtains information from a representative sample is to obtain responses from a large proportion of the individuals receiving the questionnaire. A small percentage of non-response will have little effect on the results, even if the nonresponders differ from the others. Methods to obtain high response have two general purposes: to secure a large percentage response to a given mailing and to obtain returns from those who do not respond at first.

Researchers using mailed questionnaires should start with the assumption that the questionnaire is an imposition. To overcome the natural resistance to such an imposition, it is necessary to be sure the questionnaire is well designed and laid out for easy completion and mailing (discussed in the questionnaire chapter), that the request for completion of the questionnaire is persuasive, and that a persistent follow-up is initiated to urge cooperation on those who don't respond at once.

An imaginative cover letter with a personal, friendly tone can have a major effect on the rate of response. Many experiments have been conducted to find the mechanical and procedural devices that will insure the best returns. Some of these are contradictory, but in general the following seem to be effective: official sponsorship shown by letterhead; stamped instead of metered postage both ways; airmail postage both ways; eight one-cent stamps instead of one eight-cent stamp; incentive included with mailing—25¢ probably the most productive per dollar; request immediate response; send extra copy of questionnaire; and mail on Friday. Color of paper, anonymity, and personalized salutation appear to have no definite effect.[61]

---

[59] *Ibid.*

[60] E. M. Rogers, "Characteristics of Agricultural Innovators and Other Adapter Categories," in *Studies of Innovation and of Communication to the Public,* Studies in the Utilization of Behavioral Science, Vol. 2 (Institute for Communication Research, Stanford University, 1962), pp. 63–97.

[61] See Scott, *op. cit.*, pp. 164–79; Watson, *op. cit.*; Francel, *op. cit.*; and S. D. Bachrack and H. M. Scoble, "Mail Questionnaire Efficiency: Controlled Reduction of Nonresponse," *Public Opinion Quarterly,* 31 (Summer, 1967), pp. 265–71.

Follow-up letters, telephone calls, and even personal visits are used to increase the number of returns of mail questionnaires. A quick follow-up postcard sent only two or three days after the orginal mailing increases the initial response. Most returns will be received within two weeks. A follow-up at that point will bring another wave of responses; another follow-up two weeks later will produce a third wave of responses. In general, the responses at each wave will be in roughly the same proportion of the nonrespondents still existing, but this may vary according to the stimulus used and the size of the response to the initial mailing. Table 4–5 shows the results from a mail survey with three follow-ups among members of the League of Women Voters.

TABLE 4–5. Responses to original mailing and three follow-ups

Item	Number of returns	Percent of non- respondents outstanding	Percent of total sample	
			This wave	Cumulative
First Mailing	1,278	46.2%	46.2%	46.2%
First follow-up: letter	338	22.7	12.2	58.4
Second follow-up: letter	244	19.6	8.8	67.2
Third follow-up: letter	279	28.9	10.1	77.3

SOURCE: Marjorie N. Donald, "Implications of Nonresponse for the Interpretation of Mail Questionnaire Data," *Public Opinion Quarterly,* Vol. 24 (Spring, 1960), pp. 99–114.

Analysis of data obtained in each wave of response tends to indicate that the most interested respondents answer first and that the trend of the data predict the actual situation better than the totals at any particular time.[62]

Results obtained from mail surveys are generally not considered to be as accurate as results from personal or telephone studies. With the higher rate of return now achieved in good mail surveys, this is not so clear. Studies among populations with higher than average income, education, and social status in particular probably produce as accurate results by mail as by any other method. For example, information on life insurance policies held was obtained from a national sample by personal interview at the same time that the same information was obtained from a mail panel. Data such as company with which policies were owned, amount of insurance owned, and premium payments were verified against company records. The mail panel produced more accurate results in each case.[63]

Despite the improving returns being reported on mail surveys, many such studies still have large proportions of nonrespondents. Whenever this is the case, some special attention should be given to estimating

---

[62] Scott, *op. cit.,* pp. 160–62.

[63] Robert C. Nuckols, "Personal Interview versus Mail Panel Survey," *Journal of Marketing Research,* Vol. 1 (February, 1964), pp. 11–16.

the characteristics of interest among the nonrespondents. Telephone or personal interviews among a subsample of nonrespondents are the best procedure. Information so obtained can be compared with the data collected by mail and the similarities or differences used in interpreting the results.

Of course, the same type of analysis of nonrespondents should be made with the other methods of communication if the nonresponse percentage is large. That it may often be larger than one is apt to suspect and that it may not differ much by method of communication is suggested by the data published as part of the congressional investigation of the broadcast rating services. Table 4–6 shows the proportion of the total population covered by the final data collected by each of five methods of collecting data.

TABLE 4–6. Percentage of total universe from which data obtained by each of five data collection methods used in broadcast audience research

Data collection method	Percentage of universe covered
Personal interview	52%
Telephone recall	59
Telephone coincidental	52
Meter (tape mailed in)	62
Diary (mailed in)	54

SOURCE: *Evaluation of Statistical Methods Used in Obtaining Broadcast Ratings* (Report of the Committee on Interstate and Foreign Commerce) (Washington, D.C.: U.S. Government Printing Office, 1961), p. 77.

Other considerations.   Other considerations which are important in appraising personal interview, mail, and telephone methods of communication are speed, cost, and quality control. The three are closely related.

Telephone interviews are by far the fastest of the three. With short questionnaires, as many as twenty calls an hour can be made. Interviewers calling at homes could not approach that figure, even if their calls were concentrated in a very small geographic area. Of course, more interviewers can be used to shorten the time required to complete either telephone or personal interview studies. As the number of interviewers increases, the problems of quality control increase. This is particularly true with personal interviews in studies covering large geographical areas. Telephone interviewers can be concentrated at one location, even for national studies, thus making intensive training and supervision feasible. Long-distance toll charges formerly made the costs of large telephone studies prohibitive, but WATS has brought these costs down.

Quality in data collection has some subjective elements, but the following are common indicators:[64]

---

[64] Eastlack and Assael, *op. cit.*, p. 4.

1. Percentage of refusals.
2. Percentage of completed interviews.
3. Number of callbacks required to locate respondent.
4. Average number of interviews per hour.
5. Percentage of questionnaires that have to be returned for editing.
6. Supervisor rating of interview process.

All these factors are primarily related to telephone and personal interviews. The first five can be measured in both types of studies. Field work assignments vary in personal interviews (high-rise apartments, slums, or rural areas, for example), so that comparison of interviewers is questionable and time lags between field locations and the central office make it difficult to correct weaknesses. Supervision of the actual interview process is almost impossible with personal interviews. When telephone interviewers all work at a central location, each can be given an assignment comparable with the others, and supervisors can listen to the actual interviews. Corrections can be made quickly.

A small group of workers in one location can handle a large mail survey. There are no interviewer variations in mail projects. Once questionnaires are put in the mail, however, the researcher can do nothing to change the character of the response process and little to speed it up. A period of two weeks is usually necessary to receive the bulk of the returns from one mailing. If a follow-up letter is sent, another two weeks is required. Some researchers are now finding they can speed this up by sending the follow-up after only one week.[65] Nevertheless, if great speed is needed, the mail method is probably not the best solution. Very large samples, however, can be coverd by mail in the same period required for small samples.

Time and the administrative problems of quality control lead to high costs. Therefore, the personal interview tends to be the most expensive per completed questionnaire, and the telephone interview tends to be the cheapest. This is a tendency only, however, and in many specific situations the relative costs of the three methods will be different. Some comparisons from specific studies are shown in Table 4–7, and give ideas as to how costs vary. All of the expense data are not directly comparable as it is not clear how much in the way of administrative and sample selection expenses were included in each case.

Selection of method to use. The use of either personal interview, mail, or telephone involves advantages and disadvantages. Fundamentally, however, the decision to use one or the other method is based on thinking as to the accuracy of the information which will be obtained. If the same results will be achieved by each method of collecting data, the decision can be made on the basis of cost or speed.

---

[65] W. E. Cox, Jr., "Response Patterns to Mail Surveys," *Journal of Marketing Research*, 3 (November, 1966), p. 392–97.

TABLE 4-7. Cost data from selected studies

	Method of data collection				
	Telephone[a]	Mail[b]	Personal[c]	Telephone[d]	Personal[d]
Subject of survey	Health	Unknown	Health	Health	Health
Respondents	General U.S. population	Urban households	Urban households	Doctors	Doctors
Number of completed questionnaires	456	750	1,298	24	40
Administrative costs	$ 506	—	$ 5,900	—	—
Interviewer costs	584	—	10,700	$160	$645
Telephone tolls	1,259	—	—	125	—
Mailing expense	—	153	—	—	—
Travel expense	—	—	800	—	—
Inducements	—	493	—	—	—
Miscellaneous costs	275	295	300	—	—
Total costs	$2,626	$941	$17,700	$285	$645
Cost per completed interview	$ 5.78	$ 1.25	$ 13.65	$ 11.87	$ 16.12

SOURCES: a. Kegeles, Fink, and Kirscht, *op. cit.*, p. 415.
b. Estimated from data in T. R. Wotruba, "Monetary Inducements and Mail Questionnaire Response," *Journal of Marketing Research*, 3 (November, 1966), pp. 398–400. Returns were 40 percent of those mailed.
c. J. R. Hochstim and D. A. Athanasopoulos, "Personal Follow-up in a Mail Survey," *Public Opinion Quarterly*, 34 (Spring, 1970), pp. 69–81.
d. Seymour Sudman, "New Uses of Telephone Methods in Survey Research," *Journal of Marketing Research*, 3 (May, 1966), pp. 163–67.

Comparisons of the cost per completed interview such as those given above are not always a sound basis for decision. If a particular method of communication will not reach a particular population group or will not secure accurate information from that group on the subject of interest, there is no point in considering its use no matter what its cost. Cost per unit of accuracy would be a desirable basis for comparing these three methods, but accuracy can be quantified only arbitrarily[66] Major factors affecting the decision are the homogeneity of the population to be studied, the subject of interest, the length of the questionnaire, the complexity of the questionnaire, geographical area to be covered, the time available for the study, and budgetary limitations.

OBSERVATIONAL METHOD

Observation is the second method of collecting data. It is the process of recognizing and noting people, objects, and occurrences rather than asking for information. For example, instead of asking consumers what brands they buy or what television programs they view, the researcher arranges to observe what products are bought and what programs are watched.

Advantages and disadvantages of observation

Some of the advantages of this method of collecting data as compared to the questionnaire method are obvious. If the researcher observes and records events, he does not have to rely on the willingness and ability of respondents to report accurately. Furthermore, the biasing effect of the interviewer or his phrasing of questions is either eliminated or reduced. Data collected by observation are, therefore, more objective and generally more accurate. Several comparisons of observation and questionnaire data were presented in the early part of this chapter showing the relative accuracy of the observational method.

Unfortunately, the observational method also has a number of weaknesses which keep it from being more widely used. Researchers have long recognized the merits of observation as opposed to questioning, yet the vast majority of marketing research projects continue to rely on the questionnaire. Probably the most limiting factor in the use of observation is the inability to observe such things as attitudes, motivations, and plans. Only as these factors are reflected in actions can they be observed, and then they are confounded with so many other factors as to make their identification difficult, if not impossible.

---

[66] For an interesting effort in this direction see Lester R. Frankel, "How Incentives and Subsamples Affect the Precision of Mail Surveys," *Journal of Advertising Research,* Vol. 1 (September, 1960), pp. 1–5.

Events of more than short-term duration also pose observational problems. For example, a family's use of leisure time, frequency of visits to the drug store, or the use of hotels or motels on the last trip are items which do not lend themselves to observation. Personal and intimate activities such as brushing teeth and watching TV late at night are more easily discussed with questionnaires than they are observed.

On the other hand, there are some things which can be observed, but which cannot be reported with any accuracy by respondents. Tone of voice, nervous habits, and spatial relationships in interpersonal encounters are examples of things of which most people are too unaware to report accurately, but which can be observed.

Observation eliminates much of the subjective element encountered with questionnaires, but it is not entirely objective. Observers are still necessary and, being human, are subject to error. Many times these observers are well trained and are required to record only facts in which they have no personal interest. Results under these circumstances should be objective and accurate. In other studies, however, observers may be active participants and, therefore, may not be objective reporters. For example, an observer may go into a store acting as a customer. He is to observe the activities of the salesman. This involves interaction between the two. Since another observer might interact differently with the salesman, the results obtained will have subjective elements.

In some observational studies, it is impractical to keep the respondent from knowing that he is being observed. This results in a biasing effect similar to the one found in questionnaire studies. If the respondent knows his actions are being observed, he is apt to act differently than he otherwise would.

Cost is a final disadvantage of observation. Under most circumstances, observational data are more expensive to obtain than survey data. It is necessary to station observers where they can see the pertinent phenomena. Frequently, this requires the observer to wait, doing nothing, between events to be observed. For example, to observe the consumers who ask for a specific brand of canned milk, an observer would have to wait in a store until customers came in for canned milk. This unproductive time is an increased cost.

In a large study to measure the retail sales of apples, data were collected by both direct observation of sales and by auditing of store records. The two methods produced data of equal accuracy, but the observational method was more expensive than the audit method—$35,000 versus $20,000 per market per year if a sample of one hundred stores were used in a market.[67] Another project along the same lines found the

---

[67] Peter L. Henderson and Sidney E. Brown, *Measuring Weekly Changes in the Wholesale and Retail Movement of Apples* (Washington: U.S. Department of Agriculture, 1959), p. 1.

observation of sales was cheaper for fast moving items in large stores, but auditing of records was cheaper for slow moving items in small stores.[68]

Methods of observation[69]

Observational studies can be classified usefully on five bases: (1) whether the situation in which the observation is made is natural or contrived, (2) whether the respondent knows he is observed or not, (3) whether the observation is structured or unstructured, (4) whether the factor of interest is observed directly or indirectly, and (5) whether observations are made by observers or by mechanical means. Various combinations of these bases are used to establish the following classes.

Simple direct observation. When an observer is stationed in a grocery store to note how many different brands of canned soup each shopper picks up before selecting one, there is simple, direct observation in a natural situation. If the observer looks and acts like another shopper, the regular shoppers do not realize they are being observed. If a camera is positioned to record shopping actions, the observation is by mechanical means. If the observer counts the specific cans picked up, the observation is structured; but if the observer has a less clear assignment, such as to observe how shoppers go about selecting a brand of soup, the situation is unstructured.

Structured direct observation is used when the problem at hand has been formulated precisely enough to enable the researcher to define specifically the observations to be made. An observer in a supermarket, for example, might note the number of different cans of soup picked up by each customer buying soup. Such observations are not as apt to have a subjective bias by the observer as are unstructured observations. A form can be easily printed for simple recording of such observations. Even if the observer must wait for an unnoticed moment to record each observation, he is not apt to have as much bias in his memory as with unstructured observations. Not all structured observations are as simple as this example, but experiments have shown that even observers with different points of view on a given question will tend to make similar observations under structured conditions.[70]

Unstructured direct observation is similar to unstructured questioning;

---

[68] Earl E. Houseman and Benjamin Lipstein, "Observation and Audit Techniques for Measuring Retail Sales," *Agricultural Economics,* Vol. 12 (July, 1960), pp. 61–72. Notice, however, that auditing of records may be considered a form of observation.

[69] The following discussion draws heavily on E. J. Webb, D. T. Campbell, K. D. Schwartz, and Lee Sechrest, *Unobstrusive Measures: Nonreactive Research in the Social Sciences* (Chicago: Rand McNally & Co., 1966).

[70] H. Thelen and J. Withall, "Three Frames of Reference," *Human Relations,* Vol. 2 (1949), pp. 159–76.

an observer is placed in a situation and observes whatever he deems pertinent. For example, in an effort to find ways of improving the service in a retail store, an observer may mingle with customers in the store and look for activities that suggest service problems. Such observation is subject to subjective errors in both the actual observation and recording. No one can observe everything that is going on, hence the observer must select certain things to note. The actual observation also has subjective elements because of the difficulty of separating observation from inference; a customer standing at a counter with an annoyed look on her face may be observed as irritated because of lack of service. The latter inference follows so easily from the observation that it may not be separated from it.

The following is the report of one out of a large number of observations of shopping behavior in supermarkets:[71]

A school age boy and his parents enter the aisle.

The parents hurry down the aisle, looking straight ahead and not even glancing at the cereals.

"Can't I have some cereal?" asks the boy very winningly.

"No," answers the father very sternly, and quickly continues up the aisle.

"You dirty crumb," is the boy's reply as he walks up the aisle with his head lowered.

This is a somewhat dramatic observation. Did the drama cause the observer to overlook more mundane aspects of the family's behavior? Would similar adjectives have been used by other observers to describe the behavior? The example suggests the possibilities for observer bias. In this particular study, the researchers found two major problems: (1) to get observers to record their observations in detail, and (2) to prepare permanent records of observations at the earliest opportunity. Extensive training was necessary to overcome these problems. The second problem above is common to observations where an effort is made to keep the observer unnoticed. In such cases, the observer cannot easily record the data except from memory—another invitation to error.

Sampling is another problem common to direct observation studies. Because it is necessary to let events happen as they do naturally, it is often difficult to get a cross-sectional sample. Efforts are usually made to sample at different geographical locations (e.g., different stores) and to make a representative sampling of time periods.

Contrived observation. When the researcher relies on simple direct observation, he frequently finds the observer has a great deal of waste time while he waits for the desired event to happen. To reduce this problem, it may be desirable to contrive situations so that observations

[71] W. D. Wells and L. A. LoScuito, "Direct Observation of Purchasing Behavior," *Journal of Marketing Research* (August, 1966), p. 227.

may be made more efficiently. To study the bargaining that goes on be-tween automobile salesmen and customers, for example, the researcher may have his observer pose as a customer and take various bargaining attitudes from the most eager to buy to the toughest price-seeking. In each case, the observer would note the salesman's response. As long as the salesman believes the researcher to be a *bona fide* customer, there is no bias in the observation. It is often much easier for the observer-cus-tomer to maintain a natural situation than for an intruder-observer to do so. As a result, contrived observations often have a validity advantage as well as an economic one.

Another type of contrived observation is the lost-letter technique. To measure the relative interest in a political candidate in different geo-graphical areas, sixty letters addressed to:[72]

> Educators for Senator Eugene McCarthy
> c/o A. Wicker
> Specific residential address

were "lost" in each of several areas. Another sixty letters with the same address except for the first line were lost in each of the same areas. The proportion of letters returned from both the experimental and control groups in each area was then observed.

Chinese jade merchants presumably learned to determine the inten-sity of a customer's interest in a particular piece by watching the cus-tomer's eyes carefully and noting a dilation of the pupils. This idea has been used in contrived observation studies by exposing respondents to different advertisements and observing pupil dilation—the most interest-ing advertisements are believed to bring the largest dilation. Obviously, in studies of this type, the situation is not natural and might be pre-sumed to bias the results, although it is doubtful that respondents can control eye response.

Mechanical observation. In the discussion of both simple direct observation and contrived observation, it was assumed that humans were used as observers. A number of imaginative methods of mechanical ob-servation and devices for making such observations have been developed. The most widely known device of this type is the audimeter, a device used by the A. C. Nielsen Company to record when radio and television sets are turned on and the stations to which they are tuned. The tape on which this information is recorded is mailed at regular intervals to the Nielsen Company, where it is analyzed. Another device for making ob-servations is the psychogalvanometer. This machine measures minute emotional reactions through changes in the rate of perspiration, much like a lie detector. Advertisements can be tested for relative impact by

---

[72] A. W. Wicker, "A Failure to Validate the Lost-Letter Technique," *Public Opinion Quarterly*, 33 (Summer, 1969), pp. 260–62.

showing them to respondents and measuring the emotional response of the respondent on the galvanometer.

The eye-camera is a device to record the movements of the eye. A respondent can be given an advertisement and the eye-camera can then be used to record the movements of the eye in looking at the ad—what parts are noted first, in what sequence the various copy blocks are read, and what parts attract the longest attention.

The latter two methods tend to be limited to laboratory settings and, hence, raise questions as to the bias of observation in unnatural circumstances and when the respondent knows he is being observed. The audimeter raises more subtle questions. This device is placed on the radio or TV set in a manner that has no effect on the way these appliances are used. Even though the subjects can use their radios and television sets in a normal manner, there is some question whether or not they will be "natural" if they know they are being observed. Will the family that knows its TV set has an audimeter on it watch the same programs, no more and no less, as it otherwise would? Research on this question indicates that whatever bias occurs when the audimeter is placed on the TV set soon wears off. On the other hand, a small bias does occur because some families, ones who view TV relatively little on the average, will not permit audimeters to be placed on their sets.[73]

Physical traces.   Methods discussed above are all direct observations of the factors of interest. One type of observation, however, focuses on the physical traces left by the factor of interest. These traces are of two types—accretions left or erosion that has resulted—similar in character to the delta built up at the mouth of a river as compared to a canyon carved by the same river. To define the trading area of cities, researchers have found it useful to observe the formations where farm roads enter the main highways leading to a city. Where the corners of these intersections have been rounded off the most on the side towards a given city, it is safe to assume that the majority of the time farmers entering the main highway are turning towards that city and are, in fact, a part of the city's trading area. At the point where the "round-off" begins to be more in the opposite direction, the farmers belong to the trading area of another city. When flying over an area, this breaking point between two trading areas can often be seen clearly.

Other accretion studies have involved the observation of liquor bottles in trash to estimate the liquor consumption in cities without package stores,[74] and the determination of the best radio stations on which to advertise to car-listeners by observing the stations at which radios were

[73] Cordell and Rahmel, *op. cit.,* p. 46.

[74] H. G. Sawyer, *The Meaning of Numbers* (speech before American Association of Advertising Agencies, 1961).

set in the cars brought to a car dealer for repair.[75] Brand preference studies are often based on observation of brands on consumer pantry shelves, and relative store emphasis on different brands is noted by observing the size of the inventory displayed.

Erosion observations are less frequent in marketing research, but examples are a study of the relative popularity of different museum displays done by observing the relative wear on floor tiles around the exhibits, and a study of the relative readership of different sections of an encyclopedia by measuring the wear and tear on the pages.

Observation of the results of past actions will not bias the data if done on a one-time basis. Pantry audits can determine what products have been bought previously. If such audits are made regularly, however, as with some store audits, biased data may result. It is rumored, for example, that manufacturers' salesmen attempt to find the stores which are audited and put special sales effort on these stores. In this way they hope to make it appear that they are building large stocks with their retail store customers.

Observation of records. Whenever the researcher uses data collected for another purpose, he employs the observation method in a manner very similar in character to the observation of physical traces. In one sense, the records of previous activities (e.g., sales, inventories, newspaper accounts, population census, highway usage) are physical traces of previous periods. In recent years computerized warehouse inventory and movement data have become a major source of information on brand shares. The particular problems associated with the use of secondary data are discussed at length in the chapter on that subject.

SUMMARY

If one wishes to find what people think or know, the logical procedure is to ask them. This has led marketing researchers to use the questionnaire technique for collecting data more than any other method.

It is not as easy as it might appear, however, to collect facts or opinions from people. Unless the point of interest has been impressed on the respondent's mind very recently, he is apt to have trouble remembering it exactly. Another problem is the unwillingness of some people to answer questions from strangers. Different wordings of questions will often obtain different results; yet there is no way of knowing what is the correct way to ask the question. When the survey method is properly used, these disadvantages can be minimized. The versatility of the questionnaire method, its speed, and its relatively low cost are important advantages relative to the observation method.

---

[75] "Z-Frank Stresses Radio to Build Big Chevy Dealership," *Advertising Age* (November 2, 1964), p. 35.

Interviews can be handled in various ways. The general purpose of the survey can be disclosed to respondents or it can be disguised. Interviews can follow a formal list of questions which are asked as written, or interviews can be nonstructured and proceed as the interviewer's judgment dictates. The cross classification of these two characteristics establishes four classes of interview each of which fits certain situations.

Three methods of communication are used with the questionnaire method—personal interview, mail, and telephone. Each has advantages and limitations. Personal interviews are generally superior to the other two methods, but require the use of interviewers who may bias results. Furthermore, personal interviews tend to be costly. Mail surveys are suspect because they frequently obtain only a small percentage return. Experiments indicate that this small return can bias mail survey results in many instances. In other cases, however, mail surveys obtain the same results as telephone or personal interviews.

Theoretically the observational method is superior to the questionnaire method. Observations are made at the time events occur. The collection of data by observation involves less chance for bias, with the possible exception of cases where the observer is an active participant in the event.

On the practical side, the advantages are in favor of the questionnaire method and have led to its widespread use. Almost any marketing problem can be approached with the questionnaire, whereas the observational method cannot get data of many types. The observational method also tends to be more expensive than the survey.

Many studies make use of both data collection methods. When asking questions interviewers frequently observe age, sex, indications of economic level, and other classification data. Observations are often followed with questionnaires. Observers watching to see what products consumers purchase may stop individuals after the purchase is completed to ask why the specific product was bought.

Case 4—1. ECONOMY PLUS STORES, INC.

The management of the Economy Plus Stores, Inc. was considering the need for more detailed information about the effects of unit pricing on their operations. Unit pricing had become an important topic in the consumer movement. It was defined as the listing on each package of the retail cost of the contents on the basis of some common denominator, such as "per pound" or "per ounce." This information, according to some consumer advocates, would enable buyers to compare brands more effectively. Retailers were particularly concerned about the inevitable problems associated with implementing any unit-price system. For instance, a store would have to decide for what goods unit-price data would be most appropriate and what measurement units would be most suitable—should the units be expressed in terms of the usual standards of measure or in terms of consumer utility such as number of servings or washloads.

After discussing the subject with an outside research agency, the management of Economy Plus Stores decided that discovery of consumer response to unit pricing in the marketplace was of primary concern. With this objective in mind, answers to the following questions were to be sought by means of field research:

1. To what extent does the consumer use unit-price information in making the purchase decision?
2. Do consumers who use unit-price data do so to compare prices of competitive brands and, if so, to what extent does this comparison affect brand switching?
3. Do consumers using unit-pricing information do so to compare prices of differently sized packages of a single brand?
4. To what extent does the use of unit-pricing information vary among product classes?
5. Does the implementation of unit pricing by retail outlets affect consumer store preference? Can a retailer gain customers by introducing unit pricing?

The research agency recommended setting up an experimental research design which would call for the introduction of unit pricing into four stores for 10 packaged grocery and household items regularly stocked. Frozen and refrigerated products, fresh fruits and vegetables, and fresh meats would *not* be included. The 10 product classes would be chosen at a later date. A control group of four additional company stores would also be selected. These would be carefully "matched" with the four experimental stores. Sales of the 8 individual stores by product class for the four weeks preceding and following the test as well as for the four weeks of the test itself would be obtained from company records.

Reasoning that customers would typically give normative answers to questions dealing with the usefulness of unit-pricing and their reaction to it, the research agency recommended that interviewers be stationed in each of the experimental stores to observe the behavior of individual consumers. Using a daily random number start, consumers would be selected as they entered the store and their behavior regarding unit pricing observed.

The observation form to be used appears as Exhibit I. For each product purchased, consumers would be asked several questions relating to their prior purchasing habits.

The question as to whether the adoption of unit-pricing by a retail organization would affect sales would be answered by determining to

EXHIBIT 1

UNIT PRICING QUESTIONNAIRE

INTERVIEWER _____   Store # _____

  Respondent # _____   Date _____

CONSUMER ACTION   (RECORDED BY INTERVIEWER)

PRODUCT CLASS*	Walked-by Product class	Stopped-looked Handled no items	Examined one item	Examined two items	Examined three items	Examined four or more items	Purchased one or more items	BRAND PURCHASED	SIZE	NO.
1										
2										
3										
4										
5										
6										
7										
8										
9										
10										

Interviewer comments _____

_____

_____

_____

_____

* Actual product names on separate control sheet

what extent sales increased during the four-week test period in the experimental group versus the control group as well as by the answers to question number 3 of the questionnaire.

Should the proposed research be undertaken?

Case 4—2.   CUYLER, INC.

The Cuyler advertising agency was requested by its new beer account, the Riester Beer Company, to conduct a research investigation in order to determine what kind of image men had of the Riester brand. The agency was anxious to obtain the information since work was to commence soon on the fall campaign. The spring and summer campaigns had been prepared by the client's former agency. Both the agency and the

EXHIBIT 1 (*Continued*)

For each item purchased, ask the following questions and record the answers below:

1. Do you usually buy this (specify by name) brand? (yes or no).

    a. If "no": What is the reason why you purchased it this time?
    b. If "no": What brand do you usually buy?

2. Do you usually buy this package size (point to package purchased)?

    a. If "no": Why did you buy it this time?
    b. If "no": What size do you usually buy?

3. Do you usually shop at this store? (yes or no).

    a. If "no": Why are you shopping here this time?
    b. If "no": Where do you usually shop?

PRODUCT_____

Quest. #1	Quest. #2	Quest. #3	If "no" to Q. #1: a._____
Yes No	Yes No	Yes No	_____
___ ___	___ ___	___ ___	b._____
			_____
			If "no" to Q. #2: a._____
			_____
			b._____
			_____
			If "no" to Q. #3: a._____
			_____
			b._____
			_____

PRODUCT_____

NOTE: The same format was repeated several times to provide space for each product.

Riester Company had agreed that it would not be wise to attempt any advertising changes either in copy or media until the fall. Since the agency felt the proposed study would be especially helpful to their creative staff, it agreed to underwrite its entire cost, amounting to approximately $4,500.

The agency's research director, Mr. Jacobsen, stated that the primary objective of the study would be "to find out what men think of the Riester brand of beer in contrast to other leading sellers." Because he did not feel that men could or would talk at great lengths about why they liked a certain brand of beer, Mr. Jacobsen decided not to use a depth interview approach. Rather, he felt that the use of a sentence completion test and rating scale devices would be more appropriate. "This way," he said, "I'm certain that we can get quantifiable answers which will help our creative people."

Both Mr. Jacobsen and Mr. Smith, the Riester account supervisor, felt that the research project should study Riester's present advertising programs, particularly the copy themes that were being used, in greater detail. For the past several years, Riester had featured a pretty girl in all its advertising copy. The girl, called "Miss Riester," was always the same young woman and appeared in Riester ads dressed in appropriate seasonal costumes. In the summer she wore a bathing suit; in the fall, outdoor clothing such as a turtle neck sweater, tweed skirt, wool knee socks and loafers; in the winter, a ski outfit; and in the spring, a sweater and skirt. The same girl and costume were featured simultaneously in TV and billboard advertising as well as in newspapers and magazines. The theme was maintained in radio advertising by having a woman announcer commence the commercial by introducing herself as "Miss Riester."

The message that was used in practically all advertising, and which had not been changed for several years, was "Cool—*And* Refreshingly Wonderful." The company had emphasized the quality of its product by stating that only the finest ingredients were used and that the same family had supervised the brewing operations continuously for more than 85 years.

Riester beer was sold in only four states and received heavy competition from regional, and local brands. It was priced just below the national brands. The company had marketed its brand in this region for over 85 years, and sales had grown gradually to a peak of $6 million. In the last two years, however, sales had been declining because, in the opinion of the president, the competition from national brands had become increasingly severe.

After about two weeks of work, including pretesting, the agency's research department developed what the research director termed "a workable questionnaire" (see Exhibit 1, on pages 176–79). Using this questionnaire, a total of 407 male beer drinkers were interviewed—about 100 in each of the four largest cities in which the Riester Company marketed its product. The interviews were conducted within the corporate limits of these cities, and respondents were selected from various neighborhoods with particular emphasis on upper-lower and lower-middle social class areas, since such men were reasoned to have a higher per capita consumption of beer than members of other social classes. Experienced male interviewers were used to do the field work. The highlights of the report appear below.

I. Riester girl

    A. Question: *"I think the girl in the Riester beer commercial is the kind of girl who. . . ."*
       Almost all replies to this sentence completion test were favorable. Representative favorable remarks were as follows:

```
Advertises/represents beer ..............................22%
Sells beer ..............................................11
Sings and dances ....................................... 6
Likes beer ............................................. 4
Is attractive .......................................... 2
Is type men go for ..................................... 2
Is sparkling ........................................... 1
Is refreshing .......................................... 1
Is cheerful ............................................ 1
```

A few negative associations were obtained:

```
Sells frozen food ...................................... 4%
Isn't tempting ......................................... 1
Should put more clothes on ............................. 1
```

B. Question: *"My wife thinks the Riester Beer girl is. . . ."*
In response to this question, comments were again favorable although a large portion of the men had never heard their wives say anything about her and were unwilling to guess what she might say. The following comments were representative:

```
Cute  .................................................11%
Glamour—beautiful .................................... 5
Is attractive ......................................... 4
Is tops ............................................... 1
Wonderful ............................................ 1
```

Negative associations included a relatively large number of people associating her with frozen food:

```
Sells frozen food .....................................20%
Of no importance ..................................... 1
An ad gimmick ........................................ 1
No account ........................................... 1
Tired of her ......................................... 1
Silly ................................................ 1
```

II.   Riester beer

A. Question: *"Riester beer is. . . ."*

```
Good  .................................................20%
Fair/so-so ............................................12
Best/very good ........................................ 9
All right/OK .......................................... 7
Mild .................................................. 5
Old beer .............................................. 4
Other .................................................48
```

The other descriptions included: local beer, nice, tasty, less costly, wholesome, German beer, light, etc. Definitely negative comments included:

```
Flat  ................................................. 2%
Not popular .......................................... 2
Just beer ............................................ 2
No good .............................................. 2
```

III. The Riester tavern

A. Question: *"The kind of tavern that sells Riester beer is. . . ."*

OK 10%
Average 9
Neighborhood tavern 6
Any beer tavern 6
High-grade tavern 5
Nice tavern 4
One that carries all brands 3

IV. The (a leading national brand) tavern

A. Question: *"The kind of tavern that sells (   ) is. . . ."*

Choice/tops/high class 20%
Good/all right 16
Crowded 6
Friendly 9
Average 8
Old timer 3

V. The Riester bartenders

A. Question: *"Bartenders say Riester beer is. . . ."*

Good/very good 11%
Good seller 7
Slow seller 3
Tops 3
Building up business 1

VI. The (a leading national brand) bartenders

A. Question: *"Bartenders say (name of another leading national brand) is. . . ."*

Good beer 28%
Best—premium 20
Choice product of brewer's art 8
Best seller 5
Mild 4
Local beer 3
Old beer 2

Character identification of Riester and a leading national brand

Question 7 concerned the respondent's opinion of the type of person who might be identified with different brands of beer. The following table gives the weighted scores of the various types of people with whom the respondent identified Riester and a leading national brand. All scores are in terms of a percent of the maximum possible score obtained if all respondents reported that the word or term on the list applied perfectly to the brand. To do this a rating of "would drink" was given a weight of

2 and "probably would drink" a weight of 1. Midpoint ratings were dropped.

VII. Stereotypes of individuals who would, would probably, might or might not, probably wouldn't, or would not drink Riester beer and a leading national brand.*

	Would drink†		Wouldn't drink†	
Type of person	*Riester*	*Leading national brand*	*Riester*	*Leading national brand*
Athlete	25%	34%	22%	21%
Young woman	25	28	15	23
Intellectual	23	40	21	16
Low income	32	24	29	42
Executive	26	54	24	10
Young man	52	43	8	18
Mature older man	29	46	17	9
Man who knows beer ..	35	60	20	7
Happy man	49	39	3	8
Man with high income .	31	44	21	14
Modern man	41	49	9	4
Older woman	17	26	33	35
Foreman	35	42	17	13
Accountant	27	36	14	13
Serious man	32	31	15	14
Man who would not drink hard liquor ...	38	41	29	26
Professional man	31	46	23	12

* Name omitted because of confidential nature of study.
† Percentages are based on total possible most favorable or most unfavorable scores. Only relative magnitude of scores is important in the analysis.

Each stereotype listed below indicates that the beer brand it applies to has significantly higher or lower ratings on that variable than the other brand. Variables without significant differences are not listed.

High ratings

Riester	*A leading national brand*
Man with low income	Young man (would not)
Young man	Man who knows beer

Low ratings

Riester	*A leading national brand*
Athlete	Happy man
Intellectual	
Executive (very low)	
Mature older man	
Man who knows beer	
Man with high income	
Modern man	
Foreman	
Accountant	
Professional man	

VIII.   Image characteristics of Riester and a leading national brand

Question 8 asked the respondent to rate the applicability of several words that could be used to characterize beer. The weighted scores of the various beer description words for Riester and a leading national brand appear below. All scores are in terms of a percent of the maximum possible score obtained if all respondents reported that the word or terms on the list applied perfectly to the brand. To do this a rating of "would apply" was given a weight of 2 and "probably would drink" a weight of 1. Midpoint ratings were dropped.

Description	Applies to		Does not apply to	
	Riester	A leading natl. brand	Riester	A leading natl. brand
Carbonated	34%	46%	38%	32%
Strong	23	47	41	27
Fun	54	62	8	9
Dry	32	45	28	24
Good	64	74	8	6
Active	58	60	7	2
Light	65	54	8	22
Mild	61	42	11	27
Ordinary	43	22	15	43
Young	41	21	21	42
Sweet	23	10	42	66
Aged	53	66	14	12
Bitter	14	28	49	40
Expensive	17	54	58	28
Dark	11	20	56	57
Sharp	21	37	43	30
Regional beer	50	31	28	50
For everyday drinking	53	48	17	21
Refreshing	73	76	6	5
Masculine	51	77	8	6
Tasty	60	65	9	10
Respected	57	83	11	3
Feminine	22	17	25	40
Old fashioned	27	40	29	20

Each of the words listed below indicates that the beer brand it applies to has significantly higher or lower ratings on that variable than the other brand. Variables without significant differences are not listed.

High ratings

Riester	*A leading national brand*
Ordinary	Strong
Regional beer	Dry
	Bitter
	Expensive
	Dark
	Sharp
	Masculine
	Old fashioned

Low ratings

Riester	*A leading national brand*
Carbonated	Light
Strong (very low)	Mild
Fun	Young
Good	Sweet
Aged	
Expensive (very low)	
Respected	

1. Was the research design appropriate for this problem?
2. Was the most efficient method of data collection used?

EXHIBIT 1

1. Do you drink beer? ☐ Yes ☐ No (If "No", end interview)

2. What brand of beer do you prefer above all others? _____

3. Which of the following brands of beer have you tried?

   ☐ Hamm's   ☐ Schlitz   ☐ Budweiser
   ☐ Riester   ☐ Falstaff

4. Do you ever drink draught beer?   Yes   No

   4a. If "Yes", ask: What brand of draught do you prefer? _____

5. About how many bottles or cans of beer do you think you drank last week? _____

6. I'm going to read off to you some sentences which I want you to finish. Say the first words that come into your mind.

   1) I think the girl in the Riester beer commercial is the kind of girl who . . . . .

      _____

   2) The kind of tavern that sells (a leading national brand) is . . . _____

      _____

   3) Riester beer is . . . _____

      _____

   4) My wife thinks the Riester beer girl is . . . _____

      _____

   5) Bartenders say Riester beer is . . . _____

      _____

   6) Bartenders say (a leading national brand) is . . . _____

      _____

   7) The kind of a tavern that sells Riester beer is . . . _____

      _____

EXHIBIT 1 (*Continued*)

7. I'm going to read off a list of people. I want you to tell me whether you think they would, would probably, might not, probably wouldn't, or would not drink _____ brand of beer.** (Hand respondent a scale card and tell him he need only give you a number as his answer.)

Person	Would Drink	Would Probably Drink	Might or Might Not Drink	Probably Wouldn't Drink	Would Not Drink
Athlete	1	2	3	4	5
Factory Worker	1	2	3	4	5
Young Housewife	1	2	3	4	5
Intellectual	1	2	3	4	5
File Clerk	1	2	3	4	5
Man With Low Income	1	2	3	4	5
Executive	1	2	3	4	5
Young man	1	2	3	4	5
Mature Older Man	1	2	3	4	5
Man Who Knows Beer	1	2	3	4	5
Man Who Drinks Beer With Meals	1	2	3	4	5
Conservative Man	1	2	3	4	5
Happy Man	1	2	3	4	5
Man With High Income	1	2	3	4	5
Modern Man	1	2	3	4	5
Older Woman	1	2	3	4	5
Truck Driver	1	2	3	4	5
Foreman	1	2	3	4	5
Man Who Drinks Beer Only Occasionally	1	2	3	4	5

**Respondent asked to rate one brand of beer in addition to Riester. Thus the same question (#7) was repeated two times -- each for a different brand of beer.

EXHIBIT 1 (*Continued*)

Person	Would Drink	Would Probably Drink	Might or Might Not Drink	Probably Wouldn't Drink	Would Not Drink
Serious Man	1	2	3	4	5
Farmer	1	2	3	4	5
College Student	1	2	3	4	5
Accountant	1	2	3	4	5
Man Who Does Not Drink Hard Liquor	1	2	3	4	5
Professional Man	1	2	3	4	5

8. I'm going to read off some words which some people use to describe a brand of beer. For the _____ brand of beer will you tell me whether the word applies, probably applies, might or might not apply, probably doesn't apply, or does not apply.* (Hand respondent a card showing this scale and tell him he need only give a number as his answer.)

Description	Applies	Probably Applies	Might or Might Not Apply	Probably Does Not Apply	Does Not Apply
Carbonated	1	2	3	4	5
Strong	1	2	3	4	5
Fun	1	2	3	4	5
Dry	1	2	3	4	5
Good	1	2	3	4	5
Active	1	2	3	4	5
Light	1	2	3	4	5
Mild	1	2	3	4	5
Ordinary	1	2	3	4	5
Clear	1	2	3	4	5
Young	1	2	3	4	5

* Same procedure used here as for Question 7.

EXHIBIT 1 (*Concluded*)

Description	Applies	Probably Applies	Might or Might Not Apply	Probably Does Not Apply	Does Not Apply
Relaxing	1	2	3	4	5
Sweet	1	2	3	4	5
Aged	1	2	3	4	5
Bitter	1	2	3	4	5
Expensive	1	2	3	4	5
Dark	1	2	3	4	5
Sharp	1	2	3	4	5
Regional Beer	1	2	3	4	5
For Everyday Drinking	1	2	3	4	5
Nice Aroma	1	2	3	4	5
Modern	1	2	3	4	5
Refreshing	1	2	3	4	5
Masculine	1	2	3	4	5
Tasty	1	2	3	4	5
Respected	1	2	3	4	5
Burning	1	2	3	4	5
Feminine	1	2	3	4	5
Old Fashioned	1	2	3	4	5
Green	1	2	3	4	5

Case 4—3. WALLACE COMPANY

The research director of the Wallace Company was considering ways of testing the company's aerosol spray starch product against a new similar product which had been introduced three months earlier by a large competitor. The new product, also sold in an aerosol can, was advertised as containing a special ingredient which made fabrics more resistant to scorching. Since the new product had made substantial inroads in several of the Wallace Company's key markets, the marketing vice president had requested the research director to undertake a product test to determine whether consumers, in fact, could note any differences under normal use conditions. In addition, he requested information regarding how housewives viewed the spray starch products in general with respect to price, spray pattern, effects on ironing in terms of "stickiness" and "smoothness," resistance to scorching and flaking, the manufacturer's name, and the odor.

After considerable deliberation the research director decided on a dual product placement test among current users of spray starch. He thought that a total sample of 150 "user" housewives would suffice. The sample would consist of approximately two-thirds city proper, and one-third suburban households. All interviewing would be done using local interviewers who could be supervised closely since the study would be conducted in the same metropolitan area in which the company headquarters were located. Households would be selected by interviewers on a judgment basis within specific, predetermined city and suburban blocks.

Each housewife would first be qualified as being a spray starch user (Exhibit 1). Frequency of usage and brand used most often would be determined from users, along with what they thought was the primary consideration in buying a spray starch. After obtaining the respondent's consent to participate in a placement study, the interviewer would leave with the respondent two masked containers of spray starches—the Wallace brand and the other new competitive product.

In addition, each respondent would receive a diary sheet (Exhibit 2), on which she would be instructed to record the date of usage for each product and any immediate comments she might want to add. Frequency of usage would not be dictated to respondents, other than requesting that they use each of the products alternately within their normal usage pattern. Method of application, however, would be specified in order that both products could be compared on various attributes.

The two containers left with respondents would be stripped of all brand identification, and would resemble each other as closely as possible. The only product identification would be a three-digit code number assigned to each brand and placed in small print on the bottom of the can. The same usage instructions were to be stated on the labels of each test product.

The products were to be left with respondents for a period of four weeks. Midway during the placement (after two weeks), each respondent would be reached by phone to ascertain usage and to answer or clarify any questions that might have arisen. At the end of the stated placement period, members of the panel would be personally interviewed using the suggested questionnaire (Exhibit 3). All questionnaires would be returned to the research office where they would be edited, coded, and tabulated. Results would be presented in a written report containing all tabulations. An estimated 3 to 5 percent dropout could be expected from the original panel.

What changes, if any, would you recommend making in the proposed research design?

EXHIBIT 1. Proposed placement questionnaire

Hello, my name is _____ from Business Research Associates, and we are conducting a survey among women on spray starches. Would you mind, please, answering a few short questions? Thank you.
1. How many brands of spray (aerosol) starches can you think of? (RECORD IN GRID BELOW)
2. Do you personally ever use a spray starch?
    1. Yes (SKIP TO QUES. #3)
    2. No (ASK 2a)
2a. Would you please tell me why you do not use a spray starch?

_____

_____ (TERMINATE INTERVIEW AND DO NOT COUNT IN QUOTA)
3. In buying a spray starch, what is the most important consideration to you?

_____

_____

4. What brand of spray starch do you usually use? (RECORD IN GRID BELOW)
4a. About how often do you use your spray starch? (IN TERMS OF WEEKS, DAYS. RECORD IN GRID BELOW)

Question #1 *brand awareness*	*Question #4* *usual brand*	*Question #4a* *frequency of usage*	
		days	weeks
_____	_____	"	"
_____	_____	"	"
_____	_____	"	"

I have a few statements here that we would like to have you rate on their importance in regard to buying a spray starch. Here's how this works (HAND RESPONDENT

EXHIBIT 1 (*Continued*)

EXAMPLE CARD). The higher the number you choose will indicate the more you feel that the statement is an important reason for buying a particular brand of spray starch. Likewise, a low number will indicate that you feel the statement is an important reason for not buying a particular brand of spray starch. (MAKE SURE RESPONDENT UNDERSTANDS RATING PROCEDURE)

INTERVIEWER: MAKE SURE THE CARDS ARE SHUFFLED THOROUGHLY BETWEEN EACH INTERVIEW. THEN, AS THE RESPONDENT STATES THE RATING NUMBER SHE ASSIGNS TO EACH STATEMENT, RECORD THIS NUMBER OPPOSITE THE APPROPRIATE STATEMENT. (NOTE: ALWAYS BE CERTAIN BEFORE EACH INTERVIEW TO COUNT THE NUMBER OF CARDS SO THAT YOU KNOW YOU HAVE A CARD FOR EACH STATEMENT.)

Sample of card handed respondent

Rating scale

1. Very important reason for not buying
2.
3.
4.
5.
6. Unimportant either way
7.
8.
9.
10.
11. Very important reason for buying

Statements	*Rating*
A. Its odor	_____
B. Its sizing efficiency	_____
C. Resistance to flaking	_____
D. Resistance to scorching	_____
E. Easy to use	_____
F. Makes ironing smooth and easy	_____
G. Leaves garments clean and bright	_____
H. Doesn't leave streaks on garments	_____
I. Spray doesn't clog the spout	_____
J. Not messy to use	_____
K. Plenty of power behind the spray	_____
L. Spray works no matter which way can is held	_____
M. Push button works easily	_____
N. The price	_____
O. Doesn't stain garments	_____

Classification data

Thank you very much for your cooperation, you have been most helpful. Now if I may just ask a few questions for classification purposes. . . .
A. Do you own a washing machine?   Yes ☐   No ☐
  (IF YES, ASK) What type of washer is that?
      Conventional   ☐
      Automatic tumble   ☐
      Automatic agitator ☐
      Pulsator   ☐
B. Are you (housewife) employed?   Yes ☐   No ☐
  (IF YES, ASK) Is that full time, or part time?   Full time ☐   Part time ☐

EXHIBIT 1 (*Concluded*)

C. Do you have any children?   Yes ☐   No ☐
   (IF YES, ASK) How many do you have, and how old are they?
   # Children _____ Age of each _____ _____ _____ _____
D. Occupation of head of household _____
E. Age of housewife: Under 20   ☐
                   20–34   ☐
                   35–44   ☐
                   45–54   ☐
                   55 & over   ☐
F. Total family income: Under $5,000   ☐
                        $5,000–7,999   ☐
                        $8,000–9,999   ☐
                        $10,000 & over ☐
G. Education of housewife: Some grammar school ☐, Finished grammar school ☐,
   Some high school ☐,   Finished high school ☐,   Some college ☐, Finished
   college ☐.

RESPONDENT'S NAME _____ DATE _____
ADDRESS _____ CITY _____ STATE _____
PHONE # _____ INTERVIEWER _____

We have two free samples of spray starches which we would like to leave with you.
In turn, we would appreciate it very much if you would use each of them as directed,
whenever you normally use your spray starch, and allow us to interview you again
at a later date and get your opinions of them. Would you be interested in participating?
         1. Yes ☐   2. No ☐ ("THANK YOU" AND TERMINATE)

EXHIBIT 2. Proposed usage diary

Product #	Date used	Type of fabrics used on	Type of garment used on	Comments

EXHIBIT 3. Suggested callback questionnaire

Hello, my name is _____ from Business Research Associates. We
would now like very much to interview you once again on your reactions toward
spray starches in general, and particularly toward the two spray starches that were
left with you about a month ago. Would this be a convenient time? Thank you.
First, I wonder if you would please get the two products so we can look at them
while we are talking. Thank you.

1. In buying spray starch, what do you think is the most important consideration?

_____
_____
_____

EXHIBIT 3 (*Continued*)

2. Now, generally speaking, what was your overall opinion toward each of these two products—that is, have you a preference for one over the other, or do you feel they're both about the same?

Prefer # _____ (ASK QUES. 1a)
Same _____

1a. Why do you prefer product # _____?

_____

_____

_____

_____

Now I would like to get your opinion on some specific points in regard to both products. The way we'll do this is by having you rate on this little eleven-point rating scale various product statements.

(HAND RESPONDENT EXAMPLE CARD) Here's how this works. The higher the number you choose will indicate the more you agree or the higher you rate a given statement. Likewise, the lower the number you choose will indicate the less you agree, or a lower rating of the statement. For example, let's take the statement "Easy to Store." If you thought the product was very easy to store, you would give it a high rating like an 8, 9, 10, or 11. On the other hand, if you thought it was only *fairly* easy to store you would rate it somewhere in the middle, and if you thought it was difficult to store, you would give it a low rating. Do you understand?

(MAKE SURE RESPONDENT UNDERSTANDS RATING PROCEDURE)

Now here are some cards. On each card there is a statement along with the product code identification number. Please tell me where you would rate each particular statement in relationship to the product referred to. (Note: A card is included for each statement for each of the two products.)

(MAKE SURE THE CARDS ARE SHUFFLED THOROUGHLY BETWEEN EACH INTERVIEW. THEN, AS THE RESPONDENT RELATES THE RATING NUMBER SHE ASSIGNS TO EACH STATEMENT, RECORD THIS NUMBER OPPOSITE THE APPROPRIATE STATEMENT AND UNDER THE PROPER COLUMN ON THE NEXT PAGE.)

Statement rating section

	Product identification rating	
Statement	#573	#375
A. Resisted scorching	____	____
B. Resisted flaking	____	____
C. Added sizing efficiently	____	____
D. Easy to use	____	____
E. Its odor	____	____
F. The aerosol container	____	____
G. The push button's ease of use	____	____
H. Made ironing smooth and easy	____	____
I. Made ironing sticky and hard	____	____
J. Made garments dull and dingy	____	____
K. Left garments clean and bright	____	____
L. Left streaks on garments	____	____
M. The spray clogged the spout	____	____
N. Product was messy to use	____	____
O. Good for touch-ups	____	____
P. Good for complete garment starching	____	____
Q. Plenty of power behind the spray	____	____
R. Left stains on garments	____	____
S. Spray works no matter how can is held	____	____

EXHIBIT 3 (*Concluded*)

3. Thinking of both products, would you say one cost more than the other, or would you say that both would cost about the same price?

            Both the same price   ☐

            Product # _____ cost more ☐ (ASK 3a)

3a. Why do you feel product # _____ would cost more?

    _____

    _____

    _____

    _____

4. What, if any, additional comments would you like to make about either of the two products, or spray starching in general?

    (CHECK HERE IF "NO ADDITIONAL COMMENTS") ☐ _____

    _____

    _____

    _____

    _____

    _____

Thank you very much for your cooperation, you have been most helpful.

RESPONDENT'S NAME _____

ADDRESS _____ CITY _____ STATE _____

INTERVIEWER _____

Case 4—4. WESTERN CABLE TELEVISION

The Western Cable Television Company owned and operated six cable TV (CATV) systems of which five were located in the San Francisco and Los Angeles areas. In January 1970, the company's chief executive officer decided that Western should be more concerned about environmental problems and to this end should undertake a series of public information telecasts featuring local "authorities" on particular problems. Every effort would be made to present a full picture of each problem and to provide specific information as to how individuals could help to alleviate it. As the first subject for action, he selected the problem of litter resulting from one-way beer and soft-drink containers.

An investigation of this problem area revealed that a number of state legislature bills were pending but no federal legislation was contemplated. Almost all of the bills pending before the various state legislatures fell into two categories: 1) a tax on the sale of one-way containers, or 2) a mandatory deposit on all beverage containers. Discussions with several brewers showed that none had made any preparation for the eventuality that they might be required to produce only returnable containers, and none had specific, well-articulated antilitter programs in effect. Almost all, however, gave advertising support to antilitter campaigns, and some helped by providing equipment and personnel in antilitter drives. All were very concerned about the situation and hoped for some leadership —presumably from the various governments involved—to help in solving the problem. Retailers and container manufacturers were also concerned with the subject.

Western was unable to locate any research which provided insights into how the consumer felt about the problem. Since any successful implementation of an antilitter program would necessarily require full cooperation by consumers, measurement of consumer attitudes on the subject appeared to be of critical importance. In preparation for the public interest telecasts on litter, it was decided to undertake a telephone survey of consumers to determine:

1. The level of concern with the problem.
2. The consumer's perception of how strong a role government should play in combating litter.
3. The consumer's perception of the role business should play in alleviating the problem.
4. The consumer's perception of the role individuals should play in helping to solve the problem.

The research worker assigned to design and implement the study decided to concentrate primarily on placing before each respondent a series of statements and asking him to indicate his agreement, disagreement, or neutrality towards each. In addition, the interviewer was to encourage the respondent to comment on any issues raised by the questions and to give brief reasons for his answers. This format would be used for each of the four subject areas described above.

It was decided to use a 3-point scale (agree, neutral, disagree) rather than a 5-point scale on the attitude questions, although it was recognized that the latter would permit each respondent to be more precise in expressing his opinion. This decision was made because the 3-point scale was simpler and would cause less of a problem over the telephone. The pretest questionnaire appears as Exhibit I.

Critically evaluate the questionnaire as a measuring instrument and as a way of generating information needed by Western for its telecasts on the subject of litter.

EXHIBIT 1. Litter consumer questionnaire

NOTE: The below questions are to be answered on a 3-point scale—"Agree", "Neutral", "Disagree". Circle the answer.

Part 1—Level of concern

1. Litter should be the concern of every U.S. citizen.   A N D
2. Litter is *not* one of the three most important environmental problems facing America today.   A N D
3. Unless drastic action is taken soon, litter will become a more and more serious problem in the U.S.   A N D
4. Litter is not yet a serious enough problem to bother about.   A N D
5. Strong action must be taken immediately to stop the litter of our streets, parks, and beaches with cans and bottles.   A N D

EXHIBIT 1 (*Continued*)

Part 2—Governmental Involvement

1. The government should impose a "litter tax" on each citizen to collect funds for solving the litter problem.   A   N   D
2. The government has no responsibility for sponsoring research on how to reduce the litter problem.   A   N   D
3. We cannot rely entirely on the sense of responsibility of corporations and individuals to control litter.   A   N   D
4. The government should avoid getting involved with the litter problem.   A   N   D
5. A percentage of the government's budget should be spent on fighting the litter problem.   A   N   D

Part 3—Business Involvement

1. The business community has no role to play in fighting litter.   A   N   D
2. Business should be required to use only returnable containers.   A   N   D
3. Business should help in antilitter educational efforts.   A   N   D
4. The blame for litter caused by beverage cans and bottles lies more with the general public who throw away the containers than with the beverage and container manufacturers.   A   N   D
5. Business should contribute monies to fund research for developing a "nonlittering" container.   A   N   D

Part 4—Personal Involvement

1. Avoiding litter by not discarding trash (e.g. bottles and cans) is the extent of my involvement with the litter problem.   A   N   D
2. I would not be willing to pay a 5¢ deposit (refundable if returned) on every beverage container I purchase.   A   N   D
3. I should have to pay enough "extra" for products sold in one-way (nonreturnable) containers to cover the costs of disposal.   A   N   D
4. I should not have to pick up litter that someone else has caused.   A   N   D
5. I should choose beverages in returnable containers because the containers can be reused and will not litter.   A   N   D

Part 5—Solutions

1. What do you think is the best solution to litter in general?

_____
_____
_____
_____
_____

2. To the litter caused by cans and bottles?

_____
_____
_____
_____
_____

Classification data

Tel. no. _____

1. Name of respondent _____
2. Address _____

EXHIBIT 1 (*Concluded*)

(Circle one)

3. Sex: M   F

4. Age: 18–25   26–39   40–55   56 & over

5. Education: Less than high school
              Completed high school-no college
              Some college

6. Family income: Under $6,000 $6,000–14,999 $15,000 & over

PART II

Marketing
research procedure

Research design and methods of communication have been discussed in the preceding chapters. The discussion has been general in nature, however, and the problems of organizing and carrying through a specific research project have been avoided. The following nine chapters will trace a research project from its inception to the final report on the results. Each of the major problems faced by the researcher on a typical problem will be discussed.

5

Planning the project and formulating the problem

To PLAN a research project, it is necessary to anticipate all of the steps which must be undertaken if the project is to be completed successfully. These steps are often referred to collectively as the research procedure or research process. This procedure is not a mechanically contrived sequence of independent steps. Rather it consists of a number of interrelated, frequently overlapping, activities. They are so interdependent that each step is dependent to some extent on each of the others, and the first step must be planned with the second, third, etc. in mind. For example, in developing a questionnaire one must consider not only the problem and the information needed to "solve" the problem (prior steps), but the type and caliber of the field force, the tabulation procedure to be used, and the analyses to be made of the collected data.

Despite this interrelationship, the research procedure is comprised of several rather distinct activities. In the project planning or design stage, all of these different activities must be thought through in a meticulous manner. Only in this way can the researcher be sure that, after the expenses of the project have been incurred, he will have the desired information. If the problem is ill-defined, for example, then no matter how well the other steps in the procedure are planned and implemented, the study is not likely to succeed. If the questionnaire design is faulty, then erroneous or useless information will be obtained—regardless of the skill exercised with the other steps.

Each of the research steps is a source of error, and it is the responsibility of the researcher to minimize these errors in such a way that,

191

for a given investment, he obtains the best possible overall results. In other words, he has to concern himself with the total error to which each step contributes. He has to organize his project in such a way that the data obtained will be sufficiently reliable for the problem at hand. This might mean, for example, taking a smaller sample and with it a larger sampling error in order to spend more of the budget on training to cut down errors made by the field force.

In planning and evaluating a research investigation the estimated *total* error is rarely taken into account. With but rare exceptions, sampling errors arising from random fluctuations serve as the sole basis for specifying both sample size (a major determinant of cost) and the degree of confidence one can have in the survey results. Yet such non-sampling errors as those associated with measurement and nonresponse may be considerably greater than random errors resulting from sample size. Unless one can estimate the total error generated by alternative research designs, there is no way of making a choice among them. Further, unless one can decompose the overall error into its more significant components, there is no way to determine how best to allocate resources *within* a given research inquiry. Before discussing the procedure for estimating the overall error, let us first discuss the various steps in the research process so as to get a better idea of the various sources of error as well as their interdependency.

THE RESEARCH PROCESS

The research process can be divided into seven steps as follows: (1) formulating the problem, (2) determining sources of information, (3) preparing the data collection forms, (4) designing the sample, (5) collecting the information in the field, (6) editing, coding, tabulating, and analyzing the data, and (7) preparing the research report. Each of these is discussed in considerable detail in this book. To provide the student with some insight into the complete research process, however, each step is discussed briefly here before the first step is taken up in detail.

Formulating the problem. Formulating the problem is, of course, the first step in the research process. The researcher must avoid accepting a request for information as the starting point for a research study. He should try to find out *why* the request was made. Only if the researcher knows the problem that management wants to solve can he be sure that he will design a project which will provide the pertinent information. Often it is necessary for the researcher to help management recognize just what the basic problem is.

Much marketing research is undertaken to help management recognize the existence of problems. Sales are often analyzed by product, sales district, salesmen, type of account, and major account. This information is compared with some standard such as last year's sales or this year's quota to see how the firm is progressing. If standards are not met, management can be alerted to the fact that a problem exists.

Once a problem has been noted and it has been decided that research is needed, the researcher needs to specify the objectives of the research project or projects which may be undertaken. He will then need to decide what information is needed to attain these objectives. After doing these things, he should project his thinking forward to the probable findings of the study and try to answer the question, "What will management do if these are the findings?" It is possible that the probable findings may suggest courses of action which management cannot undertake, for example, because of limited financial resources. If management can take no action regardless of what the findings are, then there is no reason to undertake a research study.

Determining sources of information. After preparing a list of the information required for the study objectives, the next step is to determine whether such information is already available, either in company records or in outside sources such as books, pamphlets, or articles. Certainly, the researcher should not collect information from the field until he has made certain that the needed data can be obtained in no cheaper way. A multiplicity of sources outside the company provide much valuable marketing information. These sources include the many bureaus of the federal government, state and local government agencies, universities, foundations, private research agencies, trade associations, and media such as newspapers and magazines.

Information obtained from such sources as the above must be examined carefully to make sure that it fits the particular needs of the researcher. Since it was obtained for another purpose, it may not be adequate. Outside data may have been gathered and tabulated using different definitions—or the information may be outdated. While it is often difficult to determine the reliability of such data, a careful check should be made for internal consistency to determine whether data have been collected and reported with care and precision. The reputation and experience of the organization collecting the data are often the best guide to the accuracy of the data.

Preparing the data collection forms. If the researcher cannot find the information he needs in internal or external records, he must plan to gather the information himself. A necessary step is to design a form for collecting the data. Preparation of data collection forms is linked to the listing of information required to achieve the project objectives. The listing is the starting point in designing these forms. The particular form to be designed will vary considerably from study to study depending upon the information needed, the kind of respondents (for example, business executives versus housewives), and the method of collecting the information (questionnaire versus observation).

If an observation study is planned, a data collection form must be designed which will make it easy to record observations accurately. If a questionnaire study is planned, special attention must be paid to designing the questionnaire, for it will influence the data obtained. Certain kinds of questions lead to interviewer bias more than others. The way in which questions are worded has a great effect on the reliability of the answers given by respondents. For example, in interviewing housewives the questionnaire must use words which all respondents will understand —words which have the same meaning to all concerned. Respondents must be able to answer the questions; questions which request information which many respondents cannot, or will not, provide must not be used.

Designing the sample.   The first task in sampling is to define carefully what groups of people, stores, etc. are to be sampled. For example, if the study calls for collecting data from appliance dealers, then it is necessary to define what is meant by an appliance dealer (are department stores selling appliances to be included?), and to define the precise geographical area which is of interest (e.g., the corporate city limits of Chicago or the metropolitan Chicago area).

Another aspect of sample design has to do with the selection of the sample. Two general methods can be used to select respondents—probability and nonprobability. In probability methods each member in the group from which the sample is drawn has a known likelihood of being chosen. Examples of the various probability techniques are simple random sampling, sampling systematically from a list of all items in the group, stratifying the group by certain characteristics and then selecting within each stratum at random, and so on. Nonprobability sampling methods include the selection of respondents by convenience, by judgment, or quota and by convenience within strata which are established from existing data.

Another important decision is determining the size of sample. Marketing research samples vary from ten or fifteen individuals to several thousand. The researcher must consider the nature and importance of the problem at hand, his budget, and the accuracy needed in the data before he can answer the sample-size question. The sampling method used and the sample size will influence the confidence in the results. For example, if 18 percent of the Houston housewives in a sample view a given television program regularly, then the question arises: "How close is this estimate to the real or true percentage existing among *all* Houston housewives?" Questions such as these can be answered with some degree of precision, *provided* probability sampling methods have been used.

Collecting the information in the field.   The field operation includes the selection, training, control, and evaluation of the members of the field force. The methods used in the field are important since they usually involve a substantial part of the research budget and are an important potential source of bias. The field methods are dictated largely by the sampling requirements and the kinds of information which must be obtained.

The field operation is a difficult one to control because of the dispersed nature of the work, the many different kinds of respondents, and the varying skills of the field workers themselves. It is a difficult, expensive, and time-consuming process just to determine whether the interviews or observations were actually made, let alone to determine whether each worker followed the field instructions to the letter.

Analyzing the data collected.   After the field work has been completed, the difficult task of processing the completed forms in a way which will enable the project objectives to be attained remains. First, the forms need to be edited to make sure that instructions were followed, that all questions were asked or observations made, and that the resulting data are consistent and "logical" within each form. Next, the data must be prepared for tabulation; for many questions this means establishing classes and assigning responses obtained to appropriate classes. When machine tabulation is used, the data must be coded so that they may be punched into cards which can be sorted and counted by electronic or mechanical means.

The data are then tabulated and analyzed. The types of information which were specified in step one of the research process (problem formulation) predetermine the analysis function. To analyze literally means to "break apart" and "examine the parts critically"—especially as they relate to each other. In analyzing the results, the researcher must compute percentages and averages and compare them for different classes. In some cases, he may use more advanced statistical procedures such as correlation analysis. He must always consider how accurate are the results. For example, when the percentage using product X varies between two income groups, the researcher must question whether the difference is "real" or a chance fluctuation of sampling.

Preparing the research report.   The report represents the end product of the research process. No matter what the proficiency with which all previous steps have been dispatched, the project will be no more successful than the research report.

The type of report will vary a great deal depending on the nature of the project and the audience for which it is prepared. Some reports should include considerable descriptive material covering the details of the research methodology used to obtain the findings. Other reports are concerned primarily with a presentation of the conclusions reached.

Each of these steps in the research process will now be considered in more detail. The remainder of this chapter is devoted to the first step —formulating the problem.

FORMULATING THE PROBLEM

Management is interested in marketing research only to the extent that it helps executives make better decisions; that is, to the extent it reduces the uncertainty inherent in specific business decisions that must be made. If the researcher is to maximize the contribution which he can make to reducing this uncertainty, he must share in the formulation of the problems on which he works. In this way he can insure that the research problem, and hence the data collected, will focus on the action decision which is to be made. Research which divorces itself from action ". . . dies within its own solid covers, too remote, or detached to influence the rapidly moving stream of events. Research which disavows any responsibility except that of being objective and non-utilitarian may well qualify as 'pure.' But it is a kind of purity which a society—particularly a society in an age of change—can overvalue."[1]

Decisions are made *only* because the decision maker wants to achieve something, that is, he has certain goals or objectives that may vary from the formation of new enterprises to the maintenance of the status quo. The researcher must know the goals of the decision maker if his studies are to be oriented most effectively towards helping the executive to attain his goals.

Anatomy of a decision

If the researcher is to provide maximum help to the decision maker, the latter's problem must be identified, dissected with precision, and ultimately translated into one or more research problems. This means that the researcher cannot accept a request for information as the starting point for a research inquiry. Such requests are typically made by individuals who are not familiar with research methods, and consequently, who are not aware of the difficulty or expense which may be associated with their requests. Since different kinds of data will frequently help "solve" the same problem, the researcher must know a great deal about the basic problem if he is to obtain the most efficient information.

The researcher cannot do an efficient job of designing a research project unless he knows the components of the decision maker's problem: (1) who the decision maker is, the environment in which he operates, and the resources he commands; (2) the objectives or goals he hopes

---

[1] *Annual Report for 1959* (New York: Twentieth Century Fund, 1960), p. 11.

to obtain (expressed in measurable terms); (3) the possible courses of action "available" for solving the problem; and (4) the consequences of each of the alternative courses of action. An understanding of these components is the key to problem formulation and effective manipulation of the subsequent research steps. Without such an understanding the researcher lacks an adequate guide for designing the inquiry.

The decision maker. Frequently, the individual who first contacts the researcher is not the ultimate decision maker. Rather than accept this person's interpretation of the problem, the researcher should strive for a meeting with the executive who has the major responsibility for making the decision. This is easier said than done, if only because of the hierarchy of command which exists in most companies and the policy of delegation. The situation is made no less difficult by the fact that frequently a number of individuals are involved in the decision process. Nevertheless, the researcher should make every effort to learn the goals of the individual or individuals who are to make the decision for which information is sought.

Knowledge of the environment within which the decision maker operates is important because it tells the researcher a great deal about the resources the decision maker has under his command. This, in turn, facilitates the establishment of realistic courses of action. If resources are not available to implement a given course of action, then it makes little sense to consider that alternative seriously.

Objectives of the decision maker. Since the identification of possible courses of action (solutions) as well as the selection of the best one can only be accomplished with reference to the objectives or goals sought by the decision maker, the researcher must give careful attention to this part of the decision process. Frequently, the objective is to maintain the status quo. It is unfortunately true that the researcher seldom receives a clear-cut statement of such objectives.

Despite a popular misconception to the contrary, objectives are seldom given to the researcher. The decision maker seldom formulates his objectives accurately. He is likely to state his objectives in the form of platitudes which have no operational significance. Consequently, objectives usually have to be extracted by the researcher. In so doing the researcher may well be performing his most useful service to the decision maker.

Direct questioning of the decision maker seldom reveals all the relevant objectives. One effective technique for uncovering these objectives consists of confronting the decision maker with each of the possible solutions to a problem and asking him whether he would follow that course of action. Where he says "no" further probing will usually reveal objectives which are not served by the course of action.[2]

---

[2] Russell L. Ackoff, *Scientific Method* (New York: John Wiley and Sons, Inc., 1962), p. 71.

Quite often the decision maker responds to an intuitive feeling that "something is wrong"—hence the existence of a problem which may require action. Frequently, there is little advance evidence to support such a conclusion. A careful study of the evidence often reveals insufficient proof that a problem requiring action does exist. A substantial part of all marketing research work is undertaken, not to help solve specific problems, but rather to determine whether a problem exists in sufficient magnitude to warrant action to define it. Such research activity is probably important even though it is difficult to assess its real value. For example, a manufacturer of an insecticide noted that one of his major competitors had brought out a similar product. The firm's marketing director was concerned about the possible impact of the competitor's new product on the sales of his product. At this point, the marketing director had evidence that a problem existed, but did not know how serious it was or how serious it was likely to become. He decided that the consequences of the action taken by the competitor might be serious enough to warrant investing funds in a study to find out the impact of the competing product on sales of the company's product.

Conversely, the decision maker may perceive an opportunity which, to him, might offer the firm a chance to gain certain rewards. Thus, opportunities, like problems, may bear investigating. Similar research would be carried out, namely, to define the extent of the opportunity.

The determination of the objective still leaves the matter of measuring the worth of the objective. Unless some such measure can be specified, one cannot judge what the "payoff" will be to the decision maker. The development of such a measure is a difficult task, if only because the impact of many decisions may spread over a long time, for example, the decision to market a new product. Still, some monetary worth must be assigned to objectives, no matter the difficulties involved. At the very minimum, the obective's value must be large enough to warrant expenditures on research.

Determining alternative courses of action. Management often proceeds on the assumption that, if the causes of the problem can be ascertained, proper remedial action can be taken. This is tantamount to saying that the "why" of the problem will determine the most relevant course of action. Usually problems are not that simple. Typically, there will be more than one reason "why" and, thus, several alternative ways of taking remedial action. Still there is no question but what understanding the problem will help in formulating realisitic alternative courses of action.[3] Exploratory research (discussed in Chapter 2) is one way of learning more about a problem (or opportunity), as well as searching out and identifying alternative courses of action.

---

[3] For an interesting case study in problem formulation and subsequent action see William R. King, "Toward a Methodology of Market Analysis," *Journal of Marketing Research* (August, 1965), pp. 236–43.

Evaluating the consequences of alternative courses of action. For any course of action taken, any one of a number of outcomes is possible. If management could measure these outcomes and if it knew which would occur, then it would not be difficult to make a decision. But this is almost never the case and, as a consequence, the researcher must spend a considerable amount of time with management assessing what the outcomes of alternative courses of action are *likely* to be and what information, with what accuracy, and at what cost is desirable to assess better the likelihood of each outcome.

Decision theory and problem solving

If one can formalize the decision process to the extent of specifying the alternative courses of action (designed to solve a given problem or to maximize an opportunity), identifying the possible outcomes of each action, and stating the likelihood of the various outcomes occurring, *then* one will, in most situations, have a better chance of solving the given problem in the most efficient manner. Bayesian decision theory provides a framework for this approach.[4]

Almost all decision making in marketing is associated with uncertainty. The decision maker usually cannot state with certainty what outcomes will follow a given action on his part. If a new product is introduced, what will be the effect on the sales and profits of present items in the line? If the price of one of the products in the line is increased, what will competition do? If advertising copy A is selected over advertising copy B, what will the effect be on the attitudes of a given segment of the market towards the brand?

Management can always make an intuitive decision as to which alternative course of action to select in a given problem situation. Or management can seek to lower its risks by collecting information which will reduce uncertainty. Such information is not always accurate and it costs money. How can management—with help from the researcher—determine the value of additional information? An illustration will help to show how this problem can be handled.

Case example. A coffee company is faced with the problem of whether to introduce a new blend. The company's management assigns an 80 percent probability to a favorable sales reaction and a 20 percent probability to a "failure." If the new blend is successful, the company expects to make $500,000 additional profit before taxes, but if it is unsuccessful, the company expects to lose $300,000. In other words, the

---

[4] For a dicussion of this subject see Howard Raiffa, *Decision Analysis—Introductory Lectures on Choices under Uncertainty* (Reading, Mass.: Addison-Wesley, 1968); John W. Pratt, Howard Raiffa, and Robert O. Schlaifer, *Introduction to Decision Theory* (New York: McGraw-Hill Book Co., 1965); Robert O. Schlaifer, *Analysis of Decisions under Uncertainty* (New York: McGraw-Hill Book Co., 1967).

company could "win" $500,000 or "lose" $300,000. Since the management has estimated the probability of a "win" (80 percent) and a "loss" (20 percent), it is possible to calculate an "expected value" or payoff from introducing the new blend. This is calculated by combining the potential gain and loss with the probability of each occurring. In the example, it equals a profit of $340,000 [($500,000 × 80% = $400,000) − (20% × $300,000 = $60,000) = $340,000].

Suppose now that the decision maker could undertake marketing research which would yield *perfect* information, i.e., the research would tell him with certainty whether or not the new product would be successful. How much would such information be worth? At present, his expected payoff is $340,000 if he introduces the new blend. If he knew *for certain* that the new blend would succeed, he would introduce it and "win" $500,000. If he knew *for certain* that the new blend would not be successful, he would not introduce it and his payoff would be zero. He believes the probabilities are 80 percent for success and 20 percent for failure; therefore, the expected value under certainty is $400,000 [(80% × $500,000) + (20% × 0) = $400,000]. The value of *perfect information*, i.e., information which would enable the decision maker to make the correct decision for certain, is the difference between the $400,000 and the expected value with uncertainty ($340,000), or $60,000. If the proposed research (e.g., a test market) would cost more than $60,000 to conduct, it should not be undertaken; the manager would do better to make his decision as to introducing the blend without the research.

Perfect information, however, is never available—no matter how carefully research is designed and executed. After the research is completed the researcher is still not certain as to how "perfect" the information is. Bayesian theory helps to cope with such real-world problems. A modification of the above coffee company case will illustrate how this subjective probability theory can be used.

Assume that instead of two possible outcomes there are three which can occur from a decision to introduce the new coffee blend, one for each of three conditions that may exist in the market (states of nature). These three outcomes and the states of nature with which they occur (S_1, S_2, S_3) are: a profit of $500,000 ($S_1$), a profit of $300,000 ($S_2$), and a loss of $500,000 ($S_3$). In the manager's judgment, the probabilities of each state of nature existing are 30 percent, 40 percent, and 30 percent, respectively. Under these new assumptions a payoff table may be developed as shown in Table 5–1.

In this situation the expected payout of introducing the new blend under certainty is $120,000 [(30% × $500,000) + (40% × $300,000) + (30% × −$500,000) = $150,000 + $120,000 − $150,000 = $120,000]. If the executive had perfect information, i.e., if he could eliminate

TABLE 5–1. Payoffs from introduction of new coffee blend

	States of nature					
	S_1		S_2		S_3	
Alternative decisions	Prob. S_1 exists	Profit if decision taken	Prob. S_2 exists	Profit if decision taken	Prob. S_3 exists	Profit (loss) if decision taken
Introduce new blend	30%	$500,000	40%	$300,000	30%	($-$$500,000)
Do not introduce	30%	0	40%	0	30%	0

all uncertainty, he could make the correct decision depending upon which state of nature existed. If S_1 or S_2 existed, he would introduce the new blend, making a profit of $500,000 or of $300,000, respectively. If S_3 were the state of nature, he would not introduce the new blend and would make a profit of zero. Since the probability of the three states of nature existing are 30 percent, 40 percent, and 30 percent, respectively, the expected value of the decision under certainty, i.e., with perfect information, is $270,000 [(30% × $500,000) + (40% × $300,000) + (30% × $0) = $270,000].

The value of perfect information would be the difference between the expected value of the decision under uncertainty and the expected value of the decision under certainty, or $150,000 [$270,000 − $120,000 = $150,000]. Therefore, no research should be undertaken in this situation if it would cost more than $150,000. No research provides perfect information, however, so the actual value of any research would be less than this figure.

To proceed with the analysis it is necessary for the research director to make some estimates of the probabilities that the research proposed will produce correct results. In the example of the new coffee blend, it has been assumed that there are three possible states of nature. It is now necessary to make this assumption more concrete, as it would be in an actual situation. Assume that the three market conditions (states of nature) are:

S_1 — new blend would obtain 6 percent of market.
S_2 — new blend would obtain 3 percent of market.
S_3 — new blend would obtain 0 percent of market.

Now, if the firm were to undertake research in the form of test marketing, it would obtain some estimate of the market share that the new blend might be able to get in the market. The estimate found in the test marketing would probably be close to the actual situation that would occur if the product were put on the market, but it is unlikely that the estimate would be exactly correct. There is some possibility that the estimate from the research would differ from the actual by a considerable degree. Assume that three different outcomes of the research are possible. One outcome would provide an estimate of the new coffee blend's market share at below 2 percent; one outcome would lead to an estimate of 2 percent to 5 percent; and the third outcome would provide an estimate of over 5 percent. Letting E stand for the estimated outcome of the research, then:

E_1 = below 2 percent market share in test market.
E_2 = 2 percent to 5 percent market share in test market.
E_3 = over 5 percent market share in test market.

The researcher must estimate the probability that the research will lead to a given estimate of the market share for the new blend if a given market condition actually exists. For each of the three actual market conditions, the researcher must estimate from his past experience the probability of getting each of the three possible (assumed here) research results. Table 5–2 presents such estimates.

TABLE 5–2. **Probabilities test market research will show various market shares**

| | Possible research outcomes | | | |
| | E_1 | E_2 | E_3 | |
If state of nature is	*Below 2% market share*	*2% to 5% market share*	*Over 5% market share*	*Total*
S_1 (6% of market)	0.20	0.30	0.50	1.00
S_2 (3% of market)	0.30	0.40	0.30	1.00
S_3 (0% of market)	0.50	0.30	0.20	1.00

Table 5–2 is read as follows: If the actual market situation is S_1 (i.e., the new blend would secure 6 percent of the market if it were introduced), there is a probability of 0.5 that the test market research will provide an estimate of over 5 percent for the new blend, a probability of 0.3 that the research will show 2 percent to 5 percent market share, and a probability of 0.2 that the research will show a market share below 2 percent. Note that for each state of nature, the sum of the probabilities of the three research outcomes is 1.0, i.e., one of the three outcomes must occur.

If the executive knew which of the three states of nature actually existed, he would not need to do research. He could make the decision to introduce, or not to introduce, the new coffee blend with certainty. What actually happens is the opposite: research is carried out, and with the new information the executive tries to make a better estimate of the acutal state of nature than he had previously been able to make. If in the above example test marketing were carried out with a result showing the new blend obtaining over 5 percent of the market, what probability would exist that the true market situation was S_1 (new blend would obtain 6 percent of the market)? This can be estimated by proceeding as illustrated in Table 5–3.

In Table 5–3 the probability that a given test market outcome will be obtained if a given state of nature exists is combined with the probability that the specified state of nature does in fact exist. This is the joint probability that a given state of nature exists and that test market research, if conducted, will provide a given result. The reader will recall that the hypothetical executive estimated the probabilities of each of the three states of nature (S_1, S_2, S_3) existing at 0.30, 0.40, and 0.30, respectively. These are shown in column (*a*) of Table 5–3.

The estimated probabilities that each of the three research outcomes would occur, if given states of nature exist, are taken from Table 5–2 and appear in columns (*b*), (*d*), and (*f*) in Table 5–3. These probabilities are multiplied by the probabilities of each state of nature existing (column *a*) to obtain the joint probabilities shown in columns (*c*), (*e*), and (*g*). These results may be interpreted as follows: The 0.15 joint probability which appears in row 1, column (*g*) indicates that there is a probability of 0.15 that S_1 state of nature exists *and* that research outcome E_3 will be obtained if research is conducted.

One may now ask: If research is conducted and the outcome is E_3 (test market share over 5 percent), what is the probability that S_1 is the true state of nature? This is the usual type of question that confronts an executive after a research study has been completed—on the basis of this research evidence, how likely is it that various actual conditions exist? If the executive has confidence in his research staff, he will usually judge that the actual market condition is close to that shown by the research, but he will recognize that small deviations from the research results have some chance of occurring, while larger deviations have less probability. In the example at hand, Table 5–3 shows that the probability of each of the three possible research outcomes (E_1, E_2, E_3) occurring is about the same—namely, 0.33, 0.34, and 0.33, respectively (totals in columns *c*, *e*, and *g*).

Considering column (*g*), one can see that, if E_3 is the research result (a probability of 0.33), any one of the three states of nature (S_1, S_2, S_3) could exist, but the probability of S_1 actually being the true state of nature is larger than the probability of either S_2 or S_3 being the true state of nature (0.15 is larger than either 0.12 or 0.06). The specific probability that S_1 is the true state of nature if E_3 is the research result obtained, is $0.15 \div 0.33 = 0.45$. Similarly, if E_3 is the research result, the probability that S_2 is the true state of nature is 0.36 ($0.12 \div 0.33$) and the probability that S_3 is the true state of nature is 0.18 ($0.06 \div 0.33$).

TABLE 5–3. Joint probabilities for given states of nature and given research outcomes to occur

States of nature	Prob. of S_x being true state (a)	E_1		E_2		E_3	
		Prob. of E_1 research outcome if given S exists (b)	Joint prob. of $E_1 \uplus S_x$ (a) × (b) (c)	Prob. of E_2 research outcome if given S exists (d)	Joint prob. of $E_2 \uplus S_x$ (a) × (d) (e)	Prob. of E_3 research outcome if given S exists (f)	Joint prob. of $E_3 \uplus S_x$ (a) × (f) (g)
S_1	0.30	0.20	0.06	0.30	0.09	0.50	0.15
S_2	0.40	0.30	0.12	0.40	0.16	0.30	0.12
S_3	0.30	0.50	0.15	0.30	0.09	0.20	0.06
	1.00	1.00	0.33	1.00	0.34	1.00	0.33

* Probabilities of E_1, E_2, and E_3 outcomes occurring with given states of nature are taken from Table 5–2.

Similar calculations can be made on the basis of E_1 and E_2 being the research result. Such calculations are shown for all nine possible situations in Table 5–4.

TABLE 5–4. Probability of a given state of nature being true state if a given research outcome is obtained.

States of nature	Possible research outcomes		
	E_1	E_2	E_3
S_1	0.06/0.33 = 0.181	0.09/0.34 = 0.265	0.15/0.33 = 0.454
S_2	0.12/0.33 = 0.365	0.16/0.34 = 0.470	0.12/0.33 = 0.365
S_3	0.15/0.33 = 0.454	0.09/0.34 = 0.265	0.06/0.33 = 0.181
	1.000	1.000	1.000

Table 5–4 is read as follows: If E_1 is the research outcome, the probability that S_2 is the true state of nature is 0.365; if E_2 is the research outcome, the probability that S_2 is the true state of nature is 0.470; and so on.

From Table 5–4 it is possible to calculate the expected profit from the decision to introduce the new coffee blend if any of the possible research results are obtained. Assume that research result E_1 is obtained. The expected value from the decision to introduce the new blend after such a result would be calculated as shown in Table 5–5.

TABLE 5–5. Expected value of decision to introduce new coffee blend if research gives result E_1

State of nature (a)	Probability that S_x is true state of nature* (b)	Profit from introducing new blend if S_x is true state of nature (c)	Calculation of expected value (b) × (c) (d)
S_1	0.181	$500,000	$ 90,500
S_2	0.365	300,000	109,500
S_3	0.454	−500,000	(− 227,000)
Expected value of decision			(−$ 26,500)

* Taken from Table 5–4.

Similarly, the expected value of the decision to introduce the new coffee blend if research outcome E_2 or E_3 were obtained would be $141,000 and $246,000, respectively. In each of the three cases, i.e., research results E_1, E_2, or E_3, the expected value of the decision *not* to introduce the new blend would be zero. Therefore, if research outcome E_1 were obtained, the new blend would not be introduced (expected value of not introducing is zero, which is better than expected value of introducing, which is a negative $27,000), but if research result E_2 or E_3 were obtained, the new blend would be introduced.

It is now possible to compute the expected value of the decision to do test market research. In Table 5–3 it is shown that the probability of each of the three research results occurring is:

$$E_1 = 0.33$$
$$E_2 = 0.34$$
$$E_3 = 0.33$$

The expected value of the decision to introduce, or not to introduce, the new coffee blend if research is carried out is calculated by multiplying the expected value of the decision to introduce, or not to introduce, the new coffee blend in the case of each possible research result by the probability of that research result occurring, and then summing the results. See Table 5–6. Note that if E_1 research result is obtained the decision will be *not* to introduce the new blend, but if E_2 or E_3 is the result, the new blend will be introduced.

TABLE 5–6. Calculation of expected value of coffee decision if test market research conducted

Research outcomes (a)	Expected value of best decision on new coffee given research outcome (b)	Probability of research outcome occurring (c)	Expected value (b) × (c) (d)
E_1	$ 0	0.33	$ 0
E_2	141,000	0.34	47,940
E_3	246,000	0.33	81,180
Expected value of decision if research is conducted			$129,120

The final computation can now be made. Earlier (Table 5–1 and following), it was shown that the expected value of introducing the new blend without research was $120,000. The expected value of the decision after research is shown here to be $129,120—only $9,120 more. In this case, it would be worthwhile to conduct the research only if the cost of the research were less than $9,120.

The reader will note that the above illustration is simplified. In practice, there would be complicating factors such as an indefinite time horizon, more possible states of nature, and more possible research outcomes. Nevertheless, this model is the basis for appraising the value of marketing research.

A more sophisticated application of decision theory occurred in a major coffee company's decision with regard to a container change which would have a major impact on the company's market share.[5]

In this example decision trees were used to structure the analysis. Six major alternative courses of action were identified:

1. Adopt the new container nationally as soon as possible.
2. Stay with the present container until a major competitor converts and then decide what action to take.
3. Convert one of the company's plants to the new container, test market, and then decide.
4. Same as 3 above, except order all needed conversion equipment now.
5. Undertake two months of consumer research and then decide.
6. Same as 5 above, but order all conversion equipment now.

The decision tree for alternative one above is shown in Figure 5–1. It reflects clearly the two major questions facing the company—namely, what action would the company's competitors take, and what effect would the new container have on the consumer's evaluation of the company's brand? Figure 5–1 shows that the company's management thought there were three possible first order consequences of their decision to adopt the new container nationally immediately. These were: (1) no reaction, major competition does not convert—branch B_1; (2) major competitor follows conversion to the new container—branch B_2; and (3) independent conversion by major competitor—branch B_3. Each of these first order consequences would be followed by decisions from the rest of the industry—branches C_1 to C_6. The last "branches" represent possible outcomes in terms of changes in the company's brand share of the market.

Probabilities were assigned to the three alternatives which pertained to the reaction of the major competitior, i.e., 0.1 that he would not convert, 0.4 that he would follow the company's action, and 0.5 that he would convert independently of action taken by the company. In the case of all three alternatives, it was considered a certainty (1.0) that some others in the industry would convert—C_2, C_4, and C_6—and a certainty (0.0) that all others would not convert C_1, C_3, and C_5. Finally, for each "branch" (C) of the tree, changes in the company's market share were estimated. Each of four possible market share changes was given a 0.25

[5] Joseph W. Newman, "An Application of Decision Theory under the Operating Pressures of Marketing Management," Working Paper No. 69 (Stanford, Cal.: Graduate School of Business, Stanford University, August, 1965).

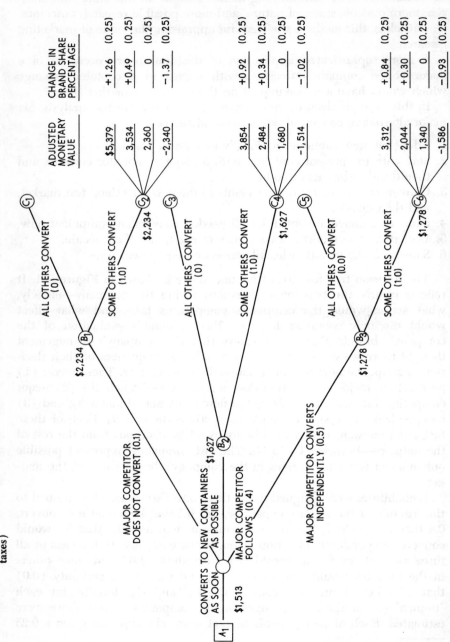

FIGURE 5-1. Expected value of decision to convert to new container as soon as possible (in thousands of dollars before taxes)

Source: Joseph W. Newman, "An Application of Decision Theory under the Operating Pressures of Marketing Management," Working Paper

	ADJUSTED MONETARY VALUE	CHANGE IN BRAND SHARE PERCENTAGE	
C₁	$5,379	+1.26	(0.25)
	3,534	+0.49	(0.25)
C₂ $2,234	2,360	0	(0.25)
	−2,340	−1.37	(0.25)
C₃			
	3,854	+0.92	(0.25)
	2,484	+0.34	(0.25)
C₄ $1,627	1,680	0	(0.25)
	−1,514	−1.02	(0.25)
C₅			
	3,312	+0.84	(0.25)
	2,044	+0.30	(0.25)
C₆ $1,278	1,340	0	(0.25)
	−1,586	−0.93	(0.25)

probability of occurring, i.e., each of the four was believed to have an equal chance of occurring.

The column entitled "adjusted monetary value" needs elaboration. The researcher reasoned that a loss in share could have important personal consequences for the decision maker and, therefore, he weighted losses in brand share more heavily than gains. Such "subjective" measures of the utility of the monetary gains and losses were used to estimate the expected value derived from each alternative in contrast to a straight "dollar per percentage of market," hence the term "adjusted monetary value."[6]

The expected value (profit before taxes) of alternative one was obtained by weighting the value of each branch by the probability assigned, and "working back." Thus, for example, the C_6 figure of $1,277,500 was obtained by multiplying each of the four adjusted monetary value figures ($3,312, $2,044, $1,340, and −$1,586) by the appropriate probability (0.25). This total is then weighed by 1.0 and combined with zero from C_5 to get the expected value of B_3—also $1,277,500. This figure in turn was weighted by 0.5 and the result combined with B_2 ($1,627,000 weighted by 0.4) and B_1 ($2,234,000 weighted by 0.1) to obtain the expected value of alternative #1 (A_1). The expected values of each of the alternatives similarly computed were:

Alternative	Expected value
1	$1,513,000
2	212,000
3	769,000
4	823,000
5	1,246,000
6	1,554,000

On the basis of the above evidence, alternative 6 would be the best choice. Analysis of the value of possible research along the lines discussed previously could be the next step, but the analysis would be considerably more complex than the simple one presented here.

Value of decision analysis of researcher. Clearly, the formalizing of the decision process in the above manner is vital in understanding a problem and should benefit both the decision maker and the researcher.

The real difference between "decision theory" and present management practice is the formalization of this "intuitive" process of choosing among various possibilities. While this may not improve the judgment of the individual decision maker, it improves his communication with others and facilitates the collection and analysis of further information. More important, it forces an executive to

---

[6] For a discussion of how decision makers view risk see Ralph O. Swalm, "Utility Theory—Insights into Risk Taking," *Harvard Business Review* (November–December, 1966), pp. 123–36.

examine his problem in concrete terms, and thus serves as a stimulus to more systematic thinking on his part.[7]

Using such a structured approach the researcher can "push" the decision maker to state what he believes will happen if a certain course of action is taken and what kinds of marketing data he would need (and with what accuracy) to change his mind. Perhaps more importantly, this approach will tend to reveal how strongly the decision maker holds certain beliefs and whether any new information would change his "convictions."

The structured approach also tends to reveal the critical point in the decision process. In the case of the coffee company faced with the need to make a decision on adopting a new container, the critical determinant was the 0.25 probability of *losing* market share. This gave the researcher a "fix" on what was needed; he could then prepare a plan for getting information which would shed light on this risk. He could even test the design with the decision maker by saying, "If I find such and such using the following research design, will you accept the evidence and revise your probabilities?" The researcher would also have a better understanding of the time pressures, the magnitude of the problem, and the identification of the individual who would ultimately make the decision.

Even if the complete structured analysis of the decision process is not used, the researcher should always hypothesize research results and ask the decision maker, "What action will be taken if the research shows—————?" By asking this question over a range of possible results, the researcher can "simulate" the action which will likely be taken in advance of the actual findings, and he can determine what degree of reliability is required.

Determining whether the best course of action was selected. The decisions which result from research findings are based on historical data, i.e., data which apply to the past—even if only a few days or weeks in the past. The action taken on the basis of these decisions, however, applies to the future. Management forecasts that a given action will achieve certain results. New and different market conditions may arise to dissipate the effectiveness of the action taken; the best course of action may not have been selected, or the implementation may not have been handled in the most efficient manner. Therefore, management's responsibility does not end with a decision as to the best course of action. Follow-through or control action is required to determine if the decision is effective. In some cases, the continuous accounting type of research, which is designed to help management recognize the existence of problems, may be sufficient to check on the results of the decision. If it is not, then some other type of follow-through research is necessary.

---

[7] Robert D. Buzzell and Charles C. Slater, "Decision Theory and Marketing Management," *Journal of Marketing* (July, 1962), p. 8.

For example, a manufacturer decided that the best way to correct an inadequate distribution of his product at the dealer level was to employ a missionary sales force. From the salesmen's call reports, it was determined that the men were successful in placing the product in about 30 percent of the stores not carrying the product previously, thereby giving the company nearly 50 percent coverage of retail outlets. This increase occurred within a period of several weeks, but the company decided that, before committing itself to an expanded marketing program, it should check to see whether the stores sold by the missionary force continued to stock the product after the force had terminated its work. The research found that more than 75 percent of the "new" stores were continuing to stock the item. On the basis of these findings, the company proceeded with its expansion plans.

MODELS IN MARKETING

The decision tree example cited earlier was, in actuality, a model. It summarized the way the decision maker thought about the "world." Marketing managers are making increased usage of models and most areas within marketing have been subjected, in recent years, to attempts at model building.[8] Models are important to a marketing researcher since he will increasingly be called upon to work with specialists in providing input data for them. In some cases he may be called upon to help develop a model. In either case he must concern himself with the decision process in order to insure that the information to be collected will be relevant and viable to the decision maker.

Models may be grouped into two classes—behavioral and normative.[9] The former is concerned essentially with attempting to describe how consumers or firms behave, while the latter type is devoted to indicating how consumers or firms ought to behave. Normative, or optimization, models are concerned with attempting to achieve some stated objective, e.g., maximizing sales or profits.

Workable optimization models have been slow to develop in marketing because so little is known about market behavior, i.e., one cannot describe it with any precision. Since behavioral models must precede optimization models, major efforts should concentrate on them at this time.

Optimization models provide the linkage between behavioral relationships and such criterion variables as profits or sales. They are designed to help decision makers use their knowledge about the world wisely. But it is important to

---

[8] For a discussion of the more common types of models in marketing see Paul E. Green and Ronald E. Frank, *A Manager's Guide to Marketing Research* (New York: John Wiley & Sons, Inc., 1967), pp. 108–50.

[9] See William F. Massy and Frederick E. Webster, Jr., "Model Building in Marketing Research," *Journal of Marketing Research* (May, 1964), pp. 9–13.

remember that the results obtainable from the best optimization model can only be as good as the behavioral information that is used as input to the model.[10]

While some progress has been made in modeling consumer behavior, it represents only a beginning. Behavior in the marketplace is an enormously complicated subject.[11]

If a formal decision model is made explicit at the outset of a project, the job of the marketing researcher is simplified because he can know more precisely what data are needed and with what accuracy. He can, therefore, do a better job in designing the research project and in evaluating the findings.

DETERMINING THE RESEARCH OBJECTIVES AND THE INFORMATION NEEDED IN DETAIL

After determining the basic problem and the overall problem setting, the researcher must specify precisely the objectives of the research and what information is needed to attain the objectives. Unless these steps are undertaken carefully, the project will be directed toward vague goals, and inadequate data probably will be obtained.

In spelling out the survey objectives, the researcher must answer the question, "What is the purpose of this study?" or "Why is the study being undertaken?" In order to avoid confusion about the study objectives, the researcher should detail them in writing. For example, a study undertaken by an advertising agency for one of its clients stated that the objective was "to ascertain the characteristics of those households in Greater New York owning an electric roaster." This statement is more like a project title than a precise statement of the study objectives. It does not indicate such pertinent requisites as what area is included in Greater New York City, what characteristics are to be measured, whether household characteristics by brand of roaster will be obtained, and most important, to what uses the information will be put.

Preparing a listing of the information needed

In practice, a detailed statement of the objectives will, to a considerable degree, coincide with a listing of the information which is needed to attain the objectives, but a listing of information needed is of little value unless it is associated with some objectives. In setting down what information is needed, the researcher must anticipate limitations of the data gathering process. For example, it does no good to list desired information which cannot be obtained because consumers cannot, or will

---

10 *Ibid.*, p. 10.

11 For an excellent summary of what is known about consumer behavior see Francesco M. Nicosia, *Consumer Decision Process* (Englewood Cliffs, N.J.: Prentice-Hall, Inc., 1966).

not, answer questions on such a subject or because dealers consider such information a competitive secret. The researcher has to know this or otherwise he will list information which realistically cannot be obtained.

In a study to determine the reasons why consumers in the New York Metropolitan Area used, or did not use, instant rice, the types of information sought were itemized as follows:

1. How many housewives have heard of instant rice, and of these, how many are current users and how many nonusers of the product?
2. What information and misinformation regarding this product, its qualities, and its uses exist among users and nonusers?
3. Why has the product not been tried by those who have heard of it but have never used it?
4. How is the product used for each major use, and why is the product used instead of substitute items?
5. Why did housewives who have tried the product but no longer use it quit using it?
6. In each of the above questions, how do the results compare among classes by age of housewife, family income, family size, education of housewife, and race?

The above listing is presented as an example of the listing of information desired in an actual research project. The reader should note improvements that could have, and should have, been made. For example, in point one, what is a "current user," and in point four, what foods will be considered substitute items?

Anticipating the possible findings of the research project

After completing the listing of data to be obtained, the researcher must anticipate the probable results. For each item of information desired, he must list what he expects to find. He should then ask the question, "What can the firm do with these findings?" If the possible courses of action indicated by the findings cannot be undertaken by the firm, a research inquiry may not need to be undertaken. Or, if it appears that regardless of the findings only *one* course of action is open to the firm— no decision, hence no research, is required.

A recent research proposal for an agricultural chemical company provides a good illustration of this point. The study objectives were to obtain a profile of the company's image versus those of Hercules, Niagara, and Shell chemical companies with regard to such attributes as research skills, aggressiveness in introducing new products, maintaining an effective dealer organization, honesty in making advertising claims, and competency of technical field staff. A number of possible findings could have been obtained, but the most likely one was that, because it was a new company, the firm's profile would not be as good as its competitors'. Given such a finding, what would management do? In this case, the management decided it would do nothing different from what it was already doing, since current actions were based on this assumption. The research director then set up a number of other alternative profiles, including one which was superior to the three competitors on all counts. Only in the latter case did management indicate it would change what it was then doing (by reducing its corporate advertising budget); since the probability of such a "superior" profile was assessed at less than 0.01, the image study was abandoned.

Another illustration of the value of this approach is provided by the case of a small manufacturer selling a canned food specialty item which was consumed primarily in the summer months. This company shared the market with a dozen other brands and estimated that it had a 2 percent share. The sales manager had the advertising agency prepare advertising copy to be run during the winter months to sell the idea of using the specialty food product during that time of the year when it was ordinarily not eaten. He then proposed that the copy be tested among consumers to learn their reactions.

In this case, the researcher should ask the sales manager, "Suppose we find that consumer attitudes are favorable toward the idea of consuming this product in the off season—are you prepared to spend the money on advertising which will be necessary to change consumer habits, knowing that our competitors stand to gain more than we from any increased demand? Can we afford to undertake the necessary brand advertising to maintain our position when competition retaliates?" Probably some cost estimates of the possible advertising job required would be necessary, but, unless the food company is prepared to take this course of action, the research project is not practical.

Thus, it will sometimes be found that a research study is not necessary. Too frequently the assumption is made that research is always desirable, when, in fact, research expenditures should only be made when a firm will be able to act on the findings. A research director will easily earn his salary by pointing out when research expenditures are not needed, either because no problem exists or because the choice of action is in reality so restricted that securing the information is pointless.

The basic purpose of defining the problem is to determine what kinds of information will be obtained from the results, if any, and what specific action will flow from the information to be gathered. Without a thorough understanding of the problem, it is not possible to decide what information to collect or what actions might result.

PROBLEM FORMULATION STUDIES

In many cases, the researcher will find it necessary to undertake research in order to help construct the decision model. Unless the researcher has conducted identical studies before and unless he can assume that the environment has not changed, he should not rely on "armchair" judgment in setting forth the details of the problem at hand.

No one can envision all of the many factors that may have a bearing on a problem. Consider the "diminishing sales" example. A company is faced with a decline in its sales—what researcher can list all of the possible causes of this decline and can then array these possible causes in order of their probable importance? Before attempting to do this, the researcher should get ideas from other sources—ideas which may support his views and/or the views of the company management or ideas which may suggest conflicting or entirely new viewpoints. When he has collected as many tentative explanations as he can, he is better able to set up hypotheses that are likely to support further research.

Research to help formulate problems is exploratory research. The researcher is looking for ideas which will help him formulate and array hypotheses. Exploratory research takes one or a combination of three avenues—study of secondary data, survey of individuals with ideas, and analyses of selected cases.

Probably the first investigation that should be done in problem formulation is research among secondary sources, including all applicable company records. An example of the value of this type of effort occurred when a firm producing commercial laundry equipment called in a research firm. The company's sales had been falling and the management was worried that the product had declined in quality or price appeal relative to competitors. The research firm charted the company's sales over the past ten-year period and then charted the industry's sales over the same period. Company sales had gone down, but the industry's sales had declined more rapidly. This changed the whole line of thinking as to the problem. Instead of suffering from competition within its industry, the firm was losing business to a change in the environment. The investigation then turned in the direction of finding new products which had growth potential.

In most cases, the researcher will want to go beyond secondary sources in his work to formulate the problem. This means that he will get into a survey of people with ideas and/or a study of selected cases. In either case he will face two major problems: (1) how to select the respondents, and (2) how to obtain ideas from the respondents selected.

Selection of respondents

If the project is concerned with finding a "best" way rather than a typical way of doing something, such as organizing a voluntary chain or laying out the main floor of a store, the exploration may well turn to analysis of a few selected cases. The cases will be selected on the basis of the researchers' judgment as to what are the most successful cases available and, possibly, the least successful for comparison. A few cases only would be chosen—perhaps four or five, maybe only one.

If the investigation turns to a survey of individuals with ideas as is common in marketing research, the effort should be to select individuals who have considerable knowledge of the subject and who are sufficiently articulate to express their ideas. A representative group is not sought in exploratory work. Respondents should, of course, be selected so as to provide some representation of the different views which exist on the subject. For example, both dealers and consumers should often be interviewed to obtain different points of view. If consumers are to be interviewed, it may be desirable to distribute the interviews among several income classes, regions, and even city sizes. If dealers are to be interviewed, both large and small dealers and perhaps both chains and independents should be included.

No easy answer is available as to how many interviews should be made in a formulative study of this type, aside from including enough to secure adequate representation of the different types of respondents. Probably the best way of determining the sample size is for the researcher to continue his interviewing until he finds that he is not obtaining any new ideas.

Obtaining ideas from respondents

If a few selected cases are analyzed, the researcher attempts to get a complete understanding of each case. This means that he must gather all types of information about the case. In some instances this will mean interviewing individuals (e.g., members of a firm); in other cases it may mean observing individuals (e.g., selected salesmen) or objects (e.g., layout of a store); or it may mean a study of records. In many cases it will mean a combination of all three.

Interviews are usually used in surveys of individuals with ideas. The interviewers must be well acquainted with the general background of the problem. Since the objective is to obtain new ideas, formal questionnaires are not used. Interviewers have in mind an outline of the issues they want discussed. Within this framework they attempt to get the selected respondents to express their views. Whenever an interesting point comes up, the interviewer explores it fully. Sometimes ideas are obtained by observation, for example, the field worker may observe a salesman in action.

Since much of what is learned from a formulative study cannot be reduced to a precise written report, it is desirable that the researcher who is in charge of the project do the interviewing. This is not always possible, since respondents may be scattered geographically. In any case, he should do some interviewing or he will not be able to evaluate the reports given him by other interviewers.

An important function of the formulative study is to provide an insight into the practical difficulties involved in conducting certain kinds of research. For example, interviews with dealers may indicate the person in the store who is best qualified to answer certain questions and the best hours to call. Further, the formulative inquiry may point up the fact that it is not possible to get certain kinds of information using certain kinds of techniques.

ESTIMATING THE TOTAL ERROR

In planning a research project, it is important for the researcher to have some idea of the accuracy needed in the information to be developed from the research. The more accuracy that is needed, the more expensive will be the research. There are several types of errors which may reduce the accuracy of the data collected, and it is necessary for the researcher to recognize all of these sources so that he can concentrate on reducing the most serious sources of error, thereby reducing the total error to the lowest level consistent with a given expense. He also needs to be able to tell the decision maker how accurate the data collected will be.

Both the research user and practitioner need some measure of credence in survey findings which takes logical account of whatever information they have available. If the survey estimates a market share, the research user is interested in assessing, say, credible limits within which the true market share probably lies. A measure of credence could help the research user appraise a survey's value or its reliability. It could also help the survey practitioner discriminate between research strategies, e.g., to pick that strategy which promises to reduce most the uncertainties that gave rise to the survey.[12]

One approach to a measure of credence is by error ratio analysis. The central idea of this analysis is that the overall error in a research measure of a variable of interest is a function of a number of errors, each arising from an independent error source.[13] The following discussion is simplified because the student at this stage is not equipped to understand all the specifics, although he can get the general idea.

Error ratio analysis

The ratio of major interest in error ratio analysis is t/r, which is a function of three major sources of error, each of which can be expressed as a ratio as follows:

$$\frac{t}{r} = \frac{t}{p} \times \frac{p}{a} \times \frac{a}{r}$$

---

[12] Rex V. Brown, "Evaluation of Total Survey Error," *Journal of Marketing Research* (May, 1967), p. 117.

[13] *Ibid.*, pp. 119–24. The following discussion draws on this reference.

t = true value of variable under study.

r = research measure of the value of the variable
under study (to be estimated from the proposed study) where

p = the true value of the variable in the planned sample

a = the true value of the variable in the final sample

$\dfrac{t}{p}$ = the sampling error

$\dfrac{p}{a}$ = the nonresponse error

$\dfrac{a}{r}$ = the measurement error.

Each of these variables and ratios will become more clear to the student as he progresses through this book. The true value of the variable under study (t) is the information sought by a research project. It might be the percentage of housewives in Denver who use nonpolluting detergents. If this information is obtained by a survey among a sample of Denver housewives, the research measure of the percentage (r) will not be exactly accurate. It is unlikely that the sample selected will be exactly like all Denver housewives in the use of nonpolluting detergents. The ratio of the true value of the percentage among all Denver housewives (t) to the true percentage among the housewives in the planned sample (p) may be called the sampling error.

Actually it is not possible to get a measurement of the true percentage in the planned sample (p), because some housewives selected for the sample will not be at home when the interviewer calls or will refuse to answer questions. Therefore, the final sample will usually have a true value (a) of the variable under study (percentages of housewives using nonpolluting detergents in the example) which is different from the true value in the planned sample (p). The ratio of p to a may be called the nonresponse error.

Even those housewives who respond to the survey questions may not respond accurately, either by mistake or on purpose. The information actually collected from those housewives reporting (r) is, therefore, different from the true value of the variable in the final sample (a), and the ratio a/r may be called the measurement error.

The reader should note that the only one of the above measures which is known is r, and it is not known until after the research is completed. Thus, in planning the research each of the above variables must be estimated by the researcher.

A better grasp of how this analysis might be used may be obtained from the following example based on a planned study to estimate the demand for parking spaces needed in a shopping center during peak hours. On the basis of the research results, the authorities would decide whether to introduce parking meters.[14] A mail survey was to be conducted to determine the number of shoppers who might need parking spaces at one time.

On the basis of preliminary work, the researcher estimated that 10 percent of the sample respondents would need parking spaces. He then needed to estimate the total error (t/r) so that he might have some idea of the possible deviation of the research results from the true value of the variable (number needing parking spaces). He estimated the three subratios as follows:

$t/p = 1.0$. The researcher planned a large sample selected in such a way that it should be very similar to the entire population. (This problem will be discussed at considerable length in the sampling chapters.)

$p/a = 0.9$. Preliminary tests indicated that about 90 percent of those in the planned sample would return the questionnaire. Those not returning it would tend to be people not needing parking spaces.

$a/r = 1.2$. In exploratory work there was evidence that respondents tended to underreport their need for parking spaces.

$$\frac{t}{r} = \frac{t}{p} \times \frac{p}{a} \times \frac{a}{r} = 1.0 \times 0.9 \times 1.2 = 1.08$$

In this example the total error ratio $(t/r = 1.08)$ is quite close to 1.0, which suggests the research results might be quite close to the true measure of parking space needs. The measurement error (a/r) is the farthest from 1.0, suggesting that more effort (expense) should be put to reducing that error before further effort is made to reduce either the sampling error or the nonresponse error. It should be emphasized again that this presentation greatly simplifies the concept of error ratio analysis and leaves out entirely the question of confidence limits which will be introduced in the sampling chapters.

Error ratio analysis is appropriate for determining the "best" estimate both before and after a survey. It is especially useful in choosing between alternative research designs and for allocating effort to the different components of a survey, e.g., reducing the sample size in order to do a better job of interviewing (thereby reducing the measurement error).

SUMMARY

In order to plan a research project, it is necessary to anticipate all the steps in the research process. These steps represent seven interre-

---

[14] *Ibid.* Only a simplified version of Brown's illustration is presented here. For the full report see *ibid.* For another example see Charles S. Mayer, "Application of Bayesian Statistics to Research Design," *American Statistical Association Proceedings* (1968), pp. 181–87.

lated activities which frequently overlap one another. They are: (1) formulating the problem; (2) determining sources of information; (3) preparing the data collection forms; (4) designing the sample; (5) collecting the information in the field; (6) editing, coding, tabulating, and analyzing the results; and (7) preparing the research report.

In formulating the research objectives the researcher should attempt to dissect the problem into its components. This means he will be working with the decision maker to learn the latter's goals, the environment in which the decision will be made, including the available resources, the alternative courses of action, and the possible reactions or outcomes to each course of action. Decision theory provides a way of structuring these components into a payoff matrix or decision model. This helps the researcher, since it establishes a priority listing for possible research projects and helps him to understand better the assumptions being made by the decision maker. The framework also provides him with perspective on the value of any research which might be undertaken.

After determining the basic problem and the overall problem setting, the researcher next needs to specify precisely the objectives of the individual study and what information is needed to attain these objectives. In detailing the objectives, the researcher must answer the question, "What is the purpose of this study?" If the objectives are spelled out in great detail, they will become a listing of the needed information. In preparing this listing, the researcher must anticipate the subsequent research steps. He must not list information which cannot be obtained.

After completing this listing the researcher must estimate the possible research findings and ask the question, "What can the firm do with these findings?" If the firm will not be able to undertake any of the courses of action dictated by the findings, there is little reason for undertaking a research project.

It is frequently necessary to undertake research in order to specify the objectives and to detail the information required. This kind of research is referred to as problem formulation research or exploratory research. It includes study of company records and published materials, surveys of people with ideas, and analysis of selected cases. Unless the research worker has conducted very similar studies before, it is wise for him to conduct a formulative inquiry before stating the precise objectives of any study.

Error ratio analysis is a procedure designed to help the researcher estimate the total survey error, including those errors associated with sampling, nonresponse, and measurement. It can be used to evaluate almost any survey design, as well as to assess which research strategy is best.

Case 5—1. GROCERY PRODUCTS, INCORPORATED*

Grocery Products, Inc. (GPI) was a medium-sized national manufacturer of consumer food products, which included dry soups, pet foods, crackers, and frozen desserts. With over 40 different products, GPI generated a sales volume of over $317 million annually.

The packaged grocery products industry was a highly competitive one, and thus the heart of GPI's marketing-oriented organization was the product manager, who was responsible for the marketing strategy, marketing expenditures, sales volume, and profitability of the product(s) assigned to him. Each product manager had to coordinate the activities of others whose specialized skills and talents contributed to a product's performance from start to finish, e.g., advertising, sales, manufacturing, R & D, etc. Although the product manager was expected to operate much as the manager of a privately-owned business, he was not always able to do so because his brand's objectives might conflict with those of the overall corporation or of another brand. Nevertheless, the product manager's job offered him a great deal of responsibility and flexibility in determining the future of his brand(s). As one product manager, Ellis Dee, put it, "The job can be frustrating at times, but it's always challenging."

Ellis Dee was product manager for Early Dawn Mushroom and two other brands of dry soup. He had an assistant product manager and two staff marketing assistants to help him devise and implement all marketing strategies for his products. The following specific problem encountered by Ellis Dee provides some insight into the nature of the product management function at GPI and into the kinds of decisions the product manager was required to make.

Early Dawn Mushroom had done very well. After four years on the market, sales had reached about 1.4 million cases annually. GPI's gross margin per case averaged $4.65.

Early Dawn Mushroom had a unique appeal to the higher income market which GPI had created through its advertising strategy. Over the four years, a stable media mix of television (65 percent of advertising expenditures), radio, and print had been used to advertise Early Dawn Mushroom; more than $3 million had been allocated for advertising Early Dawn Mushroom the current year. A copy strategy centered around the unique quality and rare type of mushroom used in the mix, which imparted a special flavor to the end result. In addition, about 15 percent of the brand's total advertising and promotion budget had traditionally been spent on promotion—primarily couponing.

* Reprinted from Stanford Business Cases 1968 with the permission of the publisher, Stanford University Graduate School of Business. © 1968 by the Board of Trustees of the Leland Stanford Junior University.

Within the last year, a competitor's new liquid soup product with an appeal similar to Early Dawn Mushroom had been introduced and test marketed in GPI's southern region. The competitive soup, Supreme Mushroom, had captured about 1.5 percent of the total soup market during the year, although it had not particularly hurt Early Dawn's franchise. The competitor had distributed samples by mail in that region and had seen its share increase to 3.6 percent, compared to about 3.0 percent for Early Dawn. Since Ellis Dee was fearful that the competitor would try the same tactic—sampling—shortly after going national with Supreme Mushroom, he considered running his own sampling program in the southern region with Early Dawn. By so doing, Dee thought he might increase the market share of Early Dawn and discourage the competitor from sampling nationally if the competitor thought that GPI would again follow suit.

To sample Early Dawn in the southern region, Dee would have to allocate $50,000 of his promotion budget. The sampling would involve putting one one-ounce package of Early Dawn into a flat box along with a 5¢ coupon to be sent to census tracts where the homes had a $6,000+ average income. The latter insured that over 74 percent of the samples would go to the target group, homes with incomes $7,500 and over, which was thought to be the group most likely to consume the product. The total cost of the sampling amounted to about $130 per thousand homes, including estimated coupon redemption costs.

A larger question in the background was what action Dee should take if and when the competitor "went national." The advertising group proposed a direct-mail promotion program. A coupon, worth 7¢ on the purchase of Early Dawn soup, would be prepared in advance and mailed to 20 million homes immediately following any attempt by Supreme Mushroom to "go national."

The expected rate of redemption for such a mailing was about 22 percent. For each coupon redeemed, GPI would have to pay the face value of 7¢ plus 2¢ for handling. Thus, Dee calculated the total cost of the mailing to be just within the limits of the $500,000 remaining in his promotional budget. Any unused portion of the budget could not be carried over to the following year, and it was improbable that additional funds could be allocated to Early Dawn during the current year.

Dee worked closely with his advertising agency to develop a media plan for Early Dawn for the following year. Because Early Dawn's appeal was to the higher-income market, he needed a media mix that reached that segment effectively. PGI typically spent 65 percent of its advertising budget on TV. Its agency had research data related to upper income audience/cost per exposure for both TV and magazines which indicated to the agency that TV would be the most effective media for Early Dawn in the coming year. Dee was concerned, however, that the

TV audience would not be as selective as magazines. Although Dee disagreed with the agency's interpretation of the research data, he was not sure whether he should defer to the agency. He was cautious about making his point too adamantly for fear the results would not bear out his interpretation, especially since he had been "burned" earlier in the year for becoming too involved in a staff-related area.

The vice president—marketing, in conjunction with all of his soup brand managers, proposed running a contest for all salesmen in the coming fall, aimed at increasing distribution of all GPI soups. The contest was to run for three months, after which time the overall results of the contest were to be evaluated. Dee was asked to determine whether he should support the contest. He would be charged $25,000 as his share of the total cost if he did.

The mechanics of the contest were as follows: Each district was awarded a point for each new placement[15] made either to a major account[16] or to one of the specifically designated large independent stores. Based on the number of points gained by a district, selected members of each district would be eligible for the prize—a week on the town in New York City under the auspices of GPI's sales department. The contest was designed so that an average of two men per district (about one out of twelve) could win the trip.

To verify the sales force reports on major account placements, before and after comparisons were made from quarterly district reports which indicated exactly which chains stocked which brands. Nielsen data were also used to verify distribution information.

In thinking about these problems, Dee realized he should set up a research program which would yield data that would help him evaluate strategy and tactics.

1. What research problems should Dee specify?
2. What specific data should he request relative to each problem?
3. How can the specified data be used to evaluate Dee's plans and actions?

Case 5—2.　LERNER PAINT COMPANY

The Lerner Paint Company was a medium-sized firm producing a high quality paint which was sold nationally through stores franchised to handle the Lerner brand. Lerner sold a complete line of paints with the various bases—oil, alkyd, water, and latex. The line included all of

---

[15] A placement was defined as either a chain or large independent store taking on a brand or a brand size which it had not carried for the last six months.

[16] There were 20–25 major accounts in each of GPI's 27 regions. They generally accounted for 70–85 percent of the total sales for a given region.

the ordinary colors and some special colors developed by Lerner. The firm was intrigued by a new type of roller for applying paint which had been brought to it by a hitherto unknown individual, Mr. Swenton.

This new roller had a chamber above the actual roller which was as wide as the roller itself—ten inches in the standard size—one inch thick, and extended about eight inches up the handle. A plastic bag of paint could be placed in this chamber. The bag was perforated at one end; when it was inserted in the chamber, a tape covering the perforation was removed to permit the paint to ooze out onto the roller. The chamber could be made smaller by squeezing the lid down tighter and tighter. A series of catches in the lid made this easy to do. As the bag was squeezed, more paint was forced out through the perforations. This made it possible to keep a constant flow of paint on the roller and, hence, made it unnecessary for the painter to stop and dip his roller in a pan of paint. The roller model which Mr. Swenton had developed held a plastic bag holding 4/5 quart of paint. All of the different base paints could be used in this manner.

The Lerner management tried the new product in the company laboratories. It seemed to perform adequately, and with a few minor adjustments was ready for the market. In appraising the possible sales of this product, management felt that it had appeal primarily for the household do-it-yourself market. Professional painters had resisted the use of paint rollers, inasmuch as such rollers speeded up painting and, thereby, presumably reduced the need for painters. This suggested to the Lerner management that this new device, which would speed painting more, would be further resisted by professional painters. The device would have a great deal of convenience for the typical consumer, however, and might be received very well by the household market.

Looking over statistics of the household paint market, the Lerner management found that there were varying estimates. One mail survey made by a trade association among six thousand consumer panel members showed that, on the average, families in the United States painted two and a fraction rooms in their homes each year. This included bathrooms, kitchens, and game rooms, as well as living rooms and bedrooms. On the average, these families had five such rooms which were painted, as opposed to being papered, in their homes. Among these families, 70 percent painted their rooms themselves, that is, some member of the family had actually put the paint on the walls.

Another survey, which had been made by mail by one of the major home magazines among its subscribers, found that 60 percent of the subscribers answering the questionnaire had painted one complete wall or ceiling or more during the past twelve months. Among this 60 percent of the families, 70 percent had done the painting themselves. Painting of interior rooms in homes was a seasonal activity. During each of the months from April to September, 10 to 14 percent of the families did some interior painting. In March and October about 8 percent of the families did such painting, while in the other four months 5 percent or less did interior painting. Both men and women did a considerable volume of interior painting. The proportion was about equal, according to replies received in the survey. The percentage of women doing the painting, however, was larger among lower income groups and among families living on farms and in smaller towns. As income rose and as the size of the city in which families were located increased, the percentage of women doing painting declined; however, there was a significant proportion of families, about 20 percent, in which women did painting even in the population groups where women were less inclined to do this work.

The most recent survey of household interior painting indicated that about 60 percent of those families doing their own painting had used rollers the last time they had done such painting. This survey, however, was several years old. Data on household painting by the members of the family showed that there were fairly common practices in this regard throughout the various sections of the United States.

The cost of producing the new type of roller which Mr. Swenton had developed was relatively small. Lerner executives believed that they could produce a medium quality roller of this type so that it would sell for about $1.00 at that retail level.

In estimating the possible profit opportunities in the new product, Lerner executives made the following estimates:

1. There were 50,000,000 families in the United States that might be considered possible customers for the product.
2. One percent of those families which painted 200 square feet or more in a year might be induced to try the product.
3. No profit would be made on the sale of the new type of roller, but one bag of paint would be sold with each roller.
4. Paint sold with rollers would be paint that would not otherwise be sold.
5. Lerner's margin on the added paint sales would be 60¢ per bag regardless of volume.
6. To complete the engineering and marketing of the product would require an investment of $100,000.
7. From the data available the best estimates Lerner executives could make of the proportion of the 50,000,000 families who were potential customers that painted 200 square feet or more in a year were as follows:

% of families painting 200 square feet or more in a year	Probability of being fact
60% or more	0.05
40–59%	0.40
20–39%	0.50
Under 20%	0.05
Total	1.00

Research to test the product in actual consumer use and to determine the percentage of families who painted 200 square feet or more a year would cost an estimated $5,000.

1. Do the secondary data available indicate a large enough market to warrant further investment in marketing research?

2. How much confidence should Lerner executives have in these data? Are they all of equal reliability?

3. Should the additional research expenditure of $5,000 be made?

Case 5—3. ESTHER BURCH, INC.

Esther Burch, Inc. was one of the largest manufacturers of shampoos, hair conditioners, and hair sprays. While many of its products were suitable for both men and women, and were in fact used by both sexes, sales efforts were aimed almost exclusively at women. Annual advertising expenditures averaged around $3 million and were about equally divided between television and magazines. Almost all of the company's ads featured one or more models whose hair had been treated with the company products. Different models were used for virtually all ads. Since a large volume of advertising was done, this use of new models meant that the selection of models was a continuing problem. Difficulties developed as a consequence since different executives of the company and of its advertising agency had different ideas as to the best model for each particular ad. As a result, the company decided to undertake some research to establish criteria for the best models for its ads.

The marketing research department at Esther Burch worked with the marketing research department of the advertising agency to set up the research to define the characteristics which models in Esther Burch ads should have. The final project involved twenty-four pictures of twenty-two models; two models were included twice in different poses. All of the pictures were of the head and shoulders only and all featured the hair to some degree. Some of the models had been used in past Esther Burch ads, but models featuring quite different types of girls and quite different hair-dos were also included to be sure respondents had a wide enough range from which to pick.

One of the copywriters at the ad agency prepared a short paragraph which described the type of girl which the Esther Burch management thought was the ideal type to use its product. While Esther Burch tried to sell to women of all ages, it attempted to maintain an image of a product especially designed for younger women. This had two purposes: (1) younger women were thought to use more hair preparations than older women; and (2) younger women were apt to continue to use over the years preparations with which they first became acquainted if such products were satisfactory. The paragraph describing the Esther Burch girl follows:

She is bright, alert and well liked. Although she leads an active and busy life, her appearance is very important to her and she makes sure that she keeps up on the latest fashions and beauty hints. She has learned to recognize and select the styles that are becoming to her instead of trying to keep up with all the latest fads. Her fresh, neat appearance is admired by all. Women and girls who see her feel "that's the way I'd like to look" or "I think I'd like that style on me."

One hundred fifty-nine women in four different cities were shown the twenty-four pictures of models and asked whether or not they thought each model fitted the girl described in the above paragraph. The results are shown in Table 1. At no time was the Esther Burch name associated with the survey.

After each respondent had indicated that she thought the models fitted or did not fit the descriptive paragraph, six of the photographs were selected at random from the twenty-four. Respondents were then asked to rate each of the six photographs on a 1 to 5 scale for each of several statements or phrases that might describe that model. The descriptive statements were given in pairs which opposed each other, for example, "Is very attractive—Not very attractive." Respondents could rate each picture any place from 1 to 5. If they thought the model was very attractive, they could rate it 5; if they thought the model pictured was unattractive, they could give a rating of 1; if their feelings were someplace in between, they could give a rating of 2, 3, or 4. The particular statements on which ratings were given were as follows:

1. Is very attractive—Not very attractive
2. Is a warm and friendly person—A cool and aloof person
3. Has a natural looking hair style—Has an artificial looking hair style
4. Is particular about her appearance—Not too particular about her appearance
5. Is honest and sincere—Not very honest and sincere
6. Is aware of the latest fashions but selects only those becoming to her—Slavishly follows each new style and fad that comes along
7. Is bright and refreshing—Dull and ordinary

TABLE 1. Photo fits Esther Burch girl description*

Photo number	Yes		No		Don't know	
	No.	%	No.	%	No.	%
24	150	94	7	4	2	1
16	148	93	11	7	—	—
10	146	92	12	8	1	1
4	141	89	17	11	1	1
17	137	86	19	12	3	2
12	135	85	22	14	2	1
2	132	83	22	14	5	3
15	132	83	27	17	—	—
11	120	76	32	20	7	4
7	120	76	35	22	4	3
8	115	72	41	26	3	2
1	111	70	45	28	3	2
5	103	65	45	28	11	7
19	101	64	50	31	8	5
20	99	62	55	35	5	3
9	86	54	65	41	8	5
21	86	54	69	43	4	3
18	85	53	69	43	5	3
13	79	50	73	46	7	4
22	74	47	81	51	4	3
14	73	46	84	53	2	1
23	58	37	94	59	7	4
3	44	28	110	69	5	3
6	33	21	123	77	3	2

* Percentages for each photo are based on a total of 159.

8. Has a hair style that could be done at home—Has a hair style that can't be done at home
9. Looks the way I would like to look—Doesn't look the way I would like to look
10. Has a hair style that I really like—Has a hair style I don't particularly like

Because the six photos used in each interview for this rating scale were selected at random, all pictures did not get the same number of reports. The lowest number of interviews on any one picture was twenty-five—the highest number of interviews was fifty-two. Results are shown in Table 2.

1. Was the research problem defined properly?
2. Was the research designed in the way to be most effective in solving the Esther Burch management's problem?

TABLE 2. Average score for each photo on each statement rating scale

Photo number	Attractive	Warm and friendly	Natural looking hairstyle	Particular about appearance	Honest and sincere	Selects fashions becoming to her	Bright and refreshing	Hair style can be done at home	Looks way I would like to look	Has hair style I like
1	4.1	3.2	2.7	4.5	3.6	4.0	4.0	2.7	2.9	2.6
2	3.7	4.4	4.6	4.2	4.4	3.7	4.6	4.8	3.3	3.4
3	3.5	2.4	3.7	3.7	3.0	3.7	2.9	4.3	2.2	1.8
4	4.5	4.3	4.3	4.5	4.3	4.3	4.5	4.2	4.2	3.4
5	3.8	3.8	4.1	3.5	3.9	3.5	4.1	4.0	3.4	3.2
6	2.6	2.5	3.7	2.5	3.1	2.8	2.6	4.5	1.6	1.8
7	4.1	3.5	2.9	4.5	3.8	4.4	4.0	2.8	3.2	3.0
8	3.9	4.4	4.6	4.2	4.3	4.1	4.1	4.6	3.5	3.3
9	3.8	3.2	3.7	3.9	3.7	4.2	3.6	4.0	2.7	2.7
10	4.5	4.4	4.8	4.8	4.6	4.5	4.6	4.5	4.1	3.9
11	4.2	4.0	3.3	4.6	4.1	4.4	4.2	3.4	3.7	4.2
12	4.5	4.7	4.8	4.6	4.7	4.3	4.6	4.7	4.0	4.0
13	2.9	3.3	3.3	4.0	3.6	3.5	3.1	3.9	2.2	2.0
14	2.9	3.5	3.6	3.7	3.7	3.6	3.4	3.6	2.1	2.2
15	4.2	3.9	4.4	4.7	4.2	4.2	4.4	4.2	3.4	3.3
16	4.6	4.6	4.7	4.5	4.5	4.4	4.5	4.3	4.0	4.0
17	4.2	4.2	4.3	4.5	4.4	4.4	4.3	4.1	3.9	4.1
18	3.3	3.0	3.1	3.4	3.1	3.4	3.4	3.3	2.1	1.8
19	3.7	3.7	3.6	4.2	3.9	3.5	3.7	4.5	2.9	2.8
20	3.7	3.9	4.1	4.1	4.0	3.8	3.7	4.3	3.2	2.8
21	3.1	4.3	4.3	3.8	4.0	3.5	4.0	4.3	2.6	2.7
22	3.3	3.0	4.2	3.6	3.3	3.8	3.3	4.3	3.3	3.6
23	3.8	2.8	3.8	3.5	3.1	3.5	3.0	3.8	2.5	2.3
24	4.7	4.8	4.8	4.6	4.6	4.4	4.7	4.6	4.2	4.3
24-picture average	3.8	3.8	4.0	4.1	3.9	3.9	3.9	4.1	3.1	3.1

Case 5—4. AMERICAN INSTITUTE OF LAUNDERING

The American Institute of Laundering was a trade association organized to provide the laundering industry with a wide range of services. These services included the preparation and dissemination of information regarding plant operations, distribution and sales, the conduct of a laundering school, maintenance of a textile-testing laboratory, and the operation of a full-scale model laundry. Over the past twenty years, the physical volume of laundry processed in power laundries had remained level, while population, disposable income, and gross national product in the United States had increased steadily. Overcapacity existed in the industry and future expectations in new textiles and home-laundering equipment indicated radical changes in laundry services. With this prospect, the American Institute of Laundering (AIL) engaged the Armour Research Foundation (ARF) to develop a long-range research program to meet the present and future needs of the laundry industry.

The ARF study team found that, although the number of power laundries (i.e., laundries using commercial laundering equipment) had not changed significantly since 1935, there had been a 50 percent increase in neighborhood laundries which were typically small establishments using family-type washers. Total dollar receipts of power laundries had doubled since 1939, but so had the consumer price index covering all consumer purchases. Estimated physical volume had apparently shown no growth and probably was declining, since the consumer laundry price index had been increasing more rapidly than the total consumer price index.

A survey of the laundry industry indicated that there had been little or no change in the operations of power laundries in the past fifteen years. Laundries picked up dirty clothes and returned clean clothes to consumers through delivery routes, or dealt with customers over the counter. Most laundries, regardless of size, did not have over two over-the-counter outlets. On the other hand, the number of delivery routes increased with the volume of business. The majority of laundries served a market area of twenty miles or less around their plants, and 80–100 percent of their business was concentrated in the area within ten miles of their plants.

There was relatively little active sales promotion by laundries. The survey indicated that more than half the power laundries spent less than 2 percent of sales for advertising and sales promotion. Newspaper ads, bundle inserts, and radio ads were most commonly used. Only 14 percent of the laundries had attempted to attract business from such institutions as motels, hotels, and hospitals.

There did not appear to be any one factor that related to profitability, but laundries specializing in family-bundle work had a slightly higher profit level than others. There was some indication that laundries that did more over-the-counter business and less pickup and delivery business tended to have a higher profit level. The survey showed that profits of 4 percent of sales before taxes were average, regardless of the size of the laundry. Overcapacity in excess of 10 percent existed.

The laundry industry leaders placed a great deal of emphasis upon the need for better quality of work and the development of revolutionary equipment to accomplish this. Some suppliers to the laundry industry were conducting research into new equipment, but most indicated that sales to the industry were not large enough to justify large-scale research programs.

Home washers and neighborhood laundries were the main competitors of the power laundries with home washers being by far the most important. Over 90 percent of all wired homes contained electric clothes washing machines. This was near the saturation point, and most washer producers aimed their sales efforts at the replacement market. Another survey indicated that a large number of washer owners still used outside laundry service on occasion, when the weather was unfavorable or they did not feel up to the general trouble of hanging clothes to dry. The percent of all wired homes which contained either an electric or a gas clothes dryer was considerably less than those owning a washer. It appeared reasonable to expect that the volume of power and neighborhood laundries would be adversely affected by increased dryer sales.

New scientific developments indicated that home washing, drying, and ironing might become even more effortless by 1980. Advances in supersonic washing and forced-air drying could cut washing and drying time to a matter of minutes. Other advances indicated the possibility of easy ironing through the use of electrostatics.

The trend toward more informal and leisure clothing was expected to continue, including more and more of the "wash-and-wear" fabrics. This would have adverse effects on the laundry industry. Disposable clothing, which could be priced so low that it would be disposed of after a couple of wearings, was also nearing commercial reality.

These factors made the future outlook for the laundry industry such that the ARF team recommended that no long-range research projects be embarked upon by the Institute. Any long-range research might be completely inapplicable before it was completed. Research in marketing and production appeared preferable to research on the development of new equipment. The former would be less expensive and could be done quicker.

Five major areas of possible research were developed by the ARF team: marketing research, production and cost-control research, technological research, communications research, and management-development research. In each of these major areas, specific projects were considered and analyzed as to cost of the research, probability of technical success, cost of development, probability of commercial success and research and development time. From these estimates an overall "measure of commercial effectiveness" was determined. This procedure is explained in Exhibit 1. The first three areas of possible research listed above were considered to be the most promising. The fourteen research projects considered most practical are shown in Exhibits 2 and 3. (Those projects which are not marketing in character are listed, but are not described in detail.)

The American Institute of Laundering could not support a large research program under current conditions. Membership dues amounted to $400,000. No idle funds were on hand. The best method for raising funds appeared to be by requesting voluntary subscriptions from members. Other methods included more extensive use of trade shows, increasing the Institute's laundry operations, raising membership dues, and short-term borrowing. There were also possibilities of getting support from allied industry associations and from government agencies and/or foundations.

1. What research, if any, should the Institute undertake?
2. Is the method of appraising the relative value of projects effective?

EXHIBIT 1. Method of estimating probability of technical success, probability of commercial success, and commercial effectiveness

Probability of Technical Success

This factor measures the chance that no unforeseen scientific or technical impasse will be encountered. A high probability of success does not necessarily indicate that the research will result in favorable findings; it simply implies that an answer will be obtained. In this study the probability of technical success is rated in terms of the following ratios: 0.9, 0.7, 0.5, 0.3, and 0.1. A ratio of 0.9 may be interpreted as indicating an excellent chance of success, 0.7 as a good chance, 0.5 as a fair chance, 0.3 as a poor chance, and 0.1 as a very poor chance.

Probability of Commercial Success

This measure considers primarily the degree and extent to which the industry will accept and implement the research recommendations. Tacit consideration is given to the probable effect of the implemented recommendations upon the laundering market. As in the case of the probability of technical success, the degree of commercial success is measured by the ratios 0.9, 0.7, 0.5, 0.3, and 0.1.

Measure of commercial effectiveness

This is predicated on several assumptions:
1. The power laundry industry is comprised of 6,500 establishments; the American Institute of Laundering membership includes approximately 3,000 power laundries.
2. Total industry sales are somewhat over $1 billion, and total sales of AIL members are about $800 million.

EXHIBIT 1 (*Continued*)

3. Operating costs and profits of the industry are distributed as shown in the accompanying tabulation.[1]

	Annual cost (millions)	Percent of total
Productive labor	$265	33
Productive supplies	80	10
Power	40	5
Buildings	16	2
Machinery	40	5
Indirect overhead	55	7
Distribution	128	16
Sales	48	6
Administration	96	12
Profits (before taxes)	32	4

4. An increase in sales volume would not materially alter the distribution of costs.
5. All the research recommendations possess the same useful life, and therefore annual or one-year savings provide a valid base for comparison (not necessarily true, but no means exist for estimating the economic life of research findings).
6. All the research programs are financed and adopted by 100 percent of the AIL membership where applicable.

Sample calculation

Effect of research: 5 percent increase in the sales of AIL members and a 5 percent reduction in distribution costs. A 5 percent increase in sales is equivalent to an increased dollar volume of $4,000,000; at a profit margin of 4 percent this results in a $160,000 increase in profits. A 5 percent decrease in distribution costs results in a $6,400,00 addition to profits.

$$\text{Measure of commercial effectiveness} = \frac{\text{Annual addition to profits resulting from research}}{\text{Cost of research and development}} = \frac{6,560,000}{190,000} = 34.5.$$

EXHIBIT 2. Evaluation of fourteen proposed research projects

1. *Market definition*
   Research cost:
   Field survey, $35,000.
   Probability of technical success:
   Excellent (0.9)—many similar studies have been previously conducted.
   Cost of development:
   A redirection of advertising effort would probably be required to implement the research findings. The preparation of illustrative copy ($10,000) and dissemination of recommendations to AIL members (3,000 members × $5/member) would result in a total cost of about $25,000.
   Probability of commercial success:
   Fair (0.5)—advertising is in a sense an intuitive art. A general reluctance on the part of individual AIL members to forego personal advertising preferences may be expected.

---

[1] Based on AIL Special Report No. 227, "Operating Cost Percentages."

EXHIBIT 2 (*Continued*)

Research and development time:

Two years—one year for research and one year for development.

Measure of commercial effectiveness:

26.7—arising from increase in sales of AIL members of about 5 percent.

2. *Diversification: new-markets study*

Research cost:

Literature and field survey, $15,000.

Probability of technical success:

Excellent (0.9)—similar studies are continuously being conducted successfully.

Cost of development:

Distribution of findings to the industry in terms of specific case studies and recommendations, $25,000.

Probability of commercial success:

Good (0.7)—the national trend toward greater leisure indicates that markets for new services exist—they remain only to be uncovered and exploited.

Research and development time:

Two years—one year for research and one year for development.

Measure of commercial effectiveness:

40.0—arising from 5 percent increase in sales of AIL members.

3. *Media research*

Research cost:

Consumer field survey, $20,000.

Probability of technical success:

Excellent (0.9)—this is a common type of advertising study.

Cost of development:

Primary costs lie in the dissemination of the research findings to AIL membership for utilization—$15,000.

Probability of commercial success:

Good (0.7)—a relatively minor effort would be required on the part of the individual laundry owner to redistribute present advertising expenditures in such a manner as to reach a large potential market. The simplicity of the effort greatly enhances its widespread acceptability.

Measure of commercial effectiveness:

4.6—resulting from 0.5 percent increase in sales volume of AIL members.

4. *Appeal research*

Research cost:

Limited consumer motivation survey, $25,000.

Probability of technical success:

Excellent (0.9)—a good deal of progress in this kind of research has been achieved in recent years.

Cost of development:

The development of several sample advertising approaches would be required. Total cost for distribution to AIL membership would approximate $45,000.

Probability of commercial success:

Fair (0.5)—appeal research is relatively new and as such its comprehension and acceptance may prove difficult for a number of laundry owners.

Research and development time:

Three years—one and one-half years for research and for development.

Measure of commercial effectiveness:

45.9—arising from estimated 10 percent increase in AIL membership sales volume.

5. *Packaging research*

Research cost:

Laboratory study and field survey, $20,000.

Probability of technical success:

EXHIBIT 2 (*Continued*)

Good (0.7)—many packaging research studies have previously been completed successfully.

Cost of development:

Dissemination of research findings to AIL membership, $20,000.

Probability of commercial success:

Good (0.7)—adoption of the recommendations would probably entail little or no additional expense. The prospect of increasing sales in this manner would have widespread acceptance.

Research and development time:

One year for research and development.

Measure of commercial effectiveness:

Nil—in the large majority of cases laundry packages come only to the attention of individuals already using laundry services. It is unlikely that the present consumer would increase his laundry use merely as a result of a packaging change.

6. *Study of route versus over-the-counter costs*

Research cost:

Field study and records analysis, $20,000.

Probability of technical success:

Excellent (0.9)—this is a relatively straightforward study.

Cost of development:

Dissemination of research findings to AIL membership, $20,000.

Probability of commercial success:

Good (0.7)—the research findings are based upon historical case data and are easily understood and applied.

Measure of commercial effectiveness:

64.0—arising from anticipated 2 percent reduction in average distribution costs.

7. *Operations research over-the-counter location study*

Research cost:

Field survey and mathematical analysis, $30,000.

Probability of technical success:

Good (0.7)—a good number of similar studies have previously been successfully completed.

Cost of development:

Mathematical analysis of individual laundryman's distribution system ($10 per AIL member × 3,000 members) plus cost of distributing the research findings ($10,000), $40,000.

Probability of commercial success:

Fair (0.5)—while it is unlikely that the research findings would result in the relocation of present outlets, they do present a workable guide for the planning of new outlets.

Research and development time:

Two years—one year for research and one year for development.

Measure of commercial effectiveness:

9.1—arising from anticipated 2 percent increase in sales of AIL members.

8. *Equipment catalogue evaluation*

9. *Equipment evaluation study*

10. *Renting versus purchasing equipment study*

11. *Industrial engineering team evaluation*

Research cost:

Field study, $40,000.

Probability of technical success:

Good (0.7)—similar studies are common, but some difficulty may be encountered in relating specific profit improvements to the recommendations of the industrial engineers.

Cost of development:

EXHIBIT 2 (*Concluded*)

    Dissemination of research findings to AIL membership and solicitations of industrial engineering firms to undertake a full-scale improvement program, $10,000.

    Probability of commercial success:

        Good (0.7)—industrial-engineering concepts are common in the industry and bear a relatively high degree of acceptance.

    Research and development time:

        Two years—one and one-half years for research and one-half year for development.

    Measure of commercial effectiveness:

        103.0—based upon anticipated 2 percent reduction in AIL members' direct labor costs.

12. *Re-evaluation of AIL publication policy*

13. *Information exchange research*

    Research cost:

        Field research, $10,000.

    Probability of technical success:

        Fair (0.5)—difficulty may be encountered in measuring the absolute effectiveness of each form of information exchanged and tested.

    Cost of development:

        Dissemination of research findings and organization costs of initiating a long-range information exchange program, $15,000.

    Probability of commercial success:

        Fair (0.5)—difficulty may be encountered in obtaining the full scale and enthusiastic support of industry necessary to the success of the program.

    Research and development time:

        Two years—one and one-half years for research and one-half year for development.

    Measure of commercial effectiveness:

        10.3—arising from anticipated 0.1 percent reduction in average direct labor costs.

14. *Evaluation of traveling information team*

    Research cost:

        Field trial, $20,000.

    Probability of technical success:

        Fair (0.5)—the accurate correlation of operational improvements with the information provided by the information team may be difficult to obtain. In many instances the laundry owner's memory would be the only source of such information.

    Cost of development:

        Dissemination of the research findings to AIL membership and the solicitation of funds to select, train, and maintain a number of information teams in the field, $40,000.

    Probability of commercial success:

        Good (0.7)—there is a strong natural tendency to accept and place relatively high value upon the direct recommendations of an expert as opposed to "wading through" printed matter.

    Research and development time:

        Three years—two years for research and one year for development. Measure of commercial effectiveness:

        22.1—arising from expected 0.5 percent reduction in average direct labor costs.

EXHIBIT 3. Summary evaluation of proposed research projects

Research and development projects	Cost of research (dollars)	Probability of technical success	Cost of development	Probability of commercial success	Research and development time (yrs.)	Effect of research*	Measure of commercial effectiveness
1. Industrial engineering team	40,000	0.7	$ 10,000	0.7	2	−2% productive labor/yr.	103.0
2. Study of route vs. over-the-counter costs	20,000	0.9	20,000	0.7	1	−2% productive labor/yr.	64.0
3. Appeal research	25,000	0.9	45,000	0.5	3	+10% sales/yr.	45.9
4. Diversification and new market study	15,000	0.9	25,000	0.7	2	+5% sales/yr.	40.0
5. Market definition	35,000	0.9	25,000	0.5	2	+5% sales/yr.	26.7
6. Equip. evaluation study	20,000	0.7	100,000	0.7	4	−1% productive labor/yr.	22.1
7. Information team	20,000	0.5	40,000	0.7	3	−0.5% productive labor/yr.	22.1
8. Equipment catalogue evaluation	35,000	0.9	3,0000	0.7	2	−0.05% productive labor/yr.	20.4
9. Reevaluation of AIL publication policy	30,000	0.5	nil	0.7	2	−0.2% productive labor/yr.	17.6
10. Renting vs. purchasing equipment study	20,000	0.7	6,000	0.7	1	−1% depreciation/yr.	15.4
11. Information exchange research	10,000	0.5	15,000	0.5	2	−0.1% productive labor/yr.	10.3
12. O.R. over-the-counter location study	30,000	0.7	40,000	0.5	2	+2% sales/yr.	9.1
13. Media research	20,000	0.9	15,000	0.7	1	+0.5% sales/yr.	4.6
14. Packaging research	20,000	0.7	20,000	0.7	1	nil	0.0

* + = increase, − = decrease.

Case 5—5. DENNY COLA CORPORATION

The Denny Cola Corporation was one of the large soft drink companies in the United States, producing a complete line of soft drinks, but specializing in the Denny Cola, which was by far its largest selling brand. The Denny Company's products were sold at soft drink stands and vending machines throughout the United States, but in recent years had been selling in larger and larger volume in the carry-home six-packs sold in supermarkets. This volume had become more than half of Denny's total sales and gave every indication of becoming an even larger proportion in the years ahead. The Denny products had traditionally sold in bottles which were returned for refilling, but there had been an increasing volume sold in cans. The latter, however, was still less than 5 percent of Denny's total sales.

Denny Cola Corporation was approached by a private individual who had invented a new type of container for soft drinks. This container was similar to a small keg in that it would contain the soft drink and would dispense it through a spigot similar to that on a keg. The container was shaped like an ordinary shoe box, though somewhat larger, and would hold the equivalent of a case of twenty-four bottles of soft drink. The proposal for this container was that the Denny Company "bottle" its drink in the new container and sell the unit to the consumer, who would put it in his refrigerator where it would be cool and where he could draw off as much as he wanted at any time. When empty, the container would be returned to the retailer from whom it had been purchased. The retailer would return it to the bottler for refilling. The working of the keg was ingenious. The soft drink was put into the container under pressure, and was kept under pressure by a compressed gas which was separated from the drink by a plastic film. This pressure kept the effervescence in the soft drink and furnished the pressure to force it out through the dispenser's spigot. The inventor proposed to sell these containers to the Denny Company at $4.80 each.

Denny management was interested in this new idea and ran a number of laboratory tests on the new container. From every indication the con-

TABLE 1. **Per capita consumption of soft drinks in the United States for selected years**

Year	Number of bottles°	Year	Number of bottles°
1919	38.4	1967	298.1
1929	53.1	1968	331.6
1939	88.6	1969	344.0
1949	162.0	1970 (est.)	354.0
1959	199.8	1971 (est.)	368.0

° Eight-ounce bottle equivalents.
SOURCE: Standard and Poor's Industry Surveys, *Soft Drinks-Candy* (April 18, 1963), p. 523 and (December 31, 1970), p. S2.

tainer worked as described. No mechanical defects were detected in the laboratory.

Consumption of carbonated beverages had been rising in the United States at a rapid, but somewhat irregular, rate for many years, as shown in Table 1. The number of bottles consumed per capita made a major jump after World War II when the carry-home market developed. This market had grown to account for more than half of all soft drink sales. The use of cans had developed in recent years and industry forecasts were for more than two billion cans of soft drinks to be sold.

Denny's major competitors, all of which were larger than Denny, were Coca-Cola, Pepsi-Cola, and Seven-Up. Their sales in 1970 are shown in Table 2.

TABLE 2. Sales of Denny Cola's major competitors (1970)

Company	Sales (million)
Coca-Cola Co.	$1,606
PepsiCo, Inc.	1,123
Seven-Up Co.	100

SOURCE: Standard and Poor's Industry Surveys, *Soft Drinks-Candy* (December 31, 1970). p. S4.

Denny typically sold syrup to private bottlers who were given franchises for particular territories, usually a city and the adjacent area. These bottlers sold Denny Cola to retailers in cases of twenty-four bottles and packs of six bottles. Retailers paid $1.30 for a case and 35 cents for a pack of six, plus a deposit of 2 cents a bottle. Consumers usually paid 49 cents plus a bottle deposit for a pack of six, or 10 cents each for individual bottles.

Raw material, bottle, and carton costs were about the same for all sizes of bottling operations. For a case of twenty-four bottles, a bottler incurred the following expenses:

Raw materials	$0.43
Bottle and carton replacement	0.07

For a bottler selling 300,000 cases a year, all other expenses (labor, selling, delivery, and overhead) averaged about 73 cents per case. This cost tended to rise slightly at lower levels of operation and to decrease slightly at higher volumes. The typical investment in bottles was about $60,000 for 900,000 bottles.

If the new container were used, the regular bottling equipment could be adapted to handle it with little trouble. Since the executives did not know how many times the container could be reused, they were reluctant to estimate the charge that would have to be made for each trip of the new container; twenty round trips was the average estimate, but the range of estimates varied widely.

The Denny executives needed to answer several other questions before they could make a final decision to try or not to try the new container. Some of these were:

1. How many of the containers would actually disappear, that is, not be returned by consumers or dealers?
2. How long would it take for the average container to make a round trip, that is, leave the local bottlers, go to the retailer, to the consumer, back to the retailer, and then back to the bottler?
3. How many of the containers would be damaged in use and how extensive would the damage be?
4. What would be the consumer and dealer reactions to the containers and to the handling of the empty containers on the return trip?
5. What effect would the new container have on total consumption of soft drinks?
6. What effect would the new container have on the consumption of Denny soft drinks specifically?
7. What effect would the new container have on sales of Denny drinks in bottles and cans?

To get some answers to these questions the Denny Company proposed to run a market test.

1. What information should be specified to be obtained from the research?
2. Prepare a complete statement of the research design.

6

Secondary data

ONCE THE PROBLEM to be studied has been defined and the specific information needed to solve the problem has been determined, the researcher should decide which sources are likely to yield the data required. A not uncommon practice is to launch immediately into a field survey. Actually, the market researcher should look upon the survey as a last resort, to be utilized only if the information can be obtained in no easier way.

Broadly speaking, the data available to the researcher are either primary or secondary. Primary data are originated by the researcher in the study at hand. If General Mills collected statistics on the sale of Betty Crocker piecrust mix when offered at different prices, such statistics would be regarded as primary data for that project. Data collected for some other purpose than the one at hand are secondary data.

Since the bulk of marketing research concerns either individual brands or proposed new marketing methods, the information needed is often not available from secondary sources and primary data must be collected. Because the problems encountered in gathering primary data are so many and so varied, most of the remainder of this book is devoted to examining the techniques of collection.

The researcher, however, should always explore the availability of secondary data before taking to the field for primary data. The use of secondary data whenever efficacious saves time and money, but it involves many problems. Proper employment of secondary data, for one thing, requires a sound knowledge of the techniques for collecting primary data. This chapter will deal with problems and opportunities connected with secondary data.

USING SECONDARY DATA

The tremendous explosion of information related to virtually every aspect of life in the United States that affects marketing precludes the possibility of keeping up with all of the sources of such information. Nevertheless, a competent researcher must be well acquainted with the major sources and should know how to go about finding the less obvious material. An imaginative researcher is likely to locate valuable data by discovering unusual sources, or to put readily available data to work by rephrasing his hypotheses.

Advantages of secondary data

Economy is clearly the greatest advantage of secondary data. Instead of printing data collection forms, hiring fieldworkers, transporting them throughout the field area, and editing and tabulating the results, the researcher, alone or with some clerical assistance, may go to the library and take information from a published record compiled by somebody else. Not only are available secondary data cheaper than primary data, but they can also be more quickly obtained. While a field project often takes sixty to ninety days or more, secondary data can be collected in a library within a few days.

A third advantage of secondary data is its availability with relation to some subjects which are totally unyielding of primary data. The Bureau of Census, for example, can require individual retailers to divulge sales, expenses, and profit information which would normally be inaccessible to the typical researcher. Moreover, data of this category, collected in the ordinary course of events, are less subject to the biases that might occur if the researcher were to gather the information for a specific purpose.

Limitations of secondary data

The two major problems encountered in using secondary data are: finding information which exactly fits the needs of the project at hand, and being sure that the data are sufficiently accurate.

Finding data to suit the project. Quite often, secondary data do not satisfy immediate needs because they are, by definition, compiled for other purposes. Even when directly pertinent to the precise subject under study, secondary data may be just enough off the point to make them of little or no use. Three variations of this type which frequently impair the value of secondary data concern: (1) units of measurement, (2) definitions of classes, and (3) currency.

Variation of units of measurement is a common drawback of secondary data. Consumer income, for instance, may be measured by individual, by family, by household, by spending unit, or by tax return, depending on the source. In view of the differences in the units of measurement, the various data can be used together only for rough approximations.

Another common variation in secondary data is the distinctive construction given to classes in different projects. A chain of stores, for example, may be defined as more than one store, four or more stores, ten or more stores, etc. Similarly, age groupings may be under twenty, twenty to thirty, and over thirty, or they may be under twenty-five, twenty-five to forty, and over forty, etc. Continued efforts are being made to establish uniform classifications, so as to avoid this sort of variation. The definitions employed by the United States Bureau of Census are often adopted by others because the Bureau probably produces more statistics than any other single body. Unfortunately, however, neither these nor any other standards, such as the breakdowns of population data suggested by the American Marketing Association as far back as 1951, have been generally accepted.[1] So long as unique classifications further the special purposes of marketing research groups, they will continue to be constructed.[2]

Yet another common variation in secondary data that is sometimes crippling is the obsolescence which characterizes so much of it. Marketing is seldom concerned with historical statistics. Data which are invaluable one year may have become useless by the next. The census, for example, contains some of the most indispensable marketing data, yet six to eight years after a census is taken, much of that information will have largely lost its value.

Finding data of known accuracy. Once the researcher has discovered appropriate secondary data, he must determine whether or not the information is accurate enough for his purposes. Before applying any secondary data, the researcher must critically evaluate them and the circumstances under which they were collected.

Of cardinal importance in this evaluation is identification of the data's source. Secondary data, which essentially means information collected by someone else, may be derived from a secondary source or from an original source. If the researcher obtains secondary data from the party who gathered them, he is going to the original or primary source. If secondary data are taken from a source which procured them from the original source, then a secondary source is being used. Secondary data should be collected, whenever possible, from original sources.[3]

---

[1] "Standard Breakdowns for Population Data," *Journal of Marketing,* Vol. XV (April, 1951), pp. 476–78.

[2] For an interesting discussion of the problems of making secondary data more widely usable, and of methods of doing so, see Maxwell R. Conklin, *The Role of the 1954 Census of Manufacturers in Overcoming Problems of Industry Data* (Washington, D.C.: Bureau of the Census, 1956).

[3] For a good discussion of original and secondary sources, see Kenneth P. Uhl

The importance of original sources. The paramount advantage of original sources is their usual explanation of how the data were collected, which facilitates an appraisal of their reliability. Secondary sources often omit this description. Moreover, secondary sources often make errors in copying data. An unwary researcher is likely to perpetuate such errors in his own work.

Some time ago, Robert S. Henry carefully documented his assertion that most of the textbooks then in use in U.S. schools gave erroneous data on the amount of land granted to the railroads.[4] One of the reproved historians, Edward Kirkland, replied that the writers of textbooks could not use original sources to check the validity of all of their data, but were often obliged to employ secondary sources to save time.[5] In this way, significant errors are prolonged and even compounded.

Not infrequently, secondary sources bobtail the information given in the original sources. Explanatory or cautionary footnotes, for example, may be omitted. Furthermore, quotations out of context often carry an implication not provided by the complete data. Another hazard in reliance upon secondary sources is their common acceptance of preliminary data as final and their failure to follow up on revised data. The federal government often releases preliminary data which are later adjusted into "final" data. Moreover, the "final" data are sometimes revised as a result of additional information or a change in procedure. These alterations are most likely to be picked up if the original source is consulted; even then, it is essential to be constantly apprehensive of such possible changes.

Evaluating secondary data. On some occasions, the researcher will be confronted with the necessity of choosing among two or more sources of data. On such occasions, but also when only one source is available, the researcher must evaluate the secondary data he is considering. Above all, he must decide whether or not the data are accurate enough for the purposes of the project.

1. PERTINENCY OF THE DATA. Having defined his problem and specified precisely the information necessary to its solution, the researcher can determine what secondary data meet his needs. To be used, the data must be measurable in the project's units and applicable to the time period in question. In addition, classes of data must be construed in the

---

and Bertram Schoner, *Marketing Research: Information Systems and Decision Making* (New York: John Wiley and Sons, Inc., 1969), chap. xiii, and Ya Lun Chou, *Applied Business and Economic Statistics* (New York: Holt, Rinehart and Winston, 1963), pp. 76 ff.

[4] Robert S. Henry, "The Railroad Land Grant Legend in American History Texts," *Mississippi Valley Historical Review,* Vol. XXXII (September, 1945), pp. 171–94.

[5] Edward Kirkland, "Comments on the Railroad Land Grant Legend in American History Texts," *Mississippi Valley Historical Review,* Vol. XXXII (March, 1946), pp. 574–76.

same way as in the project. A little flexibility and imagination may enable the researcher to redefine particular hypotheses so as to allow the use of data which could not otherwise be applied, but which promise to shed some light on the basic problem.

2. WHO COLLECTS AND PUBLISHES THE DATA—AND WHY. In evaluating secondary data, the researcher must necessarily examine the organization which collected the data and the purpose for which they were published. An organization which makes the collection and publication of data its chief function is apt to furnish accurate data, especially if it has a reputation for excellence. Obviously, the success of any firm of this sort depends on the long-run satisfaction of its clients that the information supplied is accurate.

The ability of an organization to procure the wanted information is clearly a pivotal consideration. This often reduces itself to a matter of authority and prestige. The U.S. Bureau of Internal Revenue, for instance, can obtain accurate income information more easily than any private firm because of its legal authority. In another instance, the prestige of universities as impartial and reliable institutions frequently enables them to secure information from businesses which other firms would have trouble getting. Universities are also helped in this regard by their normal abstention from competition with business organizations.

Available resources may also affect the accuracy of data. The U.S. Bureau of the Census, with an abundance of money and personnel, is apt to do a better job of collecting accurate data than a university professor with a limited grant.

If feasible, the individual in direct charge of the data collection in question should also be appraised. Reputation, experience, and degree of independence on the particular project are all germane matters for judgment. An individual working on a university research grant would be more likely to turn out an accurate report than the same individual working for an organization which is committed to one side of a question. The controversy over the relationship between cigarette smoking and lung cancer provides a continuing illustration of this point. With few exceptions, physicians, academicians, and government researchers have concluded that the available evidence indicates a positive link between smoking and the incidence of lung cancer. With unsurprising regularity, the cigarette manufacturers, including professionals in their employ, and the officials of states with important tobacco industries insist that the evidence supports no such conclusion. In seeking to choose between the two interpretations of the same data, the public must rely upon a critical appraisal of the parties involved. The obvious vested interests in the group which denies that any causal relationship between smoking and lung cancer has been proven can scarcely be expected to foster an objective analysis of this issue.

Discovering the purpose for which data are published is mandatory for an adequate evaluation of secondary data. Data published to promote the interests of a particular group, whether it be political, commercial, or social, are suspect. Media buyers, for example, see so many studies of magazine audiences, each of which "proves conclusively" that the study sponsor's magazine is the best available medium for advertising, that the buyers pay little attention to many of these studies. The weekly, *Life,* would not be prone to print a study that might show *Playboy* or some other competitor to advantage—and vice versa. At the same time, not all data derivable from sources with an "axe to grind" are biased, although great care should always be exercised with respect to information so procured.

3. METHOD OF COLLECTING DATA. If a source fails to give a detailed description of its method of data collection, the researcher should be hesitant about using the information that it yields. Only too often, shyness about procedures for the procurement of data betokens the employment of sloppy methods. Most primary sources, however, describe their methods.

When the methodology is described, the researcher should subject it to a painstaking examination. Even if the procedures appear to be sound, he must use caution, because weaknesses tend to be camouflaged. Searching questions must be answered positively before the data can be put to work.

If a sample was used, was it selected objectively? Was it large enough, particularly in the subsamples? Was it chosen from the universe of interest? Was the method of collecting data in the field sound? Was it the most objective possible? Data gathered by observation tend to be more objective (and, therefore, more accurate) than data collected through questioning. Was the method employed adequate for getting the information? Questionnaires which attempt to determine buying motives, for instance, are usually unlikely to reveal the actual motives. Accumulating data in the field requires administration. What kind of supervision did the people have who actually made the observations? Were any checks made on the accuracy of the fieldworkers' results?

4. GENERAL EVIDENCES OF CAREFUL WORK. An indispensable point of evaluation is the general evidence that the data have been collected and processed carefully. Is the information presented in a well-organized manner? Are the tables constructed properly, and are they consistent within and among themselves? Are the conclusions supported by the data?

In recent years, several efforts have been made to improve the accuracy of secondary data and to provide users with better means for judging that accuracy. The Advertising Research Foundation, for instance, has a consulting committee which will work with organizations that collect data for the use of others. The committee's "seal of approval" not only guarantees a relatively high quality of data, but also provides a full discussion of the methodology employed. Associated Business Publications has published a standard form for the reporting of research results obtained by business publications. This form includes a complete disclosure of the methods used.[6]

Conflicting data. If several sources of data relating to a researcher's problem are available, the data can be submitted to quality control analysis of the sort applied in production.[7] After dividing the data into "good" and "poor" on the basis of criteria like those mentioned in the foregoing section, correlations on points of interest can be run between the two groups, and statistical tests can be made with the results. In projects which rely heavily on secondary data, this technique is particularly valuable.

TYPES OF SECONDARY DATA

Secondary data are either internal or external relative to the company considering their use. Internal data are procurable within the company. They include such things as invoices, salesmen's reports, shipments, detailed operating statements, general and departmental budgets, and previous research reports done by or for the company. A research manager must necessarily make himself thoroughly familiar with all of the material of this type that is available within his company. He should explore company records constantly so as not to overlook possible answers to the needs of his projects.

The collection of internal data requires relatively little formal technique. It is largely a matter of knowing the company's operating procedures and establishing systematic methods for recording the desired information. Collection of external data is more difficult because the data have much greater variety and the sources are far more numerous. Every researcher should be well acquainted with the major sources of marketing information and should be well versed in the procedures of searching for other sources.

In the following discussion, external data will be divided into four classes, each of which will be considered in turn: (1) census and registration data; (2) individual project reports publicly circulated in encyclopedias, books, monographs, bulletins, and periodicals; (3) data collected for sale on a commercial basis; and (4) miscellaneous data.

---

[6] *Full Disclosure Form for Publication Research* (New York: Associated Business Publications, 1961).

[7] See Raoul Naroll, *Data Quality Control* (New York: The Free Press of Glencoe, 1962).

Census and registration data

Census data. The U.S. Bureau of Census continually produces censuses and complete counts and studies based on samples plus related surveys, many of which are indispensable tools for the market researcher. Originally limited in its reference to a count of heads for purposes of taxation, the "census" has long since come to mean enumerations of far wider variety, and the broadening of its significance promises to persist.[8]

The major uses of census data are in sales forecasting, development of market potentials, construction of sales territories and quotas, store location, and plant location.

The Census of the United States presently incorporates eight different censuses, none of which is without interest to the marketing researcher. Together with other reports issued by the Bureau, they constitute the most fruitful single source of data useful in marketing research. The experience, resources, and authority of the Bureau combine to earn its data a high reputation for validity.[9] A brief description of each of these censuses follows.

Census of Population. This census reports the count of population by state, county, city, metropolitan area, and, in large cities, by census tract. "Census tracts" are fixed areas of around 4,000 population—very convenient for marketing surveys as constant indices from one census to another. The 1970 Census of Population was not completely reported by January 1972, but most of the individual state reports on number of inhabitants were available and the more detailed reports were expected soon covering many characteristics of the population such as age, sex, race, mother tongue, citizenship, education, families and their composition, employment status, place of work, veteran status, occupation, and income. This census used new techniques for enumeration which are expected to produce more accurate data.[10]

Census of Housing. Made in conjunction with the Census of Population, this census enumerates types of structure, year built, equipment (including clothes washers, air conditioners, etc.), water source, sewage disposal, fuel used, rent paid, value, number of persons per room, occupancy and tenure, race of occupants, condition of dwelling, size, and mortgage status. The 1970 census gives reports by city block for

---

[8] Other censuses such as school censuses are made, but are relatively unimportant in marketing research.

[9] Even the Bureau of Census, however, is reproachable. No source of information should be treated as Calpurnian—a persistent scepticism is an essential posture when it comes to successful marketing research. For an example of the Bureau's lack of infallibility, see William E. Cox, Jr., "Census of Business: Some Contrary Evidence," *Journal of Marketing* (July, 1967), pp. 47–51.

[10] "Dress Rehearsal for the 1970 Census," *Management Review* (April, 1968), pp. 58–60.

those places with a population of 50,000 or more. These are some of the most useful data to market researchers. A new joint Population-Housing Report which shows demographic trends for metropolitan areas between 1960 and 1970 will also be of particular value to researchers.

In 1968, the Bureau undertook a survey of the activities in 1967 of all large construction establishments and a sample of smaller ones. The result was the first national census of construction since 1939; it includes data on contract construction, subdividing and developing, operative builders, and every type of specialty contractor and subcontractor.

The Bureau also issues a series entitled *Current Housing Reports,* which, like *Current Population Reports,* helps the researcher to keep abreast of developments between censuses. Special reports on narrower topics are issued irregularly by the Bureau in the fields of these and other censuses.

Census of Business. This census was last taken to cover operations of 1967. The report is divided into three parts: retail trade, wholesale trade, and selected services. The statistics cover total sales, number of employees, payrolls, and number of establishments for each principal type of business; the enumerations are made by state, county, metropolitan area, and city.

Retail figures encompass nearly 100 store categories for metropolitan regions and for the larger cities and counties. Retail establishments are classified by number of stores operated, number of employees, and size of sales. Each retailer was asked to report sales for 25 major lines of merchandise. Other data gathered include sales of second-hand merchandise, concessions, legal form of organization, and status of stores as self-service or not.

Wholesale statistics report the number of establishments, commodity-line sales, sales for merchant wholesalers and for all other operating types combined, sales by class of customer, payroll, warehouse space, and cold storage facilities. Also included are information on the commissions of manufacturers' agents and operating ratios.

The reports on the service sector are devoted to such services as amusement, cleaning, repairing and maintenance, blacksmiths, direct-mail advertisers, and motels, but attorneys, physicians, realtors, dentists, and marketing professors are not. The reported data comprise the size of establishment, receipts, and the legal form of organization.

Future censuses of business, as well as those of manufactures, mineral industries, and transportation will be taken at intervals of five years in the years ending in 2 and 7. Current data in all fields are furnished by monthly, annual, and in retail trade, even weekly surveys. Valuable special reports are also issued on an irregular basis.

Census of Manufactures. This census gives data on the number and size of establishments, the legal form of ownership, payrolls, manhours, sales by customer class, inventories, selected costs and book value of fixed assets, capital expenditures, industrial water use, selected metal-working operations, fuels and electric energy consumed, and value added by manufacture. The census covers all establishments in approximately 430 manufacturing industries. Area reports, industry reports, and special subject reports are also published. The key general statistics of the main census are carried forward in an annual survey. *Current Industrial Reports* which incorporates a commodity series on production, sales or shipments, and, sometimes, stocks for over 100 product groups, appears monthly, quarterly, and annually.

Census of Mineral Industries. The 1963 census lists the number of companies, mines, and preparation plants in 50 mineral industries and 13 subindustries, as well as the number of employees, principal expenses, capital expenditures, power equipment, value of shipments, and water use. The annual Mineral Industry Surveys, published by the U.S. Bureau of Mines, supply current intercensal data, as do a number of weekly, monthly, quarterly, or annual specialized reports which are also published by the Bureau of Mines.

Census of Agriculture. Compiled every five years, the latest census, covering 1969, divided the country into over 50 parts, but also tabulated data on a county basis within those divisions. Information in the report includes: number of farms, size, acreage value, farm expenditures, crops and livestock, value of products, facilities and equipment, number and characteristics of persons living in farm households, farm labor, irrigation, and the use of fertilizers. As in other censused fields, the intercensal developments in agriculture are well reported by the Bureau of Census and other governmental agencies—especially those of the Department of Agriculture.

Census of Transportation. First taken in 1963 and repeated in 1967, this survey deals with passenger transportation, truck inventory and use, commodity transportation, and bus and truck carriers.

Census of Governments. The 1967 report presented data on: the numbers and characteristics of local governments; civilian employment by federal, state, and local governments; payrolls, revenue, and indebtedness for school districts and governments; and assets and expenditures as well as other fiscal matters.

Registration data. These data are collected routinely as the result of legal requirement or as a part of administrative procedure. Most of this information is compiled by governmental agencies and is sometimes difficult to locate. Its wide variety is illustrated by the following list which is, of course, far from exhaustive.

1. Births
2. Deaths

3. Marriages
4. School enrollment
5. Income tax returns
6. Social security tax payments
7. Unemployment
8. Sales tax payments
9. Sales and prices at public markets
10. Export declarations
11. Trade association (and other organization) membership lists
12. Customers lists (particularly credit customers)
13. Automobile registrations
14. License requirements for various business activities

Finding census and registration data.[11] Perhaps the most efficacious guide to census data is the quarterly *Catalog of U.S. Census Publications,* which has monthly supplements and also appears in an annual cumulated volume. In addition, the Bureau issues Publication Programs, leaflets which contain tentative publication dates of preliminary and all other census reports. The data can also be checked by using the list of census volumes and the table of contents in each volume. A vast quantity of tabulated but unpublished data and a great many special tabulations are produced by the Bureau. The unpublished data, with the exception of individual records, are available at cost—often on magnetic tape or punchcards. The special tabulations are similarly available. If regular work allows, the Bureau will undertake individually requested tabulations at project cost; such custom-made work, however, then becomes accessible to the rest of the public. In general, registration data are harder to locate than census data because of their variety and the dispersal of their sources. Guidebooks like the *Directory of Federal Statistics for Local Areas* and the *Directory of Federal Statistics for States,* both recently issued by the Bureau of Census, help to dispel some of the confusion.

Knowing the field. Nothing can replace familiarity with the field of study. A marketing research man who works with a manufacturer for a substantial length of time inevitably becomes acquainted with the important census and registration data pertinent to that field of manufacturing. Whenever involved in problems connected with a relatively strange field, it is naturally profitable to seek out sources through discussion with veterans in the field.

---

[11] For a more extended discussion of how to locate data, see Steuart H. Britt and Irwin Shapiro, "Where to Find Marketing Facts," *Harvard Business Review,* Vol. XL (September–October, 1962), pp. 44–52; *Guide to Information Sources for Education in Distribution* (Washington, D.C.: U.S. Department of Commerce, 1961); and Robert N. Carpenter, *Guidelist for Marketing Research and Economic Forecasting* (New York: American Management Association, Research Study No. 73, 1966).

Trade associations can usually refer the researcher to all major sources of information related to their lines of business. Most associations compile data on members of the trade, and some gather additional relevant data. The National Machine Tool Builders' Association, for example, collects information on machine tool orders and shipments, while the Tanners' Council of America reports the number of cattle hides produced monthly.

Guides to census and registration data.   Besides those already mentioned, guides for helping the researcher locate census and registration data are plentiful. In view of the vast volume of data, however, no single guide can be entirely comprehensive, so that knowledge of at least the principal guides is a necessity for the competent researcher. Many of the items listed in these guides are part of the holdings of average business libraries. Those which are not are obtainable through interlibrary loan or from the original sources. Among the major guides are the following:

1. Joyce Ball, ed., Roberta Gardella, comp., *Foreign Statistical Documents* . . . (Stanford, Cal.: the Hoover Institution on War, Revolution and Peace, 1967). vii, 173 pp. Arranged by country. Limited to holdings of libraries at Stanford University.
2. Business and Defense Services Administration, U.S. Department of Commerce, *Measuring Markets: A Guide to the Use of Federal and State Statistical Data* (Washington, D.C., 1966). vi, 94 pp.
3. Robert N. Carpenter, *Guidelist for Marketing Research and Economic Forecasting,* rev. ed., (New York: American Management Association, 1966). 112 pp. ". . . descriptions of publications which contain figures and other facts often sought by the marketing research man. . . .   . . . cites many indexes, bibliographies, catalogs, and even directories of directories, which do not give numerical data but do point the way to other literature or sources of such data."
4. Chamber of Commerce of the United States, *Sources of State Information and State Industrial Directories* (New York, 1967). 19 pp. Serial listing.
5. Edwin T. Coman, Jr., *Sources of Business Information,* rev. ed. (Berkeley, Cal.: University of California Press, 1964). ix, 330 pp. This guide to the basic sources of business information is organized by subject areas.
6. Nathalie D. Frank, *Market Analysis, A Handbook of Current Data Sources* (New York: Scarecrow Press, Inc., 1964). 268 pp. Original statistical sources are particularly well represented.
7. H. Webster Johnson, *How to Use the Business Library with Sources of Information,* 3d ed. (Cincinnati: South-Western Publishing Co.,

1964). v, 160 pp. Not only provides guide to use of the library but also to the means of securing information elsewhere.

8. Library of Congress, *A Directory of Information Resources in the United States Social Sciences* (Washington, D.C., 1965). List of 600 governmental as well as other sources.

9. Library of Congress, *Monthly Checklist of State Publications* (Washington, D.C.). All state documents received by the Library are indexed by state and by department or issuing agency. An annual summary index is compiled by subject.

10. Organization for Economic Cooperation and Development, *Guide to European Sources of Technical Information* (Paris: O.E.C.D., 1964). 292 pp. Can be procured through McGraw-Hill Book Co. 487 sources.

11. Organization for Economic Cooperation and Development, *List of Official Existing Guides to Official and Semiofficial Statistics* (Paris, 1963). Obtainable from McGraw-Hill.

12. *Statistical Sources Review* (Detroit). Monthly published by the Gale Research Company. Subject index, cumulated quarterly.

13. *United Nations Statistical Yearbook* (New York: United Nations Statistical Office). Annual. Subject index. World coverage.

14. U.S. Bureau of the Census, *Guide to Industrial Statistics* (Washington, D.C.: U.S. Department of Commerce, 1964). 60 pp. Locator guide. Tells how to get special tabulations and primary source materials.

15. U.S. Office of Distribution, Department of Commerce, *Marketing Information Guide* (Washington, D.C.). This monthly guide gives an annotated list of selected current marketing material. Semiannual index and an occasional supplement.

16. U.S. Office of Statistical Standards, Bureau of the Budget, *Statistical Services of the U.S. Government* (Washington, D.C.: Bureau of the Budget, 1963). 136 pp. Part I describes the federal statistical system, and Part II gives a brief account of each of the main economic and social statistical series collected by the government.

17. Paul Wasserman and others, eds., *Statistics Sources . . .* , 2d ed. (Detroit: Gale Research Co., 1965). 387 pp. Not limited to U.S. sources. Commercial as well as governmental sources.

Summary volumes of statistics. The publications listed below summarize statistics from many sources. Valuable as sources of information in themselves, they also indicate original sources in which more detailed data can be found.

1. Board of Governors, Federal Reserve System, *Federal Reserve Bulletin* (Washington, D.C.). Monthly. Includes statistics on retailing,

prices, consumer credit, and national income. Current and trend data.

2. Chamber of Commerce of the United States, *Foreign Commerce Handbook: Basic Information and Guide to Sources,* 16th ed. (Washington, D.C., 1967). 184 pp. Comprehensive annotated bibliography which lists important sources on foreign trade.

3. Commodity Research Bureau, Inc., *Commodity Year Book* (New York). Annual. Data on the production, prices, consumption, and import and export flow are provided for a great many commodities. The commodities and their areas of production are also briefly described.

4. Standard and Poor's Corporation, *Standard and Poor's Trade and Securities* (New York). Monthly. The third section, "Statistical Section," contains data on commodity production, prices, and inventories as well as information on employment, stock price indexes, and business activity.

5. U.S. Bureau of Labor Statistics, Department of Labor, *Monthly Labor Review* (Washington, D.C.). Monthly. Statistics on employment, wages, consumer price indexes, wholesale price indexes, labor turnover, economic sectors, and so on.

6. U.S. Bureau of the Census, *Business Cycle Developments* (Washington, D.C.). Monthly. Current data on 70 different kinds of economic indicators.

7. U.S. Bureau of the Census, *County and City Book* (Washington, D.C.). Published approximately three times during a decade. 1967 edition furnishes data on education, income, housing, and many other subjects (over 140 statistical items) for every county and for every city over 25,000. Information also available on tape and punchcards.

8. U.S. Bureau of the Census, *Historical Statistics of the United States, Colonial Times to 1957* (Washington, D.C.: U.S. Department of Commerce, 1960). xi, 789 pp. Supplement extends data through 1962 (1965, iv, 154 pp.) Close to 8,000 statistical series extending back to 1610. Includes useful definitions.

9. U.S. Bureau of the Census, *Pocket Data Book USA* (Washington, D.C.). Annual summary of the *Statistical Abstract.*

10. U.S. Bureau of the Census, *Statistical Abstract of the United States* (Washington, D.C.). Annual. In the latest issue, over 1,300 subjects are covered in about 1,000 pages. Based upon ". . . most of the important statistical publications, both governmental and private."

11. U.S. Department of Agriculture, *Agricultural Statistics* (Washington, D.C.). Annual. Agricultural production, prices, consumption, costs, facilities, and so on.

12. U.S. Office of Business Economics, Department of Commerce, *Sur-*

vey of Current Business (Washington, D.C.). Monthly. Weekly supplements. Some 2,500 different statistical series are published. Comprehensive. Biennial supplement, *Business Statistics,* covers historical data.

13. U.S. Internal Revenue Service, Department of the Treasury, *Statistics of Income* (Washington, D.C.). (1) One annual gives data for individuals and unincorporated businesses by various classifications, such as source of income, size of source, and size of net income. (2) A second annual provides information on corporations.

14. U.S. Bureau of the Census, *Quarterly Summary of Foreign Commerce of the United States* (Washington, D.C.). Quantity and value of exports and imports by quarter. Annual figures given in the fourth quarter.

Miscellaneous reference aids. Possibly the most rewarding single source is a competent reference librarian. This informational factotum is to be found in almost every business library. Among the many other sources to which he might direct a researcher would be one of the forty-two field offices that the U.S. Department of Commerce maintains in major cities throughout the country. These offices are equipped to aid the researcher in finding data on any given business topic.

Special problems in using census and registration data. Census and registration data suffer from the defects common to secondary data. Above all other failings, they were not collected to meet the exact needs of the job at hand. In general, however, the data gathered by the U.S. Bureau of the Census serve as worthy standards for other data. Even so, care must be taken in their use.[12] Definitions are sometimes changed from one census to another. Moreover, different definitions may be applied to different areas within the same census. New England metropolitan areas, for example, are defined differently in the census than other metropolitan areas.

Registration data are subject to these and additional problems. Some registration data are distorted by the administrative process with which they are associated. Income tax returns, for instance, are undoubtedly biased by the desire to reduce tax liabilities. Data gathered as a by-product of other work may escape many of the biases that inevitably accompany the collection process, but, at the same time, they will be subject to all sorts of errors typical of unprofessional collectors of data. In one case, for example, a researcher who was making a study of disease and mortality statistics in a particular community was led by the peculiar totals presented to make a closer investigation. He discovered that the clerk who recorded the data habitually accumulated certificates a week

---

[12] *Ibid.* Also see "Row over Census: Will We Get the Facts?" *Nation's Business,* 56 (October, 1968), pp. 80–83.

at a time and entered the totals on the last day of each week. To save time, he recorded the cause of death on the first certificate and dittoed the entry for all of the deaths during that week.[13]

In view of the frequent alteration of the provisions under which registrations are made, they must be very carefully checked. Sales tax rates change, for example, and new classes of transactions are either made subject to, or exempted from, sales taxes. Moreover, the geographical assignment of registration data is sometimes determined primarily by administrative convenience. Sales tax returns from chain stores and mail-order houses, for instance, are often reported as though they had all been paid in one county when actually they were paid throughout the state. This makes these data difficult to use as measures of retail sales by counties.

The accuracy of registration data is also affected by the ability and motivation of the reporters, as well as by the efficacy and completeness of the reporting agency's coverage. The wide variety of registration data in accuracy and coverage makes it imperative that the researcher gauge the definitions and procedures employed in gathering the data so as to determine their suitability for his project. An example of the high importance of reportorial skill is provided by the common attribution of the rising incidence of many diseases in recent years to the improved diagnostic capacity of physicians. The influence of coverage is well illustrated by the registrations of infant births reported in the Census of 1950.[14] For the United States as a whole, 97.8 percent of all births were registered, but this ranged from 100 percent in Connecticut to 88.1 percent in Arkansas. Only 53.3 percent of the births outside of hospitals in Arizona were registered, and the percentage for the same more elusive category was 88.1 for the entire country.

Publicly circulated reports of individual projects

These reports include a broad sweep of sources and items of extremely differing value. Among the materials incorporated in this group are books, monographs, bulletins, journal articles, and sections in encyclopedias. Items are taken to be "publicly circulated" when the originator clearly sought to expose his work to a significant slice of the public.

---

[13] *Scientific Method in Business: Some Observations* (College Park, Md.: Bureau of Business and Economic Research, College of Business and Public Administration, University of Maryland, 1953), p. 3. Another example was provided in the 1950 Census of Population in which ". . . several thousand of the basic Persons cards . . . were subject to a displacement of columns when being punched." Among the results, ". . . the 1950 Census age distribution of American Indians contains more than 15 percent too many males 10–14 and 20–24. . . ." Ansley J. Coale and Frederick F. Stephan, *Journal of the American Statistical Association* (June, 1962), pp. 338–47.

[14] S. Shapiro and J. Schachter, "Birth Registration Completeness, United States, 1950," *Public Health Reports,* Vol. LXXVII (June, 1952), pp. 515–16.

Some of these items describe the results of extensive original research, others summarize research of others, and some are statements of opinion. They tend to include more discussion and less statistics than do census and registration data, although much statistical information is included in some items of this type.

Sources of publicly circulated reports of individual projects. Materials of this sort originate with almost every conceivable source. Examples follow:

1. Federal government
2. State and local governments
3. Colleges and universities
4. Foundations
5. Professional associations
6. Trade associations
7. Chambers of commerce
8. Publishing companies
9. Commercial organizations

Finding publicly circulated reports of individual projects. Quite a few guides are available for help in locating materials of this type. Many publications issued by universities, local governments, and trade associations, however, are inadequately indexed, so that combing such sources for everything of value is often difficult and sometimes virtually impossible. Guides of particular help are listed below.

A. General guides.

1. Robert W. Murphy, *How and Where to Look It Up* (New York: McGraw-Hill Book Co., 1958). xiv, 721 pp. Part I explains how to use reference works. Part II describes the major guides to reference sources. Part III deals with specific sources and tells how to find out about people, places, and things. 3,900 sources listed and indexed by subject analysis. Not limited to business.
2. Paul Wasserman, *Information for Administrators: A Guide to Publications and Services for Management in Business and Government* (Ithaca, N.Y.: Cornell University Press, 1956). xiv, 375 pp. Annotated list and evaluations.
3. C. M. White and others, *Sources of Information in the Social Sciences: A Guide to the Literature* (Totowa, N.J.: Bedminster Press, 1964). xiii, 498 pp. Bibliographical essays and annotated lists in all major fields, including "economics and business."
4. Constance M. Winchell, *Guide to Reference Books,* 8th ed. (Chicago: American Library Association, 1967). xx, 741 pp. Organized by subject. Well indexed. Each reference is described in detail. Covers about 7,500 works.

B. *Guides to books, monographs, and bulletins.*

1. *Bibliographic Index: A Cumulative Bibliography of Bibliographies* (New York: H. W. Wilson and Co., since 1937). Subject arrangement. Semiannual with annual cumulation. Books and periodicals. Almost 1,500 journals are monitored.
2. *Card Catalogue.* Every library is accessible through a card catalogue which is generally organized by subject, author, and title.
3. *Cumulative Book Index.* Published since 1928 by H. W. Wilson Co. Entries by author, title, subject. Seeks to list every book published in the English language.
4. *Dissertation Abstracts* (Ann Arbor, Mich.: University Microfilms, since 1952). Monthly. Since 1962, cumulated subject and author indexes.
5. *Index of Publications of Bureaus of Business and Economic Research.* Annual. Indexed by institution, author, and subject. Since 1949. Published under the title *Bibliography of . . . Publications of University Bureaus of Business and Economic Research* since 1963.
6. Library of Congress Catalog, *Books: Subjects, 1950–1954* (Ann Arbor, Mich.: Edwards, 1955). 20 vols. *Books: Subjects, 1955–1959* (Paterson, N.J.: Pageant Books, 1960). 22 vols. Continued by quarterly and annual cumulations. Subject arrangement.
7. *Monthly Catalog of United States Government Publications.* Published monthly since July, 1945 (published only annually from 1895 until then). Lists publications of all branches of the government. Includes subject index.
8. *Public Affairs Information Service Index.* Since 1915. Issued weekly, cumulated five times a year, and cumulated finally on an annual basis. "A subject index . . . books, documents, pamphlets, reports of public and private agencies, articles in periodicals, multigraphed material, etc. Includes selective indexing to more than 1,000 periodicals . . . in . . . English. . . ."
9. *Subject Guide to Books in Print* (New York: R. R. Bowker and Co., annually since 1957). Subject analysis of all books in print in English-speaking countries.

C. *Guides to periodicals.*

1. American Association of Law Libraries, *Index to Legal Periodicals.* Since 1908. Now indexes over 290 journals. Subject index. Includes table of cases.
2. American Economic Association, *Index of Economic Journals* (Homewood, Ill.: Richard D. Irwin). 7 vols. 1886–65. Articles from 89 journals arranged by subject under 23 main headings and 700 subheadings. To be continued.

3. *Applied Science and Technology Index.* Published since 1957 (part of *Industrial Arts Index,* 1913–57). Monthly, with cumulations quarterly, semiannually, and annually. Subject index. Covers about 200 British and U.S. periodicals.

4. *Business Periodicals Index.* Published since 1958 (part of *Industrial Arts Index,* 1913–58). Monthly (except for July), with cumulations quarterly, semiannually, and annually. Subject index. Covers about 120 British and U.S. periodicals.

5. *Economic Abstracts: A Semimonthly Review of Abstracts on Economics, Finance, Trade and Industry, Management and Labour.* Published since 1954 by Martinus Nijhoff. Covers books, governmental reports, and journal articles mainly in European languages, including English. The abstracts follow the language of the abstracted. Subject and author indexes. Cumulated annually.

6. *The Engineering Index.* Since 1884. Monthly, with annual cumulation. Selected books, reports, papers, and articles from about 1,500 journals in over 20 languages are abstracted. Subject arrangement.

7. *International Bibliography of Economics.* Since 1952. Published by the International Committee for Social Sciences Documentation since 1960. Subject classification. Author and subject index. Books, pamphlets, journal articles, governmental documents in European (including Slavic) and Asian languages.

8. *International Bibliography of Sociology.* Since 1951. Published by the International Committee for Social Sciences Documentation since 1960. Subject classification. Author and subject index. Books, pamphlets, journal articles, governmental documents in European (including Slavic) and Asian languages.

9. *International Index to Periodicals,* 1916–65. Since 1965, it has appeared as *Social Sciences and Humanities Index.* Quarterly and annual. Subject and author arrangement. Now indexes over 200 U.S. and British journals, most of which are categorized as "scholarly."

10. *Internationale Bibliographie der Zeitschriftenliteratur aus allen Gebieten des Wissens* (Osnabrück: Felix Dietrich). Since 1965. Semiannual. Subject arrangement. World literature. Over 7,600 journals are covered. Subject headings are German with cross-references from English and French.

11. Doris B. Katz and others, eds., *Guide to Special Issues and Indexes of Periodicals* (New York: Special Libraries Association, 1962). 125 pp. Almost 800 trade and technical journals. Subject index.

12. *Journal of Advertising Research.* Published by the Advertising Research Foundation. Includes reviews, résumés, and listings of the current literature.

13. *The Journal of Marketing.* Published quarterly by the American Marketing Association. "Marketing Articles in Review," a special

section, classifies selected articles from over 175 business, economic, and social science periodicals under 23 headings; the articles are summarized briefly.

14. *New York Times Index.* Since 1913. Semimonthly, with annual cumulation. Subject index.

15. *Psychological Abstracts.* Since 1927. Monthly, with annual cumulations. Author and subject indexes. Books and articles arranged under subject headings.

16. *Readers' Guide to Periodical Literature.* Since 1900. Semimonthly and annual. Subject and author arrangement. Indexes over 125 U.S. periodicals of the popular type.

17. *Sociological Abstracts.* Since 1952. Issued nine times a year since 1964. Abstracts from journal articles.

18. *Ulrich's International Periodicals Directory: 1967–68,* 12th ed. (New York: R. R. Bowker and Co., 1967). xiii, 540 pp.; xxvii, 1,315 pp. Vols. 1 and 2 to be published henceforward in alternate years; supplement to both annually. Over 12,000 entries in Vol. 1: Scientific, Technical, and Medical; over 18,000 in Vol. 2: Arts, Humanities, Business, and Social Sciences.

19. *Wall Street Journal Index.* Since December, 1957. Monthly with annual cumulations. Subject index.

   D.   *Encyclopedias.*

1. *Encyclopedia Americana.* Continually revised. Special attention paid to scientific and technological developments.

2. *Encyclopaedia Britannica.* Now published at the University of Chicago. Considered by most to be the finest general encyclopedia.

3. D. L. Sills, ed., *International Encyclopedia of the Social Sciences* (New York: Macmillan, 1968). 17 vols. Detailed subject index. Articles accompanied by bibliographies.

By no means does the foregoing pretend to be an exhaustive listing. Many indexes of ancillary or tangential worth so far as most U.S. marketing research goes have been omitted—e.g., *Canadian Periodical Index, Index to New Zealand Periodicals, British Technology Index, Employment Relations Abstracts, Accountants Index, Index to Philippine Periodicals*—to name but a very few out of a great many. As U.S. marketing research increases its scope and sophistication, more attention will necessarily be paid to sources now rarely consulted, especially those in languages other than English.

   Problems of using publicly circulated reports of individual reports. These are largely the same problems encountered when using secondary source materials. Particular care should be exercised in electing to resort to items of this type because of the extreme range in competence of writers in the field.

Commercial information

Sources of commercial data. The growing demand for marketing data in recent years has given rise to a number of companies which make a business of collecting and selling such information.[15] They exhibit significant differences in scope and in skill. One category of such companies restricts itself to research on specific problems faced by their clients. Hiring a company of this type to study a given problem is tantamount to collecting primary data directly. Consequently, consideration of these companies and their work is not relevant here.

Another category of companies collects certain marketing data on a continuing basis. This information is sold on subscription. In effect, it is secondary data to the buyer. Two of the best known companies in this category are the A. C. Nielsen Company and the Market Research Corporation of America.

A. C. Nielsen Company. This company, the largest and best known marketing research firm in the world, provides a variety of continuous services. Perhaps the most familiar of these services are the Retail Index and the Television Index.

The Retail Index service gathers continuous data on foods, drugs, cosmetics, pharmaceuticals, confectionery, tobacco, toiletries, photographic, and other products which are sold primarily through food stores and drugstores. These data are obtained by auditing inventories and sales of about 2,000 stores located in some 600 scientifically selected counties every sixty days. In return for its cooperation, each sampled store is given the information collected in it, and is paid cash as well.

The information received by a client includes total sales of the product class, sales of the client's own brands, and sales of important competing brands. The report also covers purchases made by retailers, retailer inventory and stock-turn, percentage of stores stocking an item, retail and wholesale prices, and information on sales and dealer advertising. These data are made available for the total United States and for such subdivisions as regions, city sizes, store ownership (chains versus independents), and store sales volume groups.

Consumer sales data are generally thought to be the basic part of the Retail Index service. Unless a manufacturer knows the current competitive position of his brand in the market and whether he is gaining or losing relative to the sales of competitors, it is difficult for him to make the proper marketing decisions. Consumer sales of his own product are

---

[15] See, for example, *Bradford's Directory of Marketing Research Agencies and Management Consultants in the United States and the World: 1968–69;* Bureau of Foreign Commerce, *A Directory of Foreign Advertising Agencies and Marketing Research Organizations* (1959); *The Market Research Directory: 1967* (Monaco: John Anns); *International Directory of Marketing Research Houses and Services: 1967* (New York: Marketing Review, 1967).

of unique importance to the manufacturer since he cannot determine this figure from his shipments to wholesalers and retailers because of the variations in inventory at these levels. This lag between factory and consumer sales may prevent the manufacturer from taking immediate steps to exploit an advantage or to minimize the effect of actions taken by his competitors.

The Nielsen Television Index is designed to measure the size and nature of the television audience for individual programs. These data are recorded by audimeters, electronic devices which are attached to the television receivers in a fixed sample of homes. These devices record every minute during which the sets are turned on, as well as the channels to which they are tuned.

This service furnishes a variety of information on television audiences, such as size of audience (both in percentage and number of homes with television sets), viewing habits (by months, days, hours, and even minutes, with breakdowns by income, geographical location, ages, etc.), flow of audience (to and from "off," and to and from competing programs), audience duplication among different shows, size of audience minute by minute, and cost per 1,000 homes reached. These data are used by advertisers in selecting programs, determining the best days and hours of the day in which to sponsor programs, scheduling the time of the commercial within the program, and evaluating the success of the program.

As a result of using fixed samples, both the Retail Index and the Television Index services are capable of making many valuable special tabulations. The recognition of trends is particularly facilitated by the policy of maintaining a steady sample. The actions of a specific store or household at one time can be linked with its actions at a later time.

Market Research Corporation of America. This company provides information similar to that furnished by the Nielsen Retail Index. The major difference between these two services is that MRCA data are collected at the consumer level, while Nielsen's are collected at the retail level. MRCA maintains a national consumer panel of over 7,500 families. Consumer sales by brands are reported for households classified by such factors as total family income, age of housewife, presence and age of children, occupation of family head, education of family head, and location by region and city size. Sales are also reported by the types of stores from which purchases are made, including type of ownership such as chains and independents, and kinds of stores such as food, drug, variety, general merchandise, and department stores.

Inasmuch as the bulk of the panel remains constant throughout a single year and substantially so from year to year, special reports on continuity are available. Brand loyalty, for example, can be studied to determine number and characteristics of those households continuously buying one brand as contrasted with those buying two or more brands. Brand switching as a result of special merchandising efforts, such as one-cent sales, two for the price of one sales, and couponing is also reported. Still other reports are made on the contrasting characteristics of users and nonusers of a particular brand.

This information is accumulated through a weekly diary in which the sample households register their purchases of specific food, drug, and household items. These weekly reports are cumulated in monthly ones which are issued to the client. Panel members are compensated with points which can be progressively amassed and exchanged for prizes.

MRCA also furnishes The Metropolitan Supermarket Audit. Every three months, trained interviewers visit approximately 2,000 million-dollar supermarkets in over 50 key metropolitan areas and check whether particular products are in stock, the amount of stock on hand, the price of the product, shelf-space assignment, and so on. The distribution and inventory level data are made available by regions, city-size groups, ownership types (chain or independent), store size, and store type (e.g., grocery versus combination).

Other independent research agencies. Many other agencies provide continuous marketing data. Among these are the Audit Bureau of Circulations, which supplies data on the paid circulation of newspapers and magazines; Standard Rate and Data Service, which lists advertising rates and publication data for all publications and stations in the major advertising media; Publisher's Information Bureau, which reports monthly expenditures by advertisers in various magazines and in radio and television; Media Records, which gives the newspaper linage purchased by advertisers; Daniel Starch and Staff, which measures the readership of newspaper and magazine ads; and Gallup-Robinson, which assesses the "impact" of ads in magazines. A highly useful academic agency is the Roper Public-Opinion Research Center at Williams College, where survey data from recognized research organizations which deal with public opinion are assembled from all over the world for the specific purpose of promoting research based upon secondary data.

Continuous data which indirectly relate to marketing are supplied by many other agencies. Dun and Bradstreet, for example, furnishes credit information on individual firms, the Dodge Corporation compiles construction statistics, and *Sales Management* magazine publishes annual income, sales, and population statistics for all counties and for cities of 10,000 or more population. Clearly, this list of commercial sources of data is intended to be no more than representative.

How to find commercial data. Most commercial data of the type described above are available to any subscriber. In the majority of instances, however, libraries would find subscription too expensive. The Nielsen Retail Index, for example, would cost a single subscriber from

$12,000 to $100,000 or more a year. A researcher must be sure that the information to be provided is likely to be worth the expenditure by his organization.

None of the guides to marketing research agencies is fully satisfactory. Bradford's directory, for instance, lists over three hundred firms, but many organizations which supply valuable data do not classify themselves as marketing research companies. Moreover, the services provided by any one company can often be adapted to given situations in ways that cannot be described in print. The researcher must rely on his own contact with the field to find all possible sources of this type.

Problems in using commercial data. The general problem of using data not collected with the researcher's specific problem in view applies to the use of commercial data, but to a lesser extent than to other secondary data. Although commercial agencies do not have the user's specific problem in mind, they do have a general type of problem in mind when they collect their information. As a result, the data are apt to fit the researcher's needs rather well.

In buying commercial data, the researcher must be sure the data are accurate enough for his purposes. Such a judgment is easier to make with these data than it is with most other secondary data, because detailed descriptions of the methods of data collection can be easily obtained. In some cases, essentially similar data can be bought from two or more sources which differ in their methods of collection. Much of the same information is procured by Nielsen through store audits and by MRCA through consumer diaries. The buyer must decide which of the methods more adequately meets his project's needs. The measurement of radio and television audiences is accomplished by organizations using such different techniques as audimeters, spot telephone calls, diaries, recall interviews, and combinations of these. Whoever buys such audience data must make an evaluation of these alternative techniques in the context of the problems which the data are expected to help solve.

Fortunately, most continuing services are operated by competent technicians who employ sound procedures. Even the best of these organizations, however, are somewhat hindered by the major limitations which cost places on commercial research operations; and the difficulties encountered in trying to provide accurate data are legion. This was revealed with unusual clarity by a comparative analysis of research problems undertaken as a result of a congressional investigation of broadcast ratings.[16]

---

[16] *Evaluation of Statistical Methods Used in Obtaining Broadcast Ratings* (Report of the Committee on Interstate and Foreign Commerce) (Washington, D.C.: U.S. Government Printing Office, 1961).

Miscellaneous external data

External data not discussed above consist primarily of reports of research projects which have not been publicly circulated. Most of these have been done by private businesses, but some projects done by individuals, trade associations, and state and local governments also fall in this category.

No completely satisfactory system of locating this type of information exists, and many such studies go undiscovered by needful researchers. Many libraries maintain files of such materials, classified by subject.

The *Vertical File Index,* arranged according to subject, provides a monthly list (with an annual cumulation) of current, available pamphlets, booklets, leaflets, and other processed material. Many items of this description are listed in the "Market Data Issue" which *Advertising Age* has published annually since World War II. Subscribers to the journal can obtain these items from the individual publishers.

Information of this type has a broad range of reliability and must be used with the caution that should be exercised in the use of all secondary data.

Automatic information retrieval

The modern explosion of information on virtually every subject is both a blessing and a curse to the researcher. Automatic information retrieval systems give undeniable promise of making the explosion more manageable and, therefore, more of a blessing than a curse. The use of high-speed data processing equipment for the location of information is expanding rapidly. The applications of automation to the problems of this field are certain to revolutionize it.[17]

SUMMARY

Before rushing out to collect expensive primary data, the researcher should always explore the possibilities of using secondary data. Secondary data are cheaper and more quickly available than primary data, and may also be available where primary data could not be obtained at all. It is difficult, however, to find secondary data that exactly fit the needs of a specific project and to determine the accuracy of such data. In evaluating secondary data, the researcher must consider: (1) pertinency to the problem, (2) the organization collecting the data, (3) the reasons for publishing the data, (4) methods used in collecting the data, and (5) general evidence of careful work.

[17] Donald Kraft, *Automating to Meet the Information Explosion* (speech to Chicago Chapter, American Statistical Association, April 10, 1964).

Secondary data are of two general types, internal and external. Internal data must be found through a knowledge of the record-keeping procedures of a particular company. External data are more varied, more dispersed, and more difficult to locate. External data can be classified into four groups: (1) census and registration data, (2) individual project reports publicly circulated, (3) data collected for sale commercially, and (4) miscellaneous data. Although knowing all of the sources of such information is impossible, the researcher should be acquainted with most of the basic sources and familiar with the guides to other secondary data.

Case 6—1.   AMERICAN DAIRY ASSOCIATION

The American Dairy Association, a national trade organization representing local and regional dairy groups, was formed to promote the sale of all dairy products on a nonbrand basis. This was accomplished through the development of an advertising, merchandising, research, and public relations program. About 10 percent of ADA's annual promotional budget of $4.5 million was spent on cheese. The Association, in cooperation with its advertising agency, was attempting to determine toward what kinds of people their cheese promotions should be aimed, and what kinds of advertising appeals should be used.

On a long-term basis, per capita cheese consumption in the United States had increased substantially. A report prepared by the marketing research director of the advertising agency noted that 7.7 pounds of cheese per capita were consumed, a 48 percent increase in a 20-year period. However, the U.S. Department of Agriculture reported a slight drop in per capita cheese consumption in the last year. Data from the Market Research Corporation of America (MRCA) indicated that household purchases had declined more than these per capita data indicated. According to this source, total household purchases of cheese were 4 percent less than the previous year. This decline, however, was not uniform for all kinds of cheese. Natural cheese[1] purchases actually increased by 6 percent between the two periods, but processed cheese declined 15 percent.

The advertising agency suggested several reasons for the decline in processed cheese purchases:

1. Per capita meat consumption had increased due to continued high personal income. This increased consumption cut into the use of processed cheese for sandwiches.

---

[1] Processed cheese differs from natural cheese in the way it is made. Natural cheese is made directly from milk (or whey, in a few instances), while processed cheese is made by further processing or blending of one or more kinds of natural cheese.

2. Kraft Foods Company had started to spend some of its cheese advertising money on natural cheeses and Armour & Company had started to promote its Miss Wisconsin natural cheese. This company was spending considerable sums advertising Miss Wisconsin natural cheese—$200,000 annually in home service magazines alone.

3. The number of employed people and school children who carry lunches from home had declined. School lunch programs and in-plant feeding facilities had expanded, thereby cutting down on sandwich lunches.

According to MRCA total household consumption of cheese (except cottage cheese) per year amounted to 589,680,000 pounds. Of this, 55.8 percent was natural cheese and 44.2 percent was processed. The importance of each of seven general classes of cheese is indicated in Table 1.

TABLE 1. Household purchases of cheese by types

	Lb. (000 omitted)	% of total
Total cheese (except cottage)	589,680	100.0
American natural	201,930	34.3
Processed cheese	114,110	19.4
Cheese spreads (processed)	82,640	14.0
Cheese foods (processed)	63,080	10.7
Swiss cheese	43,240	7.3
Cream cheese	42,430	7.2
All other natural cheese	42,250	7.1
Total natural cheese only	329,850	100.0
American	201,930	61.2
Swiss	43,240	13.1
Cream	42,430	12.9
All other natural cheese	42,250	12.8

SOURCE: Market Research Corporation of America.

U.S. government production figures, which were based on cheese in its natural state (that is, prior to any processing), showed that 76 percent of all cheese produced was American type, 8 percent Swiss, 5 percent Italian varieties, and 5 percent cream cheese. The remaining 6 percent consisted of all other varieties, including Limburger, brick, Muenster, and blue.[2]

---

[2] These types differ from each other as follows:

American—a hard, smooth-textured cheese with a sharp flavor; the sharpness and texture vary with the type, such as cheddar or colby.

Swiss—a mild cheese with a nutlike, sweetish flavor; known for the holes or eyes that occur as a part of the aging process.

Italian varieties—include parmesan, romano, provolone, and scamorze cheeses, which originated in Italy.

Cream—a soft, mild, rich cheese made of cream or cream and milk.

TABLE 2. Family population and cheese consumption, by regions

Region	Family population	Total cheese	Natural American	All other natural	Processed
Total U.S.	100%	100%	100%	100%	100%
Northeast	28	34.2	24.1	53.2	32.9
North central	31	28.3	25.7	24.1	31.9
South	20	16.5	22.8	12.5	13.8
Pacific	11	12.2	17.1	7.0	11.2
Mountain and southwest	10	8.8	10.3	3.2	10.2

° These 5 regions include the following states:
Northeast—Maine, New Hampshire, Vermont, Massachusetts, Rhode Island, Connecticut, New York, New Jersey, Pennsylvania
North Central—Ohio, Michigan, Indiana, Illinois, Wisconsin, Minnesota, Iowa, Missouri, North Dakota, South Dakota, Nebraska, Kansas
South—Delaware, Maryland, District of Columbia, West Virginia, Kentucky, Tennessee, Virginia, North Carolina, South Carolina, Georgia, Florida, Alabama, Mississippi, Louisiana, Arkansas, Oklahoma, Texas
Pacific—Washington, Oregon, California
Mountain and southwest—Montana, Wyoming, Colorado, New Mexico, Arizona, Nevada, Utah, Idaho
SOURCE: Market Research Corporation of America.

Per capita consumption of cheese varied considerably between regions of the United States. These variations are shown in Table 2, along with data on population size.

MRCA data showed that cheese consumption was greater among those families living in large cities who had no children. Conversely, cheese consumption was lightest among rural families who had small children. Processed cheese was more universally used than was natural American cheese or other types of natural cheeses. MRCA family purchase data showed fewer differences in per capita consumption of processed cheese than of natural cheese. Table 3 presents more detail on the consumption of processed and natural cheese by selected family characteristics.

The advertising agency could offer no logical reason why families with small children used less cheese than families with no children. The agency research director pointed out:

Cheese is as readily available to them as to other families, and it is a relatively inexpensive food, particularly if used as a meat substitute. We have no evidence that parents do not consider cheese a good food for children.

Studies undertaken by Alfred Politz Research, Inc.[3] for the American Dairy Association revealed that on an average day more people ate cheese

Limburger—a semisoft cheese with a strong flavor and aroma, a gray-colored surface, and a creamy-white interior.
Brick—a semisoft, mild cheese, creamy-yellow in color; one of the few cheeses of American origin.
Muenster—similar to brick cheese in flavor and color.
Blue—a white, crumbly, semisoft cheese with blue mold veins and a tart, salty flavor. Roquefort cheese is similar, except that it is made from sheep's milk, while blue cheese is made from cow's or goat's milk.

[3] These studies used a nationwide sample of over 4,000 respondents.

TABLE 3. Per capita cheese consumption by selected family characteristics

	Total natural and processed cheese (lb.)	Natural American (lb.)	All other natural cheese (lb.)
Average for all persons	2.245	0.549	0.526
Families with no children	3.103	0.902	0.796
Families with children	1.648	0.332	(not available)
Families with children 5 years of age and under	(not available)	0.250	(not available)
Families living in cities of 500,000 and over	2.383	(not available)	0.785
Families living in cities under 2,500	1.738	(not available)	0.182
Families living in rural areas	(not available)	(not available)	0.108

SOURCE: Market Research Corporation of America.

in a sandwich than in any other way. The second most frequent use was as a snack—alone or with crackers or bread. The third most frequent use was in a cooked dish; fourth, in a salad; and last, as a dessert. The Politz studies also showed that cheese dishes, when used as substitutes for meat, were not as popular as egg and fish dishes. One reason given by the housewife for not preparing cheese dishes more frequently was that cheese was not always available. She did not keep it on hand because of fear of spoilage. The Politz studies also found that although one out of three adults ate cheese on an average day, knowledge about cheese, including its varieties, uses, and keeping qualities, was low. Most varieties of cheese were unknown to more than half the housewives. The better known varieties were American cheddar, Swiss, packaged spreads, Limburger, and Roquefort or blue. By far the greatest number of housewives (95 percent) had heard of American cheddar, over 85 percent had heard of Swiss and the packaged spread varieties, while 75 percent had heard of Limburger, and 65 percent of Roquefort or blue.

On the basis of this information, the ADA and its advertising agency were trying to determine the market for cheese and the main advertising appeals to use.

1. On what market segment or segments should the American Dairy Association concentrate in its cheese program?

2. What main advertising appeals should it use?

Case 6—2.   TvQ

Home Testing Institute offered to clients a service which measured the appeal of television shows. The name of the service was TvQ. TvQ permitted subscribers to place questions on product-brand usage, intensity, of usage, etc. on the TvQ questionnaire. Thus, subscribers could relate television program appeal to buying or living habits. It was in this connection that the Valient Cereal Company considered buying the TvQ service.

Valient Cereal Company was one of the large companies of the United States and was a major factor in the food industry. The management was considering the purchase of the TvQ service for use in planning its television advertising of breakfast cereals. Valient had a complete line of breakfast cereals, both hot and cold, including products made from wheat, corn, barley, and oats. Its advertising budget for these cereals totaled several million dollars and was concentrated heavily in network television. Most of the shows sponsored were during the day, especially late afternoon for children, but one major evening show was included. Like most other companies investing similar amounts in television time, Valient was constantly bothered by the problem of selecting the best programs to sponsor. Ratings of the various shows, prepared by various firms, were the common basis for comparing the value of different shows, but the Valient management was not entirely satisfied with these ratings.

TvQ offered data on the relative appeal of different shows to specific family members—a figure which was stated to be different from set tuning ratings. The data were obtained from a nationwide panel of more than 20,000 families which was maintained by Home Testing Institute for conducting all manner of consumer surveys and product tests. Twelve times a year questionnaires were mailed to a different sample of one thousand families. Each family member six years old or older filled out his own questionnaire. The questionnaire listed every network show on the air during the report period. Over 250 programs were surveyed each time. Each respondent was asked to rate each program in one of six ways:

1. One of my favorites
2. Very good
3. Good
4. Fair
5. Poor
6. Never have seen the program.

TvQ produced two basic scores—a familiarity score and a TvQ score. Familiarity was the percentage of the total respondents which gave the show a rating other than "never have seen the program." It was a measure of the public's awareness of a show. The Q-score was the percentage of respondents familiar with the program who rated it "one of my favorites." It was an index of appreciation of the show.

These scores were broken out by the total sample; males and females six years and over; adults, men and women eighteen years and over; and

TABLE 1. Proposed analysis of TvQ data on program "A" showing hypothetical data

	Opinion groups				Totals		Scores	
	Favorite	Very good and good	Fair and poor	Never seen	Total familiar	Total sample	Famil- iarity	TvQ
Total sample	750	1250	1000	1000	3000	4000	75	25
Total adult smokers	310	500	430	410	1240	1650	75	25
Total filter smokers	216	275	229	160	720	900	80	30
Adults	139	200	141	120	480	600	80	29
Adult males	65	95	80	60	240	300	80	27
Adult females	74	90	76	60	240	300	80	31
Major filter brands								
Brand 1	26	28	26	20	80	100	80	33
Brand 2	22	28	22	18	72	90	80	30
Brand 3	19	23	22	16	64	80	80	29
etc.								
Nonfilter brands	147	300	288	315	735	1050	70	20
Brand 1	18	30	22	30	70	100	70	26
etc.								
Menthol brands	25	25	20	30	70	100	70	35
Brand 1	8	7	6	9	21	30	70	40
etc.								

five age groups—six to eleven, twelve to seventeen, eighteen to thirty-four, thirty-five to forty-nine, and fifty and over. A special annual study reported familiarity and TvQ scores by sex within age, and adult favorites by sex, by size of family, education of individual, market size, income of family, occupation of head of household, and other breaks.

Studies conducted by advertising agencies and TvQ indicated "favorites" got more out of the program and its commercial message than nonfavorites. Specifically, favorites:

1. Viewed more frequently (see data in Table 4).
2. Gave the program more uninterrupted attention.
3. Viewed more of each episode.
4. Recalled commercials better.
5. Recalled commercial sales points better.
6. Enjoyed commercials more.

The Valient Company was interested in a special study relating TV program appeal to cigarette usage. Home Testing Institute had added the following questions to its regular questionnaire:

1. Do you ever smoke cigarettes?
2. If you do, about how many cigarettes (not packs) do you smoke per day?
3. What one brand of cigarettes have you smoked most regularly during the past two months?
4. Is this a filter or nonfilter cigarette?

In the brochure which announced the special study on cigarettes, Home Testing Institute indicated some of the tabulations that might be made with the data. These are shown in Table 1 to 3 below. (Total sample has been rounded to four thousand in the hypothetical Table 1.)

Table 2 shows a type of analysis that might be common. A given company might study the percentage using its brand among those with various opinions of the TV program it sponsored. In Table 2, the overall usage of brand "X" is increasing, but similar analyses could be made if the overall usage of the brand were dropping or holding steady.

Another type of analysis is suggested by Table 3. If cigarette brand "Y" sponsors program "B," should cigarette brand "X" sponsor program

TABLE 2. Percentage using brand "X" among those with various opinions of program "A" at successive periods

Period	Total sample	Favorite	Very good and good	Fair and poor	Never seen
October	10%	10%	10%	10%	10%
December	10	11	10	10	9
February	11	12	11	10	9
April	12	13	11	10	9

TABLE 3. Cross classification of respondent opinions of programs "A" and "B"

Program "B"	Program "A"			
	Favorite	Very good and good	Fair and poor	Never seen
Favorite	70%	50%	30%	10%
Very good and good	10	20	20	20
Fair and poor	10	15	20	30
Never seen	10	15	30	40
Total	100%	100%	100%	100%

"A"? The type of table shown below was designed to help answer the question.

TABLE 4. Average number of eight most recent telecasts viewed of selected programs by opinions of the same programs

Program	Favorite	Very good	Good	Fair	Poor
A. Hitchcock	4.8	3.2	2.5	2.0	1.3
Colt .45	4.6	3.8	2.7	1.8	1.7
Dragnet	4.4	3.2	2.1	1.7	1.6
Loretta Young	4.7	3.2	2.4	1.6	1.5
Peter Gunn	5.2	3.9	3.1	1.9	1.6
Restless Gun	5.0	4.0	3.0	2.1	1.3
Rifleman	5.5	4.2	3.0	2.2	1.8

NOTE: Respondents were queried about the number of the last eight telecasts of specific programs they viewed. Responses were cross tabulated by program opinion. The higher the program opinion, the more telecasts were viewed.

1. Are the data furnished by TvQ valid and reliable enough to serve as a basis for Valient's advertising decisions?
2. If Valient spent $2 million on TV advertising annually, how much could it afford to pay for the TvQ data?

Case 6—3. FRO-GOLD PACKING COMPANY[1]

Fro-Gold frozen orange juice was one of the best-known brands in the industry. Annual sales exceeded $18 million—approximately 12 percent of all frozen orange juice sales according to company estimates. There were many different brands on the market, however, and competition was stiff.

In the period following 1946, the frozen orange juice industry had grown from almost nothing to a major food industry. This rapid growth of the entire industry made it difficult for Fro-Gold to tell whether it was

---

[1] All charts in this case are presented through the courtesy of Market Research Corporation of America.

maintaining its percentage of the market or was gaining or losing position. Fro-Gold sales had grown every year since the company's inception in 1946, but the executives often wondered if competitors might not be growing more rapidly. This problem was particularly acute in various regions of the United States. Regional and local brands were continually being introduced. Many of them had attained considerable success in their market areas. Company executives could guess at the Fro-Gold brand position in these local markets only on the basis of salesman and wholesaler reports. Thus, when they came to allocating sales and advertising budgets, Fro-Gold executives always felt they were "working in the dark."

Fro-Gold frozen orange juice was sold through food brokers to wholesalers and chain store organizations. These channels of distribution made it difficult for Fro-Gold even to tell how its own brand was selling to consumers. The sales manager pointed out that changes in inventories held by wholesalers and retailers could make Fro-Gold sales at the factory go up when sales to consumers were actually decreasing or, of course, vice versa. This meant that during any selling season, despite its own sales, the company could not be sure what was happening to its consumer sales.

This channel problem also created difficulties for Fro-Gold of another type. In Florida, many of the orange growers had banded together in cooperative bargaining associations for purposes of selling their oranges to the frozen-juice packers. During the harvest season the packers would purchase oranges almost every day. The purchases during this harvest period exceeded sales during the period because oranges for the entire year's pack had to be purchased at that time. The more a packer was willing to pay, the more oranges he could get. If he bought too many, however, he would be left with more orange juice than could sell at a profit during the year. Thus, Fro-Gold needed to know how rapidly consumers were buying frozen orange juice in general, and its brand in particular, if it was to estimate accurately how much it should pack and how much it could afford to pay for fresh oranges. In the absence of such information, the executives had to guess.

A vice president of Market Research Corporation of America met with the top executives of Fro-Gold to discuss the information which MRCA could furnish which might help the Fro-Gold executives in some of their decisions. The following is a summary of the vice president's presentation.

MRCA serves many of the largest and best-known firms in the United States including General Mills, Quaker Oats Company, General Foods, and Swift & Company. The basic service which it would provide for Fro-Gold would be similar to that furnished its other clients.

Each month it would deliver to Fro-Gold a report for the preceding month showing total consumer purchasing of frozen orange juice in the

EXHIBIT 1. Food product—volume and brand shares U.S. total

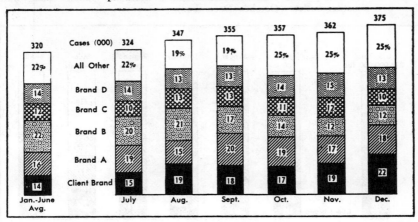

United States and consumer purchasing of each important brand individually. A study of this information over a period of months would enable Fro-Gold to tell whether it was gaining or losing in market position. Exhibit 1 shows the type of analysis that might be made.

In addition to this basic consumer purchasing information, the monthly report would include analyses of such things as deal versus nondeal purchases and average prices paid by consumers. This monthly report would be delivered within ten to fifteen days after the end of the month.

Every three months a separate quarterly report would be submitted.

EXHIBIT 2. Food product—volume and brand shares client company's sales regions (April–December)

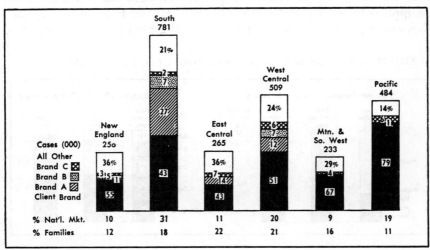

EXHIBIT 3. Food product—market and brand performance major chains and other outlets (October–December)

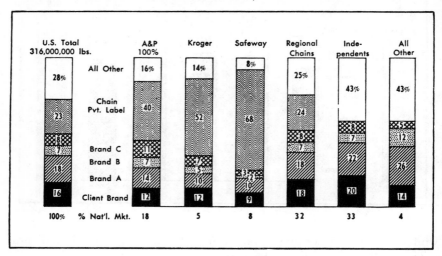

This would include analyses of purchases by regions and by type of retail outlet as shown in Exhibits 2 and 3 and, on occasion, it would include other special analyses such as concentration of purchases among families as shown in Exhibit 4.

Other special studies would be made on an annual basis, such as a study of the trend in product types (fresh, canned, and frozen) as shown in Exhibit 5.

The cost for the services described above would be $2,700 a month with the following provision: 10 percent or $270 each month would be applied to special analyses of the basic data such as those suggested above or otherwise requested by Fro-Gold. If other special studies costing

EXHIBIT 4. Drug product—market concentration (six months' period)

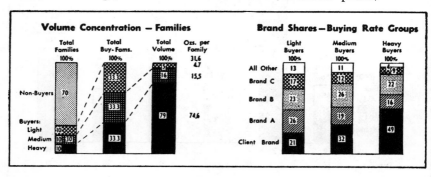

EXHIBIT 5. Food product—consumer purchases by type (October through March each year)

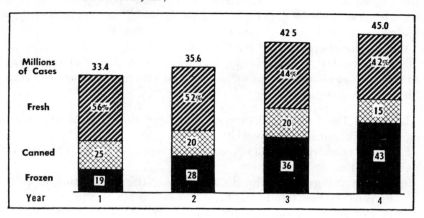

more than $270 a month were desired, Fro-Gold could order them on a cost basis.

In addition to this service, MRCA had a fast weekly service that Fro-Gold could purchase for an additional $100 per week. These weekly reports would show total sales of frozen orange juice and sales of each of the major brands. The reports would be delivered within five days after the week under study.

If Fro-Gold chose to buy the MRCA service, it would have to contract for a minimum of one year—a total cost of $32,400. After the one year, however, Fro-Gold could cancel the contract at any time on ninety-days' notice. The weekly service could be purchased for any four-week period or more as long as Fro-Gold was purchasing the regular service.

The MRCA data are obtained from a consumer panel of approximately 7,500 families throughout the United States. These families keep "diaries" which they send in each week. Each family records the requested food and drug purchases as they are brought home. Thus, any "memory error" is reduced or eliminated. For each purchase the following information is recorded:

Date and day of week
Brand name
Type of container (glass, tin, etc.)
Number of items purchased
Exact weight or quantity
Where purchased (including store name)
Normal transaction or deal (one-cent sale, coupon, etc.)
Price paid

The 7,500 families used in the sample are carefully selected on a probability basis and are representative of the total population on major characteristics such as geographic region, city size, income, presence of children, education, size of family, and age of housewife.

When a family is selected for the panel, a member of the MRCA staff calls on it, enlists its cooperation, and trains it in the procedures. Each family receives compensation in the form of points which are exchangeable for merchandise.

1. Should the Fro-Gold Company purchase the MRCA services? If yes, should it also buy the weekly service?

2. What marketing decisions could be made more accurately with this information at hand?

3. In attempting to appraise the accuracy of the information supplied:

    a. What factors should the Fro-Gold executives consider?

    b. For what additional information should the executives ask?

Case 6—4. HENRY PAPER COMPANY

The Henry Paper Company manufactured a variety of branded paper products of which its consumer table napkin was an important item. Annual sales of the napkin were over $8 million. Company salesmen working out of district offices sold to institutions, wholesale grocers, food chains, and hotels. The company estimated that about 80 percent of its sales were through retail food outlets. The marketing director of the company was faced with the decision of whether to subscribe for the paper napkins to the Nielsen Retail Index, a service of the A. C. Nielsen Company, at an annual cost of about $42,000.

The Henry Company spent over $750,000 in advertising its paper napkins each year. Advertising was concentrated largely in the urban areas since the company and its advertising agency thought that per-family usage was like to be substantially higher in such areas than in rural areas. The firm concentrated most of its advertising in newspapers. Sunday newspaper supplements, and local radio spots. Company officials believed that consumer demand for paper napkins would probably increase, but they anticipated increased competition as more firms entered the field.

The A. C. Nielsen Company provided a variety of fact-finding services. One of these was the Nielsen Retail Index. This index measured consumer sales continuously (every sixty days) by personally conducted audits of invoices and inventories in 1,600 typical chain and independent food stores. The consumer sales figures obtained from the sample were expanded to a total for the U.S. These stores were selected in such a manner that their sales furnished a representative cross section of the sales of all stores. The sample stores were located in 600 counties selected on a probability basis. Contracts were signed with each store and with chain headquarters under which Nielsen auditors had the privilege of taking inventories, and auditing the invoices for all goods coming into the store. Cooperating stores are compensated with cash and general marketing information.

The Nielsen Company used a highly trained, permanent full-time auditing staff. Most of the auditors were college graduates and their average length of service with the firm was approximately eight years. A field supervisor was employed for every eight auditors to insure accuracy in the field work. Essentially the same stores were included in the bi-monthly audits, and thus trend data showed the long-term direction of the total market as well as for each important brand. The basic data obtained as a result of these audits are shown in Exhibit 1. These data were charted every two months and a presentation made to the client. The company maintained a trained group of client service men who analyzed and interpreted the data regularly.

The Nielsen service determined the consumer sales of competitors and

EXHIBIT 1. Complete list of data secured every 60 days in food and drug stores

1. Sales to consumers
2. Purchases by retailers
3. Retail inventories
4. Average monthly sales
5. Store count distribution
6. All commodity distribution
7. Out-of-stock stores
8. Prices (wholesale and retail)

9. Special factory packs
10. Dealer support (displays, local advertising, coupon redemption)
11. Total food store sales (all commodities)
12. Major media advertising (from other sources)

SOURCE: A. C. Nielsen Co.

Data breakdowns available

Brand, Type, & Size	Territory	Client Areas		County Sizes	Store Types	
	New England	1	10	Metro New York	Drug	Grocery
All Other Brands	Metro New York	2	11	Metro Chicago	Chain (4 or More)	Chain (4 or More)
Private Label	Mid. Atlantic	3	12			
D	East Central	4	13	Metro Los Angeles	Independents	Independents
C	Metro Chicago	5	14	A Counties	Large ($200M & Over)	Large (Over $500M)
B	West Central	6	15			
	South East	7	16	B Counties	Medium ($100M to $200M)	Chain & Large Combined
A	South West	8	17	C Counties	Small (Under $100M)	Medium ($100 to $500M)
	Metro Los Angeles	9	18			
Client Brand	Rem. Pacific			D Counties		Small (Under $100M)

SOURCE: A. C. Nielsen Co.

provided an index of a client's competitive progress which was expressed as a percentage of the total market. These are illustrated in Exhibit 2.

The service was thought to be especially valuable in noting the difference between factory and consumer sales. It was pointed out that, since a manufacturer may be spending large sums of money for various advertising and merchandising efforts to increase the flow of his goods at the point of consumption, he needs to know promptly the volume of his consumer sales. He cannot use factory sales as a measure of the success or failure of his efforts since the trend of such sales is generally slow in reflecting the ups and downs of consumer sales trends. Exhibit 3 illustrates this point.

EXHIBIT 2. Consumer sales—all brands
(add 000 to dollar figures)

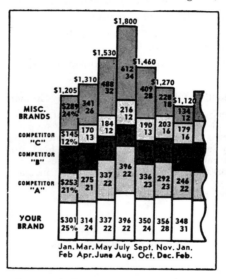

SOURCE: A. C. Nielsen Co.

The Henry Company was particularly interested in the possibility of using the service to detect profitable and unprofitable promotional methods. Since the Index measured consumer sales of a product (and its share of total consumer sales) both before and after any change in promotional effort, it was thought that much could be learned about the company's promotional activities. Exhibit 4 illustrates the situation in which, if factory sales had been used to judge the success of an advertising switch, a serious mistake would have been made.

The Nielsen Company also indicated to the Henry Company that its service could separate the consumer take-away of regular merchandise from the one-cent combinations. The company used the latter as an "in-

EXHIBIT 3. Consumer sales in percent of total market versus factory sales

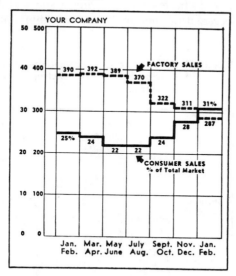

SOURCE: A. C. Nielsen Co.

EXHIBIT 4. A change in advertising (quantity, type, copy, media)

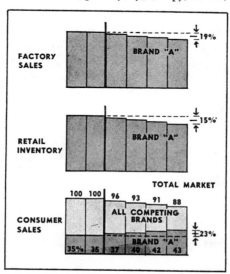

SOURCE: A. C. Nielsen Co.

troductory offer" twice a year. The Nielsen client-service executive illustrated what his company could provide in this respect by referring to two specially prepared charts—one showing a successful promotion and the other an unsuccessful promotion. These two charts are reproduced in Exhibits 5 and 6.

EXHIBIT 5. A successful promotion—case 328—brand "H" metropolitan Chicago

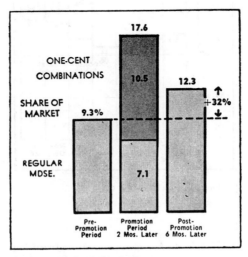

SOURCE: A. C. Nielsen Co.

Nielsen also made available to its clients a means of testing new products, changes in existing products, changes in advertising or merchandising, etc., by employing several "test" cities and making special area breakdowns of existing store panels and auditing special test stores, either to supplement regular test cities or areas or for use on a special standalone basis.[1] The Nielsen Company had experience in testing the following types of promotion:

1. Advertising quantity
2. Advertising media (e.g., radio, television, newspaper, outdoor)
3. Cooperative advertising
4. Push money
5. Displays
6. Deals
7. Retail sales effort

---

[1] The charge for the test city audits was $8,600 per year. It was not necessary for the Henry Company to subscribe to the regular Nielsen Retail Index in order to purchase the test city audit data.

EXHIBIT 6. An unsuccessful promotion—case 508—brand "T" metropolitan Chicago

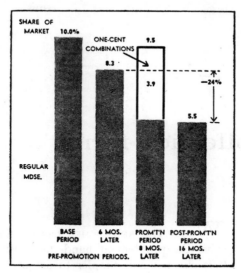

SOURCE: A. C. Nielsen Co.

8. Detailing of dentists, physicians, etc.
9. Sampling
10. Price changes
11. Package changes
12. Product or formula changes

Several executives of the Henry Company believed that the company should subscribe to the Nielsen Food Index on paper napkins since the data provided would enable the company to do a better job of directing its marketing activities. Others, however, argued that instead of spending about $42,000 for such information, the company would be better off to hire additional salesmen whose efforts would be directed toward increasing distribution of paper napkins in food outlets or to step up the advertising in low-volume areas.

Should the marketing director of the Henry Company subscribe to the Nielsen Food Index Service?

7

Data collection forms

W HEN THE RESEARCHER has specified the information he needs to solve the problem at hand, he must proceed to find that information. It is cheaper and simpler to use secondary data, data which someone else has collected previously, if such data are available. If secondary data cannot be found, the researcher is faced with the necessity of collecting original information himself, or of doing without. This collection and analysis of primary data occupy most of the time of marketing researchers. Accordingly, the next several chapters are devoted to consideration of primary data problems.

Questioning and observing are the two basic methods of collecting primary data. The general advantages and weaknesses of each of these methods were discussed in Chapter 4. Regardless of which of these data collection methods is used, some procedure must be developed to standardize the process and, thereby, standardize the data accumulated. If the researcher goes out to ask people questions and asks each person somewhat different questions, he will get answers that are not directly comparable. If fifty different field workers in cities and rural areas throughout the country are sent out to observe salesmen in retail appliance stores, they will be extremely unlikely to observe the same things unless they are given a guide to follow. Thus, some standardized procedure must be developed if the data collected in the field are to be comparable.

A second reason for needing a standardized procedure is to achieve speed and accuracy in recording data. If the field workers have an established pattern to follow in their work and a standardized form on which to record the data collected, they can proceed more rapidly and more accurately. A third reason for standardized data collection procedures is to achieve speed and accuracy in handling the data in the office. If all the information coming into the central office from the field workers comes in a common form, it can be summarized more quickly and with less error than if each field worker reports data in whatever form he chooses.

To collect good primary data, then, it is necessary to develop standardized forms to guide the procedure. These forms are one of the main sources of error in the typical marketing research project. This is particularly true in the case of questionnaire studies where verbal communication is involved. Since questionnaire studies are also more prevalent than observation studies, the major part of this chapter will be devoted to the problems encountered in constructing good questionnaires. Some of this will also be pertinent to observation forms; however, a brief section at the end of the chapter will take up the latter specifically.

IMPORTANCE OF QUESTIONNAIRE

When information is to be collected by asking questions of people who may have the desired data, a standardized form called a questionnaire is prepared.[1] The questionnaire is a list of questions to be asked respondents and spaces in which to record the answers. Each question is worded exactly as it is to be asked, and the questions are listed in an established sequence. Figure 7–1 shows a page from a typical questionnaire.

At first, one is inclined to think that the construction of a questionnaire is simple. All that is necessary is to write down the questions that are to be asked and have them printed on sheets of paper. Unfortunately, the problem is deceptive. It is easy to write down questions, but are they the right questions? Will a question mean the same thing to Mrs. Longstreet in Fort Collins, Colorado, as it does to Mrs. Vanderbilt in New York City? Will it mean the same to either of them as it means to the researcher? Slight variations in question wording may make a considerable change in the answers obtained. Which is the "correct" alternative? If one question is asked before another, it may get a different

---

[1] All data collected by verbal communication are not collected through the use of standardized questionnaires. The reader will recall the four types of questionnaire studies discussed in Chapter 4—structured-nondisguised, structured-disguised, non-structured-nondisguised, and nonstructured-disguised. The structured studies involve the use of standardized questionnaires, but the nonstructured studies use forms which vary from fairly formal questionnaires to the roughest of outlines. The discussion presented here will apply only indirectly to nonstructured studies.

Questionnaire studies may be conducted by personal interview, mail, or telephone. The discussion here is in terms of questionnaires to be used in personal interviews, but will apply almost equally to mail or telephone interviews. Special comments are made at points where variations would occur in mail or telephone studies.

FIGURE 7–1. Page from steam iron questionnaire

16.   Some steam irons also have a spray device on them which sprays water from the
front of the iron. This is in <u>addition</u> to the steam which comes out through the
holes in the soleplate or bottom of the iron. Does your steam iron have a spray
device like this on it?

71–	
72–	
73–	
74–	
80–	

            Yes – 1   No – 2   Don't know/not sure – 3 | 4 |

                              SKIP TO Q. 18a

17a.   Do you use the spray device on your iron always, sometimes, or never when you
iron?

            Always – 1   Sometimes – 2   Never – 3 | 5 |

IF "SOMETIMES" OR "NEVER," ASK:

    17b.   Why don't you use the spray device on your steam iron (more often)?
            . . . Why else don't you use it? (PROBE)

                                                                        | 6– |
                                                                        | 7– |

18a.   Aside from using a spray device on your iron, do you <u>ever</u> sprinkle or pre–dampen
your clothes before ironing them with your steam iron?

                Yes – 1   No – 2

                              SKIP TO Q. 19a

IF "YES," ASK:

    18b.   Do you <u>always</u> sprinkle or pre–dampen your clothes in that way before you | 8 |
            iron them <u>with</u> your steam iron, or do you sometimes do it and sometimes
            not?

                Always – 4   Sometimes – 5

19a.   In addition to the electric cord attached to the iron, do you <u>usually</u> use an extension
cord with your steam iron?

                Yes – 1   No – 2 | 9 |

    b.   Would you prefer that the cord that comes attached to your iron be longer, or
shorter, or is it about the right length as it is?

    Would prefer longer – 1   Would prefer shorter – 2   About right as is – 3 | 10 |

Courtesy: Elrick and Lavidge, Inc.

answer than if it is asked after the other. If some questions are asked,
respondents may refuse to answer them at all. On the other hand, respondents may knowingly answer other questions incorrectly.

How much difference can questionnaire problems of this type make
in the final results of a survey? In one public opinion survey, the follow-

ing question was asked with the results shown:[2] *Which of the following statements most closely coincides with your opinion of the Metallic Metals Act?* Thirty percent of the respondents had no opinion; the other 70 percent distributed their answers as follows:

It would be a good move on the part of the U.S. (21.4 percent).
It would be a good thing but should be left to the individual states (58.6 percent).
It is all right for foreign countries but should not be required here (15.7 percent).
It is of no value at all (4.3 percent).

If these data were included with other information and presented in a leather-bound report, they would be impressive evidence in favor of the second alternative. Of course, the point is that there is no such thing as a Metallic Metals Act. Questions will get answers, but do the answers mean anything?

Political differences over American involvement in Vietnam in the late 1960's and early 1970's led many politicians to conduct polls among their constituents to determine the latter's attitudes on the question. Two such polls, both conducted in New York City at about the same time, asked the following questions with the results shown:[3]

Do you approve of the recent decision to extend bombing raids in North Vietnam aimed at oil reserves and other strategic supply depots around Hanoi and Haiphong?

Yes	66%
No or don't know	34%

Do you believe the United States should bomb Hanoi and Haiphong?

Yes	14%
No or don't know	86%

While the wording of these questions differs slightly, they seem to be getting at the same issue. They leave one less than sure what the "true" sentiments of the public are on this question.

The preceding examples are extreme cases, but they illustrate factors which the researcher must consider in preparing a questionnaire. Other problems are so many and so varied as to lead one outstanding researcher to conclude after a major project ". . . that error or bias attributable to sampling and to methods of questionnaire administration were relatively

---

[2] Sam Gill, "How Do You Stand on Sin?" *Tide,* Vol. XXI (March 14, 1947), p. 72.
[3] Leo Bogart, "No Opinion, Don't Know, and Maybe No Answer," *Public Opinion Quarterly,* 31 (Fall, 1967), p. 332.

small as compared with other types of variation—especially variation attributable to different ways of wording questions."[4]

QUESTIONNAIRE CONSTRUCTION PROCEDURE

Questionnaire construction is still much more of an art than a science. No procedures have been established which will automatically lead to a good questionnaire. Most of what is known about making questionnaires is the result of general experience. No basic theory has been developed, nor even a fully systematized approach to the problem. Nevertheless, the extensive experience of many researchers and a limited number of organized experiments have led to a considerable understanding of the problem and to a long list of "dos and don'ts" and rules of thumb. These can help a beginning researcher avoid many pitfalls; they cannot be substituted for creative imagination in designing a questioning procedure. In the following discussion, the generally accepted "rules" are organized so as to provide a step-by-step approach to the development of a questionnaire.[5]

Determine what information is wanted

Basically a questionnaire must serve two functions: it must translate research objectives into specific questions the respondent can answer, and it must motivate the respondent to cooperate with the survey and to furnish the information correctly. Therefore, before a questionnaire can be formulated, a specific statement of the information which is needed must be made. The complete analysis must be anticipated. For example, it is not enough to know that the objective is to find what type of person forms the market for the product. The specific characteristics that are thought to be important must be stated. Thus, a deodorant soap company wishing to define its market might specify that the survey determine the proportion of individuals using the soap within the groups shown in Table 7–1. With such a listing, the questionnaire framer could develop a series of questions that would elicit the information needed for the proposed analysis. This statement of objectives is part of the problem definition step. It is repeated here to emphasize that a questionnaire cannot be started until the precise information sought is known.

---

[4] Samuel A. Stouffer, *et al.*, *Measurement and Prediction, Studies in Social Psychology in World War II* (Princeton, N.J.: Princeton University Press, 1950), Vol. IV, p. 709.

[5] The best single effort to systematize the problem of questionnaire construction is still Stanley L. Payne, *The Art of Asking Questions* (Princeton, N.J.: Princeton University Press, 1951).

TABLE 7–1

Age	Sex	Income	Geographical area	City size
Under 20	Male	Under $3,000	Northeast	Over 1,000,000
20–29	Female	$3,000–$4,999	North central	50,000–1,000,000
30–45		$5,000–$7,499	South	2,500–49,999
Over 45		$7,500 and over	West	Rural

Determine the type of questionnaire to be used

Questionnaires can be used by personal interview, mail, or telephone. The choice among these alternatives is largely determined by the type of information to be obtained and by the type of respondents from whom it is to be obtained. The situations for which each is best adapted were discussed in Chapter 4. It is necessary to decide on the type of questionnaire at this point since the questions asked, the way in which they are asked, and the sequence in which they are asked will all be influenced by this decision. The influence of the type of questionnaire on these factors will be brought out in the following discussion.

Determine the content of individual questions

Once the specific information needed is known and the method of communication is decided, the researcher is ready to begin formulating his questionnaire. A first problem is to decide what to include in individual questions. The following points are in the nature of standards against which to check possible questions; obviously, they leave much to the originality of the researcher.

Is the question necessary? It seems an obvious point that no question should be included in a questionnaire unless it is necessary;[6] however, there is a strong tendency to include "interesting" questions which have no particular value for the study objectives. Other questions may be asked in more detail than is necessary and could be replaced with one summary question. Extra questions add to the expense of the survey and increase the demands made on respondents, thus decreasing the likelihood of their cooperation. It is reported that the addition of one question to a United States Census questionnaire adds approximately $1 million to the total cost of the census. While the typical marketing research project is extremely small compared to the census, this example indicates the problem.

To determine whether a question is necessary or not, the researcher

---

[6] There is one exception to this statement. Occasionally a "useless" question is asked to gain respondent interest.

must turn back to the objectives of the study. Is the information definitely called for? Will something actually be done as a result of the information obtained? If the answer to either of these is "no," the question should be eliminated.

Similarly, the value of detailed questions should be checked. Is it necessary to know the age of each member of a family, or would the number under twenty and the number twenty and over do just as well in the analysis? The latter could be obtained with fewer questions.

Are several questions needed instead of one? This point is essentially the reverse of the previous one. Some questions may have two or more elements. If these are left in one question, interpretation of the answers becomes impossible. In a survey on laundry detergents one might ask: *Do you think Tide gets clothes clean without injuring the fabric?* A "yes" answer would presumably be clear, but suppose the housewife says "no." Does she mean Tide doesn't get clothes clean, or that it injures fabrics? Or suppose she thinks Tide damages silks and rayons but doesn't hurt other fabrics. A series of two or more questions could clarify these points.

A more subtle example of the multielement question is the "why" question. *Why do you use Trend detergent?* One can imagine answers such as "to get the clothes clean," "it's easier on my hands than others," and "my neighbor recommended it." Actually, each of these answers is a reply to a different element in the question. The first answer tells why the woman uses a detergent; the second answer tells what the woman likes about Trend as compared to other detergents; and the third answer tells how she happened to get acquainted with Trend. Thus, the three answers cannot be compared. Useful comparisons might be obtained if the question were changed into separate questions:

1. *What do you like about Trend as compared to other detergents?*
2. *How did you first happen to use Trend?*

Question 1 finds the characteristics of the product women like in comparison to other brands, while question 2 refers to the influences which led them to try it. Almost any "why" question about the use of a product involves these two elements: (1) attributes of the product, and (2) influences leading to knowledge of it.[7]

Does the respondent have the information requested? The trick question quoted previously on the Metallic Metals Act shows that people will answer questions that they do not understand. Similar tests, in which dummy advertisements are inserted in magazines, find people who report having seen the ads before. Such answers do not necessarily

[7] For a more complete discussion of this point see American Marketing Association, *The Technique of Marketing Research* (New York: McGraw-Hill Book Co., Inc., 1937), chap. iv.

stem from dishonesty. Many result from confusion. In any case, it is easy to get answers to questions, but it is another thing to get answers that are meaningful. Results of the type discussed above emphasize the importance of asking only questions for which the respondents have the necessary information to answer. Several aspects of this point, which the researcher should consider in planning his questions, are discussed in the following paragraphs.

Is the point within the respondent's experience? Even questions which seem quite ordinary may not fall within a given respondent's experience.

How do you think All compares with other packaged soaps and detergents? This question seems straightforward. Unless the respondent has used All, however, her answer is not apt to mean much. It would be better to determine in advance whether or not the housewife has ever used All. Even then some respondents will be comparing All with Tide and Trend, while others will be comparing it with Ivory and Lux. It is important, then, to determine whether or not the question is meaningful in the respondent's experience. When there is doubt, "filter" questions should be used. In this example, the researcher might ask: *What packaged soaps and detergents have you used during the last year?* If All is reported among others, the next question might be: *How do you rank these in order of your preference?* The filter question shown here is indirect. It is probably preferable to a direct question in this case, since the latter might introduce some bias. If an indirect question is not feasible, however, a direct filter question should be used. For example: *Have you used All during the last year?* More people will say "no" to such a question than will volunteer that they have not used All if asked a question which assumes they have used it, such as, *"How do you think All compares with other detergents?"*

Can the respondent remember the information? How many can name the brand of shirt they are wearing, the license number of their car, or the amount of the deductions from their pay check? The typical person has known all these points at one time or another, but he is not apt to remember them when questioned specifically. Many things that one might expect everyone to know are not remembered. In fact, where memory is involved at all, the researcher must be cautious not to overestimate the accuracy with which respondents will remember the information he wants.

A great many questions asked in marketing research involve memory in varying degrees. What brand of soap do you use? Have you seen this advertisement before? What stories did you read in this magazine? What TV programs did you watch yesterday? Memory of such events is influenced by four factors: (1) the event itself, (2) the individual remembering, (3) the length of time since the event, and (4) the stimulus given to the individual's memory. The first two of these factors are beyond the researcher's control, but he must consider them in deciding what questions to include in his survey. The last two factors he can affect.

When the prosecuting attorney asks his classic question, "Where were you on the night of January 3, 1972?" the witness always seems to know. This may be the result of prior coaching, but, if the witness saw a murder on that night, it is quite likely that he would remember it for the rest of his life. Thus, the importance of the event has much to do with its recollection. Few consumers will recall the brand of canned peas purchased three weeks ago, but most can remember the brand of car bought years ago. Unusual events are remembered well. Most people have trouble remembering all of the TV shows they watched the night before, but everyone who saw the first game of the World Series probably remembered it for at least several days. Events which are part of an established pattern or which interrupt an established pattern are remembered better than unrelated events. The person who always buys Colgate toothpaste will remember what brand he bought last time better than the person who has no established favorite. This is true even if the Colgate man took Crest the last time.

When he is unable to remember the answer to a specific question, a respondent will often attempt to guess or to come up with a logical answer, as was shown in the Metallic Metals Act example. This usually means that the best advertised brands and the most popular magazines and TV shows are reported. Leading national brands often have their brand share doubled by responses in recall surveys.[8]

Any woman remembers her wedding date, but most of the bridesmaids would be unable to recall it a few years later. The difference is in the importance of the event to the individual. The researcher cannot change the ability of a person to remember things, but he can try to ask the person most apt to remember. Thus, the housewife is usually sought as the respondent on questions about household purchases. She makes most of them and, since she often establishes habits, she is more apt to remember them than are other members of the family.

The researcher can control the length of time between an event and the date of his questioning only by limiting his questions to events that have happened recently. This means that questions on purchases are usually limited to the most recent purchase; questions on TV programs watched are limited to the previous day, the immediately preceding hours, or even to the current moment; and questions on the readership of magazines are asked on the latest issue.

Ability to remember is influenced by the stimulus which calls for

---

[8] Seymour Sudman, "On the Accuracy of Recording of Consumer Panels: II," *Journal of Marketing Research*, 1 (August, 1964), p. 76.

the remembering. Thus, it is easier for the respondent to recognize a past event if it is presented to him than it is for him to recall the same event without any clues. The latter is referred to as unaided recall. This is the procedure used when the respondent is asked, "What radio programs did you listen to last night?" Experiments have shown that such a question may locate as little as 10 percent of those who actually listened to a program. Many more can recall the same programs if they are given a list of the programs from the previous evening and asked which ones they heard. This is called aided recall.

Even aided recall methods may not be enough to insure accurate recollection. Some things are forgotten with time, even short periods of time, and confusion becomes greater as more events intervene. A common method of measuring magazine reading audiences, for example, is to show a series of cards on which the names of various magazines are reproduced in their unique forms. Respondents are to indicate which magazines they have looked at in the last several months. For those mentioned, the following question is asked: "When was the last time you looked at a copy?" If the answer is within the last thirty days for a monthly magazine, the respondent is considered a reader. In one study of this type, 9.2 percent of the respondents were readers. When a much more intensive interview was conducted with all respondents later, the conclusion was reached that at least 14.8 percent should have been classified as readers. Even more importantly, only about 5.2 percent of the respondents were identified as readers in both surveys. Assuming the latter study was correct, the first study identified only about one third of the actual readers, and also identified almost as many nonreaders as readers.[9]

Why was the second study considered more accurate? Every effort was made to reconstruct the actual situation. Copies of the magazine were studied with the respondent; both the issue in question and others, the occasion for reading the magazine, and how it was obtained were discussed; and individual stories were reviewed. A thorough reconstruction of the event, going from one circumstance surrounding it to another, is a major help to a respondent in attempting to remember something that was of not much importance to him at the time.

The considerable advantage of aided recall which comes with these stimuli to the respondent's memory is, at least partially, offset by the bias resulting from the suggestions offered by each such stimulus. Every multiple choice question is subject to suggestion bias of this type. The extent of this bias and methods of reducing it are discussed in the section on multiple choice questions.

An extreme of the aided-recall approach is the "recognition" method

---

[9] Harry Henry, "Belson's Studies in Readership," *Journal of Advertising Research,* Vol. 2 (June, 1962), pp. 9–14.

of stimulating recall. Instead of describing possible answers, the researcher shows the respondent the actual items in which he is interested. For example, the researcher trying to determine purchases of Jell-O might show respondents actual boxes of Jell-O. To determine the readership of advertisements, researchers often go through magazines with respondents, showing them each ad and asking if they remember having seen it before. This recognition method furnishes an excellent stimulus to memory, but it is also subject to suggestion bias as is all aided recall.

Will the respondent have to do a lot of work to get the information? In a survey for a trucking firm, traffic managers of manufacturing plants and department stores were shown a map of the United States with a section equivalent to about eight states outlined in red. The traffic managers were then asked: *What annual volume in tons do you ship to or from the area outlined in red on the map?* It is likely that most of the traffic managers had this information, but it is also likely that most of them would have had to compile the data from written records to give a very accurate report. Few respondents will take a lot of time to collect the information needed to answer a questionnaire. They may make the best guess they can. If it is a mail questionnaire, they are apt to drop the questionnaire in the wastebasket. Such questions, even if answered, tend to irritate respondents and, hence, to damage cooperation with the rest of the survey. In most instances, such questions should be avoided.

Will respondents give the information? Even though they know the answer, respondents will sometimes not answer questions. There are two reasons for this: (1) they are unable to phrase their answers, or (2) they do not want to answer. It goes without saying that such questions hurt cooperation for the rest of an interview and, therefore, should be eliminated. It is often possible, however, to change such questions so as to secure the desired information.

General Motors developed a classic questionnaire to get consumer opinions on car styling. Few consumers could describe the type of car grill work that they liked best, but if they were shown pictures of ten cars they could point out the grill they liked best. The pictures made it possible for the respondent to report his answer.

The interviewing situation as seen by a respondent is quite different than as seen by the interviewer. The respondent has no particular interest in the accuracy of the survey as such. She sees a situation in which a person is asking her questions; her answers will, in her opinion, influence the interviewer's opinion of her. Thus, she may be hesitant to answer accurately if she sees the question as embarrassing or as one which relates to her social status. Such questions, therefore, will elicit incorrect answers which are worse than useless. A questionnaire on magazine readership, for example, showed relatively little readership of pulp magazines in the upper-income groups. On the theory that these people might feel it was degrading to admit reading such "trash," the study was revised. People were asked to contribute their old magazines to charity. A count of these magazines showed that the number of women contributing certain magazines exceeded the number who reported reading them by 50 percent.[10]

Questions of this type should be omitted unless a way can be found to ask for the information that will obtain correct responses. When asked on what matters they were least willing to be interviewed, one group of respondents reported money matters, family life, political beliefs, and religious beliefs, in that order.[11] Some income classification, however, is desirable on many research projects. Other embarrassing or status-damaging questions may be necessary for particular surveys. Numerous techniques, of which the following are examples, have been developed for the purpose.

1. The question .may be included in a group of others that are more innocuous and the whole list asked quickly.
2. The interviewer may make a statement indicating that the behavior in question is not unusual and then ask the specific question of the respondent. The statement tends to make the respondent feel that his own behavior is not out of place.
3. The question may be phrased to refer to "other people." For example, the respondent may be asked if most people report errors on their bills that are favorable to themselves. He will presumably answer in terms of his own practice.
4. A special ballot may be provided which the respondent can complete personally and drop in a sealed box.
5. Probably the most useful approach is that of handing the respondent a card with alternatives listed and identified by letters or numbers. He can then respond in terms of the letter or number. For example, the interviewer may hand him a card on which the following information is entered and ask him in which class his annual income falls:

Class A . . . . Under $5,000
Class B . . . . $5,000–$10,000
Class C . . . . Over $10,000

It may be desirable to have enough classes so that both extremes are so extreme that few will be in those groups.

Determine the type of question to use

Once the content of individual questions is decided, the researcher is ready to begin forming the actual questions. Before he can work on

---

[10] American Marketing Association, *op. cit.*, p. 66.

[11] Gideon Sjoberg, "A Questionnaire on Questionnaires," *Public Opinion Quarterly*, Vol. 18 (Fall, 1954), pp. 423–27.

the wording of each question, he must decide on the type of question to use. He may choose from three major types: (1) open, (2) multiple choice, and (3) dichotomous.

Open questions. *What industries are your best potential markets for hydraulic equipment? How many families occupy this home? How long have you had this piano? Why do you smoke Marlboro cigarettes?* Each of these is an example of an open, or free-answer, question. The respondent is free to answer in his own words and to express any ideas that he thinks pertinent. No alternatives are suggested. Three of the four examples would probably result in short answers. The question on cigarettes might draw a length discussion which the interviewer would have to record verbatim or attempt to digest according to his instructions.

Open questions are good as first questions. They introduce the subject and obtain general reactions which are relatively uninfluenced by the question itself. If the question is left especially wide open, almost every respondent will be able to give some answer and will thus begin to warm up to the questioning process. In a survey on color television the following was the first question: *In general, how do you feel about color TV?* This question acquaints the respondent with the subject of the survey, gets general attitudes which may be helpful in later interpretation of results, and opens the way for more specific questioning on color television.

Open questions do not suggest any alternative answers from which the respondent can choose. Therefore, they influence the answers obtained less than multiple choice or dichotomous questions. A survey on shaving habits among men might ask: *With what type of instrument do you shave?* Or a multiple choice question might be used: *Do you shave with a safety razor, straightedge razor, or electric shaver?* The latter suggests alternatives and may, as a result, influence the answers obtained. The open question does not suffer from this weakness.

Since the open question suggests no answers, the variety of answers obtained is often extreme. Take the question: *What are the things you look for in buying a suit?* The researcher could list a number of the answers that would be forthcoming—color, style, price, etc. But some respondents will mention items that are not likely to occur to the researcher. Thus, the open question is particularly useful in exploratory research where new ideas and relationships are sought. On the basis of the replies received in the exploratory study, the researcher may be able to establish the alternative answers that appear and use them in a multiple choice question in further research.

The specific points, side comments, and explanations which are included in answers to open questions are often helpful to the study director in interpreting the final results of a survey. By reading over such answers, he gets a "feeling" for the general attitudes of respondents. Direct quotations from these answers often add concreteness and life to the final report.

Despite these advantages of the open question, certain disadvantages limit their usefulness. A principal weakness is the large degree of interviewer bias which they permit. The interviewer may be instructed to record answers to open questions verbatim or to set down the main points mentioned by the respondent. In either instance, the interviewers' reports will vary. An interviewer skilled in shorthand will get down every word; other interviewers will have to ask respondents to give their answers phrase by phrase if they are to get each word. Obviously, in the latter case the interview will drag and respondents will lose interest. Answers given a few words at a time will differ from answers which are given in more or less normal conversation. If interviewers are told to digest replies, bias is even more likely. Each interviewer interprets the replies he receives in terms of his own ideas. The result is a mixture of interviewer and respondent, rather than respondent alone. Where verbatim reporting is important, tape recorders may be used.

The length of answer received will also vary by interviewer. Some interviewers will pause expectantly after a respondent's comment, thus encouraging further comment. Other interviewers will move on to the next question at the first pause, thereby limiting the extent of the answer. The answer recorded is also influenced by the amount of space left for recording. If a small space is left, short answers are recorded; if a larger space is left, longer answers are recorded. This suggests that few interviewers actually record all answers on a verbatim basis.

A second main disadvantage of open questions lies in the difficult and time-consuming tabulation problems which they pose. Since each respondent answers in his own words, each answer is unique. For some questions, answers may run several sentences or more in length. If generalizations are to be drawn from such answers, some way must be found for summarizing them. This is usually done by having an editor read some or all of the answers and establish classifications. Then he must go over each answer and mark it to indicate into which class or classes it falls. A tabulator can then go over the answers and count the number in each classification. The process is time-consuming and open to subjective errors on the part of the editor. Since answers differ in wording and degree of explanation, it is difficult to classify all answers in any given categories. In a survey on packaged soaps for automatic washing machines the question, *What do you like about "X" soap for washing clothes?* brought the frequent answer, "suds." Usually housewives like lots of suds from a soap, but in automatic washers too much suds flow over and are a nuisance. Some soaps make a point of a fact that they make little suds. The answer "suds" could mean the respondent thought the soap produced either a lot or a little suds. Classification is almost impossible.[12]

This expensive job of editing can be eliminated or reduced without losing the advantages of the open question when the subject is well formulated and the possible answers are limited in variety. The probable answers can be set down so the interviewer can check the one given. This speeds up the field work and eliminates the editor's job of classification. The following question illustrates the method: *For how many months or years have you been buying gasoline at this station?*

Less than 6 months ————
6 months to 1 year ————
1 to 5 years ————
5 years or more ————

The alternatives listed are not mentioned to the respondent or the question becomes a multiple choice one. Whenever possible, lists of answers, as shown above, should be used with open questions because of the time saving both in field work and tabulating.

Another disadvantage of the open question is the implicit weighting which it may give to the upper-income, better-educated segment of the population. Individuals in these groups are more articulate than others and, hence, tend to mention more points in answering open questions. For example, this group might mention three reasons for liking "X" soap on the average, while the average for others might be one. Then, if one hundred from the articulate group and one hundred others are interviewed, four hundred reasons for using "X" soap will be recorded. Three out of every four, however, will be reasons given by the articulate group. If the two groups differ in attitude, the resulting summaries will be biased.

Answers to open questions can be limited to fairly specific areas in some cases by phrasing the question properly. In one study, a bottle of orange drink was shown to respondents who were asked: *How much orange juice do you think it contains?* Among the answers obtained were the following:[13]

One orange and a little water and sugar
25 percent orange and 75 percent carbonated water
Juice of one-half dozen oranges
Three ounces

---

[12] The question used in this example is also a leading question unless it has been preceded by a series of questions that established that the housewife liked "X" soap for washing clothes.

[13] *U.S.* v. *88 Cases* (Bireley's Orange Beverage), 5 FRD 503 (U.S. D.C.N.J., 1945).

Full strength
A quarter cup
None
Not much
Small amount
One fourth
Very little, if any
Doubt it
Don't know
Not very much
Part orange juice
A pint
Most of it
About a glass and a half

The answers in this case reflect so many different frames of reference that they are relatively useless. They would have been more comparable if the question had been worded: *What percentage of this drink do you think is orange juice?*

Researchers are coming more and more to the conclusion that open questions are useful in exploratory research and as a means for opening up topics, but that otherwise their disadvantages outweigh their advantages in large surveys. The best study of the open question has concluded:[14]

1. Average response to open questions is three times as long as to closed questions.
2. The meaningful, relevant, nonrepetitive response was no more in open than in closed questions.
3. Pertinence of responses was the same in both types of questions.
4. Factual reporting was less accurate in open questions.
5. Open questions get less valid responses on subjective topics.
6. Self-revelation was greater on factual topics but less on attitudinal topics when open questions were used.

Multiple choice questions. Questions of this type offer the respondent a number of specific alternatives from which he is to choose one or more, as the case may be. The following are examples: *Do you buy this brand of motor oil exclusively, more than any other brand, or just occasionally?*

Exclusively ————

---

[14] B. S. Dohrenwend, "Some Effects of Open and Closed Questions on Respondents' Answers," *Human Organization*, 24 (Summer, 1965), pp. 175–84, as reported in Stanley L. Payne, "Are Open-ended Questions Worth the Effort?" *Journal of Marketing Research*, 2 (November, 1965), pp. 417–18.

More than any other ————
Just occasionally ————
Don't know ————

Which of the following reasons do you think explain your patronage of this service station?

It's closest to my home ————
It's clean and attractive ————
It sells the brand of gasoline I prefer ————
Its prices are lower ————
It gives complete service ————
The personnel are courteous ————
They are good mechanics ————
They are personal friends ————
Other reasons ————
Don't know ————

Notice in each case the alternatives are actually repeated to the respondent. If the second question were asked without actually mentioning the alternatives, it would be an open question rather than a multiple choice.

The two questions above illustrate some of the difficulties in using multiple choice questions. In the first question, the three alternatives are mentioned in the question proper. In the second question, there are too many alternatives to mention in the question proper; instead, they are listed at the end. But the list is so long that respondents would not be able to remember it when it was read to them. Whenever the list of alternatives is as long as this, the choices should be listed on a card which can be handed to the respondent.

In the first illustration above, it is clear that the respondent is to select one alternative only. In the second question, this is not so clear. If uniformity of response is to be obtained, it is necessary to make clear to the respondent how many choices may be selected.

In the second illustration above, the last alternative is "other." It is common practice to give this choice, since some alternative may have been omitted. A respondent who had an answer not listed might be confused or feel forced to select another choice if he didn't have this escape. Actually, any alternative that is not listed will usually be mentioned so seldom as to amount to little. Therefore, it is imperative to list all alternatives that may be of any importance at all. For example: *Approximately which of the following percentages of the total gasoline purchases for your car are made at this station?*

25 to 50% ————
50 to 75% ————
75 to 100% ————
100% ————

Someone who bought less than 25 percent of his gasoline at the designated station would be unable to select one of the alternatives. This question also illustrates another problem. Suppose the respondent estimated he bought 50 percent of his gasoline at the designated station. Would he select the first or second alternative? This is particularly troublesome in cases where the overlap is in the round numbers in which answers will probably be formulated. Thus, care should be taken to avoid overlap among alternatives.

It is also desirable in questions with quantitative answers to select alternatives so that the most probable answers will fall in the middle of a class. In the above example 25, 50, and 75 percent would be frequent answers and so should be near the middle of classes instead of at extremes. As it is, most of the answers in the second class would probably be at one extreme or the other—50 percent or 75 percent. The class average of 62.5 percent, however, would be used to represent the class. But this would be an answer few would give.

Multiple choice questions overcome some of the disadvantages of open questions, but incur some new ones. Open questions are subject to interviewer bias in the recording of answers. This is not nearly as important with multiple choice questions where answers are in one or more of the stated alternatives. All the interviewer has to do is check the applicable reply. Thus, the multiple choice question is faster and less subject to bias in the field.

Similarly, the multiple choice question simplifies the tabulating process. The difficult and time-consuming editing process is reduced to a rapid check for mechanical accuracy.

Multiple choice questions give a list of alternative answers. It was pointed out above that this list must include all alternatives or there will be a bias against those omitted. The alternatives identified in a multiple choice question will be reported by more respondents than would mention them if an open question were used. In one experiment respondents were asked who should manage unemployment and health benefit funds. Three alternatives were given—company, union, and government. Only 15 percent of the respondents suggested combinations of these. But, when combinations were suggested as other alternatives, the number choosing these alternatives jumped to 52 percent.[15] This greater mention of suggested alternatives may be the result of aided recall—the listing helps the respondent recall pertinent points. This is good. On the other hand, the listing of alternatives may suggest ideas to respondents that seem logical, and so the respondent selects them even though they are not correct. If this happens, the results are obviously biased.

Multiple choice questions also tend to bias results by the order in

---

[15] Payne, *op. cit.,* p. 87.

which the alternative answers are given. When ideas are involved, the first item in the list of alternatives has a favorable bias. More respondents pick a given idea when it is first than will pick it when it is in another position. In an experiment to test this, four ideas were presented as alternatives to a multiple choice question. Each of the four was shown alternately in each of the four positions. Each was selected more times when it was in the first position than in any other. In total, the percentage of respondents selecting a choice when it was first on the list was 6 percent larger than the percentage selecting the idea when it was in one of the two central positions and 4 percent above the percentage picking it when it was last.[16]

This bias of position can be overcome by alternating the order in which alternatives are listed. If six choices are offered, six different groups of cards are printed. The order of listing is different on each card. Each item appears first on one of the six different cards, second on one, etc. Thus, in one sixth of the interviews, item A is first, in one sixth it is second, etc. This, of course, does not eliminate the bias, but it averages the upward and downward bias of the various positions.

When the alternatives in a multiple choice question are numbers, this bias of position changes. Central positions are chosen more than either extreme. Respondents guess that the answer expected is apt to be near the middle. They are usually correct. It is common in constructing questionnaires to put down the likely answer and to add one or two alternatives on either side of it. Unfortunately, it is not easy to rotate positions when numbers are used. If a series of numbers is involved, it is logical to put them in order from small to large or vice versa. Even if they are out of this order, the respondent will tend to sort them into a sequence. An effort should be made to have a class at each end that is more extreme than any respondent is apt to be. This will enable all respondents to report accurately without being in an extreme category.

Dichotomous questions. The dichotomous, or two-way question, is an extreme of the multiple choice question. The idea is to offer only two choices—yes or no, did or didn't, cash or credit, railroad or airline, etc. Such questions are the most widely used of the three basic types. The following are examples of dichotomous questions: *Would the service proposed by "X" Lines make motor freight service more useful to you? Is any of this discount normally passed on to others? Did you buy it or was it a gift? Was it new or used when you got it?*

Close examination will indicate a basic difference between the first

---

[16] *Ibid.*, pp. 84–85. Another student cautions that position bias is more complex than ordinarily believed. He thinks that it is also influenced by where the interview is conducted, the length of the check list, and the length of the questionnaire. See Sam L. Becker, "Why an Order Effect?" *Public Opinion Quarterly*, Vol. 18 (Fall, 1954), pp. 271–78.

two and the last two questions above. In the last two, the two alternatives are both stated; in the first two, one alternative is stated, while the other is implied. In the second question it seems obvious that the other alternative is that none of the discount was passed on or, putting it another way, that all of the discount was kept by the firms reporting. Probably there would be no confusion as to what the two alternatives were in this case. It is also likely, however, that different results would have been obtained had both alternatives been stated explicitly. For example: *Is any of this discount normally passed on to others or is all of it kept by your firm?*

An experiment to test the effect of stating only one alternative used the following two questions:[17] *Do you think the United States should allow public speeches against democracy? Do you think the United States should forbid public speeches against democracy?*

The following results were obtained:

First question		*Second question*	
Should allow	21%	Should not forbid	39%
Should not allow	62	Should forbid	46
No opinion	17	No opinion	15

Since the two questions ask exactly the same thing—one in a positive way and one in a negative way—the answers should be directly comparable. Those who say the U.S. should allow such speeches should also report that these speeches should not be forbidden. The results show that this did not occur. Only 21 percent wanted to allow speeches against democracy, but 39 percent were against forbidding them. A closer estimate of the true feeling on the subject would probably have been obtained if the question had stated both alternatives: *Do you think the United States should allow or forbid public speeches against democracy?*

Dichotomous questions have about the same advantages as multiple choice questions. They are quick and easy for the field worker to handle. Editing and tabulation are relatively simple. They offer less opportunity for interviewer bias to creep into the results.[18] The straight yes-no type of answer makes it easy for the respondent to reply. But dichotomous questions may be deceptive in their seeming simplicity. Few dichoto-

[17] Donald Rugg, "Experiments in Wording Questions: II," *Public Opinion Quarterly,* Vol. 5 (March, 1941), pp. 91–92.

[18] Not all researchers agree with this point. One study reports particular interviewer bias in dichotomous questions which include explicit alternatives because they permit undue stress in stating the alternatives, and dichotomous questions which permit a volunteered third answer because interviewers who themselves would give a third answer are more aware of the respondents leaning in this direction. Don Cahalan, Valerie Tamulonis, and Helen W. Verner, "Interviewer Bias Involved in Certain Types of Opinion Survey Question," *International Journal of Opinion and Attitude Research,* Vol. 1 (March, 1947), pp. 63–77.

mous questions, for example, are actually only two-way. Take the following question: *Do you expect to buy another piano some day?* Undoubtedly some people definitely plan to buy another piano and others definitely plan not to, but a large middle group may have no definite plans either way. Some of these might properly report, "don't know." Others might be in a "maybe" class. Even the "maybes" might fall into distinct groups—those who probably would but were not sure and those who probably would not but were not sure. This would mean that instead of two possible answers there would be five: yes, no, probably, probably not, and don't know. If the piano question were reworded to include explicit statement of both of the original alternatives and to take into account the five alternatives actually existing, it might appear as follows: *Do you expect to buy another piano some day, or not?*

Yes ———

Probably ———

Probably not ———

No ———

Don't know ———

The five alternatives would not be suggested to the respondents, but if one of them qualified his answer, the interviewer could then check the appropriate space. At the very least, the "don't know" category should be provided.[19] Then the "probablys" would be classified in the "yes" category and the "probably nots" in the "no" category. As was pointed out in the discussion of multiple choice questions, however, if the alternatives are not actually stated to the respondent, fewer persons will report them than would otherwise. Therefore, if the "probably" answers are not actually indicated to the respondent, the number reporting them will have a downward bias and the number saying "yes" and "no" will have an upward bias.

Dichotomous questions may be more than two-way questions for another reason—instead of one or the other of the two alternatives, the correct answer may be both. In a survey on shaving habits among college men, the question was asked: *Do you shave with an electric razor or a safety razor?* As it turned out, many college men use both. They use an electric razor for everyday shaving, but when they have a date and want an especially close shave, they use a safety razor. It would be better in this case to have the "both" category available for the interviewer to check, or to make the question multiple choice by including the "both" possibility in the actual question.

---

[19] The importance of the "don't know" category is amplified in international surveys, as it has been shown that nationalities differ considerably in their tendencies to respond "don't know." Andrzej Sicinski, " 'Don't Know' Answers in Cross-National Surveys," *Public Opinion Quarterly*, 34 (Spring, 1970), pp. 126–29.

Summary. The researcher must consider the advantages and disadvantages of each of the three basic types before deciding which type to use for each question in his survey. In general, the expense of editing open questions militates against their use if it is at all possible to avoid them. If preliminary work has pretty well established the answers which will be forthcoming, the open question may well be changed to a multiple choice question. Even if the question is left open, it may be possible to set down the various answers which will be given and, thus, to permit the interviewer to check one or more of the alternatives rather than to record the answer verbatim. If the open question is used, the question should direct answers to a particular framework so that they will be comparable. Otherwise results as useless as those in the orange drink questionnaire may be obtained.

If a multiple choice question is used, all alternatives should be stated and should be mutually exclusive. A "don't know" category should be left on the questionnaire even though it may not be suggested to the respondents.

If dichotomous questions are used, they must actually be two-way questions. If qualified answers or combination answers are possible, space should be left for recording them, and also for a "don't know" answer.

Decide on wording of questions

In the preceding discussion of question content and types of questions, much has been said on question wording. A number of other important ideas, however, should be considered. Unfortunately, these ideas are more rules of thumb which have been developed from experience than they are underlying concepts.

Define the issue. Beginning newspaper reporters are admonished to include in their lead paragraphs the six points: who, where, when, what, why, and how. This can also serve as a guide to the researcher preparing a questionnaire. Each question should be checked against these points to be sure that the issue is clear. Who, what, where, and when are particularly important. The why and how may be applicable in some questions.

Take the question: *What brand of cigarettes do you smoke? Who?* In this case the "you" seems clear, but in some cases this word may leave confusion as to whether it applies to the individual, his family, his company, or some other plural application. *What?* "Brand of cigarettes" and "smoke" are stated. The word "brand" may be slightly confusing, but otherwise the "what" in this question is clear. *When?* This is not clear. Does the question mean usually, always, last time, ever, or what? The question makes the fundamental error of assuming something. It assumes that all respondents smoke one brand of cigarettes to the exclusion of all others. Of course this is not true. A better way to get at the same information might then be to ask: *What brand of cigarettes did you buy the last time you bought cigarettes?* This makes the "when" specific. In this question the where, how, and why are not applicable.

Should question be subjective or objective?   Many questions can be stated in either subjective or objective form. *Do you think the Ford is a better car than the Chevrolet? Is the Ford a better car than the Chevrolet?* The first phrasing is subjective; it puts the question in terms of the individual and is apt to elicit a response in terms of the individual's feelings. The second phrasing tends to cause the respondent to think more in terms of what people in general think. One study of the effect of subjective-objective statements used questions of the following type:[20] *Did you see a demonstration of Foley Kitchen Utensils in the housewares department? Was there a demonstration of Foley Kitchen Utensils in the housewares department?* The results of this study indicated that subjective, rather than objective, questions tended to give more reliable results. The researcher has no available rule to follow in deciding whether to make his question subjective or objective. He must be aware, however, of the fact that the choice will influence his results.

Positive or negative statement.   In a survey to determine the attitudes of executives towards advertising, every question was stated in both a positive and a negative way. Two different questionnaires were prepared, one using half of the positive and half of the negative wordings in an interspersed way, and the second using the other half of the questions. Several issues were presented in either positive or negative statements and respondents were to indicate one of five alternative reactions to each statement: agree generally, agree partially, can't say, disagree partially, and disagree generally. Presumably one who agreed with a favorable statement of one issue would disagree with an unfavorable statement of the same issue. While this was generally true, considerable variation obtained, as shown in Table 7–2.[21]

This study used positive and negative statements alternately to average out the effect of each wording. Another approach would have been to state both alternatives, the positive and the negative in each question, as follows: *Do you think advertising should be increased or decreased to hasten recovery in a recession?*

Use simple words.   Words used in questionnaires should be words which have only one meaning, and that meaning known by everyone.

20 Alfred W. Hubbard, "Phrasing Questions," *Journal of Marketing*, Vol. 15 (July, 1950), pp. 48–56.

21 Stephen A. Greyser, "Businessmen Re Advertising: 'Yes, but . . .'," *Harvard Business Review*, Vol. 40 (May–June, 1962), p. 28.

TABLE 7–2. Effect of positive and negative wording of questions on attitude towards advertising

Nature of question	Agree		Can't say	Disagree	
	Generally	Partially		Generally	Partially
Effect on standard of living:					
Raises it	51%	34%	6%	6%	3%
Lowers it	2	1	5	14	78
Effect on products for the public					
Better ones	47	30	6	9	8
Poorer ones	2	6	6	20	66
Most efficient way to stimulate mass buying:					
Advertising	66	23	4	4	3
Other methods	3	10	16	16	55
To hasten recovery in a recession:					
Substantially increase advertising	18	36	14	13	19
Substantially decrease advertising	2	3	7	9	79
Advertising effect on prices:					
Lower prices	30	24	13	14	19
Higher prices	14	14	10	17	45

SOURCE: S. A. Greyser, "Businessmen Re Advertising: 'Yes, but . . .'," *Harvard Business Review*, Vol. 40 (May–June, 1962), p. 28.

Unfortunately, it is not easy to find such words. Many ordinary words have different meanings listed in the dictionary, and even other meanings among certain groups of the population or in certain sections of the country. What is "soda pop" in some sections is "tonic" in others, and "root beer" and "sarsaparilla" are the same thing.

Do you require all prospective salesmen to go through training? In this question, "prospective" can readily be picked out as an unusual word which might not be understood by everyone. But what about "require"? It is a common enough word. The dictionary, however, shows eight different meanings. Does it mean that all new salesmen must, or do, go through a training program? If so, why not ask: *Do all new salesmen go through training?*

Several lists of common words may help in selecting words which will be known by most respondents. One that is of value appears in *The Teacher's Word Book of 30,000 Words*.[22] It is best to err on the side of simplicity if doubt exists. There are many examples of misunderstandings

---

[22] E. L. Thorndike and Irving Lorge, *The Teacher's Word Book of 30,000 Words* (New York: Columbia University Press, 1944).

of what seem to be everyday words. One study found less than half the population knew the meaning of such common terms as filibuster and tariff.[23]

Avoid ambiguous questions. Ambiguous questions mean different things to different people. Naturally, comparable replies cannot be received from respondents who take a question to mean different things. The following question was cited above: *Do you require all prospective salesmen to go through training?* This question would be ambiguous because of differences of opinion as to what constitutes training. Is one trip with an experienced salesman training? Or is a formal program of classes extending over a period of several weeks the type of training that the researcher had in mind?

Questions which use such terms as usually, normally, frequently, and regularly are ambiguous: *What brand of cigarettes do you smoke regularly?* What does regularly mean—always, almost always, more than any other, or what? Some respondents will interpret it one way and some another. When the researcher wants to find out typical behavior, it is probably best to inquire about a specific time, such as the last time: *What brand was the last cigarette you smoked?* The last brand smoked by some respondents will be different from the one they usually smoke, but, if the sample is adequate, this will average out.

While the authors hold to the above view, a French study of magazine readership suggests that words such as "regularly" and "occasionally" may have a more consistent meaning than has been thought. After asking respondents if they read different magazines regularly, occasionally, or never, the researcher then undertook intensive investigation to discover how extensive each respondent's readership was. The results showed the following:[24]

Reported read magazine	Probability of reading a given issue
Regularly	0.89
Occasionally	0.24
Never	0.02

This study concluded that for repetitive studies of this type it would be useful to determine the meaning of words such as the above in terms of probabilities and then to use questions involving such words.

Avoid leading questions. In a study to evaluate the service of automobile insurance companies, a series of questions on claim service was preceded by a statement which began as follows: "It has been alleged

---

[23] Mildred Parten, *Surveys, Polls and Samples* (New York: Harper & Brothers, 1950), p. 201.

[24] J. M. Agostini, "The Case for Direct Questions on Reading Habits," *Journal of Advertising Research,* 4 (June, 1964), p. 31.

that some low-rate companies are much tougher in adjusting claims than standard rate companies, and that you are more likely to have to go to court to collect the sum due you."[25] It is obvious that this statement would influence the answers to the questions on claim service which followed. Most marketing research studies do not have the obvious bias of the above, but it is easy to lead respondents toward one answer unless care is taken not to do so.

Do you have a General Electric refrigerator? This question will result in more reports of GE refrigerators than will a question: *What brand of refrigerator do you have?* When respondents get an idea that a survey is being made for a particular company or product, they have a tendency to respond favorably toward the sponsor. In a mail survey among FM radio owners in the area covered by a small FM radio station, respondents were asked to list the four FM stations to which they listened most. The sponsoring station came out on top by far. A study of the individual questionnaires, however, showed that many of the respondents had associated the survey with that station, apparently through the address to which the questionnaire was mailed. Many of the returned questionnaires had additional comments such as, "We think you're wonderful," and "We like your station but not quite as well as X."

Do not ask questions in a way that will involve generalization. Questions should always be stated in specific terms. If generalizations are desired, the researcher should make them from the specific data obtained. Consider the following question: *How many machine tool salesmen have called on you in the last year?* The only way the respondent could answer this question would be to estimate about how many salesmen came in during a typical week or possibly a month and then to multiply. The results would be more accurate if the question asked: *How many machine tool salesmen called on you last week?* The researcher could then multiply by fifty-two.

Avoid questions which may seem unreasonable to the respondent. In many marketing research projects it is desirable to know the income of the respondent so that comparisons can be made among income groups. It is generally believed, however, that a sudden question *What is your income?* may impress the respondent as being too personal. A brief explanation as to the reason for asking such a question is often used to ease the respondent's reaction. The interviewer may explain, for example, that he would like to get some personal information to help classify respondents. Then the request for income data may seem more reasonable to the respondent.

Consumer surveys have become commonplace enough in recent years that difficulties of the above type may be less important than in the past.

---

[25] J. Stevens Stock and Barbara K. Auerbach, "How Not to Do Consumer Research," *Journal of Marketing*, Vol. 27 (July, 1963), p. 21.

To test this point, a survey that inquired about insomnia alternated three different introductory remarks: *"I would like to ask you about . . .*

1. *. . . certain ailments."*
2. *. . . certain common ailments."*
3. *. . . certain common ailments which most people have."*

No difference was found in the response to the question which followed as to whether the respondent had insomnia. On the other hand, when "buffer items" (questions as to the incidence of colds and allergies) were introduced between the above introduction and the question on insomnia, 23.2 percent of the respondents reported insomnia as compared to only 12.5 percent when no "buffer items" were used.[26]

Use split ballot wherever possible. No one wording is the correct one for a question. Different wordings may get different answers, yet no one can say one wording is right and the others wrong. It is important for the researcher to realize this situation exists and to understand what effect a particular phrasing may have on the results. To do this the split ballot technique can be used. Whenever there are two wordings from which to choose but no basis on which to pick one over the other, one can be run on half the questionnaires and the other on the other half. Comparison of the two halves of the questionnaires will permit a better interpretation of the results than would be possible were only one wording used.

Decide on question sequence

Once the wording of the individual questions has been determined, it is necessary to set them up in some order. The sequence can influence the results obtained.

A questionnaire has three major sections: (1) the basic information sought, (2) classification information, and (3) identification information. Since questions pertaining to these sections tend to be of declining interest to the respondent, the sections are usually put in the order shown. Questions relating to the basic information sought form the body of the questionnaire. To help in analyzing this information, it is usually necessary to be able to classify respondents on such bases as age, sex, income, education, and nationality. Questions on these points form the classification section. The identification section identifies all parties involved. This includes the name and address of the respondent, and the names of such individuals as the interviewer, editor, and card puncher. These are used to verify that the actual respondents shown were interviewed and to assign responsibility for and to evaluate the quality of the tasks done.

---

[26] Frederick J. Thumin, "Watch for Those Unseen Variables," *Journal of Marketing,* Vol. 26 (July, 1962), p. 59.

Opening questions must win respondent's interest. When a respondent agrees to be interviewed, he has made a concession—often partly out of curiosity. The questionnaire must capture his interest at once or he may break off the interview. Therefore, the first question should be an interesting one, even if it is necessary to insert a question which is not strictly necessary for the survey. The opening question in a shopping habits survey was: *Who lives here?* This could hardly be expected to excite the respondent. Undoubtedly the next few questions were received rather coldly. Compare this with the survey opener: *Do you own a horse?* The latter seems sure to create curiosity among most people.

It is also important to make the first few questions particularly simple —questions that everyone will be able to answer easily. This builds the confidence of the respondent so he feels he can handle the project. If the opening questions "stump" the respondent, he is apt to say something like, "I don't know. I'm not the type of person you should be talking to anyway," and the interview may be lost.

Place questions which are apt to cause difficulty in the body of the questionnaire. Questions which might embarrass the respondent and those which may have little interest for the respondent should be well down in the questionnaire so that the questioning process is well established before they are reached. After the respondent has answered a number of questions, he is more at ease with the interviewer and is less apt to balk at personal questions such as those relating to income, knowledge, ability, and status.

Consider influence of questions on succeeding questions. In discussing leading questions, it was pointed out how mention of the product sponsoring the survey would bias answers. Thus, if it is necessary to mention the product specifically in some questions, those questions should be left to the end of the questionnaire.

In another study to test the effect of question sequence, a researcher set up five different question sequences before asking respondents how interested they would be in buying a new product described as a combination pen and pencil selling for 29¢. One set of respondents was asked their buying interest immediately after the product was described to them; a second set was first asked what advantages they saw in the product; a third set was asked the disadvantages; a fourth was asked both advantages and disadvantages in that order; and a fifth, disadvantages and then advantages. The results are shown in Table 7–3.[27]

It is clear that mention of the advantages of the product increased the expressed buying interest, whereas mention of the disadvantages decreased the interest. Other types of question sequence bias may be more subtle. Interestingly, several experiments testing the effect of chang-

---

[27] Edwin J. Gross, "The Effect of Question Sequence on Measures of Buying Interest," *Journal of Advertising Research,* 4 (September, 1964), p. 41.

TABLE 7–3. Effect of question sequence on reported buying interest

Degree of buying interest		Interest in buying questions asked			
	Immediately	After asking advantages	After asking disadvantages	After asking advantages & disadvantages	After asking disadvantages & advantages
Very much interested	2.8%	16.7%	0.0%	5.7%	8.3%
Somewhat interested	33.3	19.4	15.6	28.6	16.7
A little interested	8.3	11.1	15.6	14.3	16.7
Not very interested	25.0	13.9	12.5	22.9	30.6
Not at all interested	30.6	38.9	56.3	28.5	27.7
Total	100.0%	100.0%	100.0%	100.0%	100.0%

SOURCE: Edwin J. Gross, "The Effect of Question Sequence on Measures of Buying Interest," *Journal of Advertising Research*, 4 (September, 1964), p. 41.

ing the sequence in which major sections of questionnaires have been presented have found little evidence of any effect.[28]

Arrange questions in logical order. Questions should follow one another in some logical order, i.e., logical to the respondent. Sudden changes in subject confuse the respondent and cause indecision on his part. In an experiment to test the effect of sudden shifts in thought, a survey asked a given group of questions in a series of related questions, and then in between a series of unrelated questions. In the second case, the number of indecisive answers such as "don't know" ran 7 to 13 percent higher than in the first case.[29]

Mail questionnaire a special problem. Mail questionnaires raise unique problems in question sequence. Since the mail questionnaire must sell itself, it is particularly important that the opening questions capture the respondent's interest. Questions should then proceed in logical order. It is not possible, however, to take advantage of sequence position in the same way as in personal interviews. Questions that are at the end to avoid biasing the answers to other questions will still bias the others because respondents can go back and change their responses to earlier questions. Recent research suggests this bias may be overestimated. A

[28] See, for example, Reuben Cohen, "The Position Effects Problem," *Public Opinion Quarterly*, 29 (Fall, 1965), p. 456, and N. M. Bradburn and W. M. Mason, "The Effect of Question Order on Responses," *Journal of Marketing Research* (November, 1964), pp. 57–61.

[29] Albert B. Blankenship, *Consumer and Opinion Research* (New York: Harper & Brothers, 1943), pp. 77–78.

deliberate effort was made to create such bias in a survey on gasoline brand purchases. Only a slight difference was found.[30]

Decide on layout and reproduction

The physical layout and reproduction of a questionnaire can influence its success with respondents and can affect the problems encountered in handling it in the researcher's office. Three major points should be considered in planning the layout and reproduction of the questionnaire: (1) securing acceptance of the questionnaire by respondents, (2) making it easy to control the questionnaires, and (3) making it easy to handle the questionnaires.

Securing acceptance of the questionnaire. The physical appearance of a questionnaire influences the attitude of the respondent towards a survey. If the questionnaire is mimeographed on a poor grade of paper, the respondent is apt to think the project doesn't amount to much. Printing on a good quality of paper, however, makes the questionnaire appear to be of some value.

The name of the firm sponsoring the project and the name of the project should appear at the top of the first page or on the cover if the questionnaire is in book form. Most companies use fictitious names on their questionnaires in order to prevent biased answers from respondents, and also to forestall phone calls from respondents asking information about the survey.

Ease of control. To make it possible to control the questionnaires in the field operation and in the editing and tabulating procedures, the questionnaires should be numbered serially. This enables the research director to verify that all questionnaires are accounted for or to determine which ones are lost. Mail questionnaires are an exception. If these are numbered, respondents will assume that the number identifies a given questionnaire with them personally. It is generally believed that some respondents will refuse to reply or will answer differently under this condition. Recent research, however, suggests that the loss of anonymity influences results very little, if any.

Similarly, the questions on the questionnaire should be numbered serially. This makes reference to individual questions more simple and helps eliminate mistakes in editing and tabulating.

Ease of handling. Proper reproduction of a questionnaire can facilitate the field work and the office work on surveys. The size of the questionnaire is important. Small forms the size of a post card are easy to

---

[30] William F. O'Dell, "Personal Interviews or Mail Panels?" *Journal of Marketing*, Vol. 26 (October, 1962), p. 36.

carry in the field and easy to sort, count, and file in the office. It is not wise, however, to crowd material into a small space. If the questionnaire is crowded, it makes a bad appearance and leads to errors in data collection. If small spaces only are available for answers to open questions, interviewers will digest the answers received to make them fit the space available. When interviewers have to crowd answers into small spaces, it is frequently hard to read the answers and tabulation errors appear.

Questionnaires that are too large become awkward for the interviewer to handle. Something near letter size, 8½ by 11 inches, is probably about the right size.

When a questionnaire runs to several pages, it should be made into a booklet form rather than a number of sheets of paper clipped or stapled together. A booklet is easier for the interviewer to handle, and does not come apart with use as do clipped and stapled papers.

Questions should be laid out so as to make it easy for the field worker to follow the sequence. Numbering the questions in sequence helps, but confusion is particularly apt to come on filter-type questions. If question 4 is to be asked only of those respondents who answered "yes" to question 3, it is helpful if the layout of the questionnaire guides this procedure. Sometimes subquestions are indented or numbered 3a, 3b, etc., to indicate they are to be asked only under certain circumstances. When one series of questions is to be asked of those saying "yes" to a previous question and another series is to be asked of those saying "no," the two series can be put on different sides of the paper. The following is an illustration: 1. *Does your family own a piano?*

Yes		*No*
If "yes" ask:		If "no" ask:
2.		3.
2a.		3a.
2b.		3b.

Many opportunities exist for improving the average questionnaire in layout in such a way as both to improve the quality of data collected and to reduce costs. One of the few reported efforts along these lines resulted in a reduction in printing costs for the questionnaires in a study from $1,150 to $214.20.[31]

New equipment is making possible a more mechanized system of tabulating data with accompanying improvements in both accuracy and cost. One of these, the optical scanner, requires that responses be recorded by code, which requires special questionnaire layout and may introduce

---

[31] David F. Wolfe, "A New Questionnaire Design," *Journal of Marketing*, Vol. 21 (October, 1956), pp. 186–90.

errors in the recording. Answers are recorded with a heavy pencil similar to that used by many students in standardized tests and usually must be recorded on a sheet separate from the questionnaire proper. While this system has been used successfully, it is still experimental in nature.[32]

Pretest

Before a questionnaire is ready for the field, it needs to be pretested under field conditions. No researcher can prepare a questionnaire so good that improvements cannot be discovered in field tests. Researchers have reported pretesting, changing, and pretesting again for as many as twenty-five times before they were satisfied with some questionnaires. One pretest is as much, however, as most questionnaires get.

Pretests are best done by personal interview even if the survey is to be handled by mail or telephone. Interviewers can note respondent reactions and attitudes which cannot otherwise be obtained. After any pertinent changes in the questionnaire have been made, another pretest can be run by mail or telephone if those methods are to be used in the survey. This latter pretest should uncover any weakness peculiar to the method of communication.

The people interviewed in a pretest should be roughly similar to those who will be covered in the final study. Ordinarily, the number of interviews in a pretest is small—perhaps twenty, but, if major changes are made as a result, the new questionnaire should be pretested again. Only the best interviewers should be used in pretest work, since they must be able to perceive uneasiness, confusion, and resistance among respondents. Poor interviewers may not be aware of these difficulties.

Interviewers in pretests should watch particularly to see if the issue in each question is clear to the respondent. Any requests for explanation, comments, or other reactions by the respondents should be noted. After an interview is over, the interviewer may discuss it with the respondent to get explanations of what meaning he got from individual questions and why he answered "don't know" where he did.

Wording of some questions should be improved as a result of the pretest. Interviewers should note words which are not understood by all respondents. If there is any doubt as to the wording of a question, interviewers can try alternate wordings and compare reactions of respondents to the different phrasings.

As a result of the pretest, some questions may be eliminated from the questionnaire and others may be added. Interviewers will observe ques-

---

[32] F. Q. Sessions, R. J. Epley, and E. O. Moe, "The Development, Reliability, and Validity of an All-Purpose Optical Scanner Questionnaire Form," *Public Opinion Quarterly*, 30 (Fall, 1966), pp. 423–28.

tions which cause embarrassment or resistance, the point at which respondents begin to get bored and impatient, and the places where relaxed cooperation seems to break down.

Pretests should also test questions sequence. Do the first questions catch the respondent's interest? Are some answers influenced by the questions which precede them? Interviewers should report mechanical difficulties encountered, such as confusion in following question sequence and difficulty in squeezing answers into the spaces allotted.

Revision and final draft

After each significant revision of the questionnaire, another pretest should be run. When the last pretest suggests no new revisions, the researcher is ready to print the actual questionnaires to be used in the survey.

Summary

Questionnaire construction has been discussed in nine steps. These steps may vary in importance in individual projects, but each one must be thought through in each case. The nine steps are: (1) decide what information is wanted, (2) decide what type of questionnaire (personal interview, mail, telephone) to use, (3) decide on the content of individual questions, (4) decide on the type of question (open, multiple choice, dichotomous) to use, (5) decide on the wording of the questions, (6) decide on question sequence, (7) determine form, layout, and method of reproduction of questionnaire, (8) make a preliminary draft and pretest it, and (9) revise and prepare the final questionnaire.

ATTITUDE MEASUREMENT[33]

In the preceding discussion, attention has been focused on the problems of designing questionnaires for use in obtaining factual information such as the brand last purchased or the price paid. Increasingly, however, marketers are wanting to measure attitudes—primarily attitudes of consumers toward products, companies, advertising, the state of the economy, and other similar items, but also the attitudes of employees, such as that of salesmen toward their jobs, or of other businessmen, such as retailers, toward the supplier. The great interest in recent years in

[33] For more extended discussions see: Allen L. Edwards, *Techniques of Attitude Scale Construction* (New York: Appleton-Century-Crofts, Inc., 1957); Warren S. Torgerson, *Theory & Methods of Scaling* (New York: John Wiley & Sons, Inc., 1958); and Clyde H. Coombs, *A Theory of Data* (New York: John Wiley & Sons, Inc., 1964).

brand and company images has focused attention on the problems of measuring such images and, currently, the concern with measurement of advertising effectiveness has spurred further efforts to improve the measurement of consumer attitudes as the factor most influenced by advertising. While images and attitudes are not exactly the same thing, problems of measuring them are similar and similar measuring devices are used.[34] The following discussion applies to both.

Measuring scales

What has been said about questionnaire design is pertinent to the development of questionnaires for measuring attitudes, but the latter involve special problems which deserve attention. These problems stem from the fact that no standardized counting or measuring scales to measure attitudes have been developed. Direct questioning of respondents on their attitudes is not effective, as many are not aware of their own attitudes or cannot articulate a statement of the attitude that is a compound of many conflicting feelings. Observation is not an efficient method of studying attitudes, as it is difficult to observe enough aspects of an individual's behavior to get a good sampling, and behavior often disguises true feelings. The researcher, therefore, must construct his own measuring instrument or adapt other scales to his specific purpose.

Suppose, for example, a coffee company wants to know the attitude of consumers toward the color of coffee in the cup (preference for light, dark, or in between), and toward bitterness, aroma, and flavor. No standard "yardsticks" exist for measuring these factors; the researcher must develop his own in his questionnaire. The term *scaling* has been applied to the process of developing measuring devices for purposes such as the above and using them to measure the attitudes of individuals.

Ordinal scales are the simplest used in marketing research. They serve to rank respondents according to some characteristic such as favorability toward a certain brand, or to rank items such as brands in order of consumer preference. Such scales make no attempt to measure the degree of favorability of the different rankings, i.e., the distance between the different rank positions may vary widely. All the scale tells is that the individual or item has more, less, or the same amount of the characteristic being measured as some other item. This is the most widely used type of scale in marketing research.

Interval scales not only separate individuals or items by rank order, but measure the distance between rank positions in equal units. Such a scale permits the researcher to say that position 4 on the scale is above position 5, and also that the distance from 5 to 4 is the same as the dis-

---

[34] Attitude implies an evaluation of an object or concept, whereas image suggests description with no value judgement.

tance from 4 to 3. Such a scale, however, does not permit conclusions that position 6 is twice as strong as position 3 because no zero position has been established. If one measures the distance between two points as four feet and between two other points as two feet, it is possible to say that the one distance is twice that of the other because each distance is measured from an absolute zero. A scale which permits such measurements is called a *ratio* scale. While ratio scales are common in the physical sciences, the measurement of attitudes is still so crude that they are of no significance in marketing research.

Ordinal scales are the most widely used in marketing research, although interval scales have had some minor use. The more common variations of these different basic types are discussed in the following paragraphs.

Rating scales

The simplest ordinal scale is the rating scale on which the respondent rates himself in one of two categories. This may result from a dichotomous question such as: *Do you like or dislike TV commercials?* In answering this question, respondents classify themselves in one of two categories—those who like TV commercials and those who don't. A possible third category would include those who refuse to take a position saying they neither like nor dislike commercials.

A refinement of this approach would result from asking a similar question in an open fashion: *What do you think of TV commercials?* The following answers might result: "I enjoy them"; "They are a terrible bore"; "They are clever"; "I always get a drink during commercials"; "I think they sell the products"; "They stink."

All of these comments express something of the respondent's attitude toward TV commercials. If they are to be used to measure attitudes towards TV commercials, however, the researcher must classify them. One might, for example, put them into two categories, those that are favorable and those that are unfavorable; or the classes could be broken more finely and become very favorable, favorable, neutral, unfavorable, and very unfavorable. It is readily apparent, however, that it is quite difficult to determine whether some of these comments should be in the unfavorable or very unfavorable category. For that matter, in some cases it may not be clear whether a comment is either favorable or unfavorable, such as, "I think they sell the products." To overcome these difficulties, rating scales have been developed which help the respondent rate himself more accurately. Two of these, the graphic rating scale and ranking procedures, are discussed here.

Graphic rating scales. The most widely used scale in marketing research is that in which the respondent is asked to rate himself by checking the point at which he would fall on a scale running from one extreme of the attitude in question to the other. In a study to determine attitudes toward private brands as compared with national brands, respondents were given the following task:[35] *Suppose that a large, new A & P store has recently opened up in your neighborhood and you have decided to shop there. Listed below are several brands of products that the store carries. Check in one of the spaces beside each brand how you think you might feel about using the brand.*

	USE REGULARLY 1	USE OCCASION- ALLY 2	MIGHT USE 3	PROBABLY NEVER USE 4	WOULD NEVER USE 5
LIBBY'S CANNED PEAS	├————	————	————	————	————┤
CAMEL CIGARETTES	├————	————	————	————	————┤
BRECK SHAMPOO	├————	————	————	————	————┤
A & P ASPIRIN	├————	————	————	————	————┤

Many different scaling devices can be used with this type of rating scale; sufficient evidence is not yet available to determine whether or not the particular method of presenting the scale or the number of gradations influences the results obtained. The four devices shown on p. 320 were used in a project in which respondents were asked to rate their opinions on the following question:[36] *Listed below are several brands of each of two household products. For each brand place an "X" in the one box which best indicates how much you dislike or like that brand. The more you dislike, the smaller the number you should give it. The more you like it, the bigger the number you should give it. There are no right or wrong answers. Only your opinion counts.*

Analysis of the results from using these scales was made in two ways, by computing an average score for each of the brands in the study and by computing the percentage of the respondents who placed each brand in one of the two top positions. The results were as shown in Tables 7–4 and 7–5.

The scales were quite consistent in both methods of analysis; in each case Brand F was rated the highest and Brand C the lowest, except in the case of Scale #2, on which Brand E rated slightly lower than Brand C in both methods of analysis.

In the study from which the above data are taken, the author tried

---

[35] John G. Myers, "An Investigation of Socio-Psychological Variables as Determinants of Brand Imagery and Brand Choice" (unpublished manuscript, Northwestern University, 1964).

[36] Jack Abrams, "An Evaluation of Alternative Rating Devices for Consumer Research," *Journal of Marketing Research*, 3 (May, 1966), pp. 189–93. The question wording was slightly varied in the original to fit the different scaling devices. Each scale was repeated for each brand.

SCALING DEVICE 1

DEFINITELY
DISLIKE
                                                                DEFINITELY
                                                                LIKE

1   2   3   4   5   6   7   8   9   10

□   □   □   □   □   □   □   □   □   □

SCALING DEVICE 2

DISLIKE COM- PLETELY	DISLIKE SOME- WHAT	DISLIKE A LITTLE	NEITHER LIKE NOR DISLIKE	LIKE A LITTLE	LIKE SOME- WHAT	LIKE COM- PLETELY
1	2	3	4	5	6	7
□	□	□	□	□	□	□

SCALING DEVICE 3

DEFINITELY
DISLIKE
                                                                DEFINITELY
                                                                LIKE

-5   -4   -3   -2   -1   0   +1   +2   +3   +4   +5

□   □   □   □   □   □   □   □   □   □   □

SCALING DEVICE 4

BELOW AVERAGE	ABOUT AVERAGE	A LITTLE BETTER	A LOT BETTER	ONE OF THE BEST	NONE BETTER
□	□ □	□ □	□ □	□ □	□ □

to relate the attitudes measured to actual purchase of the brands involved by checking respondents three months after they completed the attitude scales to determine which brands they had on hand. From such inventory data, the researcher concluded that Scale #4 measured attitudes in a way that was the best predictor of the respondent's actually having the brand three months later. The assumption that favorable attitude towards a brand leads to its purchase would indicate that Scale #4 was the best of the four scales used at measuring attitudes towards brands. The differences among the various scales in this regard were not large, however, so further tests of different scales are needed. This is particu-

TABLE 7–4. Average score by scale type

	Scale			
Brand	1	2	3	4
A	7.5	5.6	2.5	6.3
B	7.2	5.5	2.1	5.9
C	6.8	5.3	1.6	5.4
D	7.6	5.7	2.6	6.3
E	6.8	5.2	1.7	5.4
F	8.5	6.1	3.3	7.1

TABLE 7–5. Percentage of respondents who rated in one of top two positions

Brand	Scale			
	1	2	3	4
A	52%	62%	48%	16%
B	43	61	38	10
C	36	56	30	6
D	48	67	47	13
E	41	55	37	10
F	69	79	64	24

larly true since there is no accepted theory as to why one scale, #4 in this case, may be better than others.

The researcher in this study concluded that the effectiveness of a particular scaling device was related to the subject under study. He suggested, for example, that Scale #4 would be particularly useful for measuring changes in attitudes because it had fewer respondents clustered in the most favorable positions. This assumes that attitude changes would be towards a more favorable position and, hence, could be measured by this scale. Without further evidence, the present authors are doubtful that this argument shows that Scale #4 will be more sensitive than the others, and sensitivity is the key factor in a scale for measuring changes in attitudes. Clearly, much more needs to be learned about why scaling devices work as they do.

Graphic scales generally are relatively simple to construct, use, and interpret, and they permit the use of various degrees of gradation as the researcher may choose. When descriptive terms are used, it is important to keep them reasonably closely related to the numerical points on the scale, but even so it cannot be assumed that the points represent equal intervals.

Ranking. In the graphic rating scales just discussed, the respondent rated himself or some item on a scale without reference to other respondents or items. From the results it would be possible to rank companies, brands, or respondents with respect to the particular attitudes being measured. (In the example given, all three firms ranked at the same point on each of the four devices, although the same firms scored differently on different devices.) Another way to approach the problem, if rankings are desired, is to ask respondents to rank the subjects of interest according to the attitude being studied. In the previously mentioned study of attitudes toward private and national brands, the following technique was used:[37] *Beside each of the products listed below are four brand names. Mark a 1, 2, 3, or 4 alongside each brand according to how*

---

[37] Myers, *op. cit.*

often you use the brands. If the brands you use are not shown, choose those that you would be most likely to use.

1. Canned peas	____	Del Monte	____	Green Giant	____	Libby's	____	Jewel
2. Cigarettes	____	Kent	____	Camel	____	Benson & Hedges	____	Salem
3. Liquid shampoo	____	Prell	____	Breck	____	Halo	____	Pamper
4. Headache remedy	____	Aspirin Bayer	____	Bufferin	____	Walgreen	____	Excedrin

Rankings of this sort separate the items in the group studied, but of course give no absolute rating—all the items could be considered good or bad. This technique is also limited by the number of items that a respondent can consider meaningfully at one time.

Rating scales of the graphic and ranking variety are simple in concept and use, yet seem to give results, in most cases, comparable with those obtained with more complex techniques. Several studies have shown very similar results from various graphic and ranking scales.[38] The most significant problem in using such scales has to do with their validity, i.e., do they measure what they are presumed to measure? It is difficult to find standards against which to measure validity. The most common effort has been to compare opinions of products with their market shares or with purchases following the opinion measurement. These tests tend to support the validity of various attitude measures, but the correlation is far from perfect.[39] Price is a confusing factor in these validity tests, as the most expensive brand is often considered the best even though many consumers may not choose to pay the high price.

Indirect scales

Attitudes are complex and difficult to measure, as the above discussion has indicated. Few people spend much time analyzing their own attitudes. This means that when an individual is asked to mark the point on an attitude scale that accurately indicates his attitude on the subject in question, he must make a judgment under difficult circumstances. It would be strange if such judgments were uniformly accurate. In an effort to improve the measurement of attitudes, indirect approaches to the problem have been developed. Rather than ask an individual for a self-assessment, a series of statements related to the attitude is developed and the individual is asked to indicate agreement or disagreement with

---

[38] See Abrams, *op. cit.*, and H. H. Kassarjian and M. Nakanishi, "Study of Selected Opinion Measurement Techniques," *Journal of Marketing Research*, 4 (May, 1967), pp. 148–53.

[39] Abrams, *op. cit.*

them. On the basis of the responses, a score is determined which is a measure of the individual's attitude. The entire series of statements is called an attitude scale. Some of the several different types of indirect scales will be discussed below.

Thurstone or method of equal-appearing intervals.[40]   On the assumption that, even though people could not assign quantitative measurements to their own attitudes, they could tell the difference between the attitude represented by two different statements and could identify items that were approximately halfway between the two, Thurstone developed his method of equal-appearing intervals. The procedure is as follows:

1. Collect a large number of statements (perhaps as many as several hundred) related to the attitude in question.
2. Have a number of judges (perhaps twenty or more) sort the statements independently into eleven piles which vary from the most unfavorable statements, to neutral statements in pile six, to the most favorable statements in pile eleven.[41]
3. Study the frequency distribution of ratings for each statement and eliminate those statements that have widely scattered ratings, i.e., that are in a number of different piles.
4. Determine the scale value of each of the remaining statements, i.e., the number of the pile in which the median of the distribution falls.
5. Select about two statements from each of the eleven piles for the final scale. Those items with the narrowest range of ratings are preferred as being the most reliable.

The statements in the final scale are then mixed up in sequence and the respondents whose attitudes are to be scaled are asked to indicate their agreement or disagreement with each statement. Presumably each respondent will agree with only one or a few of the items that are immediately adjacent to each other in scale position; for example, a respondent might agree with the items in position 9 (pile 9) or positions 8, 9, and 10, but if the scale is a good one, he should not agree with, say, items 1, 4, 7, and 11. Each individual's score is computed as the median of the item positions with which he agrees. If a respondent agrees with items at random points on the scale, it is assumed that he does not have an organized attitude toward that subject. The following statements are taken, one from each of the eleven positions, from a scale to measure

---

[40] L. L. Thurstone and E. J. Chave, *The Measurement of Attitude* (Chicago: University of Chicago Press, 1929).

[41] Thurstone recommended a large number of judges, one hundred or more, but current work indicates such a large number is not necessary for reliability. See Allen L. Edwards, *Techniques of Attitude Scale Construction* (New York: Appleton-Century-Croft, Inc., 1957), pp. 168–69.

attitude toward TV commercials. They give an idea of the range covered by such a scale.

1. All TV commercials should be prohibited by law.
2. Watching TV commercials is a complete waste of time.
3. Most TV commercials are pretty bad.
4. TV commercials are monotonous.
5. TV commercials do not interfere too much with enjoying TV.
6. I have no feeling one way or the other about most TV commercials.
7. I like TV commercials at times.
8. Most TV commercials are fairly interesting.
9. I like to buy products advertised on TV whenever possible.
10. Most TV commercials help people select the best products available.
11. TV commercials are more fun to watch than the regular programs.

As the scale was originally developed by Thurstone, eleven positions were used; this number is still commonly used. Actually, there is no particular reason for this number and either more or less could be used. An odd number is preferred by most so that a central, neutral position can be identified.

Thurstone scales are not widely used in marketing research, probably because of the time-consuming task of preparing them. The preparation of long lists of statements and the rating of these statements by a number of judges is more easily adapted to the classroom than to commercial field operations. Some interesting examples are available, however, such as the readiness-to-buy scale used to indicate the degree to which consumers are ready to purchase various brands of convenience goods.[42]

A number of questions have been raised as to the value of the Thurstone scaling technique. The scale position of each item is determined by a group of judges; their ratings may be influenced by their own attitudes. Many experiments have shown these ratings to be independent of the judges' opinions,[43] but more recent studies indicate that, at least on some subjects, a definite correlation exists between the judges' attitudes and their ratings.[44] Even where this correlation is clearly shown, however, judges with different attitudes themselves still arranged the statements in the same rank order. This suggests that Thurstone scales should not be used as interval scales as originally intended, but as ordinal scales.

---

[42] William D. Wells, *Readiness to Buy* (paper delivered to AAPOR-WAPOR Conference, May 6, 1960).

[43] See, for example, H. J. Eysenck and S. Crown, "An Experimental Study in Opinion-Attitude Methodology," *International Journal of Opinion and Attitude Research*, Vol. 3 (Spring, 1949), pp. 47–86.

[44] R. T. Granneberg, "The Influence of Individual Attitude and Attitude-Intelligence Interaction upon Scale Values of Attitude Items," *American Psychologist*, Vol. 10 (August, 1955), pp. 330–31.

Another problem with the Thurstone scale comes from the fact that different individuals can obtain exactly the same scores from agreeing with quite different items. A respondent who agreed only with item 7 would have a score of 7, but so would a respondent who agreed with items 3, 7, and 11. Some would argue that an individual who could agree with items as extreme as number 11 couldn't possibly have the same attitude as one who could agree with no item above number 7. The contrary argument would be that attitudes are a composite of reactions to a large number of factors; no two people have been exposed to the same factors or have reacted exactly the same way to all of them. Each person's attitude, therefore, is an average of a number of factors and the same average (attitude) can result from many different combinations of factors.[45]

A final criticism of Thurstone scaling is that it does not obtain information as to the degree or intensity of agreement with the various statements. It is this criticism that leads to the next type of scale to be considered, the Likert scale.

Likert scales. As with Thurstone scales, Likert scales involve a list of statements related to the attitude in question. Instead of checking only those statements with which they agree, however, respondents are asked to indicate the degree of agreement or disagreement with each of the statements. Each degree of agreement is given a numerical score and the respondent's total score is computed by summing these scores from all the statements. The following example on attitudes towards hot cereal will illustrate. Respondents were given a card on which the following was shown:

1. Agree very strongly
2. Agree fairly strongly
3. Agree
4. Undecided
5. Disagree
6. Disagree fairly strongly
7. Disagree very strongly
X. Don't know

The respondents were then given a list of statements about hot cereal and asked to select one of the above answers for each statement. Some of the statements were as follows:

1. Hot cereal has a taste I like.
2. Hot cereal is a mess to make.
3. Hot cereal sticks to your ribs.

---

[45] Claire Selltiz, Marie Jahoda, Morton Deutsch, and Stuart W. Cook, *Research Methods in Social Relations* (New York: Henry Holt and Co., 1959), pp. 369–70.

4. Hot cereal is expensive.
5. Hot cereal is high in vitamins.

The responses were scored from one to seven, as indicated above, except that the values were reversed for statements unfavorable to hot cereal. The sum of scores from all the statements made the total score for the respondent.

Likert scales are developed in a manner similar to that used for Thurston scales:

1. Collect a large number of statements relevant to the attitude in question which can be clearly identified as either favorable or un- favorable.
2. Select a series of responses that represent various degrees of agree- ment or disagreement. Five variations such as agree strongly, agree, undecided, disagree, and disagree strongly are often used, but vari- ous other numbers can be used. It is doubtful that respondents can make meaningful distinctions among more than seven or nine varia- tions. An odd number is usually used in order to have a middle, or zero point, but this is not necessary. If a respondent is forced to choose between a favorable or unfavorable response when he in fact has no opinion, he should pick the mildest degree of agreement and disagreement about an equal number of times.
3. Administer the collected statements to a group reasonably repre- sentative of the universe to be studied and have them check one of the classes of agreement or disagreement for each statement.
4. Compute each individual's score by summing the scores of the re- sponses to each question. The responses must be scored so that the most favorable response has the same rating for each statement. Since some statements will be favorable and some unfavorable, this will mean reversing the ratings of the responses for one of the groups of statements.
5. Eliminate those statements that do not discriminate between the high and low scorers on the total test. This can be done by selecting the high and low quartiles of respondents according to total score. Determine the average score on each statement among those in the high quartile and similarly among those in the low quartile. Those statements on which these averages differ by the largest amount are the most discriminating.

Likert scales are of the ordinal type; they enable one to rank attitudes but not to measure the difference between attitdues. They take about the same amount of effort to create as Thurstone scales and are con- sidered more discriminating and reliable because of the larger range of responses typically given in Likert scales. They have the same disadvantage as the Thurstone scales—similar scores can be achieved through varying combinations of responses. In this connection, the same argument as was presented in the discussion of Thurstone scales is pertinent to Likert scales.

Semantic differential[46]

The semantic differential has come to be used widely in marketing research. Perhaps its main use has been in connection with brand and company image studies; it permits the development of descriptive profiles that facilitate comparison of competitive items.[47] For example, the following profiles of three beer companies were developed with this technique:[48]

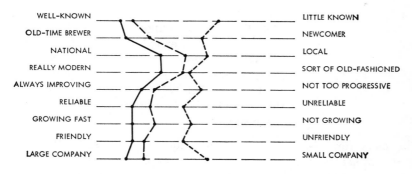

WELL-KNOWN							LITTLE KNOWN
OLD-TIME BREWER							NEWCOMER
NATIONAL							LOCAL
REALLY MODERN							SORT OF OLD-FASHIONED
ALWAYS IMPROVING							NOT TOO PROGRESSIVE
RELIABLE							UNRELIABLE
GROWING FAST							NOT GROWING
FRIENDLY							UNFRIENDLY
LARGE COMPANY							SMALL COMPANY

The unique characteristic of the semantic differential is the use of a number of bipolar scales, such as those shown above, to rate any product, company, or concept of interest. Respondents are given a group of these scales and asked to check on each one the point that indicates their opinion of the subject in question. As originally developed, each scale consisted of two opposing adjectives, such as good-bad and clean-dirty, which were separated by a continuum divided into seven segments. Each segment is assumed to represent one step in moving from the meaning of the adjective at one end to that at the other. Respondents check the segment which represents the degree of the characteristic involved which most closely coincides with their opinion of the product or other item being rated. There is no reason why the space between the opposing adjectives must be divided into seven

---

[46] C. E. Osgood, G. J. Suci, and P. H. Tannenbaum, *The Measurement of Meaning* (Urbana: University of Illinois Press, 1957).

[47] R. Gatty and C. Allais, *The Semantic Differential Applied to Image Research* (New Brunswick: Rutgers University, undated).

[48] W. A. Mindak, "Fitting the Semantic Differential to the Marketing Problem," *Journal of Marketing*, Vol. 25 (April, 1961), pp. 28–33.

segments; any number will work if it does not get so large as to represent distinctions too small to be meaningful to respondents. In one project, the entire scale was omitted and respondents were asked to pick one or the other of the polar adjectives, whichever most nearly coincided with their opinion of the subject.[49] Many researchers now use an even number of segments to force respondents to take a position. The neutral midpoint in a semantic differential seems to attract many respondents, thus resulting in nondiscriminating scores.

Although the original semantic differential scales could presumably be used for rating any item, most researchers develop their own scales for specific projects. For example, in a study to determine how people viewed a picture which was to be used in an ad, the following pairs of adjectives were used:

Rich—Poor
Intelligent—Unintelligent
Worried—Unworried
Honest—Dishonest
Healthy—Unhealthy
Likable—Unlikable
Wholesome—Unwholesome
Cheerful—Sad

The basis for selection of opposing adjectives to use is the purpose of the project at hand. In the above example, the ad was for an insurance company which was particularly concerned that the man pictured should not be thought to be worried or sad. Opposing adjectives must be such as to be readily understood as opposites by respondents.

Semantic differential scales can be used to obtain total attitude scores similar to those obtained by the Likert method. Pairs of adjectives must be selected that are relevant to the attitude to be measured. In a study to determine the relative favorability of consumer attitudes toward two brands of the same product, pairs such as fair tasting-excellent tasting, average value for money-excellent value, and very healthful-not very healthful were used.[50] The adjectives were separated by a six-segment scale; the least favorable location on each scale was given a value of 1, the next least favorable a value of 2, etc. After all the scales had been completed for each brand, these values were summed to obtain an attitude score for each brand. It should be noted that the paired adjectives in this project did not represent opposing extremes in each case. It was apparently reasoned that few people

---

[49] Louis Cheskin Associates as quoted in *Advertising Image* (Richmond: *Richmond News Leader,* 1963).

[50] William D. Barclay, "The Semantic Differential as an Index of Brand Attitude," *Journal of Advertising Research,* Vol. 4 (March, 1964), pp. 30–33.

would consider any food product on the market as less than fair tasting. The use of a total score obtained in this manner as an indication of the overall attitude toward a brand assumes that all the important factors that determine consumer attitude toward a brand have been included and that they are all of relatively equal weight. In the study cited above, a positive correlation was found between attitude scores so determined and brand purchases.

When the semantic differential is used to develop an image profile, it provides a good basis for comparing images of two or more items. When it is used as in the last example above, it is presumably serving as a scale on which some underlying attitude is measured. If it is to be used in this manner, some procedure must be inserted to sort out the nondiscriminating adjectival pairs in a manner similar to that suggested in step 5 of the Likert scale procedure.[51] The one big advantage of the semantic differential is its simplicity, while producing results comparable with those of the more complex scaling methods. The method is easy and fast to administer, but is also sensitive to small differences in attitude, highly versatile, reliable, and generally valid.[52]

Multidimensional scaling[53]

The scaling methods discussed above all enable the researcher to measure to some degree consumer attitudes towards products and brands. In general, they permit one to determine such things as that one brand is perceived by consumers as more economical than another, less glamorous, more old fashioned, and so on. Two or more brands can thus be compared on as many different characteristics as the researcher considers significant or is imaginative enough to bring into consideration. But the various brands are measured against each characteristic one at a time. The measurement process tells nothing about the relative importance of the different characteristics or how the characteristics relate to each other in reference to the various brands.

Multidimensional scaling is concerned with spatial representation of consumer perceptions and preferences. The dimensions of the "space" are "multi" in number, one for each of the significant characterics used to measure the perception or preference.

---

[51] Factor analysis has been used to find the major dimensions of the attitudes measured by the semantic differential, but this procedure is beyond the scope of this book.

[52] R. F. Carter, W. L. Ruggels, and S. H. Chaffee, "The Semantic Differential in Opinion Measurement," *Public Opinion Quarterly,* 32 (Winter, 1968–69), pp. 666–74.

[53] This discussion is based primarily on Paul E. Green and Frank J. Carmone, *Multidimensional Scaling* (Boston: Allyn and Bacon, Inc., 1970). For an interesting application see Ronald E. Turner, "Market Measures from Salesmen: A Multidimensional Scaling Approach," *Journal of Marketing Research,* 8 (May, 1971), pp. 165–72.

An example may clarify the idea. Suppose a consumer is asked to compare each of a group of cars with each of the others and to specify the two he perceives as being the most similar, the pair that is next most similar, and so on. The respondent is to use any criteria he chooses. For the following eleven cars this would mean ranking on similarity all possible 55 pairs:

1. Ford Mustang 6
2. Mercury Cougar V8
3. Lincoln Continental V8
4. Ford Thunderbird V8
5. Ford Falcon 6
6. Chrysler Imperial V8
7. Jaguar Sedan
8. AMC Javelin V8
9. Plymouth Barracuda V8
10. Buick Le Sabre V8
11. Chevrolet Corvair

This could be done by putting each of the pairs on one of 55 cards. The respondent could separate these into two groups—those that have pairs that tend to be similar and those with pairs that tend to be different. He could then take the "similar" pile and separate it into those that are very similar and those not so similar. Within one of these groups, the respondent would then choose the most similar, the next most, and so on. In this step-by-step procedure a complete ranking on similarity would eventually be obtained. One respondent came up with the results shown in Table 7–6.

Analysis of these results by multidimensional methods is at a level of sophistication beyond this book. In general, the procedure is somewhat akin to factor analysis and requires the power of a computer to be

TABLE 7–6. Pairs of cars ranked by similarity*

Car no.	1	2	3	4	5	6	7	8	9	10	11
1	—	8	50	31	12	48	36	2	5	39	10
2		—	39	9	33	37	22	6	4	14	32
3			—	11	55	1	23	46	41	17	52
4				—	44	13	16	19	25	18	42
5					—	54	53	30	28	45	7
6						—	26	47	40	24	51
7							—	29	35	34	49
8								—	3	27	15
9									—	20	21
10										—	43
11											—

* Read as follows: Pairs 3 and 6 are most similar, 3 and 5 least similar.
SOURCE: Green and Carmone, *op. cit.*, p. 33.

FIGURE 7–2. Illustration of similarities space of eleven cars

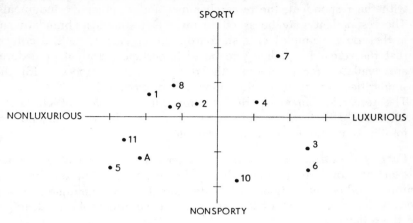

SOURCE: Green and Carmone, *op. cit.*, p. 23.

practical. Assume that the respondent had only two criteria that were important in his judgment—luxuriousness and sportiness. Figure 7–2 shows a plotting in two-dimensional space of the results of one analysis of the data in Table 7–6.

Those cars that are the closest to each other on the chart are the most similar, and those farthest away from each other are the most dissimilar in the perception of this respondent. For example, 3 and 6 (Lincoln Continental and Chrysler Imperial) are relatively similar, while 1 and 3 (Ford Mustang and Chrysler Imperial) are perceived as quite dissimilar.

Note in Figure 7–2 an additional point A has been added. This is assumed to be a point representing the ideal combination of luxuriousness and sportiness for the respondent. If the point representing Ford Falcon (#5) is closer to the ideal point A than is the point representing Jaguar (#7), we would say that individual A prefers the Ford Falcon to the Jaguar.

In the above example it was assumed that luxuriousness and sportiness were the characteristics (dimensions) of importance to the respondent. Unfortunately, these "labels" are *not* found by the analytical technique. One may well question how these "labels" are determined. This question is rendered even more difficult when it is noted that undoubtedly there are more than two criteria of significance in comparing cars, or in comparing brands of most other products. Much research is still to be done before this phase of multidimensional analysis is well established, but three different approaches, all heavily dependent on the judgment of the researcher, are used:

1. On the basis of the general pattern of the data, and perhaps discussion with the respondent, the researcher may make subjective judgments.
2. The respondent may be asked to rate each stimulus (brand of car in the above example) on a standard scale on each of several criteria that the researcher believes to be of importance. Formal procedures are available for combining the data from this process with the similarities data to determine important criteria.
3. The researcher may experiment with different levels of characteristics he believes to be important, e.g., with different horsepowers for the same car in the above example.

Uses of multidimensional scaling. There are many possible uses for this method of scaling which have already been glimpsed, but undoubtedly other applications will be developed as the technique becomes more widely used. Some of the uses which have already been identified are the following:

1. *Market segmentation.* If brands are located as points in preference-space, as in the example, and consumers are located as ideal points, market segments might then be viewed as subspaces in which consumers had similar ideal positions and perceived the brands similarly.

2. *Product life cycle.* By analyzing respondent perceptions at different times, the researcher might be able to relate movement along various dimensions (characteristics) to some measure such as market share and, thus, develop a new concept of product life cycle.

3. *Vendor evaluations.* Industrial purchasing agents must choose among vendors who differ, for example, in price, delivery, reliability, technical service, and credit. How purchasing agents summarize the various characteristics to determine a specific vendor from whom to purchase would be information that would help vendors design sales strategies.

4. *Advertising media selection.* What magazines should be used for an advertising campaign to reach a given audience? Different possible media could be identified as points in similarity-space (as were cars in the example) and members of the audience located as ideal points. This would be similar to the market segmentation process. A similar aproach might be taken to locate the best media for specific ads.

Limitations of multidimensional scaling. In the above discussion, it has been suggested that many problems remain to be solved before the apparent full potential of multidimensional scaling is achieved. Some of these problems are significant limitations in current use of the technique. One analysis of these limitations classifies them in the following three categories:

1. *Conceptual problems.* Definitions of "similarity" and "preference" that are conceptually clear and that can be communicated accurately

to respondents have not been developed and may not be achievable. Criteria on which similarities are gauged may vary during an interview with one respondent; they may vary by the context in which the respondent is thinking, such as a purchase for himself or as a gift; and small variations in one criterion may be more important than large variations in another. None of these factors is fully understood or amenable to control at present.

Current studies assume that each stimulus (brand in the example) is a first choice. If the preferred brand were not available, it is assumed the consumer would take the second choice. But what if the consumer purchases two, e.g., two cars. After the first choice has been bought, will the order of preference change for the second car?

How do preferences change over time? Do they change frequently, or are they relatively stable? The answers to these questions would have much to do with the operational use which a firm would make of a multidimensional analysis.

2. *Empirical problems.* In the discussion of the multidimensional scaling process, it was pointed out that the "labeling" of the various dimensions (criteria) of importance to respondents is subjective and, hence, open to question.

The data collection process is as open to bias in multidimensional scaling projects as in any other, but the relative impact of such biases is less well known. Procedures for collecting data and the general background conditions or "scenarios" in which a project is presented have yet to be standardized.

The example presented here was for one respondent. The problem of aggregating responses over a large group of people has not been worked out.

3. *Computational problems.* All analyses of the type discussed here require computer programs. Several different ones are used, but it is not known how, if at all, they vary in results according to variation in such inputs as number of points and experimental error.

Many researchers believe that multidimensional scaling is a powerful tool that has the potential of adding a new level of understanding of consumer behavior. The concepts and procedures involved are highly technical and complex and have not yet been fully developed. Hopefully, extensive experimentation with this new tool will make it more useful in the future.

Summary

The different types of attitude scales involve different methods of construction, different methods of response, and different methods of interpreting the results. All try to get at the same problem—measurement of an underlying attitude. For many subjects and under many circumstances, they produce similar results. None of the scaling methods, however, has been validated to the degree needed. Ranking of individuals according to a given attitude is the best that the present scaling methods can accomplish. Reliable interval and ratio scaling methods are not now available in marketing research. The semantic differential is generally the simplest of the scaling methods and produces results comparable with the more intricate methods; as a result, it is rapidly becoming a favorite in marketing research.

FORMS FOR OBSERVATIONAL STUDIES

Forms for the recording of observational data are much more simple to construct than are questionnaires. The psychological impact of the form on the source of the information does not need to be considered. All that is necessary is to develop a form which makes it simple for the field worker to record the desired information accurately, which identifies the information properly, and which makes tabulation of the results easy. Figure 7–3 is an example of a page from a form used in collecting data on retail store displays, prices, inventories, purchases, and sales of Purina Dog Food during a market test.

This page is one actually used by a field worker in collecting data in a store. The figures entered by hand were put there by the field worker. Note that a separate column is provided for each package size. Spaces are provided for each observation to be entered separately, e.g., shelf location, width of the face of the display, price, inventory, and each delivery. Calculation of net purchases, current sales, and sales last period is made in the office where the environment and equipment are available for doing an accurate job.

A good observation form permits the researcher to record individual observations, but does not force him to make a summary of his observations, which would be subject to error.

Physical layout and reproduction of observation forms should follow the same rules discussed for questionnaires.

Recording of disguised and unstructured observations is more difficult. Usually in such situations it is not feasible for the observer to record observations at the moment they are made for fear of influencing the event of interest. In a shopping observation, for example, where the observer is posing as a prospective customer in an appliance store, he can hardly stop after each exchange with the salesman to note what took place. The salesman would begin to wonder what was going on. Under such circumstances, the observation must be written up as soon after the event as possible—in the example, as soon as the customer-observer leaves the store. To help in remembering what has taken place, it is

FIGURE 7–3. Example of form for recording observational data

Item No. (11-14)	0	3	0	1	0	3	0	2	0	3	0	3	0	3	0	4								
Item Description Page 4	Purina Dry Dog Food 2 lb.				Purina Dry Dog Food 5 lb.				Purina Dry Dog Food 10 lb.				Purina Dry Dog Food 25 lb.											
Shelf Loc. (15-16)	1 of 3				1 of 3				3 of 3				3 of 3				of				of			
Inches Fac. (17-18)	2				3				2				2											
Quantity (19-20)	1				1				1				1											
For Price (21-23)	3	7	//		6	9	//		1	2	9	//	2	7	9	//			//				//	
Other Inv. (24-27)	1	2																						
Display Inv.(28-31)																								
Shelf Inv. (32-35)	2	1			4	9			2	2			1	7										
Total Inv.	3	3			4	9			2	2			1	7										
Prev. Inv. (76-80)	1	3			3	4			1	0			1	4										
Difference + -	- 2 0				- 1 5				- 1 2				- 3											
Deliveries: Date - Amount	4/15-12 / 6/22-12 / 7/6-12				6/15-20 / 6/22-20				6/15-5 / 6/22-10 / 6/27-10				6/15-4 / 6/22-10 / 6/29-10											
Product Credits																								
Net Purch. (36-39)		3	6			4	0			2	5			2	4									
Current Sales S/Days	1	6			2	5			1	3			2	1			S/Days				S/Days			
Sales Last Period (Date)		21				46				20				1 5										
Sales 2 Periods Ago (Date)																								

Courtesy: Market Facts, Inc.

useful to have an outline of the desired observations in mind before undertaking the actual observations. The observer might have in mind to note: (1) the salesman's opening; (2) the number of sales points made; (3) if certain major sales appeals were brought up; (4) the method of handling selected objections; (5) the salesman's understanding of the mechanics of the product; (6) how the question of price was handled; and (7) how the salesman attempted to close the sale. With these as a framework for observation, the observer would be able to recall what occurred if he recorded it immediately. In some cases, it may be possible to record some of the observations by checking items on a list, e.g., did salesman demonstrate the automatic ice cube maker; did salesman volunteer price?

Mechanical recording of observations is accomplished in some cases by such devices as the Nielsen audimeter or the eye camera. Moving pictures are used to record consumer action in such shopping activities as picking products from supermarket shelves. These mechanical methods give accurate records of the factors recorded, but the factors may be limited to only part of the total activity.

Case 7—1. OUTBOARD MOTORS, INC. (A)

Outboard Motors, Inc., one of the leading manufacturers of outboard motors, used boat shows as one of its major methods of promoting its motors to retail dealers. At one time there had been only two significant annual boat shows in the country, one in New York and one in Chicago. With the growth of boating as a recreation following World War II, the number of shows increased rapidly. In the past year, Outboard Motors had displayed its product line at 26 different shows, and company executives were aware of a number of other shows at which they had not been represented.

The typical boat show was a promotional device for attracting consumers to look at the items offered by the boating industry. Manufacturers of motors, boats, boat trailers, and miscellaneous boating items such as life jackets and horns displayed their new models at the annual shows. Pretty girls and entertainment features were often added to attract a larger crowd.

For a day or two prior to the opening of the larger shows in the major cities, the shows were open only to marine retailers. At this time the retailers looked over what the manufacturers were offering and often placed orders. Most retailers handled only one brand of motors and the boat shows were an occasion at which each manufacturer would try to secure new dealers. At the smaller boat shows, the trade activities took place while consumers were also attending the shows.

Outboard Motors had tried for a number of years to display its line at each significant boat show and to compete aggressively at these shows for new dealers. As the number of shows increased, this became more and more expensive, and in the past year Outboard had spent over $400,000 on such shows. Executives in the firm had different opinions as to the value of the shows. To get some added information with which to review the existing policy, it was proposed that a telephone survey be made among a sample of 50 retailers handling all brands of motors. The following information was to be obtained:

I. What boat shows, if any, has the retailer (or his representative) attended in the last three years?
   A. Name of the shows
   B. Location of shows
   C. Dates of shows
   D. Who in the firm attended
   E. Reasons for attending
      1. Buy merchandise
      2. See new models
      3. Appraise competition
      4. See friends
      5. Obtain a new franchise
         a. Motors
         b. Boats

      c. Trailers

      d. Other

    6. Get general industry information

    7. Talk with manufacturer

    8. Exhibit for self or for manufacturer

  F. Were any of objectives in E accomplished

  G. Rate each show attended on scale from important to unimportant

  H. Did family attend with individual

II. What changes would
he like to see in shows

  A. Number of shows

  B. Dates of shows

  C. Length of shows

  D. Trade only versus trade and consumers

  E. Other changes

III. Classify dealers by:

  A. Annual dollar volume in total sales

  B. Type of dealer

  C. Motor volume

  D. Marine lines carried

    1. Motors

    2. Boats

    3. Trailers

    4. Accessories

  E. Location

Design the questionnaire for the above information.

Case 7—2.   FOSTER, HARKWELL & BEHL, INC.

The Foster, Harkwell & Behl advertising agency had received an invitation to solicit the Big-Value Apple Juice Company's advertising account. Initially this company had considered eight agencies but, from conversations held with the principals of these eight, a committee had eliminated four of the agencies. Each of the four remaining agencies had been asked to present their advertising recommendations to the agency selection committee. One of the four had declined this invitation, thereby leaving three in final contention for the Big-Value account, which billed approximately $200,000.

Mr. James, vice president in charge of new business for the Foster, Harkwell & Behl agency, felt strongly that his agency's presentation should not only include a copy platform but specific ads as well. He said, "This is the best way I know of to show this prospective client

just exactly what we have to offer. We can say we're good, we can tell
him about all the clients we've got, and we can even give them a copy
platform in generalized terms. But if we give them some really good
ads, then we'll get the account."

A copywriter was assigned to work with Mr. James to develop the
appeals to be used in the advertising copy. They reviewed the prospective
client's past and present advertising and the advertising being done by
competitors. They went out to supermarkets and talked to women about
apple juice, and they talked to two food economists. They were not,
however, able to come up with what they considered adequate and
stimulating appeals to use in their advertising copy. Mr. James then
turned to the marketing research department for help. Specifically, he
requested the marketing research director to conduct a study among
housewives to try to get answers to the following:

1. The relative popularity of clear vs. pureed apple juice.
2. The average number of bottles purchased per month per family.
3. What benefits housewives expected from drinking apple juice.
4. How and when apple juice is served.
5. Which members of the family do not drink it and why.
6. How housewives rank apple juice in competition with other canned
   or bottled fruit juices with regard to taste, flavor, and healthfulness.

The research director turned this assignment over to one of the analysts
in his department. Several days later the analyst presented the research
director with his plan for accomplishing the study. Because of the problem
of locating users, he recommended that all interviewing be done in
grocery stores near the fruit juice shelves. Interviews were to be made
with women who bought apple juice in that store or with women who
recalled having bought apple juice within the past two weeks. He had
selected ten supermarkets scattered throughout the city and suburbs,
which he felt catered to different income groups. He planned to interview
twenty women in each for a total of 200. He had prepared and pretested
a questionnaire which he submitted for clearance. The research director
agreed with the survey design and questionnaire, and cleared the proposal. The questionnaire used in making the study appears as Exhibit 1.

Approximately two weeks later the analyst presented the detailed
findings in tabular form to Mr. James and the copywriter. Each of the
tables was discussed in some detail, and following this meeting Mr.
James asked the research analyst to prepare the summary of findings
which appears below.

SUMMARY OF FINDINGS

1. There is a clear-cut preference for the clear type apple juice, based
on brands purchased.

2. The average number of bottles of apple juice purchased per month by users is approximately two, and these women have been buying apple juice for an average of two years.

3. When asked what benefits they expect from drinking apple juice, almost 20 percent said it acts as a laxative; the remainder of the answers were concerned with "healthfulness."

4. In about 65 percent of the families using apple juice, it is served at one of the meals, with breakfast accounting for 45 percent of this total. Almost as many serve it between meals (56 percent), and 10 percent serve it as a cocktail before dinner. Obviously, apple juice is not a one-function beverage. Eight-five percent serve it cold or chilled, 13 percent at room temperature, and the remainder serve it both ways. Only about 5 percent of these users dilute apple juice with water.

5. Women comprise the largest group of nondrinkers: 12 percent of the wives and 15 percent of the other females. Only 7 percent of the husbands, 3 percent of the girls, and none of the boys are nondrinkers of this juice.

6. With regard to taste and/or flavor, it was found that apple juice ranks a very strong second, with a weighted preference rating of 30 percent as contrasted with 31 percent for pineapple juice, 16 percent for orange juice, and 8 percent for grapefruit juice. In regard to healthfulness, apple juice ranks first, with 33 percent of the votes. Orange juice is a close second, with 25 percent, followed by grapefruit juice with 12 percent.

1. Is the questionnaire constructed in the most effective form?

2. Could the findings summarized in the case have been drawn from data obtained with this questionnaire?

EXHIBIT 1. Apple juice user questionnaire

1. What brand of apple juice did you buy then? _____
   What type is it, clear _____ or pureed _____?
2. Do you buy this brand regularly?   Yes ☐   No ☐
   a. (IF YES) How many bottles/cans do you buy per month? _____
   b. (IF NO) What is the name of your regular brand? _____
      What type is it, clear ☐ or pureed ☐?
      How many bottles/cans do you buy per month? _____
3. How long have you been buying apple juice? _____
4. What benefits do you think you get from drinking apple juice? _____
   _____

5. How do you serve apple juice to your family?
   a. Cold ☐ or at room temperature ☐?
   b. As it comes in the bottle/can ☐ or diluted ☐?
      (IF DILUTED) With what do you dilute it? _____
      Why do you dilute it? _____
      _____

   c. Other methods of serving it? _____

EXHIBIT 1 (*Continued*)

6. When do you serve apple juice to your family?
    a. Breakfast ☐
    b. Lunch ☐
    c. Dinner ☐
    d. Between meals ☐
    e. At bedtime ☐
    f. Other answers: _____

7. What members of your family drink apple juice?

	Do	*Don't*
Husband	☐	☐
Wife	☐	☐
Ages of boys		
_____	☐	☐
_____	☐	☐
_____	☐	☐
Ages of girls		
_____	☐	☐
_____	☐	☐
_____	☐	☐
Others _____	_____	

8. Which members of your family *do not* drink apple juice? (SEE DON'T ABOVE.) What are the reasons they do not drink apple juice? _____

9. Do you serve your family other kinds of canned or bottled fruit juices?   Yes ☐
   No ☐
   (IF YES) What kinds of fruit juices? _____ _____
   _____ _____ _____ _____

10. Do you serve any of these more often than apple juice?   Yes ☐   No ☐
    Which ones? _____ _____ _____
    Why? _____

11. How would you rank these canned or bottled fruit juices, according to: (SHOW CARD TO RESPONDENT)

Taste/Flavor		*Healthfulness*	
Orange juice	☐	Orange juice	☐
Prune juice	☐	Prune juice	☐
Grapefruit juice	☐	Grapefruit juice	☐
Lemon juice	☐	Lemon juice	☐
Pineapple juice	☐	Pineapple juice	☐
Apple juice	☐	Apple juice	☐
Grape juice	☐	Grape juice	☐
Orange and grapefruit juice	☐	Orange and grapefruit juice	☐

NAME_____DATE_____

ADDRESS_____PLACE_____

CITY_____STATE_____INTERVIEWER_____

Case 7—3.   NORTHWEST PETROLEUM COMPANY

Northwest Petroleum Company was one of the large advertisers in the United States and, as such, had for many years been concerned with the virtual impossibility of measuring the effectiveness of its advertising. The management was particularly frustrated with the problem of deciding whether or not a particular advertising campaign should be run. The advertising agency would present a proposed campaign to the firm's executive committee for approval and the executives realized that their approval or disapproval was based primarily on whether the campaign in question appealed to them personally or not. While the agency often presented research data on the ability of certain ads to catch consumer attention, the sales points remembered by consumers who read the ads, and consumer preferences among different ads, the Northwest executives did not believe these data indicated the real sales effectiveness of the ads.

To get a new approach to this problem of predicting advertising effectiveness in advance, Northwest retained a psychology professor from a nearby university as a consultant. After some study, the consultant suggested that, since one of the main objectives of advertising was to create a favorable attitude towards a product, an effort should be made to develop an instrument for measuring small changes in attitude. If such an instrument could be devised, it could be used to measure changes in attitude resulting from exposure to proposed ads.

As a first step in developing a measuring scale for attitudes toward brands of gasoline, the consultant developed a list of statements that might be made about a gasoline—some of them favorable in various degrees and some unfavorable. An effort was made to make the statements clear and simple and to have each statement relate to one idea only. The following are examples:

"This is the finest gasoline made."
"I have confidence in this gasoline."
"This gasoline will ruin your engine."

When he had obtained a list of about 150 statements about gasoline, the consultant listed them in random order and set up an eleven-point scale of favorability on which each statement was to be rated. Point number one on the scale indicated extreme unfavorability; number 6 was neutral, i.e., neither favorable nor unfavorable; and number 11 was extreme favorability. One hundred adults selected on a convenience basis by ten interviewers in the city where Northwest's home office was located were asked to rate each of the 150 statements on the eleven-point scale. Respondents were told to check one of the eleven points on the scale for each statement; the point checked was to indicate the degree of favorability of the statement, not the respondent's acceptance or rejection of the statement.

Median ratings and interquartile ranges were computed for each statement. All statements for which the interquartile range was more than two were eliminated. Others were eliminated if they had a significant number of extreme variations in the ratings or if the ratings did not tend to a bell-shaped distribution. Only thirty-five statements were left after the above process. These statements were then classified as having favorability-scale values from one to eleven, depending on the location of the median rating. The thirty-five statements were then placed in random order and another convenience sample of 100 asked to check the degree of agreement with each statement as it pertained to the Northwest brand of gasoline. Five alternatives were offered: agree strongly, agree, neither agree nor disagree, disagree, and disagree strongly. For those statements that had been classified on the favorability scale between one and five, i.e., as unfavorable statements, weights for degree of agreement were assigned as follows:

Degree of agreement	Weight
Agree strongly	1
Agree	2
Neither agree nor disagree	3
Disagree	4
Disagree strongly	5

For those statements that had been classified on the favorability scale between six and eleven, i.e., as neutral or favorable statements, weights for degree of agreement were assigned as follows:

Degree of agreement	Weight
Disagree strongly	1
Disagree	2
Neither agree nor disagree	3
Agree	4
Agree strongly	5

To compute the attitude of each respondent towards Northwest gasoline, a score was computed for each statement and then the scores for all thirty-five statements added. Computations were made as follows:

1. The statement, "This is the finest gasoline made," had a favorability-scale value of 11—the most favorable possible value.
2. Suppose one respondent checked the degree of agreement with this statement as "agree." For a statement with a favorability-scale value of six, or more, this degree of agreement had a weight of four.
3. Multiplying the favorability-scale value (11) by the degree of agreement weight (4) gave a score of 44 for that statement.
4. Similar scores were computed for all thirty-five statements and added to give the total score for the respondent.

Total scores varied from 422 to 810. Respondents were divided into upper, middle, and lower thirds on the basis of these scores. The average score for each statement was then computed separately for each of these three groups. Those respondents in the "upper" group were assumed to be the most favorable to Northwest brand gasoline; therefore, their average score on any statement should be higher than the average of the respondents in the "middle" group, and the middle group should have a higher average score than the respondents in the "lower" group. If respondents in one group averaged higher scores on a particular statement than did respondents in a group higher by total score, it was assumed that the particular statement was not a valid measuring device for attitude toward brands of gasoline. On this basis twelve more statements were eliminated, leaving twenty-three which were used as a final scale for measuring attitudes towards gasoline brands. The statements with their scale values were as follows:

Scale value	Statement
1	No one in his right mind would want this gas.
1	This gasoline will ruin your engine.
2	At the same price there are at least a dozen other gasolines I'd prefer.
2	Anyone who really cares about his car wouldn't use it.
3	I'd drive past a station with this gasoline to get another.
3	I doubt that it is the best buy.
4	It's not as good as the company claims.
4	They should be required to have some independent laboratory test this brand.
5	There's something about it I don't care for.
6	All gasolines have the same chemical makeup.
7	It's all right.
7	This is a friendly company.
7	I would like to try this brand.
8	This gasoline is made with the newest formula.
8	The people selling this gasoline know their business.
9	It rates pretty high with me.
9	This gasoline is efficient.
9	This gasoline gives excellent performance.
10	Everything that can be done to make a gas good has been done to this one.
11	Money can't buy a better gasoline.
11	This is the finest gasoline made.
11	I prefer this to other brands no matter what the price.

Working with Northwest's marketing research department, the consultant hypothesized that those people who bought a particular brand of gasoline should have more favorable attitudes toward that brand, regardless of which brand it was, than others who did not use the brand. A second hypothesis was that, in the city at large, the attitude scores toward all brands sold in the city would be in order of each brand's share of the market. These hypotheses were used as a basis for testing the overall validity of the attitude scales; it was assumed that, if the attitudes measured confirmed the hypotheses, this would show the scale was a valid measuring instrument. Tests were then conducted and the results supported both hypotheses except that one brand failed to fit the second hypothesis. The third ranking brand of the city was a cut-price gasoline; it ranked sixth on the attitude scale among ten brands tested. (See Exhibit 1 for scale as used in these tests.)

A third hypothesis was that exposure to a "good" ad for a gasoline would raise the attitude toward that brand among those so exposed. To test this hypothesis, the consultant asked students in his classes at the university to volunteer for an experiment. Those that volunteered were numbered serially; the odd numbers were told to report to one room at the given time and the even numbers were told to report to another room. Actually thirty-four reported to one room and thirty-seven to the other. In the room with thirty-seven, the students were asked to complete the attitude scale which had previously been used among the general population. In the other room, the students were shown a movie which was really a one-minute TV commercial for Northwest gasoline. No explanation was made except that they were asked to watch "this short movie" and then to complete the questionnaire. The questionnaire was not handed out until after the "movie." In both rooms, the students were asked not to talk with each other and this request was observed. The scores from the two groups are shown in Table 1.

TABLE 1. Scores on attitude scale for students exposed to TV commercial and for students not exposed

Students exposed to commercial		Students not exposed to commercial	
483	411	430	422
416	455	393	389
446	404	410	462
388	490	448	447
417	415	325	524
436	365	450	423
488	381	380	336
407	395	420	397
450	468	444	463
467	434	412	420
459	384	442	377
455	377	427	361
478	403	429	314
382	343	448	
392	406	423	426
438	438	427	399
475	403	458	440
		482	497
		366	467
Total students ..	34	Total students ..	37
Total score	14,449	Total score	15,578
Average score ..	420.8	Average score ..	424.7

1. Does the scaling procedure have enough promise to warrant further financial support by Northwest Petroleum Company?
2. What are the limitations of this scaling method?
3. Are there any ways in which the procedure could be improved?

EXHIBIT 1. Scale for measuring attitudes towards gasolines
In this list, you will probably agree with some statements and not agree with others as far as the brand of gasoline shown is concerned. Will you check the square after each statement that best indicates the degree to which you agree or disagree with that statement for this particular brand of gasoline.

Brand—Northwest

Statement	Agree strongly	Agree	Neither agree nor disagree	Disagree	Disagree strongly
1. No one in his right mind would want this gas.					
2. Everything that can be done to make a gas good has been done to this one.					
3. It rates pretty high with me.					
4. It's not as good as the company claims.					
5. This gasoline will ruin your engine.					
6. Money can't buy a better gasoline.					
7. All gasolines have the same chemical makeup.					
8. I have confidence in this gasoline.					
9. At the same price there are at least a dozen other gasolines I'd prefer.					
10. This gasoline is made with the newest formula.					
11. I'd drive past a station with this gasoline to get to another.					
12. I doubt that it is the best buy.					

EXHIBIT 1 (*Continued*)

Statement	Agree strongly	Agree	Neither agree nor disagree	Disagree	Disagree strongly
13. I prefer this to other brands no matter what the price.					
14. It's all right.					
15. This gasoline gives excellent performance.					
16. Anyone who really cares about his car wouldn't use it.					
17. This gasoline is efficient.					
18. The people selling this gasoline know their business.					
19. This is a friendly company.					
20. They should be required to have some independent laboratory test this brand.					
21. I would like to try this brand.					
22. There's something about it I don't care for.					
23. This is the finest gasoline made.					

Case 7—4. DEAN MILK COMPANY

The Dean Milk Company of Chicago, Illinois, was one of the largest dairies in that region. It sold a complete line of dairy products in the Chicago area and in a three-state area surrounding Chicago. Although the firm sold a small amount of milk through a regular home delivery service, the bulk of its sales were to retail stores. In retail stores it was the leading dairy brand in the area. Dean products were all sold under the Dean brand name. Dean's milk accounted for about 10 percent of all milk sold in the Chicago metropolitan area. Other Dean products such as cottage cheese and ice cream maintained considerably larger brand shares—most of them having between 20 and 30 percent of their markets.

Dean had been a consistent advertiser in local newspapers and on radio and TV for a long period of time; in fact, it was the largest such advertiser among dairies in the Chicago area. Since milk accounted for more than half of the firm's sales, the bulk of the advertising was devoted to featuring Dean Milk. Some of each year's budget, however, was given to the related products. While looking at the market share figures one day, one of the Dean executives was again impressed with the fact that the company's market share was considerably larger for the related products than it was for the basic product, milk. This suggested to him that it might be advisable to concentrate the advertising program on cottage cheese, ice cream, yogurt, whipping cream, and other such products. Customers who bought these secondary products might then switch to Dean milk.

Such an advertising approach would be new for the dairy industry, as it was standard practice to feature milk in the hope that the other products would "ride on milk's coattails." The new plan, however, had some logic to it. The market share figures suggested that Dean's secondary products ranked higher relative to competitive products than did Dean milk. This suggested that consumers generally liked these products and could be induced to buy them and to continue to buy them. The management believed that, if consumers once became sold on Dean products, of whatever type, it was likely they would begin to use other Dean products until they were relying on Dean for most of their dairy needs.

Before deciding to use the new idea for their advertising program, the Dean executives decided to make a market study. It was proposed that an observer be stationed in a sample of stores throughout the Chicago area where Dean milk was sold. The observer would station herself near the check-out counter and would observe customers as they were having their purchases checked before leaving the store. The observer was to note what dairy products the customer had purchased and which brand of each product. The products to be checked included milk, cream, whipping cream, ice cream, sour cream, cottage cheese, yogurt, and a low fat content milk.

Another study was to be made among a representative sample of housewives in their homes. This study was to be made with a questionnaire which was to obtain the following items of information:

1. Whether milk was bought at a retail store or was delivered to the home.
2. What brand of milk was used, regardless of how purchased.
3. What brand of other dairy products was used—cream, whipping cream, ice cream, cottage cheese, yogurt, and low fat content milk.

4. If two or more Dean brand items were purchased, which of these was bought first; that is, historically, which of the products had the family first tried in the Dean brand.

Prepare a form for collecting the observation data and a questionnaire form for the survey.

8

Introduction to sampling

SAMPLING is a commonplace idea. Everyone is accustomed to drawing conclusions about a large group on the basis of a small sample. For example, we test the warmth of our coffee by taking a sip or we decide if we want to read a book by scanning paragraphs here and there throughout the book. Almost every day newspapers report the results of studies in which public opinion on some question is estimated by collecting opinions from a few selected individuals. Much marketing information is obtained in a similar manner, i.e., through the use of samples. It is important, therefore, that the student of marketing research understand the advantages and limitations of collecting data through samples. This discussion of sampling will be limited to an examination of basic concepts. The reader is assumed to have only a limited knowledge of mathematics.[1]

Lower cost is the major reason why data are collected by sampling in place of complete enumerations. However, samples possess other advantages. For example, to make a census of all housewives in the United States it would be necessary to recruit, train, and supervise a very large number of field enumerators if the work were to be completed within a reasonable period of time. This would be a difficult administrative

---

[1] The reader who is interested in more technical discussions of sampling is referred to the following: W. G. Cochran, *Sampling Techniques* (New York: John Wiley & Sons, 1963); W. E. Deming, *Sample Design in Business Research* (New York: John Wiley & Sons, 1960); M. H. Hansen, *et al., Sample Survey Methods and Theory,* Vols. I and II (New York: John Wiley & Sons, 1953); P. V. Sukhatme, *Sampling Theory of Surveys with Applications* (Ames, Iowa: Iowa State College Press, 1954); F. Yates, *Sampling Methods for Censuses and Surveys* (London: Charles Griffin and Company, Ltd., 1960); and Leslie Kish, *Survey Sampling* (New York: John Wiley & Sons, 1965).

task. A sample would require fewer field workers. Therefore, better personnel could be selected and trained, and their work could be more closely supervised.

These considerations are nonstatistical in character. They are important, however, because in practice the researcher is *not* concerned exclusively with the problem of sampling per se. He is concerned with the total research process instead of any particular aspect. He may find, for example, that the lesser administrative problems encountered in collecting data from a sample lead to more accurate data than could be obtained by collecting data from all units. The procedure which leads to the greatest accuracy in the final data is the procedure desired.

Confusion between sampling errors and data collection errors

Any data collected from a sample or from all units in the group under study are a function of two factors, the "underlying reality" and the method used to collect the data. The researcher is interested in estimating this "underlying reality"; therefore, he must be aware of the possible errors in his data collection method. When data are collected from a sample, an additional source of error is introduced—that of sampling. In sampling studies these factors are often confused. If the results of a sampling study are found to be incorrect, the tendency is to assume that the sample was in error. Actually, the method of collecting data from the sample might have been inaccurate, or both factors may have been involved. For example, assume the problem of finding the percentage of households in Denver, Colorado owning a television set. If a count of all households were made, an incorrect answer might still be obtained because the method of determining whether the household owned a TV set might be inaccurate. If only a sample of households was studied, the inaccurate method of measuring TV ownership would still be present but, in addition, there would be error because the sample would not be exactly representative of the universe. Both of these two types of error —the sampling error and the data collection error—must be considered in designing a research project. The following discussion of sampling deals primarily with sampling error. The reader must keep in mind that the final choice of sampling method will involve consideration of the nonsampling factors as well.

BASIC SAMPLING PROBLEMS

Definition of the universe being studied

The first problem in any sampling operation is to define the universe, or population, being studied.[2] The universe is the entire group of items

---

[2] Some statisticians make a distinction between the terms *universe* and *population*. In this book the terms are used synonymously.

which the researcher wishes to study and about which he plans to generalize. For a given project, the universe might consist of all house-wives over forty years of age residing in the United States, all drug-stores east of the Mississippi River, all families within the corporate limits of the city of Chicago, or all grocery stores in the New York metropolitan area. Thus, the definition of the universe, in any particular case, is determined solely by the research objectives of the particular study.

Many decisions usually must be made if the universe (or population) is to be sharply defined. For example, to define the universe of grocery stores located in the New York metropolitan area, such questions as the following must be answered: What is a grocery store? Are both chains and independents to be considered? Are stores which sell primarily cooked foods(delicatessens) to be considered? What point or period of time is involved? Exactly what geographical area is to be considered? This problem of defining the universe is not unique to sampling inves-tigations; it is also present when a complete enumeration is planned.

Definition of the variables being studied

The second problem to consider is the definition of the variables to be studied. For example, assume a bottler wishes to determine whether New York metropolitan area grocery stores stock a particular brand of soft drink. In this case, only one variable is being studied and it may be given a strict definition—a store either has the drink in stock or it does not. It is easy to imagine an investigator determining the presence or absence of the particular brand with a high degree of accuracy for every grocery store in the defined universe.

In practice one often studies universe characteristics which are less sharply defined and, therefore, are difficult to measure accurately. For example, it is difficult to define precisely the attitude of housewives to-ward home permanents. Since this attitude is difficult to define, it is difficult to measure, because it is not exactly clear what one is trying to measure. This problem of "variable definition" is also present when a complete census is planned.

Sample design

Sample design is the third question raised in any sampling operation. This subject may be divided into: (1) determining sampling units, (2) selecting the sample items and determining sample size, and (3) esti-mating universe characteristics from sample data.

The sampling section of this book will be devoted to an examination of these topics, with particular emphasis on methods of sample selec-tion.

Choice of sampling unit.   Consider the problem of finding the proportion of grocery stores in the New York metropolitan area which stock Pepsi-Cola. Here grocery stores would be the units observed and, therefore, it would be reasonable to consider a *direct* sampling procedure. Given a list of all New York metropolitan area grocery stores, it would be relatively easy to choose a sample. If no such list were available, however, it would be necessary to resort to some *indirect* method of sampling stores. One might, for example, choose a sample of areas (such as city blocks) and observe all, or a specific fraction, of the grocery stores located in the chosen blocks. Thus, where a list of the units to be studied is not available, sampling units (such as blocks) which are not coextensive with the particular units being studied (such as stores), but for which a list does exist, can be used. This method will be discussed in some detail in the section on area sampling.

Selecting the sample.   Another part of the sample design problem is the method of choosing the sample items. Two general classes of methods exist for selecting samples: probability methods and non-probability methods. *Probability sampling methods* are those in which every item in the universe (for example, every grocery store in the New York metropolitan area) has a known chance, or probability, of being chosen for the sample. This implies that the selection of sample items is *independent* of the person making the study, that is, the sampling operation is controlled objectively so that the items will be chosen strictly at random. *Nonprobability sampling methods* are those which *do not* provide every item in the universe with a known chance of being included in the sample. The selection process is, at least partially, subjective. Someone, usually a field worker, decides what items to interview or observe.

The Pepsi-Cola distribution example provides an illustration of each of these two general classes of sampling methods.

1. *A probability sampling method.*   From a list of all New York metropolitan area grocery stores, select a sample of fifty stores at random, i.e., in such a way as to give each store an equal chance of being selected.[3] Field workers visit all fifty stores and observe whether Pepsi-Cola is in stock.

2. *A nonprobability sampling method.*   Each of ten New York metropolitan area field workers visits five "average" grocery stores near her home, and observes whether Pepsi-Cola is in stock.

Each method will provide a sample of fifty stores. The first method will cost more because the sample stores will likely be distributed throughout the New York area. The use of such a method, however,

---

[3] This makes the selection of a random sample sound deceptively easy. Actually, it is necessary to establish a formal procedure to insure that the selection is really random. This will be discussed in some detail later in this section.

would guarantee that every store had an equal chance of being included in the sample. The second method of sample selection would cost less, since the stores would be near the observers' homes and the observers would not spend as much time traveling among them. But there is no rigorous way of determining whether the sample is representative of all the stores in the New York area.

In this book, the major emphasis will be placed on methods of probability sampling. One cannot think intelligently about nonprobability samples without using probability sampling theory as a reference point. However, several nonprobability sampling techniques are widely used in marketing research. They will be discussed in a later section.

Estimating universe characteristics from sample data. Marketing researchers are usually interested in summary numbers which describe particular properties of a given universe, for example, the arithmetic mean or the percentage of observations which show a given characteristic. In practice the researcher does not usually know these summary values for the universe. He estimates them by measuring the given characteristics in a sample. Thus, the researcher is forced to rely on *estimates* of the universe values, which will generally be different from the true universe values. It is important to note that any universe value (e.g., mean or percentage) is a fixed number—even though generally it is not known. In contrast, the estimate of the universe value obtained from a sample will vary from one sample to the next. Thus, if a researcher were to take one hundred independently selected samples of X items, each from the same universe, he would expect to obtain a different sample mean or percentage each time—even though there was only one real universe mean or percentage.

As an example consider the universe that exists when all face cards are removed from an ordinary deck of fifty-two playing cards. Such a universe contains forty items. Each element of such a universe can be classified in three ways: numerical value, suit, and color. Some characteristics of this universe are:

1. The arithmetic mean (5.5).
2. The proportion of cards represented by any suit (0.25).
3. The proportion of red cards (0.50).

It must be emphasized that in the usual marketing study the researcher does not know the value of the characteristics of the universe with which he is dealing. It will help develop the reader's understanding of the behavior of sample values, however, to consider samples drawn from a universe for which he knows the true values.

From the universe of forty cards described above, fifty independent random samples of five cards each were drawn. After each sample was selected, those five cards were replaced in the universe of forty before the next sample was selected.

For each of these fifty samples, the proportion of red cards was determined. This proportion was taken to be an estimate of the proportion of red cards in the universe (which was known to be 0.50). In each sample this proportion could take any one of six values; .00, 0.20, 0.40, 0.60, 0.80, or 1.00. The results of this experimental sampling from a known universe are given in Table 8–1.

TABLE 8–1. Distribution of 50 sample proportions taken from samples of 5 cards each (universe proportion of red cards = 0.50)

Sample proportion of red cards	Number of times proportion occurred
0.00 (all black)	2
0.20 (1 red, 4 black)	3
0.40 (2 red, 3 black)	14
0.60 (3 red, 2 black)	21
0.80 (4 red, 1 black)	8
1.00 (all red)	2
Total	50

A first observation that can be made about these data is an obvious one: *all samples do not lead to the same estimate of the universe value.* In this case, sample estimates of the proportion of red cards varied from 0.00 to 1.00, when in fact the universe proportion was 0.50. Unless all items in a universe are identical, different samples may lead to different estimates. That some sample estimates differ in extreme fashion from the universe value being estimated (in the above illustration the 0.00 and 1.00 values are examples) is an inevitable consequence of sampling. It is the price which must be paid for generalizing about a universe characteristic on the basis of a sample.

A second observation from the example is that *most of the estimates tend to cluster around the true universe proportion of red cards.* It is this property which gives faith in sampling. Unless there were some reason for believing that a sample estimate would ordinarily be close to the true value, there would be little point in using samples. Actually, there is no objective basis for supposing that this will happen unless probability sampling methods are used in selecting the items for the sample. In the above example, of course, it is possible to verify the existence of this tendency for the sample estimates to cluster around the universe value. But, in general, the universe value is unknown and, therefore, it is impossible to verify directly that a sampling process gives estimates which are close to the true value.

It should be emphasized that the sampling illustration presented above is artificial in other respects besides the fact that the universe value being estimated is known. Under practical research conditions, the universe would ordinarily consist of more than forty items; usually only one sample is chosen; and the sample generally consists of more than five items. Nevertheless, the experiment demonstrates in rough terms some of the main features of the sampling process.

SIMPLE RANDOM SAMPLING—SAMPLE SELECTION

Probability sampling is the *only* sampling technique available which will provide an objective measure of the reliability of the sample estimate. The simplest possible probability sampling method is called *simple random sampling*—or unrestricted random sampling. Simple random sampling is a special case of probability sampling. In probability sampling, every possible sample of a given size drawn from a specified universe has a known chance of being selected. In simple random sampling, every possible sample has a *known and equal* chance of being selected.

Simple random sampling is considered in some detail for two reasons:

1. It is the easiest probability sampling method to understand. Therefore, it will serve as a vehicle for introducing some of the more complicated ideas involved in drawing inferences from samples.
2. It serves as a good approximation to some of the more complex sampling methods used in practice, many of which are elaborations of simple random sampling.

What is a simple random sample?

Assume a universe for which there is a list identifying each item in the universe. How can one select a simple random sample from such a universe? The sample must be selected in such a way that every possible sample has an equal chance of being picked.

It may be helpful if this general problem is translated into a concrete, though oversimplified, situation. Consider a universe composed of six housewives. A simple random sample of two housewives is to be chosen from the universe. If the six housewives are identified by the letters *A*, *B*, *C*, *D*, *E*, *F*, the fifteen possible samples of two each which can be drawn from such a universe are:

Sample	Housewives in sample	Sample	Housewives in sample	Sample	Housewives in sample
1.........*AB*		6.........*BC*		11.........*CE*	
2.........*AC*		7.........*BD*		12.........*CF*	
3.........*AD*		8.........*BE*		13.........*DE*	
4.........*AE*		9.........*BF*		14.........*DF*	
5.........*AF*		10.........*CD*		15.........*EF*	

By definition, if a simple random sample of two is to be selected, each of these fifteen possible samples must have the same chance of being selected. Of course, only one sample will be chosen at a particular time. How can one sample be selected so that "each possible sample has the same chance of being chosen"? Suppose that in the example being considered a very large number of independent samples of two housewives each (say several thousand) were drawn from the universe of six housewives. If each of the fifteen possible samples turned up with approximately equal frequency, it would seem logical to conclude that the sampling had been done in such a way that every possible sample had the same chance of being chosen. This will be used as an operational definition of the expression: "Each possible sample has an equal chance of being chosen." It follows that simple random sampling is a procedure whereby, if a large number of samples were drawn, *each individual item* in the universe would be represented equally often.

So much for the meaning of "simple random sample." The term applies only to the method of selecting the sample—not to the characteristics of the sample actually obtained. Strictly speaking, there is no such thing as a "simple random sample," but only a sample derived by a simple random sampling method. Remarks of this kind apply with equal force to probability sampling in general. There is no such thing as a "probability sample," but there are samples selected by probability sampling techniques. For simplicity, however, the terms "simple random sample" and "probability sample" will be used. The reader must keep in mind exactly what is meant.

Basic techniques for selecting a simple random sample

How can one select a simple random sample? Some technique is needed which will, in repeated sampling, insure that every item in the universe will have an equal chance of being included in the sample.

Selecting from list of all possible samples. One method which meets this requirement for the housewife example is this:

1. Number fifteen poker chips serially from one to fifteen, one number corresponding to each possible sample.
2. Place the chips in a bowl and mix thoroughly.
3. Make a "blind" drawing of one chip and select as the sample the pair of housewives corresponding to the number on the selected chip. If this procedure were repeated a large number of times, each time replacing the chip before the next draw and mixing the chips thoroughly, then each possible sample would tend to occur with the same frequency.

Selecting sample items one at a time. In practical work it is usually impossible to make direct use of the method given above. However, use is made of methods which are equivalent in theory to this process. One modification is to select sample items individually from the universe instead of choosing the entire sample in one draw. In the housewife illustration this could be done as follows:

1. Number six poker chips serially from one to six, one number corresponding to each of the universe items, *A* through *F*.
2. Mix the chips thoroughly in a bowl and choose one "blindly." The housewife corresponding to that chip will be one of the two sample housewives.
3. Mix the remaining five chips thoroughly (*without* replacing the chip chosen in step 2) and select another chip by a "blind" drawing. The housewife chosen this time will complete the sample of two housewives.

Ordinarily it is more convenient to choose sample items one at a time instead of picking the entire sample at one draw. This will become obvious if one considers the very large number of possible samples, often in the millions, which may arise in a practical situation. Using the technique of drawing one item at a time, rather than the entire sample, eliminates the necessity for enumerating all possible samples, a step required by the technique described first.

Both methods—selection of one element at a time and selection of the whole group at once—give equivalent results. This is easily seen in the example of choosing two housewives from the universe of six housewives. By direct enumeration it was shown that there are fifteen possible samples in this situation. Now consider the alternative technique of drawing one sample item at a time. The first item can be any one of six since there are six items in the universe. The second item, once the first has been chosen, can be any one of five. Together there are $6 \times 5 = 30$ arrangements of two items, each of which has the same chance of occurring. But only fifteen of these possible thirty samples are distinct —the other fifteen are merely the same housewives selected in reverse order. For example, included among the thirty possible samples are both sample *AB* and sample *BA*, which for our purposes are the same. Similarly, both *BC* and *CB* are counted among the thirty, and so on. Thus, there are $30 \div 2$ or 15 possible samples which might be obtained by this technique. Each of these has the same chance of being chosen as it had with the other technique.

The use of tables of random numbers. In the practical selection of a simple random sample, *tables of random numbers* are used rather than choosing chips from a bowl. The reader will readily recognize the practical problems which would be encountered if an attempt were made to select, say, 10,000 poker chips individually from a bowl containing

175 million chips. Other problems besides sheer magnitude are encountered—the chips must be extremely well mixed, they must be almost exactly alike in shape and weight, and so on. Table 8–2 is a short table of random numbers.

The table consists of four hundred digits arranged in ten columns of four digits each in ten rows. There is no pattern to the occurrence of any particular digit. If, for example, the pattern of occurrence of the digit 7 in the first row is studied, it is found that this digit occurs in the columns 14, 28, 30, 31, and 37. If the 7's are traced throughout the remaining columns of the table, one finds no systematic pattern of their occurrence. The 7's occur "at random" in the table, and make up approximately 10 percent of the digits in the table.

It may be helpful to visualize how such a table of random numbers might be constructed. Number ten poker chips with the digits 0, 1, 2, 3, 4, 5, 6, 7, 8, 9 and put them in a bowl. After thoroughly mixing them,

TABLE 8–2. Short table of random numbers

Row no.	Column no.									
	1–4	5–8	9–12	13–16	17–20	21–24	25–28	29–32	33–36	37–40
1	3125	8144	5454	6703	2444	1518	3387	8772	6538	7532
2	1496	9980	1454	3074	3889	9230	2398	1598	3947	6917
3	4905	4956	3551	6836	6512	8312	9283	6663	8606	9580
4	9967	5765	1446	9288	0555	2591	8307	5280	5948	7869
5	5414	9534	9318	7827	5558	8651	7679	9983	5528	8922
6	5750	3489	9914	5737	6677	8288	7957	0899	1918	7684
7	9867	7825	0690	3990	2075	5402	8168	1601	0830	7544
8	4099	0087	9042	8818	0716	0373	6561	0855	3654	5997
9	2082	0918	8491	6480	8460	9663	2426	2816	1263	8430
10	7884	3991	1608	1489	7127	0563	1140	8816	9437	0495

SOURCE: M. G. Kendall and B. Babington Smith, *Tables of Random Sampling Numbers* ("Tracts for Computers") (Cambridge, England: Cambridge University Press, 1946), p. 33. The fact that the digits are shown in groups of four has no significance. This grouping is to make it easier to read the numbers.

select one chip and record the number given on the chip. This would be the first random digit in the table. Replace the chip and repeat the process. The next number obtained would be the second random digit, and so on.

To illustrate the use of a table of random numbers in the selection of a random sample, start with the simple problem of choosing two housewives from the universe of six housewives. The first step is to number each universe item:

Housewife	Number		Housewife	Number
A	1		D	4
B	2		E	5
C	3		F	6

The next step is to choose two random numbers from one to six, using Table 8–2. Suppose that before examining the table it is agreed to take as the first random number the digit located in column 1, row 6, and then to proceed systematically across row 6 until a sufficient number of digits is obtained. The first number in row 6 is five. Therefore, the housewife corresponding to that number, *E*, will be in the sample.

Proceeding across row 6, the next random digit is seven. Since no housewife in the universe corresponds to seven, this number is ignored. The next digit is five again. Since the housewife corresponding to this digit has already been chosen, this second selection is ignored. The next digit is zero. No housewife corresponds to this figure, so it is ignored. The following digit is a three, so housewife *C* will be the other sample housewife. This completes the selection of a simple random sample of two housewives.

As a variation, suppose it were desired to choose a simple random sample of fifteen furniture stores from a universe of eighty-three furniture stores. The first step would be to assign the numbers one to eighty-three to the universe items. Then, beginning at a preselected place in a table of random numbers, select two-digit random numbers between one and eighty-three until fifteen furniture stores are identified. Suppose, for example, the digits in columns 10 and 11, row 1, are selected as a starting point. The sample of furniture stores would then consist of the stores numbered as follows: 45, 46, 70, 32, 44, 41, 51, 83, 38, 78, 77, 26, 53, 21, and 49. The reader will observe that: (1) two-digit random numbers where chosen since the universe had more than ten but not more than one hundred members; (2) once a particular random number had been chosen it was ignored thereafter; (3) random numbers exceeding the last element on the list (83) were ignored.

Generalizing from these examples, the procedure for choosing a simple random sample with the use of a table of random numbers may be summarized as follows:

1. Number each item in the universe serially from 1 to *N* (the total number in the universe). The arrangement of the list itself is immaterial.

2. Beginning at some preselected place in a table of random numbers, proceed systematically through the table untilizing as many rows as are needed. If the universe has between one and ten items, take one digit at a time; if the universe has between eleven and one hundred items, take two digits at a time; and so on. Enough digits must be selected each time so that the highest numbered item in the universe could be selected.[4]

---

[4] The table of random numbers that has been provided here is not large enough for most marketing research applications. Tables of adequate size can be found in any of the following publications: H. B. Horton and R. T. Smith, *Table of 105,000*

3. The sample will be comprised of those universe items whose numbers are chosen.

ESTIMATION AND THE CONSTRUCTION OF CONFIDENCE LIMITS

After selecting a simple random sample, how does one estimate universe values from the sample data? Many such values might be of interest, but the treatment here will emphasize the estimation of the two most commonly used, the *arithmetic mean* and a *percentage*.

Sample values as estimates of universe values

Assume one is interested in the total sales of Colgate toothpaste in Detroit grocery stores during a given week. For each of the grocery stores the value of this characteristic (sales of Colgate toothpaste) could be measured. The sum of these values would be the total sales of Colgate in Detroit grocery stores during the given period. The arithmetic mean would be the average sales of Colgate toothpaste per store for the given week, i.e., the total sales divided by the number of stores.

Another parameter of common interest is the *percentage*, or proportion, of items in the universe possessing a particular characteristic. For example, in the toothpaste study one might be interested in the percentage of grocery stores stocking Colgate toothpaste or the percentage of self-service stores stocking Colgate.

How does one estimate a universe mean from sample data?[5] Intuition suggests that the mean of the sample might be a good estimate of the universe mean. In this, intuition tends to be correct. If all possible simple random samples of a given size are drawn from a universe and the mean computed for each sample, the average of these sample means will be the same as the universe mean. This indicates that the sample mean is an unbiased estimate of the universe mean, i.e., sample means do not tend, on the average, to be higher or lower than the universe mean. This does *not* mean that each sample mean will be exactly equal to the

---

Decimal Digits (Washington, D.C.: Interstate Commerce Commission, 1949); R. A. Fisher and F. Yates, *Statistical Tables for Biological, Agricultural and Medical Research* (Edinburgh, England: Oliver and Boyd, Ltd., 1948); M. B. Kendall and B. Babington Smith, *Tracts for Computers No. XXIV* (Cambridge, England: Cambridge University Press, 1946); The Rand Corporation, *A Million Random Digits with 100,000 Normal Deviates* (Glencoe, Ill.: Free Press, 1955). In addition to supplying random digits, these sources also provide direction for their use in sample selection, including special techniques for minimizing the work involved.

[5] The discussion here is centered on the mean because it is the most widely used measure of central tendency. Other such measures, particularly the median, are sometimes important.

universe mean. Only rarely will this happen; in general, the two will differ.

It may be helpful to illustrate this lack of bias in sample means as estimates of a universe mean. Consider a universe of four items with the values of $A = 1$, $B = 3$, $C = 4$, and $D = 8$. Assume all possible samples of size three are selected from this universe. The possible sample means would be:

Sample	Sample mean	Sample	Sample mean
A,B,C	$2\frac{2}{3}$	A,C,D	$4\frac{1}{3}$
A,B,D	4	B,C,D	5

In this case only one of all the possible sample means is equal to the universe mean, but the average of all possible means

$$\frac{2\frac{2}{3} + 4 + 4\frac{1}{3} + 5}{4}$$

is equal to the universe mean of 4. The sample mean, then, affords an unbiased estimate of the universe mean, but any one sample mean is unlikely to be exactly the same as the universe mean.

Since the sample mean can be used as an estimate of the universe mean, it offers a method of estimating the universe aggregate or total. If the sample mean is multiplied by the number of items in the universe, the result is an unbiased estimate of the universe total, but it is not likely to be exactly the same as the actual total.

The proportion (or percentage) of the universe items having a particular attribute is simply a special case of the arithmetic mean.[6] Hence, a sample proportion (or percentage) provides an unbiased estimate of the corresponding universe proportion (or percentage). For example, from a simple random sample of two hundred drugstore owners, it was found that one hundred and fifty preferred to buy directly from the manufacturer, i.e., a sample percentage of 75 percent. This percentage is an unbiased estimate of the universe percentage which prefers to buy directly. If a large number of simple random samples were drawn

---

[6] By this we mean that the *proportion* of items having a particular characteristic is equal to the *arithmetic mean* of the items, when items having the characteristic are given the value of 1, and those without it are given the value of 0. As an illustration, suppose there are five items, of which four have a specified characteristic. The proportion with this characteristic is 0.8. This is identical with the arithmetic mean when the four items with the characteristic are scored 1, and the item without it is scored 0:

$$\frac{4(1) + 1(0)}{5} = 0.8.$$

The fact that this so-called "scoring system" (0,1) enables us to regard a proportion as a special kind of mean simplifies the theory, since it permits immediate attribution of properties of the mean to a proportion.

from this universe, and the sample percentage computed each time, then the average value of these sample percentages would tend to equal the universe percentage which prefers to make direct purchases.

Although both the sample mean and proportion are unbiased when based on simple random sampling, not all sample values provide unbiased estimates of the corresponding universe values. A conspicuous example is a group of estimates called *ratio estimates* which, as often used, are biased estimates of their population counterparts. Structurally, estimates of this type involve a ratio of quantities, *both* of which vary from sample to sample.

An example is provided by brand share. Suppose we have a universe of five stores, with sales of Brand X and the product class of which it is a part, as follows:

Store	Sales of Brand X	Total product class
A	1	10
B	5	10
C	16	20
D	14	30
E	14	30
Total	50	100

Using samples of size two, it will be shown that the average brand share for all possible samples is not equal to the brand share for the universe as a whole. The ratio estimate of brand share is a biased estimate of universe brand share. The possible samples, and the brand share for each, are as follows:

Possible sample	Sample total of: X	Product class	Sample brand share
A B	6	20	6/20
A C	17	30	17/30
A D	15	40	15/40
A E	15	40	15/40
B C	21	30	21/30
B D	19	40	19/40
B E	19	40	19/40
C D	30	50	30/50
C E	30	50	30/50
D E	28	60	28/60

The average of all ten possible sample brand shares is 0.493, compared to 0.500 for the universe. Hence, the sample value in this case is a biased estimate.

The above example has been used mainly to illustrate the fact that not all estimates derived from simple random samples provide unbiased estimates of the analogous universe values. The sample mean and proportion are unusual in this regard, as previously demonstrated.

Despite the bias in sample ratio estimates, such estimates find frequent application in sample surveys, particularly in more complex forms of probability sampling. Although they will often be biased estimates, in many situations the bias will be small (as in the above example) and other considerations will recommend their use. The space available here does not permit further discussion of ratio estimates, though many of the ideas expressed later in this chapter apply to them with modifications.

Interval estimation

Different samples from the same universe will give different estimates of the universe value. The estimate obtained from a particular sample will differ from the universe value because of "sampling error," that is, because the sample selected by chance is not exactly representative of the universe. If the researcher took another random sample from the same universe, the resulting estimate might differ a little, somewhat, or a great deal from the estimate he obtained from his first sample. He is then faced with the problem of determining how precise, or reliable, his sample estimates are.

The investigator would like to determine a range of values within which he can be fairly sure that the true value lies. That is, he would like to be able to construct an *interval estimate.* Fortunately, the theory of simple random sampling (and of probability sampling in general) provides methods for establishing such a range or interval estimate, thereby permitting evaluation of the reliability of sample estimates. Thus, with simple random sample data it is possible to measure the sampling error associated with such estimates as the mean or a percentage, and to set bounds within which the universe value being estimated will likely fall. This is a great advantage of probability samples over nonprobability samples.

The sampling distribution concept. It has been emphasized that different samples from the same universe will lead to different estimates of the universe mean or a universe percentage. For example, assume one chooses all possible simple random samples of two each from a college student universe of six students. Each student has monthly income as follows: $A = \$20$, $B = \$80$, $C = \$100$, $D = \$100$, $E = \$100$, and $F = \$200$. The universe mean is $100. Sample means ranging from $50 (Sample AB) to $150 (Samples CF, DF, and EF) would be obtained. The fifteen possible sample means would occur as follows:

Sample mean	*Relative number of occurrences*	Sample mean	*Relative number of occurrences*
$ 50	1 out of 15	$110	1 out of 15
$ 60	3 out of 15	$140	1 out of 15
$ 90	3 out of 15	$150	3 out of 15
$100	3 out of 15		

Such a listing of the possible random sample means together with their relative frequencies of occurrence is called the *random sampling distribution of the mean* for samples of two each from the given universe. Any such distribution of sample values under random sampling is called a sampling distribution.

Given a sampling distribution, one can predict the average behavior of the sample estimate under study. In this case, for example, if repeated simple random samples of two each were drawn from the universe of six students and a sample mean computed each time, on the average 60 percent (9 out of 15) of these sample means would lie between $60 and $100, inclusive. Again on the average, about 73 percent (11 out of 15) of the sample means would be within $40 of the universe mean ($100), and so on.

The fact that a knowledge of the sampling distribution makes it possible to predict the sampling behavior of the mean or a percentage is of fundamental importance in statistical inference. If one knew only that a particular sample estimate would vary under repeated sampling and had no information as to *how* it would vary, then it would be impossible to devise a measure of the sampling error associated with that estimate. Since the sampling distribution of an estimate describes how that estimate will vary with repeated sampling, it provides a basis for determining the reliability of the sample estimate.

Sampling distribution of the mean in large samples. In practical sampling work, the composition of the universe from which the sample is drawn is seldom known. Therefore, the sampling distribution of an estimate based on observations from the universe will also be unknown. On the face of it this would seem to rule out the possibility of constructing interval estimates of the type discussed above.

Although this fact does make it impossible to make estimates whose sampling properties are known *exactly*, it does not preclude the making of estimates, the sampling behavior of which is known approximately. Mathematicians have derived a theorem called the Central Limit Theorem, which makes it possible to construct interval estimates whose properties are known sufficiently well for most practical purposes. In rather crude terms, the Central Limit Theorem states: The sampling distribution of the mean, for a large sample, will be approximately a *normal distribution.*[7]

This large sample distribution of sample means will be distributed symmetrically around the true universe mean as shown in Figure 8–1. The sample means tend to cluster around the universe mean.

FIGURE 8–1. Distribution of large sample means around universe mean

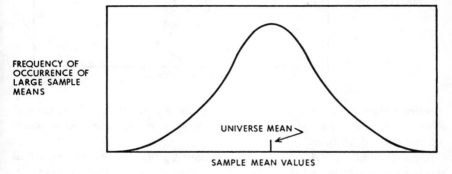

FREQUENCY OF
OCCURRENCE OF
LARGE SAMPLE
MEANS

UNIVERSE MEAN

SAMPLE MEAN VALUES

Small deviations from the universe mean are more frequent than large ones. Sample means that deviate very widely from the universe mean are rare. Positive and negative deviations of equal magnitude occur with equal frequency.

If a number of samples of a large size is drawn at random from the same universe, the means of the samples will tend to form a normal curve around the universe mean. The larger the individual samples, the more closely will the sample means cluster around the universe mean. That is, the larger the sample, the greater the reliability of the sample mean. This accords with common sense since it would be expected that a large sample would be more similar to the universe than would a small sample.

Figure 8–2 illustrates the closer clustering of sample means around the universe mean when very large samples are used. Compare this distribution with that shown in Figure 8–1. Note that both are distributed symmetrically, but the distribution of sample means for larger samples has fewer values that deviate widely from the universe mean. The larger the samples, the more closely the sample means will cluster around the universe mean. However, no matter how large the sample, unless it approaches the size of the universe, some sample means will be different from the universe mean. If a universe is normally distributed, the pro-

---

[7] Cochran, *op. cit.,* gives a discussion of the validity of the normal approximation in sampling from a finite universe.

FIGURE 8–2. Distribution of sample means around universe mean for very large samples

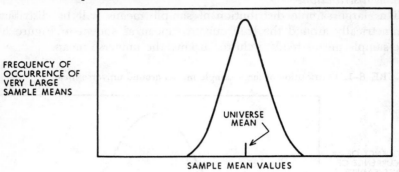

portion of the universe items located between any two limits is determined by the distance of those limits from the universe mean, measured in terms of standard deviations.[8]

In a normally distributed universe, about 68 percent of the items will be within one standard deviation of the mean, about 95 percent within two standard deviations of the mean, and virtually all (99.7 percent) within three standard deviations of the mean. These facts are exhibited geometrically in Figure 8–3.

FIGURE 8–3. Area under the normal curve

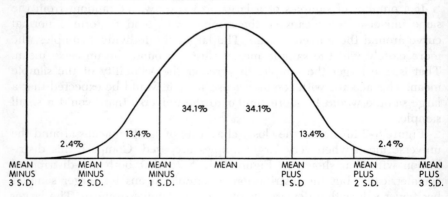

_____
[8] The standard deviation of a universe is a measure of the dispersion of the items in the universe around their mean. The standard deviation of a finite universe may be defined by the formula

$$\sigma = \sqrt{\frac{\Sigma x^2}{N - 1}}$$

where

σ = standard deviation.

x = deviation of an item from the universe mean.

N = number of items in the universe.

Since sample means will be approximately normally distributed about the universe mean, it is possible to make analogous statements about the deviation of sample means from the universe mean. When applied to the sampling distribution of the mean, however, the term *standard error of the mean* is used instead of standard deviation. The following statements apply.

a. About 68 percent of sample means will fall within one standard error on either side of the universe mean.

b. About 95 percent of sample means will fall within two standard errors on either side of the universe mean.[9]

c. Practically all sample means will be located within three standard errors on either side of the universe mean.

This leaves the problem of determining the actual size of the standard error of the mean. For a simple random sample, this is obtained from the following formula:

$$\sigma_{\bar{x}} = \frac{\sigma}{\sqrt{n}}$$

where

$\sigma_{\bar{x}}$ = standard error of the mean.

σ = standard deviation of the universe.

n = number of observations in the sample.

This formula applies if less than 5 percent of the universe is included in the sample.[10]

Nothing has been said as to how large the sample must be before the Central Limit Theorem may be applied. The question can be answered only by a knowledge of the universe being sampled. For fairly symmetrical universes, the sample can be as small as ten and the approximation

---

[9] Technically, 95 percent of the sample means will fall within 1.96 standard errors on either side of the universe mean. The 1.96 is rounded to 2 to simplify the illustrations used in this section and to conform to common usage.

[10] If more than 5 percent of the universe is included in the sample, then the standard error may be computed as:

$$\sqrt{\frac{(N - n)}{N}} \cdot \frac{\sigma}{\sqrt{n}}$$

where N is the universe size and n is the sample size. The factor

$$\sqrt{\frac{N - n}{N}}$$

is called the "finite population correction." It takes account of the fact that a sample from a finite population partially exhausts that population. That some such correction is necessary becomes clear when one considers the limiting case $n = N$, i.e., when a complete census is done. If no finite population correction were made, this would make the standard error of the mean equal to $\sigma/\sqrt{N}$, an obviously erroneous result. With the correction factor, the standard error of the mean based on a complete enumeration of the population becomes will hold very well. On the other hand, for very skewed universes (which are common in marketing), the approximation may be a relatively poor one, even for a sample as large as several hundred. For most applications it is probably satisfactory to assume that means based on samples of thirty will be approximately normally distributed.

Construction and interpretation of confidence intervals

How does the researcher construct an *interval estimate* of the universe mean? This procedure will be illustrated by the construction of what is called a 95 percent *confidence interval* estimate of the mean. Consider the following hypothetical situation. The mean of a certain universe (M) is unknown, but the standard deviation of that universe (σ) is known. A sample mean which is based on a sample of $n = 100$ observations is available.

Our knowledge of the sampling distribution of the mean tells us that the interval

$$M \pm 2\frac{\sigma}{\sqrt{n}} = M \pm 2\frac{\sigma}{\sqrt{100}} = M \pm 2\frac{\sigma}{10}$$

will include about 95 percent of all possible sample means of samples for which $n = 100$. That is, 95 times out of a 100, we will be right if, *before* the sample of 100 is chosen, we assert that the sample mean we will obtain will lie between

$$M - 2\frac{\sigma}{10} \quad \text{and} \quad M + 2\frac{\sigma}{10}.$$

After the sample is known, we *assume* that the sample mean actually obtained is one of those which does lie in this interval. If this is true (and by definition it will be true in 95 percent of repeated samplings), then the sample mean will be located between

$$M - 2\frac{\sigma}{10} \quad \text{and} \quad M + 2\frac{\sigma}{10}.$$

Denoting the sample mean that was actually obtained by $\bar{x}$, the statement: "M lies between

$$\sqrt{\frac{N - N}{N}}\,\frac{\sigma}{\sqrt{n}} = 0,$$

as it should, since the estimate contains no sampling error when a census is conducted.

There is nothing magical about the use of 5 percent as the division point for the use of the finite correction factor. Some writers recommend 10 percent. Ignoring the correction factor is conservative, since it results in an overestimate of the standard error.

$$\bar{x} - 2\frac{\sigma}{10} \quad \text{and} \quad \bar{x} + 2\frac{\sigma}{10} \text{,''}$$

will be correct 95 percent of the time, if we draw a large number of samples.

In a practical situation, a particular sample mean will have been obtained so that we can solve numerically the two equations

$$M = \bar{x} - 2\frac{\sigma}{10}$$

$$M = \bar{x} + 2\frac{\sigma}{10}.$$

This will give us a range of values within which the population mean M may, with 95 percent confidence, be presumed to lie. More precisely, if a large number of random samples of size 100 is drawn from this universe, and each time the statement is made that M lies between

$$\bar{x} - 2\frac{\sigma}{10} \quad \text{and} \quad \bar{x} + 2\frac{\sigma}{10}$$

(where x is computed afresh for each sample), then 95 percent of these statements will be correct. This is the meaning of the expression "95 percent confidence interval."

By the same reasoning, a confidence interval which is "almost certain" to cover the universe mean may be computed using the limits

$$M = \bar{x} - 3\frac{\sigma}{\sqrt{n}}$$

$$M = \bar{x} + 3\frac{\sigma}{\sqrt{n}}.$$

Three standard errors are used because almost all of the observations in a normal distribution are located within three standard deviations of the universe mean.

It must be emphasized that this interpretation of "confidence" in a particular interval estimate is defined in terms of what will happen if a large number of samples is drawn. Any particular confidence interval either will or will not cover the universe mean. After the sample has been drawn it is a matter of fact whether or not the particular interval estimate does cover the universe mean. What is guaranteed is that, for example, 95 percent of such statements about the location of the universe mean will be correct if a 95 percent confidence interval is used.

Up to this point it has been assumed that the standard deviation of the universe is a known quantity. In practical marketing research problems this value will almost never be known. Therefore, an estimate must be substituted in the formula if the standard error is to be estimated. The standard deviation of the sample is used for this purpose, resulting in the estimated standard error[11]

$$s_{\bar{x}} = \frac{s}{\sqrt{n}}$$

where

$s_{\bar{x}}$ = estimated standard error of the mean.

s = standard deviation of the sample.

n = number of observations in the sample.

This estimate tends to distort the accuracy of the estimation of confidence limits, but for practical purposes it will be satisfactory if the sample is large. An illustration may be of value in illustrating the concepts expressed relative to confidence intervals.

Example 1. A random sample of four hundred housewives provided the following information about the amount of money spent during a six-month period on food items:

$$\text{Sample mean } (\bar{x}) = \$400.$$

$$\text{Sample standard deviation } (s) = \$80.$$

The problem is to estimate the mean of the universe with a 95 percent confidence interval and to interpret the result. The algebraic expression for this confidence interval is:

$$\bar{x} \pm 2 \left(\frac{\$80}{\sqrt{400}} \right) = 400 \pm 2 \left(\frac{\$80}{20} \right) = 400 \pm 2(\$4) = 400 \pm \$8.$$

We are 95 percent confident that the universe mean will be between \$392 and \$408. This finding is interpreted in the following way: If a very large number of samples of four hundred housewives each was selected at random from this universe and for each such sample the confidence interval

$$\bar{x} \pm 2 \frac{s}{\sqrt{n}}$$

---

[11] If the sample represents 5 percent or more of the universe, this expression may be revised downward. Multiply the expression given for s_x by the factor

$$\sqrt{\frac{N-n}{N}}$$

See footnote 10.

was computed, then about 95 percent of the intervals so computed would include the universe mean.

It is to be emphasized that the interpretation did not say the particular interval, \$392–\$408 (as calculated from a single sample), will bracket the universe mean. Rather the interpretation said that, if a large number of random samples were selected and the interval computed each time, then about 95 percent of the intervals would cover the universe mean.

Confidence limits for percentages. As in the case of the universe mean, the researcher may also wish to construct confidence limits for population percentages. Fortunately, the theory is identical to that used to construct confidence limits for the universe mean since a percentage is but a special case of the mean. It follows that the sampling distribution of a percentage is, for large samples, approximately normally distributed. The standard error of a percentage, σ_p, from a simple random sample is estimated by the formula $\sqrt{\dfrac{pq}{n}}$, where p is the percentage of items in the sample possessing a given characteristic, q is the percentage of items not possessing the characteristic, and n is the sample size. Suppose that a simple random sample of one hundred families shows forty own a dog and sixty do not, i.e., the dog ownership level is 40 percent. The estimated standard error, s_p, would be computed as follows:

$$s_p = \sqrt{\frac{(40)(60)}{100}}\%$$

$$= \sqrt{\frac{2400}{100}}\%$$

$$= 4.9\%.$$

The 95 percent confidence interval would be

$$p \pm 2s_p = 40\% \pm 2(4.9\%), \text{ or } 30.2\% \text{ to } 49.8\%.$$

Thus, one would be 95 percent confident that the true percentage of dog ownership is between 30.2 and 49.8 percent.

One caution is in order with regard to this method of constructing a confidence interval for percentages. For values of p less than 30 percent or more than 70 percent, a sample of more than one hundred is needed if the normal approximation to the sampling distribution of a percentage is to be a good one. If, for example, one were sampling an infrequent attribute, one which only 2 percent of the universe had, he could not realistically assume that the sample percentage would be distributed normally under repeated random sampling unless a very large sample were used.

ESTIMATION OF SAMPLE SIZE NECESSARY FOR SPECIFIED RELIABILITY

When estimating a mean

Consider the following problem. A marketing executive wishes to estimate the average monthly sales of a particular brand of cat food in chain grocery stores. After some discussion, he decides that an estimate which is correct within 15 percent will be of serviceable precision. If simple random sampling is used, how big a sample of chain stores is needed?

Recall the earlier theory that indicated that a sample mean is virtually certain to be within 3 standard errors of the universe mean. Applying this fact to the 15 percent precision requirement, the sample size needed, n, must be a number such that

$$3\sigma_{\bar{x}} = 0.15 \text{ of the mean } (M)$$

$$3\frac{\sigma}{\sqrt{n}} = 0.15\,M$$

$$\frac{\sigma}{M}\left(\frac{1}{\sqrt{n}}\right) = 0.05.$$

Let the symbol $C = \sigma/M\,(100\%)$. Then

$$C \cdot \frac{1}{\sqrt{n}} = 5\%$$

where the quantity $C = \sigma/M\,(100\%)$ is called the *relative standard deviation* (standard deviation relative to the mean, in percentage), or *coefficient of variation*.

To solve this equation, it is necessary to have an adequate estimate of C. In practice, this will come from a pilot test or perhaps from knowledge of the relative variation in a similar situation. Let us suppose that, in this case, $C = 100$ percent, i.e., $\sigma = M$. Then

$$(100\%)\frac{1}{\sqrt{n}} = 5\%$$

$$\text{or } \sqrt{n} = 20$$

$$n = 400.$$

The required sample size, assuming simple random sampling, is four hundred.

On inspection of this result, it might be decided that the required sample size is too large, i.e., it will cost more than the results will be worth. Instead of being virtually certain (3 standard errors) of getting an estimate within 15 percent of the mean, one might be willing to take a 1 in 20 chance (2 standard errors) that the sample will provide an estimate that is not within 15 percent. Maintaining the same value for C, the indicated sample size becomes the value of n, for which

$$2 \frac{\sigma}{M} \left(\frac{1}{\sqrt{n}} \right) = 0.15$$

$$= 2C \cdot \frac{1}{\sqrt{n}} = 15\%$$

$$= 200\% \cdot \frac{1}{\sqrt{n}} = 15\%$$

or $n = 178$, approximately.

The general sample size formula implicit in these examples is

$$n = \frac{k^2 C^2}{r^2}$$

where
   n = necessary sample size, assuming simple random sampling.
   k = 2 or 3, depending on whether one wishes to take a 1 in 20 chance of not having an adequate sample size ($k = 2$), or wishes to be virtually certain of the result ($k = 3$). Other values of k may be used, but these will be adequate for most applications.
   C = universe coefficient of variation, expressed in percentage.
   r = percentage within which universe mean is to be estimated.

   It should be remarked that the above formula (and the preceding examples given) are based on the assumption that the universe size (N) is large relative to the projected sample size (n). If the indicated sample size is an appreciable proportion of the universe (more than 5 percent), this formula overestimates the sample size required. If the ratio n/N exceeds 0.05, the indicated sample size should be revised downward using the formula

$$n^1 = \frac{n}{1 + \dfrac{n}{N}}.$$

As an example of this refinement, suppose that in the first cat food example (page 372), the relevant universe size is $N = 1000$ chain stores. Then, since $n/N = 0.40$, the required sample size should be reduced to

$$n^1 = \frac{400}{1 + .40} = 286.$$

Determining sample size when estimating a percentage

To determine the necessary sample size when estimating a percentage, one again uses the basic sample size formula given in the last section. In this situation, if P percent of the elements in the universe have the characteristic under study and the analyst wishes to estimate this universe percentage within r percent, the formula becomes

$$n = \frac{k^2}{r^2} \left(\frac{100 - P}{P} \right) 10,000.$$

As as example of application of this formula, suppose one wishes to estimate the percentage of families which serve a specific hot cereal during a particular week. He speculates that $P = 40$, i.e., 40 percent serve it. This percentage is to be estimated within 4 percentage points ($r = 4/40 = 10\%$). If he is willing to take a 1 in 20 chance that the estimate will be more than 10 percent away from the true universe percentage, the formula says that n should be

$$n = \frac{4}{100} \left(\frac{100 - 40}{40} \right) (10,000)$$

$$= \left(\frac{4}{100} \right) \left(\frac{3}{2} \right) (10,000)$$

$$= 600.$$

Note from the formula that extremely large samples are needed to estimate small values of P, even when a large relative error is permitted. For example, if P is estimated in advance at 1 percent, and it is considered satisfactory to have a relative error of 50 percent ($\frac{1}{2}$ percentage point), the sample size required to guarantee this precision level is

$$n = \left(\frac{9}{2500} \right) \left(\frac{100\% - 1\%}{1\%} \right) (10,000) = 3564.$$

A more efficient sampling method than simple random sampling would be indicated for this problem.

As was the case when determining sample size for a mean, the size indicated by the basic formula for a percentage should be revised downward if the indicated sample comprises over 5 percent of the universe. The same formula for the revised sample size as was given in connection with the mean (page 373) should be used.

Additional remarks on the determination of sample size

The actual application of the sample size formulas given in this section requires consideration of a number of related issues. These include:

1. The formulas given are applicable strictly to only *simple random sampling*. Sampling systems which are more efficient statistically (such as stratified random sampling, to be discussed later) will require fewer observations for equally satisfactory results. Similarly, there are other sampling systems, commonly used in practice, for which the simple formulas provided will underestimate the actual number of observation units which must be contacted.

2. These formulas relate to the sample size needed for one particular characteristic of interest. Hardly ever is a survey done to answer only one question. Typically, several values are of interest and each of these may require a different sample size. One consequence is the necessity for compromise on this question, some estimates being provided with less precision than is really wanted and others having greater reliability than is necessary.

3. In addition to varying reliability requirements for different universe characteristics of interest, various universe segments may have different precision needs. For instance, in chain stores, it might be necessary to have results that are correct within 10 percent; in independent stores, this requirement might be relaxed to 30 percent. In general, simple random sampling would not be the best approach to this problem, but, regardless of sampling method, the broad problem of differential reliability needs must be considered in most cases.

4. In order to be useful, the sample size formulas must be based on adequate estimates of the relevant coefficients of variation. In statistics, as elsewhere, information begets information, and the more that is known of a universe, the more efficiently it can be sampled. Ingenuity, as well as full examination of related data, must often be exercised in order to obtain satisfactory estimates of universe variability.

5. The administrative requirements on precision of results required must be realistic. Executives sometimes overestimate the reliability with which estimates must be provided. Because of the importance of this factor in affecting the sample size needed, it is critical that a realistic appraisal be made.

The student of marketing research should also be aware that the sample size determination method described above is not the only approach to the problem. If a given research project is designed to answer a highly specific decision problem, and certain information is available, then it may be possible to arrive at a formally optimal (or near-optimal) solution to the sample size problem. The methodology used is generally described as the "Bayesian" or "decision theory" approach to the question. Although detailed discussion is beyond the scope of this book, in general this alternative approach requires that the analyst be able to specify the (prior) probability of various parameter values, sampling costs, and the consequences of the various decisions that might be made.[12] The Bayesian approach is probably most useful when a study is being designed to answer a single, specific decision problem; the approach we have sketched is perhaps of greatest value when general information is sought on a variety of questions for multiple and possibly incompletely specified purposes.

PRACTICAL PROBLEMS IN USING SIMPLE RANDOM SAMPLING

Although simple random sampling serves well to introduce the basic ideas of sampling, it is not suitable for most of the sampling problems encountered in marketing research. Its use is severely limited by a number of difficulties: cost of the procedure, the necessity for having a complete list of individual universe elements to be sampled, its lesser statistical efficiency relative to certain alternative sampling systems, and the administrative problems met with in its use.

Cost

One of the most important factors limiting the use of simple random sampling is the cost. Since the method guarantees that every possible item in the universe has the same chance of being chosen, the actual sample selected often consists of universe items which are widely dispersed geographically. With a field survey, this means that interviewers may have to travel considerable distances, thereby increasing the costs of the field operation.

Availability of a current listing of population elements

A second major limitation to the practical use of simple random sampling is the necessity of having a list identifying every individual universe element. It is sometimes very difficult to obtain even reasonably accurate lists of relatively fixed items, such as grocery stores, but the problem is especially acute when sampling human universes.

Suppose it were desired to draw a simple random sample of Detroit families. To do so would require an accurate and up-to-date listing of Detroit families. Compilation of such a list would likely require a greater expenditure in time and money than could reasonably be allocated for the purpose. The problem of developing an adequate list of elements in a less geographically compact area, say a region or the entire United States, would be even more difficult.

---

[12] The basic reference is R. Schlaifer, *Probability and Statistics for Business Decisions* (New York: McGraw-Hill Book Co., Inc., 1959), especially Chapter 35. See also H. V. Roberts, "Bayesian Statistics in Marketing," *Journal of Marketing*, Vol. 27 (January, 1963), pp. 1–4.

Statistical efficiency

A third difficulty associated with simple random sampling is that it is often *statistically inefficient*. One sample design is said to be statistically more efficient than another when, for the same size sample, a smaller standard error is obtained. Given some knowledge, or perhaps just "educated guesses," about a universe, one may ordinarily improve the reliability of his estimates by imposing certain restrictions on the sampling procedure. For example, if it is known that in a grocery store universe 20 percent of the stores are chain stores and that kind of ownership may influence the characteristic being studied, then it may be more efficient to specify that 20 percent of the sample consists of chain stores. If simple random sampling were used, it is unlikely that exactly 20 percent of the sample would turn out to be chain stores, and the sample data would have an additional component of error from this source. Thus, the estimate obtained would vary more in repeated simple random samples than it would if this restriction on number of chain stores were imposed.

Administrative difficulties

A number of difficulties are associated with the administration of simple random samples. One is the conceptually simple, but sometimes troublesome, problem of selecting the sample. The random selection of, say, five thousand names from a list of two million would be a difficult job if errors were to be avoided.

Another administrative problem inherent in simple random sampling is the difficulty of maintaining supervisory control over the field interviewers. The geographic dispersion of sample units to be contacted makes interviewer supervision difficult and expensive.

Simple random sampling occasionally a feasible method

In spite of the difficulties enumerated above, some use is made of simple random samples in practical marketing research. Sometimes one wishes to sample a universe with the following properties:

1. It is small.
2. A satisfactory list of universe items exists.
3. The cost per interview is practically independent of the location of the sample items.
4. The only information available about the universe is the list of items.

In such a case, simple random sampling might be a practical procedure. An example of such a situation would be a telephone survey of dentists in Chicago.

In general, however, the practical limitations of simple random sampling are severe enough to limit seriously its application in marketing research. Accordingly, various alternative probability and nonprobability sampling schemes have been devised. In subsequent sections a few of these alternate methods will be considered. Particular attention will be paid to their relationship to simple random sampling. It will be found that a knowledge of simple random sampling provides the basis for understanding some of the other sampling techniques that are available.

SUMMARY

The first two steps in sampling are to define the universe and to specify the variables to be studied. Next, the sample must be designed. This involves a determination of sampling units, planning the selection of sample items, and preparing to estimate universe characteristics from sample data.

The two basic methods of selecting sample items are probability and nonprobability methods. Probability sampling methods are the only ones which enable the researcher to measure objectively the precision of sample estimates. Simple random sampling is the simplest type of probability sampling. In simple random sampling, the sample mean provides an unbiased estimate of the universe mean. This does not mean, however, that any particular sample mean will be the same as the universe mean. Moreover, not all sample analogues of population values (most notably certain ratio estimates) enjoy this property of being unbiased.

The sampling distribution of a mean or percentage describes how that value will vary under repeated sampling. While in practical sampling work the sampling distribution is not known, it is still possible to make use of an approximate sampling distribution and so to construct confidence limits.

If a large number of samples is drawn from a given universe, the means of these samples will tend to form a normal distribution around the universe mean. The larger the samples, the more tightly are the sample means clustered around the universe mean. Therefore, the larger the sample, the greater the reliability of the sample mean.

In simple random sampling, the distribution of sample means is approximately normal. Thus, if a great many samples of the same size are selected at random from the same universe, about 68 percent of the sample means will fall within one standard error of the universe mean, 95 percent within 2 standard errors, and practically all within 3 standard errors. From this information one may construct a confidence interval estimate of a mean or a percentage which will, with a given confidence, include the universe value of the mean or percentage.

By substituting desired values of the standard error and an estimated value of the universe mean into the standard error formula, it is possible to determine the sample size required for a specified reliability. The question of sample size determination may be approached alternately via decision-theoretic considerations.

Simple random sampling is infrequently employed in marketing research because of the problems associated with its use. It tends to cost more than other sampling methods because the sample items are widely dispersed geographically. A second limitation is the necessity for having a list which identifies all items in the universe. Such lists are expensive and often unattainable. A third difficulty is that simple random sampling is not always statistically efficient, and a fourth, that the selection of a large random sample is administratively difficult to carry out.

Case 8—1.   MAUER, HARE AND GILLESPIE

The Mauer, Hare and Gillespie advertising agency billed $14 million annually, of which 60 percent was spent in television. The agency had several large accounts which used TV heavily, including a local beer account, an airline, a cosmetic company, and a candy firm. The agency maintained a research department composed of seven persons, one of whom specialized in print copy research. No research evaluation of any of the agency's radio or TV commercials had been attempted to date. The agency was being solicited by the Institute for Advertising Reseach to subscribe to their research service for the evaluation of television commercials.

The representative from IAR pointed out that the increasing cost of television, the cancellation effects of competitive advertising, and the growing apathy of the television viewer were forcing more and more advertisers to place greater emphasis on the production of better TV commercials. He went on to say that research must evaluate the commercials *before* the money is spent to show them.

IAR, after eleven years of studying television and TV commercials, had formulated a completely new plan to aid advertisers and agencies in the development of more effective TV commercials. This research centered around the depth of penetration, the effect of the sales claims on the mind of the viewer, and the recall meanings. In other words, the total communication of the commercial and the clarity of the communication were the subject of the inquiry, as contrasted to an attempt to pinpoint quantitatively the percentages of people recalling the sponsor's name and the prime sales claims.

The research was designed to assist the creative man and not to serve as a judge of his final efforts. For that reason, the staff of IAR was prepared to work closely with the agency's creative people in all stages of creating TV commercials. In studies of finished commercials, it was thought important to understand what the writers and producers were attempting to express and communicate, in order to evaluate the commercial properly as a communication piece.

The research was designed to test the details as well as the total effect of the commercial through three particular services as follows:

1. Testing selling themes.
2. Testing story boards and/or components.
3. Testing completed film commercials.

The research was also designed to answer such questions on the commercial as:

1. What basic theme or selling idea should be used?
2. What type of treatment should be used? Animation? Live action? Singing jingle? High pressure? Low key? Demonstration?
3. Whose face and voice should be used? Dick Stark? Art Linkletter? Betty Furness? Donald Duck? What testifier will carry authority?
4. Is a singing jingle going to be a hit?
5. Which way of showing the product is best?
6. Which way of showing the logo or trademark is best?
7. Which method of demonstrating the product is best?
8. What kind of voice is best? Male? Female? Strong? Quiet?

Evaluations were also offered of the total effect of the commercial. This part of the research service was designed to answer the following questions:

1. What is the image of the product in the mind of the viewer—before and after the commercial?
2. What do the sales claims in the commercials communicate to the viewer?
3. What are the symbolic meanings communicated to the viewer by the manner of presenting the product in the commercial?
4. Does the viewer identify himself or herself with the product and its use?
5. Does the commercial seem to create effective attitudes toward the brand?
6. How does the viewer identify with this product in this commercial versus competitors' products in their commercials?
7. What specific components of the commercial caused what reactions in the viewer's mind?

Yet another service provided by IAR was designed to measure the total effect of a commercial (or commercials) versus the total effect of the commercials being run by competitors, as well as the length of time a commercial should run.

This service could be used periodically, on a continuing basis, or whenever changes in consumer attitudes, new product competition, and/or changes in competitors' commercials created new conditions and hazards for commercial effectiveness.

The service contract would be offered only on a continuing basis to a limited clientele, because it was felt that only those who participated continuously, with frequent consultation, would reap the maximum benefits. Therefore, IAR required users to pay a basic retainer of $1,000 a month. Against this would be credited whatever services were ordered from time to time, at the rate card prices, with no limit on the number of services ordered. After ten months the contract was cancellable on sixty days' notice. Delivery would be scheduled from two to four weeks after testing, depending upon the magnitude of the job.

The rate card offered by IAR is presented below:

SERVICE 1.	TESTING BASIC THEMES Up to 3 basic themes on one product—$1,000. *Sample:* 50 people selected according to specifications as to appropriate consumer types, with a range of age and socio-economic status, where one type only is needed (e.g., house-wives). Where types fall into several categories (e.g., women, men, teenagers) an additional 50-sample unit is added for each category. Add $500 for each category of 50.
SERVICE 2.	TESTING STORY BOARDS OR COMPONENTS Up to 3 story boards, or 15 components—$1,150. *Sample:* as above.
SERVICE 3.	TESTING COMPLETED FILM COMMERCIALS 1 commercial—$1,450. *Sample:* 70 of one specified consumer type. Individual interviews with at least 20. Group interviews, in addition, with at least 50. For each additional type category, add $800 for each sample unit of 70.
SERVICE 4.	TESTING VS. COMPETITIVE COMMERCIALS 1 commercial $1,450, or special rates according to the complexity of the comparisons desired. *Sample:* as in service 3.
CONSULTATION:	There will be a conference on each research report. Additional consultation will be available at a charge of $50 per hour. Consultation will be handled by senior staff members experienced in cooperating with creative agency personnel.

IAR regarded certain research measures as being superficial, such as like-dislike scores, the percent of viewers who could recall certain sales claims, or viewer statements as to the believability of claims. Direct questions were also regarded as less useful in the main than indirect questions. This position was based on the belief that most people cannot express their real, meaningful feelings about commercials.

A fact-gathering session would precede each test interview. In this situation, the respondent would describe his product and brand preferences, his social involvement, and his general purchasing habits. These data were thought to provide a baseline on which to evaluate test results and to study impact and meanings.

Brand images would be checked before and after the testing was completed. Changes would be measured and studied to further systematize interpretations. Several indirect methods would be used here, such as a list of words appropriate to the product to elicit free association.

Because some interviews would be with individuals and some with small groups, IAR planned to use different techniques to cope with the two types of interview situations. These testing situations would be subject to a carefully planned observation system. Trained people would note and record informal, nonverbal clues such as attentiveness, restiveness, indifference, discontent, etc. In the group interviews, interactions and their quality would be noted and recorded. Thus, each interviewee would have forms which he alone would fill out. Among such forms would be those which called for the respondent to describe the kind of person who would most likely be interested in the commercial or would be most likely to use the product.

Other research methodology to be used by IAR included story telling, semantic differentials, sentence completions, and picture completions. All work would be done under the supervision of IAR's senior consultants, who included personnel with doctorate training in cultural anthropology, sociology, and psychology.

1. Are the samples proposed for the various services of the proper size?

2. Should the agency subscribe to this service?

Case 8—2. OUTBOARD MOTORS, INC (B)

Outboard Motors, Inc. was one of the large manufacturers of outboard motors and for many years had held between 15 percent and 25 percent of the U. S. market. The bulk of its sales were made under its own brand, but in recent years a growing proportion of sales were in private brands sold by the large mail-order chains. Outboard was one of the pioneers in the outboard motor field, and had grown to its current size as the industry had grown.

For many years outboard motors were relatively small—most of them under 10 horsepower. With the advent of lighter, stronger boats and with the great growth in popularity of water skiing, the demand for much larger motors skyrocketed, although a significant demand continued for the smaller motors. The proportion of total unit sales by all manufacturers accounted for by motors of 35 and over horsepower had grown each year for ten years. Outboard Motors, Inc. shared in the growth of large motor sales, but to a smaller degree than did some of its newer competitors who had developed images identified with powerful motors.

Although the large mail-order chains had become significant factors in the retailing of outboard motors, most manufacturers, including Outboard Motors, Inc., relied primarily on independent dealers for retail sales. Most of these dealers were located in resort areas on lakes and were quite small in annual motor sales. A relatively few outlets were much larger, some selling as many as 1,000 units. Almost all dealers handled the motors of only one manufacturer. The following table shows the company's estimate of the general distribution of retail outlets by annual sales.

Annual volume in no. of motors	Estimated no. of retailers
1–9	7,000
10–24	4,500
25–99	3,200
100 and over	300

The smaller dealers were believed to have annual stock turnovers of about 2, but this figure was probably 8 or 10 for the larger dealers.

Annual model changes were customary in the outboard motor industry. Changing patterns of demand by size of motor and variations in the stock of motors carried over from one year to the next made it difficult for Outboard Motors to forecast sales and, hence, production for each new year. To help in this regard the firm decided to make an annual survey of dealers' inventories of motors prior to the major sales forecast on which production schedules would be based.

The information to be obtained was the total U.S. inventory of new motors broken down as follows:

I. Current year models
   A. By horsepower
      1. Under 4.0 horsepower
      2. 4.0–6.9 horsepower
      3. 7.0–9.9 horsepower
      4. 10.0–14.9 horsepower
      5. 15.0–19.9 horsepower
      6. 20.0–34.9 horsepower
      7. 35.0 and over
   B. By annual sales volume of outlet
      1. 1–9 unit sales
      2. 10–24 unit sales
      3. 25–99 unit sales
      4. 100 and over

II. Noncurrent models
   A. By horsepower as above
   B. By sales volume of outlet as above

III. Current and noncurrent models combined
   A. By each of 6 regions
   B. By above horsepower breakdowns in each of 6 regions

While Outboard Motors had little accurate information on which to base estimates of the inventory of motors by size of motor, the marketing research director finally settled on the following "best guesses."

Size of motor in horsepower	Estimated inventory in retail outlets (units)
Under 4.0	14,000
4.0–6.9	15,000
7.0–9.9	2,000
10.0–14.9	16,000
15.0–19.9	9,000
20.0–34.9	12,000
35.0 and over	24,000
Total	92,000

What size of sample of retail outlets should be selected?

Case 8—3.   TRANSIT RADIO, INC. (A)

Transit Radio, Inc. was negotiating for the franchise to install FM radio loudspeakers on buses in Eastville, an eastern city of 95,000. If it got the franchise, Transit Radio would broadcast music over the loudspeakers and would sell time to advertisers for commercials. The amount of income it might obtain from such advertising would determine how much it could afford to offer for the franchise.

Officials of Transit Radio believed they would have to pay approximately $50,000 for the franchise, but they were not sure this was a price they could afford to pay. The equipment to be installed on each bus would cost about $200. Since there were 48 buses on the city line, the total investment in equipment would be about $9,600.

To help in arriving at an estimate of the potential advertising income, the company executives decided to make a survey among Eastville residents of 15 years of age or more. They engaged a consultant to plan the details of the research. He developed a questionnaire which included the following questions:

1. Have you ridden on an Eastville city bus in the last seven days?
2. (IF YES TO QUESTION 1) On which day, or days, of the last seven did you ride an Eastville bus?

3. (FOR THE MOST RECENT DAY ON WHICH RESPONDENT RODE BUS) When you rode the bus on (NAME DAY), did you ride it to work, to school, to go shopping, to go visiting, or for some other purpose?
4. What is your approximate age?
5. What was your total family income last year?
6. (INTERVIEWER TO CHECK) Male ——— Female ———

Pretesting of the questionnaire and discussions with bus line officials led the research consultant to the following estimates of the answers that would be obtained to these questions:

Q#1: 70 percent will have ridden a bus in the last seven days.
Q#2: Riding would be distributed fairly equally over the five work days of the week, but Mondays and Thursdays would be 5 percent to 10 percent larger than the other three because Eastville stores were open on those nights. Bus riding on Saturday would be 30 percent below the Tuesday, Wednesday, Friday level, and on Sundays would be 80 percent below that level.

Q#3: Work 35%
     School 10%
     Shopping 25%
     Other 30%
Q#4: 15–19 ....10%
     20–29 ....20%
     30–45 ....30%
     Over 45 ....40%
Q#5: Under $4,000 ....40%
     $4,000 to $6,000 ......20%
     Over $6,000 ....40%
Q#6: Male 50%
     Female 50%

Eastville was divided into 22 census tracts of approximately equal population. There were 846 blocks and 26,211 dwelling units in the city according to the *Census of Housing*. The number of dwelling units per block varied from 0 in some business and industrial blocks to 308 in one block which had a number of large apartment houses.

1. How large a sample should the research consultant draw?
2. Should a probability or a nonprobability sample be used?
3. If a probability sample is used, how should it be drawn?
4. If a nonprobability sample is used, how should it be drawn?

Case 8—4.   THE BISSELL COMPANY

Scuff'n Wax Remover, a new product developed in the Bissell laboratory to remove the scuff marks and wax from all types of floors, was ready for test marketing. The marketing research department proposed to introduce it in three test markets and to measure sales in those markets by auditing sales in a sample of stores.

It was very difficult to estimate how much of the new product might be sold. No directly comparable products were on the market, although one or two brands of wax remover were available. These did not work with the ease of Scuff'n Wax Remover and had not been aggressively promoted. The product most closely similar seemed to be consumer floor waxes which had developed into large volume products. The Scuff'n Wax Remover was not expected to sell in volume even approaching the leading wax brands, but Bissell's management believed that most floors would benefit in appearance and durability if the old wax were removed at least once every six months. Otherwise, unsightly wax accumulated in corners and the grit which became embedded in these accumulations was abrasive on the floor. Most commercial and industrial buildings had regular schedules for wax removal.

Very little was known about the sales of the floor wax removers on the market. These were sold primarily through hardware stores. Bissell planned to sell its new product through food stores in conjunction with the waxes and other floor care products sold there. By promoting the idea of removing old wax from the floor, the management estimated that it could get one tenth of all families to use the product. Each of these families was expected to use two quart containers of wax remover per year. Scuff'n Wax Remover would be the first brand aggressively pushed in the market and was, therefore, estimated to obtain 50 percent of the market. For a city of one million, the above estimates would lead to the following sales of Scuff'n Wax Remover:

Total population	1,000,000
Number of families	250,000
One tenth who use wax remover	25,000
Two units per year per family using	50,000
Scuff'n Wax Remover 50% of market	25,000
Sales of Scuff'n Wax Remover per week	500

The three cities selected for test marketing were in different parts of the country. The population and food stores in each of these cities was as follows:

City X—population 375,000

Chain stores	Number of stores	Percentage of market
A	12	19
B	10	14
C	8	11
D	9	10
E	1	—
Voluntary group	38	7
Retailer cooperative	106	35
Total	184	96%

City Y—population 230,000

Chain stores	Number of stores	Percentage of market
A	5	22
B	7	20
C	1	12
D	3	10
E	4	9
F	3	6
Voluntary groups		
A	19	9
B	20	4
Total	62	92%

City Z—population 550,000

Chain stores	Number of stores	Percentage of market
A	52	35
B	29	22
C	11	12
D	11	8
E	7	3
Voluntary groups		
A	12	3.5
B	50	2.5
Retailer cooperative	151	14
Total	323	100%

Bissell's sales manager believed they could get distribution in virtually all the chain stores and the larger independents.

The research plan was to audit the stocks in a sample of stores just prior to the start of the advertising campaign; to audit them again two weeks later; a third time a month after the campaign started; and a fourth time two months after the start of the campaign. The first audit in each store would cost $15; subsequent audits would be $10 each.

Sales of Scuff'n Wax Remover in the test cities would be used as a basis for making more accurate estimates of potential national sales and, from this, would indicate the size of the advertising campaign that could be used.

How many stores should be included in the sample?

9

Application of sampling methods to marketing problems

ALTHOUGH SIMPLE RANDOM SAMPLING has the important advantage of simplicity, it is not appropriate for many problems in marketing research. Some alternative sampling designs which, while more complex, have more general applicability are considered in this chapter. The first to be examined is *stratified random sampling*.

STRATIFIED RANDOM SAMPLING

This procedure may be summarized as follows:

1. The universe to be sampled is subdivided (or *stratified*) into groups which are mutually exclusive, but which together include all items in the universe.
2. A simple random sample is then chosen independently from each group—or stratum.

This sampling procedure differs from simple random sampling in that with the latter the sample items are chosen at random from the *entire* universe. In stratified random sampling the sample is designed so that a designated number of items is chosen from *each* stratum. In simple random sampling there is no way of knowing exactly how many of the sample items will have the characteristics of stratum 1, how many of stratum 2, and so on; the distribution of the sample among strata is left entirely to chance.

388

Reasons for stratification

Greater reliability. Stratification is often used in marketing research. Although several reasons obtain for the widespread use of this procedure, the leading one is that it usually will lead to sample estimates which have a greater reliability than would otherwise be obtained. The basic idea involved may be grasped by reference to Figures 9–1 and 9–2. Suppose the curve depicted in Figure 9–1 represents the distribution of the number of cases of Wheaties stocked in United States grocery stores. The objective is to estimate the average number of cases of Wheaties in stock per store.

FIGURE 9–1. Graphical representation of the universe

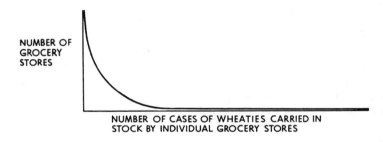

NUMBER OF GROCERY STORES

NUMBER OF CASES OF WHEATIES CARRIED IN STOCK BY INDIVIDUAL GROCERY STORES

The universe represented by this curve is typical of many encountered in marketing research. A very small proportion of the universe "contributes" heavily to the mean. A relatively few large stores account for a high percent of the total inventory. The presence or absence in a simple random sample of a few extreme items would determine whether or not the sample mean would be reasonably close to that of the universe. Unless a very large simple random sample were used, there would be reason to expect that the extreme members of this universe would be represented somewhat more or less than their actual proportion in the universe.

Now, suppose information were available which made it possible to partition this universe into subuniverses, A, B, C, etc., as indicated in Figure 9–2.

A relatively small sample taken within each subuniverse would provide a good estimate of the mean of that subuniverse because of the similarity of the items included in that partition. If the proportion of the universe included within each subuniverse were known, the estimated means of these subuniverses could be weighted together so as to provide an estimate of the mean of the entire universe.

If the variable being studied varies little among items in the same stratum but a great deal among strata, this stratifying procedure will

FIGURE 9–2. Partitioning of universe into subuniverses

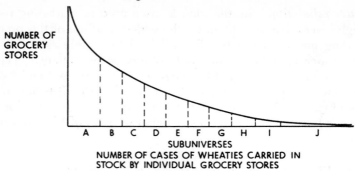

ordinarily provide a better estimate of the mean than could be obtained by using simple random sampling. In practice, the researcher usually does not know enough about the universe to subdivide it in quite this way. However, information will often be available about a variable which is highly correlated with the variable of interest. This may be used to make up the strata.

Obtaining information about parts of the universe. A second reason for stratification is that information may be desired about the component parts of a universe. For example, in a national study of coffee consumption, information might be wanted as to how the rate of consumption per family varies among geographic regions, city sizes, family sizes, and the like. Similarly, in a study of pancake mix sales in grocery stores, data might be wanted separately for chains and independents, and by store sizes. If individual estimates are desired for each of the component subuniverses, these subuniverses may be regarded as strata and an independent random sample drawn from each.

Estimation of the universe mean, with a stratified random sample

Since a stratified random sample is just a group of simple random samples, the sample mean of each stratum is unbiased. The means of the individual strata can be combined (weighted) into an unbiased estimate of the overall universe mean. Thus, the estimate of the universe mean is simply a weighted average of the strata means. For example, assume a two-stratum universe. From each stratum, the following observations are made using simple random sampling.

Stratum number	Number of observations	Value of each observation	Total value of all observations
1	2	10, 30	40
2	4	50, 100, 150, 200	500

In Stratum 1 the arithmetic mean is 20 ($40 \div 2$), while in Stratum 2 it is 125 ($500 \div 4$). The weight assigned to each stratum is the proportion of universe items included in that stratum. Assuming each stratum was sampled proportionate to its weight in the universe, the mean of Stratum 1 would receive a weight of 2 and the mean of Stratum 2 a weight of 4. The universe mean would be estimated by multiplying each stratum mean by its assigned weight, adding the results, and dividing by the sum of the weights. In the case at hand, the estimate for the universe mean would be

$$\frac{(20 \times 2) + (125 \times 4)}{2 + 4} = 90.$$

In the general case, one wishes to estimate the universe mean when there are k strata, where k can be any number greater than one. For each of the k strata, the following data must be obtained:

1. The mean of the sample for that stratum.
2. The ratio of the total number of items in that stratum to the total number in the universe. This is the relative "weight" of that stratum, denoted by W.

The data can be summarized as follows:

Stratum	Sample mean in stratum	Relative weight of stratum
1	$\overline{X}_1$	W_1
2	$\overline{X}_2$	W_2
3	$\overline{X}_3$	W_3
.	.	.
.	.	.
.	.	.
k	$\overline{X}_k$	W_k

With the information in the above table, the universe mean is estimated by the formula

$\overline{X}_{sr}$ (estimated mean based on stratified random sampling)

$$= W_1\overline{X}_1 + W_2\overline{X}_2 + - - - - - + W_k\overline{X}_k.$$

Note that this formula provides a weighted sample mean, each stratum mean being weighted in proportion to its share of the total number of elements in the universe. For the two-stratum example on page 390, the calculation is

$$\overline{X}_{sr} = W_1\overline{X}_1 + W_2\overline{X}_2$$
$$= \tfrac{1}{3}(20) + \tfrac{2}{3}(125)$$
$$= 90$$

the same answer obtained before.

As another example, suppose the researcher has these data:

Store stratum	Sample mean unit sales per store	Number of stores in stratum
Large stores	200	20,000
Medium stores	100	30,000
Small stores	50	50,000

Then the estimated universe mean sales per store would be

$$\overline{X}_{sr} = W_1\overline{X}_1 + W_2\overline{X}_2 + W_3\overline{X}_3$$
$$= (.2)(200) + (.3)(100) + (.5)(50)$$
$$= 40 + 30 + 25 = 95 \text{ units.}$$

Interval estimation with stratified random samples

Little new theory is required to develop confidence limits for a universe mean estimated from a stratified random sample. As in the case of simple random sampling, an estimated standard error of the mean is first secured. Then the appropriate multiple of this figure (2 for 95 percent confidence, 3 for virtual certainty) is added to and subtracted from the estimated mean. The resultant two numbers are the confidence limits.

To estimate the standard error of the mean of a stratified random sample, the data required are these:

Stratum	Sample variance in stratum	Sample size in stratum	Weight of stratum
1	s_1^2	n_1	W_1
2	s_2^2	n_2	W_2
3	s_3^2	n_3	W_3
. ...	.	.	.
. ...	.	.	.
. ...	.	.	.
k	s_k^2	n_k	W_k

The quantity s_1^2 is the variance (standard deviation squared) of the sample in Stratum 1, and n_1 is the number of observations in that stratum. For Stratum 2, the sample variance is s_2^2 and the sample size is n_2, and so on. The W's are the same numbers used in estimating the universe mean.

To estimate the standard error, first calculate the quantity,[1]

$$s_{\bar{x}_{sr}}^2 = \frac{W_1^2 s_1^2}{n_1} + \frac{W_2^2 s_2^2}{n_2} + - - - - + \frac{W_k^2 s_2^2}{n_k}.$$

The estimated standard error sought is $s_{\bar{x}_{sr}}$, the square root of $s_{\bar{x}_{sr}}^2$.

As an illustration of the calculations, suppose that in the store sales example (page 392), the stratum sample variances and sample sizes are these:

Store stratum	Sample variance in stratum = s^2	Sample size in stratum = n	Weight of stratum = W
Large stores	4,000	100	0.2
Medium stores	1,400	70	0.3
Small stores	400	80	0.5

The square of the estimated standard error is

$$s_{\bar{x}_{sr}}^2 = (.2)^2 \left(\frac{4000}{100}\right) + (.3)^2 \left(\frac{1400}{70}\right) + (.5)^2 \left(\frac{400}{80}\right)$$

$$= (.04)(40) + (.09)(20) + (.25)(5)$$

$$= 1.60 + 1.80 + 1.25 = 4.65.$$

So the estimated standard error of the mean is

$$s_{\bar{x}_{sr}} = \sqrt{4.65} = 2.2 \text{ units, approximately.}$$

Multiplying this standard error by 2, and adding and subtracting the resulting quantity to the estimated mean of 95 units, gives a 95 percent confidence interval for the population mean of 90.6 to 99.4 units. An interval which is virtually certain to cover the population mean is 95 units $\pm$ 3 (2.2) units, or, 88.4 to 101.6 units.

In working through the above example, the reader will have noticed that the calculation was based on the estimated *within-stratum* variances.

---

[1] For each stratum in which the sample size exceeds 5 percent of the number of universe elements, a finite population correction factor needs to be applied to the appropriate term in the expression given for $s_{\bar{x}_{sr}}^2$. Although this situation is fully analogous to the corresponding correction for simple random sampling, this refinement will be ignored here for simplicity.

Differences among strata means do not enter into the sampling error of the mean in a stratified random sample, as they would in a simple random sample. It is this fact that renders stratified random sampling a generally more precise procedure than a simple random sample containing the same number of elements.

Issues in the selection of stratified random samples

The preceding part of this chapter has dealt with how to make certain simple estimates from the data secured by a stratified random sample. It is now necessary to consider some of the issues involved in setting up a stratified random sample:

1. *Bases of stratification*—What characteristics should be used to subdivide the universe into strata?
2. *Number of strata*—How many strata should be constructed, and what stratum boundaries should be used?
3. *Sample sizes within strata*—How many observations should be taken in each stratum?

Logically, these questions should perhaps have preceded the discussion on estimation. In a practical situation, they must be answered before data can be gathered and the estimates prepared. They are considered at this point, rather than earlier, because it is easier to discuss them after the general procedure of stratified random sampling and estimation has been sketched out.

Bases of stratification

An early decision in the development of a stratified random sample is the selection of bases of stratification. How should the total universe of interest be subdivided into component subuniverses?

Intuitively, it seems clear that the best basis would be the frequency distribution of the principal variable being studied. For example, in the earlier Wheaties inventory illustration, it is plausible that creation of strata on the basis of inventory would provide an optimal stratification. However, two difficulties arise in attempting to proceed this way. First, there is usually interest in many variables, not just one, and stratification on the basis of one may not provide the best stratification for the others. Secondly, even if one survey variable is of primary importance, current data on its frequency distribution will not be available. If they were, the study would not be needed.

Under these circumstances, a reasonable approach is to create strata on the basis of variables, for which information is available, that are believed to be highly correlated with the principal survey characteristics of interest. The stratification may be on the basis of a single, simple variable (e.g., store dollar volume), or a compound variable (e.g., store dollar volume *within* geographic region), depending on such matters as availability of detailed information and number of strata to be used.

In general, it is desirable to make up strata in such a way that the sampling units within strata are as similar as possible. The effect of this is that a relatively limited sample within each stratum will provide a generally precise estimate of the mean of that stratum. Similarly, it is desirable to use a stratification system which will maximize differences in stratum means for the key survey variables of interest. The accomplishment of this goal is desirable since stratification has the effect of removing differences between stratum means from the sampling error.

In practical marketing research, one or more of a few stratification bases will often be found useful. For example, such stratification variables as geography and population density will typically be of value if either human or institutional populations are being sampled. When human populations are being studied, it may be possible also to stratify on demographic characteristics (age, income, etc.), provided these are known in advance of the sampling. (If they are not, it is also possible to stratify after selection, although this cannot be discussed in detail here.) In the case of institutional samples, it will virtually always be desirable to stratify on some measure of size (dollar volume, number of employees, etc.), since stores, wholesalers, etc. may exhibit enormous variability in such important characteristics as sales, inventories, and the like.

Number of strata

When modes of stratification have been chosen, the questions of number of strata and construction of stratum boundaries remain. As regards number of strata, preliminary evaluation suggests that as many as possible be used. If each stratum could be made as homogeneous as possible, its mean could be estimated with high reliability and, in turn, the universe mean could be estimated with high precision.

However, some practical problems limit the desirability of a large number of strata:

1. No stratification scheme will completely "explain" the variability among a set of observations. Past a certain point, the "residual" or "unexplained" variation will dominate, and little improvement will be effected by creating more strata.
2. Depending on the costs of stratification (both for sample selection and

subsequent tabulations), a point may be reached quickly where creation of additional strata is economically unproductive.

More than six strata may be unprofitable when a single overall estimate is to be made.[2] If estimates are required for universe subgroups (e.g., by region or city size), then more strata may be desirable.

As far as stratum boundaries are concerned, the issue is this. Given a certain number of strata to be made up, what "cut-off" points should be used to establish stratum boundaries? If the stratification is done on the basis of a quantitative variable (e.g., grocery store dollar volume), then rules are available.[3] In the case of qualitative stratification variables (e.g., geographic regions), decisions as to strata definition must ordinarily be made on a judgmental basis. Often, the decision in either instance will be partially dictated by the need to provide estimates for particular universe subgroups. For example, it may be necessary to provide data by company sales divisions, for particular store size categories, etc.

Sample sizes within strata

Once strata have been established, the question of how big a sample should be drawn from each must be decided. To illustrate the problem, and some ways of approaching it, consider one particular situation which is of fairly common occurrence in marketing research. Suppose a budget has been fixed and that the cost per observation is known and equal for all strata. This amounts to saying that the total sample size (for all strata combined) is fixed. How should this total sample size be allocated among strata—how many observations should be taken from the first stratum, how many from the second, and so on?

As a concrete example, suppose the researcher wishes to estimate the mean value of some characteristic in this two-stratum universe:

Stratum	Number of items in stratum
A	10,000
B	90,000

Suppose further that the budget for the job is $3,000 and that the cost per observation is $6 in each stratum, so the available total sample size is 500. With this total sample size, there are 499 possible sample allocations between the two strata:

---

[2] W. G. Cochran, *Sampling Techniques* (New York: John Wiley & Sons, Inc., 1963), pp. 133–35.

[3] *Ibid.*, pp. 128–33. This section gives a summary of recent results and references.

Allocation	Sample size in stratum: A	B
1	1	499
2	2	498
.		
. ...	.	.
.		.
499	499	1

The problem is to decide which of these allocations is to be used.

Proportioned allocation. One intuitively plausible approach would be to sample the same proportion of items in each stratum, i.e., to sample all strata at the same rate. In the example being considered, the overall sampling fraction is

$$\frac{\text{Sample size}}{\text{Universe size}} = \frac{500}{100{,}000} = 0.5\%$$

so that this method of sample allocation would provide a sample of 50 in Stratum A (10,000 × 0.5%) and a sample of 450 in Stratum B (90,000 × 0.5%).

This method of allocation, sampling each stratum at the same rate, is called *proportional sampling*. It is probably the most widely used method. As a general rule, it is also the preferred procedure when the objective is to estimate the overall universe mean and the only statistical data available on the strata are their sizes (number of items in each).

The major practical advantage of proportional allocation is that it leads to estimates which are computationally simple. In general, as noted earlier, it is necessary to weight the estimated stratum means in order to provide an estimate of the overall universe mean:

$$\bar{X}_{sr} = W_1 \bar{X}_1 + - - - W_k \bar{X}_k.$$

With proportional allocation, this formula reduces to just

$$\frac{\text{sum of sample observations}}{\text{total sample size}}.$$

That is, no special weighting is needed; all one has to do is add up the sample observations for all strata and divide by their number. Proportional allocation automatically weights the stratum means in their correct proportions. The reader may verify that this process works in the simple example considered on page 390. For that case, the sum of the sample values is $40 + 500 = 540$, and it is based on $2 + 4 = 6$ observations. Since this was a proportionally allocated sample, the above formula leads to $540/6 = 90$, which is the same estimated mean obtained by using the general formula involving weights.

Optimal allocation. As a rule, proportional allocation is recommended when all one knows of the strata is their sizes. If, in addition, the standard deviation of the observations in each stratum is known, then a *disproportionate allocation* may be desirable.[4]

To illustrate a situation where a disproportionate allocation would be clearly indicated, suppose all the observations in Stratum B of the above example had the same value. In this instance, a sample of one from Stratum B would be sufficient and the remaining 499 observations would be taken from Stratum A. This allocation would be optimal, in the sense of giving the most information possible about the overall universe mean for a total available sample size of 500. It would obviously be wasteful, in this situation, to take a proportional sample (450) from Stratum B.

In general, an allocation of a total sample size among strata is said to be the *optimal allocation* if, for that sample size, it provides the smallest possible standard error of the estimated mean.[5] In any specific situation where the stratum standard deviations are known, it would be possible to identify the optimal allocation by going through the following process:

1. First enumerate the possible allocations, as in the illustration on page 397.
2. Then, for each allocation, calculate the standard error of the mean, using the formula given on page 393, with the known standard deviations substituted for the estimated values in that formula.
3. Finally, select the allocation which leads to the smallest standard error. This is the optimal allocation.

Fortunately, it is not necessary to go through the steps indicated above to identify the optimal distribution of the sample. Mathematical analysis provides formulas which give the answer at once. For the two-stratum case, the optimal sample size (n_A) in Stratum A, is

$$n_A = \frac{nN_A\sigma_A}{(N_A\sigma_A + N_B\sigma_B)}$$

where n = total available sample size.

N_A = number of items in Stratum A.

N_B = number of items in Stratum B.

σ_A = standard deviation of the observations in Stratum A.

σ_B = standard deviation in Stratum B.

---

[4] If the unit *costs* of sampling vary among strata, a disproportionate sampling may similarly be desirable. Although account may be taken of these variations in arriving at optimal sample sizes, this facet is ignored here for simplicity.

[5] A different definition would be appropriate if the possibility of differential costs of sampling among strata were also considered.

The optimal sample size in Stratum B will be $n_B = n - n_A$.

Note in the above formula that the optimal allocation depends on two factors:

1. *The sizes of the strata, N_A and N_B.* In general, the larger the stratum, the larger the sample from that stratum.
2. *The variabilities within strata.* As a rule, the stratum with the larger standard deviation is sampled more heavily.

Observe also that, if the strata standard deviations are equal ($\sigma_A = \sigma_B$), then the formula says to take a proportional sample from each stratum. That is, proportional allocation is optimal when the strata are equally variable.

Consider the problem originally posed:

$$n = \quad 500$$
$$N_A = 10,000$$
$$N_B = 90,000$$

if

$$\sigma_A = 50$$
$$\sigma_B = 10$$

then in Stratum A

$$n_A = 500 \left(\frac{(10,000)(50)}{(10,000)(50) + (90,000)(10)} \right)$$
$$= 179 \text{ observations.}$$

In Stratum B, $500 - 179 = 321$ observations would be taken. With this allocation, the standard error of the estimated universe mean would be 0.63. This is about one fourth less than the standard error that a proportionally allocated sample would provide (0.83), as may be verified. This represents a substantial increase in statistical efficiency, considering that just the allocation of the sample among strata was involved.

Application of optimal allocation. It is not anticipated that many of the readers of this book will have occasion to use the formula for optimal allocation that has been given. Its practical application requires consideration of a number of factors, the development of which is beyond the scope of this book. For example, stratum standard deviations will not be known exactly and it must be decided whether adequate approximations exist; the optimal allocation for one survey question will not be the same for other equally important questions and a compromise must be made; and so on.

Despite these limitations, the reader should be broadly familiar with the idea of optimal allocation and have some understanding of its basis.

The principle is applied fairly often in practical marketing research, especially where institutions (e.g., stores) rather than families or individuals are being sampled. It is also of greater importance when measurement data (sales, inventories, etc.) are being gathered rather than attribute data (simple presence or absence of a characteristic).

A good illustration of the use of this general principle in practical application is provided by the Nielsen Retail Index (page 261). Although the Nielsen sample comprises about 0.5 percent of the food stores in the Continental United States, its stores account for more than 1.5 percent of the grocery store business. Because large food stores have more variable sales of almost any product, Nielsen samples them at a disproportionately heavy rate. This results in a much more efficient sample than would be obtained with a proportionally allocated sample.

Concluding remarks on stratum sample sizes.   This discussion on sample sizes within strata has been confined to the problem of allocating a fixed overall sample size among strata. Through the use of optimal allocation, it is possible to maximize reliability for a given total sample size.

Sometimes, instead of allocating a fixed sample size, the problem is to decide what stratum sample sizes are needed in order to achieve a specified level of reliability in the estimated population value. For example, the objective might be to estimate the population mean within 20 percent, and the problem would be to determine the minimal stratum sample sizes necessary to reach that goal. This problem is an extension of that dealt with on pages 372–76, where the object was to determine the size of a simple random sample necessary for specified reliability.

It is not feasible, within the limits of this book, to present a discussion of this problem.[6] However, a few useful general comments can be made on the basis of what has been said so far:

1. For a fixed reliability requirement, an optimally allocated stratified random sample will require fewer observations than the corresponding proportional design. In turn, a proportionally allocated stratified random sample will demand a smaller sample size for a given reliability than will a simple random sample.
2. Therefore, the sample size necessary assuming simple random sampling may be a useful "upper limit" to that required with more efficient sampling methods, such as optimally or proportionally allocated stratified sampling.

Concluding remarks on stratified random sampling

In general, stratified random sampling is subject to many of the same practical limitations as are encountered with simple random sampling.

---

[6] For a more detailed treatment, see Cochran, *op. cit.*, pp. 95–97.

For example, a listing of all universe items must be available before the sample is drawn, just as was the case with simple random sampling. In addition, the number of universe items in each stratum must be known if full advantage of stratification is to be taken.

Again, as was true of simple random sampling, the costs of this method may be high per sampled item because of the likelihood of wide geographic dispersion of the sample within strata. However, more control of this factor may be exercised with stratified random sampling than with simple random sampling because of the possibility of using geographic location as one basis of stratification. This enables the investigator to determine in advance the number of items to be sampled in any particular area and to plan his field work accordingly.

Stratified random sampling will almost always provide more reliable estimates than simple random sampling. The gains achieved by this method will typically be moderate rather than extremely large. It is always worthwhile, however, to consider the possibility of stratification and, if it can be done cheaply, it is usually worth doing. In certain situations, it may be worth sampling the more variable and larger strata at a disproportionately heavy rate. Stratification and optimal allocation are most valuable when sampling from highly skewed universes such as are often found in studies of marketing institutions.

CLUSTER SAMPLING

In the sampling methods discussed so far, each observation is chosen individually. In some probability sampling methods, however, groups or clusters of observations are chosen at random. A simple example will illustrate the idea. Consider the following universe of sixteen items arranged arbitrarily into four groups:

Group	*Elements*
1	X_1, X_2, X_3, X_4
2	X_5, X_6, X_7, X_8
3	$X_9, X_{10}, X_{11}, X_{12}$
4	$X_{13}, X_{14}, X_{15}, X_{16}$

Suppose it is desired to choose a probability sample of eight elements from this universe.

One way of proceeding would be to choose a simple random sample of eight items. But suppose that for some reason it is not feasible to carry out such a sampling method. An alternative way would be to select two of the four groups at random and enumerate their items *completely*. Clearly such a sampling technique would be a probability sampling scheme, since every element would have a known chance of being chosen, namely, a chance of one in two. Every possible combination of universe items, however, would *not* have the same chance of being chosen. This is true since the selection of one item in a cluster automatically means the inclusion of the other items in the cluster. Thus, with this sampling procedure (called *simple, one-stage cluster sampling*), it is impossible for some random samples to be chosen. For example, in the cluster sample described above the following combination, among others, could not occur: X_1, X_2, X_5, X_6, X_9, X_{10}, X_{13}, and X_{14}.

This procedure amounts to sampling from a universe of groups or clusters of items rather than sampling from a universe of individual items. The original universe of sixteen items has been redefined as a universe of four clusters and a random sampling of two clusters has been made. Probability sampling techniques of this kind in which clusters of items are chosen with known chances, are called *cluster sampling methods* and are widely used in the sampling of human populations. In this chapter, some of the basic ideas involved in cluster sampling will be explored, although the complexity of the subject will not permit a detailed discussion.

Relative efficiency of simple one-stage cluster sampling and simple random sampling

How does the sampling behavior of an estimate obtained by simple, one-stage cluster sampling compare with that obtained by simple random sampling? A comparison of the two methods will indicate the circumstances under which cluster sampling will be more precise than simple random sampling, and vice versa.

Relative statistical efficiency. Consider the statistical efficiency of the mean of a simple, one-stage cluster sample relative to that of a simple random sample. One method will be regarded as superior to the other if it has a smaller standard error for the same total number of items sampled. The relative efficiency of the two sampling systems depends on the degree of similarity among items in each cluster. The greater the similarity of the observations in a cluster, the *less* efficient will be cluster sampling. The greater the dissimilarity among the observations in a cluster, the *more* efficient will be cluster sampling.

Suppose that two clusters of four elements each are to be selected from a universe with the following numerical values: four items with a value of 1, four with a value of 2, four with a value of 3, and four with a value of 4. Next, consider the two extreme ways of grouping the sixteen elements into four clusters as shown below. The first clustering method gives a maximum of similarity within each cluster. The second method gives a minimum of similarity within each cluster.

Degree of similarity within cluster	Cluster number	Values of the observations in cluster
Maximum	1	1111
	2	2222
	3	3333
	4	4444
Minimum	1	1234
	2	1234
	3	1234
	4	1234

With the first of these clustering methods, the standard error of the mean of the cluster sample will be *more* than that of a simple random sample because, regardless of which two clusters are chosen, information will be obtained on only two of the four different values. One observation in each cluster in the sample gives information. The other six observations in the sample do little more than repeat this information. Thus, simple random sampling would be more efficient. With the minimum similarity clusters the standard error of the means of the cluster samples is zero, i.e., each cluster has the same mean. Cluster sampling will be more efficient than simple random sampling in this case.

This example illustrates the basic principle that the statistical efficiency of cluster sampling depends on how the clusters are constructed—that is, on the degree to which each cluster can be made to include all the values in the universe. If the observations within a cluster represent only a few of the values in the universe, a simple cluster sample will be less efficient statistically than a simple random sample having the same total number of items. Clusters are often constructed in such a way that the items within a cluster are relatively homogeneous. This implies that in practice cluster sampling is often less efficient statistically than simple random sampling.

Relative net efficiency

The preceding discussion has been in terms of statistical efficiency only, that is, in terms of the relative magnitude of the standard errors under the two sampling systems. When *economic efficiency,* the relative cost per observation, of the two systems is considered, it will often be found that simple cluster sampling is the superior method. In a practical situation one will generally be interested in *net efficiency,* which consists of maximizing the information obtained per dollar of cost. A consideration of this latter criterion will often lead to the adoption of cluster sampling, since the gain in economic efficiency will usually offset the decline in statistical efficiency which may result from cluster sampling.

At this point in the discussion some of these ideas may seem rather abstract. For the moment, the essential conclusions are these:

1. Simple cluster sampling may be either more or less efficient statistically than simple random sampling. This depends on the degree of intracluster heterogeneity which is obtained.
2. In practice clusters are often constructed in such a way that the observations within a cluster are relatively homogeneous. When this is the case, simple cluster sampling will be less efficient statistically than simple random sampling.
3. The lower relative cost of obtaining observations in cluster sampling often offsets the loss in statistical efficiency. The net efficiency is often greater for cluster sampling.

The reasoning behind the second and third conclusions will become more clear when a special type of cluster sampling, called *area sampling*, is discussed. Some idea of the interplay between statistical efficiency and economic efficiency in a practical situation will also become clear at that time.

Systematic sampling

One type of cluster sampling is called systematic sampling. An illustration will show how such a sample is drawn. From a list of one hundred food stores, it is desired to choose a probability sample of twenty stores. One way of doing this as as follows:

a. Draw a random number between 1 and 5. Suppose the number chosen is 2.
b. Include in the sample the stores numbered 2, 7, 12, 17, 22 . . . 97; i.e., starting with the number 2, take every fifth number.

The above is an illustration of *systematic sampling*. That this is a particular kind of cluster sampling is readily seen if the possible samples produced by this procedure are considered. This particular example has only five possible samples:

Sample	Identification of stores in sample	
1	1, 6, 11, 16, 21	96
2	2, 7, 12, 17, 22	97
3	3, 8, 13, 18, 23	98
4	4, 9, 14, 19, 24	99
5	5, 10, 15, 20, 25	100

Each of these samples amounts to a *cluster* of stores and each has a chance of 1 out of 5 of being included in the sample. In effect, the original universe of one hundred stores has been redefined as a universe of five clusters of stores and each cluster is given an equal chance of being chosen by the sampling process. A *single* random number determines all twenty sample stores. As a consequence, the twenty sample stores are not independently chosen. Once random number 2 is chosen, the whole sequence of stores 2, 7, 12, 17, 22, and so on is *automatically* included in the sample.

To choose a systematic sample, the first step is to determine the total number of items in the universe. Divide this figure by the desired sample size. The result is called the sampling interval. Next select a random number between 1 and the sampling interval figure. This identifies the first element on the list to be included in the sample. Add to this random number the sampling interval. The result identifies the second item to be included in the sample. Continue adding the interval and taking the items so identified until the sample is drawn.

Advantages of systematic sampling.   In one form or another, wide use is made of systematic sampling. The principal advantage of this technique is its simplicity. When sampling from a list, it is easier to choose a random start and select every *n*th item thereafter than to make a simple random selection. The technique is faster and less subject to error than simple random selection. Hence, systematic sampling is often used in place of simple random sampling. For example, it might be used instead of random sampling for selecting items within strata in a stratified design.

In common with simple random sampling, the mean of a systematic sample is an unbiased estimate of the universe mean.[7] This property is clear in the example used to introduce systematic sampling on page 404. Since each of the five possible samples shown has the same chance of being chosen, and their average is equal to the universe mean, the sample mean provides an unbiased estimate.

It is often found that systematic sampling is somewhat more efficient statistically than is simple random sampling. This will be the case when "nearby" universe items on the listing are similar and items widely removed from one another are dissimilar. For example, if a list were made up by listing grocery stores in order according to dollar sales volume and the variable being sampled was correlated with sales, then it would be expected that systematic sampling would be more precise than simple

---

[7] Technically, for this to be true, it is necessary that the ratio of the number of universe elements to the sample size (i.e., the sampling interval) be a whole number. The small variations from this that are usually encountered generally will not bias the estimate to an appreciable extent.

random sampling. The ordering of stores by dollar volume in this case would set up an implicit stratification, and the systematic sampling would operate much like a stratified random sampling, with a single store chosen out of each stratum.

To illustrate the basic ideas of systematic sampling, it has been assumed that a listing of all universe items was available. It is not necessary that a complete listing be available at the time the sampling is begun. For example, one might sample systematically through time by collecting the carbon copy of every fifteenth sales slip in a store, or one could sample systematically through space by interviewing at every ninth dwelling unit on a block, even though a list of the dwelling units was not available beforehand.

Difficulty in estimating sampling error of a systematic sample.   One difficulty arising from systematic sampling is that an unbiased estimate of the sampling error attached to the estimated mean cannot be obtained without making some assumptions, because the selection process only identifies *one* cluster (even though this may contain several items for observation). At least two independently chosen sampling units (here, clusters) are needed to evaluate sampling error.

One might, for example, assume that the universe items were listed in random order. If this were the case, a systematic sample would be equivalent to a simple random sample and the usual formulas would apply. In some situations it may be quite reasonable to make this assumption—for example, when the list is in alphabetical order.

Another procedure is sometimes used to provide an estimate of sampling error. The sample items are considered in pairs, 1 and 2, 3 and 4, etc. Each pair is assumed to be a random sample of two from a stratum. Thus, if the one hundred food stores in the earlier example were listed in order of dollar volume, one could assume that the first two sample stores came from one stratum of ten stores, the next two from another stratum of ten stores, and so on. The twenty sample observations would then be analyzed like a stratified random sample consisting of two observations from each of ten strata. Ordinarily, this procedure will result in an overestimate of sampling error, but it may provide a satisfactory upper limit to the standard error.

In some situations, it may be possible to obtain an unbiased estimate of the sampling error by drawing a number of systematic samples instead of just one. For instance, instead of drawing one systematic sample of five hundred, it might be feasible to draw ten independent systematic samples of fifty each. The variation among sample estimates yields a measurement of sampling error.

Danger of periodicities in universe listing.   Another basic difficulty may arise in systematic sampling when the universe listing contains "hidden periodicities." An example will again clarify the point. Suppose the problem is to sample from a list of one hundred grocery stores consisting of twenty chains and eighty independents. The list of stores is made up as follows:

$$I,I,I,I,C,I,I,I,I,C, \ldots\ldots\ldots\ldots.I,I,I,I,C.$$

I denotes an independent store and *C* denotes a chain store. A systematic sampling of one out of five stores on this list is to be made.

With a systematic sampling scheme, one would obtain either all independent stores in the sample (4 times out of 5) or all chain stores (1 time out of 5). Because the list contains a periodicity equal to a multiple of the sampling interval (1 in 5), such a sampling procedure would yield an estimate with a greater standard error than would simple random sampling. If the sampling interval were 1 in 10, 1 in 20, or any other multiple of 5, the difficulty would still persist.

In the illustration cited, if the characteristic being surveyed were independent of the type of store ownership, no difficulty would arise. Where periodicities do exist, however, it will often be found that the characteristic studied will *not* be independent of the periodically recurring phenomenon. For example, in sampling department store sales through time one would not choose to study sales every seventh day because of the weekly sales cycle. In a practical situation, it will not always be easy to determine whether a periodicity is present or to evaluate its significance if it is suspected. The sample data themselves do not help to show the presence of such problems. All one can do is to give some attention to the possibility and, where periodicity seems likely, to adopt some alternative sampling system.

Area sampling

Up to this point the discussion has been concerned with sampling from a list which identifies every individual item in the universe. In many marketing problems, either no such list is available, or what is available is badly out of date or otherwise inadequate. To meet problems of this kind a very ingenious method of cluster sampling known as *area sampling* has been devised. Although the basic principles of area sampling are easy to understand, their application to particular problems requires considerable experience and ingenuity. Only the more important basic principles will be considered here.

Suppose it is desired to estimate the number of packages of Jell-O in households located within the corporate area limits of Philadelphia, and that no accurate listing of these households is available. How might one deal with this problem? One approach is to:

1. Choose a simple random sample of (n) city blocks from all those (N) which make up the city of Philadelphia.
2. Determine the number of Jell-O packages in all households located

on the sample blocks. Add up these data to obtain the total inventory for all households located on sample blocks.

3. Multiply the total sample inventory by N/n, which is the reciprocal of the sampling ratio. The resulting figure will be an unbiased estimate of the total inventory of Jell-O in Philadelphia households.

Such a sampling procedure is a probability sampling method, since each Philadelphia household has a known chance (n/N) of being included in the sample. However, in this illustration the universe (Philadelphia households) was not sampled directly. A universe of *areas* (city blocks) was first defined and a sample of those selected. Then, the households located on the sample blocks were audited, and the total inventory of these households was used to estimate the inventory for all Philadelphia households.

Reasoning back of area sampling. Consider in detail the reasoning behind this particular procedure. Philadelphia may be defined precisely in terms of a particular area. Further, it is possible to subdivide this area into a number of blocks such that (1) each block is clearly defined in terms of location and extent, and (2) the total number of blocks, N, is known. Since this operation is possible, Philadelphia may be considered a universe of areas (in this case, blocks). Because all of these blocks are identified and their total number is known, it is possible to draw a probability sample from this block universe.

Thus, the original universe (for which no list was available) is transformed into a universe of areas for which a listing (in the form of maps) does exist. The existence of a list for this block universe permits the selection of a probability sample of blocks. Since a rule of association between households and blocks has been established, the investigator may regard the households located on the sample blocks as a sample of households. This sample of households will be a probability sample because the cluster of households associated with each block has a known chance of being selected. This chance is equal to the chance that the block with which it is associated will be selected.

Simple, one-stage, area sampling. The above example of area sampling is an illustration of simple, one-stage, area sampling. The distinguishing feature of this process is that the areas chosen for the sample are completely enumerated; for example, every household on each block selected was included. A one-stage area sample of, say, one thousand households (stores, etc.) may not be as efficient as a simple random sample of the same size. The principal reason for this is that the elements in the same area cluster may tend to be alike. For example, the families living on a particular city block will in general be relatively similar with regard to such characteristics as income, race, occupation, family size, and social class. Similarity in these socioeconomic characteristics makes it likely that the families on a block will give relatively similar responses on attitude surveys, will buy the same general types of merchandise, and will respond similarly in other ways of interest to the marketing researcher.

These statements do not imply that all families on a block will respond *exactly* alike. They do imply that the households, or other units in an area cluster, are probably more alike than would be the same number of elements chosen at random from the entire universe. Because of this intracluster similarity, the statistical efficiency of a one-stage area sample will ordinarily be less than that of a simple random sample having the same number of units.

Simple, two-stage, area sampling. In the previous section, a method of area sampling was discussed in which all households (stores, etc.) associated with the areas selected in a sample were enumerated. Actually, it is not necessary to enumerate all the items associated with a selected area; the elements associated with a sample area may be subsampled. This method of sampling, in which the sample units are themselves sampled, is called two-stage sampling. For example, in sampling households in a city, one might first choose a sample of blocks and then choose a sample of households on the selected blocks. Such a technique would be a two-stage sampling scheme since there would be two stages of sampling, first blocks and then households on the chosen blocks.

An illustration of two-stage area sampling. The basic idea involved in two-stage sampling may be illustrated as follows. Consider a universe of 40 blocks. Suppose that each block contains 8 households. Assume further that a sample of 20 households is to be chosen by sampling blocks and then subsampling households on the selected blocks. Since there are 320 (40 × 8) households in the universe, this amounts to saying that the overall sampling ratio for households is to be 20/320, or 1 out of 16.

One way of selecting this sample would be to sample blocks at the rate of 1 in 8, and then to subsample the households on the selected blocks at a rate of 1 in 2. This procedure would identify 20 households since 5 blocks would be selected (⅛ × 40) and 4 households would be chosen on each block (½ × 8). The steps involved in this process are illustrated schematically in Figure 9–3.

This particular scheme is not the only way of choosing 20 households within the two-stage framework. Some other examples which indicate the possibilities are:

1. Choose blocks at a rate of 1 in 2 and households on selected blocks at a rate of 1 in 8.
2. Choose blocks at a rate of 1 in 4 and households on selected blocks at a rate of 1 in 4.

**FIGURE 9–3. Diagrammatic representation of the selection
of a two-stage, area sample of 20 households**

A. The universe of 40 blocks.

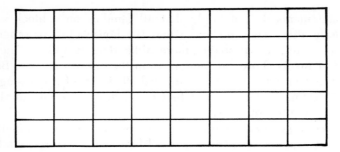

B. The first stage: Choose 5 blocks—1 out of 8—at random.

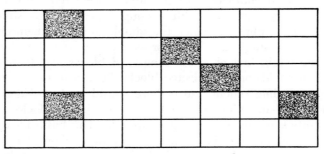

C. The second stage: Subsample households on the blocks
chosen randomly at a rate of 4 per block—1 out of 2.

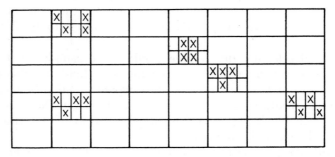

In all of these cases, it will be observed that the product of the block
sampling fraction and the intrablock subsampling fraction is equal to
$\frac{1}{16}$. This is an essential requirement in this example because the overall
sampling ratio is established at $\frac{1}{16}$.

In general, if the researcher wishes to sample second-stage units at a
rate of 1 in *ab,* this can be accomplished by choosing first-stage units at

a rate of 1 in *a* and second-stage units, in the selected first-stage units, at a rate of 1 in *b*. The overall selection probability for second-stage units is the product of the first- and second-stage sampling fractions:

$$\frac{1}{ab} = \frac{1}{a} \cdot \frac{1}{b}.$$

In the example being discussed,

$$\frac{1}{ab} = \frac{1}{16}.$$

Possible combinations for securing the desired overall sampling rate are ($a = 8$, $b = 2$), ($a = 2$, $b = 8$), and ($a = 4$, $b = 4$).

The general two-stage sampling scheme outlined above is called *simple two-stage area sampling*. Its distinguishing features are these:

1. Each first-stage unit has the same probability of being selected for the sample (1 in *a*).
2. All second-stage units in the selected first-stage units have the same chance of being selected for the sample. In any selected first-stage unit, each second-stage unit has a selection opportunity of 1 in *b*.

Further comments on simple two-stage area sampling. The preceding discussion of two-stage area sampling conveys the flexibility of the method. However, it gives no indication as to which combination of first-stage and second-stage sampling fractions should be used. Based on economic efficiency alone, it would be desirable to concentrate the sample in as few first-stage units as possible. Considering sampling error by itself, the opposite would be indicated—dispersion of the sample among as many first-stage units as possible. These generalizations arise from the following facts:

1. Concentration of the field work in fewer first-stage units reduces travel costs. Also, the costs involved in "listing" the selected first-stage units—i.e., identifying the second-stage units they contain—is less.
2. But concentration in fewer first-stage units is less efficient statistically, because of the tendency for observations in the same area cluster to be similar.

Statistical theory points the way to an effective compromise between these conflicting factors, assuming certain data on costs and the homogeneity of observations are available. This is, in fact, another variation of the problem of "optimal allocation" which was discussed in connection with stratified sampling.

The problem of optimal choice of the two sampling fractions will not be carried further here except to indicate its existence and the availability of a solution under certain conditions.[8]

Regardless of the choice of first- and -second-stage sampling rates, two general statements can be made about simple two-stage area sampling:

1. *A two-stage area sample will practically always be less efficient statistically than a simple random sample with the same number of observational units.* One implication is that the formula given for evaluating the sampling error of, for example, a mean, based on a simple random sample, can *not* be applied to a two-stage area sample. The erroneous application of simple random sampling formulas in this situation will generally underestimate the actual sampling error, and hence overstate the precision of the estimate. In this respect, two-stage area sampling is typical of area sampling generally. Area sampling is almost always less efficient statistically than is a simple random sample containing the same number of observational units.

More complex formulas are needed to evaluate sampling error when area samples are used.[9] In the two-stage illustration, the appropriate standard error formula takes account of the sampling error which arises at both stages in the sampling process:

a. A component of sampling error resulting from the sampling of first-stage units.
b. A component of sampling error due to the sampling of second-stage units associated with the first-stage units in the sample.

2. *If each first-stage unit contains the same number of second-stage units, then the mean of the sample for second-stage units is an unbiased estimate of the population mean for second-stage units.* To verify this, consider the following universe of three blocks with four households per block. Household observations are as shown:

Block A	Block B	Block C
2	6	10
4	1	11
4	7	11
10	6	12

Consider the following two-stage sampling plan:

a. Select blocks randomly at a rate of 1 in 3.
b. Choose three households randomly from the selected block (a within-block sampling fraction of ¾).

---

[8] See M. H. Hansen, *et al.*, *Sample Survey Methods and Theory,* Vol. I (New York: John Wiley & Sons, 1953), pp. 284–302.

[9] *Ibid.,* pp. 252–57.

Note that this procedure will provide samples of three households since the overall sampling fraction will be $\frac{1}{3} \cdot \frac{3}{4} = \frac{1}{4}$.

The possible samples with this system, and the sample mean generated by each, are as follows:

Block selected	Possible samples of 3 households	Sample mean
A	2, 4, 4	$3\frac{1}{3}$
	2, 4, 10	$5\frac{1}{3}$
	2, 4, 10	$5\frac{1}{3}$
	4, 4, 10	6
B	6, 1, 7	$4\frac{2}{3}$
	6, 1, 6	$4\frac{1}{3}$
	6, 7, 6	$6\frac{1}{3}$
	1, 7, 6	$4\frac{2}{3}$
C	10, 11, 11	$10\frac{2}{3}$
	10, 11, 12	11
	10, 11, 12	11
	11, 11, 12	$11\frac{1}{3}$

Since the average of the twelve possible sample means is 7, the same as the population mean, the sample mean is verified as an unbiased estimate. The reader should show that this property holds for some other simple two-stage plans in this illustration. For example, enumerate all possible means from a plan in which two blocks and two households per block are taken.

The property of unbiasedness illustrated above depends on the fact that equal numbers of second-stage units are in each first-stage unit. If the number of second-stage units per first-page unit varies greatly, then the sample mean may be appreciably biased. An example of how this bias arises and a device for overcoming it, by varying the probability of selection for first-stage units, are given later in this chapter.

Some additional techniques in area sampling

Proceeding from the simple one- and two-stage area samples dealt with previously, this section considers some additional techniques that are in common use on large scale area samples in marketing research:

1. Selecting first-stage units with variable probabilities.
2. Sampling in three or more stages.
3. Stratification in area sampling.

Although typically two, or all three, of these devices will be used jointly in an actual survey, they are treated here more or less independently for purposes of exposition.

Selecting first-stage units with variable probabilities. The distinguishing feature of simple two-stage area sampling is this: at each stage, sampling units are selected with *equal* probabilities. With this system, all first-stage units have the same chance of being chosen and the same applies to second-stage units within selected first-stage units.

A difficulty with simple two-stage sampling. This procedure works well if all first-stage units contain the same, or nearly the same, number of second-stage units. Often, however, first-stage units will vary greatly in size (number of second-stage units). In such circumstances a problem may arise, as illustrated by the following extreme example. Suppose a universe is made up of five blocks, containing widely varying numbers of households.

Blocks	Number of households
1	120
2	40
3	20
4	10
5	10
	200

The researcher wishes to estimate the mean value per household for some characteristic. The sample design is to be simple two-stage sampling. One of the five blocks is to be selected at random and, in order to secure an average sample size of eight households, the within-block sampling fraction is set at $1/5$ ($8/200 = 1/25 = 1/5 \cdot 1/5$). The mean value of the characteristic measured in the sample households will be used to estimate the universe mean per household for that characteristic.

Use of this sampling and estimation design here would lead to two generally undesirable consequences:

a. Although the *average* number of households in the sample would be eight, the number would vary greatly from sample to sample. The actual number of sample households identified could range from twenty-four (when Block 1 was selected) to two (when either Block 4 or 5 was chosen).

b. The sample mean per household would be a *biased* estimate of the population mean, unless the mean value of the characteristic studied were the same in each block—a highly unlikely circumstance. To verify this, suppose the actual means of the various blocks were as follows:

Block	Average value of characteristic
1	10
2	5
3	1
4	1
5	1

Then the true population mean would be 7.2. The sampling system under consideration, however, would, on the average, produce an estimated mean of

$$\tfrac{1}{5}(10) + \tfrac{1}{5}(5) + \tfrac{1}{5}(1) + \tfrac{1}{5}(1) + \tfrac{1}{5}(1) = 3.6,$$

since each of the five blocks would have a chance of 1 in 5 of being selected, and the sample mean per household is an unbiased estimate of the household average in that block.

Actually, it would be possible to obtain an unbiased estimate of the population mean even with this method of selection. However, since this would involve a weighting process which might produce a highly "unstable" estimate—one with large sampling variability—it will be ignored.

Sampling first-stage units with probability proportional to size. The difficulties illustrated by the example can be overcome by a device known as sampling with *probability proportional to size.* This is a way of choosing first-stage units in such a manner that the sample mean of a characteristic per second-stage unit will be an unbiased estimate of the corresponding population mean. Probability-proportional-to-size sampling is a special, but very important, case of the general procedure of sampling with *variable (unequal) probabilities.* The principle of the former sampling method is widely used in large scale area surveys in marketing research.

The illustration used to exemplify the practical difficulties associated with simple two-stage sampling, when first-stage units vary greatly in size, will help to clarify the idea. Suppose that block selection probabilities are assigned to the population of blocks in proportion to the number of households contained on each:

Block	Probability of selecting given block
1	120/200
2	40/200
3	20/200
4	10/200
5	10/200

First, the procedure for selecting a block with the specified probabilities will be explained and then it will be shown that this procedure leads to an unbiased estimate of the population mean.

To choose one of the five blocks in proportion to its size, the initial step is to form a "cumulative size" table like this:
Select a random number between 1 and 200. The block corresponding to that number in the "cumulative size" column is the block selected. For example, if the random number were 47, Block 1 would be selected; if it were 191, Block 5 would be identified.

Block	Size (number of households)	Cumulative size
1	120	120
2	40	160
3	20	180
4	10	190
5	10	200

All that has been done here is to assign selection numbers to each block, and to choose the block corresponding to the random number drawn:

Block	Selection numbers assigned
1	1 to 120
2	121 to 160
3	161 to 180
4	181 to 190
5	191 to 200

Note that, if this procedure for selecting a block were repeated a large number of times, Block 1 would be chosen 120/200 of the time, Block 2 would be chosen 40/200 of the time, and so on. Each block would be selected with a relative frequency proportional to its size.

Once a particular block has been identified by this method, a fixed number of second-stage units (eight households in the example) would be chosen at random from that block. Observe that, with this method, the probability of selecting a particular houshold varies from block to block. If Block 1 were selected, the chance of picking a specified household on that block would be $8/120 = 1/15$. If Block 4 were selected, then the chance of selecting any particular household on that block would be $8/10 = 4/5$. The inequality among blocks in these household selection probabilities is compensated for by the differential selection probabilities assigned to the various blocks.

To demonstrate that the procedure just described will generate an unbiased estimate of the population mean, consider the hypothetical mean values ascribed to the population of blocks on page 414.

Block	Average value of characteristic
1	10
2	5
3	1
4	1
5	1

Now, if one block is selected with probability proportional to size, the chance of choosing each block will be:

Block	Probability of selection × 200
1	120
2	40
3	20
4	10
5	10

Therefore, if the sampling and estimation procedure were repeated a large number of times, the average value of the sample mean would be:

$$10\frac{(120)}{(200)} + 5\frac{(\ 40)}{(200)} + 1\frac{(\ 20)}{(200)} + 1\frac{(\ 10)}{(200)} + 1\frac{(\ 10)}{(200)} = 7.2.$$

Since this is also the population mean, the estimate obtained via this selection system is unbiased.

General procedure for selecting one first-stage unit with probability proportional to size. Having applied the technique of sampling with probability proportional to size in a specific example, now consider the general procedure when one first-stage unit is to be selected. There is a universe of k first-stage units, the ith of which contains N_i second-stage units:

First-stage unit	Number of second-stage units
1	N_1
2	N_2
3	N_3
.	.
.	.
.	.
.	.
i	N_i
.	.
.	.
.	.
.	.
k	N_k

The researcher wishes to choose one first-stage unit with probability proportional to the number of second-stage units it contains (size). A sample of n second-stage units will be chosen at random from the first-stage unit that has been selected.

To choose the first-stage unit, first form a "cumulative size" table, assigning selection numbers to the first-stage units as shown in the table following:

Table for choosing a first-stage unit with probability proportional to size

First-stage unit	Number of second-stage units (size)	Cumulative size	Selection numbers assigned
1	N_1	N_1	1 to N_1
2	N_2	$N_1 + N_2$	$(N_1 + 1)$ to $(N_1 + N_2)$
3	N_3	$N_1 + N_2 + N_3$	$(N_1 + N_2 + 1)$ to $(N_1 + N_2 + N_3)$
.	.	.	.
.	.	.	.
.	.	.	.
k	N_k	$N_1 + N_2 + \cdots N_k$	$(N_1 + N_2 + \cdots + N_{k-1} + 1)$ to $(N_1 + N_2 + \cdots + N_k)$

The last step is to select a random number between 1 and $N_1 + N_2 + \ldots N_k$. The random number selected corresponds to one of the selection numbers in the right-hand column. The first-stage unit corresponding to this selection number is the one selected for the sample.

The procedure outlined above may appear formidable when expressed in terms of the N's. This feeling will be dispelled by writing out the table, one row at a time, for the numerical illustration used to introduce the subject. Since $N_1 = 120$, the first row will be:

First-stage unit	Number of second-stage units (size)	Cumulative size	Selection numbers assigned
1	120	120	1 to 120

The second row, omitting column headings, will be:

2	40	120 + 40	$(120 + 1)$ to $(120 + 40)$
or,			
2	40	160	121 to 160

The other rows follow similarly. Of course, if the number of first-stage units is large, the job may become laborious.

Selecting a first-stage unit with estimated probability proportional to size. The use of probability-proportional-to-size sampling to choose a single first-stage unit has been illustrated and the general procedure outlined. A difficulty with the method as sketched is that, in practice, the *actual* sizes of first-stage units will seldom be known. Much of the benefit of this sampling method, however, can often be salvaged by using *estimated* sizes, so that a first-stage unit is chosen in proportion to its estimated size. In the example discussed, the measures of size used might represent the numbers of households per block as of a recent census, and would be more or less inaccurate as of the survey date.

Two consequences of choosing a first-stage unit with only estimated probability proportional to size may be noted:

a. In general, the sample mean value of a characteristic per second-stage unit is no longer an unbiased estimate of the corresponding population value.

b. However, the combined bias and sampling error of selecting a first-stage unit with estimated probability proportional to size will often be less than that of simple two-stage sampling, if the estimated measures of sizes are reasonably accurate.

In practical marketing research, a measure of size that· is often used is *population,* even if an ultimate sample of institutions (such as drug stores) is wanted. Population is frequently used for this purpose because current population data may be more readily available for small areas than other measures, and population may be highly correlated with the ultimate observational units of interest. For example, population may be highly correlated with number of drug stores in a given area. For these reasons, published accounts of market research often refer to the selection of first-stage units with probability proportional to population.

Some other comments on sampling first-stage units with variable probabilities. The discussion has been confined to the selection of a *single* first-stage unit with probability proportional to actual or estimated size. Such a situation might arise, for example, in choosing a single county to represent a group of 75 sparsely populated counties in the southwest (e.g., a stratum defined as "small counties in the XYZ Company Southwestern Sales Division"). The method outlined is often used in area sampling to select a single county or a group of counties from a stratum consisting of an aggregate of counties and groups of counties judged to be more or less homogeneous for survey purposes. It has been found to be very useful for problems of this kind.

The reader should be aware, however, that the particular device illustrated is not the only way of choosing first-stage units with variable probabilities. It is not necessary to confine the selection to a *single* first-stage unit; two or more may be selected. However, the theory in such cases may get very complex, and much recent work in sampling theory has been concerned with ways of dealing with the situation.[10]

---

[10] For a brief overview of recent developments in sampling with variable probabilities (as well as other recent innovations in sampling theory and practice), see M. N. Murthy, "Some Recent Advances in Sampling Theory," *Journal of the American Statistical Association* (September, 1963), pp. 737–55.

Also, first-stage units may be selected with probabilities other than equal probabilities and estimated probabilities proportional to size. For example, first-stage units may be chosen with probabilities in proportion to the *square root* of estimated sizes, representing a halfway house between equal and estimated proportional-to-size probabilities. In general, however, the use of equal and estimated proportional-to-size probabilities represents the overwhelming majority of practical applications.

Sampling in three or more stages.   Although this discussion of area sampling has emphasized one- and two-stage sampling, a need for three-or-more-stage sampling often arises in marketing research. The basic extension involved in three-stage sampling is that the second-stage units are themselves subsampled, instead of being completely enumerated.

As an illustration, suppose a sample of households was wanted to represent all households in a group of cities. The sampling might proceed through these three stages:

1. A sample of cities is chosen.
2. Within each sample city, a subsample of blocks is selected.
3. On each sample block, a subsample of households is chosen.

At each level in a multi-stage sample, various alternative selection methods may be used. First-stage units will often be chosen with probability proportional to estimated size. The actual selection system used in any particular situation—kinds of sampling units used, number of stages, method of choosing sampling units at each stage—will depend on the individual circumstances of the problem.

Stratification in area sampling.   Practically all area samples use stratification in their structure. At the minimum, geographic stratification will be used. When feasible, other data will be built into the stratification scheme.

Geographic stratification in a household sample design for a city might involve subdividing the area of the city into groups of geographically proximate blocks. Then one or more blocks might be selected from each of the geographic strata so defined, and a subsample of households selected from these.

If relatively current data on block sizes were available in the above illustration, this variable might be built into the stratification as follows:

Stratum	Geographic area	Size of blocks
1	A	Small
2	A	Medium
3	A	Large
4	B	Small
5	B	Medium
6	B	Large
etc.		

The use of block size as a stratification device in this case would eliminate some of the benefits of selecting blocks with probability proportional to size. In general, if first-stage unit size is controlled by stratification (so that the first-stage units in any stratum are roughly equal), then there will be little value in varying the selection probabilities for first-stage units.

Another variation of stratified area sampling is illustrated by a national area design in which the researcher might first group the three thousand-odd U.S. counties into, say, fifty strata, consisting of counties that are more or less homogeneous with regard to such characteristics as geographic region, degree of urbanization, and other relevant attributes for which data are available by county. When these strata had been constructed, one or more counties would be selected from each, perhaps with probability proportional to population since modes of stratification other than county population would most likely be used in making up the strata. The chosen counties might themselves then be stratified into urban and rural areas, before the ultimate subsample of households (or whatever) was chosen.

These examples will indicate in rough terms how the principle of stratification is utilized in area samples. As with any specific application of statistical ideas, the way the principle is applied will depend on the particular problem posed and the available resources. In general, the same kinds of issues must be considered here as were mentioned in connection with stratified random sampling.

Concluding remarks on area sampling

The review of area sampling presented here has dealt with only a few of the basic ideas involved in this important approach to large scale sampling problems in marketing research. The limits of this book have precluded examination of many aspects of the subject which are critical to the effective planning, execution, and analysis of area designs. For instance, it has not been possible to discuss the evaluation of sampling error in complex designs, or to consider in depth the questions involved in the "tactics" of design—selection of the best overall sample design considering requirements and resources. It has also been necessary to skip the many operational problems involved in the application of area designs, e.g., procurement and processing of maps and data and development of rules for associating observational units with areas.[11]

---

[11] For a comprehensive treatment of the principles of area sampling, the reader is referred to Hansen, *et al.*, *op. cit.* For a detailed discussion of various materials used in area sampling, plus an illustration of their use, consult John Monroe and A. L. Finkner, *Handbook of Area Sampling* (Philadelphia: Chilton Co., 1959).

NONPROBABILITY SAMPLING

The methods of sampling previously discussed have all been probability sampling methods. In each case discussed, the basic requirement for probability sampling has been fulfilled: namely, every element in the universe sampled has a known chance of being chosen for the sample. Some methods of sampling in which this condition is not met will now be discussed. For lack of a better term, these will be called *nonprobability sampling methods* and will be defined to include any sampling method in which the chance of choosing a particular universe element is unknown.

As so defined, nonprobability sampling includes a great variety of techniques ranging in complexity from a sample chosen purely on the basis of convenience to an elaborate "quota sample" in which respondents are chosen on the basis of several socioeconomic characteristics. Also included are techniques which use "expert judgment" to choose what is believed to be a "representative sample." Any sampling procedure which does not specify the chance of selecting any universe element is a nonprobability sampling method, no matter what else is included in the specifications.

Convenience sampling

As the name implies, a "convenience sample" is chosen purely on the basis of convenience. The items of such a sample are chosen simply because they are accessible or articulate or otherwise easy to measure. "Man on the street" interviewing is an illustration of this general approach.

For obvious reasons, this method of sampling should only be used in special cases in marketing research. The items of the universe to be sampled may occasionally be sufficiently homogeneous so that any kind of sample will suffice. A convenience sample may be of value during the pretest phase of a study to improve the questionnaire, but it should rarely be used in any serious effort to estimate values of a universe.

In general, it will be found that the "convenient" items of a universe differ substantially from the less convenient items, thereby introducing a bias of unknown magnitude and direction into any estimate based on a convenience sample.

Judgment sampling

A second method of nonprobability sampling which is sometimes advocated is the selection of universe items by means of "expert judgment." Using this approach, a specialist in the subject matter of the survey chooses what he believes to be the best sample for that particular study. For example, a sales manager might select a group of grocery stores in a city that he regarded as "representative" in some sense. A difficulty with this approach is that it has been found empirically to produce unsatisfactory results. And, of course, there is no objective way of evaluating the reliability of sample results under such circumstances. Despite these limitations, this method may be useful when the total sample size is extremely small. Such uses should be rare.

Quota sampling

Perhaps the most commonly used sampling technique is a nonprobability technique called *quota sampling.*[12] Although the elaborateness of quota samples varies considerably, they all embody three basic steps:

1. *Selection of the "control characteristics" and determination of the proportion of the universe having each set of characteristics.* This step involves the subdivision of the universe into component subuniverses and is similar to the stratification described earlier. The resultant subuniverses are usually called "cells" and the bases for the stratification are called "controls." These controls are usually chosen on two bases: (1) they are believed to be correlated with the characteristic to be studied, and (2) reasonably up-to-date information is available on their distribution within the universe.

Suppose that two control characteristics, age and family income, have been decided on for a survey of housewives in a particular city. The resulting cells for the universe would then appear somewhat as in Table 9–1.

TABLE 9–1. Cells in two-control quota sample

Family income	Age of housewife		
	Under 35 years	*35 years and over*	*Total*
Under $10,000	21%	27%	48%
$10,000 and over	12	40	52
Total	33%	67%	100%

In the universe to be sampled, 21 percent of the housewives are under thirty-five years of age and have family incomes under $10,000, 12 percent are under thirty-five years and have incomes of $10,000 and over, and so on.

---

[12] An extensive discussion of quota sampling is given in F. Stephan and P. McCarthy, *Sampling Opinions* (New York: John Wiley & Sons, 1958).

424   *Marketing research: Text and cases*

It is not necessary that the number of control variables be restricted to two or that the subdivisions within each control variable be two. Often more than two control characteristics will be used although the number of subdivisions within each control variable is generally restricted to four or five. If very many controls and subdivisions are used, the number of cells multiplies rapidly. For example, assume five controls are used:

Age—3 subdivisions, under 35, 35–50, and over 50.
Education—3 subdivisions, two years of high school or less, completed high school, and some college.
Race—2 subdivisions, white and nonwhite.
City size—4 subdivisions, over 50,000, 2,500 to 50,000, rural nonfarm, and farm.
Geographical region—4 subdivisions, northeast, midwest, south, and west.

These controls and subdivisions within each would result in 288 different cells $(3 \times 3 \times 2 \times 4 \times 4 = 288)$.

2. *Allocation of the sample among cells.* Once the strata or cells have been established, the next step is to decide how large a sample should be taken from each cell. Usually, but not necessarily, a proportional sample is taken, i.e., each cell is given the same proportion of the sample that it represents of the universe. In the two-control example given, if a total sample of two hundred were wanted, a proportional distribution of interviews by cell would be as follows:

Description of homemaker	*Number in sample*
Under 35 years, family income under $10,000	42 (21%)
Under 35 years, family income $10,000 and over	24 (12)
35 years and over, family income under $10,000	54 (27)
35 years and over, family income $10,000 and over	80 (40)
	200 (100%)

3. *Selection of the sample items.* When the total number of respondents in each cell has been decided on, the next step in the sampling procedure is to assign a "quota" to each field worker. That is, each field worker is told to secure X observations with items having one set of characteristics, Y observations with items having another set of characteristics, and so on until the total sample has been allocated. In the housewife illustration, one interviewer might be told to secure a quota of eight interviews with housewives under thirty-five having a family income under $10,000 and fourteen interviews with housewives under thirty-five having a family income of $10,000 or over. This is the origin of the adjective "quota" in the name quota sampling.

The field representatives then seek out and interview or observe items (e.g., housewives) who appear to have the characteristics specified by their quotas. Usually, the interviews are obtained in the most expeditious way possible, but sometimes additional restrictions are placed on the way in which the respondents are chosen. For example, it may be specified that respondents must be found in certain areas.

Some difficulties with quota sampling. Quota sampling and stratified random sampling are similar. In both methods, the universe to be studied is partitioned into subuniverses, and the total sample is allocated among the subuniverses. At this point, however, the two procedures diverge radically. In stratified random sampling, the sample within each stratum is chosen at random. In quota sampling, the sampling within each cell is not done at random; the field representatives are given wide latitude in the selection of respondents to meet their quotas.

This distinction between quota sampling and stratified random sampling is important. The two sampling systems are sometimes mistakenly thought to be equivalent, and the data from a quota sample are sometimes treated as if they were derived from a stratified random sample. The two systems would in fact be equivalent *if* it could be assumed that the within-cell samples of a quota sampling represented simple random samples. However, experience indicates that this assumption is not warranted. In using a quota sample, the implicit assumption is almost always made that the selection within cells is random or that the differences between items within cells is so small that even if a sample is drawn from extremes, it will not seriously affect the estimates. Thus, some researchers incorrectly apply the same principles to determine sample size and sampling error of a quota sample as they use with probability sampling.

Because the choice of respondents within a cell is left to the field representatives and is not governed by a random selection, the more accessible and articulate people within a cell will usually be the ones who are interviewed.

It will often be found, in addition, that quota samples differ from stratified random samples in ways other than the nature of the within-stratum sampling. For example, the "quotas" may be based on out-of-date or otherwise inaccurate information. Frequently, census information is used in establishing quotas, and this may be outdated at the time of use. The desired control characteristic data (such as family size within income groups) may not be available for some controls or subdivisions, thereby necessitating approximations. As a matter fact, when several controls are used, data on cross classifications of these controls are seldom available.

Another problem occurring in the execution of quota samples arises in connection with the field workers' identification of the eligible respondents. Even though the field representatives may be conscientious and alert, it is often difficult to determine such control characteristics as age, occupation, and income in interviews. As a result, the interviews conducted to meet a particular quota may not in fact be restricted to respondents having the characteristics specified by the quota. For example, a group of interviews ostensibly conducted with housewives under thirty-five years of age having an annual family income under $10,000 may actually include housewives who are over thirty-five years old and/or have family incomes exceeding $10,000 per year.

An additional fundamental methodological difficulty with quota sampling pertains to the nonstandardized, essentially idiosyncratic character of each quota sample: "Quota sampling is not one defined scientific method. Rather, each one seems to be an artistic production, hard to define or describe. Hence, a general critique cannot be detailed, and a specific critique of one procedure may not fit another."[13]

The "validation" of quota samples.   Most researchers are aware that quota sampling may lead to the selection of a sample having properties different from the universe ostensibly sampled. In an effort to determine the nature and importance of such biases, a device called "validation" is often used. This involves a comparison of the sample and the universe with regard to various characteristics not used as control variables. For example, in the housewife illustration the two hundred respondents might be compared with the universe sampled with respect to characteristics like number of children, husband's occupation, and race.

If the sample and the universe differ significantly with regard to one or more of these validation characteristics, this constitutes evidence that the sample is biased in these respects. This fact must then be considered in the interpretation of the sample data. If the validation indicates no large differences between sample and universe in the characteristics compared, it is commonly assumed that the sample is representative of the universe. It is important to note, however, that this does not *prove* that the sample corresponds with the universe in all respects. Just because a sample corresponds with the universe in respect to age, race, and family size, it is not conclusive evidence that the two will also correspond with regard to kind of automobile owned, type of shoe polish used, usual weekly expenditure for entertainment, or any other subject of interest. Properly used, validation is an important technique for studying the characteristics of quota samples. This procedure, however, can only be of value in spotting potential weaknesses; it cannot serve as evidence of strength.

---

[13] Leslie Kish, *Survey Sampling* (New York: John Wiley & Sons, 1965), p. 563.

PROBABILITY AND NONPROBABILITY SAMPLING IN MARKETING RESEARCH

In this book considerable emphasis has been placed on probability sampling techniques. Nonprobability sampling techniques have received relatively little attention, and have been criticized. This has been done even though nonprobability sampling is a useful tool in marketing research and is used more often than probability sampling.

Advantages of probability sampling

There are three basic advantages in probability sampling:

1. Probability sampling is the only sampling method that provides estimates which are essentially unbiased and have measurable precision.
2. It is possible to evaluate the relative efficiency of various sample designs only when probability sampling is used.
3. Probability sampling does not depend on the existence of detailed information about the universe for its effectiveness.

Each of these reasons will be discussed briefly.

Probability sampling is the only sampling method that provides estimates which are essentially unbiased and have measurable precision. The use of probability sampling enables the investigator to compute from the sample data: (1) essentially unbiased estimates of the relevant universe values, and (2) measures of the sampling error associated with these estimates. If certain conditions are met, interval estimates may be constructed which, with measurable confidence, will include the applicable universe values.

In contrast, the estimates derived from nonprobability samples may contain bias of unmeasurable size. It is not necessary that this be the case, but there is no guarantee that, for example, the average of a large number of quota-sample means from the same universe will approximate the true universe mean. In fact, there is evidence to the contrary. Because the nonprobability sample respondents are often chosen in the ways most convenient to the field workers, samples secured in this manner usually contain a disproportionate number of readily available respondents who are willing and able to discuss the survey subject matter.

The data obtained from a nonprobability sample do not by themselves enable the investigator to evaluate the accuracy of his estimates.[14] He can, of course, go through the mathematics of calculating confidence

---

[14] Stephan and McCarthy, *op. cit.*, Chapter 10, discuss the question of the meaning of a "sampling distribution" in the case of quota sampling. They discuss methods for estimating quota sampling variability under certain assumptions.

limits, but he has no measurable confidence that the limits so derived will include the universe values being estimated. Under certain favorable conditions, he may be able to assess roughly the biases inherent in his sampling scheme and to make crude corrections for these, but he has no objective basis for doing this.

It is possible to evaluate the relative efficiency of various sample designs only when probability sampling is used.   An important advantage of probability sampling is that the relative efficiency of various possible designs may be evaluated. For example, one can compare simple random sampling with simple cluster sampling and deduce the conditions under which the sampling error of one will be less than that of the other. Similarly, one can contrast the relative costs and statistical efficiency of simple random sampling with those of simple cluster sampling and thereby arrive at a near-optimum design in terms of maximizing the information obtained per dollar of expenditure.

On the other hand, no objective way exists of comparing the relative merits of possible nonprobability sampling designs. One has no objective way of knowing, for instance, whether a quota sample of a particular type will be superior to an "expert judgment" selection in a certain situation. Again, no objective method exists for determining the conditions under which a quota sampling procedure will be more effective than a convenience sampling.

The effectiveness of probability sampling does not depend on the existence of detailed information about the universe.   Typically, nonprobability sampling requires the existence of considerable information about the population to be sampled. Quota sampling, in particular, requires that fairly accurate information about the universe be available for: (1) establishing controls, and (2) estimating the total number of universe items which possess the characteristics of interest. In the absence of such information, the resulting universe estimates may be biased, even if the values for each cell are estimated without substantial error. This dependency on external information may be more or less important, but the possibility of trouble from this source is always present.

Probability sampling requires relatively little information about the universe. Basically all that is needed is (1) a way of uniquely identifying every universe element, and (2) knowledge of the total number of universe elements. As previously noted, it is not even necessary that the universe elements sampled be coextensive with the items of the universe. If correspondence can be established between units of area and items of the universe and if maps of the area units are available, a probability sample can be selected.

The sampling efficiency of a probability sample can be improved if detailed information about the universe is available. However, this additional information is not necessary for the successful execution of a probability sample. Given only limited information about a universe, one may still obtain essentially unbiased estimates having calculable precision if he uses probability sampling.

Disadvantages of probability sampling

Even though probability sampling possesses the important advantages enumerated above, it is probably not yet used in a majority of cases in marketing research. There appear to be three main reasons for this: (1) the level of skill and experience required for its use, (2) the time required for its planning and execution, and (3) the relative cost of the method. Each of these obstacles will be considered briefly.

Skill and experience required for probability sampling. In this book only a few of the basic ideas underlying probability sampling have been discussed. As a result, the reader has been presented with an oversimplification of the actual problems involved in the efficient design and execution of probability sampling. For any but the simplest types of problems, this work demands highly specialized skill and experience. Since probability sampling techniques have been developed only recently, comparatively few people are equipped to deal with such problems. Relatively few marketing research agencies, and still fewer marketing research departments, are properly staffed to handle complex probability sampling problems. The end result is reliance on more simple sampling methods.

The design and execution of nonprobability sampling schemes are comparatively easy. Here too, of course, the more experience the sample designer has, the better the results are likely to be. Since these designs are generally simpler to handle, however, persons of lesser training and experience are required.

Time requirements. Except for very simple surveys, the time required to plan and implement a probability sample is usually greater than for a nonprobability sample of the same general scope. There are a number of reasons for this, but they all may be ascribed to the greater care and preparation required for the probability sample. For example, in the planning of an area probability sample, time must be allowed for such general steps as procurement of maps, delineation and numbering of areas, stratification, and selection of sample areas. The execution of such a sampling plan is also time-consuming because the proper units to be contacted must be identified in the field, callbacks must be made for not-at-homes, and so on.

By way of comparison, the typical nonprobability sampling plan may be prepared and executed rather quickly. The sacrifice in rigor will usually lead to large savings in time which, in marketing research, may sometimes outweigh the possible losses due to the introduction of biases into the sample estimates. Frequently management will need an "answer" so quickly that time is not available to set up a probability sample. Since management will make a decision, the choice is one between management's judgment and that of a sample which can be comprised of a number of segments from the universe. In such a situation, a gain may be made in using a nonprobability sample as compared to no sample at all.

Cost considerations.   A probability sample will usually cost substantially more than a nonprobability sample of the same size. The advantage of securing essentially unbiased estimates, the precision of which may be evaluated, must be paid for in increased cost per observation. A probability sample is more expensive to design because of the need to structure the sampling plan in such a way that every universe item has a known chance of being selected. The execution of a probability sample is more expensive because of the necessity of contacting pre-designated units for observation and of guaranteeing that substantially all the items identified for the sample are, in fact, observed.

It should be emphasized that this cost comparison is strictly on a *per-observation* basis and does not take the quality of results into account. Since the reliability of the results obtained from a nonprobability sample cannot be measured, it is impossible, therefore, to compare the costs of the two systems for a fixed degree of reliability.

The relatively low cost of nonprobability sampling per observation is an important advantage in marketing research. Because many studies must be conducted with a small budget, nonprobability sampling may be the only practical alternative. Also, the cost must be associated with the accuracy demands of the problem. A store owner who wanted to find the factors that cause customers to go into his establishment or to go to competitors might use a nonprobability sample. If he knew very little about these factors, a rough ranking of their importance would satisfy him. It would be hard to justify a refined and expensive sampling technique for this purpose. On the other hand, of course, where the decision which will be made is of considerable importance, a probability sample should be used. For example, if an unreliable sampling design leads to an erroneous conclusion that a particular product can be marketed successfully, the company may dissipate many thousands of dollars. It must be recognized that no sampling design is without risk, but a probability design involves less risk.

The choice between probability and nonprobability sampling methods in practice

In the preceding pages, the principal theoretical advantages and disadvantages of probability and nonprobability sampling are outlined.

In practical marketing research these advantages and disadvantages must be continually balanced in selecting sampling procedures. *Nonsampling errors* (broadly defined as those *not* reduced by increasing sample size, such as nonresponse, data collection errors, and inadequate universe definition) may loom large in many projects and so offset the advantages of particular sampling methods.

The basic choice of sampling method is relatively clear-cut where the survey must provide essentially unbiased estimates, the precision of which may be objectively evaluated, and where sampling errors are expected to be the dominant source of total survey error. Some form of probability sampling would be indicated in such a case. An example would be the choice of a sample to audit sales of a particular product in retail stores for a trade association. In such circumstances, objectivity would be especially important because multiple survey sponsors (members of the association) would be involved. Total survey error would probably be primarily sampling error, since nonsampling errors (due to store and auditing errors, lack of retailers' cooperation, etc.) could probably be kept relatively small. In contrast, sampling error could be substantial, owing to the typically large variation in size of outlets comprising almost any retail store universe.

At the other extreme, nonprobability sampling may be indicated if rough estimates are adequate, if resources are very limited, or if total survey error is expected to be composed primarily of nonsampling errors and it is desired to focus limited resources on the reduction of these nonsampling errors. An example of this situation might be a survey of consumer finances in a high-income household universe, where the researcher would be willing to sacrifice results that would permit objective measurement of precision in order to maximize accuracy of responses from cooperating respondents.

In the majority of applications, the above generalizations (while probably agreed on by most researchers) may provide only limited guidance. Most administrators want maximal reliability, and resources are always limited.

An important practical consideration in the choice of sampling method is that a "pure" probability sample (in the sense that *100 percent* of the sample-identified units provide data) is seldom, if ever, achieved.[15] A "pure" probability sample must be regarded as an ideal limiting case rather than a practically attainable goal, particularly where sensitive information is sought from mobile sample units. If nonresponse is high, or other kinds of nonsampling errors are important, the nominal virtues of probability sampling can be largely vitiated and theoretical confidence limits rendered of limited value.[16]

---

[15] For some data on nonresponse, see Kish, *op. cit.*, especially pp. 536–47.

[16] Some studies by Robert Ferber and collaborators illustrate this point. See R. Ferber, "The Reliability of Consumer Surveys of Financial Holdings: Time Deposits,"

In specific research projects, one partial solution to the problem is to adopt, to the extent possible, at least some of the features of probability sampling. This may be done in various ways. For example, in a national sample of urban adults, one might use probability sampling methods down to the block level and then assign age and sex quotas on the sample blocks. Again, one might take a probability sample from a segment of the population of interest, assuming results would be applicable to the entire population. For example, one survey of premium buyers was restricted for economy purposes to Chicago premium buyers having telephones. A random sample, with callbacks, of telephone interviews among this group yielded results assumed to be representative of premium users generally, regardless of geographic location and telephone ownership.

Confronted with incomplete and only informal guidance as to the "best" sampling method in particular situations, some researchers have advocated a subjective, but closely reasoned and consistent, approach to the general problem.[17] These individuals perceive the issue as one of selecting the best of several survey research "strategies," rather than the narrower problem of choosing a sample selection procedure. They formally recognize the multiple sources of nonsampling error in generating survey results and attempt to quantify the consequences of these, as well as of random sampling error. They argue that, in many situations, random sampling error is only one component of total survey error, and that realism demands explicit recognition of this. In the simplest version of this model, the measure of interest is visualized as the (mathematical) product of a "reported survey value" multiplied by a series of ratios, each reflecting an independent source of survey error. Using whatever objective or subjective information is available, the analyst assesses the mean and variability associated with each independent error source. The total error for a given survey research strategy is then compared with that of other possible strategies. The survey strategy with the smallest total "error index" is the one recommended under this general approach.

The present authors take the following general position with regard to the choice of probability versus nonprobability sampling in a particular situation. For most large scale survey situations, probability sampling should be regarded as the *tentative initial choice*. The objectivity afforded

Journal of the American Statistical Association (March, 1965), and R. Ferber, *et al.,* "Validation of Consumer Financial Characteristics: Common Stock," *ibid.* (June, 1969).

[17] See Chapter 5, pp. 217 ff; R. V. Brown, "Evaluation of Total Survey Error," *Journal of Marketing Research,* Vol. IV (May, 1967); and C. S. Mayer, "Integrating Non-sampling Error Assessments into Research Design," *Marketing and the New Science of Planning,* R. L. King, ed., 1968 Fall Conference Proceedings, American Marketing Association.

by this approach is a powerful advantage if, as is usually the case, study results must be communicated to, and accepted by, many people for effective use. Yet, it is unrealistic and unwise to insist that objective measurement and control of sampling error alone should be the sole determinant of sampling methodology. Proceeding from probability sampling as a theoretically desirable approach, the researcher must confront the practical implications of both sampling error, the only error controllable by probability sampling, and nonsampling errors. In some circumstances, it may be possible to arrive at a formally consistent choice, utilizing quantitative assessment of the error possibilities inherent in alternative approaches. In many cases, however, the final choice will depend on intuitive judgment. The researcher will often be able to adopt some, if not all, of the features of probability sampling.

Case 9—1. ABCO CEREAL COMPANY

The Abco Cereal Company had introduced a new brand of cereal called Powie! In its advertising, Powie! had been positioned as a highly nutritious product designed particularly for very young children. As a part of the earlier promotional strategy, various children's premiums, including mail-in offers, had been used to help achieve trial and to sustain repeat purchases.

About six months after national product introduction, Abco management raised questions concerning mothers' perceptions of Powie! There was specific interest in whether or not mothers perceived Powie! as a highly nutritious cereal for their children.

To help answer this question, the firm proposed a survey among mothers of young children. The research was to determine whether or not mothers were familiar with the brand Powie! and, if so, what impression they had of its nutritional value. As the research director began to plan the project, he discovered that the data collection method was going to be influenced by the method he used to select a sample of mothers of young children. Two alternative methods of selecting a sample were considered:

1. The first method involved a telephone survey, using a systematic sample from phone directories in California, where the product had been launched initially. Whoever answered the telephone would be asked if there were children under six living at the residence. If the answer were "yes," the interviewer would then ask to speak to the mother of the children.

2. The second method involved sending a mail questionnaire to all homes (about 2,400) from which someone had written the company to receive a particular mail-in offer premium. This premium, more

expensive than most, required that the consumer send in five Powie! box tops, along with $1.00 in cash.

1. Which, if either, of these two sample identification methods should be chosen?

2. Under what circumstances would the other method be used?

3. What other ways of dealing with this problem are there?

Case 9—2.   NEWHOUSE AND ASSOCIATES

Newhouse and Associates was a land development corporation which specialized in developing industrial parks, small to medium size shopping centers, and housing developments. The company opened a shopping center in a suburb of Los Angeles consisting of a total of 68 stores including such store types as specialty shops, service establishments, eating establishments, a variety store, a supermarket, and a hardware store. The total cost of this shopping center was in excess of $10 million.

With but a few exceptions, all locations within the center had been rented two months prior to the announced opening date of September 1. Beginning August 15, Newhouse and Associates undertook an advertising campaign which featured not only the opening of the new center but the many attractive shops which collectively formed "a convenient and exciting environment for shoppers from all walks of life." The advertising consisted of a full page (black and white) in each of the four local newspapers on Wednesdays, Thursdays, and Fridays. The company planned to continue this advertising until approximately September 10.

Late in August, the sales promotion manager of Newhouse and Associates received a call from a committee of men who purported to represent about half of the rentors of space in the new shopping center. The purpose of their call was to complain that the opening of the center was not receiving adequate advertising support. Their statement was not based on any study, but rather on what they claimed to have found out from friends and relatives.

At the end of the discussion the sales promotion manager agreed to conduct a phone study among housewives residing in the four suburbs contiguous to the new center to determine whether they knew about the opening, what they knew about the kinds of stores in the center, and, if possible, the sources of their information.

The problem of selecting the sample was turned over to the assistant sales promotion manager. He decided that a sample of two hundred completed calls would be satisfactory and proposed to select these from the phone books as follows:

1. Count the number of phone listings contained in the first twenty columns in the suburban phone book. Since there were four columns per page this would mean covering five pages. The phone book to

be used was the directory for the largest suburb involved. Actually it made little difference which phone book was used, since they were all the same size and used the same size type face. No distinction was to be made between the residential and commercial listings.

2. Divide the total number of phone listings by twenty to get the average number per column.

3. Count the number of columns in each of the four suburban directories and by multiplying the number of columns in each by the average number of listings obtain the total listings for each suburb.

4. Based on the results obtained from step 3, the relative weight or worth of each suburb would be determined. For example, if suburb A had 14,000 phone listings out of a total of 50,000 (for all four), then suburb A would receive 28 percent of the sample (or 56 interviews).

5. The number of interviews thus assigned to each suburb would be divided into the total number of listings for that suburb. This would provide a "sampling interval." In the illustration given in step 4, this would mean dividing 14,000 by 56 and obtaining a sampling interval of 268.

6. The sampling interval would then be applied to the phone listings and the final sample selected. Since the average number of phone listings per column was known, it would not be necessary to count each listing in order to make the sample selection. The sample selection numbers would be obtained by cumulating the sampling interval (268, 536, 804, 1072, etc.) and dividing them by the average number of listings per column. This would indicate the column number involved as well as how far into the column the researcher had to count. For example, assume an average column contained 53 listings. Sampling interval number 268 would fall in the 6th column and would be the third listing in that column ($268 \div 53 = 5$ with 3 left over).

7. If the listing indicated was "commercial," the next residential listing in the column would be selected for inclusion in the sample.

8. If a "no answer" were obtained, up to three callbacks would be attempted. If a completed call had not been accomplished with these efforts, the next residential listing in the column would be selected and the same procedure repeated.

9. Refusals were to be handled in a similar fashion, that is, the next residential number in the column would be selected.

The assistant sales promotion manager was confident that the sampling procedure described above would provide an unbiased sample of housewives residing in the four suburbs.

Was the proposed sampling design adequate for the study being undertaken? What biases, if any, were present? How can these biases be eliminated?

Case 9—3. HAYWOOD COMPANY

The Haywood Company was a large meat packer which sold fresh, cured, and canned meats. The company sold its fresh meats regionally, but its cured and canned meat products were sold nationally. The sales manager of the cured meat division authorized the company's research department to undertake a national survey to determine consumer attitudes toward bacon.

After numerous conferences with personnel of the sales division, the advertising department, and the advertising agency, the research director formulated the objectives of the study as follows:

1. To provide data on the relative rankings of reasons for consuming bacon at breakfast.
2. To provide a classification of consumers into motivational types with regard to the use of bacon in general and the Haywood brand in particular.
3. To provide data on the state of consumer information and misinformation about bacon as a meat product with special reference to the direction of misinformation (i.e., is misinformation favorable or unfavorable) and the existence of fallacies.
4. To determine what stereotypes consumers have of those individuals who eat bacon and those who don't.

These objectives were to be sought for the entire United States. In addition, it was planned to analyze several subgroups such as those who eat various quantities of bacon, different sexes, geographic regions, city size, type of work done, presence of children in the home, and income. Where appropriate further analyses would be made, for example, consumption groups might be analyzed *within* age groups or city size groups.

The problem of designing the sample was assigned to the department's statistician. Working from the above stated objectives, he recommended the use of a disproportionate quota sample in which interviewers would be restricted to areas selected on a probability basis. He decided that a total of 96 cells would be required as follows: three age groups within two sex groups within four city size groups within four geographic regions. He estimated that a total sample size of about 2,400 would be required and that this number of interviews should be divided equally among the four regions. The breakdown within a typical region would, therefore, be as shown in Exhibit 1.

The statistician stated this number of cells and the number of interviews assigned to each would permit an analysis of the following major groups:

I. Age
   1. Unmarried—13–20 years of age living at home
   2. Head of household—21–49 years of age
   3. Head of household—50 years and over
II. Sex
   1. Male
   2. Female
III. City size
   1. 50,000 and over
   2. 2,500–49,999
   3. Rural nonfarm
   4. Rural farm
IV. Region
   1. Northeast
   2. North central
   3. South
   4. West

EXHIBIT 1

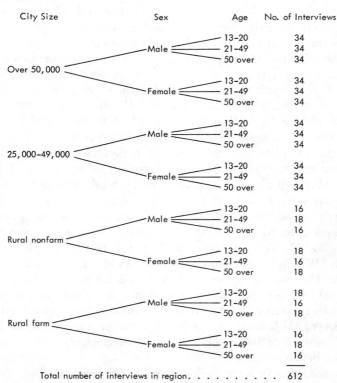

City Size	Sex	Age	No. of Interviews
Over 50,000	Male	13–20	34
		21–49	34
		50 over	34
	Female	13–20	34
		21–49	34
		50 over	34
25,000–49,000	Male	13–20	34
		21–49	34
		50 over	34
	Female	13–20	34
		21–49	34
		50 over	34
Rural nonfarm	Male	13–20	16
		21–49	18
		50 over	16
	Female	13–20	18
		21–49	16
		50 over	18
Rural farm	Male	13–20	18
		21–49	16
		50 over	18
	Female	13–20	16
		21–49	18
		50 over	16

Total number of interviews in region. 612

In addition, the sample was designed to permit analyses such as age within sex, city size and region; sex within city size and region; and city size within region.

Within each region the statistician planned to select eighteen major sampling points—six cities of 50,000 and over population and twelve cities with population of 2,500–49,999. Close to each of the latter cities a town of less than 2,500 was to be selected as a minor sampling point. Also in the neighborhood of each city of 2,500–49,999 population, a rural area was to be selected in which the farm interviews were to be made.

The statistician did not designate the cities to be included in the sample. He recommended that the following selection criteria be used: (1) availability of a good interviewer, (2) dispersion of the cities within a region, and (3) dispersion by size (population) within the city size class. He stated he would be glad to pick the sample cities after conferring with the interviewing agency chosen to do the field work.

The within-place sampling plan for cities of 50,000 and over population called for a selection of census tracts, then a selection of blocks within tracts, and finally a selection of dwelling units within blocks. Since 34 interviews were required in each of these cities and no more than two persons per block were to be interviewed, 17 blocks were to be chosen. The selection procedure was as follows.

Census tracts. All tracts within a single city were to be listed and numbered consecutively. Since one block and only one block was to be chosen within a tract, a total of 17 tracts was required. Thus, the total number of tracts was to be divided by 17 to provide a sampling interval. For example, if a city contained 170 tracts then the sampling interval would be 10 ($170 \div 17$). The list of tracts would be entered with the use of a random number chosen between one and the upper limit of the sampling interval. The tract designated by this number would come into the sample. Next, the sampling interval would be added to this number and the tract indicated by the total of these two numbers would be the second tract selected for the sample. The sampling interval would again be added and the applicable tract chosen. For example, if the sampling interval was 10 and the random number 3, census tracts 3, 13, 23, 33, 43, 53, etc. would be included in the sample.

Blocks. Within each sample tract it would be necessary to select one block. This was to be accomplished in a manner somewhat similar to that used to select the census tracts, that is, all blocks would be listed and a random number selected between one and the upper limit of the blocks present. This number would identify the sample block. For example, if there were 100 blocks then a random number between 1 and 100 would be chosen.

Commercial blocks were excluded from the block listings. For each block chosen for the sample, the statistician recommended that two contiguous alternate blocks be selected. If the number of interviews assigned to a specific block could not be accomplished, the interviewer would be instructed to go to the first alternate block to complete her work and, if this failed, to proceed to the second alternate. Interviewers were to be told to start at the northwest corner of the block and travel around the block in a clockwise fashion. The starting point within the block was to be determined by selecting a random number between the total number of dwelling units (from the Census of Population) divided by two. For example, if 60 dwelling units were located on the block, a random number between 1 and 30 would be selected—say 12. Starting from the northwest corner the interviewer would count off 11 dwelling units and attempt to interview the 12th, 13th, 14th, etc., until the necessary two respondents had been interviewed.

Each interviewer was to be assigned a quota. The quota would call for half the interviews to be conducted with men and half with women. Within each of these cells the interviews were to be divided equally between the three age groups. Interviewers were not given a quota within any specific block, but rather for their entire assignment.

In cities of 2,500–49,999 population, block statistics were not available and the plan called for obtaining block maps from each city. These were to be "gridded" and the sections so indicated to be treated as census tracts. The procedure from this point on was identical to that recommended for use in the 50,000 and over population cities.

For the rural nonfarm towns (those of 2,500 and under), it would again be necessary to obtain maps. From the map of each city four blocks would be selected at random. The interviewer would call on all households in these blocks until she obtained her quota. No limit was to be set on the number obtained in any one block.

To select the rural farm quota, maps would again be used. Routes would be drawn on this map and a starting point indicated. All farms on both sides of the route were to be interviewed until the quota was obtained.

The statistician stated that, if this sample design were acceptable, he would work with the interviewing agency to implement it and would be responsible for assigning the quotas to the individual interviewers as well as for drawing up the applicable interviewer instructions.

1. How was the sample size determined? Could any improvements be made?

2. Do you agree with the way in which the sample was allocated among the various cells? Discuss.

3. Would the results from this sample give an accurate picture of the

entire United States? If not, could the results be adjusted to provide an accurate measure?

4. Would the method of selecting the sample result in any biases?

Case 9—4.   DANIEL RESEARCH COMPANY

In February 1968, the Daniel Research Company, which was located in a medium-sized metropolitan area, successfully bid on a research project originated by one of the local TV stations to set up a consumer panel which would report all household TV viewing as well as products purchased. The study would cover only those households residing in the metropolitan area, even though the station's coverage exceeded that area.

The project called for the Daniel Research Company to compile up-to-date population and household statistics for the metropolitan area. Following this, a consumer panel of some 500 households would be recruited and made operational. It was reasoned that a sample census was strongly needed because the only local data currently available were derived from the 1960 Census of Population.

The research group assigned to the project agreed that the sampling universe would consist of the metropolitan area as defined by the U.S. Bureau of Census. This area would include all dwelling units in both the incorporated and unincorporated parts of this area. The group also agreed that the study would employ a multistage probability area sample which would be representative of the area and would yield results capable of being projected to the total area. The universe would be stratified in three ways, as follows: (1) by geographic location; (2) by "new" and "old" areas; and (3) by "small" and "large" blocks.

The total metropolitan area was to be divided into five parts—the city proper (corporate area), the three major suburban cities, and the remainder of the area. By means of the 1960 Census of Population the blocks of the city proper and the three suburban cities were to be divided into those with less than 50 dwelling units and those with 50 or more dwelling units. A further stratification would be effected by dividing blocks into "new" and "old" to ensure the inclusion of new building—especially housing developments. This was to be done by obtaining information from various governmental agencies and local utilities on new dwelling units built since 1960. For these four cities, a total of 9,900 blocks would be classified by size and newness.

The remainder of the sampling universe was to be fragmented by using the 1960 enumeration districts, which boundaries were obtained from the Bureau of the Census. These were not classified by size because the census had laid them out in such a way as to provide equal work loads for their census enumerators. They were, however, to be stratified by "old" and "new" based on information provided by the local utilities. Later work revealed a total of 735 enumeration districts as "old" and 83 as "new."

The next step would be the selection of primary sampling units from 9,900 blocks in the four major cities and the 818 enumeration districts. These units would be areas in which complete enumerations would be made and from which sampling units would be selected. The final sample called for approximately 2,000 dwelling units, and in an effort to control costs it was decided to use an average cluster size of 5 units. Thus, some 400 primary sampling units were to be selected.

The four major cities contained about 75 percent of all dwelling units in 1960, and thus 75 percent of the primary sampling units were to be selected from these cities. All blocks within each of the four strata were to be consecutively numered (old-small, new-small, old-large, and new-large). For the first stratum (old-small) every 50th block was to be selected after a random start. In the other strata, every 25th block was to be selected after a random start. This process would yield about 291 blocks.

Using essentially the same procedure, 100 from the total of 818 enumeration districts were to be selected: 1 out of 8 was the sampling rate to be used. Out of the 100 districts, 90 would be old and 10 new. Each of the 100 districts was to be further divided into subunits consisting of approximately 30 dwelling units each following a visual counting of units in each district. One subunit would be selected from each of the 100 districts on the basis of proportion to size (in dwelling units). Thus, a segment with 50 dwelling units would have twice the chance of being selected as one with 25. The 100 segments within the 100 districts plus the 291 blocks would constitute the 391 primary sampling units. The latter would be distributed approximately as follows:

Old-small	105
Old-large	176
New-small	9
New-large	1
Total	291

Inasmuch as the sample was to be self-weighting, with each dwelling unit in the universe having an equal chance to be included in the sample, all dwelling units located in the 391 primary sampling units were enumerated, and the sample of 2,000 was selected (systematically with a random start). This would mean using an overall sampling rate of one in 450. Since primary sampling units were selected with different probabilities, it was necessary to apply different probabilities in the final selection of dwelling units to arrive at the uniform overall rate of 1/450. Thus, for the old-small stratum, the rate was 1/9; for the other three, 1/18.

For the subunits within the enumeration districts, a different sampling rate would have to be determined in order to arrive at the same overall rate of 1/450. This procedure would be as follows:

1. Every enumeration district would have a 1/8 chance to be selected.
2. If a subunit had 50 units in a district of 250, it had a second stage chance of 50/250 or 1/5 chance to be included.
3. After a random start, every 11.25th dwelling unit should be selected because $1/8 \times 1/5 \times 1/11.15 = 1/450$.

The sample findings would be readily projectable to the universe using an inflation factor of 450.

Critically evaluate the proposed sampling design.

Case 9—5. BOYINGTON RESEARCH AGENCY

The Boyington Research Agency serviced a substantial number of large manufacturers and advertising agencies on a variety of research inquiries. While the agency performed a great many different research activities for its clients, it specialized in national consumer surveys.

For one of these projects to determine the characteristics of users and potential users of a prepared food product, the agency drew a national probability sample of 25,000 households. A general description of this sample follows.

The sample was allocated proportionately among the four main census geographic regions. The Census of Population served as the basis for allocating the sample. The sampling universe consisted of all households within the continental United States. Thus, persons residing in quasi-households (transient hotels, institutions, military camps, etc.) were not included in this plan.

Within each region the sample was stratified by metropolitan versus nonmetropolitan counties. All metropolitan areas as defined by the census were included in the sample. Where metropolitan areas extend across state lines and into another region, the entire area was assigned to only one region. The basis of allocation was the relative amount of the area's population contained in each of the two regions. Whichever region had the largest share received credit for the entire area.

The 25,000 households were assigned on a proportionate basis to the two strata indicated above. Within each of the metropolitan counties the sample was again allocated on a proportionate basis. For example, the metropolitan Chicago area represented 5.9 percent of the population residing within all metropolitan areas and thus 5.9 percent (874 households) of this part of the sample was allocated to this area. Cook County contained 81 percent of this area's population and so 708 households were assigned to it.

Within each region it was decided to select approximately 50 non-metropolitan counties. These 50 were selected on a probability proportionate to population basis. The procedure was as follows:

1. The population for all nonmetropolitan counties was totaled for each region.
2. This total was divided by 50. Those counties which had a population greater than the resulting quotient automatically were included in the sample.
3. All nonmetropolitan counties having a population of less than 1/50 of the total were then listed by states. The sample selection was made by using 1/50 of the total as the sampling interval. The list was entered at random. A simplified example of this procedure follows:

Assume a situation in which it is desired to select five counties from the following list of thirteen Wisconsin counties.

County	Population
Washburn	11,665
Forest	9,437
Dunn	27,341
Pepin	7,462
Pierce	21,448
Sawyer	10,323
Rusk	16,790
Bayfield	13,760
Eau Claire	54,187
Price	16,344
Taylor	18,456
Clark	32,459
Ashland	19,461
Total	259,133

The sampling interval would be 259,133 ÷ 5 or 51,826. Eau Claire County comes in with certainty since its population is larger than the sampling interval. This county is then deleted from the list and the remaining twelve counties listed and their populations cumulated as follows.

County	Population	Cumulated population
Washburn	11,665	11,665
Forest	9,437	21,102
Dunn	27,341	48,443
Pepin	7,462	55,905
Pierce	21,448	77,353
Sawyer	10,323	87,676
Rusk	16,790	104,466
Bayfield	13,760	118,226
Price	16,344	134,570
Taylor	18,456	153,026
Clark	32,459	185,485
Ashland	19,461	204,946

This list is entered at random by selecting a random number between 1 and 51,826—say 23,121. The sampling interval of 51,826 is added to the random number start and cumulated through the rest of the list. The four counties of Dunn (23,121), Pierce (74,947), Price (126,773), and Clark (178,549) are selected in this manner.

Selection of places within metropolitan counties

The sample size allocated to each metropolitan county was determined by the proportion of its population weight to the total U.S. metropolitan population. Within each county a total of three places was desired. These were selected with a probability proportionate to population in the same fashion as were counties. The "within-place" sampling rate was determined by the relative importance of the place. For example, assume that the following three towns were selected from DuPage County in Illinois.

| | Population | |
Town or city	*Number*	*Percent*
Downers Grove	11,900	27.8
Elmhurst	21,200	49.7
Glen Ellyn	9,500	22.5
Total	42,600	100.0

DuPage County had 2.8 percent of the population of the Chicago metropolitan area which was assigned a sample of 874 (see earlier discussion). A sample of 24 was allocated to DuPage County (2.8 percent of 874). These 24 would be distributed among the three towns or cities in proportion to their relative population: Downers Grove would receive 7, Elmhurst 12, and Glen Ellyn 5.

Selection of places within nonmetropolitan counties

The sample size allocated to each nonmetropolitan county is determined on the basis of the relative importance of that county in population to the total of all sample nonmetropolitan counties in the region. If a sample county had 4 percent of this population, then 4 percent of the region's nonmetropolitan sample would be allocated to that county.

The selection of the three places within each county was handled in a manner analogous to the selection of places within metropolitan counties. The "within-place" sample size was also determined in a similar fashion.

Selection of blocks

The average number of interviews per block for any given survey was set at two. Since the sample size for the place had already been established, the number of sample blocks was determined by dividing the sample size by two. Thus, if the sample size were one hundred, the number of blocks to be selected would be fifty.

Blocks were selected with equal probability; that is, each block had the same chance of being selected as any other block regardless of its size (number of dwelling units). A listing of all blocks within the place was obtained and each block was assigned a number. The total number of blocks was divided by the sample size desired to obtain the sampling interval. The list was entered at random through the use of a random number which identified the first sample block. The sampling interval was next added to the random number and the total identified the second sample block, and so on. For example, if there were 100 blocks within a place and 25 were to be selected for the sample, then the sampling interval would be four (100 ÷ 25). A random number between 1 and 4, taken from a table of random numbers, might be 3. Then the 3rd, 7th, 11th, 15th, 19th, 23rd, etc., blocks on the list would be included in the sample.

All households within the sample blocks were enumerated and the sample households selected by establishing a sampling interval, entering the list at random, and cumulating through the list in a manner similar to the way blocks were selected.

In order to obtain block listings it was necessary to obtain maps from any possible source such as city clerks, assessors, police departments, commercial map firms, and the Bureau of the Census. For open county segments (small rural towns and farm areas) it was not possible to obtain a block listing and, therefore, there was no alternative but to require that all dwelling units within the specified area be enumerated. From this listing the desired number to be included in the sample was obtained by using a sampling interval after a random number start.

1. What was the reasoning behind selecting counties and cities or towns on a probability-proportionate-to-population basis?

2. Why were blocks within cities selected on an equal probability basis?

3. Did the sample design employ proper stratification?

4. Is the final sample a true probability sample, i.e., does every household in the United States have an equal and/or known chance for selection?

10

Statistical design of experiments

THE PRECEDING two chapters have outlined the principles of sampling as typically used in marketing research. These methods apply particularly to conclusive research of the descriptive type; they are the methods most widely used in marketing research. In the chapter on the design of experimental research studies (Chapter 3), it was pointed out that experiments are effective in measuring cause and effect relationships between two or more variables. It is often difficult and expensive to design experiments to provide the information needed in a particular situation, but such studies are nevertheless becoming more widely used in marketing.

The principles of sampling discussed in the previous chapters are applicable to experimental research, but the statistical design and analysis of experiments has a special body of principles, theory, and methods. This chapter will introduce the student to the ideas.[1]

---

[1] The reader interested in general technical discussion is referred to the previously mentioned book by R. A. Fisher, *The Design of Experiments,* 6th ed. (New York: Hafner Publishing Co., 1951); W. G. Cochran and G. M. Cox, *Experimental Designs,* 2d ed. (New York: John Wiley and Sons, Inc., 1957); D. R. Cox, *Planning of Experiments* (New York: John Wiley and Sons, Inc., 1958); O. Kempthorne, *The Design and Analysis of Experiments* (New York: John Wiley and Sons, Inc., 1952); O. L. Davies, ed., *The Design and Analysis of Industrial Experiments* (New York: Hafner Publishing Co., 1954).

A text on experimental design in marketing is provided by Seymour Banks, *Experimentation in Marketing* (New York: McGraw-Hill Book Co., 1965). For an overview article on promotional experiments, see W. S. Hoffnagle, "Experimental Designs in Measuring the Effectiveness of Promotion," *Journal of Marketing Research,* Vol. II (May, 1965), pp. 154–62.

Basic principles pertaining to experimental design have been discussed in Chapter 3. It is worth repeating that the use of a randomized experiment provides the marketing researcher with a powerful tool for appraising cause and effect relationships. The key element is the use of randomization in applying the experimental variable. This provides the basis for statistical evaluation following the same principles discussed in sampling. The randomization assures the experimenter that, apart from sampling error, the groups of experimental units will respond identically to the application of experimental variables except for the differential effects of different variables. By using methods of the sort to be described in this chapter, the experimenter can utilize the observed data for estimating the fallibility of his conclusions.

Experimental designs to be discussed here differ from those described earlier in Chapter 3, principally in the use of *random sampling* in determining which units receive the experimental variables. Otherwise, the basic ideas are the same. The discussion of randomized experiments will depend heavily on the idea of random sampling introduced in Chapters 8 and 9.

EXPERIMENTAL GOALS AND GENERAL PROCEDURE

Assume that the researcher wishes to evaluate the effects of two or more alternative marketing variables and that he has a random sample of experimental units from some relevant population. For example, he may wish to assess the comparative effectiveness of three display methods using a sample of grocery stores. The experimenter will typically proceed as follows:

1. Assign test variables (display methods in above example) to experimental units, using some method of randomization.
2. Apply variables, observing and recording the appropriate response variable for each experimental unit (e.g., sales in the above example).
3. Combine the results from each experimental variable, ordinarily by a simple averaging process (average sales for all stores receiving the same display variable).
4. Compare the average responses to the various treatments. Typically, such evaluations will involve the construction of confidence intervals.

Various methods of assigning experimental variables to experimental units will be considered. The method of allocating these variables (the *statistical design*) and the conceptualization of the effects of the design (the *mathematical model*) are critical because they determine the analysis of the experimental results. The discussion will use the basic experimental designs developed in Chapter 3, but will focus on statistical problems that could not be introduced there. Only a few basic designs can be discussed here. The approach will be to describe the conceptual background of a particular experimental design, illustrate its application to a marketing problem within the four-step framework sketched above, and discuss its usefulness in marketing experimentation generally.

THE COMPLETELY RANDOMIZED LAYOUT

The simplest experimental design that uses the principle of randomization in assigning treatments to experimental units is called the *completely randomized layout* (abbreviated hereafter as CRL). The researcher may use two or more treatments in this layout. For simplicity, the discussion is limited to the two-variable case and to the situation where there is an *equal* number of observations (or "replications") for each treatment. This is the simplest design—the "after only with control group" design.

To illustrate, suppose one wishes to evaluate the effect on sales in drug stores of two price levels, 89¢ vs. 99¢, for a new hair spray. There are 14 stores available for the experiment, so that each price will be assigned to 7 stores, and sales will be recorded over a suitable time period, perhaps 6 months. A completely randomized layout (CRL) is the experimental design to be used. Either price may be considered the experimental variable and the other the control.

The first step in a CRL is to assign the variables (here, price levels) at random to the available experimental units (here, the 14 drug stores). This would be done as follows in the example:

1. Randomly select 7 of the 14 stores to receive one of the two variables (arbitrarily, either 89¢ price or 99¢ price). This would be done by numbering stores from 1 to 14 and choosing 7 random numbers between 1 and 14 to identify those to receive the first price. Although identification of the first price is arbitrary, it must be done before the sample is chosen.
2. Designate the remaining 7 stores as those to receive the other price treatment.

This pattern of variable assignment is called a *completely* randomized layout because no restrictions are placed on the random assignment of treatments. As a result, before the randomized assignment of the variables, every possible sample of 7 units (stores) has an equal probability of being assigned to either of the two price treatments. This guarantees that, *on the average*, in advance of applying the treatments, the two groups of 7 stores will be equivalent in all respects. As a result, *after* treatments (prices) have been applied and responses (sales) measured, differences between the average sales in the two groups of stores will tend to reflect *true* differences in the effects of the different prices, rather than merely differences in subgroup composition.

Of course, genuine differences in the effects of the different prices still can be obscured by random variations, and, conversely, apparent differences in the effects may be purely random in origin. The point is that, in a CRL, the use of randomization in assigning treatments guarantees that, on the average, sample experimental units will reflect what would have been obtained if the experimental treatments could have been applied independently to all experimental units in the population sampled (in this case, all drug stores). This characteristic is equivalent to the unbiasedness property of a sample mean derived by simple random sampling in the case of sample surveys (Chapter 8).

The mathematical model for a CRL

Assume that the two experimental treatments (prices) have been applied to the appropriate experimental units (stores), as identified by the randomization process. Suitable measurements, depending on the experiment objectives, are then made for each test unit (store sales of hair spray). The experimental data then consist of one response measurement (hair spray sales) for each experimental unit (store).

To make sense of the data, the experimenter must make explicit assumptions about the mathematical connection between the observed data and the essential features of the experimental design used. Before discussing this structure, or "mathematical model," for the CRL, it will be useful to develop some shorthand notations.

The general symbol for any observation in a CRL is:

$$y_{ij}$$

where the two subscripts i and j have these meanings:

1. The subscript i identifies the *variable* (price in the example) being referred to. If it is variable #1, then $i = 1$; if variable #2, then $i = 2$.
2. The subscript j identifies specific observations (sales in a specific store in the example). If the reference is to the observation in experimental unit #1 (sales in store #1), then $j = 1$; if the reference is to the observation in unit #7, then $j = 7$.

Some examples will clarify this notation further. Refer to the hair spray example, where there are 7 sales observations for each of the two price treatments, or 14 observations in all. Using the above notation: y_{11} refers to the first observation ($j = 1$) on price treatment #1 ($i = 1$). This is hair spray sales in the first store receiving price #1 (89¢). y_{12} is the second observation ($j = 2$) on price treatment #1 ($i = 1$), i.e., hair spray sales in the second store assigned price #1. y_{13} symbolizes the third observation ($j = 3$) on price treatment #1, or sales in the third store assigned the first price.

The last observation for the first price treatment would be y_{17}, since there are 7 observations (store sales) for treatment #1. Similarly, the following notation will identify the observations on price treatment #2 in the hair spray example: y_{21} is the first observation $(j = 1)$ on price treatment #2 $(i = 2)$. This is hair spray sales in the first store receiving price #2 (99¢). y_{22} identifies the second observation on the second price treatment, i.e., hair spray sales in the second store assigned treatment #2.

Using the y_{ij} notation, consider the assumed structure (mathematical model) for a CRL. There are two aspects to the model: the individual *components* of the model, and the manner in which they are assumed to *combine* to generate the experimental response observation. The CRL model for any observation consists of two components, and they are assumed to combine by simple addition. Specifically, any observation (y_{ij}) in a CRL is assumed to be made up this way:

$$y_{ij} = M_i + e_{ij}$$

where
  y_{ij} is the jth observation for treatment i.
  M_i is the *population mean* of all observations subjected to treatment i.
  e_{ij} is the *experimental error*, or deviation from the population mean M_i, associated with the jth observation.

Examples will clarify the meaning of this model. Refer to the hair spray test. The first sales observation on price #1, namely y_{11}, is, according to the model, composed of two additive parts:

$$y_{11} = M_1 + e_{11}.$$

M_1 is the population mean sales of hair spray per store under price #1; e_{11} is the deviation of y_{11} from that population mean (M_1); and e_{11} is associated with the first store $(j = 1)$ receiving price #1 $(i = 1)$.

Similarly, the observation on the second store receiving price #1 is:

$$y_{12} = M_1 + e_{12}$$

where M_1 is again the population mean sales per store under price #1, and e_{12} reflects the experimental deviation associated with the observation of sales in the second store. The remaining hair spray sales observations related to price #1 are similarly comprised:

$$y_{13} = M_1 + e_{13}$$
$$y_{14} = M_1 + e_{14}$$
$$y_{15} = M_1 + e_{15}$$
$$y_{16} = M_1 + e_{16}$$
$$y_{17} = M_1 + e_{17}$$

Notice that all the price #1 observations have the same M_1, the population mean for treatment #1. They differ from each other because of random fluctuations, the experimental errors arising from uncontrolled variations in the experiment. These will be explained more fully a little later. The CRL model specifies that each observation for treatment #1 is a sum of two components: a common population mean, M_1, and a random experimental error associated with each experimental unit in the test.

The observations on the second treatment (price #2 in the example) are assumed to be similarly comprised of: (1) a common component, plus (2) a random experimental error which varies from one experimental unit to the next. In the hair spray test, the observations on price treatment #2 are assumed to be made up as follows:

$$y_{21} = M_2 + e_{21}$$
$$y_{22} = M_2 + e_{22}$$
$$y_{23} = M_2 + e_{23}$$
$$y_{24} = M_2 + e_{24}$$
$$y_{25} = M_2 + e_{25}$$
$$y_{26} = M_2 + e_{26}$$
$$y_{27} = M_2 + e_{27}$$

where M_2 is the population mean sales per store for price #2. The error terms e_{21}, e_{22}, e_{23}, etc. reflect, respectively, the random fluctuations associated with the first, second, third, etc. stores receiving price #2 in the test.

The experimenter would like to *know* the values of the two population treatment means, M_1 and M_2, for these are the measures of the effects of the two prices which he is seeking. The effect of the experimental errors, the e_{ij}, is to obscure the experimenter's vision of these unknown means. Much of the methodology of statistical experimental design is concerned with reducing the magnitude of the experimental errors, thereby permitting the experimenter to achieve the "best estimates" of such means as M_1 and M_2 with measurable precision. In this regard, the goals and tactics of statistically designed experiments are similar to those identified earlier in connection with the purposes and methods of probability sampling for surveys.

Assumptions about the experimental errors

To complete the CRL model, some assumptions about the nature of the experimental errors (the e_{ij}) are required. Mathematically, it is *necessary that, for each treatment, the experimental errors be con-*

ceived as normally and independently distributed about the population mean so that, if they are measured plus and minus from the mean, they will have an average value of zero, and the distribution of each set of experimental errors around its population mean will have the same standard deviation.

Although technically complete discussion of these assumptions is beyond the scope of this book, a few comments about them will be helpful.

1. If randomization is used to assign treatments, then for the purposes described in this chapter the experimenter can often assume that the errors will be "close enough" to a statistically normal distribution. Use of randomization assures that the errors will be "independent" of each other. Randomization guarantees that the average value of the experimental errors will be zero—there will be no systematic tendency for a favorable bias toward either of the two experimental treatments.

In summary, the use of randomization tends to validate, for many practical purposes, the assumptions that the experimental errors are normally and independently distributed with a mean of zero. This serves roughly the same purpose as described for random sample selection in Chapter 8, and is why the need for treatment randomization has been emphasized.

2. Possibly the most vulnerable assumptiion is that *all the experimental errors in a CRL have the same standard deviation.* In the present context, this means that the standard deviation of the treatment #1 observations should be the *same* as the standard deviation of the treatment #2 observatiions. Intuitively, it would seem the variation of the treatment #1 observatiions about their sample mean should be about the same as the variability of the treatment #2 observations around their sample mean. Unfortunately, this is often not the case, particularly in the instance where one experimental variable has a much larger effect than the other. There are methods of coping with this failure to meet the basic assumptions, but they are beyond the level of this book.[2] Fortunately, it has been demonstrated empirically that the experimental designs described in this chapter provide enormously useful results, despite some departures from the mathematical assumptions.

The nontechnical reader exposed to the above ideas for the first time will probably have experienced difficulty in understanding them completely. From the standpoint of the practical marketing researcher, the major conclusion is that randomization is a powerful device for helping to validate many of the assumptions about the experimental errors that are needed for a simple analysis of CRL experimental data. Few actual market experiments fulfill exactly all of the assumptions cited above.

---

[2] How to deal with the specific problem of unequal standard deviations in a two-treatment CRL is described succinctly in G. Snedecor and W. G. Cochran, *Statistical Methods* (Ames: Iowa State University Press, 1967), pp. 114–16.

Since experience has shown that experiments nevertheless produce highly useful results, the following discussion will assume that the assumptions are sufficiently fulfilled by the procedures described to make the possible error of little importance.

Data analysis in a completely random layout: First steps

Having identified the structure of a CRL, we next illustrate the analysis of CRL data using some information from an actual experiment. Two alternative packaging designs for a new cat food brand were tested. The experimental units were 24 grocery stores, reasonably typical of the population of grocery stores. Package design #1 (treatment #1) was assigned to 12 stores randomly chosen from among the 24 available for the experiment. Package #2 was assigned to the remaining 12 stores, so that there were 12 replications of each treatment. The sales observed in each store over a one-month period of the test are shown in Table 10–1.

TABLE 10–1. Results of two package designs tested in a CRL (one-month dollar sales of cat food)

Package #1	Package #2
$y_{11} = \$24.70$	$y_{21} = \$29.30$
$y_{12} = 32.40$	$y_{22} = 23.10$
$y_{13} = 32.00$	$y_{23} = 27.00$
$y_{14} = 30.30$	$y_{24} = 18.60$
$y_{15} = 24.90$	$y_{25} = 23.00$
$y_{16} = 38.10$	$y_{26} = 25.40$
$y_{17} = 23.30$	$y_{27} = 15.60$
$y_{18} = 25.90$	$y_{28} = 22.80$
$y_{19} = 32.80$	$y_{29} = 25.00$
$y_{110} = 24.60$	$y_{210} = 40.00$
$y_{111} = 36.20$	$y_{211} = 29.00$
$y_{112} = 25.80$	$y_{212} = 19.90$

Table 10–1 is read as follows: $y_{11} = \$24.70$ means that the first store receiving package #1 had sales for the cat food brand of $24.70. In the second store assigned package #1, sales were $y_{12} = \$32.40$. Among stores assigned package #2, the first had sales of $y_{21} = \$29.30$, the second store had sales of $y_{22} = \$23.10$, etc.

The experimenter was interested in estimating two population values (parameters):

1. *Each population treatment mean.* He wished to estimate M_1 and M_2, the population treatment means for package #1 and package #2. The population treatment mean M_1 is the average value that would be obtained if all experimental units (stores) in the sampled population had package #1. In the cat food packaging test, M_1 is the average dollar

sales per store of the cat food brand that would have been obtained over the test period if all stores in the universe had used package #1.

2. *The difference between the two population treatment means.* The researcher wanted to estimate the difference between the two universe treatment means $(M_1 - M_2)$. In the cat food experiment, this difference is the "true" (population) difference in the average sales per store between stores handling package #1 and those handling package #2.

In comparative experiments such as the cat food package test, where one is contrasting the comparative effectiveness of two treatments, the principal focus is on the *difference*, $M_1 - M_2$, rather than on either M_1 or M_2 considered individually.

The best estimate of M_1, the *population* treatment #1 mean, is the mean of the *sample* observations for treatment #1. In the cat food example, the best estimate of M_1, the population mean sales per store for package #1, is:

$$\bar{y}_1 = \frac{1}{12}(24.7 + 32.4 + \text{-} \text{-} + 25.8)$$

$$= \frac{1}{12}(351.0) = \$29.25 \text{ per store.}$$

The best estimate of M_2, the other population treatment mean, is similarly calculated to be $24.89 per store.

As one would expect, the best estimate of the difference between the two population treatment means, $M_1 - M_2$, is simply the difference between the two sample treatment means. With the cat food results, this becomes

$$\bar{y}_1 - \bar{y}_2 = \$29.25 - \$24.89$$

$$= \$4.36 \text{ per store.}$$

This says that, based on this experiment, the best estimate of the comparative effectiveness of the two packages is that package #1 generates $4.36 more sales per store per month than package #2.

What has been illustrated so far is the analysis of CRL data to provide single-valued (point) estimates of M_1, M_2, and their difference, $M_1 - M_2$. It should be noted that: In a CRL, the sample treatment mean is an unbiased estimate of the corresponding population mean. To relate this to the discussion in the preceding chapters on sampling, recall that the mean of a simple random sample is an unbiased estimate of the corresponding population mean. If a large number of simple random samples is drawn and a sample mean computed each time, then the average of these will tend to equal the mean of the entire population. The analogous result in a CRL is that the *sample* treatment mean is similarly an unbiased estimate of the corresponding population treatment mean.

There remains the question of how to construct *confidence interval* estimates of these parameters, i.e., ranges of numerical values within which each of these parameters may be presumed to be located.

Interval estimation of each treatment mean

The procedures described above provide estimates of treatment means and their difference for a two-treatment CRL. These alone are usually not sufficient, since such estimates are subject to sampling error. Ordinarily, the analyst also wants to put *confidence intervals* on such estimates, to provide an indication of the precision of the results. In the packaging experiment, for example, he wanted to specify intervals within which which he could be reasonably confident that the population means for package #1 and package #2 were located.

The problem here is similar to the situation encountered earlier in connection with simple random sampling in surveys. To see the similarity, consider again the packaging data of Table 10–1, and suppose that one wishes to put a 95 percent confidence interval on the package #1 population mean. If (*contrary to fact*) the experiment were based on a large sample, the analyst could construct a 95 percent confidence interval on this population mean in the same manner as described in Chapter 8. The approximate confidence limits for treatment #1, assuming a large sample, would be

$$\bar{y}_1 \pm 2 \frac{s}{\sqrt{n}}$$

where
  $\bar{y}_1$ = package #1 sample mean.
  s = estimated standard deviation of observations (store sales) on package #1.
  n = number of observations (stores) for package #1.

This method would be equivalent to confidence interval construction for sample survey means based on simple random sampling. No new theory would be involved. Such an approach would not be adequate here, however, because it assumes that the *sample* standard deviation is identical with the *population* standard deviation. With the small samples characteristic of experimental data, this approximation is no longer close enough to be satisfactory.

Use of the *t*-distribution in constructing interval estimates

This small-sample problem is dealt with by using the *t-distribution*, which takes into account the fact that small samples provide data that vary more widely than data from large samples. Since the formula above requires an estimate of the standard deviation of the observations based on the sample data (population data are not available), the greater un-certainty inherent in the use of the small-sample estimate of the standard deviation is accommodated by using a variable confidence interval of the form

$$\overline{y} \pm t \frac{s}{\sqrt{n}}$$

where the multiplier t is taken from the t-table and varies with: (1) the desired confidence level and (2) the number of independent observa-tions on which the estimated standard deviation, s, is based.

The latter number is called the *degrees of freedom* associated with the estimated standard deviation. For a two-treatment CRL, the de-grees of freedom associated with s are always $2 (n - 1)$, where n is the number of observations per treatment. The origin and meaning of the number $2(n - 1)$ are described later, when the determination of the sample standard deviation, s, is discussed.

TABLE 10–2. Values of t for selected confidence probabilities and error degrees of freedom

Error df	Confidence probability			
	80%	90%	95%	99%
10	1.37	1.81	2.23	3.17
11	1.36	1.80	2.20	3.11
12	1.36	1.78	2.18	3.06
13	1.35	1.77	2.16	3.01
14	1.34	1.76	2.14	2.98
15	1.34	1.75	2.13	2.95
16	1.34	1.75	2.12	2.92
17	1.33	1.74	2.11	2.90
18	1.33	1.73	2.10	2.88
19	1.33	1.73	2.09	2.86
20	1.32	1.72	2.09	2.84
21	1.32	1.72	2.08	2.83
22	1.32	1.71	2.07	2.82
23	1.32	1.71	2.07	2.81
24	1.32	1.71	2.06	2.80
25	1.32	1.71	2.06	2.79
30	1.31	1.70	2.04	2.75
∞	1.28	1.64	1.96	2.58

SOURCE: Rounded values from R. A. Fisher and F. Yates, *Statistical Tables for Biological, Agricultural and Medical Research* (New York: Hafner Publishing Co., Inc., 1963).

In the Table 10–1 packaging experiment, error $df = 22$. Reference to Table 10–2 shows that t would have these values for the confidence probability levels given:

For error $df = 22$	
Confidence	t value
80%	1.32
90	1.71
95	2.07
99	2.82

Since, in the problem introducing these ideas, the researcher was seeking a 95 percent confidence interval, the appropriate value of t for 22 error df would be $t = 2.07$. Hence, a 95 percent confidence interval on the population value of the package #1 mean would be given by

$$\bar{y}_1 \pm t \frac{s}{\sqrt{n}} = \bar{y}_1 \pm (2.07) \frac{s}{\sqrt{12}}.$$

To complete the calculation of the confidence interval, a value for s, the estimated standard deviation of the experimental errors in this experiment, is needed. For the package data in Table 10–1 this value is 5.67 (calculation will be shown in the next section).

Substituting this value for s and the previously obtained $29.25 for y_1, from the Table 10–1 data, a 95 percent confidence interval on the population mean for package #1 is given by solving

$$\bar{y}_1 \pm t \frac{s}{\sqrt{n}} = \$29.25 \pm (2.07) \frac{5.67}{\sqrt{12}} = \$29.25 \pm 3.39.$$

This result is interpreted as follows: the experimenter is 95 percent confident that applying package #1 to all experimental units (stores) in the population under study would yield an average sales per store between $25.86 and $32.64. The precise technical meaning of this result is the same as given in the discussion of confidence interval interpretation in Chapter 8.

Calculation of the confidence interval for package #2 would follow the same procedure. To illustrate the difference caused by choice of different confidence levels, the following calculation is for a 99 percent confidence interval for the population mean for package #2.

$$\$24.89 \pm \frac{2.82 \,(5.67)}{\sqrt{12}} = \$24.89 \pm 4.62$$

Confidence interval on a treatment difference

The remaining confidence interval to be calculated is that for the "treatment difference," i.e., the average *difference* in response between the two treatments in a CRL. The best estimate of this difference is $(y_1 - y_2)$. A confidence interval on the difference in population means for the two package designs is

$$(\bar{y}_1 - \bar{y}_2) \pm \sqrt{2} \frac{t\,s}{\sqrt{n}}$$

where the only new term is $\sqrt{2}$. This additional factor takes account of the fact that the sampling error of a difference in sample treatment means reflects a combination of the error inherent in *both* sample means.

Using the Table 10–1 data for illustration, a 90 percent confidence interval on the difference in population values of the two packaging means is given by

$$(\bar{y}_1 - \bar{y}_1) \pm \sqrt{2}\frac{ts}{\sqrt{n}} = \$29.25 - \$24.89 \pm$$

$$\sqrt{2}\,(1.71)\frac{(5.67)}{\sqrt{12}} = 0.42 \text{ to } 8.30.$$

The analyst would be 90 percent confident that the population treatment difference was between these two limits. Since this difference excludes the value zero, the analyst may say that he has 90 percent confidence that this difference is "statistically significant."

Determining s, the estimated error standard deviation

In the preceding discussion, the value of s, the estimated standard deviation of the experimental errors, was provided without explanation as to how it was calculated. In a practical problem, the evaluation of s precedes construction of confidence intervals. This section describes its calculation for a two-treatment CRL with n observations per treatment, using data from Table 10–1 for illustration.

To understand the calculation of s, it is desirable to have an intuitive grasp of its general nature. The experimental errors in an experiment reflect the uncontrolled variations present and s is a measure of such random "noise." In a CRL, s is derived from the variations in response (sales in the above example) of experimental units subjected to the same treatment. Variations in the observations *within a treatment* (e.g., among observations of sales of package #1) reflect the uncontrolled variation (i.e., experimental errors) associated with the experiment. If a given treatment yields widely variable results, s will be large. If responses to a treatment are quite uniform, then s will tend to be small.

The determination of s in a two-treatment CRL may be described in four stages. It is calculated from the formula $s^2 = \frac{1}{2}(s_1^2 + s_2^2)$. The first step is to obtain the *experimental error variance* (the *square* of the estimated standard deviation of the errors) from the variation in results observed from the application of treatment #1. This estimated experimental error variance, denoted by s_1^2 for package #1 in the example, is obtained from the formula

$$s_1^2 = \frac{\Sigma(\bar{y}_{ij} - \bar{y}_1)^2}{n-1}.$$

In words, this is the sum of the squares of the deviations of the observations from their sample mean, $\bar{y}_1$, divided by one less than the number of observations $(n - 1)$. Calculation of s_1^2 from Table 10–1 would proceed as follows:

$$s_1^2 = \frac{(24.7 - 29.25)^2 + (32.4 - 29.25)^2 + \text{----} + (25.8 - 29.25)^2}{11}$$

$$= \frac{1}{11}(277.59) = 25.24.$$

In calculating this result, notice that the *numerator* in the expression for s_1^2 namely

$$\Sigma(\bar{y}_{ij} - \bar{y}_1)^2$$

is a measure of the variation of the treatment #1 observations about their sample mean, y_1. If this quantity is small, then most of the treatment #1 observations are similar, reflecting limited experimental error in the results. If this quantity is large, then for the same number of observations this implies that the experiment was subject to relatively larger uncontrolled variability (higher experimental error).

The *denominator* in this formula, $(n - 1)$, is called the *error degrees of* freedom contributed by treatment #1. It can be thought of as the number of *independent* observations involved in the calculation of the numerator. This is one less than the total number of observations (12, in the example) because mathematically one observation loses its independence in the calculation of the mean around which the deviations are measured. In the example, $n = 12$, so that there are said to be $(n - 1) = 11$ degrees of freedom for error associated with, or contributed by, s_1^2.

To review the meaning of the results above: In the Table 10–1 data, $s_1^2 = 25.24$ based on 11 degrees of freedom. The quantity s_1^2 is the variance (standard deviation squared) of the treatment #1 observations and is a measure of their variability about their sample mean. Thus, it is a measure of the experimental errors (uncontrolled variability) associated with the observations from treatment #1. In theory, the treatment #1 observations differ among themselves only because of experimental error. The experimental error variance, $s_1^2 = 25.24$, has 11 degrees of freedom, because it is based on $n = 12$ observations, of which only $(n - 1) = 11$ are independent.

The second step in the determination of s is the calculation of the estimated experimental error variance, s_2^2, based on the variation of treatment #2 observations. This proceeds in the same manner as above:

$$s_2^2 = \frac{(29.3 - 24.89)^2 + (23.1 - 24.89)^2 + \,\text{----}\, + (19.9 - 24.89)^2}{11}$$

$$= \frac{431.29}{11} = 39.21.$$

This estimated error variance similarly has 11 degrees of freedom.

The third step of estimating s is to combine these independent values (s_1^2 and s_2^2) to obtain s^2 which for the packaging data is

$$s^2 = \frac{1}{2}(s_1^2 + s_2^2) = \frac{1}{2}(25.24 + 39.21) = 32.22.$$

It is possible to average these two sample variances, s_1^2 and s_2^2, because it has been assumed that the observations on treatment #1 and those on treatment #2 are both subject to the same level of experimental error. That is, the standard deviation (or, equivalently, variance) of the treatment #1 observations is assumed to be the same as for the treatment #2 observations. The reader will recall that this is one of the CRL model assumptions.

The final, combined estimate of the experimental error variance, s^2, is based on $2(n-1)$ degrees of freedom because each of its two components is based on $(n-1)$ degrees of freedom. Thus, in the examples, $s^2 = 32.22$ and the error df for this estimate are $(12-1) + (12-1) = 22\ df$.

The concluding step in the process of determining s, the estimated standard deviation of the experimental errors, is to take the square root of s^2. In the packaging data, this is

$$s = \sqrt{s^2} = \sqrt{32.22} = 5.67, \text{ with } 22\ df.$$

This is the value of s used earlier in the construction of confidence intervals for the packaging experiment.

This tedious development of the details of estimating s is provided to help the reader understand its origin. In practice, a computational device called the *analysis of variance* is used to estimate the error variance, and its square root, s, is taken to estimate the error standard deviation.

THE RANDOMIZED PAIRED COMPARISON

Although the CRL is the most basic design in the experimenter's tool kit and provides the foundation for understanding the statistical design of experiments, it is not widely used in marketing research because more sophisticated designs provide more precise results. The results come because experimental variables (treatments) are applied wholly at random in this design. Consequently, the groups of experimental units (stores in previous examples) randomly assigned to receive treatments may differ importantly in composition on characteristics that affect the results. For example, in a small CRL where two prices for a brand are tested in drug stores, the number of stores is usually small and one would anticipate that the group of stores assigned one price might differ greatly from the other group in such characteristics as store size, socioeconomic level of customers, relative emphasis given different departments, and national background of customers, etc. All such uncontrolled variables contribute to variability in the observations, thereby increasing experimental error and lowering the precision of experimental findings.

The marketing experimenter naturally wishes to guard against a circumstance in which test groups differ importantly (even though randomly) in characteristics that affect his observations and, therefore, his experimental conclusions. He usually has some knowledge about the characteristics of the experimental units that cause variability, and this knowledge can be used to design the experiment more efficiently. The situation is similar to that described in Chapter 9 with regard to the greater efficiency of stratified random sampling as compared to simple random sampling. It was noted there that stratification of sampling units before sample selection would usually increase the statistical precision of sample estimates over the results obtained via simple random sampling. Similar applications of stratification will improve the precision of experimental studies.

The randomized paired comparison: Basic ideas

The simplest design which utilizes the stratification principle for evaluating two experimental treatments is called the *randomized paired comparison* (abbreviated RPC). Before assigning treatments to experimental units, the researcher *pairs* the experimental units to be used on the basis of some factor (or factors) known to contribute to the variability in experimental results. That is, he stratifies the test units into groups of two each so that the members of each pair will be similar with regard to the factor known to influence results. Therefore, the two units in each pair may be expected to give the same results if subjected to the same treatment.

For example, an experimenter doing a store sales test of two variations of a new brand might first pair the stores on the basis of store size (total dollar volume, perhaps). His reasoning would be that stores similar in size (members of the same pair) would be expected to generate roughly the same sales volume if they were subjected to the same treatment. If the pairings were perfect, observed differences in response to the two experimental treatments would reflect only the true difference in the comparative effectiveness of the two treatments. To the degree that pairing is effective, the precision of the test results comparing the two product variations will be greater than in a CRL.

Once the pairing has been done in an RPC, one member of each pair is randomly selected to receive treatment #1; the other automatically gets treatment #2. Various methods discussed in Chapter 8 may be used to do this; one would be as follows:

1. For the first pair, flip a coin. If "heads," assign treatment #1 to the first member of the pair. If "tails," assign treatment #1 to the second member of the pair. The other member of the pair is allocated treatment #2. Designation of the pair members as "first" and "second" is arbitrary, but must precede the coin flip.
2. Repeat this treatment randomization separately for each of the available pairs.

A typical end result of such treatment randomization for an RPC with six pairs of experimental units is shown in Table 10–3.

TABLE 10–3. Illustration of the results of treatment randomization in an RPC with six pairs

Pair identification	Treatment (#1 or #2) assigned to members of pairs	
	First member	*Second member*
1	2	1
2	1	2
3	2	1
4	2	1
5	1	2
6	2	1

This plan would mean that treatment #1 was assigned to the second member of the first pair, the first member of the second pair, the second member of the third pair, etc. Such a plan resulted from flipping a coin six times as described above.

Structure of RPC data

After treatments have been randomly assigned to members of pairs and the treatments applied, an appropriate response variable (sales in the example) is measured on each experimental unit. For an RPC with $2n$ experimental units grouped into n pairs, the data consist of a set of n paired measurements for which the differences are calculated:

	Observations of experiment results		
Pair	Treatment #1	Treatment #2	Difference between #1 & #2
1	y_{11}	y_{21}	$y_{11} - y_{21}$
2	y_{12}	y_{22}	$y_{12} - y_{22}$
3	y_{13}	y_{23}	$y_{13} - y_{23}$
, ...	,	,	,
, ...	,	,	,
, ...	,	,	,
, ...	,	,	,
n	y_{1n}	y_{2n}	$y_{1n} - y_{2n}$

In this new notation, the first subscript identifies the treatment (#1 or #2), and the second subscript identifies the pair as the first, second, etc.

As an example, assume that two different packages are to be tested in $n = 5$ pairs of stores. The experimental sales results might look as follows:

	Observations of experiment results		
Pair	Treatment #1	Treatment #2	Difference between #1 & #2
1	$y_{11} = 16$	$y_{12} = 11$	$+5$
2	$y_{12} = 12$	$y_{22} = 4$	$+8$
3	$y_{13} = 20$	$y_{23} = 17$	$+3$
4	$y_{14} = 8$	$y_{24} = 4$	$+4$
5	$y_{15} = 14$	$y_{25} = 17$	-3

In this RPC the observation on treatment #1 in the first pair is $y_{11} = 16$, the observation on treatment #2 in that first pair is $y_{12} = 11$, and the difference between them is $(y_{11} - y_{12}) = +5$. Similarly, within the second pair, the observations on treatments #1 and #2 are $y_{12} = 12$ and $y_{22} = 4$, respectively, so that their difference is $12 - 4 = +8$, and so on for the remaining pairs.

Comparison of RPC with CRL

The following general points summarize the comparison of the RPC design with the CRL design:

1. The pairing process is intended to "equate" or "match" the two members of each pair on factors that otherwise (in a CRL) would increase the variability in the observed results. Thus, the experimenter attempts to *control* the experimental results by use of a stratification factor. To the extent that pairing is successful, within-pair comparisons

of the two treatments will be more precise than could be obtained with a CRL of the same total sample size. As an illustration, pairing on store size in a pricing experiment will (approximately) remove store size as a source of experimental error. This is because the price effect will be evaluated *within pairs* of stores which have been approximately equated in size.

2. The RPC is the simplest design in which the random assignment of treatments is done subject to a *restriction*, namely that both treatments shall be represented within each pair of experimental units. This contrasts with the CRL, where there is no pairing and, hence, no similar restriction on the treatment randomization. The experimental error standard deviation is, therefore, estimated *differently* than in a CRL with the same total number of observations, and the degrees of freedom for error are computed differently.

3. Although the treatment randomization is restricted in an RPC, the procedure leads to unbiased estimates of treatment means and their differences, just as in the CRL. The reason is that, before treatment assignment, each experimental unit within every pair has an equal chance (determined by an objective procedure, such as a coin flip) of being assigned either treatment.

Initial steps in RPC data analysis

With RPC data, the experimenter is concerned with constructing confidence interval estimates of the two treatment means and, particularly, of their difference. Thus, the goals are similar to those in analysis of data from a two-treatment CRL; but the difference in experimental design requires a different method of analysis.

The data in Table 10-4 were obtained from an RPC experiment which was designed to evaluate two alternative retail prices (price #1 and price #2) suggested for a new packaged dog food. Before the test began, dog food sales were audited for 48 experimental stores selected at random in a test market. The stores were then grouped into 24 pairs, such that dog food sales were as similar as possible within each pair. This was done by ranking the stores on the basis of dog food sales, from highest to lowest, and then assigning the first two stores to pair #1, the next two to pair #2, etc. A coin flip for each pair determined which store would receive price #1, the other automatically being assigned price #2. After treatment assignment, the gross margins on sales of the new product were audited in each store, precautions being taken to maintain shelf stock and correct pricing.

The data in Table 10-4 represent dog food gross profits for a one-week period. Gross profits in the store receiving price #1 in the first pair $(j = 1)$ were $y_{11} = \$1.49$. The gross profits in the pair #1 store receiving

TABLE 10-4. Results of two price levels tested in a RPC (one week dog food dollar gross profits)

Pair (j)	Price #1 (y_{1j})	Price #2 (y_{2j})	Difference between #1 & #2 (z_j)
1	$1.49	$0.70	$0.79
2	1.36	0.96	0.40
3	0.77	1.02	−0.25
4	1.10	0.74	0.36
5	0.79	0.95	−0.16
6	0.83	1.14	−0.31
7	0.85	0.84	0.01
8	0.58	0.58	0.00
9	0.70	0.85	−0.15
10	1.17	0.81	0.36
11	0.58	1.00	−0.42
12	0.98	0.96	0.02
13	0.81	0.78	0.03
14	0.77	0.64	0.13
15	0.78	0.41	0.37
16	0.82	0.74	0.08
17	0.54	0.55	−0.01
18	0.46	0.33	0.13
19	0.52	0.22	0.30
20	0.52	0.48	0.04
21	0.67	0.51	0.16
22	0.49	0.51	−0.02
23	0.55	0.58	−0.03
24	0.56	0.33	0.23

price #2 were $y_{21} = \$0.70$, and the difference in profits between the two experimental prices in the first pair of stores was $z_1 = y_{11} - y_{21} = \$1.49 - 0.70 = \$0.79$. Similarly, in the second pair ($j = 2$), gross profits at the first and second price levels were, respectively, $y_{12} = \$1.36$ and $y_{22} = \$0.96$, and their difference was $z_2 = \$0.40$.

The first step in analyzing RPC data is to obtain unbiased estimates of the two population treatment means and their difference. These are simply the corresponding sample values:

Population value to be estimated	Unbiased estimate
Treatment #1 mean	Sample treatment #1 mean, $\bar{y}_1$
Treatment #2 mean	Sample treatment #2 mean, $\bar{y}_2$
Treatment difference	$\bar{y}_1 - \bar{y}_2$

For the data in Table 10-4, these values are $\bar{y}_1 = \$0.779$, $\bar{y}_2 = \$0.693$, and $\bar{y}_1 - \bar{y}_2 = \$0.086$. These values are, respectively, the experimenter's *best estimates* of:

1. The population mean gross profit per store that would be obtained if price #1 were used in all stores of the population sampled.
2. The population mean gross profit per store that would be obtained if price #2 were applied to all stores of the population sampled.
3. The difference in population mean gross profit per store between price #1 and price #2. This is the comparative advantage, in gross profit per store, of price #1 over price #2. It is the quantity of principal interest in a comparative experiment like this one.

Estimation of experimental error standard deviation in an RPC

The next step is to estimate the standard deviation of the experimental errors associated with the test results. This quantity will be denoted by s_p to differentiate it from the corresponding error standard deviation, s, in a CRL. The estimated error standard deviation, s_p, is calculated from the formula

$$s_p = \sqrt{\frac{\Sigma(z_j - \bar{z})^2}{2(n-1)}}$$

where:

n = number of pairs.

$z_j = y_{1j} - y_{2j}$ = the difference in response between treatment #1 and treatment #2 in the jth pair.

$\bar{z}$ = sample mean of the z_j values (paired differences)

$$= \frac{\Sigma z_j}{n}.$$

The z_j values (paired differences) are shown in the right-hand column of Table 10–4. For these $\bar{z} = 2.06/24 = 0.086$. Therefore:

$$s_p = \sqrt{\frac{\Sigma(z_j - 0.086)^2}{2(24-1)}}$$

$$s_p = \sqrt{\frac{(0.79 - 0.086)^2 + (0.40 - 0.086)^2 + \text{---} + (0.23 - 0.086)^2}{46}}$$

$$s_p = 0.186.$$

This result may be found most easily by noting that

$$\Sigma(z_j - \bar{z})^2 = \Sigma z_j^2 - \frac{(\Sigma z_j)^2}{n}.$$

In the example,

$$\Sigma z_j^2 = (0.79)^2 + (0.40)^2 + \cdots + (0.23)^2$$
$$= 1.7764$$

$$\frac{(\Sigma z_j)^2}{n} = \frac{(2.06)^2}{24} = 0.1768$$

so that

$$\Sigma(z_j - \bar{z})^2 = 1.7764 - 0.1768 = 1.5996$$

and

$$s_p = \sqrt{\frac{1.5996}{2(23)}} = 0.186.$$

Finally, in an RPC, the estimated standard deviation of the experimental errors, s_p, has $(n-1)$ degrees of freedom, instead of $2(n-1)$ as in a CRL of the same total experiment size (i.e., one with $2n$ observations). In Table 10–4, s_p has $(n-1) = (24-1) = 23$ degrees of freedom. The reason for the reduced error *df* in the RPC is that $(n-1)$ *df* are "used up" by the pairing process. Because the randomization process is *restricted*, i.e., both treatments must be represented in every pair of experimental units, there are fewer *independent* observations with which to estimate s_p.

Confidence intervals in an RPC

Having estimated the population treatment means, their difference, and the experimental error standard deviation, the concluding step in RPC analysis is to construct confidence intervals. These calculations parallel those for the CRL, with the exception that s_p replaced s and the error *df* for determining the value of t are now $(n-1)$ instead of $2(n-1)$, as with the CRL.

An example of the calculations for a 90 percent confidence interval for the price treatment #1 population mean in Table 10–4 is:

$$\bar{y}_1 \pm \frac{t\,s_p}{\sqrt{n}} = 0.779 \pm \frac{(1.71)(0.186)}{\sqrt{24}} = 0.779 \pm 0.065 = \$0.714 \text{ to } \$0.884$$

where y_1 = sample mean = 0.779, t = 1.71 for 90 percent confidence and 23 error *df*, s_p = 0.186, and n = 24.

In a randomized paired comparison, the main focus is on constructing a confidence interval for the treatment difference. In the example summarized in Table 10–4, an 80 percent confidence interval on the price treatment difference is given by

$$(\bar{y}_1 - \bar{y}_2) \pm \sqrt{2}\frac{t\,s_p}{\sqrt{n}} = 0.086 \pm (\sqrt{2}\frac{(1.32)(0.186)}{\sqrt{24}} = \$0.015 \text{ to } 0.157.$$

The interpretation of these results parallels that given earlier for confidence intervals in general.

The RPC versus group-wise pairing

The RPC should be contrasted with an alternative experimental design for two treatments that is widely used in marketing research. This design is called "group-wise pairing," for reasons that will be evident. Its basic characteristics are as follows:

1. The experimental units to be used are grouped into two sets on the basis of some variable believed to be predictive of the response variable. On the basis of judgment, the experimenter assigns experimental units to each group in such a way that the two groups appear to be matched as closely as possible on the basis of the desired control variable. In the price test example, the experimenter would attempt to sort the 48 stores into two groups of 24 each that were as equal as possible in terms of total dog food sales.
2. After the groups have been constructed, one is assigned treatment #1 and the other receives treatment #2. The assignment of each treatment is done simultaneously to one *whole group* of experimental units, rather than independently from pair to pair of units as was done in the RPC design.
3. After the treatments have been applied, the treatment difference is estimated and a confidence interval constructed *as though a CRL design had been used*.

Although group-wise pairing is widely used, it is not recommended for the following reasons:

1. Subjective allocation of experimental units to treatment groups should be avoided, because there is no way to measure the possible bias that could result. An objective randomization process is preferred for reasons previously discussed.
2. The group-wise matching process essentially creates just two large "super" experimental units, *one* of which is assigned each treatment. If the design is conceived this way, it is impossible to evaluate experimental error, since a minimum of two independent experimental units per treatment is required for such a measure.
3. The common use of CRL analysis for dealing with data developed

from group-wise pairing tends to *overestimate* seriously the experimental error standard deviation associated with the data. Appropriate analysis is considerably more complicated and, even if attempted, rests on the dubious assumption that the assignment of units by judgment has resulted in random assignment.

For these reason, the RPC is preferred over group-wise pairing as a design for testing two marketing variables.[3]

Concluding remarks on the RPC, and its extension to more than two treatments

The RPC is a recommended design for evaluating two variables in marketing research experiments. It is superior in precision to the CRL, and this is bought at only a small price in increased complexity of design and analysis. The RPC is recommended over the more widely used group-wise pairing because of greater design objectivity and analytical simplicity.

The general principle used in the RPC design—stratification of experimental units on some basis before randomization—may be applied when there are more than two test variables. If there are k variables, the procedure is to group experimental units into "blocks" or groups of k units each, on the basis of a relevant stratification variable. Within each block, the k treatments are randomly assigned, one to each of the k experimental units. After treatment application and response measurement on each unit, analysis of treatment differences is conducted along lines similar to those described for the $k = 2$ case of the RPC design.

This extension of the RPC to more than two treatments is called a *randomized block design*. The reader interested in this design and its analysis is referred to the references in footnote 1.

THE LATIN SQUARE LAYOUT

The RPC and its extension to more than two treatments (the randomized block design) involve a stratification of the experimental units into homogeneous groups on the basis of a *single* grouping variable (store size in the examples). Often, the marketing experimenter is aware of multiple sources of extraneous variation that he would like to remove from the experimental data to improve further the precision of the results. An example of the simplest design for achieving this goal will introduce the idea.

---

[3] See D. J. Finney, "Stratification, Balance, and Covariance," *Biometrics,* Vol. 13, No. 3 (September, 1957). What here is called group-wise pairing, Finney calls "balancing."

Suppose an experimenter wishes to evaluate the effects of three alternative shelf arrangements (A, B, and C). He proposes to do so by observing sales generated by each variation in three stores in three time periods. He designs the experiment so that each treatment is applied once, and only once, in each store and in each time period. An arrangement meeting these needs is this:

Time	Store		
period	*1*	*2*	*3*
1	A	C	B
2	C	B	A
3	B	A	C

Such a geometric pattern, in which each Latin letter is represented once and only once in each row and each column of a square, is called a *Latin Square.* Its utility in experimentation arises from this balance property, from the fact that comparisons among treatments will be free from differences between "rows" (here, time periods) and between "columns" (here, stores). Thus, the Latin Square removes from experimental error *two* sources of extraneous variation in an experiment, one associated with rows, the other with columns. The effect of this is that the experimental error standard deviation will be smaller than it would have been without the Latin Square arrangement. The end result is that comparisons between treatments are almost always evaluated with greater precision than in the experimental designs described previously.

Size and number of Latin Squares

The Latin Square above for three treatments is said to be of size 3×3, referring to the number of rows and columns in the square. Latin Squares of any size exist; in marketing research, 2×2 to 6×6 squares are the most useful, since the experimenter generally does not attempt to evaluate more than half a dozen different treatments at once. Because the number of treatments must equal the number of rows (and columns) in a Latin Square, this range determines the most useful square sizes. With small Latin Squares (say, 4×4 or less) a single square will usually not provide adequate precision of results. A solution is to use more than one square, a procedure which will be discussed later.

Treatment randomization in Latin Squares

As with the other experimental designs discussed, it is essential that randomization be used to decide which treatment in a Latin Square is to be assigned to which experimental unit. As before, this process provides the experimenter with unbiased estimates of treatment means and their differences, plus the opportunity to construct confidence intervals for these.

With a Latin Square, the treatment randomization is done subject to the double restriction that every treatment be represented once only in each row and once only in each column in every square of the experiment. One may either construct a random Latin Square or refer to general tabulations that have been published.[4]

A 3 × 3 Latin Square will be used to illustrate the construction of such a design. The process is as follows:

1. Assign the three treatment symbols (A, B, C) at random to the three test treatments (e.g., alternative shelf arrangements).

2. Choose one of the three letters at random to occupy the first cell of the first row in the 3 × 3 square. Suppose B is picked. Then randomly select between the remaining letters (A and C) to determine the second position in the first row. Suppose this choice is A. The third position must be occupied by C. The resulting first row is:

	Column		
Row	1	2	3
1	B	A	C

3. Because B already occupies the first column of the first row, the treatment in the second row and first column must be either A or C. Randomly choose one of these; suppose it is A. This yields:

	Column		
Row	1	2	3
1	B	A	C
2	A		

The remainder of this square is determined by the Latin Square requirement that every letter occur once only in every row and column. The end result is:

	Column		
Row	1	2	3
1	B	A	C
2	A	C	B
3	C	B	A

---

[4] R. A. Fisher and F. Yates, *Statistical Tables for Biological, Agricultural and Medical Research* (New York: Hafner Publishing Co., Inc., 1963).

Should more than one square be used, a fresh randomization should be made for each.

A commonly used Latin Square structure

The analysis of Latin Square data derives from the specific mathematical model underlying the design. In marketing research experiments using the Latin Square principle, the following structure is relatively common.

1. There are *several repetitions* of the Latin Square arrangement, i.e., several squares of the same size used to provide adequate total sample size.
2. In each square, the *columns* represent different marketing units (for example, geographic areas or individual stores).
3. In each square, the *rows* represent time periods, these being common to all the squares in the experiment if more than one is used.

In the following discussion, attention is confined to this use of the Latin Square design. The reader should be aware, however, that other applications of this principle are used in marketing experiments.

Table 10–5 shows results of a Latin Square store test in which five

TABLE 10–5. Sales volumes in units from a test of three shelf arrangements (A, B, and C) obtained from five 3×3 Latin Squares with common rows (months) and different columns (stores)

	Square 1			Square 2			Square 3		
Month	*1*	*2*	*3*	*4*	*5*	*6*	*7*	*8*	*9*
1	C-202	B-246	A-1047	B-603	C-428	A-283	C-511	B-899	A-940
2	B-218	A-185	C-186	C-556	A-518	B-210	A-328	C-321	B-678
3	A-203	C-183	B-343	A-647	B-457	C-271	B-390	A-639	C-393

	Square 4			Square 5		
Month	*10*	*11*	*12*	*13*	*14*	*15*
1	A-119	B-346	C-203	B-291	C-319	A-600
2	C-143	A-390	B-269	C-267	A-363	B-614
3	B-245	C-397	A-190	A-164	B-243	C-716

squares were used to test three alternative shelf arrangements (A, B, and C) during three months, the same months being used in each of the five squares. The data shown are unit sales volumes for a breakfast cereal under the specified circumstances. Shelf arrangement C was used in store 1, in square 1, during month 1, and sales for that period were 202; the other tabular entries are similarly identified. The results of this typical experiment will be used to illustrate some of the basic ideas of Latin Square analysis.

The analysis of Latin Square data: Point estimates

Once Latin Square observations have been made, the researcher typically wishes to develop point and interval estimates of treatment means and their differences. For example, in the experiment tabulated in Table 10–5, the researcher will wish to estimate the average (mean) sales volume generated by arrangements A, B, and C. He will be especially interested in contrasting the differences in average sales volumes generated by A versus B, A versus C, and B versus C, i.e., he will want to know which shelf arrangement produces the most sales.

Estimation of population treatment means proceeds in the same way as with the other designs that have been discussed. The sample shelf arrangement A, mean $\bar{y}_A$, is the sum of the A observations divided by their number (15):

$$\bar{y}_A = \frac{1}{15}(203 + 185 + 1047 + \text{-- -} + 600)$$
$$= \frac{6616}{15} = 441 \text{ units.}$$

This is the best estimate of the mean sales per store per month, if arrangement A had been used in all universe stores over the three-month test period. Similarly, best estimates for the other arrangement means are:

$$\bar{y}_B = \frac{1}{15}(218 + 246 + \text{-- -} + 614)$$

$$= 403 \text{ units.}$$

$$\bar{y}_C = \frac{1}{15}(202 + 183 + \text{-- -} + 716)$$

$$= 340 \text{ units.}$$

The differences in population treatment means are best estimated by the corresponding differences in sample means, as was the case with previous designs:

$$\begin{array}{lll} \text{A vs. B} & \bar{y}_A - \bar{y}_B = 441 - 403 = 38. \\ \text{A vs. C} & \bar{y}_A - \bar{y}_C = 441 - 340 = 101. \\ \text{B vs. C} & \bar{y}_B - \bar{y}_C = 403 - 340 = 63. \end{array}$$

These are the best (point) estimates of the differential sales effectiveness of the three experimental shelf arrangements. For example, the data show that, on the average, arrangement A produced sales of 38 more units per store per month than arrangement B during the three-month period of the test. Therefore, it is estimated that if all the stores in the universe had used shelf arrangement A during the period, they would have averaged 38 more unit sales per store per month than if they had used shelf arrangement B.

The reader should note that the estimating methods described above are entirely similar to the methods used earlier with the CRL and the RPC designs. As before, sample treatment means and their differences represent the best estimates of the corresponding population values.

Construction of interval estimates with Latin Square data

Since the "best estimates" of average sales and differences in average sales are unlikely to be exactly correct, the experimenter's next concern is the computation of confidence intervals for the treatment means and their differences, as was the case with other designs. This involves two steps: (1) the calculation of the experimental error standard deviation (corresponding to s in a CRL, and s_p in an RPC), and (2) the combination of this information with the sample means to provide confidence intervals.

The detailed procedure for evaluating the standard deviation of the experimental errors in a Latin Square, while arithmetically straightforward, is too cumbersome to be described in depth within the scope of this book.[5] Conceptually, the process, in this example, amounts to estimating the standard deviation of the observations after allowing for the variability in results associated with treatment differences (differences in effectiveness of the different shelf arrangements), with row differences (month-to-month variation), and with column differences (store-to-store variation). Because the experiment was arranged in a series of Latin Squares controlling for month and store differences, and because the test treatments were randomly assigned within this structure, the response variability associated with these "sources" can be identified in the analysis. The components of variation in results identified with these sources are then taken account of in estimating the experimental error standard deviation. The end result is an estimate of the standard deviation of the experimental errors (uncontrolled variation) present in the data after allowance for these other sources of variability (store, month, and shelf arrangement).

In the shelf arrangement example, the Latin Square design provided for a balancing of the experimental treatments (A, B, C) over stores and months. The calculation of the experimental error standard deviation in this example, therefore, takes account of this "balancing out" of

---

[5] For a description of the analysis appropriate to the data in Table 10–5, see C. I. Bliss, *Statistics in Biology*, Vol. 1 (New York: McGraw-Hill Book Co., 1967), pp. 310–12.

treatments over stores and over months. Hence, experimental variability attributable to these sources is, in effect, eliminated as an influence in the experiment. The consequence is that the experimenter obtains a more precise estimate of treatment means and their differences than would have been possible had these factors not been explicitly built into the design.

Once the experimenter has obtained an estimate of the experimental error standard deviation, the usual final step will be the actual calculation of confidence intervals. In the shelf arrangement test, for example, one would probably want to construct a confidence interval on the difference in average sales per store per month generated by arrangement A versus arrangement B, by A versus C, and by B versus C to assist in determining how confident to be that one shelf arrangement did produce more sales than the others.

The general procedure for constructing confidence intervals with Latin Square data is similar, but not identical, to what has been described earlier in connection with the CRL and RPC designs. In particular, the degrees of freedom for error are determined differently. Special problems also arise when two or more pairs of treatment means are being compared, as in the present example in which the three shelf arrangement means are compared two by two. For discussion of the details of confidence interval construction with Latin Square data, the reader is referred to the standard references cited earlier.

Additional remarks on Latin Squares

Marketing research data are characterized by high variability from one physical unit to another (e.g., high variation in sales from one store to another). In these circumstances, experimentation involving the application of different treatments to the same physical unit during different time periods via a Latin Square is an attractive prospect for improving precision. For this reason, the Latin Square involving time periods as one control and physical marketing units (stores, geographic areas, etc.) as the other control, as illustrated by the experiment of Table 10–5, is potentially of great use in marketing. Therefore, the Latin Square is a desirable experimental design wherever it is feasible and desirable to control two sources of experimental variability.

Like any design, the Latin Square is subject to limitations. These were discussed in general in Chapter 3. One already mentioned here is that the number of experimental treatments in this design must equal the number of rows and number of columns in the layout. One could not, for example, test four treatments using five time periods and eighteen stores in a Latin Square arrangement.

The ordinary Latin Square layout involving time periods and physical units as the two controls is subject to an additional important limitation. It assumes that there are *no treatment after effects*, e.g., that the application of a given treatment to a particular store in time period #2 has no effect on the sales response of that store to a different treatment during period #3. In some marketing experiments, this assumption may be untenable, since the effects of a treatment (e.g., advertising) may persist beyond the time period during which it was applied. For this reason, caution must be used in recommending the ordinary Latin Square in marketing experiments involving time as one of the Latin Square dimensions.[6]

PROBLEMS IN THE STATISTICAL DESIGN OF EXPERIMENTS

In the preceding discussion and in Chapter 3, some of the problems encountered in conducting marketing experiments have been mentioned. It is now appropriate to look at some of the general difficulties involved in the statistical design and analysis of experiments and the practical problems of using experiments.

Statistical design difficulties

For ease of communication, the various designs described in this chapter have been presented as though the choice among them and other designs not discussed was a simple matter. In practice, selection of an appropriate design will be more complex. It will depend on the exact nature of the experimental questions to be answered, availability of time and other resources, knowledge about the variability of experimental units, magnitude of treatment differences to be identified by the test, and so on. In addition, there are questions as to the necessary size of experiments (number of observations) and stratification criteria to be used.

This discussion has simplified the problems of analyzing experimental data. While the analysis associated with a given experimental design model is to an important degree unique to that design, several problems occur frequently:

1. *Selection of response variables for analysis.* The researcher will often want to analyze several response variables, rather than a single one (e.g., both sales and market share). Should these give discrepant results, a choice of the most important will need to be made.

2. *The problem of "outliers."* Often the marketing researcher will be confronted with observations that look "too high" or "too low" to be plausible within the experimental context. He must decide whether such "outliers," as they are called, should be kept in the analysis or rejected.

---

[6] Various extensions of the Latin Square idea deal with this problem. See, for example, Cochran and Cox, *op. cit.*, pp. 133–42 and Banks, *op. cit.*, Chapter 6.

Given the large variability characteristic of marketing data, this question may be hard to answer. If it is known that something went awry to produce a particular outlier, then the data should be rejected. However, matters are seldom that straightforward. The issue is important, since one or two observations that are widely discrepant may influence the results considerably.

3. *The "missing data" problem.* For one reason or another, it is common to "lose" one or more response observations in an experiment. A store may burn down, experimental treatments may have been grossly misapplied to some experimental units, and so on. The missing data consequent to such situations create additional analytical difficulties. The reason is that most experimental designs rely for analytical simplicity on their "balance" properties (e.g., the fact that every treatment in a Latin Square is represented once in every row and column).

Discussion and guidance on the technical problems noted above are provided by the statistical literature. In some situations, access to expert advice is necessary.

Practical problems in application

Practical problems arise in the application of experimental designs to marketing. Several of these were discussed in Chapter 3—specifically, the lack of theory on which to base hypotheses, the tendency for market conditions to change, thus invalidating previous experimental results, the high cost of experimentation, and the administrative problems of controlling experiments so that they are conducted under reasonably realistic conditions. Another major practical problem can now be considered—the problem of large variation in response among experimental units.

Effective experimentation requires that the results obtained be sufficiently definitive, in terms of their statistical reliability, to lead to useful conclusions. For example, the confidence interval on a treatment difference must not be so wide as to be practically uninformative. As has been emphasized, the reliability of experiments depends on their structure, size (number of observations), and method of analysis. Reliability also depends on the uncontrolled variation remaining in the experiment—the magnitude of the experimental error standard deviation.

Although definitive evidence on a broad scale is nonexistent, the available information indicates that there is often large, uncontrolled variation in the results observed in experimental units receiving identical treatments. Even the same experimental unit (store, family, etc.), may exhibit bewildering response variability over time when there is no apparent trend, seasonal, or other identifiable cause of the variability.

The magnitude of the effect of the variables the researcher is studying may be small compared to such random "noise" present in an experiment.

There are some statistical techniques beyond the sophistication of this book which may be helpful with this problem, but the best the experimenter may sometimes do is to increase the total number of experimental units in a given test. This method of improving the precision of results is, of course, expensive, and introduces additional administrative complexities. However, it may be the only available alternative. The cost must then be balanced against the value of the information.

SUMMARY

The statistical design of experiments is based on random sampling and enables the researcher to improve the quality of inferences from experimental studies.

The basic statistical design, analogous to simple random sampling, is the completely randomized layout. In its simplest version, the experimental units are randomly divided into two equal groups, one of which receives the first treatment (experimental variable), while the other receives the second treatment (second experimental or control variable). A mathematical model is used to relate the principal features of the design to the experimental observations. By using randomization to validate the basic model assumptions, the experimenter establishes a statistically sound basis for constructing point and interval estimates of the two treatment means and their difference.

Because the CRL is comparatively imprecise, more complex designs are usually used in practice. One such design for testing two treatments is the randomized paired comparison. This design uses stratification before treatment assignment. The experimental units are arranged in matching pairs. Within each pair, one of the two treatments is assigned randomly to one unit, the other unit receiving the other treatment. Statistical theory again provides analytical methods for drawing inferences about the two treatment means and their difference.

Group-wise pairing is an alternative design for testing two treatments. The RPC is recommended over group-wise pairing because of its greater objectivity and analytical simplicity.

Another statistical experimental design is the Latin Square. This design controls the assignment of treatments to experimental units on two bases (or stratifications), in contrast to the RPC, which assigns treatments with only one control—namely, that both treatments be represented in each pair of experimental units. The Latin Square may be thought of as a geometric pattern of rows and columns in which each treatment is represented once, and only once, in every row (corresponding to the first control variable) and once, and only once, in every column (corresponding to the second control variable). Treatments are assigned to experimental units at random within the designated restrictions. Again, statistical theory provides methods for constructing estimates of treatment means and their differences based on the data provided by the Latin Square.

In general, the Latin Square is recommended for consideration when there are two important sources of extraneous variability that the experimenter would like to control. The use of physical marketing units (e.g., stores, areas) as the "column" control variable and "rows" as a time (days, weeks, months) control variable is common in marketing research applications.

Both operational and statistical problems arise in the practical application of these and other experimental designs to marketing problems. Nevertheless, the use of statistical experimental designs for solving complex marketing research problems is increasing.

Case 10—1.   LUCKY PUP PET FOODS COMPANY

Just prior to test marketing a new "flavor flanker" in their established dog food line, officials of Lucky Pup learned that an error had been made in costing the product. The earlier anticipated retail price of 73¢ would no longer generate required revenues, and a question was raised concerning initial consumer acceptance of the product at 79¢.

To evaluate relative consumer acceptance at the two price levels, the company's marketing research department designed an experiment which took only two weeks to run. A Latin Square, arranged as follows, was used:

1. In the initial test week, the new product was displayed in ten test stores designated as "A." A special bin was set up in each store, away from the regular dog food section, and the new product was displayed in the bin at a 73¢ price on Thursday and at a 79¢ price on Friday. In ten additional test stores (called "B"), the prices were switched, so that on Thursday the price was 79¢ and on Friday 73¢. In all test stores, the new product was available only on Thursday and Friday, and only in the special display locations. The first test week coincided with the breaking of the advertising campaign for the new product.

2. The following week, prices were reversed so that the A stores had 79¢ prices on Thursday and 73¢ on Friday, while the B's were assigned 73¢ on Thursday and 79¢ on Friday.

3. Test results from the research were as follows (in unit sales):

Total package sales

Sold at	Number	%
73¢	228	50%
Thursday sales	94	21
Friday sales	134	29
79¢	230	50%
Thursday sales	102	22
Friday sales	128	28

1. Show that this design consists of 20 repetitions of a 2 × 2 Latin Square.

2. What was the rationale for using a Latin Square here?

3. Based on these results, would you conclude that the 79¢ price should be used? Why?

4. What information does this experiment provide on repeat buying at the two price levels?

5. What other statistical experimental designs could be used here? Which would be the best?

Case 10—2. WHOLGRANE FOODS COMPANY

Over a ten-year period, Wholgrane, a leading grain processor, had introduced a number of new ready-to-eat cereals with varying success. Some introductions had used mail coupons as part of the initial marketing effort, others had delivered sample packages to consumers' homes, and still others had involved no additional marketing effort beyond the usual trade deals and consumer advertising. Since no formal plan for measuring the effectiveness of the various methods of introducing new products had been developed, the company had no clear viewpoint as to which method was best. Therefore, it was decided that when the next new cereal was introduced nationally, an experiment would be arranged that would provide clear evidence on the impact of each method.

The opportunity for experimentation came with the introduction of a new brand called "Eaties." The national marketing plan for this new product did not involve either couponing or sampling, so that special efforts were required to introduce these "treatments" into an experiment.

Wholgrane regularly subscribed to the service of an agency that maintained a consumer panel and provided monthly reports on purchases of cereal products. The research director found it would be possible to use experimental subsamples from the consumer panel. He arranged for three subsamples of 400 families each to be selected at random from among the total consumer panel of 8,000 families. One of these experimental groups served as a "control," i.e., it received no special attention. A second group, the "coupon" group, received a 15¢-off coupon via mail. The remaining group of experimental families received a home-delivered sample of Eaties. The coupons and samples were delivered about four weeks after the advertising campaign opened. Thus, three experimental groups were identified in advance of the product introduction and each subjected to a different experimental treatment. Purchases of Eaties by these families were reported in the regular panel reports over a six-month period.

The effects of these experimental treatments were measured by repeat buying, which was considered the key measure. Results are shown below for the six-month period:

	% who bought Eaties		
Treatment	Twice	3 times	4 or more times
Control	14%	10%	6%
Received coupon	23	14	7
Received sample	37	12	7

1. What interpretation should be made of these results?
2. Was the design used the most efficient available?
3. How could the experiment have been designed to show the impact of sending both coupons and samples to the same homes?

Case 10—3. ALPHA HOUSEHOLD PRODUCTS COMPANY

Alpha was a very large household products company, specializing in the sale of household cleaning products via grocery stores. The company had a retail sales force of 500 men calling on 40,000 grocery stores located in 25 company "districts." Each district had approximately an equal number of grocery stores, so that the territories ranged from small geographical areas in metropolitan locations to relatively large areas in the sparsely populated parts of the country.

In planning for the next year, the sales department recommended that the retail sales force be increased in size. At the same time, another group within the company was advocating a reduction in the size of the retail sales force, pointing out that seven districts had been understaffed for six months with no apparent loss in sales. This conflict brought out the fact that the firm had no clear evidence as to what the optimum sales force was. To help bring information to this issue, the market research department proposed an experiment to determine the effect of varying sales-call frequencies on the retail exposure of the company's products. The basic structure of the plan was as follows:

1. The company classified its "carded" stores (those called on) into three groups: A, B, and C, based on volume potential. The research department proposed that, within each of these volume potential categories, the current sales-call frequencies be halved in a sample of retail stores, kept at the present level in another sample, and doubled in a third sample.

2. To measure the effect of the three "treatments" (half level, present level, and double level), it was proposed that the retail salesmen check the number of stores normally stocking each product and the number of stores out of stock in the experimental groups once in January (before the test began) and again in August, six months after the February test start, i.e., the beginning of the new call frequencies. It would then be possible to evaluate the three treatments by the number of stores handling the product and the "out-of-stocks" before the test start and six months after the test programs had been in effect. The data generated for each company product in the test would then be put in a format like this:

While there was general agreement on the idea of the test, there was disagreement as to how the treatment samples for the experiment should be drawn. It was proposed by the research department that 75 stores be selected in each volume potential group. This would mean a total sample of 225 stores. The sales manager felt that his district managers should choose the 225 stores that would be used in the test, since they knew more about the stores than anyone else in the firm.

The research director urged that the 225 stores be selected wholly at random from the 40,000 "carded" stores. The chosen 225 would then be identified as to volume potential (A, B, or C). When this classification was completed, a third of the stores in each volume potential sample would be arbitrarily designated by the research director's secretary to receive each of the treatments.

A third sampling method was proposed by the research statistician. His scheme involved the following steps:

1. Develop lists of stores in each volume potential category (a list for A stores, one for B's and one for C's).
2. Arrange the list for each category in more or less geographic order, beginning with New England, proceeding to New York, and so on.
3. Divide each list into 25 "blocks" of equal size. (For example, if there were 1,000 A stores, this would mean 25 blocks of 40 A stores each.)
4. Within each of the blocks of 25 (separately for each volume potential category), identify three stores at random, one to be assigned each of the three experimental call-frequency patterns.

	Percent of stores receiving each treatment								
	High potential stores			Medium potential stores			Low potential stores		
	Sales level			Sales level			Sales level		
	Half	Regular	Twice	Half	Regular	Twice	Half	Regular	Twice
Normally handling product									
Before test	X%	X%	X%	X%	X%	X%	X%	X%	X%
After 6 months	X	X	X	X	X	X	X	X	X
Out-of-stocks									
Before test	X	X	X	X	X	X	X	X	X
After 6 months	X	X	X	X	X	X	X	X	X

1. Which of the proposed methods is most satisfactory?
2. What practical problems should be anticipated in each method?
3. How should the data be analyzed?
4. The information to be gathered in this experiment relates to retail exposure conditions rather than to sales as such. Can one justify this emphasis on an "intervening" variable, rather than on the end result variable of "sales"? If sales measurements as such were desired, how, if at all, might the design differ and what information would be needed in its construction?

Case 10—4. ZONOLITE COMPANY

The Zonolite Company of Chicago, having established itself in the building industry and gained some recognition in the lightweight fertilizer industry, was interested in developing new markets for its mineral products, vermiculite and verxite.[1] One of its efforts in this direction was the inauguration of its seminar plan for the agricultural, chemical, and animal food processing industries. After a year and a half's experience, the marketing vice president was asked by the president to evaluate the results and present his recommendations concerning the future of the seminars.

During 1961 and 1962 seven seminars were held at an estimated total cost of $10,000, including the time of company personnel. Each was especially arranged for selected employees of a potential customer to gain acceptance of vermiculite and verxite in product formulation or as a processing agent. The seminars were planned and staged by two Ph.D.'s, one a food technologist and the other an entomologist. Several man-days of relatively high-priced technical and executive talent were required to prepare for each seminar, in addition to travel and actual seminar time. The seminars were held in the offices of the prospect company, lasted several hours, and were usually attended by Zonolite's president or a vice president in addition to the food technologist and entomologist who presented the vermiculite story. The plan for a

---

[1] Vermiculite is a lightweight micaceous mineral that exfoliates or expands when heated. It is hydrated magnesium-aluminum-iron silicate. Expanded vermiculite—a free flowing, highly absorptive, inorganic material—comes in a wide range of forms and particle sizes. Low density, chemical inertness, fireproof and dielectric properties make it suitable for insulating, packaging, accoustical, absorbent, carrier, and filler-extender uses. It is used in agricultural chemical formulations, particularly as a chemical carrier for lightweight fertilizers, pest control products, and weed control products.

Verxite is a highly refined mineral, technically known as "exfoliated hydrobiotite," which Zonolite developed for the animal feed industry. Because of its mineral characteristics, chemical inertness and nontoxic character, verxite is an unusually effective carrier of biologicals and essential nutrients such as vitamins. It may be used as a pelleting aid and bulking agent to reduce calorie intake.

seminar included a description of the somewhat unusual characteristics and known uses of vermiculite and, where appropriate, verxite; a presentation of case histories of the successful use of vermiculite in solving difficult technical problems; the remainder of the time was given to discussion of questions raised by participants from the company for which the seminar was staged.

Customer reaction to the seminars was not easily determined, but seemed to be favorable. The seminar discussions generally revealed a high level of interest. Technical questions were sometimes received days and months after some of the seminars. Samples for laboratory testing had been requested following two of the seminars. Nevertheless, there was no evidence that any orders had been or were about to be received as a direct result of the seminars.

Following one seminar two of the research men who had been in the seminar visited the Zonolite laboratory to obtain further information. They left the impression that vermiculite would be specified in one of their products. Later it was learned that their favorable recommendation to their management had been blocked by the marketing department because it was not sure of their customers' reaction to the change. This case highlighted a possible weakness in the seminar plan. Zonolite's arrangements with the chemical and animal food companies for the seminars had been made by technical people with technical people. Few commercial research or marketing people had attended, even though Zonolite had suggested they be invited. In a few cases they were present at the opening but were called away or left during the more technical phases of the presentation. One of the guest participants indicated that vermiculite had many potential but no immediate applications in his company's operations.

Limited investigation of the use of seminars by other firms for promotional purposes revealed the following:

1. The number of companies using them was increasing, especially when demonstrations involved equipment which was relatively immobile or it was important for prospects to see a plant or laboratory.
2. They were usually held at the sponsoring company's plant and lasted from one to three days.
3. The host company usually paid expenses incurred at the seminar but participants usually paid their own transportation expenses.
4. Seminar guests were usually from a number of different companies.
5. Sales pressure at the seminars was soft when market development was sought and more intensive when orders were sought.
6. A customer under your roof was a captive, but under his own he was a commander.
7. The host might learn much about his own product.

8. Seminars opened doors for salesmen.
9. Failure to 'include some concerns could make enemies instead of friends.
10. Few companies cared to make any estimates of practical dollar returns from such programs.

During a discussion of the seminar problem, it was suggested that the company might more effectively reach the chemical industry through *Chemical Week*, with a paid circulation of 50,000, and the feed formulators and mixers through *Feedstuffs*, with a paid circulation of 14,000. A black-and-white page in *Chemical Week* could be bought for $1,000 and one-third page for $500. The rates for *Feedstuffs* were even less—the full black-and-white page rate was $450. Lower rates could be earned if several pages were bought.

1. How could an experiment be designed to test the effect of the seminars?
2. Can an experiment be designed to measure the relative effectiveness of the seminars and advertising in the trade papers?

Case 10—5. LONG-LIFE BATTERY COMPANY

The Long-Life Battery Company, one of the largest car battery manufacturers in the United States, distributed its products mainly through gasoline service stations. One of the company's major accounts was a national gasoline company with almost 20,000 stations. For several years the Long-Life Battery Company had spent over $100,000 annually to make available to these filling stations direct mail pieces featuring batteries and the oil company's major products. The advertising manager of the battery company requested the firm's marketing research director to undertake a project to measure the effectiveness of this direct mail advertising expenditure.

The Long-Life Battery Company spent over $3 million in advertising. The company used all media and was considered by the trade to be a heavy spender in direct mail. Its program with the national gasoline company consisted of making available at no cost a 4-page 4-color 12 × 15-inch direct consumer mailing piece. Page 1 of the mailing piece featured a "SAVE" headline surrounded by dollar signs, space for the retail filling station's name, address, and phone number (which would appear directly below the headline), and a picture of the company's battery with the company's trademark and name beside it. This picture took up most of the first page. The inside two pages featured pictures of each of the batteries produced by the company with the sale prices duly noted. The consumer was urged to "trade in now and save big money." The back page consisted of a reproduction of the national gasoline company's latest magazine ad, which was institutional in character. The ad showed a family about to take off for a drive and the copy emphasized how the company's service stations could make the trip safer, less time-consuming, and more economical.

The Long-Life Battery Company, through the national gasoline company, offered the latter's service stations the following:

1. An unlimited supply of these 4-page consumer mailers at no charge.
2. A listing of all car owners, including name and address, within a certain distance of the individual service station.
3. An addressing and mailing service whereby the Long-Life Battery Company would arrange with an independent direct mail firm to mail the 4-page piece to any given number of customers.

A charge of 5½ cents per mailing piece was made by the battery company to cover the preparation of the list, the addressing, handling, and postage. Those filling stations which desired to cooperate merely indicated on a map the area they wanted covered. This map was then sent to the direct mail house, which prepared the list and handled the mailing. Over 2,500 service stations had agreed to cooperate.

The research director decided to test the effectiveness of the company's direct mail campaign by setting up an experimental survey. He selected at random 20 gasoline stations throughout the country that had not agreed to cooperate in the current program. For each station he drew a circle on a map around the station approximately a mile in diameter with the station as the center. For each station he selected from a city directory the names of 100 homes located inside the circle. This constituted the "control" group. He next selected, again at random, 20 gasoline stations from the list of 2,500 stations who had agreed to cooperate and selected at random 100 names from their individual lists. This was the "test" group. Thus a total of 2,000 names and addresses were obtained for each sample.

The respondents from the cooperating dealers received the 4-page mailing piece *three* times. The mailings were made one week apart. Telephone calls were made to the homes of the 4,000 respondents included in both samples one week after the third mailing. The questionnaire used in making these telephone calls appears as Exhibit 1.

In analyzing the results (shown in Tables 1 to 13), the research director saw little difference between the two groups, that is, those who had received the direct mail pieces versus those who had not received any literature. The research director summed up his written report to the advertising manager as follows: "The results of the survey show no conclusive evidence that our direct mail advertising helps either us, our national gasoline account, or their local dealers. I therefore suggest to

EXHIBIT 1. Telephone interview (direct mail advertising)

PHONE NO.: _____

SERVICE STATION NO.: _____

1. Hello, is this (REPEAT PHONE NUMBER TO VALIDATE DIALING)? I'm doing a quick survey among car owners. I have (name from list)'s name as being the owner of a car. (He, she) does own a car, doesn't (he, she)?

   (IF LIST NAME DOES NOT OWN CAR, DISCONTINUE INTERVIEW)

2. What make and year of car is that?   (Make) _____ (Year) _____
   (Make) _____ (Year) _____ (Make) _____ (Year) _____

3. This is a research study. I have to talk with the person who takes care of servicing for that car. I'm not selling anything. Would (name from list) or someone else buy most of the gasoline for that car? May I speak to (him, her)? (TALK WITH PERSON RESPONSIBLE FOR SERVICING AND BUYING BATTERIES FOR CAR REGISTERED IN NAME ON LIST. IF NOT IMMEDIATELY AVAILABLE, MAKE TELEPHONE APPOINTMENT)

   (THE REST OF THE INTERVIEW IS WITH A QUALIFIED RESPONDENT)

4. If you were buying a new battery for your car today, what brand would you buy? _____

5. Have you bought any new batteries within the past year?   No ☐   Yes ☐
   a. (IF YES)   What brand did you buy last? _____
   b. From what dealer did you buy it?   Study dealer ☐   Other ☐
                                            Don't recall ☐

6. What brand of gasoline do you buy most often? _____

7. Where do you usually buy it?   Study dealer ☐   Other ☐   No answer ☐

8. I'd like to see how good a job your local battery and gas dealers are doing in letting you know where their businesses are located. Would you tell me if you know where you could buy each of the following products in your area?
   a. Do you know where you can buy brand A batteries?
                            Know for sure ☐   Don't know, not sure ☐
   b. Do you know where you can buy Long-Life batteries?
                            Know for sure ☐   Don't know, not sure ☐
   c. How about brand B batteries?   Know for sure ☐   Don't know, not sure ☐
   d. Now, do you know the location of brand A (gasoline)* station?
                            Know for sure ☐   Don't know, not sure ☐
   e. Do you know the location of a brand B (gasoline) station?
                            Know for sure ☐   Don't know, not sure ☐

9. Have you recently received any advertisement through the mail from local service stations?   No ☐   Yes ☐

10. Now just a couple of questions about a particular service station in your area and then we're through. Do you know of a service station at (dealer's address)?
    No ☐   Yes ☐
    a. (IF YES)   What is the name of that station?   Study dealer ☐   Other ☐
                                                          Don't know ☐
    b. Do they sell batteries?   Yes ☐   No ☐   Don't know ☐
    c. (IF YES)   What brand? _____

11. NAME: _____
    ADDRESS: _____
    CITY: _____   STATE: _____
    INTERVIEWER'S INITIALS: _____   DATE: _____

    * Sells Long-Life batteries.

you that our extensive expenditures on direct mail advertising be carefully reappraised and consideration be given to the use of these advertising funds elsewhere."

1. Do you agree with the research director's conclusion?
2. What changes, if any, would you have made in the experimental design?

TABLE 1. Question 2 (What make and year of car is that?)

Year	Control group no mail	Test group mail
1961	4%	5%
1960	14	16
1959	15	17
1958	16	18
1957	10	11
1956	13	12
1955	7	6
1954	7	8
1953 or earlier	24	21
	✿	✿

✿ Exceeds 100 percent because of multiple answers.

TABLE 2. Question 4 (If you were buying a new battery for your car today, what brand would you buy?)

Brand	Control group	Test group
Long-Life	12%	10%
Brand A	18	17
Brand B	21	23
All others	56	53
Don't know	54	5
	✿	✿

✿ Exceeds 100 percent because of multiple answers.

TABLE 3. Question 5 (Have you bought any new batteries within the past year?)

	Control group	Test group
Yes	28%	31%
No	72	69
Total	100%	100%

TABLE 4. Question 5a (What brand did you buy last?)

Brand	Control group	Test group
Long-Life	9%	6%
Brand A	14	12
Brand B	12	16
All others	47	50
Don't recall	18	16

TABLE 5. Question 5b (From what dealer did you buy it?)

	Control group	Test group
Study dealer	6%	9%
Other	51	43
Don't recall	43	48

TABLE 6. Question 6 (What brand gasoline do you buy most often?)

	Control group	Test group
Brand sold by study dealer	9%	11%
Other	87	82
No answer—don't know	4	7

TABLE 7. Question 8a-c (Do you know where you can buy brand A batteries? Long-Life batteries? Brand B batteries?)

	Brand A		Long-Life		Brand B	
	Control group	Test group	Control group	Test group	Control group	Test group
Know for sure	52%	56%	43%	47%	25%	27%
Don't know— not sure	48	44	57	53	75	74

TABLE 8. Question 8d-e (Do you know the location of a brand A and brand B [gasoline] station?)

	Brand A*		Brand B	
	Control group	Test group	Control group	Test group
Know for sure	77%	75%	60%	82%
Don't know—not sure	23	24	20	18

* Sells Long-Life batteries.

TABLE 9. Question 9 (Have you recently received any advertisements through the mail from local service stations?)

	Control group	Test group
Yes	38%	48%
No	62	52

TABLE 10. Question 10 (Do you know of a station located at [dealer's address]?)

	Control group	Test group
Yes, know of station	86%	90%
No, don't know	14	10

TABLE 11. Question 10a (What is the name of that station?)

	Control group	Test group
Dealer named on direct mail	36%	38%
Others—wrong answers	14	14
Don't know	50	48

TABLE 12. Question 10b (Do they sell batteries?)

	Control group	Test group
Yes	92%	93%
No	4	4
Don't know	4	3

TABLE 13. Question 10c (What brand?)

	Control group	Test group
Right answers—(Long-Life)	14%	17%
Wrong answers—(other brands)	34	36
Don't know	52	47

11

Data collection and
the field force

RESEARCH RESULTS depend largely upon data collected in the field. No matter how carefully a sample is drawn or a
questionnaire designed, the data collected will not be accurate unless
the field force executes its job properly. As it is usually performed, however, field work is one of the major sources of error in the typical research project—especially in questionnaire studies. There seems to be
considerable agreement among social scientists that the interview is a
perilous undertaking and one which is likely to produce unreliable
data.[1] Some go so far as to say that ". . . it is indefensible to assume the
validity of purportedly factual data obtained by interview."[2]

There are many reasons why the interview is suspect as a way of obtaining data, but one of the most important is the complex nature of the
memory process. Despite good intentions on the part of the respondent,
he may not be able to recall past behavior accurately. Events which
intervene between the interview and the time of the past behavior may
cause the respondent subconsciously to "juggle" the facts. Respondents
also experience selective recall. Memory for all events does not decay

---

[1] See, for example, Natalie Harris and Gordon M. Connelly, "Introducing a Symposium on Interviewing Problems," *International Journal of Opinion and Attitude
Research* (Spring, 1948), p. 69; Robert H. Hanson and Eli S. Marks, "Influence of
the Interviewer on the Accuracy of Survey Results," *Journal of the American Statistical
Association* (September, 1958), p. 635; Ernest A. Haggard, Arne Brekstad, and
Ase G. Skard, "On the Reliability of the Anamnestic Interview," *Journal of Abnormal
and Social Psychology*, 61 (1960), p. 311.

[2] David J. Weiss and Rene V. Davis, "An Objective Validation of Factual Interview Data," *Journal of Applied Psychology*, 44 (1960), p. 384.

at the same rate, since those elements which were most pleasant or most unpleasant tend to be remembered longest.[3] Memory is further complicated by the fact that most people begin with selective perception in which they note only certain parts of an event—typically those parts which they expected to note.[4]

In addition to encountering memory difficulties, interviewing ". . . contains many unknowns or only partially understood sources of bias. It is necessary to know what occurs in the interviewing process in order to appraise the validity and reliability of the information. Knowledge of the factors which produce bias may help . . . overcome many of these factors by appropriate interviewer selection and training."[5] This chapter is devoted to an examination of these biasing factors, as well as to a discussion of the selection, training, and control of the interviewer.

FIELD WORK PROCEDURE[6]

A research director has two major alternatives for getting his field work done—he can do it himself, or he can contract with a fieldwork agency to do the job. In either case it is a difficult and costly step in the research process. Field work involves the selection, training, supervision, and evaluation of individuals who collect data in the field.

Before field workers can be selected, the research director must prepare a complete job specification for the specific project. He decides what type of field worker will be able to meet the job requirements, and must then try to find interviewers of this type. Since the sample design often calls for data to be collected at many different places, one or more field workers with the desired characteristics often must be found at each of these places. Most firms which use interviewers frequently keep a file of such workers by geographical location. The sampling sites are matched against these files and qualified workers selected. Letters are sent to the selected interviewers telling them about the pending work and asking them to indicate by return mail their availability. Usually it is necessary to recruit some new workers for each job, since qualified interviewers may not be available at all locations and some may not be

---

[3] Jerome M. Levine and Gardner Murphy, "The Learning and Forgetting of Controversial Material," *Journal of Abnormal and Social Psychology*, 38 (1943), pp. 507–17.

[4] Roy E. Carter, Jr., "Field Methods in Communication Research" in Ralph O. Nafziger and David M. White, eds., *Introduction to Mass Communications Research* (Baton Rouge: Louisiana State University Press, 1963), pp. 78–127.

[5] J. Allen Williams, Jr., "Interviewer-Respondent Interaction: A Study of Bias in the Information Interview," *Sociometry*, 27 (1964), p. 338.

[6] Field work may involve either interviewing or observing or a combination. Interviewing is the more common and involves more problems; therefore, much of the discussion is in terms of interviewing, and the term "interviewer" is frequently used where the more general term "field worker" could be substituted.

available for the specific job. This recruiting is often done with the help of such local sources as newspapers and educational institutions.

After field workers are selected they have to be trained. Since most field work must be done within a limited time period and interviewers are widely dispersed, training is usually done by mail. Under such conditions the training program consists of written instructions which the interviewer is asked to study carefully to learn the purpose of the study, how to locate and approach respondents, to establish rapport, to ask questions, and to obtain and record accurate answers. On some projects this training is given by supervisors in person at one or a few central locations.

Following the training program, the interviewers commence the field work. During this time interviewers need to be controlled, at least to the extent of making certain that they are proceeding on schedule and that their work is satisfactory. Since factors such as sickness or bad weather may prevent some interviewers from completing their assignments on time, the director needs to keep tight control on the day-to-day field operations and must be ready to replace individual interviewers quickly, if necessary.

After the field work is completed and the completed forms are returned to the home office, a verification check is made to make certain that the interviews were actually made, i.e., to insure that interviewers did not cheat. The work of each interviewer is then evaluated. The questionnaires or other data forms turned in are checked for completeness, compliance with instructions, and apparent ability of the worker to obtain useful data. Such information helps the research director to select the best field workers for future projects.

ERRORS IN FIELD WORK[7]

While most marketing researchers are aware of the need for good field work, there is little evidence that much is done on the typical project to insure it. On most projects, part-time interviewers with unknown capabilities are used. The only home office contact with them is likely to be through a written set of instructions which may be studied with varying degrees of care. Completed interviews are "edited" for mechanical procedure, and routine checks for cheating are made. The collected data are then tabulated and assumed to be correct.

Although there has been increasingly frank discussion ". . . in research reports and professional journals, of difficulties and weaknesses in the survey procedures, including the proportion of interviews that could not

---

[7] See W. Edwards Deming, "On a Probability Mechanism to Attain an Economic Balance between the Resultant Error of Response and the Bias of Nonresponse," *Journal of the American Statistical Association,* 48 (December, 1953), p. 745.

be completed and the losses due to difficulties in finding respondents or their unwillingness to cooperate, net additions to our knowledge of how to obtain better data accumulate rather slowly. Moreover, this knowledge does not readily coalesce into a set of simple and directly applicable principles for the reduction of error and the improvement of the reliability of source material."[8] Despite these difficulties the survey leader must make every effort to be aware of and understand the kinds of interviewer errors which may occur for, by so doing, he may be able to take preventive action.

The remainder of this chapter discusses the field operation as it applies to personal interview situations. Most of what is discussed, however, applies also to the collection of data by the observational method.

Nonresponse errors

In almost every study, no response is obtained from a certain part of the sample, that is, from those who refuse cooperation, those who cannot be located, and those who are unsuitable to interview, such as the ill, deaf, and senile. In most studies, it is assumed that the replies from those who are interviewed are also representative of the nonresponse group. In some cases this may be so, but in many instances the nonresponse group differs markedly from the group which cooperates. If this nonresponse group is large, it may easily bias the results of the study. Deming says ". . . the bias of nonresponse is probably so serious in many if not most surveys that the specification of the number of recalls, and the adjustment of the original size of the sample . . . to balance the bias of nonresponse against the variance . . . are an essential part of sample-design. . . ."[9]

Not-at-homes. The percentage of not-at-homes varies by city size, day of the week, time of day, season of the year, and the sex of the respondent, as well as with the provisions made to control not-at-homes in individual studies. It is, however, almost always surprisingly large. In one study of national area samples, the interview completion rate on the first call was 31 percent, but this varied from 20 percent in large metropolitan areas to 42 percent in rural areas.[10] On week days (Monday through Friday) the first call completion rate in large metropolitan areas was 19 percent, but for Saturday and Sunday it rose to 25 percent.[11]

---

[8] Frederick F. Stephan, "The Art of Inquiry," *Public Opinion Quarterly* (Summer, 1963), pp. 266–67.

[9] W. Edwards Deming, *op. cit.*, p. 766.

[10] Charles S. Mayer, "The Interviewer and His Environment," *Journal of Marketing Research* (November, 1964), pp. 24–31.

[11] *Ibid.*, p. 25.

Failure to include not-at-homes may cause considerable bias. For example, married women who work and families with no children are not as apt to be home as unemployed women and larger families. The probability of finding someone at home is greater for low economic status units than for those of higher economic status, and it is greater in rural than in urban areas.[12]

Undoubtedly, many not-at-homes occur regardless of the interviewer, but one experiment comparing experienced and inexperienced interviewers found the latter had 15.9 percent not-at-homes compared to 10.4 percent for the former. In this study, the interviewers made as many as three callbacks to reach the respondent. The number of not-at-homes was the same for the two groups on the first call, but the experienced interviewers scheduled their callbacks more productively.[13]

Regardless of the skill of the interviewer there is still an "unavailability" problem present in most research studies. The Bureau of the Census estimates that nonwhite men in the age group 25–44 years were undercounted by about 16 percent and those in the 45–64 years group by 13 percent in the 1960 censuses of population and housing.[14] Not-at-homes occur less frequently in studies involving low-income, nonwhite respondents where the sample designates only housing units for interview and no specification is made as to which member of the household is to be interviewed.[15]

With quota samples, the survey director usually has no knowledge of the percentage of not-at-homes. When probability samples are used, the director is aware of the not-at-homes and must decide how much effort is desirable to get more of them into the sample. Because of the differences between the at-homes and not-at-homes, it is usually wise to make some callbacks to interview the original not-at-homes. Two callbacks are planned in many studies, but even so the interview completion rate rarely exceeds 70–75 percent.[16]

Refusals.   Refusal rates vary from project to project and may range up to 25 percent on typical studies. Since refusals are often the result of personality and mood, it can be argued that they will occur randomly and will not bias results. There is evidence, however, that refusals are

---

[12] John B. Lansing and A. T. Eapen, "Dealing with Missing Information in Surveys," *Journal of Marketing* (October, 1959), pp. 21–28.

[13] J. Durbin and A. Stuart, "Differences in Response Rates of Experienced and Inexperienced Interviewers," *Journal of the Royal Statistical Society,* 114, Part II (1951), p. 173.

[14] Conrad Taeuber and Morris H. Hansen, "A Preliminary Evaluation of the 1960 Censuses of Population and Housing" (paper presented at the American Statistical Association in Cleveland, Ohio, 1963). Cited in Carol H. Weiss, "Interviewing Low-Income Respondents," *Welfare in Review* (October, 1966), pp. 1–9.

[15] *Ibid.*

[16] Charles S. Mayer, *op. cit.*

concentrated among the high- and low-income groups.[17] In addition to general refusals, refusals may occur on specific questions, particularly those relating to income. In one study, those who refused to answer an income question were compared to those who did. The group not reporting income had a larger percentage of upper-income households (as inferred from rental data), highly educated persons, small families, older family heads, managerial and professional people, American born, Protestants, and Jews.[18]

Treatment of nonresponse bias. Proper field methods can reduce substantially the nonresponse rate—both refusals and not-at-homes—but they cannot eliminate the problem completely. Since most students are agreed that the bias of nonresponse is usually considerable, definite provisions to reduce it are almost always warranted. The most common procedures are substituting neighboring dwelling units and making callbacks. It is clear that substituting does not solve the problem if the universe is thought of as consisting of two strata—one from which information will be obtained if its members are included in the sample and one from which no response will be obtained. The substitution of neighboring dwellings for nonresponses adds to the size of the sample of one stratum, but provides no information about members of the other stratum. Callbacks are necessary to secure information about the members of the nonresponse stratum. For most studies, small samples with four to six callbacks are more efficient than large samples without callbacks, unless the percentage of initial response can be increased considerably above the normally anticipated level.[19]

One ingenious way of getting the not-at-homes into the sample without making callbacks calls for contacting a random sample of persons at a time chosen at random. The universe is considered to be comprised of a number of different strata which are homogeneous with respect to the probability of finding a person at home. Thus, interviewers will contact 100 percent of those respondents who are home all day, 75 percent of those who are home on the average 75 percent of the time, and so on. By having field workers determine the probability of finding each respondent at home, the results can be weighted to be representative of the entire sample. A weight of one is assigned to the data obtained from respondents who are always at home, a weight of two for respondents who are home 50 percent of the time, etc.[20]

---

[17] Mildred B. Parten, *Surveys, Polls and Samples* (New York: Harper & Brothers, 1950), pp. 412–14; and John Harding, "Refusals as a Source of Bias," in Hadley Cantril, *Gauging Public Opinion* (Princeton, N.J.: Princeton University Press, 1947), p. 120.

[18] Parten, *op. cit.*, p. 417.

[19] Deming, *op. cit.*, pp. 766–67.

[20] Alfred Politz and W. Simmons, "An Attempt to Get the 'Not-at-Homes' into the Sample without Callbacks," *Journal of American Statistical Association* (March,

An experiment in which a self-administered questionnaire with a stamped, self-addressed envelope was left at the dwellings of all not-at-homes obtained responses from only 28 percent. The method has merit, however, since, at the very minimum, it reduces the size of that part of the sample not reached initially and does so at a low cost.[21] The cost of this method per completed interview is reported as being about half that of personal interview callbacks.[22] The use of the telephone to make appointments for personal interviews does not usually affect the cooperation rate, but does reduce the total amount of travel time spent by interviewers by between 10 and 15 percent. The telephone is useful in reducing the cost of locating, screening, and interviewing relatively unique populations.[23]

A weighting system to minimize the problem of nonresponse may be developed if the subject area under study is believed to vary by certain population groups for which it is possible to estimate the different rates of response. For example, in a given study the subject may be thought to vary among income groups. Interview results show a response rate of 90 percent for low-income dwellings, 85 percent for middle-income dwellings, and 80 percent for high-income dwellings. The results from each of these groups can be weighted to approximate the original proportions of the three strata in the sample.[24]

RESPONDENT SELECTION ERRORS

Selection errors with quota samples

In quota samples, interviewers select the individuals to be included in the survey, subject only to quotas for various population groups. This interviewer control of the selection of respondents is unlikely to result in the equivalent of a random sample. Interviewers tend to follow the paths of least resistance and of greatest convenience. One study showed that even when interviewers were given economic level quotas, they tended to underselect in both the high- and low-income classes. Errors or falsification also occur in classification; two interviewers who classified the same respondents on an income basis differed in 30 percent of

---

1949), pp. 9–31. Also see Tore Dalenius, "Treatment of the Non-Response Problem," *Journal of Advertising Research* (September, 1961), pp. 1–7.

[21] Richard L. Edsall, "Getting 'Not-at-Homes' to Interview Themselves," *Journal of Marketing* (October, 1958), pp. 184–85.

[22] Seymour Sudman, Andrew Greeley, and Leonard Pinto, "The Effectiveness of Self-Administered Questionnaires," *Journal of Marketing Research* (August, 1965), pp. 293–97.

[23] Seymour Sudman, *Reducing the Cost of Surveys* (Chicago: Aldine Publishing Co., 1967), pp. 58–67.

[24] Lansing and Eapen, *op. cit.*, p. 23.

the cases.[25] Another study showed that interviewers tended to select households they "liked" and which they thought had higher incomes, even when some controls were used to discourage this.[26]

An effort is often made to overcome this respondent selection bias by setting up more elaborate controls or quotas. This can create biases of another type. When the number of controls gets beyond three or four, the field worker finds difficulty in locating respondents who meet all the characteristics prescribed. As a result the interviewer tends to "push" a 35-year old into the 40-and-over age group or "force" his quota in some other way.

Selection errors with probability samples

One of the common reasons given for the use of probability samples is that they eliminate the bias that comes from interviewer selection of respondents as described above. The use of a probability sample, however, provides no guarantee *per se* that respondent selection bias will be eliminated. The use of such a design may cause different biases such as errors in listing dwelling units, in selecting dwelling units, and in selecting individuals within dwelling units.

Evidence indicates that in listing dwelling units interviewers tend to underenumerate in low-income blocks. One study found a 13 percent underlisting in such blocks. Once dwelling units have been listed, the specific dwelling units to be included in the sample must be selected. When field workers make their selections in the field from listings, they tend to avoid lower-income households as contrasted to when random selections are made in the office.

Interviewers also tend to select the more accessible individuals in the household. Despite instructions which indicate the random procedures to follow in selecting respondents within the household, interviewers will "rig" the selection system to prevent making callbacks for the not-at-homes.[27]

The difficulty of listing and locating households is severe in the lower-income neighborhoods, as indicated in the following comment:

The Central Harlem Adult Survey conducted in 1964, which encountered problems in the listing and location of housing units, as well as in contact, had an interview completion rate of only 63 percent. Comparison with the 1960

---

[25] A. B. Blankenship, "A Source of Interviewer Bias," *International Journal of Opinion and Attitude Research*, 3 (Spring, 1949), pp. 95–98.

[26] Roy E. Carter, Jr., Verling C. Troldahl, and R. Smith Schuneman, "Interviewer Bias in Selecting Households," *Journal of Marketing* (April, 1963), pp. 27–34.

[27] Dean Manheimer and Herbert Hyman, "Interviewer Performance in Area Sampling," *Public Opinion Quarterly*, 13 (Spring, 1949), pp. 84–85.

census figures revealed that the uninterviewed were heavily concentrated in the lowest income category (under $3,000 a year). The National Opinion Research Center interviewers reported the persistent feeling that people were reluctant to answer the doorbell.[28]

ERRORS IN STIMULATING RESPONSES

Stating the question

In asking questions, interviewers are usually expected to follow certain rules. A typical set of such rules runs as follows:

1. Each question must be asked exactly as worded.
2. The interviewer must not comment on the meaning of the question or indicate in any way what kinds of answers might be acceptable.
3. Every question must be asked unless the interviewer is instructed to do otherwise.
4. Questions must be asked in the same sequence as given on the questionnaire.

There is considerable evidence that even with a relatively simple, straightforward, structured questionnaire, interviewers do not follow the above rules. In one study which used "planted" respondents, a high number of deviations from instructed behavior were found.[29] In another case tape recorders proved that ". . . one-third of the . . . interviewers deviated frequently and markedly from their instructions, sometimes failing to explain the key terms or to repeat them as required, sometimes leaving them out altogether, shortening questions, or failing to follow up certain ambiguous answers in the manner required."[30] Standardized interviewer performance is particularly difficult to obtain when using open-ended questions.[31]

If a question is not easily understood by respondents, interviewers will rephrase it in ways which will cause less confusion. Since no two interviewers are apt to rephrase a question in the same way, different respondents get different stimuli which produce variations in replies. A variation of this problem occurs when interviewers are instructed to probe with additional questions to secure more complete answers. In either case, the addition of a comment by the interviewer raises the possibility that the respondent will be influenced in a different way than

[28] Carol H. Weiss, *op. cit.*, p. 3.

[29] Bo W:Son Schyberger, "A Study of Interviewer Behavior," *Journal of Marketing Research* (February, 1967), p. 32.

[30] W. A. Belson, "Increasing the Power of Research to Guide Advertising Decisions," *Journal of Marketing* (April, 1965), p. 38.

[31] See Barbara Snell Dohrenwend, "Some Effects of Open and Closed Questions on Respondents' Answers," *Human Organization* (Summer, 1965), pp. 175–84.

other respondents.[32] Failure to probe adequately, when probing is necessary to obtain a meaningful answer, is one of the most serious sources
of interviewer error. In a laboratory-type study to determine the amount
and quality of probing, interviewers failed to probe at all in 40 percent
of the instances in which they should have, and used inappropriate or
inadequate probes in an additional 12 percent of the cases.[33]

Questions which state the alternative answers, such as multiple choice
questions, are particularly subject to interviewer bias. This bias occurs
because the interviewer puts too much emphasis on one alternative in
stating the question. The interviewer's method of asking questions will
also influence results in other, more subtle, ways. For example, slight
variations in tone of voice will change the entire meaning of some questions.

Some field-interviewing organizations require the interviewer to indicate on the questionnaire what additional comments were made in
order to elicit satisfactory answers. Presumably, these are evaluated later
to determine whether they biased the respondent sufficiently to warrant
elimination of that questionnaire from tabulation.

Under certain conditions, two interviewers may be useful in reducing
bias—for example, in executive interviews. In one such study using two
interviews, it was found that they were able to reduce the time of the
interview; that when one interviewer failed to gain rapport the other
almost always did; that one interviewer served as a check on the other
with regard to the understandability of individual questions as well as
with regard to the asking of leading questions; and that better recording of answers took place.[34]

In some interviewing situations, such as in group interviews, a tape
recorder may prove helpful in reducing bias by recording both questions
and answers verbatim. Experiments have shown that, contrary to general
expectations, respondents will accept the use of tape recorders. The
most critical element in gaining acceptance of the recorder is the inter-

---

[32] See Sam Shapiro and John C. Eberhardt, "Interviewer Differences in an Intensive Interview Situation," *International Journal of Opinion and Attitude Research*, I
(June, 1947), pp. 1–17. The authors found deviations from good performance on
attitude questions on: (1) incomplete recording, (2) too heavy reliance on initial
response with failure to follow through, and (3) failure to ask certain questions. On
informational questions, bias resulted from (1) accepting "don't knows" too readily,
(2) incomplete reporting of questions where multiple answers were possible or where
detailed answers were given, and (3) failure to obtain proper classification data. Also
see Don Cahalan, Valeria Tamulonis and Helen Verner, "Interviewer Bias Involved
in Certain Types of Opinion Survey Questions," *International Journal of Opinion and
Attitude Research*, I (March, 1947), pp. 63–77.

[33] Herbert H. Hyman, William J. Cobb, Jacob J. Feldman, Clyde W. Hart, and
Charles Herbert Stember, *Interviewing in Social Research* (Chicago: The University
of Chicago Press, 1954), p. 237.

[34] Harry V. Kincaid and Margaret Bright, "The Tandem Interview: A Trial of the
Two-Interviewer Team," *Public Opinion Quarterly*, 21 (Summer, 1957), p. 304.

viewer's own attitude toward it and his resulting behavior. The recorder, however, may introduce bias. One study found that tape recording increased the accuracy of reported responses of lower-class respondents, but reduced the reported accuracy of middle- and upper-class respondents.[35]

Respondent's perception of the interviewer

Interviews involve a social relationship between two persons, and the respondent adjusts his conduct to what he considers to be appropriate to the situation. "The way each member perceives his relative ability to influence the other affects his action. The greater is one's perceived power, the greater will be the initiative one takes in trying to influence the behavior of a less powerful partner."[36] An interviewer, whether he likes it or not, will be cast into some role by the respondent. He must be conscious of the alternative roles at his disposal and attempt to establish the role which will best further the purposes of his study. "Interviewers, as the primary link between the researcher and the respondent, are instrumental in setting the level of a respondent's desire to cooperate. Interviewers who obtain the most complete personal interviews do so because they are able to induce respondents to work hard. . . ."[37]

When interviewing takes place on a subject about which there is some expectation regarding social approval or disapproval, or in which there is a strong ego involvement, respondents err by idealizing their behavior.[38] A low-income respondent, in particular, tends to ". . . give the kinds of answers he thinks that society, through the interviewer, wants to hear."[39] In interviews among Negroes, white interviewers obtain significantly higher proportions of what may be called "proper" or "acceptable" answers than do Negro interviewers.[40] Middle-class interviewers find more conservative attitudes among lower-income groups

[35] William A. Belson, "Tape Recording: Its Effects on Accuracy of Response in Survey Interview," *Journal of Marketing Research* (August, 1967), pp. 253–61.

[36] Eugene J. Webb and Jerry R. Salaneck, *The Interview or the Only Wheel in Town* (Austin, Texas: Association for Education in Journalism, 1966), p. 10. Also see George Leowger, "The Development of Perceptions and Behavior in Newly Founded Social Power Relationships," in Darwin Cartwright, ed., *Studies in Social Power* (Ann Arbor: University of Michigan Press, 1959), pp. 83–98.

[37] Charles F. Cannell and Floyd J. Fowler, Jr., "A Note on Interviewer Effect in Self Enumeration Procedures," *American Sociological Review* (April, 1964), p. 270.

[38] Eleanor Maccoby and Nathan Maccoby, "The Interview: A Tool of Social Science," in Gardner Lindzey, ed., *Handbook of Social Psychology* (Cambridge, Mass.: Addison-Wesley, 1954), Vol. I, pp. 449–87.

[39] Carol H. Weiss, *op. cit.*, p. 4.

[40] Hyman, *et al.*, *op. cit.*, p. 159. Also see E. R. Athey, Joan E. Coleman, Audrey P. Reitmans and Jenny Lang, "Two Experiments Showing the Effect of the Interviewer's Racial Background on Responses to Questionnaires concerning Racial Issues," *Journal of Applied Psychology* (August, 1960), p. 244.

than do working class interviewers."[41] The greater the social distance between the interviewer and the respondent, the greater the likelihood of bias.[42]

Whenever interviewer and respondent are from different social classes, accurate communication between them is difficult because they have different ways of perceiving and thinking. The respondent ". . . is used to talking about personal experiences only to listeners who share a great deal of experience and symbolism with him and with whom he can safely assume that words and gestures are assigned similar meanings. But in the interview, these assumptions break down."[43]

Age and sex of the interviewer affect the data obtained. It has been found that:[44]

1. Older female interviewers are little disposed to question the validity of anyone's responses.
2. Males are critical of their own peers while women are not.
3. The least effects of age and sex are found with middle-aged women interviewers who, fortunately, constitute the bulk of all interviewers.
4. The age of interviewers has more effect on results than does the sex of interviewers.
5. Young interviewers tend to get answers oriented toward their age group.[45]
6. Interviewers over 50 are perceived as authority figures and responses are modified accordingly.[46]

In view of the evidence showing the influence on information obtained of class, race, age, sex, authority, and deference of the interviewer to the respondent, extensive efforts to control these effects would be expected. Unfortunately, the composition of the field staff can usually be modified only slightly for individual studies. Typically, the same interviewers are used to do many different kinds of projects; they work by assignment within a given geographical sampling area and interview all types of respondents. Most interviewers are middle-aged, middle-

---

[41] Gerhard E. Lenske and John C. Leggett, "Caste, Class, and Deference in the Research Interview," *The American Journal of Sociology* (March, 1960), p. 467.

[42] J. Allen Williams, Jr., "Interviewer-Respondent Interaction: A Study of Bias in the Information Interview," *Sociometry*, 27 (1964), pp. 338–52.

[43] C. H. Weiss, *op cit.*, p. 6.

[44] Mark Benney, David Riesman, and Shirley A. Star, "Age and Sex in the Interview," *The American Journal of Sociology* (July, 1956), p. 143. Also see W. I. Kinkel, "Sex of Observer and Spousal Roles in Decision-Making," *Marriage and Family Living* (May, 1961), p. 186. He found that wives report exerting more influence on family decisions when they report to female interviewers than when they report to male interviewers.

[45] June Sachar Ehrlich and David Riesman, "Age and Authority in the Interview," *Public Opinion Quarterly*, 25 (Spring, 1961), p. 41.

[46] *Ibid.*

class women, while respondents are drawn from all classes. There is no relatively simple and economical way of matching interviewer and respondent nor of correcting for the biasing effect of given interviewer characteristics.

A basic condition for optimum communication is that the respondent perceive the interviewer as one who is likely to understand and accept him and what he has to say. The interviewer must be perceived as "within range"—that is, he must be seen as a person to whom the respondent's statements and experience will not be foreign or offensive. This does not mean that the respondent needs to see the interviewer as similar to himself, but he must view the interviewer as capable of understanding his point of view, and of doing so without rejecting him.[47]

In general, the more characteristics the interviewer and respondent have in common, the greater the probability of a successful interview. An economically feasible method of achieving this pairing has not been developed.

Errors in interpreting and recording answers

Not only can the interviewer bias survey results by her impact on the respondents, but she may influence results by the way she reacts to respondents. Differences in the characteristics of interviewers such as experience, attitudes, and opinions also affect the recorded answers. Interviewers are commonly faced with the problem of recording answers by writing on clip boards while trying to keep the interviewee interested. The result is frequently a number of clerical errors. One research worker has found serious mistakes being made by interviewers in recording things not said, as well as not recording things which were said. These errors, however, were not as serious as errors resulting from failure to press for further comment on incomplete or "don't know" answers.

Interviewers also vary in the answers they record according to the amount of space available on the questionnaire. If a large amount of space is left for an answer, more will be recorded than if a small space is provided.

Cheating

It is difficult to know to what extent cheating is a serious problem—partly because cheating is hard to define. The most glaring example of cheating is the interviewer who fills out questionnaires without making interviews. More frequently, cheating is confined to falsification of cer-

---

[47] Robert L. Kahn and Charles F. Cannell, *The Dynamics of Interviewing* (New York: John Wiley & Sons, Inc., 1957), p. 47.

tain data within the questionnaire. It may be present at any point in the interviewing process, including enumeration of dwelling units, selection of dwelling units, and selection of respondents within dwelling units.

Although the field force used on a typical marketing research project probably is not selected with great discretion and is given a minimum of training, very little follow-through is made to detect cheating of any but the crudest type. Under such conditions it seems likely that cheating is an important source of interviewer bias. There are many causes for cheating other than those personality characteristics inherent in the interviewer herself. Study design and implementation influence the predisposition to cheat. If respondents are difficult to locate and interview, cheating increases.[48] Other "causes" are unreasonable deadlines and difficult-to-complete questionnaires.

Many investigators are coming to the conclusion that cheating is as much a problem of morale as of morals. "Fabrication . . . does not as a rule originate in the minds of these interviewers until they are faced with situations that are puzzling, unexplained, overly difficult, impracticable, unprofitable, or badly managed."[49] Insofar as this is true, research directors can take steps to reduce these errors.

SELECTION OF INTERVIEWERS

In some fields of business much scientific work has been done on the selection of personnel, including the use of intelligence and aptitude tests. Considerable attention is given to describing job requirements and to measuring applicants' abilities to do the job. Firms engaged in marketing research, for the most part, have not adopted these scientific selection techniques because the working conditions in the field do not lend themselves to such procedure. Some of these working conditions are as follows:

1. Workers are part-time employees.
2. The pay is relatively low—typically, interviewers receive $2.00 to $2.50 per hour plus expenses.
3. The assignments often call for night or weekend work.
4. The work is not repetitious. Even on a given survey, conditions vary from interview to interview.
5. Interviewers work without direct supervision and, hence, the quality of work is difficult to discern.

---

[48] Franklin B. Evans, "On Interviewer Cheating," *Public Opinion Quarterly* (Spring, 1961), pp. 126–27.

[49] Archibald S. Bennett, "Observations on the So-Called Cheater Problem among Field Interviewers," *International Journal of Opinion and Attitude Research,* 2 (Spring, 1948), p. 89.

Selection criteria

Much can be done to eliminate the less desirable field workers. The first step in the selection process is to draw up a set of job requirements. Such factors as the following will have an obvious effect on what kind of interviewers will be considered acceptable on a specific job: (1) sample design (for example, if a probability sample is to be used, interviewers must know how to read maps, follow enumeration instructions, etc.); (2) the sample sites (interviewers should be located as near to the interviewing sites as possible to avoid excessive travel costs); (3) race, sex, and age of respondents (interviewers should "match" respondents as much as possible); (4) occupation of respondents (if executives are to be interviewed, then specially trained interviewers are necessary); (5) the nature of the questions to be asked (the use of open-end questions which necessitate probing requires highly experienced interviewers); and (6) the need for a car.

A comprehensive analysis of the relation between experience and performance among National Opinion Research Center (NORC) interviewers found that on the average women had better ratings than men, married women were superior to single women, interviewers between the ages of thirty and thirty-nine had the highest ratings, and interviewers with college majors in psychology, sociology, and anthropology showed up best. As a group, NORC interviewers did better over time, that is, they improved as interviewers from year to year. Most of the poorer interviewers remained on the staff less than one year.[50]

Frequently selection is based almost exclusively on pleasant appearance and pleasing personality, which is assumed to reflect ability to generate and maintain rapport. Experience indicates this is not a good basis. "Although social skill plays some part in the survey interviewer work, it is not closely related to the other skills demanded by the job; an excessive social orientation of the interviewer is not conducive to superior performance."[51]

Selection procedures

After the job requirements have been prepared the next step is to hire the field force. Selection of interviewers is usually more a matter of rehiring than of original hiring. Most individuals are selected on the basis that they appear to have the necessary qualities for the job as evidenced by the information submitted on their application forms, or from their past performance as recorded in company files. Most com-

---

[50] Paul B. Sheatsley, "An Analysis of Interviewer Characteristics and Their Relationship to Performance, Part III," *International Journal of Opinion and Attitude Research*, 5 (Summer, 1951), pp. 193–97.

[51] Hyman, *et al., op. cit.,* p. 282.

panies which use interviewers maintain a file by interviewer. This file contains the application form plus a record and rating of work previously done for the company. If the work has been satisfactory in the past, the individual is likely to be rehired. The criteria for satisfactory work usually are that the work was completed on schedule, the cost per completed interview was not excessive when compared with other interviewers working in similar sampling places, the number of refusals is not out of line when compared to similar interviewing sites, and the completed questionnaires did not need much editing.

Selection tests

Several attempts have been made to correlate interviewing performance with scores on various tests. Such interviewer characteristics as agreeableness, cooperativeness, social orientation, and emotional stability correlate negatively (although not to a great degree) with interviewer effectiveness, while objectivity, self-sufficiency, and introversion appear to be positively correlated.[52] In some cases, more effective interviewers have shown significantly higher test scores on dominance, self-confidence, and attention to detail and lower scores on needs associated with support required from others.[53]

The Bureau of the Census has developed a special Enumerator Selection Aid (ESA) Test of one-hour duration which is comprised of questions dealing with reading, comprehension, map reading, and ability to follow census-type instructions. Definite correlation has been found between ESA test scores and performance in the field.[54]

A study at the National Opinion Research Center to determine what nondemographic personality characteristics were most related to high-quality, low-cost performance by interviewers found that:

1. Performance increased and costs decreased as intelligence increased.
2. High need achievement was the variable most strongly related to the quality of interviewing and to low cost.
3. High career orientation was related to high quality but also to high costs.

---

[52] See Lester Guest and R. Nuckols, "A Laboratory Experiment in Recording in Public Opinion Interviewing," *International Journal of Opinion and Attitude Research,* 4 (1950), pp. 346–52; Lester Guest, "A Study of Interviewer Competence," *International Journal of Opinion and Attitude Research,* 1 (1947), pp. 17–30; Paul B. Sheatsley, "An Analysis of Interviewer Characteristics and Their Relation to Performance, Part III," *International Journal of Opinion and Attitude Research,* 5 (1951), pp. 193–97; and Hyman, *et al., op. cit.*

[53] Stanley W. Steinkamp, "Some Characteristics of Effective Interviewers," *Journal of Applied Psychology* (December, 1966), pp. 487–92.

[54] Robert H. Hanson and Eli S. Marks, "Influence of the Interviewer on the Accuracy of Survey Results," *Journal of the American Statistical Association* (September, 1958), pp. 635–55.

4. Interviewers who perceived themselves as having heavy family commitments were less likely to be high cost interviewers and likely to do high quality work.
5. High planning scores were reflected by lower interviewing costs.
6. Interviewers with high manipulative (Machiavellian) scores were not high cost interviewers. Apparently such interviewers tended to manipulate respondents rather than their own organization.
7. Such variables as happiness, financial need, membership in other organizations, religious behavior, perfectionism, and size of place where raised did not appear to be related to quality and cost.[55]

Selection tests are probably most useful in eliminating obviously unqualified applicants and in reducing the number to be interviewed. They are also valuable when used with the personal interview. In the latter case, they may provide information on things that the personal interview cannot uncover, such as the ability to write legibly, read maps, and understand complex instructions.

Selection interviews

Many organizations use a personal interview to select field workers. If the individual doing the interviewing is familiar with the work requirements and is a skilled interviewer, this selection approach is likely to meet with some success. The interview can be conducted in such a manner as to "test" the applicant on a number of important factors. For example, the applicant's knowledge and reasoning can be tested, her ability to meet people can be examined by having her meet a number of "new" persons, and her flexibility can be evaluated by posing a number of case studies and getting her to evaluate them. The person conducting the interview can also rate the applicant on appearance and personality. However, the personal interview as a selection device is no better than the skill of the person conducting the interview. This person's ratings are, of course, subjective and have to be considered on a relative basis. The final selection is made on the basis of the relative rankings of the applicants.

TRAINING

Objectives of the training program

Before any research project can be put "in the field," the field workers must be trained in what is expected of them. If interviewers who have had no previous experience are used, it is desirable to give them some training in basic field work concepts. Usually, however, interviewers

---

[55] Sudman, *op. cit.*, pp. 100–53.

have had previous experience. The training for a specific job, then, has two main objectives: to train the interviewers on the procedures to be used in the project at hand and to provide interviewers with the necessary attitudes and motivation.

Interviewers must be convinced that the study is worth doing—that the results will be useful. If interviewers feel that the study will not produce the desired results, or that the results will not be used, then they have little incentive to do a thorough job. Another factor which has a direct bearing on motivation is the reasonableness of the assignment. The interviewer needs to be convinced that the work load is reasonable. This requires an explanation of the length of time required to execute the sampling instructions, to conduct the actual interviews, and to meet unforeseen events. This explanation must be based on a first-hand knowledge of the interviewing situation.

Training methods[56]

Planning for the training program must start with the development of the questionnaire. In preparing and testing the questionnaire, the research director usually finds a number of problems which will "bother" the field force. Where feasible, he modifies the questionnaire to eliminate such problems. When this cannot be done, he notes the problems so that he can give interviewers special training on how to handle them. Similarly, in designing the sample he notes points on which specific training should be given.

Once the project is ready for the field, the research director will organize a training program to cover these difficult points and to acquaint the field workers with the entire procedure. This training is best done in person, but for cost reasons is usually done by mail.

Written instructions.   In all research projects the interviewers should have a set of written instructions to carry for reference. When training is by mail, these written instructions are usually the only training given the interviewers. In some projects interviewers are required to complete one or a few practice interviews after reading the instructions. These are typically returned to the home office for approval before the actual field work is started.

Written instructions should state clearly the purpose of the study; describe the materials which will be used by the interviewer (such as the questionnaire, maps, expense forms, daily time sheet, and mailing materials); describe the interviewing methods generally and describe specifically how each question is to be asked, what kinds of answers are "satisfactory," and how and when to probe; explain the sampling

---

[56] For a detailed discussion of the principles of interviewer training see Kahn and Cannell, *op. cit.*, pp. 235–41.

procedures; and specify administrative details such as the deadline for completing the field work. Instructions should be well organized and easy for the interviewer to read. All terms must be defined and realistic examples used wherever possible. The instructions should be prepared in such form as to make it easy for the interviewer to carry them with her in the field. Interview instructions should be pretested before their final use. This can usually be done at the same time the questionnaire is pretested by noting the mistakes made by the interviewers and comparing them with the specific instructions.

Some organizations incorporate many of the important instructions in the questionnaire. No matter how thoroughly the interviewer understands the instructions, there is always a likelihood of confusion at some point during an interview. The inclusion of instructions in the questionnaire is sound, if it does not make the questionnaire too long or complicated.

Training in person.   If interviewers can be brought together at one place, e.g., where a survey is concentrated in one metropolitan area, the survey leader can give instructions orally. Such a training session would cover the same points as written instructions, but all interviewers should get written instructions as well. Questions can be answered in such meetings, but the main advantage of them is in the opportunity they give for additional work in role playing and case study.

Role playing requires interviewers to play the parts of interviewers and respondents, thereby simulating the interviewing procedure. Members of the training staff start by playing the parts of interviewers and respondents to demonstrate good and bad procedure. After such a demonstration, the interviewers evaluate the procedure. Interviewers then play the roles and go through complete interviews. Role playing has the advantages of introducing reality into the training program, stimulating interest in the project, and focusing attention on problems which will be encountered by interviewers. Since the process involves the interviewer in actual interviewing, it leaves more lasting impressions than lectures or written instructions alone.

When training is done by the case method, trainees are given written descriptions of situations they are apt to face. Then, as a group, they discuss how each situation should be handled. Like role playing, this technique has the advantage of forcing the trainee to think actively about the problems she will face.

Practice interviewing.   Interviewers may be required to complete a number of interviews in the field on a practice basis. Usually they are given some instruction by one of the preceding methods before going into the field. After the practice interviews are completed, the interviewers reassemble and discuss their experiences. Practice interviews may be graded and each interviewer's shortcomings discussd with her individually. This is the most expensive of the normal training procedures, but is also the best.

Contents of training program

A discussion of the contents of the training program is essentially a discussion of the interviewer's entire job. A good training program should not assume that the field workers can handle any part of the job without specific instructions. The following points should be covered.

Locating the respondent. The first step in the interviewer's job is to find the individuals to be interviewed. This is difficult to explain simply when a probability sample is involved; the procedure must be outlined precisely and in detail.

Introduction and establishing rapport. Interviewers must be told how to introduce themselves and how to establish rapport, i.e., how to put the respondent at ease so that she will cooperate fully on the interview. The interviewer usually states her name and the purpose of the call. Usually it is desirable to give a specific short statement for the interviewer to use in introducing herself.

If the respondent is suspicious, it may be necessary to take more time to set her at ease and to reassure her that the interview subject is meaningful. If only experienced interviewers are being used, no special training on this point is needed. Inexperienced interviewers should be given ideas on how to develop rapport. They may be told how to show their identification card, to assure the respondent that her replies will be held in confidence, and to make conversational comments on such things as the respondent's home and family.

Asking the questions. Interviewers are usually told to ask each question in exactly the form it is given on the questionnaire. If respondents do not understand a question, the interviewer must know how far she can go in explaining or whether she must just repeat the question. If any questions are to be asked only of certain respondents, this procedure should be explained carefully.

Obtaining adequate answers. Regardless of the simplicity of the questions some respondents will provide partial answers, will indicate they "don't know," or will evade the question by giving an answer which is so general as to be meaningless. The interviewer must be told in advance what constitutes an adequate answer and given illustrations of such answers. The answer "economy" would be given by many, for example, in answer to the question, "What factors do you consider in deciding what brand of a car to buy?" In this case the word economy can mean many things—good gas mileage, few repairs, low price, or good trade-in. This may be unsatisfactory for the project at hand. It is one thing to recognize an unsatisfactory answer, however, and another to do something about it. In general, the best thing to do is to repeat the question. If this fails, the interviewer will need to probe further. Neutral phrases are useful to obtain a more complete response, for example, "Why do you feel that way?" "Anything else?" "How do you mean?" and "I'd like to know more about what you're thinking." Since some probes may produce biases by suggesting an answer, it is desirable to provide specific statements that may be used as probes or to have interviewers record the exact wording of any probes.

Recording the answers.   Interviewers must be told how they are to record answers. For example, should explanatory remarks be recorded if the question is of a multiple choice type where the main answer can be recorded with a check mark? For open-end questions, it should be made clear whether answers are to be recorded verbatim or in summary form. It is probably desirable to instruct the interviewer to check the entire questionnaire for completeness before leaving the scene of the interview.

Measuring the interviewer's understanding of the survey specifics

Before interviewers are sent into the field, it is important to be sure that they understand how they are to proceed. If practice interviews are used, they offer an excellent way of determining whether interviewers understand the training instructions. Some organizations make use of a quiz which is filled out by the interviewer after the instructions have been studied. These examinations usually contain true-false and multiple choice questions and are relatively brief. The more difficult aspects of the interviewing and sampling process should be covered. Such a quiz accomplishes two purposes: first, it forces the interviewer to pay strict attention to the instructions and, second, the results show areas of confusion which need correction. The quiz is also a helpful selection device in identifying careless or unintelligent interviewers.

INTERVIEWER CONTROL

Field supervision

Whenever possible, on-the-spot field supervision should be employed. This means supervisors work directly with individual interviewers in making first calls or until the interviewers work is considered satisfactory. Once the interviewer is on her own, the supervisor should still check the completed questionnaires frequently to pick up any bad habits that the interviewer develops. Such a program of supervision has obvious selection, training, and evaluation values, since there is no substitute for direct observation of the way the worker performs her duties. It is also a morale factor since it personalizes the central office to the interviewer and lets her know that management is interested in the caliber of her work.

Personal supervision has its limitations, since the interviewer can be expected to put her "best foot forward" when in the presence of the supervisor and there is no assurance that the interviewer will not revert to undesirable practices as soon as the supervisor leaves. Despite this limitation, field supervision undoubtedly improves the quality of field work.

Preliminary home office edit

Another control method is a preliminary home office edit. This requires the interviewers to send completed questionnaires to the central office daily. Here they are carefully scanned to determine whether the interviewer has made any serious mistakes. The questionnaires are checked for legibility, completeness, and whether instructions have been carried out—such as recording the use of probes, accepting unsatisfactory answers, and recording full, not partial answers.

This procedure has several advantages. First, the exact status of the progress of the field work can be determined. Second, the more obvious mistakes can be caught by this edit and the appropriate corrective action taken. Third, the editing work gets an earlier start, thereby cutting down the elapsed time required for this step; for example, two hundred questionnaires may be received and edited each day for a period of ten days instead of having two thousand questionnaires arrive on the tenth day. This procedure is especially applicable where a sizable and dispersed field force is employed and when all contact is by mail.

EVALUATION

Some evaluation can be made by supervisors in the field, but, since most interviews are made without supervision, much of the evaluation must be based on examination of the completed questionnaires. Interviewer evaluation provides pertinent information about the reliability of the data collected in a specific project, it gives a basis for evaluating selection and training procedures, and provides a basis for determining whether each interviewer should be rehired.

Detection of cheating

The first step in the evaluation process is to determine whether the interviews were actually made. Since interviewers work without direct supervision, the task of detecting all cheating is a difficult one. However, one can spot much of the cheating that takes place in a number of different ways. One way is to send another interviewer to the respondent's home to ask if the interview took place on the specific subject on a specified date. When this is done on a sample basis by another interviewer, it is expensive and time consuming and for these reasons is not often used.

Another similar method is to call respondents by phone, again on a sample basis. This is the most frequently used checking procedure where a study is local. It has the limitation that only those respondents with telephones can be contacted. A further difficulty often arises in determining whether the telephone respondent is the same person who was interviewed by the field worker. This method is too expensive for use with regional or national studies unless local supervisors can do the checking. A third method is to send a letter with a return post card to a sample of each interviewer's respondents asking if they were interviewed. This procedure takes considerable time and usually the tabulation of results cannot wait this long. Many respondents fail to reply to such inquiries, leaving the question of how to interpret the nonresponses. Some research directors argue that those who have not been interviewed tend not to reply, but this is a difficult assumption to make. The only real advantage of the post card system is that it may, in extreme cases, pick up cases of interviewer cheating. For example, assume that an interviewer completed twenty-five questionnaires and that post cards were mailed to ten respondents. If one-half, or five replied—all in the negative, i.e., that they were not interviewed—there would be good evidence of interviewer cheating. However, in less extreme cases, negative replies may mean that the respondent did not remember the interview or that another person in the household filled out and returned the card. Unless the results are consistently against the interviewer, it is difficult to draw any precise conclusions without further inquiry.

Determination of quality of work

Completed questionnaires can be used as the basis for rating the quality of work done. In fact, they offer the only practical base on which to evaluate interviews. Reinterviewing is too expensive and, because of the respondent's prior exposure, does not provide a completely reliable base for comparison.

An interviewer can be rated on several factors. The more important ones are:

1. Cost. Total cost (expenses and salary) per completed interview is a basis for comparison of interviewers. Since these factors differ by city size, such comparisons should be made only among interviewers working in similar locations. Since some interviewers cover city, suburban, and rural areas in the same assignment, it may be necessary to tabulate the costs by interviewing site within each interviewer assignment in order to make a realistic analysis. The detailed cost data necessary for such an analysis, however, are seldom obtained.

2. Refusals. The percentage of refusals can be compared among interviewers. This comparison should also be limited to interviewers working in similar areas.

3. Following instructions. Each interviewer can be graded on the basis of the number of mistakes made. It is usually desirable to weight the various kinds of mistakes since some are more serious than others. Thus, the interviewer's performance on open-ended questions, as evidenced by the relevance of the responses recorded, should receive a heavier weight than many other types of work performance. The acceptance of an unsatisfactory answer, such as an ambiguous or partial answer, is more important than failure to date or sign the questionnaire. After totaling the number of points "off" for each interviewer, a rating can be assigned, for example, the number 10 can be assigned to those interviewers who on the basis of their score fall into the upper 10 percent of all interviewers. This would mean that such individuals had fewer mistakes than 90 percent of all other interviewers.

The National Opinion Research Center supplies its coders with error sheets which are used to note the following types of interviewer error:[57]

Type of error	Error weight
Answer missing	3
Irrelevant or circular answer	3
Lack of sufficient detail	2
"Don't know"—with no probe	2
Dangling probe	1
Multiple codes in error	1
Superfluous question asked	1

The interviewer's rating on each project should be made part of the records maintained for each interviewer. Results on a particular study may fit a trend and indicate what should be done about rehiring or retraining a particular interviewer. Upon the completion of a survey, each interviewer should receive a report which indicates her completion and refusal rate, grade, and how well she did relative to interviewers working in comparable areas.

The entire procedure outlined above suffers in that only a relative rating is obtained and, if the results are uniformly bad, it would only reveal that some interviewers were worse than others. It is not a completely satisfactory method, since it lacks objective standards; however, since absolute standards are usually not available and since each study is

---

[57] Seymour Sudman, "Quantifying Interviewer Quality," *Public Opinion Quarterly* (Winter, 1966–67), pp. 664–67.

likely to differ from the next, a relative comparison is of considerable value.

SUMMARY

Errors originating with interviewers are undoubtedly a major source of error in most surveys. These interviewer errors can be classified in five major groups: (1) nonresponse errors, (2) respondent selection errors, (3) errors in stimulating responses, (4) errors in interpreting and recording answers, and (5) cheating.

Research directors differ as to the relative importance of the cheater problem, but agree generally that the problem is serious. Proper management can reduce this error to a relatively low level, but many marketing research studies probably have a significant bias because of cheating.

The fact that the field worker is a part-time employee working without supervision under varying conditions makes the use of scientific personnel selection techniques impractical. In most cases the selection of field interviewers is more a matter of rehiring than of initial hiring. Interviewers previously used are considered on the basis of their past performance.

Interviewer training programs may be implemented on a face-to-face basis, by mail, or by a combination of the two. The training program has two main objectives, to train for the specific job and to provide the interviewer with the necessary attitudes and motivation.

Personal field supervision is the best way of controlling the field force. Another control method—and one which should be used in addition to personal supervision—is to maintain a continuous preliminary edit. Such a procedure keeps a control on whether interviewers are keeping to the schedule and whether their work is generally satisfactory.

Completed questionnaires are the basis for evaluation of interviewers. The first step in the evaluation process is to determine whether the interviews were actually made. Interviewers should then be rated on a number of factors, including cost per completed interview, percentage of refusals to the total number of interviews assigned, and mistakes made. If such data are made part of the interviewer's permanent record, a basis exists for deciding what interviewers should be rehired and what additional training is needed.

Case 11—1.   FRUSTROM RESEARCH COMPANY

The Frustrom Research Company was an independent marketing research agency which specialized in field survey work. The company was founded by Mr. Charles Frustrom in 1951 and had prospered to a point where it employed over thirty individuals. The company had an extensive field force which was used on Frustrom studies and on studies originated by other organizations as well. In the latter case the company merely provided field workers and accepted no responsibility for either the sample or the questionnaire. It did, however, guarantee that the work of its field force was reliable, that is, that all work completed was in accordance with the written instructions.

In its own survey work, the Frustrom Company employed a national probability sample with over 200 primary sampling points. Over the years the company had succeeded in building up a field interviewing force of approximately 150 women to handle the interviewing work done in these primary sampling locations. These women had been selected and trained by company personnel. Usually they could handle the field work for an entire study, but sometimes, when a large sample was used, it was necessary to use them as supervisors and to hire other interviewers. In addition to the 150 staff interviewers, the company had access to over 500 interviewers scattered throughout the United States. Most of these were women who were not known personally to the company. With but a few exceptions they had not been personally selected or trained by anyone connected with Frustrom.

It was the policy of the company to use its 150 staff interviewers as much as possible and to fill in with other interviewers only as necessary. Typically, for those jobs not involving the use of the company's national probability sample, the staff interviewers accounted for about half of the completed interviews. When Frustrom hired a new field supervisor, Mrs. Hazen, the firm charged her with upgrading the quality of the field force.

Mrs. Hazen, after studying the geographical dispersion of the 150 staff interviewers, decided to establish them as area supervisors. Each, initially, would be responsible for the selection and training of all "new" interviewers. In time it was hoped that each area supervisor would be able to select and train interviewers located strategically throughout her area, thereby giving the company a much more capable field force. The dispersion sites within each area had been worked out by the company's sampling statistician.

In her letter to each area supervisor, Mrs. Hazen set forth certain selection criteria and pointed out that they applied only to those individuals who were to be hired in those dispersion points where the company had no designated field worker or where present employees were not considered satisfactory. That part of the letter setting forth selection procedures is reproduced in Exhibit 1.

What changes, if any, should be made in the selection criteria and training procedures recommended by Mrs. Hazen?

EXHIBIT 1. Portion of letter from Mrs. Hazen to area supervisors specifying selection criteria for new interviewers

You are well aware of the many demands placed on a field interviewer working for our company. But being aware of these job requirements is not enough. We must use, as best we can, objective selection criteria. So as to leave no doubt as to what criteria to use, I have set forth below what to consider—although not necessarily in order of importance.

1. How good is the health of the potential interviewer? Remember that field workers often have to work in the rain and snow and to work for long hours. Can the candidate "take it"?
2. Has the person any physical defects which may prevent him or her from doing a satisfactory job—such as ability to take notes, read fine print, or hear?
3. What is the reason back of the applicant's desire to be a field interviewer? Is it purely money? Is she interested in people?
4. What job skills does the applicant have, such as typing and shorthand, teaching, etc.? Why doesn't she use these skills to get a job as a secretary, a teacher, etc.?
5. Does the applicant appear to lead a normal, well-ordered life? Is she well organized? Is she so involved in different activities that there is little or no "extra" time in which to do satisfactory interviewing work?
6. Has the applicant a good job record? How many part-time and/or full-time jobs has the individual held over the past several years? Why did she leave each of these jobs? Is she overly critical of her past employers? Does her job record indicate instability?
7. Would you say that the applicant has a pleasing personality that will enable her to establish rapport with respondents?
8. Does the prospective interviewer express herself well? Is her diction such that she will be easily understood?
9. Does the individual appear to have a good native intelligence coupled with mature judgment?

You should emphasize repeatedly that our work is only part-time, but that we are interested *only* in people who want this kind of employment over a relatively long number of years.

The prospect should not be "too young" or "too old." Probably the best age is between thirty and forty. Being part of a stable home is important. Make certain that she knows that evening hours are part of the job—so is the availability of a car both during the week and over the weekend.

If it is at all possible, try and interview the prospect in her own home. You can often tell a great deal about a woman just by "being in her home." Try and meet the husband—if there is one. Tell him about the kind of obligations his wife will be accepting if she becomes an interviewer. A disapproving husband often means a short-term worker!

If you think the candidate is a good prospect, then test her ability by having her interview you using a questionnaire from your most recent or current assignment. If at all possible, have her then conduct an interview with a respondent who is a neighbor. If you are doing any interviewing in the area, take the prospect along and let her see for herself the nature of the work.

Check her references.

If, as a result of all this, you have any serious doubts about the applicant being a good interviewer, *do not hire her!* We *must* set and maintain high selection standards.

Case 11—2. MORRIS RESEARCH COMPANY

The Morris Research Company was the largest independent marketing research service in its city. Its reputation was excellent. Among its clients were leading national and local manufacturers and several large department and specialty stores. The company employed eighteen full-time people including the president and owner, Mr. Morris. The staff also included a full-time field supervisor, Miss Stevens, who had served the company in that capacity for almost ten years. Her work had always been considered to be of highest quality.

The company was approached by the executive vice president and the advertising manager of one of the large department stores located in the same city. The store executives wanted to make a buying habit survey among their customers, and were considering having the Morris Company do the work. After a series of conferences, and after checking with some of the company's clients about the caliber and cost of work done, the two executives were convinced that the Morris Company had the necessary experience, ability, and facilities to undertake the proposed study. At the same time, the store executives decided to split the study into two parts: (1) the planning, sampling, and development of forms, and (2) the field work, tabulation, and analysis.

Mr. Morris pointed out to the store executives that this division was not only illogical but would make it difficult to obtain the best results. He argued that part 1 could not be done properly without consideration of part 2, and that this splitting of the project would result in divided responsibility for the final results. Mr. Morris' line of reasoning did not prevail. He decided not to labor his point of view when he observed that the store executives did not want to commit themselves beyond the developmental stage of the study until they were assured that the Morris Company could do good work. This situation led Mr. Morris to handle the study himself.

After numerous conferences and false starts, the objectives of the study were defined. These objectives were the subject of a letter sent to the executive vice president of the store. Written approval of them was requested and received. The objectives agreed on were:

1. To determine the geographical distribution of the store's women customers by city district, by suburb, and by county.

2. To determine the characteristics of the store's women and family customers by such items as age, marital status, and income. (These classification questions were worded or phrased exactly the same as those in a previous [six months] government sample census so that a direct comparison of results could be effected.)

3. To determine where (store name, store location, type of store) the store's women customers bought each of fourteen different shopping items. (Only those shopping items which involved considerable discretion in purchase were used.)

Mr. Morris then devoted himself to the preparation of the questionnaire and other field forms. The sampling problem was delegated to his statistician, Mr. Igor, who was directed to use a probability sample. Mr. Igor proceeded as follows:

1. He investigated the store records to determine how he could obtain a recent list of store customers from which to select the sample. His first problem as to find an acceptable definition for "woman customer." The definition of a woman customer, "one who has purchased any item or service, either by charge, C.O.D., or cash, from the store within the last six months," was accepted. But charge account records could not be used as a source from which to select the sample for several reasons which were obvious to Mr. Igor. After more than a week of querying store personnel who were familiar with the various store records, he found the tissue copies of the sales books completed during February of the current year to be the best source of information. This was true because store records were incomplete prior to February, and March records were still in process. The sampling universe which was selected was far from satisfactory. Mr. Igor pointed out that "it contained sales for only one month, that cash register sales were excluded, that many slips were illegible, that over 200,000 slips were involved, and that sales to women were often registered under a man's name."

After much discussion on the limitations of using these records, it was decided that there was no alternative within a reasonable cost. Therefore, the February sales slips had to be used. They did possess the advantages of showing such information as the department number, the merchandise sold, the price, the type of sale (charge, C.O.D., or cash), whether it was to be delivered, and the full name and address of the buyer. A final sample of 2,000 completed interviews was decided upon. This size sample was thought to be sufficient to yield the required precision for the overall sample as well as for the various subsamples.

2. The sample was obtained by applying random numbers to the tissue copies of sales books which had been completed during February. The mechanics of this involved counting all the slips (212,423) and selecting the first 3,000 numbers falling between 1 and 212,423 from tables of random numbers. These 3,000 random numbers were then applied to the sales slips. It was necessary to exclude the following types of sales:

1. Sales to employees.
2. Sales to commercial and charity institutions.
3. Illegible slips.
4. Exchange merchandise slips.

When one of the excluded sales slips was selected by random numbers, the next acceptable sales slip was substituted for it.

Mr. Igor stated later in his report on the sampling methodology that "this method of selection insured that each of the 212,423 sales transactions (less those labeled as nonacceptable) had an equal chance of selection and inclusion in the sample."

3. The following information was taken from the tissue sales slips forming the sample:

1. Name and address.
2. Type of sale (cash, charge, C.O.D.).
3. Department number.
4. Dollar amount of sale, excluding tax.

It was necessary to exclude 496 names and addresses from the 3,000 drawn because they resided too far away to be economically called on.

4. Random numbers were used to select 2,000 names from the remaining 2,504. The 504 "surplus" names were to be used in making substitutions for refusals or cases where respondents could not be reached because they had moved or died. The 2,000 names and addresses were separated into applicable districts and suburbs to facilitate control of investigators.

Prior to and during the selection of the sample, extensive work was done in developing the questionnaire. Several pretests were made in the field. Not only were the individual questions pretested, but careful attention was given to question sequence, physical layout, and precoding of the entire form for machine tabulation. The final draft was approved by the store.

By early June the survey was ready to go into the field. On the basis of the quality of work performed to date, the store executives decided that the remainder of the survey should be done by the Morris Company. The controller decided that the store should ask Mr. Morris for a detailed statement on field costs in advance. The latter refused to sign a contract on a fixed cost per completed interview. He stated that his company had always worked on a cost-plus agreement. He did agree, however, to submit a written statement of estimated costs to the store, and stated verbally that this figure would be met with a plus or minus allowance of 10 per cent. He set a figure of $5.65 per completed interview. The costs of supervision, training, the field edit, supplies, and verification were not included in this estimate. It did, however, include all direct expenses of making original calls and callbacks. In determining this cost, Mr. Morris and his field supervisor, Miss Stevens, took into account the following factors:

1. The sample included suburban calls and was selected at random; therefore, calls were scattered geographically.
2. An average interview took about twenty minutes to complete.
3. A number of respondents would refuse to cooperate. Mr. Morris

estimated this would run about 10 percent of the number of calls made.

4. Callbacks would be necessary and expensive. Mr. Morris estimated that 25 percent of all calls made would necessitate callbacks. This included callbacks on callbacks. The decision had been made to make three attempts to contact a respondent. If all three failed, a substitute respondent would be selected from the 504 "surplus" names.

5. Pay per hour for interviewers would be $2.60, plus expenses. Mr. Morris estimated expenses would average 50 cents per hour. These expenses would include mileage for the six women who were using their cars for suburban work. In those cases where night or weekend calls were necessary, the company planned on paying $3.00 per hour instead of $2.60.

6. A profit of 10 percent on the total interviewing costs was desired.

7. An average of eight completed calls per field interviewer per day was expected.

The controller thought the figure of $5.65 per completed interview was too high. This would mean that field work costs alone would be $11,300. After analyzing in detail the factors affecting the cost, however, he decided to accept the estimate.

During the second week in June, the Morris Company's field supervisor, Miss Stevens, selected sixteen women from her file of experienced interviewers. These women agreed to work a minimum of thirty hours a week for a maximum period of five weeks. They also agreed to do some night and weekend interviewing. Six of the women agreed to use their cars whenever they were instructed to do so by the field supervisor. In addition to the sixteen women interviewers, an assistant field supervisor was hired to handle the clerical work in the office pertaining to this survey. Miss Stevens' secretary was assigned to work full time on verifying the completed calls by telephone.

The training program for interviewers occupied two full days. Interviewers were, of course, paid for this time. This program included lectures and group discussions designed to acquaint the women interviewers with the objectives of the survey as well as its methods. An important phase of the training program included practice interviews which were required of all workers. These practice interviews were made in the field among housewives not included in the sample. At the end of the training period all interviewers were required to take a written examination based on the instruction period. All the women passed this examination.

Miss Stevens gave instructions that all completed questionnaires should be mailed to her office each day. The women were to call in every morning and report the number of completed interviews for the previous day, the number of calls made, and the number of refusals. The assistant field supervisor was assigned the job of preparing the daily and weekly summary reports of this information. Miss Stevens planned on spending a majority of her time in the field working with the individual interviewers.

The summary report at the end of the first week (Monday-Friday) is shown in Table 1.

TABLE 1

Interviewer	Calls made	No. of completed interviews	No.° of refusals	No.† of hours	Cost‡ per completed interview
1	62	20	3	33	$4.55
2	55	19	2	31	4.48
3	96	31	8	36	3.20
4	66	20	1	37	5.10
5	96	18	14	31	4.73
6	81	33	12	30	2.50
7	60	27	6	32	3.25
8	69	26	2	32	3.33
9	70	26	3	34	3.60
10	40	14	1	30	5.90
11	0	0	0	0	
12	47	12	1	36	8.25
13	51	22	2	39	4.88
14	36	9	0	30	9.18
15	58	14	6	36	7.08
16	48	15	1	31	5.68
Total	935	306	62	489	$4.48§

NOTE: Interviewers 11–16 worked in the suburban areas and used cars. Interviewer 11 was sick for the entire week.
° Includes "refused to cooperate," deceased, moved, etc.
† No evening or weekend hours.
‡ Does not include any expense.
§ Average cost per completed interview.

Miss Stevens was very concerned over the first week's results—especially in view of the cost and time commitments that Mr. Morris had made to the store executives. She felt that the work would go faster in the following weeks, since the first week involved some orientation. But an increase of 25 percent would have to be realized if the five weeks' schedule was to be met. She decided to send the tabulated results to Mr. Morris with a short note appended. This note was her request for an appointment with Mr. Morris, after he had studied the report, so that she might discuss it in detail with him.

Immediately after examining the report, Mr. Morris called Miss Stevens for a conference. He felt that the report was not as complete as it should be. For example, the report failed to show the number of callbacks, and expenses were not added to the field salaries before cost per completed interview was determined. He also stated that a daily report on the weather should be included. Miss Stevens agreed that all of these should be included and stated that all following reports would be complete. Mr. Morris suggested that Miss Stevens write him a complete report regarding the steps that should be taken to improve the efficiency of the field force.

What action should Miss Stevens recommend?

12

Analysis of data collected

A̲ᴸᴸ ᴘʀᴇᴠɪᴏᴜꜱ ꜱᴛᴇᴘꜱ in the research process have been undertaken solely for the purpose of the analysis step from which conclusions, recommendations, and decision will eventuate. Thus, to a considerable extent, the framework for analysis is set *prior to* the collection of the data. The extent to which the prior steps affect the analysis varies from project to project, but typically an experimental design more than any other predetermines the nature and scope of the analysis function. Where a decision model is involved, the data must, of course, be collected to fit specific requirements.

The analysis function consists of a number of steps typically undertaken in the following sequence:

1. *Ordering the data into meaningful categories.* The data have to be organized to give them meaning, that is, the raw data have to be tabulated, which requires that categories be established. For example, in a nationwide study among households to determine what brands of ready-to-eat cereals were used, categories might consist of various types of cereals (e.g., sugar coated versus nonsugar coated brands), geographical regions, city sizes, ages of housewives, family incomes, presence of children, ownership of television, and occupation of the male head.

2. *Summarizing the data contained in the categories.* Summary measures are necessary to describe the data within a category as well as to facilitate further data manipulation.

3. *Determining whether significant differences exist between categories.* Observed differences between categories are tested to determine whether they are significant or could have occurred by chance because of sampling variations.

4. *Explaining "why" differences exist.* Too often it is assumed that the analysis function stops with the execution of step three. It is imperative, however, that an attempt be made to explain the reasons *why* any significant differences exist. This "why" information requires that hypotheses—tentative explanations—be set up and tested through a further examination of the survey data with other information. The importance of using other information cannot be overstressed, since it may provide a more specific meaning to the results obtained from a single research study.

It may be that this "why" information cannot be obtained from either the specific project or from other data and that further research will be needed. However, it would be unwise to contemplate additional research until the possibility of getting answers from the project at hand was exhausted.

Failure to explain differences incurs the danger of overlooking important findings. This would represent a failure to maximize the return on the investment made in a particular study. Since later studies may be influenced by the findings, the failure will project itself into the future—often with serious consequences. Further, if systematic searching does not take place, unwarranted conclusions may be drawn.

5. *Making recommendations.* After drawing statistical conclusions, the analyst needs to translate them into action in the form of recommendations. Making recommendations usually requires an understanding of the practical details surrounding a given operation and so may not be the responsibility of the researcher. In general, however, when a researcher is qualified by general knowledge of the operation, he should make recommendations.

It would be a mistake to infer that the analysis function *always* follows precisely the five-step procedure outlined above. In many projects the steps will tend to overlap since, for example, the analyst may generate new hypotheses which require a recycling of earlier steps. All of the steps, however, are involved to some degree in each analysis. They will each be considered in more depth.

ORDERING THE DATA INTO CATEGORIES

Editing and coding

The primary purposes of editing and coding are to eliminate errors in the raw data and to process the data into categories so that tabulation may take place. Too often, these procedures are considered mechanical when, in reality, they require considerable skill. The effectiveness of the entire analysis function may be hampered because of poor editing and coding. For example, an editor may place a different interpretation on the data than was intended and make "wrong" classifications, or when a number of editors are employed, the same data may be classified in a number of different ways.

But other important reasons obtain for studying these subjects. Editing plays an important role in helping to evaluate the field force, the effectiveness of the questionnaire, and the survey operation in general. Thus, editing provides valuable information about how the research procedure can be improved in the future. The time and costs involved in editing and coding are sufficient reasons alone to warrant intensive study of the process. The authors have participated in a number of studies in which the editing and coding costs were more than 25 percent of the total survey costs.

The editing and coding functions are usually accomplished by the same individuals and often in the same operation. The essential difference between the two is that editing is required to eliminate errors or points of confusion in the raw data, whereas coding assigns the data to pertinent categories, thereby expediting the tabulation.

Planning the editing-coding work. The preparation of the questionnaire should anticipate the editing and coding work, since the physical arrangement of the form must allow editing and coding space. If the data are to be machine tabulated, codes, where possible, are assigned to the alternative answers and included in the questionnaire format. This is referred to as precoding.

The persons who are to do the editing and coding work should be of high caliber and familiar with field interviewing procedures. They should, if at all possible, be exposed to the interviewer training program and participate in the interviewer control work.

The editing and coding procedures need to be written and must explain, in detail, how the answers to each question are to be handled. These instructions are prepared only after a thorough study of a sizable number of questionnaires. Considerable thought must be given to what tabulations will be required. The instructions, where applicable, must be specific about the proper categories for general answers and the standards to use for those answers involving such units of measurement as time, distance, and weight. Examples of how to edit and code the raw data are included. These examples must be typical and of such a nature as to distinguish between the alternate categories in which answers might be placed. Adequate checks must be built into the editing and coding procedures. These checks are more intensive during the early stages of the work when the editing and coding personnel are still learning their work. Only rarely can the editing and coding instructions anticipate all the problems which will arise, and, therefore, the survey leader must maintain constant contact with the work in progress.

All editing is done using a writing instrument with a color other than the one used by the interviewers. Unless this is done there is no way to distinguish between "original" and "edited" data. Editors must not destroy original data by erasure. Rather, where necessary, original entries are deleted by drawing a light line through them.

A study of the written instructions does not constitute the entire training program for complex surveys. The instructions pertaining to the handling of difficult questions, for example, open questions, are discussed in detail and illustrated with examples taken from the particular study. Following this, the editors "practice" on a sample of questionnaires and their work is reviewed critically. The results of the practice work indicate whether it is necessary to revise the editing and coding instructions.

Making a preliminary check.   After receiving all questionnaires from the field, a preliminary check is made before they are subjected to the detailed editing and coding work. Thus, even though the questionnaires have been checked as part of the procedure for controlling the field force, they are rechecked for the following:

1. *Adherence to sampling instructions.*   If the interview was not made with the proper respondent, it is rejected. For example, if the sampling universe consisted of housewives, only interviews with such respondents are acceptable. Interviews with unmarried women must be eliminated. To the extent that he can, the editor makes sure that the sampling requirements have been met. In many cases he can do little since there is no way of determining whether the field worker followed precisely the sampling instructions. If random sampling procedures were used with the interviewers selecting the households, it is impossible to determine if the "right" households were selected. But if households were selected from prepared lists, the editor can verify the sampling procedure.

2. *Legibility.*   If the handwriting is not clear, the editors can do nothing to make the questionnaire usable. Where time permits, questionnaires may be returned to the interviewer for "translation." In any case, the editor decides what the recorded information is or what action to take.

3. *Completeness.*   All questions are expected to be answered since "blanks" can mean different things—no answer or refusal; the question was not applicable and, therefore, was not asked; or the interviewer failed to record the answer. When possible, the interviewer may be asked to review such "blanks," but it is dangerous to let the interviewer insert what he thinks should have been the entry. Except in unusual situations, interviews are too similar to permit accurate memory of a given one at a later date. Again, the editor must decide to tabulate the question as a "no answer," to drop the entire questionnaire, or to attempt to find the correct information.

4. *Consistency.*   Each questionnaire is examined to determine if it is internally consistent. An example of inconsistency would be on a travel questionnaire where the respondent reports not using a car and later, in answer to another question, mentions driving to a particular site. If in-

consistencies exist on any questionnaire which cannot be "edited," the editor must decide to eliminate the applicable questions from tabulation, to reject the entire questionnaire, or to attempt to reinterview the respondent.

5. *Understandability.* Answers to open-end questions are often difficult to understand. The interviewer may have abbreviated the answer to such an extent that it is not clear what the respondent meant. Or, the answer may have been recorded verbatim and still not be clear. It is often impossible to know what such words as "this" or "it" refer to. It may be that the interviewer can interpret these ambiguous answers, but such a way of correcting the data is dangerous since the interviewer may try to cover up the ambiguities. The editor must determine what shall be done.

Preliminary inconsistency and understandability checks will not reveal all such errors; some may be detected only at the time detailed editing and coding take place. However, a preliminary check often makes it possible to obtain missing data or to clear up other difficulties while the field force is still intact and the survey fresh in the interviewers' minds.

Establishing categories.   To set up an effective set of tabulation categories, the survey leader must consider the survey objectives. Without reference to these objectives, it is impossible to select the most appropriate categories. For example, a variety of answers would be given in response to the question, "What do you dislike about the car you drive most frequently?" The answers to this question might be grouped according to the various parts of the car, such as engine, body, and interior, or according to what these dislikes mean to the respondent, such as inconveniences, discomfort, expense, pride, and fear. These are but two of the many classifications which might be set up. The classification to use depends on which is most relevant to the purpose of the inquiry.

It is extremely difficult to establish categories for data obtained through the use of open-ended questions. This is especially true with exploratory studies, since such studies do not typically start with well-stated hypotheses. The first step in setting categories, regardless of the type of study involved, is to develop a set of working hypotheses that will, in effect, help decide what factors are most pertinent or relevant. If, for example, one is trying to find out why women buy a certain brand of hand lotion, one should first develop a set of hypotheses as to the "why" aspects of the problem. This does not mean that he would not be sensitive to data which suggest other hypotheses, but rather that he would start with some hypotheses as the rationale for the study.

The researcher must also concern himself with establishing categories which deal satisfactorily with the different dimensions of the problem. In a hand lotion problem, the researchers involved were concerned with the following dimensions: (1) product qualities; (2) specific problems which led the respondent to use the particular brand; (3) the image of the product with respect to what types of individuals were thought to use it; (4) what source induced the respondent to try the product; (5) the regularity of use by the respondent; and (6) the use of the product by other members of the household. Within these generalized dimensions, specific categories were established.

In classifying data with regard to any specific objective, it is essential that the categories established be mutually exclusive and at the same time cover all possible answers. Ideally, each category should contain similar responses so that overall there will be homogeneity *within* categories and differences *between* categories.

Setting up a useful classification scheme is difficult because most marketing problems require the classification of objects (e.g., consumers) by more than one characteristic. It is extremely difficult to classify objects on the basis of more than three characteristics at a time, and yet it is sometimes necessary to do so (e.g., in the establishment of market segments for a product category or a brand). Numerical taxonomy—a technique borrowed from biology and very new to marketing researchers—holds considerable promise for improved classification work. The nature and scope of this technique are well described by Ronald E. Frank and Paul E. Green.

Assume that there is a set of objects, such as people, products, advertisements, and marketing channels, each of which can be characterized by a measurement (or more generally, by an attribute score) on each of a set of characteristics. The researcher has no external criterion for grouping the objects into subsets of similar objects; instead, he wants to identify natural groupings in the data, after which more formal models might be developed.

More formally stated, the problem is: How should objects be assigned to groups so there will be as much likeness within groups and as much difference among groups as possible? From this question four others arise: (1) what proximity measure is to be used to summarize the likeness of profiles, (2) after these likeness measures have been computed, how should the objects be grouped, (3) after the objects have been grouped, what descriptive measures are appropriate for summarizing the characteristics of each group, (4) are the groups formed really different from each other (the inferential problem)?[1]

Because there are numerous taxonomic procedures and because of the general complexity of the subject it will not be possible to elaborate further.[2]

---

[1] Ronald E. Frank and Paul E. Green, "Numerical Taxonomy in Marketing Analysis: A Review Article," *Journal of Marketing Research* (February, 1968), pp. 84–85.

[2] For further information on this subject the reader is referred to *ibid*, and especially to their reference section, which lists 96 sources. For a discussion of the use of a Bayesian classification procedure which takes into account the risks of misclassification in its effort to determine the optimal number of characteristics see Paul E. Green, "Bayesian Classification Procedures in Analyzing Customer Characteristics," *Journal of Marketing Research* (May, 1964), pp. 45–50.

Detecting incorrect answers.   It is possible to detect incorrect answers when answers to two or more questions are inconsistent. The handling of such answers depends upon the nature of the inconsistency. For example, a survey was conducted to find out what percent of those families owning a television set had purchased it below list price. After finding out whether a television set was in the home, the interviewer asked the brand and model. The answers were verified by observation. A later question asked the price at which the set had been purchased. A number of answers were received which indicated a price *substantially higher* than the known retail list price. Such answers were deleted, since the answer was obviously incorrect and there was no way it could be "edited in." In another study, respondents were asked whether they bought a majority of their groceries at a chain or at an independent store. Later in the questionnaire, they were asked the name of the grocery store they patronized "more than any other." A number of respondents who had answered earlier that they bought primarily from a chain store gave the name of an independent store. After this fact had been verified in the central office (the study covered only the Chicago area, so store type verification was not difficult), the earlier chain store answer was altered to independent.[3]

Completing incomplete answers.   Very little can be done with many incomplete answers. Only where a question ties in with other questions is it possible to fill in the missing data. For example, a study determined what brands of refrigerators respondents could name without help from the interviewer. Later questions asked what brand of refrigerator the respondent owned and what brand or brands the respondent had owned prior to the present brand. In a number of cases, respondents did not include the brand(s) they owned or had owned in the initial recall question. These brands were added to those mentioned in the earlier question, although it could be argued that the association is not precisely the same.

It is impossible to specify rules for handling incorrect and incomplete answers. Each survey is different and the only safe editing rule to follow is that of being conservative. Only where one is absolutely certain as to the intent should the raw data be altered.

"Don't know" and "no answer."[4]   Such categories as "don't know" and "no answer" may contain sufficiently few cases to warrant disregarding them, except to include them to make the statistical tables complete.

---

[3] Had this study been designed to determine the extent of confusion existing in the consumer's mind about the type (chain versus independent) of store patronized, then no editing problem would have existed. This indicates how the objectives of the study can affect the editing process.

[4] The contents of this section were suggested by Hans Zeisel, *Say It with Figures* (New York: Harper & Brothers, 1957), pp. 42–66.

However, these categories assume considerable importance in some situations. Thus, it might not be possible to state what the most prevalent or common answer was—or the ranking of the answers—if a large number of "don't knows" was received. For example, in the following situation the "don't knows" are so numerous as to prevent the analyst from drawing any sound conclusions as to which type of outlet is most important or what the rank order of outlets is in the purchase of a TV set. The answers were received from a mail questionnaire. *"At which type of outlet did you purchase your TV set?" (Check one of the following store types.)*

Type of outlet	Percent of respondents
Appliance store	26%
Furniture store	16
Mail-order house	6
Department store	6
Discount house	3
All others	15
Don't know	28
Total	100%

In this illustration, it is clear that the high percent of "don't knows" is largely a function of poor questionnaire construction. Many individuals did not know what was meant by the different outlet terms and, therefore, replied they didn't know the type of outlet at which they purchased their TV sets. A high percent of "don't knows" or "no answers" may also be caused by poor field interviewing techniques.

Legitimate "don't know" answers. Not all "don't know" answers represent a problem. Such a thing as a legitimate "don't know" exists. In general, a "don't know" answer is legitimate if the question is aimed at finding out whether the respondent possesses certain information or has made a decision relevant to a certain event. The questions below could produce legitimate "don't know" answers.

1. What is the name of the product advertised on the Laugh-In television program?
2. What are the names of some English automobiles?
3. Do you plan on buying a new electric refrigerator in the next six months?
4. Do you think that food prices will be higher next year?

In these examples, it would be safe to assume that most, if not all, of the "don't know" answers were legitimate. However, such an assumption could not be made safely in other situations. Often considerable difficulty is experienced in determining whether the "don't know" answer is a function of the respondent's lack of information or the wording of the question. Thus, the "don't knows" received from the question, "Should the Congress of the United States vote to continue the Patent Law in its present form?" could have been caused by the following:

1. The respondent was not familiar with the facts surrounding the law.
2. The respondent knew the facts about the law, but had not formulated a definite attitude about the desirability of its continuance.

Other reasons for "don't know" answers.   In addition to the legitimate and "I'm confused" "don't knows," there are two other types, as follows:

1. *The respondent really means, "I don't want to answer this question" when he says, "I don't know."*   Questions dealing with personal matters or with socially unacceptable symbols often evoke a "don't know" answer. In such cases, the respondent is merely evading the necessity of giving an answer (including a "no answer") and is hiding behind a "don't know."

2. *The respondent by his "don't know" answer means "too unimportant to warrant a specific answer."*   If a question dealing with a subject which the respondent thinks unimportant is asked, some respondents will give a "don't know" answer. For example, if respondents are asked to indicate their relative satisfaction with two products or with the same product at two different times, it is possible that some will answer "don't know." What they may mean is that the difference in favor of one product is so negligible that it is not important for them to decide in either direction. It is a natural tendency for some individuals to answer a comparison question with "I don't know," and then perhaps to add "They're about the same." The interpretation of a "don't know" answer as meaning "of little significance" should be used with caution.

Ways of handling "don't know" answers.   There are three ways of handling the illegitimate "don't know" problem—none of which represents a fully satisfactory solution.

1. *Distribute the "don't knows" proportionately among the other categories.* This is the simplest way of dealing with the "don't know" problem. The procedure is quite simple: the "don't knows" are eliminated in counting the total number of responses which becomes the base for calculating the percentages of the other answers. This has the effect of distributing the "don't know" answers proportionately throughout the other categories. This procedure assumes that, if these individuals were eliminated from the sample, the remainder (those who gave an answer other than "don't know") would be representative of the universe. This assumption may not be correct, and therefore, if the extent of the "don't knows" is not shown, the reader may be misled.

2. *Show the "don't knows" as a separate category.* This procedure is similar to the one just discussed, but differs in that the number of "don't knows" is shown even though they are eliminated from the percentage base. This is the best procedure since it does not mislead anyone as to what happened. It is a difficult decision to make because it is an admission of failure either in terms of the questionnaire design, the inter-

viewing force, or in assuming that certain information could be obtained.

3. *Estimate answers from other data contained in the questionnaire.* Occasionally the "don't know" answer can be inferred by studying other information contained in the questionnaire. For example, family income might be estimated by referring to the number of individuals in the family who are working and the occupations of each. Another way might be to cross-tabulate the answers to certain questions with the answers to the questions producing the "don't knows." In a rice-purchasing study, 12 percent of the housewives failed to indicate an answer to the income question. The researcher cross tabulated answers to the question, "Do you usually buy rice in bulk, branded, or both ways?" with income and obtained the results shown in Table 12–1.

TABLE 12–1*. Housewives buying rice in bulk or branded (by income)

	Under $1,000	$1,000– $1,999	$2,000– $2,999	Over $3,000	Income not stated
Brand	32%	43%	49%	56%	55%
Bulk	49	34	25	15	16
Both	19	23	26	29	29
Total	100%	100%	100%	100%	100%
(Number of cases)	(237)	(715)	(364)	(266)	(212)

* SOURCE: Hans Zeisel, *Say It with Figures* (New York: Harper & Brothers, 1957), p. 63.

This table shows a clear relationship between income and buying rice branded or in bulk. The higher the income the greater the proportion of housewives who buy branded rice; the lower the income the more bulk rice is bought. Since bulk rice is cheaper, this result is not surprising.

Those who did not state their income buy in almost exactly the same percentages as the group with incomes over $3,000. The income identity is so striking that the failure to classify on income can be interpreted as a desire not to divulge a high income.[5]

Regardless of what efforts are made, the "don't know" and "no answer" categories will always be present to some degree. The best approach to this problem is to recognize it as an important one and to anticipate it at the time the questionnaire is prepared and the field force selected and trained.

Tabulation

Tabulation consists of counting the numbers of items which fall into the established categories. It is a technical operation and often requires considerable time and money. Like coding, it is subject to errors which may impair the validity of the findings.

[5] *Ibid.*, pp. 62–63.

Before tabulation can take place the plan of analysis must be thought through clearly—that is, it is necessary to have a plan which prescribes how the data are to be counted. The objectives of the survey and the size of the sample will determine the tabulations to be made. Generally speaking, the data should be "broken down" as much as possible. For example, assume a national distribution survey to determine the percent of stores stocking Folger's brand of coffee. The study reveals that 35 percent of the food stores in the United States stock this brand. Such a tabulation would be "interesting" information, but not very useful, since it fails to reveal the percent of stocking by the company's sales regions and districts. Nor does it reveal anything about the percent stocking by city size groups. And probably most important, the question would be raised as to what kinds of stores do and do not stock this brand. Thus, the data would need to be tabulated by dollar volume ratings of stores and by chains versus independents. Finally, the kinds of stores stocking would need to be related to geographical "breaks" so that within any sales territory the percent of high-volume stores and chain stores stocking could be ascertained. Only if the distribution data were tabulated by such categories could the survey results be of maximum value.

Planning the tabulation.   The tabulation plan specifies exactly how the tabulations are to be made. It is a detailed blueprint for action. It consists of "dummy" tables—that is, tables with complete headings and stubs plus a description of the data to be included. Often it is impossible to draw up at the outset all the detailed tables which will be of value. A common procedure is to set up general tables, to have them tabulated, and to use these tables to determine the form of the final tabulations. For example, it might not be possible to indicate in advance how all the data should be counted because the sample size by various population subgroups is not known. General tables with a large number of categories show the sizes of the subgroups in the sample.

Even as a result of this two-stage tabulation, it is probably still not possible to specify all the tables which ultimately will be desired, since in trying to explain certain relationships, additional tabulations will become important.

Planning which leads to a reduction of the number of times the data are tabulated will reduce costs. It is usually possible to make tabulations by additional "breaks" at a small additional cost, provided these tabulations are made at the same time. This is especially true with machine tabulation. For example, in counting the answers to a single question it would cost very little more to separate the answers by the different income groups.

Manual versus machine tabulation.[6]   Counting may be done by using

---

[6] For an informative discussion of the application of computers to marketing problems see David B. Montgomery, "Computer Uses in Marketing Research: A Proposal," *Journal of Marketing Research* (May, 1967), pp. 195–98.

manual or machine methods. The latter consists of using electronic machines which sort, count, and perform various arithmetic operations such as adding, subtracting, and multiplying. Virtually all large studies are now tabulated by machine. Computers are important for speed and economy and they also provide results more accurate than work done by hand. "Extensive analysis has shown that the human will make at least five errors in 100 hand calculations, making him at best 95 percent effective. The computer closely approaches 100 percent accuracy (99.99+ percent). When an error does occur, it is usually sensed and its presence is indicated to the operator."[7] Computers also make possible the use of new mathematical techniques to solve complex problems.[8]

Both manual and machine methods possess unique advantages and disadvantages. Manual tabulation is applicable when a relatively small number of cases has to be counted (several hundred or less) and when only a few cross tabulations are planned. In comparing the two methods (machine versus manual), it is important to remember that machine tabulation requires additional preparatory work since the data have to be coded and put into the machine. When computers are used, extensive time is required to program the operations.

In general, the most important determinant in selecting between the two methods is the number of cross tabulations to be run. When a large number of questionnaires is involved (five hundred or more) and each contains many questions, the speed of the electronic machines more than offsets the additional preparatory work required. If retabulations are required, they will be cheaper and faster if the data have been put on cards or tapes at the beginning.

Handling multiple answers.   Multiple answers to a single question are a frequent experience in marketing research. For example, an open-end question such as, "What magazines did you read during the past week?" will result in multiple answers from some respondents. They may be tabulated in several different ways depending on the objectives of the study. Four types of treatment may be applied to multiple answers.

1. *Share of respondents.* By share of respondents is meant the percent possessing a particular attribute. Thus, in analyzing answers to the questions, "What magazines did you read during the past week?" one might be interested in the percent of respondents reading any given magazines during this specified time period. The tabulation might be set up as shown in Table 12–2.

Note that no total is given for the percentage column because it would

[7] Daniel N. Leeson and Donald L. Dimitry, *Basic Programming Concepts and the I.B.M. 1620 Computer* (New York: Holt, Rinehart and Winston, Inc., 1962), p. 1.

[8] For an excellent discussion of the use of computers in business see Donald H. Sanders, *Computers in Business: An Introduction* (New York: McGraw-Hill Book Co., 1968).

TABLE 12–2. Percentage of persons reading each magazine

Magazine	Percent of persons
1	20.1
2	18.3
3	14.7
4	13.5
5	18.8
6	10.4
All other	23.2
None	9.7

be meaningless. It obviously exceeds 100 percent because of multiple answers.

2. *Number per respondent.* From Table 12–2, valuable information has been secured, but additional data can be obtained. One would probably want to know the number of persons reading none, one, two, three, and so on, magazines. Table 12–3 shows the number of magazines read per respondent.

TABLE 12–3. Number of magazines read

Number of magazines	Percent of persons
Zero	9.7
1	28.2
2	16.7
3	15.4
4	10.8
5	9.2
6 and over	10.0
Total	100.0

Note that the percentage column adds to 100 percent because each respondent is counted only once.

3. *Duplication analysis.* The answers to the magazine question could be tabulated to determine what combinations of magazines were read by respondents. Such a tabulation is often referred to as a duplication analysis. From this kind of tabulation, the "overlap" or duplication between various magazines is ascertained. Such an analysis would answer the question, "How many respondents who read magazine A also read magazine B, C, D, and so on?" From the answers to this question, the number of additional or unduplicated respondents who might be reached if other magazines were added to an advertiser's media list could be determined.

4. *Distribution of items (answers).* Here the distribution of answers (not respondents) is tabulated. For example, on a radio-brand ownership

study, the percent (or share of each brand to the total) would be determined. Table 12–4 presents this type of information.

TABLE 12–4. **Distribution of radio brands in metropolitan area X (based on replies from 427 respondents)**

Brand	Number of sets	Percent of all sets
1	110	18.3
2	93	15.5
3	83	13.8
4	70	11.7
5	48	8.0
6	36	6.0
7	28	4.8
8	21	3.5
All other brands	21	15.2
Made by hand	19	3.2
Total sets	600	100.0

Note that the number of sets exceeds the number of respondents, since many respondents reported owning two or more.

Multiple answers may be derived not only from single questions but from a combination of single answer questions. For example, in a study to determine readership of daily newspapers, a single answer question about each daily paper might be asked as follows: "Did you read or look at The *Tribune* newspaper during the past week?" Assuming there were four such questions (one for each daily newspaper), the replies from all four could be grouped and treated as multiple answers to a single question such as, "What daily newspaper or newspapers did you read or look at during the past week?"

SUMMARIZING THE DATA AND DETERMINING SIGNIFICANT DIFFERENCES

If the results from a marketing study are to be of maximum usefulness, they must be organized and summarized in such a way as to enable the researcher to see clearly the important points relative to the study objective. This requires the use of summary statistical measures such as the arithmetic mean and percentages. Since most marketing data are collected through the use of a sample, the reliability of these summary estimates must be determined. Data for different groups must be compared and the significance of any observed differences determined.

Summary statistics

Statistical measures which are used to typify the group are referred to as measures of central tendency. Of the several measures of central tendency, the arithmetic mean and median are the most common. Such statistics are of great help to the researcher, but they can also be misleading. Often it is forgotten that the various "averages" are only summary statistics and substitutes. In effect, these statistics enable the researcher to generalize about the universe surveyed, but they are only helpful if they reflect this universe accurately. In reducing a mass of data to an average, the researcher must realize that he is losing certain details. In shedding such detail, he must be careful not to overlook or obscure important information. Often, frequency distributions are of greater importance than averages, yet the general tendency is to push toward the use of a single figure to typify the group.

Each of the various measures of central tendency suffers certain deficiencies in describing a particular distribution. For example, two counties may have the same average income per household, but one county may have a range from zero to $350,000 while the other has a range from zero to $58,000 per household. Problems of this type demand statistical measures which reveal something about the degree to which the values in a series vary with respect to a particular average. Such measures are called measures of dispersion. The smaller the dispersion in a set of data, the greater the homogeneity of the data. The standard deviation is the most widely used measure of dispersion.

Percentages.   Percentages are a special kind of ratio and are highly useful in facilitating a comparison between two or more series of data. They have many uses, the more common of which are presented below.

Describing relationships.   Often a figure is obtained which has significance only when it is related to another figure. Thus in all sampling situations the number of cases falling into a category is meaningless unless it is related to some particular base. If, for example, 1,000 households are interviewed and it is determined that 642 have a TV set, the figure of 642 is meaningless unless it is related to the base of 1,000—in this illustration 64.2 percent.

Comparing in relative terms the distribution of two or more series of data.   For example, assume the distribution of the sales of car A and car B in four separate metropolitan markets shown in Table 12–5. The analyst would have difficulty in trying to get any meaning out of the absolute differences in the distribution of the two makes of cars, but

TABLE 12–5. Sales of two cars in four metropolitan areas

Metropolitan area	Car A	Percent	Car B	Percent
A	3,742	21.1	1,596	13.7
B	1,006	5.6	2,711	23.1
C	12,231	69.1	6,201	52.9
D	732	4.2	1,214	10.3
Total	17,701	100.0	11,722	100.0

when relative differences are shown by the use of percentages the distribution pattern of car A versus car B is more clearly seen.

Misuse of percentages. Confusion often exists in the use of percentages; it is important to describe briefly the more common types of such confusion.

1. *Averaging percentages.* Percentages cannot be averaged unless each is weighted by the size of the group from which it is derived. Thus, in most cases, a simple average will not suffice and it is necessary to use a weighted average.

2. *Use of too large percentages.* This often defeats the purpose of percentages, which is to simplify. A large percentage is difficult to understand and tends to confuse. If a 1,000 percent increase has been experienced, it is better to describe this as a ten-fold increase.

3. *Using too small a base.* Percentages hide the base from which they have been computed. A figure of 60 percent when contrasted with 30 percent would appear to indicate a sizable difference. Yet if there were only six cases in the one category and three in the other, the differences would not be as significant as it had been made to appear through the use of percentages.

4. *Percentage decreases can never exceed 100 percent.* This is obvious, but this type of mistake occurs frequently. The higher figure should always be used as the base. For example, if a price were reduced from $1.00 to 25¢ the decrease would be 75 (75/100) percent.

Sampling statistics

The meaning and use of the standard error and confidence limits have been discussed in the sampling chapters. An understanding of these terms and their applicability to the problem of determining differences is essential. Different types of sample designs require the use of different formulas for calculating the standard error. For example, small samples (say under twenty-five) are easily affected by atypical items and, thus, the theory of the normal distribution cannot be used, since it is based on a sample sufficiently large to balance out the extreme cases. The means of small samples follow the *t* distribution. This distribution increases the number of standard errors needed to obtain a certain level of confidence.[9] In the following discussion, large samples will be assumed for simplicity.

Determining whether "statistically significant" differences exist. The problem here may be illustrated by two examples:

Example A. The ABC Corporation, a large food manufacturer, is considering the acquisition of a regional dog food manufacturer, the

---

[9] For a more thorough discussion of this subject see Hubert M. Blalock, *Social Statistics* (New York: McGraw-Hill Book Co., 1960), pp. 144–49.

Lucky Pup Company. Officials of Lucky Pup assert that their brand is carried by at least half the grocery stores in their marketing area. To check the validity of this claim, the ABC Corporation selects a random sample of one hundred stores in Lucky Pup's area, and finds that thirty-five are carrying the brand. Is the claim of the Lucky Pup management credible?

Example B. Before a special advertising campaign, 48 percent of a random sample of soft drink users had heard of brand X. After the campaign, 55 percent of a new sample are familiar with the brand. Was the campaign effective?

Both of these examples have in common these characteristics:

1. In each case, there are one or more estimates of population values, based on random samples.
2. Because of sampling variation, the question arises as to whether the observed sample differences are "statistically significant" in the sense of reflecting actual differences between population values, or whether they merely reflect the variability of estimates inherent in random sampling.

For instance, in example A the observed sample proportion of stores stocking Lucky Pup is $p = 0.35$. Is this sufficiently smaller than the minimum hypothesized proportion, $P = 0.50$, to cast doubt on the Lucky Pup claim, or could such a deviation be attributable to sampling variation? Even if the actual universe proportion of stores stocking the brand were 0.50, a sample proportion stocking *exactly* 0.50 would hardly ever be found. The question is whether the observed sample proportion of $p = 0.35$ is "statistically significant," in the sense of indicating beyond reasonable doubt that the universe proportion stocking is less than 0.50.

Problems of the kind illustrated above arise whenever analytic conclusions are drawn on the basis of sample evidence—a situation of frequent occurrence in marketing research. Clearly, the existence of genuine differences must be established before inferences as to causality or appropriate action can be made.

To illustrate the kind of reasoning that is used in problems of this general type, example A will be analyzed in more detail.

Discussion of example A. In order to solve this problem, it is necessary to consider a specific hypothetical value for p, the proportion of stores carrying Lucky Pup. The specific hypothesis, $P = 0.50$, will be considered, since this is the minimum value in the range cited by the Lucky Pup management.

Now suppose this hypothesis is true, i.e., $P = 0.50$. Is the observed sample proportion, $p = 0.35$, consistent with the hypothesis that $P = 0.50$? If the chance of getting a sample proportion at least as small as the observed value is unlikely, one concludes that the hypothesis $P = 0.50$

is incorrect, i.e., that P is actually less than the hypothetical value of 0.50. If, on the other hand, random sampling variation would often produce a sample proportion at least as small as that observed, there is no reason to doubt the truth of the hypothesis, $P = 0.50$. The conclusion, then, hinges on how frequently a sample proportion at least as small as 0.35 would be excepted if P is really 0.50. If a sample proportion this small or smaller would occur only rarely, this constitutes evidence against the hypothesis that $P = 0.50$; otherwise, the hypothesis that $P = 0.50$ is accepted.

The following calculation shows, for example, how often a sample proportion this small or smaller would be expected if $P = 0.50$. In the introduction to sampling, it was shown that the sampling distribution of p will be approximately normal with a mean of $P = 0.50$. If, as hypothesized, $P = 0.50$, the standard error of estimate would be:

$$s_p = \sqrt{\frac{pq}{n}}$$

$$= \sqrt{\frac{0.50(0.50)}{100}}$$

$$= 0.05$$

where

s = standard error of estimate.

p = percentage of universe with characteristic under study.

q = 100 percent minus p.

n = size of sample.

Since the observed sample percentage ($p = 0.35$) is three standard errors below the hypothesized mean,

$$\frac{0.50 - 0.35}{0.05} = 3$$

the chance of a sample proportion at least this small is approximately 1 in 1,000. (Tables of the area under the normal probability curve show that the probability of an observation more than three standard errors below the mean is about 13/10,000.)

Confronted with this result, the ABC Corporation would almost certainly conclude that Lucky Pup did not have distribution in 50 percent of the stores. It is possible, however, that the observed value of 35 percent could have been obtained even though the real distribution was 50 percent. The analysis given for Example A is illustrative of the kind of reasoning used in problems of this general sort. It is not clear where the line should be drawn between differences which are "significant" and those which are not. The decision on this point is often somewhat arbitrary in marketing research; the choice should take account of the risk involved.

Discussion of example B. The 48 percent who had heard of Brand X *before* the advertising campaign and the 55 percent who had heard of the brand *after* the campaign were derived from two independent samples of 100 each. The question to be answered is whether the percentage of respondents who had heard of the brand *after* the advertising (55) is significantly greater than the percentage of respondents who had heard of it *before* the advertising commenced (48). The standard error of the difference formula for the difference between two percentages is

$$s_{\text{difference}} = \sqrt{s_a^2 + s_b^2}$$

where

$s_{\text{difference}}$ = standard error of difference.

s_a = standard error of percentage A.

s_b = standard error of percentage B.

The standard error of a percentage is determined by the formula

$$s = \sqrt{\frac{pq}{n}}.$$

Substituting in the previous formula,

$$s_{\text{difference}} = \sqrt{\left(\sqrt{\frac{p_a q_a}{n_a}}\right)^2 + \left(\sqrt{\frac{p_b q_b}{n_b}}\right)^2}$$

$$= \sqrt{\frac{p_a q_a}{n_a} + \frac{p_b q_b}{n_b}}$$

$$= \sqrt{\frac{0.55 \times 0.45}{100} + \frac{0.48 \times 0.52}{100}}$$

$$= \sqrt{\frac{0.2475}{100} + \frac{0.2496}{100}} = \sqrt{\frac{0.4971}{100}}$$

$$= \sqrt{0.004971} = 0.0705 = 7.05\%.$$

When the difference between the two percentages is divided by this value, $(55\% - 48\%)/7.05\% = 1$ approximately, i.e., the difference between the two sample percentages is about equal to one standard error of the difference. The probability of such a difference occurring by chance, even though no real difference existed, is 32 out of 100. Thus, it is concluded that the difference between the before and after measurements is not very significant, i.e., the observed difference could easily have occurred as a result of chance.

Bayesian analytical approach

In Chapter 5 some discussion of the Bayesian approach to decision theory was presented in the context of problem formulation. This approach also provides an effective way of looking at the analysis of data. The following is a simplified example which gives a general idea of the concept involved.

Using the above hypothetical example of ABC Corporation considering the purchase of Lucky Pup Dog Food, make the following assumptions:

1. There are 50,000 grocery stores in the market area which are potential outlets for the dog food.
2. The average store handling Lucky Pup Dog Food buys $500 of the brand per year, providing the manufacturer with a margin beyond variable costs of $50.
3. ABC Corporation projects an annual margin beyond variable cost of $1,000,000 as the minimum which it requires to make the purchase profitable.

On the basis of the above assumptions, if Lucky Pup is handled by 20,000 grocery stores (40 percent of those in the area), the return to ABC beyond variable costs would be $1,000,000, the break-even point. Each store beyond 20,000 which handled the product would provide, on the average, $50 in annual profit. The conditional payoff from buying the Lucky Pup brand is stated by the equation

$$CPO = (\$50 \times 50,000p) - \$1,000,000$$

where CPO = conditional payoff and p = percentage of stores stocking Lucky Pup.

If ABC Corporation buys Lucky Pup and if $p = 40$ percent, the CPO $= 0$; if $p =$ more than 40 percent, the CPO will increase by $25,000 for each percentage point p is above 40 percent. Similarly, for each percentage point p is below 40 percent, the CPO will become negative by $25,000. If ABC does not buy Lucky Pup the CPO will be zero.

There is another way, however, to look at this problem. Suppose $p = 50$ percent, but ABC does not buy Lucky Pup; the CPO would be zero, but the opportunity to make a profit of $250,000 would have been missed. Such a loss may be called a conditional opportunity loss (COL) from not buying Lucky Pup, and may be stated by the equation COL (from not purchasing) = [$50 × 50,000 $(p - 40)$] when p exceeds 40; if p is less than 40 there is no opportunity loss from not purchasing Lucky Pup.

Now suppose that ABC decides to conduct a survey of 20 stores to determine what percentage of them handles Lucky Pup. As has been seen in the sampling chapters, such a survey is unlikely to give the precise percentage that exists in nature, but is more likely to give an answer fairly close to the true state of nature than one that is widely different from the true state. Before making the survey, the researcher should decide what percentage in the sample stores he will accept as sufficient evidence to warrant recommending purchase of Lucky Pup by ABC. The researcher might decide that if 50 percent or more of the sample stores handled Lucky Pup, he would recommend purchase of the company. Further suppose that in fact only 30 percent of all the stores in the market area handle Lucky Pup (of course, this true state of nature is not known, or no problem would exist). What is the probability that 50 percent or more of the sample will stock Lucky Pup? The problem may be summarized as follows: if 30 percent of the stores in the universe handle Lucky Pup and if a random sample of 20 stores is taken from this universe, what is the probability that 50 percent or more of the stores in the sample will have Lucky Pup?

The answer can be calculated from the binomial formula, but is more easily read from prepared tables.[10] In this case, the tables show the probability of finding 50 percent or more of the sample stocking the dog food would be only 0.048.

If the true state of nature were 40 percent, what would be the probability of finding 50 percent or more of the stores handling the product? The answer is 0.245. On the other hand, suppose the true proportion of stores stocking the dog food were 60 percent. What is the probability that a sample of 20 stores would show 50 percent or more stocking Lucky Pup? The table shows 0.873.

The conditional expected loss from these different circumstances is shown in Table 12-6.

Notice that the expected losses are of two types—loss from buying the Lucky Pup firm if the true percentage of stores stocking the product is 30 percent (loss = $12,000), and loss (opportunity loss) from *not* buying the firm if the true percentage is 50 percent (loss = $103,000) or

---

[10] Tables of cumulative binomial distribution are found in most statistics books. See, for example, Robert Schlaifer, *Analysis of Decisions under Uncertainty* (New York: McGraw-Hill Book Co., 1967).

TABLE 12–6. Conditional expected loss if decision to purchase Lucky Pup firm (based on sample of 20 stores showing 50% or more of stores stocking dog food)

Sample outcome (a)	Decision (b)	Conditional payoff or loss (c)	Probability of sample outcome occurring (d)	Expected value or loss (c × d) (e)
If true percentage is 30 percent				
$P_s \geqslant 50\%$	Buy firm	− $250,000	0.048	− $ 12,000
$P_s < 50\%$	Not buy	$ 0	0.952	$ 0
If true percentage is 40 percent				
$P_s \geqslant 50\%$	Buy firm	$ 0	0.245	$ 0
$P_s < 50\%$	Not buy	$ 0	0.755	$ 0
If true percentage is 50 percent				
$P_s \geqslant 50\%$	Buy firm	$250,000	0.588	$147,000
$P_s < 50\%$	Not buy	− $250,000	0.412	− $103,000
If true percentage is 60 percent				
$P_s \geqslant 50\%$	Buy firm	$500,000	0.873	$436,000
$P_s < 50\%$	Not buy	− $500,000	0.127	− $ 63,000

60 percent (loss = $63,000). It will be desirable for the next part of the discussion to concentrate on the expected losses, ignoring the expected values from "correct" decisions. The objective will be to find the decision rule which will reduce the expected loss to the lowest level.

Similar calculations to those shown in Table 12–6 could be made using other possible decision rules, e.g., recommend buying the firm if the proportion of the sample stocking the item is 45, 55, or 60 percent. Calculations for each of these decision rules could be developed following the same pattern as shown in Table 12–6. Different expected losses would, of course, be found.

To determine which decision rule is the best of those available, it is necessary to establish a probability distribution of the various "states of nature" that could exist. The decision maker must do this based on his experience and any other pertinent information which he may have. Obviously, the number of different possible states of nature is very large if fine differences are drawn, such as 41.0793 percent and 41.0794 percent. To keep the problem within manageable proportions and to simplify the illustration, it is assumed that the decision maker in this case believes the true state of nature (the percentage of stores stocking Lucky Pup) is someplace between 30 percent and 60 percent and that the probability of each of 7 points within that range is as follows:

State of nature (S_x)	Probability of existence
30%	0.05
35	0.15
40	0.40
45	0.20
50	0.10
55	0.05
60	0.05

In Table 12–7 these "prior probabilities" are shown in column *b*. In the next four columns four decision rules are shown, with the probability that each will lead to a wrong decision, i.e., a decision that will result in a loss. Any decision to buy Lucky Pup will be wrong if the percentage of stores stocking Lucky Pup is below 40 percent, and any decision not to buy the firm will be wrong if the percentage of stores stocking the brand is over 40 percent. The four decision rules to be studied are:

Rule #	*Buy Lucky Pup if percentage of stores in sample stocking the brand is equal to or exceeds*
1	45%
2	50
3	55
4	60

Table 12–8 shows the situations in which losses will be incurred by buying Lucky Pup and those in which the loss will be the opportunity loss from not buying. This table should be read as follows: if the true state of nature (i.e., stores stocking Lucky Pup) is 30 percent and the firm is purchased, a loss of $250,000 will be incurred; if the true state of nature is 55 percent and the firm is not purchased, an opportunity loss of $375,000 will be incurred.

Referring to Table 12–7, it will be seen in column *c* that decision rule #1 would lead to a probability of 0.113 that a wrong decision would be made and the firm would be purchased (probability of 0.113 that a sample of 20 stores would show 45 percent or more stocking Lucky Pup even if the universe percentage were only 30 percent). Similarly, column *e* shows that decision rule #3 would have a probability of 0.444 of providing a wrong decision in leading ABC not to purchase the dog food company (probability of 0.444 that less than 55 percent of the 20 sample stores will be stocking Lucky Pup even if the universe percentage is 55 percent).

The question then arises: how likely is it that a given state of nature exists *and* that a given decision rule leads to a wrong decision? This is the joint probability of the two and is determined by multiplying the two probabilities. The results for each of the four decision rules under

TABLE 12–7. Calculation of joint probability of opportunity loss incurred by selected decision rules (Lucky Pup example)*

State of nature (S_x) (a)	Prior probability S_x exists (b)	Probability that sample result will cause opportunity loss if decision rule followed				Joint probability that S_x exists and that sample result will cause opportunity loss if decision rule followed			
		Rule #1 (c)	Rule #2 (d)	Rule #3 (e)	Rule #4 (f)	Rule #1 (b × c)	Rule #2 (b × d)	Rule #3 (b × e)	Rule #4 (b × f)
30%	0.05	0.113	0.048	0.017	0.005	0.006	0.002	0.001	†
35	0.15	0.238	0.122	0.053	0.020	0.036	0.018	0.008	0.003
40	0.40	0	0	0	0	0	0	0	0
45	0.20	0.414	0.591	0.751	0.869	0.083	0.118	0.150	0.174
50	0.10	0.252	0.412	0.588	0.748	0.025	0.041	0.059	0.075
55	0.05	0.112	0.249	0.444	0.586	0.006	0.012	0.022	0.029
60	0.05	0.043	0.127	0.245	0.404	0.002	0.006	0.012	0.020

* Joint probability is probability that a given state of nature exists and that the sample will lead to a decision resulting in a loss.
† Less than .0005.

TABLE 12–8. Loss incurred with given decisions if various states of nature exist (Lucky Pup example)

State of nature	Loss if decision is to	
	Buy	Not buy[b]
30%	$250,000	$ 0
35	125,000	0
40	0	0
45	[a]	125,000
50	[a]	250,000
55	[a]	375,000
60	[a]	500,000

[a] A profit would be obtained.
[b] When a "loss" results from not buying, it is an opportunity loss.

consideration and for each of the states of nature considered are shown in the last four columns of Table 12–7.

Data from Tables 12–7 and 12–8 can now be combined to determine the expected loss incurred with each of the four decision rules. This is shown in Table 12–9.

The results shown in Table 12–9 indicate that the lowest expected loss would be incurred if decision rule #1 were followed, i.e., buy Lucky Pup firm if the sample percentage of stores stocking the dog food brand is 45 percent or more. The pattern of the results suggests that a better decision rule might be at a percentage below the 45 percent level. Additional calculations would be necessary to check this out. The procedure provides no direct calculation of the "best" decision rule.

Obviously, the above example is greatly simplified as compared to normal business problems. Many additional states of nature could have been considered; other decision rules could have been tested; the basing of the decision on the percentage of stores stocking the brand is too simple. But the procedure illustrates how to formulate a decision when the executive has some opinions based on his experience and then adds some new information. This form of decision making is done all the time, with no clear understanding as to how the old and new information are combined. The procedure described here provides a formal analytical method for handling this type of situation.

Chi square analysis.   Some of the proceding material dealt with the significance of a difference where only two statistics were involved. Chi square analysis enables the researcher to determine whether a significant difference exists between two or more *sets* of data. The approach here is similar to the earlier discussion on significance tests, that is, the objective is to determine the maximum differences that normally could be expected to occur because of sampling variations. If the measure of difference falls within the acceptable sampling variation limits, then the differences are attributed to sampling. But if the measure falls outside these limits, then the differences are thought to be real.

For example, assume the problem of determining whether a real difference exists between the magazine reading preferences of New York City males versus all other males. The data are given in Table 12–10.

What is needed is a measure of relative variation between the two sets of data. This measure is Chi square (X^2). If the magazine reading preferences of New York City males and all other males were the same, then the proportion of males preferring any specific magazine would be expected to be the ratio of all males preferring the magazine to the total size of the sample. The proportion of either New York City males or all other males preferring magazine A, then,

TABLE 12–9. Expected losses from selected decision rules (Lucky Pup example)

State of nature (a)	Loss if wrong decision made (taken from Table 12–8) (b)	Joint probability that S_x exists and that wrong decision made (taken from Table 12–7)				Expected losses			
		Decision rule #1 (c)	Decision rule #2 (d)	Decision rule #3 (e)	Decision rule #4 (f)	Decision rule #1 (b × c)	Decision rule #2 (b × d)	Decision rule #3 (b × e)	Decision rule #4 (b × f)
30%	$250,000	0.006	0.002	0.001	0	$ 1,500	$ 500	$ 250	$ 0
35	125,000	0.036	0.018	0.008	0.003	4,500	2,250	1,000	375
40	0	0	0	0	0	0	0	0	0
45	125,000	0.083	0.118	0.150	0.174	10,375	14,750	18,700	21,750
50	250,000	0.025	0.041	0.059	0.075	6,250	10,250	14,750	18,750
55	375,000	0.006	0.012	0.022	0.029	2,250	4,500	8,250	10,875
60	500,000	0.002	0.006	0.012	0.020	1,000	3,000	6,000	10,000
Total						$25,875	$32,250	$48,950	$61,750

TABLE 12–10. Magazine reading preferences of New York City males and all other males

Magazines	N.Y. City males	All other males	Total
A	60	280	340
B	40	170	210
C	30	40	70
All others	70	310	380
Total	200	800	1,000

would be expected to be 340/1,000; magazine B, 210/1,000; etc. In this manner, the number of all other males preferring magazine A in the sample would be estimated at 340/1,000 × 800; and the number of New York City males preferring magazine A would be estimated at 340/1,000 × 200. These data appear in Table 12–11.

TABLE 12–11. Expected proportions of New York City males and all other males regarding magazine reading preferences

Magazine	N.Y. City males	All other males	Total
A	340/1000 × 200 = 68	340/1000 × 800 = 272	340
B	210/1000 × 200 = 42	210/1000 × 800 = 168	210
C	70/1000 × 200 = 14	70/1000 × 800 = 56	70
All other	380/1000 × 200 = 76	380/1000 × 800 = 304	380
Total	200	800	1,000

The Chi square test is devised to determine the probability of occurrence of the actual values obtained (Table 12–10), if the "expected" values were those shown in Table 12–11. The value of Chi square is computed from the formula

$$X^2 = \sum_{i=1}^{s} \left[\frac{(X_i - \theta_i)^2}{\theta_i} \right].$$

The subscript i denotes the ith cell in a table where there is a total of $i = 1, 2, \ldots, s$ cells. (In Table 12–10, $s = 8$ cells.) X_i is the observed value for cell i, and θ_i is the computed or expected value for cell i.[11]

The value of X^2 in the problem at hand is computed as follows:

$$X^2 = \frac{(60 - 68)^2}{68} + \frac{(40 - 42)^2}{42} + \frac{(30 - 14)^2}{14} + \frac{(70 - 76)^2}{76}$$

---

[11] Robert Ferber, *Statistical Techniques in Marketing Research* (New York: McGraw-Hill Book Co., Inc., 1949), pp. 257–79. For the application of Chi square see R. Clay Sprowls, "Sample Sizes in Chi-Square Tests for Measuring Advertising Effectiveness," *Journal of Marketing Research* (February, 1964), pp. 60–64.

$$+ \frac{(280 - 272)^2}{272} + \frac{(170 - 168)^2}{168} + \frac{(40 - 56)^2}{56} + \frac{(310 - 304)^2}{304}$$

$$= \frac{64}{68} + \frac{4}{42} + \frac{256}{14} + \frac{36}{76} + \frac{64}{272} + \frac{4}{168} + \frac{256}{56} + \frac{36}{304}$$

$$= \frac{16}{17} + \frac{2}{21} + \frac{128}{7} + \frac{9}{19} + \frac{4}{17} + \frac{1}{42} + \frac{32}{7} + \frac{9}{51}$$

$$= 24.799.$$

In a 4×2 contingency table (e.g., Table 12–10) the values of all eight cells are determined automatically when the values of three cells in a column are fixed, hence in this illustration three degrees of freedom are involved. A statement is now needed of the probability associated with a X^2 of this size with three degrees of freedom. Fisher has worked out such associations and, using his table, one gets a probability of less than 0.01 that a value of X^2 larger than 24.799 would occur as a result of random variations. Thus, one can say that the differences in magazine readership preferences between New York City males and all other males are significant.

Analysis of variance

Analysis of variance is a technique for determining what each of various sources of variation contributes to a total variance. It is an important technique to use in analyzing the results obtained from experiments. Its purpose is ". . . to test the statistical significance of differences among *average responses* caused by the control variables, after making allowance for influence on responses caused by uncontrolled variables. The label *analysis of variance* is appropriate because if the mean responses of the test objects are different *among* treatments, then the variance among groups will exceed the (independently computed) within group variance."[12] By using an analysis of variance, one can determine the effects of such factors as, for example, the age of housewife, occupation of husband, total family income, and presence of children on the purchase of brand X detergent. Or one can determine the effects of such factors in sample design as region, city size, and within-county sampling rates.

An example in which four different advertising copy platforms were tested for the same product will illustrate the use of analysis of variance.[13] Each was tried in each of five cities with only one approach being

---

[12] Ronald E. Frank and Paul E. Green, *Quantitative Methods in Marketing* (Englewood Cliffs, N.J.: Prentice-Hall, Inc., 1967), p. 33.

[13] Gwyn Collins, "Analysis of Variance," *Journal of Advertising Research*, Vol. 1 (December, 1961), pp. 40–46.

used in one city at a time. In terms of unit sales (overall average sale of 49.5 units in all cities), the results given in Table 12–12 were obtained.[14] The concern here is with measuring the effect of the cities and the effect of the copy approaches on the total variance. A measure is needed of the between-cities variation and of the between-copy approaches variation. The analysis is performed by taking the sum of the squared differences between each number and the average of the set and

TABLE 12–12. Unit sales of product X by city and by copy platform

Copy platform	City				
	A	B	C	D	E
I	62	46	56	55	37
II	59	41	59	48	33
III	58	40	61	51	32
IV	63	43	58	54	34

dividing by the number of independent members in the sets (degrees of freedom). In the "between cities" calculation, compute the average for set (row I)

$$\frac{(62 + 46 + 56 + 55 + 37)}{5} = 51.25.$$

Square the deviations of each number in this set (row) from its average, $(62 - 51.25)^2 + (46 - 51.25)^2 + (56 - 51.25)^2$, etc. Repeat this procedure for all four sets (rows) and sum the four totals together. A similar procedure would be followed for the between-copy approaches except that calculations would be made on the column basis. The results would be as follows:

Variation source	Sum of squares	Degrees of freedom	Variance estimate*
Between cities	1990	4	497.50
Between copy platforms	35.8	3	11.93
Residual	59.2	12	4.93
Total	2025	19	514.36

* Obtained by dividing column 1 by column 2.

The total variance estimate (514.36) was obtained by summing the deviations of each number from the overall average of 49.5. The residual variance estimate (4.93) was computed by subtracting the sum of the two estimates from this total. The F ratio is now obtained by dividing the variance estimate between cities (column 3) by the variance estimate

---

[14] *Ibid.*

of the residual. Similarly the variance estimate from between copy approaches is divided by the residual. By consulting the probability distribution table used in analysis of variance problems (the F distribution table), it is determined that an F ratio of 100.9 (497.5 ÷ 4.93), the probability of the variance between cities occurring by chance is less than one in a thousand. With an F ratio of 2.42, the variance between copy approaches could have occurred by chance about one time in ten. This would lead to the conclusion that the copy approach did not have a statistically significant influence on sales, but that cities did.

EXPLAINING WHY DIFFERENCES EXIST

Cross tabulations

Causal analysis requires the use of cross tabulations which represent an attempt to explain certain relationships through the introduction of additional factors. Thus, cross tabulations should be regarded as further attempts to discover those factors which influence the overall results. They represent an extension of one-dimensional tabulation which merely shows a distribution of a variable or an attribute between groups. For example, assume a recent survey obtained the distribution of answers to the question, *"Did you go to see any university football games during the last season?"* shown in Table 12–13.

TABLE 12–13. Attendance at university football games

Attendance	Percent of respondents
Yes	56
No	44
Total	100

This distribution of answers raises the question of why the 56 percent went to see a game—or why did the 44 percent *not* go to see a game? What factors determined whether a person did or did not go to see a game? To try and answer this question, additional tabulations are required; for example, if the attendance data are broken down by the educational level of the respondents, Table 12–14 is obtained.

TABLE 12–14. Attendance at university football games by educational level of respondents

Attendance	Years of formal education completed	
	13 years or more	Less than 13 years
Yes	60%	52%
No	40	48
Total	100	100

This table shows that the proportion of those attending a university football game is larger among individuals who have completed one or more years of college than it is among individuals who have not completed one or more years of college. Thus, education appears to be one factor determining the attendance at university football games.

Too frequently, the researcher attempts to clarify the analysis by using other factors as the basis for alternative tabulations; for example, in the football attendance analysis an income breakdown *in addition to* an educational breakdown. Such alternative tabulations may be misleading. Each additional factor should be introduced not as an alternative to, but simultaneously with, the other factors so that interrelationships of the factors can be studied. An example will illustrate this point. Assume that by a simple cross tabulation the ownership of electric razors is found to be substantially more frequent among men forty years of age and under than among men over forty.

TABLE 12–15. Ownership of electric razors by age

	40 & under	*Over 40*	*Total*
Own electric razor	20%	10%	15%
Don't own electric razor	80	90	85
Total	100	100	100

Next assume that the analyst thought of income as an additional factor which might have an influence on the ownership of an electric razor. Rather than repeat the procedure which resulted in the data presented in Table 12–15 (except using income in lieu of age), the better procedure would be to break by two or more groups within income groups. If two income groups were used, a total of eight cells would result. Table 12–16 shows these tabulations:

TABLE 12–16. Ownership of electric razors by age and income

	Income $5,000 & over		*Income under $5,000*	
	40 & under	*Over 40*	*40 & under*	*Over 40*
Own electric razor	30%	15%	10%	5%
Don't own electric razor	70	85	90	95
Total	100%	100%	100%	100%

Table 12–16 presents the relationship of age and ownership for those individuals with an annual income of $5,000 and over and for those individuals with an annual income of less than $5,000. These additional breakdowns (as contrasted to those shown in Table 12–15) show that there is a greater correlation (of age and ownership) for those with a higher income than for those with a lower income. Thus, the results of the

initial cross tabulation (which showed age and ownership) have been refined.

Cross tabulations—valid and spurious explanations. Often the use of an additional factor will explain the results of a simple cross tabulation. For example, a simple cross tabulation showed that a larger proportion of male drivers have an automobile accident than female drivers. This finding seemed contrary to the general belief that a male driver is better than a female driver. By adding a third factor—number of miles driven per year—the results shown in Table 12–17 are obtained.

TABLE 12–17. Automobile accidents of male and female drivers by number of miles driven

	Male drivers		Female drivers	
	Drove more than 1,000 miles	Drove 1,000 miles or less	Drove more than 1,000 miles	Drove 1,000 miles or less
Had at least one accident while driving	52%	25%	52%	25%
Never had an accident	48	75	48	75
Total	100%	100%	100%	100%
No. cases	(5,010)	(2,070)	(1,915)	(5,035)

Source: Zeisel, *op. cit.,* p. 192.

The contents of Table 12–17 show that the relationship between sex and accident rate has, in effect, disappeared since for drivers who drove approximately the same distance, there is no difference between men and women. But drivers who "drive more" have a greater chance of having an accident.[15]

A spurious relationship can be illustrated by reference to the illustration dealing with attendance at university football games. If the attendance data are broken down by multiple television set ownership, the results presented in Table 12–18 are obtained.

TABLE 12–18. Attendance at university football games by TV ownership

	Multiple TV set ownership	
Attendance	Owning more than one set	Owning one set
Yes	60%	52%
No	40	48
Total	100%	100%

This table shows that the proportion of attendance is greater among those owning more than one television set than it is among those owning only

---

[15] Zeisel, *op. cit.,* pp. 192–95.

one. Assuming these differences to be significant, this appears to be a spurious relationship, since it does not seem logical to attribute causality to the ownership of more than one TV set. It would likely be hypothesized that a third variable might be operating to affect both multiset ownership and attendance. Of course, it may be that only a combination of several other factors will explain the results. For simplicity, assume that the results can be explained in terms of income. The data from Table 12–18 would be broken down by income as shown in Table 12–19.

TABLE 12–19. Attendance at university football games by TV ownership and income

	Income over $10,000		Income $10,000 and under	
Attendance	Multiple TV set ownership	Single TV set ownership	Multiple TV set ownership	Single TV set ownership
Yes	70%	65%	40%	38%
No	30	35	60	62
Total	100%	100%	100%	100%

By controlling for income, the relationship between multiple television set ownership and football attendance is at least partially eliminated. Among persons with an income of over $10,000 (or among those having an income of less than $10,000) there are but slight differences in attendance between those having more than one television set and those not having more than one television set. Among the higher-income persons, attendance is high for both types of TV owners, and among lower-income persons attendance is low for such subgroups. It is likely that other variables may also help to explain attendance. For example, whether the respondent attended a given university may be correlated with football attendance and, if such information is available, it could be tested for its effect on football attendance. The procedure to follow in using additional variables would be the same as illustrated above. Obviously the tables will become more complicated and the data more difficult to analyze as additional dimensions are added, and the size of sample necessary to get meaningful numbers in the subgroups will become quite large.

Value of causal analysis. While cross tabulations do not reveal absolute causal relationships, they help explain relationships. The introduction of a third variable may confirm or reject the original relationship. In either case, the analyst has learned more about the survey data and is in a better position to proceed with his investigation.

The introduction of additional variables for analysis can continue for as many variables as there are data, providing the sample is large enough so that the "breakdowns" remain meaningful. Therefore, the analyst must use his time and money cautiously just to tabulate the more meaningful relationships. It is often a temptation to run numerous cross tabulations because theoretically they might be of interest. The objectives of the study must always be kept in mind in specifying what cross tabulations to run. The analyst must be careful to avoid spurious relationships. Often, additional cross tabulations cannot be made to check causality, and the analyst has to rely on common sense and experience in accepting or rejecting a relationship between two or more variables.

Setting up cross tabulations. In constructing these tabulations, the analyst must decide which way to run the percentages, that is, percentages may run either up and down (vertical) or across (horizontal). "There is a simple rule we can often use when we face this problem. It can usually be employed when one of the two factors we are cross-tabulating may be considered as the cause of the distribution of the other factor. It is the rule that the percentages should be computed in the direction of the causal factor. It is not a question of which factor is the cause of the other one, but which factor we wish to consider as affecting the percentage distribution which the other factor assumes."[16]

An illustration of this rule is contained in Tables 12–20 and 12–21, which deal with the relationship of ownership of electric razors with age. Table 12–20 reveals the proportion in each age group owning an electric razor. In the younger group, this proportion is 1 out of 5 while in the

TABLE 12–20. Ownership of electric razors by age (percentages run vertically)

Group	Under 40 years		40 years and over		Total	
	Number	Percent	Number	Percent	Number	Percent
Own electric razor	40	20	20	10	60	15
Own other type	160	80	180	90	340	85
Total	200	100	200	100	400	100

older group the ratio is 1 in 10. Table 12–21, on the other hand, reveals something different. It shows that, of those owning an electric razor, 67 percent are under forty years of age and 33 percent are over forty—or a ratio of 2 to 1. In this illustration, the first table is more meaningful, since it clearly reveals the effect of age on ownership of types of razors. However, something was gained by running percentages in both directions. Before deciding which way to set up a table the analyst should ask himself what he is trying to reveal.

Naturally in setting up cross tabulations the analyst must make certain that the differences (if any) are significant. This means that he must use

---

[16] *Ibid.,* p. 24.

TABLE 12–21. Ownership of electric razors by age (percentages run horizontally)

Group	Under 40 years		40 years and over		Total	
	Number	Percent	Number	Percent	Number	Percent
Own electric razor	40	67	20	33	60	100
Own other type	160	47	180	53	340	100
Total	200	50	200	50	400	100

the various statistical procedures discussed earlier. The determination of why differences exist is tied to whether the differences are significant. This fact merely indicates that the analysis procedure does not consist of a neat series of mutually exclusive steps which can be followed automatically. Rather, it consists of a constant searching for possible answers to a series of questions, of arranging and rearranging the data, and of applying statistical tests to observed differences.

Correlation analysis

Correlation analysis is a technique which provides a way of determining the degree of linear association which exists between a dependent variable (e.g., sales) and one or more independent variables (e.g., advertising and price). As such it is an extension of the discussion dealing with cross tabulations and analysis of variance. Correlation analysis is important in such areas as sales forecasting, determining the degree of relationship between various household characteristics and purchase behavior, and what factors are most useful in stratifying a sample. The availability of computers to do the laborious calculations involved has led to wide use of correlation analysis in recent years.

The simple correlation coefficient (r) is the measure of the degree of linear association existing between two variables and always has a value ranging between minus one and plus one. A coefficient of plus or minus one means that one variable explains all the variation in the other variable. A coefficient of zero means that neither variable explains the variation in the other. In linear correlation, a unit change in one variable is associated with a constant change in the other variable which extends over the whole range of observations. This means the relationship can be plotted in a straight line. This is an assumption used in much correlation work, and will be used here. Nonlinear relationships are much more complex and are beyond the scope of this book.

It is best to start most correlation problems by constructing a scatter diagram, which is nothing more than a graphic presentation of the relationship between variables. In Figure 12–1, an obviously high positive correlation exists between two variables (simple correlation). While a chart of this type tells the researcher of a high correlation between the variables (X and Y), it does not give him an accurate measure of the relationship. The coefficient of correlation does this.

FIGURE 12–1. Illustration of high correlation

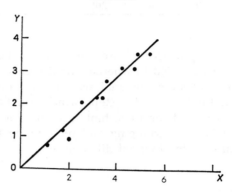

A coefficient of correlation is nothing more than the ratio of two standard deviations. For each value of the X variable (see Figure 12–1), a value of Y is calculated by finding the value of Y that corresponds with the intersection of the X variable with the graphic correlation line. The standard deviation of these calculated values of Y is computed and becomes the numerator of the ratio. The denominator standard deviation is that of the observed values of Y in the sample.[17] The formula for obtaining the coefficient of correlation is therefore $r = \dfrac{\Sigma XY}{\sqrt{\Sigma X^2 \ \Sigma Y^2}}$ where X and Y represent the deviations of the variables from their means. In an attempt to measure the effect of advertising on sales, one firm computed the correlation between sales of hair spray by county with advertising expenditures by county. Other firms have measured correlation of sales with population, number of cars, number of retail stores, value added by manufacturing, and numerous other variables.

Multiple correlation. Multiple correlation is concerned with the relationship among three or more variables. The objective is to explain the variation in one of these variables, the dependent variable, in terms of two or more independent variables. The principle behind multiple correlation is essentially the same as that for simple correlation ". . . namely, to fit a regression curve (really a surface) between the observed relation-

---

[17] Ferber, *op. cit.*, p. 347.

ships and to measure the correlation between the variables on the basis of the ratio of the variance explained or eliminated by the regression line to the total, original variance in the dependent variable."[18] The formula for computing coefficients of multiple correlation is available in most statistics books.

The use of multiple correlation is illustrated by a study of 492 households to determine the degree of association between a household's proneness for purchasing private brands within a variety of product classes and fourteen socioeconomic characteristics, plus the proportion of the household's total grocery purchases made at each of the five major grocery chains in the Chicago Metropolitan Area. The dependent variable (Y) was the proportion of the product class purchases accounted for by private brands (PBP). In the case of regular coffee the coefficient of correlation, r, was 0.46 and the coefficient of determination, r^2, was 0.21, i.e., only 21 percent of the variation in the dependent variable (PBP) was associated linearly with *all* the independent variables.[19]

It may also be useful to know the relationship between a specific independent variable and the dependent variable with all the other independent variables held constant. This enables the analyst to determine which of the various independent variables has the greatest "effect" on the dependent variable. The measure for describing such a relationship is called the partial correlation coefficient. In the study cited above, the chain at which the household shopped was more important than any other independent variable in affecting the household's private brand proneness. The partial correlation coefficient which relates the PBP and the proportion of purchases made in A & P stores was 0.39. This means that 15.2 (0.39^2) percent of the variance in PBP with respect to regular coffee could be accounted for by the variation in the degree to which households shopped in A & P stores, holding all the other independent variables constant.[20]

Dangers in correlation analysis. Of the pitfalls inherent in the use of correlation analysis, the first, and foremost, is the possibility of assuming that correlation implies a causal relationship when, in fact, correlation merely shows the degree to which variables vary together. Such an "error" is termed a spurious correlation. The second danger is that factors other than those introduced into the analysis are correlated with those introduced and may even better explain the relationship.

Regression analysis. A correlation coefficient is a summary measure

---

[18] *Ibid.*, pp. 346–79. More details on multiple correlation techniques including the graphic method are given.

[19] Ronald E. Frank and Harper W. Boyd, Jr., "Are Private-Brand-Prone Grocery Product Customers Really Different?" *Journal of Advertising Research* (December, 1965), pp. 27–35.

[20] *Ibid.*

which indicates the degree of linear relationship. It does not permit one to predict the average change in a dependent variable associated with a change in the value of the independent variable(s). To determine the value of the dependent variable which will be associated with a given value of the independent variable, a regression equation is needed. Multiple and partial regression analyses have five important values.[21]

1. To determine the relationship between one variable and a criterion factor while simultaneously removing the influence of other factors. Example: What is the relationship between family size and the sale of Scotties when the influence of income, size of city, availability, and price are eliminated?
2. To determine which of a set of factors is most related to the criterion factor. Example: Which of the following factors is most closely related to the sale of Ford cars: number of Ford dealers in the market, size of city, effective buying income, or percent of families owning a car?
3. To "match" two groups so that they are equivalent in important respects. Example: Differences between viewers and nonviewers in terms of ages, family size, previous buying habits, etc. can be eliminated when studying the relationship between viewing and buying of the advertised product.
4. To formulate a predictive equation which allows for the calculation of expected levels of the criterion factor, given any combination of values of the independent factors. Example: Estimates can be made of probable sales levels of Kodak cameras in various markets, knowing the average income level, sales in previous years, economic conditions, etc.
5. To gain inferences about additional factors which may be related to the criterion variable. Example: By examining the cases in which actual sales for Kodak do not agree with the estimates, inferences can be made about other factors which affect camera sales.

When only two variables are involved, the regression equation is $Y = a + bX$, where Y and X are the two variables and a and b are unknown parameters; X is the independent variable and Y is the dependent variable. The problem is to find the values of a and b. This can be done by use of the graphic method where a straight line is fitted to the data by inspection (see Figure 12–1). The values of a and b are then obtained from the line (by reading off the coordinates at any two points) and substituted for Y and X in the equation which can then be solved

---

[21] Jack B. Landis, "On Methods: Multiple Regression Analysis—The Easy Way," *Journal of Advertising Research* (March, 1962), p. 36. Also see G. David Hughes, "Developing Marketing Strategy through Multiple Regression," *Journal of Marketing Research* (November, 1966), pp. 412–15.

by the method of simultaneous equations. The least squares method is a more rigorous way of obtaining the values of *a* and *b*. The mechanics involved in the use of this method can be obtained from most basic books on business statistics. The least squares method determines values of *a* and *b* which define a line such that the sum of the differences between the actual values of *Y* and the values of *Y* obtained from the regression line are zero and the sum of the squares of the deviations from the regression line are less than for any other straight line.

Regression equations enable the researcher to estimate the value of the dependent variable for any value of the independent variable. Such estimations, however, assume linearity regardless of the level of the independent or dependent variables—a difficult assumption to make many times. They also assume that the relationship will exist regardless of the level of any other independent variable. To illustrate, assume a regression equation in which dollar sales is the dependent variable while advertising expenditure is the independent variable. Further assume that the regression analysis indicates that an increase of one in advertising dollars increases sales by 0.3. This "conclusion" says, in effect, that the 0.3 increase will occur *regardless* of the change in any other variable such as price.

Discriminant analysis.   This type of analysis is designed to indicate what independent variables have the greatest effect on the dependent variable, that is, which discriminates best among a number of alternatives. An example of its use would be the attempt to find out which product characteristics have the greatest effect on product sales, and the relative importance of each characteristic. Discriminant analysis differs from the standard type of multiple regression analysis in that it deals with the independent variable on a zero or one basis, for example, will or will not buy a product. Standard multiple regression analysis deals only with measured variables such as sales or market share.[22]

Factor analysis.   Another advanced form of analysis, factor analysis, seeks to condense a large number of variables to a smaller number (without losing too much information) by investigating the *intercorrelations within* the set of variables. By enabling the researcher to eliminate variables from further analysis, factor analysis simplifies the whole analytic procedure, thereby saving both time and money. It is particularly important in effecting regression analyses.

An illustration of the use of factor analysis is found in a study to determine what attributes of a brand of coffee are most salient in explaining brand preference. A list of 14 coffee attributes was first developed through open response questioning. These were then rated by a

---

[22] For an example of the use of discriminant analysis including the computational procedures see William F. Massy, "Discriminant Analysis of Audience Characteristics," *Journal of Advertising Research* (March, 1965), pp. 39–48.

sample of 94 consumers using a 10-point scale. A factor analysis revealed that collectively four factors—comforting quality, heartiness, genuineness, and freshness—accounted for 83.3 percent of the total variance observed in the respondent's ratings of the 14 attributes. Comforting quality alone accounted for 22.9 percent of the total variance.[23]

MAKING RECOMMENDATIONS

Thus far the discussion has centered mainly around the procedures required to draw valid statistical conclusions. However, it is still necessary for these conclusions to be translated into action. Conclusions have meaning only in terms of the objectives of the study, which were formulated because of the existence of a particular problem.

How far should a researcher go in making recommendations? This question has no simple answer. The researcher's action is contingent upon a number of factors, the most important of which are his standing in the firm, what his superiors want and expect from him, his knowledge of the problem, and his knowledge of the ramifications of the recommendations. In general, it is desirable for the researcher to make recommendations, assuming he is qualified to do so. Making recommendations requires an understanding of, and appreciation for, many of the practical workaday details of a given business operation.

It is difficult to give any precise rules which, if followed, will insure the evolution of logical and precise recommendations. The problem is essentially one of logic, and a person can only develop this by experience and training. However, a few pitfalls exist which the researcher must avoid if he is to draw logical recommendations.

Facts must support recommendations

The researcher must be certain that the facts do support the recommendations. If a recommendation is based on several different pieces of evidence, it is, of course, more likely to be correct than if based on only one. It is sound research to seek out sources other than the immediate survey for evidence which will help support a given recommendation. This is not to say that one makes a recommendation and then attempts to prove it—rather, all sources of information available to the researcher should be used in arriving at recommendations.

In arriving at a given recommendation, the researcher must weigh the advantages and disadvantages of alternative recommendations. He must think through each alternative to see whether it is feasible for the

---

[23] Bishwa Nath Mukherjee, "A Factor Analysis of Some Qualitative Attributes of Coffee," *Journal of Advertising Research* (March, 1965), pp. 35–38.

company to undertake such a move, what is to be gained by taking the action, and what risk is involved. He must at all times be certain that the facts from a given survey support his recommendation—and that this recommendation is better supported than any alternative. For example, assume a study were conducted to determine the size of the audiences reached by a company's TV program and by competitors' programs. Further, assume that it was found that the company's program had a significantly lower rating than did the programs of competitors. What recommendation should be made? In this case, a recommendation that the company drop its current program and attempt to pick up another show could hardly be supported by the evidence at hand. It would be necessary to know the size of the cumulative audience for the various shows; what kinds of persons watched each program; the costs of putting on these programs; the effect of the day of the week, the hour of the day, and the popularity of the preceding program on the ratings; the availability of alternative programs; etc. Perhaps, after additional evidence was collected, it would be possible to recommend dropping the program, but such a recommendation would be unwise with just the survey data.

SUMMARY

The analysis function has been anticipated from the very inception of the study and this anticipation continues through all the research steps. Consideration of the analysis was divided into five parts: ordering the data into meaningful categories, summarizing the data contained in the categories, determining whether significant differences exist between categories, explaining "why" differences exist, and making recommendations.

The first step covers the editing, coding, and tabulation of the data. The purpose of editing is to eliminate errors in the raw data prior to coding and tabulation. This requires uniform handling of incomplete and incorrect answers. Editing instructions should be prepared carefully and the personnel assigned to this work trained thoroughly. Written editing instructions explaining how to handle each question must be prepared. Another part of the editing process consists of establishing categories for the raw data. In doing this the analyst must consider the objectives of the study. Categories must be mutually exclusive and exhaustive. Coding is the process whereby the data are assigned numerical designations so that they may more easily be fitted into the appropriate categories. Coding is necessary where machine tabulation is used.

Tabulation consists of counting the number of cases which fall into the established categories. Before tabulation can take place the plan of analysis must be thought through. A tabulation plan which specifies the precise counts to be obtained needs to be prepared. Usually the plan consists of setting up dummy tables complete with headings and stubs plus a description of the data to be included. Tabulation may be accomplished using manual or machine methods. Both possess unique advantages and disadvantages. Machine tabulation is preferable when a large number of questionnaires is involved and where cross tabulations are planned. Computers provide ways of processing vast quantities of data and performing certain mathematical operations functions at high speeds.

After the tabulation step has been completed it is necessary to determine whether any differences exist between groups and whether these differences are statistically significant. If the results from a marketing study are to be useful, they must be organized and summarized in such a way as to enable the objectives of the study to be achieved. This requires the use of those summary statistical measures which typify the group, such as the arithmetic mean and percentages, and the use of those measures which indicate dispersion, such as the standard deviation. All of these measures have their advantages and disadvantages, and the analyst must be cognizant of these in selecting the most appropriate measure to use.

Since most marketing data are collected using a sample, the reliability of the summary estimates must be determined. The standard error, confidence limits, Chi square, and analysis of variance, are common measures used for this purpose.

To determine the significance of any difference existing between a sample estimate and a similar estimate from another sample requires the use of tests of significance. Such tests indicate the probability of the difference having occurred because of random sampling variations. All these tests make use of the standard error and confidence limit concepts.

The next step in the analysis procedure consists in trying to explain "why" differences exist. This is accomplished by attempting to identify a causal relationship between two or more variables. Causal analysis requires cross tabulations. This procedure introduces one or more additional variables into the analysis by dividing the sample into subgroups. In introducing additional variables, the analyst must consider the size of the sample in the various subgroups and also be on guard against spurious correlations. Correlation analysis and regression analysis are important analytical techniques.

The last step requires that the conclusions be translated into recommendations. Whether the researcher should make recommendations depends mainly upon what his superiors want and expect from him and his knowledge of the ramifications or implications of the recommendations. In general, it is desirable for him to make recommendations, assuming he is qualified to do so.

Case 12—1. STYLE-RITE HOSIERY, INC.

Style-Rite Hosiery, Inc. had been one of the leading brands of women's stockings for many years. Sales had grown slowly and steadily to approximately $20 million. Style-Rite executives had been confirmed advertisers from the beginning, relying primarily on ads in the women's service magazines with some point-of-sale display material for retail stores. The stockings were sold in better ladies' wear and hosiery shops throughout the United States.

For a number of years the management had been interested in television advertising, but had not done any because it was difficult to show stockings in television ads without the ad's becoming objectionable to many viewers. New developments had led to the use of a type of TV commercial, called the ectoplasm commercial, in which the product could be shown without the model's actually appearing. In this way, stockings could be shown as they would be worn; how they stretched and snapped back into shape could be brought out clearly without the commercial's being offensive in any way. As a result of this development, Style-Rite management thought that it would be possible to use television as an effective advertising medium.

Before putting any of the company's annual million-dollar advertising budget in television, however, the management decided to run some experiments. They selected four cities: Houston, Kansas City, Pittsburgh, and Seattle. Two or three leading department stores in each city were selected as the points for the experiment. In September, Style-Rite stationed an interviewer in each of the stores selected for the experiment with the instructions that the interviewer was to observe the first one hundred customers entering the store to buy stockings after the time the observer took her position. The observer was to note whether or not the customer asked for Style-Rite stockings. The results are shown in Table 1. Following this set of observations, Style-Rite conducted an advertising program over local television stations. Twenty-four one-minute spot commercials were presented each week for a period of twelve weeks. Following this three-month period, another set of observations was taken in the same way. These results are also shown in Table 1.

After analyzing the data obtained from these two studies, the management found that it was unable to decide whether or not the television advertising had had any beneficial effect on sales. As a result, it was decided to run a similar test again. February and May were selected as the months, and the same testing methods were used. The only difference was that the interviewers stationed in the individual stores were told to spend four days in each store and to make as many observations as developed during that time. In some cases this was more than one hundred and in some cases less. The data from these two sets of observations are also shown in Table 1.

TABLE 1. Results of experiments to test effectiveness of TV advertising

| | First test | | | | Second test | | | |
| | September | | December | | February | | May | |
Store	Total obser-vations	Style-Rite requests*	Total obser-vations	Style-Rite requests*	Total obser-vations	Style-Rite requests	Total obser-vations	Style-Rite requests
Houston								
State Dept. Store	100	39	99	21	174	18	405	35
Hazelton & Son	100		100		96	13	144	31
Kansas City								
Andersons	100		103		412	13	264	15
E. J. Palmer	100	59	100	42	134	11	81	5
Olson & Greavy	99		100		119	27	105	25
Pittsburgh								
J. H. Myers & Co.	100	42	107	43	70	9	54	12
Edison Dept. Store	100		103		119	25	68	24
Seattle								
Sedwicks	101	23	105	39	85	34	89	34
Cranston Co.	101		100		182	24	218	21

* In the first study, the results were computed for each city, but not for each store.

In each of the two tests, Style-Rite had spent something over a quarter of a million dollars on television advertising in the four cities selected. In addition to this advertising, the regular magazine advertising was continued as it had been in the past.

On the basis of the data shown in Table 1, should the management continue television advertising on a larger scale? Should further experiments be conducted? If so, how should the experiments be designed?

Case 12—2.   A. E. STALEY MANUFACTURING COMPANY

The A. E. Staley Manufacturing Company of Decatur, Illinois, produced a varied line of industrial and consumer goods. Estimated annual sales of the company approximated $168 million. A significant portion of the company's sales was made with two popular laundry aids, Sta-Flo, a liquid starch, and Sta-Puf, a liquid fabric softener rinse. Distribution of these items was made through the conventional channel of distribution, manufacturer-wholesaler-retailer-consumer. The company also sold these items directly to large scale retailing establishments such as chain store systems, voluntary chains, and cooperatives.

The laundry aid industry was highly competitive, and to obtain the high-ranking sales position enjoyed by its brands, the Staley Company allocated over $2 million annually for advertising and promoting Sta-Flo and Sta-Puf. The media used in advertising these brands included network TV, spot radio, network radio, nationally circulated women's magazines, metropolitan newspapers, Sunday supplements, point-of-purchase material, and display signs. A major portion of the advertising budget on the Sta-Flo and Sta-Puf account consisted of sponsoring a network radio program featuring Peter Lind Hayes and his wife, Mary Healy. These two entertainers were reputed to have an extensive listener audience and, furthermore, were known as "good salesmen" for products sponsored on their programs. The sponsorship began in January and was estimated to have cost about $750,000. After it had run for nine months, the company's advertising manager asked its agency, Erwin Wasey, Ruthrauff & Ryan, Inc. to make a study evaluating the sales impact of the Hayes-Healy program. At this time neither the agency nor the client had studied any other radio or TV shows.

The study, which was done by the company's advertising agency, was designed to obtain information on the following:

1. Listenership
2. Awareness of the program's sponsor and brands

3. Product and brand usage
4. Date of first purchase of the product and brand
5. Comparison of items 1–4 above with alternative programs

In order to hold the cost of the study to a reasonable budget, information was obtained from three metropolitan areas: Chicago, Philadelphia, and Dallas. These market areas were selected as representative of strong, intermediate, and weak markets, respectively, for the brands involved. The survey was made by telephone interviews. A total of 1,716 usable responses was obtained (a total of 3,752 calls was required to obtain 1,716 usable responses). Responses were distributed as follows: Chicago 707; Philadelphia 537; Dallas 472. All phone numbers were selected at random.

Each respondent was asked about listenership to the following radio programs:

1. The Art Linkletter House Party
   A half-hour program with multiple sponsorship.
   Among the products advertised was a cosmetic lotion, BEAUTY ICE.
2. Arthur Godfrey Time
   An hour program with multiple sponsorship.
   Among the products advertised was a detergent, CHIFFON.
3. Hayes-Healy program
   A fifteen-minute program sponsored exclusively by A. E. Staley in behalf of STA-FLO, a liquid starch, and STA-PUF, a liquid fabric softener rinse.
4. Backstage Wife
   A fifteen-minute program with a single sponsor, one product, a hair shampoo, HALO.
5. One Man's Family
   A fifteen-minute program with a single sponsor, one product, a hand lotion, TRUSHAY.

In addition to listenership, the respondents were questioned about their usage of each of the products sponsored on the respective programs and also about the length of time that they had been using the particular brand identified on the program (see Exhibit 1). The survey was made in September. By this time the Hayes-Healy program with Staley sponsorship had been on the air for about nine months. Many of the other programs named in the survey had been on the air for much longer periods of time.

The findings of the telephone survey disclosed data which the agency's research department considered valuable. Thus, respondents indicated their listenership of the five programs as follows:

Listenership	Percentage
Backstage Wife (Halo)	80%
One Man's Family (Trushay)	55
Art Linkletter's House Party (Beauty Ice)	44
Arthur Godfrey Time (Chiffon)	39
Hayes-Healy Program (Sta-Flo and Sta-Puf)	18

Findings (see Tables 1–3) indicated that listeners to the Hayes-Healy program rated high in identification of the sponsor; that Sta-Flo usage among listeners was significantly higher (45 percent) than usage among nonlisteners to this program; that among Sta-Flo users a larger proportion of listeners (13 percent) had started using the product during the January–September 1958 period than had nonlisteners. The latter was considered to be evidence that the Hayes-Healy program was a factor in introducing Sta-Flo to new customers.

The survey findings provided further analyses by each of the three market areas studied: Chicago, Philadelphia, and Dallas. In all of these, the Hayes-Healy program listenership correlated highly with usage of Sta-Flo. There appeared to be no significant differences between listeners and nonlisteners as to the usage of fabric rinses. However, it was noted that 41 percent of the listeners to the Hayes-Healy program who used a fabric rinse used Sta-Puf. Also, 42 percent of the nonlisteners to this program who used a fabric rinse used Sta-Puf. (See Table 2.)

Should the agency recommend continuation of the Hayes-Healy program?

EXHIBIT 1. Radio listenership survey (Chicago)

Hello, my name is _____, and I'm doing a short survey on radio programs. . . .
(RECORD ANSWERS TO Q. 1, 2, AND 3 IN UPPER HALF OF GRID)
1. Have you ever heard (ASK FOR EACH OF THE FOLLOWING RADIO PROGRAMS LISTED AND EMPHASIZE THAT THESE ARE RADIO PROGRAMS, NOT TV SHOWS)
    a. The Art Linkletter House Party on WBBM at 2 to 2:30 in the afternoon?
    b. Arthur Godfrey Time on WBBM at 9 to 10 in the morning?
    c. The Peter Lind Hayes and Mary Healy Program at ten after eleven in the morning, following the news broadcast by Larry LeSeur?
    d. Backstage Wife on WBBM at 11:15 in the morning?
    e. One Man's Family on WMAQ at 1:30 in the afternoon?
(ASK Q. 2 AND 3 FOR EACH RADIO PROGRAM RESPONDENT SAID SHE LISTENED TO IN Q. 1)
2. About how often would you say you listen to _____?
3. What brands of products are advertised on _____?
(RECORD ANSWERS TO Q. 4 THRU 9 IN LOWER HALF OF GRID; ASK Q. 4 THRU 8 FOR EACH PRODUCT AT A TIME)
4. Do you ever use (ASK FOR EACH PRODUCT LISTED)?
(ASK Q. 5 THRU 8 ONLY FOR EACH PRODUCT THAT RESPONDENT SAID SHE USED IN Q. 4)
5. What brand of (PRODUCT) do you usually use?
6. About how often do you buy (BRAND OF EACH PRODUCT USED IN Q. 5)?

Top half of grid for Exhibit 1

NAME _____ PHONE _____ CITY _____ Not home or line busy ☐

INTERVIEWER _____

Radio program	Question 1		Question 2			Question 3
	Has heard	Hasn't heard	Almost always	Often	Sometimes	Seldom	Brands adv.
Art Linkletter House Party							
Arthur Godfrey Time							
Peter & Mary (Hayes-Healy)							
Backstage Wife							
One Man's Family							

Bottom half of grid for Exhibit 1

| Product | Q. 4—Usage | | Q. 5 | Q. 6 | Q. 7 | Q. 8 | Q. 9 |
	Yes	No	Brand	Frequency	Size	Length used	Previous brand
Liquid laundry starch							
Skin conditioner							
Liquid detergent							
Fabric softener/rinse							
Liquid hand lotion							
Shampoo							

Q. 10 Just for general classification purposes, please tell me . . . are you over 30 years old?   Over 45?

1. 30 or Under _____   2. 31-45 _____   3. Over 45 _____

Voluntary comments: _____

_____

_____

_____

EXHIBIT 1 (*Concluded*)

7. And what size do you usually buy?
8. About how long have you been using (BRAND OF EACH PRODUCT USED IN Q. 5)?
9. What brand of (PRODUCT) did you usually use before you started using (BRAND MENTIONED IN Q. 4)?
10. Just for general classification purposes, please tell me . . . are you over 30 years old? (IF OVER 30, ASK:) Are you over 45? (RECORD ANSWERS AT BOTTOM OF GRID.)

Thank you very much for your time, you've been very helpful, Mrs. _____.

TABLE 1. Brand usership of liquid starch analyzed by listenership to Hayes-Healy program

	Total		Listeners		Nonlisteners	
	No.	%	No.	%	No.	%
Total respondents	1,716	100	305	100	1,411	100
Do not use liquid starch	858	50	133	44	725	51
Do use liquid starch	858	50	172	56	686	49
Sta-Flo	280	33	76	45	204	30
Perma-Starch	57	7	6	3	51	8
Quick Elastic	17	2	1	1	16	2
Linit	105	12	19	11	86	13
Texize	11	1	4	2	7	1
Easy Monday	47	6	12	7	35	5
Blue Monday	11	1	3	2	8	1
Zippy	74	9	15	9	59	9
Thrifty	28	3	4	2	24	3
Jiffy	19	2	2	1	17	2
Unity	17	2			17	2
Don't know brand used	96	11	16	9	80	12
All others	96	11	14	8	82	12

TABLE 2. Brand usage of fabric rinses analyzed by listenership to Hayes-Healy program

	Total		Listeners		Nonlisteners	
	No.	%	No.	%	No.	%
Total respondents	1,716	100	305	100	1,411	100
Do not use fabric rinse	1,385	81	239	78	1,146	81
Do use fabric rinse	331	19	66	22	265	19
Sta-Puf	137	42	27	41	112	42
Nu-Soft	80	24	10	15	70	27
All other brands	103	31	27	41	76	29
Don't know brand used	11	3	2	3	7	2

TABLE 3. Product usage and brand advertised analyzed by listenership of each of the five daytime network radio programs

Art Linkletter House Party (Beauty Ice, cosmetic lotion)

	Total		Listeners		Nonlisteners	
	No.	%	No.	%	No.	%
Number of respondents	(1,716)		(749)		(967)	
Do not use cosmetic lotion	1,330	77	564	75	766	79
Do use cosmetic lotion	386	23	185	25	201	21
Use Beauty Ice	—	—	—	—	—	—
Use another brand	364	94	173	93	191	95
Don't know	22	6	12	7	10	5

Arthur Godfrey Time (Chiffon, detergent)

	Total		Listeners		Nonlisteners	
	No.	%	No.	%	No.	%
Number of respondents	(1,716)		(668)		(1,048)	
Do not use detergent	655	39	199	30	466	44
Do use detergent	1,051	61	469	70	582	56
Use Chiffon	21	3	8	2	13	2
Use another brand	1,017	96	453	96	564	97
Don't know	13	1	8	2	5	1

Hayes-Healy Program (Sta-Flo, liquid starch)

	Total		Listeners		Nonlisteners	
	No.	%	No.	%	No.	%
Number of respondents	(1,716)		(305)		(1,411)	
Do not use liquid starch	858	50	133	44	725	51
Do use liquid starch	858	50	172	56	686	49
Use Sta-Flo	280	32	76	44	204	30
Use another brand	482	56	80	47	402	58
Don't know	96	12	16	9	80	12

Backstage Wife (Halo, shampoo)

	Total		Listeners		Nonlisteners	
	No.	%	No.	%	No.	%
Number of respondents	(1,716)		(313)		(1,403)	
Do not use shampoo	353	20	46	15	307	22
Do use shampoo	1,363	80	267	85	1,096	78
Use Halo	138	10	32	12	106	10
Use another brand	1,198	88	227	85	971	89
Don't know	27	2	8	3	19	1

One Man's Family (Trushay, hand lotion)

	Total		Listeners		Nonlisteners	
	No.	%	No.	%	No.	%
Number of respondents	(1,716)		(343)		(1,373)	
Do not use hand lotion	751	44	100	29	651	47
Do use hand lotion	965	56	243	71	722	53
Use Trushay	36	4	10	4	26	4
Use another brand	895	93	225	93	670	93
Don't know	34	3	8	3	26	4

Case 12—3. THE DUPORT COMPANY

The Duport Company manufactured the concentrate for Genii, a bottled carbonated grapefruit drink. The company had franchised bottlers in forty-four states but had varying coverage of the population of these states. In planning future expansion and franchising of new bottlers, Mr. Herbert Walker, president of Duport, felt that the company should have some idea of the potential of each state. By concentrating on those areas where the potential was the greatest, Mr. Walker felt that Duport could make the greatest gains at the least cost.

The Duport Company was not a bottling company. It manufactured concentrated flavors which were used in making carbonated soft drinks. Bottlers purchased the concentrate and mixed it with carbonated water to produce a soft drink. This was then bottled for distribution. Besides the Genii concentrate, Duport also sold assorted flavors, ginger ale, root beer, orange, etc., for bottling in 24-ounce bottles under the Walker label. The Walker brand was not nationally advertised but had a strong following in several of the major metropolitan markets.

Duport had 150 bottlers franchised to bottle Genii in the United States. The company also had bottlers in South America, Canada, and Western Europe. Duport had established a distinctive bottle design and labels which all bottlers used. An 8-ounce bottle was used for Genii. The terms of the franchise required bottlers to use only concentrate purchased from Duport for bottling Genii, to use the bottle and label specified for Genii by Duport, and to maintain certain standards of quality. The bottlers were required to send periodic samples of bottled Genii to Duport for quality checks. The franchise granted the bottlers an exclusive territory.

The bottlers were also expected to promote Genii in their area through sales effort and advertising. Duport participated in cooperative advertising with the bottlers. Most of the franchised bottlers had an advertising account with Duport. The bottler paid an extra charge of one dollar for each gallon concentrate. This was matched by Duport and set aside in the advertising account. The bottler would then forward any bills for advertising Genii to Duport for payment out of his advertising account. Also, the cost of displays and other promotional materials provided the bottler by Duport were deducted from this account. Duport allowed the bottlers, particularly newly franchised bottlers, some latitude in drawing against future accruals in their advertising account.

Duport conducted a national advertising campaign for Genii. It advertised regularly in *Life* and had occasional television spots. Also, regional campaigns were conducted from time to time, primarily through newspapers. Duport provided bottlers with mats and ideas for local advertising.

The first step in determining potentials was to attempt to isolate those factors which affected soft drink sales. Mr. Walker had learned of studies by other soft drink companies which had found that temperature and income were factors that affected soft drink sales. He asked his statistical department to do a correlation analysis involving per capita consumption in bottles of all soft drinks, mean annual temperature, and per capita income, by states. (See Table 1.) They found that a significant correlation existed between these factors, but that temperature was by far the most important factor. Appendix A is a summary of their results.

From the estimating equation developed in the calculations, the statistical department calculated what the expected demand by states was, based on the mean annual temperature and per capita income. This was then compared with actual demand to determine what states were above or below the expected demand. (See Table 1.)

Having these data on hand, Mr. Walker asked that Duport sales in bottles per capita be analyzed with temperature and income to see what correlation existed. Since Duport in no case had 100 percent coverage of a state, per capita consumption in bottles was based only on that portion of the population that was reached by franchised bottlers. The results of this analysis were somewhat disappointing. No significant relationship existed between Duport sales and temperature and income, either individually or together. A summary of the results is shown in Appendix B.

1. Was the analytic procedure appropriate to the problem? Could it be improved?

2. Where should Duport plan to locate new franchises?

APPENDIX A. Correlation analysis of bottles of all soft drinks consumed per capita (X_1), mean annual temperature (X_2), and per capita income (X_3), by states[1]

Simple correlation—bottles of all soft drinks consumed per capita (X_1), mean annual temperature (X_2), by states:

Estimating equation:	$Y_{12} = 6.81X_2 - 206.7$
Standard error of estimate:	$S_{1.2} = 40.5$
Coefficient of correlation:	$r_{12} = 0.804$

Simple correlation—bottles of all soft drinks consumed per capita (X_1) and per capita income (X_3) by states:

Estimating equation:	$Y_{13} = 257 - 5.51X_3$
Standard error of estimate:	$S_{1.3} = 78.4$
Coefficient of correlation:	$r_{13} = 0.29$

Multiple correlation—bottles of all soft drinks consumed per capita (X_1), mean annual temperature (X_2), and per capita income (X_3) by states:

Estimating equation:	$Y_{123} = 6.46X_2 - 2.37X_3 - 145.5$
Standard error of estimate:	$S_{1(23)} = 39$
Coefficient of correlation:	$r_{1.23} = 0.814$
Coefficients of partial correlation:	$r_{12.3} = 0.784, r_{13.2} = 0.258$

[1] Forty-seven states only. New Hampshire eliminated from calculation because of extreme variation. Alaska and Hawaii did not have accurate data.

TABLE 1

State	Bottles of all soft drinks consumed per capita[1] X_1	Mean annual temperatures[2] X_2	Income per capita[3] X_2 (100's)	"Expected" demand Y_{123}	Actual demand less expected demand $X_1 - Y_{123}$	Bottles of Genii consumed per capita[4] X_4	Expected demand Y_{423}	Percent of state population under franchise by Duport
Alabama	200	66°	$13	253	− 53	1.8	4.1	63.9%
Arizona	150	62	17	216	− 66	9.4	3.9	18.8
Arkansas	237	63	11	236	+ 1	3.3	4.2	55.9
California	135	56	25	158	− 23	8.2	3.5	8.4
Colorado	121	52	19	146	− 25	3.3	3.7	83.4
Connecticut	118	50	27	114	+ 4	2.1	3.3	4.9
Delaware	217	54	28	138	+ 79	—	—	
Florida	242	72	18	277	− 35	3.7	4.0	23.4
Georgia	295	64	14	277	+ 18	1.3	4.1	18.0
Idaho	85	46	16	114	− 29	5.5	3.7	70.8
Illinois	141	52	24	134	+ 7	3.0	3.5	75.8
Indiana	184	52	20	144	+ 42	2.2	3.6	28.9
Iowa	104	50	16	140	− 36	3.0	3.8	30.3
Kansas	143	56	17	177	− 34	3.7	3.8	18.6
Kentucky	230	56	13	186	+ 44	5.1	4.0	66.4
Louisiana	269	69	15	265	+ 4	3.1	4.1	33.9
Maine	111	41	16	82	+ 29	2.4	3.7	88.3
Maryland	217	54	21	154	+ 63	14.4	3.6	5.4
Massachusetts	114	47	22	107	+ 7	2.8	3.5	38.6
Michigan	108	47	21	109	− 1	1.0	3.5	75.6
Minnesota	108	41	18	77	+ 31	4.2	3.6	85.6
Mississippi	248	65	10	251	− 3	4.8	4.2	57.2
Missouri	203	57	19	178	+ 25	3.6	3.7	35.2
Montana	77	44	19	94	− 17	4.0	3.6	89.0

State							
Nebraska	97	49	16	133	− 36	2.7	3.8	39.0
Nevada	166	48	24	108	+ 58	2.8	3.4	16.3
New Hampshire	177	35	18	38	+139*	3.7	3.5	67.9
New Jersey	143	54	24	147	− 4	.9	3.5	66.2
New Mexico	157	56	15	181	− 24	—	—	30.2
New York	111	48	25	106	+ 5	4.0	3.4	42.3
No. Carolina	330	59	13	205*	+125*	6.4	4.0	68.7
No. Dakota	63	39	14	74	− 11	2.5	3.7	24.3
Ohio	165	51	22	133	+ 32	1.9	3.6	66.1
Oklahoma	184	62	16	218	− 34	1.0	4.0	74.3
Oregon	68	51	19	140	− 72	2.4	3.7	28.1
Pennsylvania	121	50	20	131	− 10	1.8	3.6	73.0
Rhode Island	138	50	20	131	+ 7	—	—	44.5
So. Carolina	237	65	12	247	− 10	3.3	4.2	96.6
So. Dakota	95	45	13	115	− 20	7.8	3.8	36.6
Tennessee	236	60	13	212	+ 24	4.0	4.0	81.3
Texas	222	69	17	261	− 39	3.7	4.0	26.7
Utah	100	50	16	140	− 40	5.7	3.8	38.6
Vermont	64	44	16	101	− 37	—	—	65.2
Virginia	270	58	16	191	+ 79	5.8	3.9	55.2
Washington	77	49	20	124	− 47	3.4	3.6	18.6
W. Virginia	144	55	15	174	− 30	1.2	3.9	
Wisconsin	97	46	19	107	− 10	2.2	3.6	
Wyoming	102	46	19	107	− 5	2.5	3.6	

* Unusually large.

1 SOURCE: "The Soft Drink Industry—A Market Study," National Bottler's Gazette.

2 SOURCE: U.S. Weather Bureau, Climatological Data—National Summary.

3 SOURCE: U.S. Department of Commerce, Office of Business Economics, U.S. Income and Output, a supplement to the Survey of Current Business.

4 Based on percentage of population under franchise in each state.

APPENDIX B. Correlation analysis of bottles of Genii consumed per capita (X_4), mean annual temperature (X_2), and per capita income (X_3) by states

Simple correlation—bottles of Genii consumed per capita (X_4) and mean annual temperature (X_2) by states:

Estimating equation:	$Y_{42} = 0.019X_2 + 2.74$
Standard error of estimate:	$S_{4.2} = 2.48$
Coefficient of correlation:	$r_{42} = 0.065$

Simple correlation—bottles of Genii consumed per capita (X_4) and per capita income (X_2) by states:

Estimating equation:	$Y_{43} = 4.33 - 0.032X_3$
Standard error of estimate:	$S_{4.3} = 2.48$
Coefficient of correlation:	$r_{43} = 0.053$

Multiple correlation—bottles of Genii consumed per capita (X_4), mean annual temperature (X_2), and per capita income (X_3) by states:

Estimating equation:	$Y_{4(23)} = 3.764 + 0.0136X_2 - 0.0409X_3$
Standard error of estimate:	$S_{4(23)} = S_{4.23} = 2.46$
Coefficient of correlation:	$r_{4.23} = 0.081$

Case 12—4. TRANSIT RADIO, INC. (B)

In trying to determine how much it could afford to offer for the franchise to install FM radio loudspeakers on the Eastville city buses, Transit Radio, Inc., conducted a survey to find what proportion of Eastville residents rode on the bus line during a week. A probability sample of seven hundred was selected, and personal interviews were made. As many as two callbacks were attempted where necessary, but, even so, thirty-four individuals specified for the sample were not interviewed.

Two questions asked were: Have you ridden on an Eastville city bus in the last seven days? What is your approximate age? The following tabulation was made of the replies to these two questions.

Number of individuals in various age groups who had ridden an Eastville city bus in the last seven days

Age	Rode bus	Did not ride bus	Don't know	Total
15–19	26	20	0	46
20–29	43	81	3	127
30–45	98	129	2	229
Over 45	104	125	3	232
No answer	14	17	1	32
Total	285	372	9	666

1. How should the "don't knows" and "no answers" be handled in analyzing these results?

2. If the analyst wants to compare the use of the city buses by various age groups, what percentages should he compute?

3. If the analyst wants to determine the make-up of bus riders by age groups, what percentages should he compute?

4. What consideration should the analyst give to the thirty-four individuals selected for the sample but not actually interviewed?

5. Is there a significant difference among the age groups in respect to riding city buses?

Case 12—5.   FOREMOST DAIRIES, INC.*

Mr. Fred Fornia, product manager for frozen desserts, faced the problem of determining what new flavors of ice cream should be offered by Foremost Dairies, Inc. in the year ahead and how they should be promoted.

The company followed the practice of introducing special new flavors one at a time, and promoting them for periods of one to three months by means of newspaper, magazine, and point-of-purchase advertising. Eighty percent of the promotional budget for frozen desserts had been devoted to the special flavors which were offered in the top two of the five quality grades of frozen dessert produced. The special flavors were in addition to the eight or nine flavors offered continuously in each grade and several seasonal flavors offered for limited periods during the year. For example, Foremost marketed 14 flavors of "regular" grade ice cream on the San Francisco Peninsula. Seven were offered throughout the year: vanilla, chocolate, strawberry, marble fudge, rocky road, neapolitan, and maple nut. Five were seasonal flavors offered only that fall: strawberry parfait, black walnut, spumoni, butter brickle, and banana and coffee combination. Two were special promotion flavors: milk chocolate chip and candy cane.

The special flavor promotions were regarded as a means of stimulating sales for all grades and flavors of Foremost ice cream. The special flavors themselves accounted for about 5 percent of Foremost's ice cream sales volume in the past.

While flavor preferences varied somewhat by geographic region, Fornia planned to run the same special flavor promotions in all of the company's markets. Nationwide special flavor promotions had not been Foremost's practice in the past. Ideas for new flavors had come either

---

* Reprinted from Stanford Business Cases 1966, Volume II with the permission of the publishers, Stanford University Graduate School of Business. Copyright © 1966 by the Board of Trustees of the Leland Stanford Junior University.

from the company's production department or from suppliers which offered flavors on a franchise basis. The product manager selected those flavors which he regarded to have a promising sales outlook by exercising his judgment based on knowledge of historical sales activity.

In a search for an improved approach to identifying flavors for profitable special promotions, Fornia consulted Robert Stark, the company's marketing research manager. Stark suggested the use of concept research in which flavor ideas would be tested in consumer interviews in order to obtain a measure of probable market acceptance. After discussing this course of action, Fornia and Stark agreed to proceed with the research.

Stark suggested getting names for which appealing flavor concepts could be developed. He believed that the name and the romance or aura built around it probably contributed more heavily to a flavor's sales success than the more tangible characteristics of flavor itself. The next step would be to test the concept for probable acceptance. If the results were favorable, a new ice cream would be developed to match the flavor concept.

NAMES FOR FLAVORS

Fornia asked the account executive at the advertising agency handling the Foremost account to suggest names for new ice cream flavors; he placed no limitations on what kinds of names would be acceptable. The agency offered a list of 200 names which then was reduced to 38. Eliminations were made because of possible trademark infringement, a probable lack of consumer acceptance as indicated by Foremost's past experience, and inability to manufacture an ice cream of the suggested concept.

A SCREENING SURVEY

To further screen the 38 names for probable market acceptance, they were submitted to 270 adults (112 men and 158 women) in personal interviews. The interviewing was done outside large supermarkets during the heavy shopping hours by approaching people as they were entering or leaving the stores. The interviews were distributed equally among 18 supermarkets: 12 in the Los Angeles area and 6 in the San Francisco Bay Area. (See Exhibit 1 for further information on the sample as well as one of the two forms of questionnaires used.)

Because of the large number of names being tested, they were divided into two lists. The lists were compiled by grouping names according to the fruit or flavor extract they suggested. It was hoped the grouping of names would increase the usefulness of the results, since ice creams with certain flavors were known to be generally preferred when compared with other flavor combinations. The order in which the names were presented was rotated to minimize sequence bias. Each list was shown to 135 respondents. Each respondent was asked whether she (or he) served ice cream in the home. If she replied affirmatively, she was shown a list of five names for new flavors of sherbet and 19 names for new flavors of ice cream.[1] She was asked which names she felt were especially appealing and which she found unappealing. The last two questions asked about the volume of ice cream the respondent used in an average month and what shape of ice cream package she preferred.

SURVEY RESULTS

The survey results of the two samples of 135 interviews, each sample having tested 19 different names for ice cream, were combined into two lists of 38 names. On one list the names appeared ranked by percent of respondents who found them "especially appealing." On the other list the names appeared ranked by percent of respondents who found them "unattractive" or "unappealing." (See Exhibits 2 and 3.) Party Parfait and Pecan Dandy received a high number of favorable responses ("especially appealing") and a relatively low number of unfavorable responses ("unappealing").

Nine of the 38 names were selected for more intensive research because their flavor concepts could be more easily visualized and would contrast with the more common flavors of ice cream. They were Party Parfait, Pecan Dandy, and seven others. Five additional names also were selected for further research. Two of them, Cherry Cherie and Wild Mountain Blackberry, had been used successfully in the past by Foremost. Chocolate Brazil and two others were submitted by the product manager. On the basis of his judgment, he considered two of the names, Chocolate Brazil and one other, to be desirable and the third name undesirable. He reasoned that these three names along with Cherry Cherie and Wild Mountain Blackberry would be useful in evaluating the results for the other nine names. A flavor concept then was developed for each of the 14 names by the advertising agency which prepared appropriate descriptive copy and art.

FLAVOR CONCEPT TESTING

The 14 flavor concepts then were given to Market Facts, Inc., a marketing research firm headquartered in Chicago, for testing to determine which ones were most likely to meet with sales success. The basis for

---

[1] Only the 38 names of new flavors of *ice cream* have been considered in this case.

making the determination would be a measure of initial consumer interest. Concepts lacking in this respect could be eliminated from consideration before further development and market testing were undertaken. In addition to attempting to learn which of the 14 flavor concepts consumers found most appealing, Market Facts also sought to measure geographic differences in flavor preferences as a basis for considering whether certain flavors should be offered on a regional basis.

Eight hundred personal interviews were conducted in nine geographically dispersed cities as follows:

Area	Cities	Sample size*
Northeast	Philadelphia, Pennsylvania	100
	Hartford, Connecticut	100
Southeast	Jacksonville, Florida	100
	Atlanta, Georgia	100
Southwest	Springfield, Missouri	65
	Kansas City, Missouri	70
	Amarillo, Texas	65
Far west	San Francisco, California	100
	Los Angeles, California	100
		800

* Twelve of the 800 interviews were discarded during editing.

Half of the interviews were with persons considered to be "users" of special flavor ice cream. A user was defined as one who had purchased flavors other than vanilla, chocolate, strawberry, or neapolitan within the last two or three months. The remaining interviews were with persons who had purchased any flavor other than special flavor ice cream in the last two or three months.

To obtain interviews, Market Facts conducted a probability sample of household residents in the nine cities. City blocks were selected at random and a fixed starting point was established in each block for the first interview. A constant interval between houses was maintained for all successive interviews in that block. As substitutes for occupants not at home or refusing to participate, and for nonqualified respondents, members of the adjacent household were interviewed. The housewife was the reporter and the family the sampling unit. Interviewing was conducted in the evenings and on weekends as well as during weekdays to insure the inclusion of working housewives in the sample.

Each respondent first was asked whether she had purchased ice cream for home use within the previous three months. If she had not, the interview was discontinued. If she had and if any of the ice creams had been special flavors, she was asked to identify the persons to whom she served these special flavors. If guests were served, she was asked on what occasions she served special flavors. Next, 14 color photographs and accompanying descriptive copy were shown one at a time. When the respondent had become familiar with each flavor concept, all of the photos were spread on a table. The interviewer asked her to imagine that all of the pictures represented cartons of ice cream stocked in the frozen dessert section of a supermarket and that she was trying to decide which to purchase. The interviewer then asked these questions in turn:

"Are there any flavors here that you would definitely consider buying?"

"Which ones?"

"Which flavors would you be most likely to buy?"

"Are there any flavors here that you would definitely not consider buying?"

"Which ones?"

"Which flavor would you be least likely to buy?"

See Exhibit 4 for questionnaire.

The finds from the Market Facts study are shown in Exhibits 5 through 10.

What conclusions should Foremost Dairies have drawn from analysis of these findings?

EXHIBIT 1. Form A (interview guide for names of ice cream flavors survey, field research company)[1]

How do you do. I'm working on a survey to help a dairy company choose names for some new flavors of ice cream and sherbet. Do you ever serve ice cream or sherbet at home? (IF NO, DISCONTINUE INTERVIEW) I wonder if I could just ask you briefly to look at some of these names and give me *your* opinion—
1. First, here are the names of some sherbets. (CARD A)
   a. Which of the names on that list do you find *especially appealing* as a name for a sherbet?
   b. Are there any names on the list that you find *unattractive* or *unappealing* for a sherbet? Which ones?

Sherbets[2]	Especially appealing	Unattractive
50	1	1
51	2	2
52	3	3
53	4	4
54	5	5

[1] Form B was identical to form A except it listed five different sherbet names and 19 different ice cream names.
[2] Numbers refer to names tested which had not yet been used in the marketplace.

EXHIBIT 1 (*Continued*)

2. Next, please turn the card over (CARD B). Those are the names of some ice creams.
   a. Which of the names on that list do you find *especially appealing* as a name for an ice cream?
   b. Are there any names you find *unattractive* or *unappealing* for an ice cream? Which ones?

Ice creams°	Especially appealing	Unattractive
1	1	1
2	2	2
3	3	3
4	4	4
5	5	5
6	6	6
7	7	7
8	8	8
9	9	9
10	1	1
11	2	2
12	3	3
13	4	4
14	5	5
15	6	6
16	7	7
17	8	8
18	9	9
19	0	0

° Numbers refer to names tested which had not yet been used in the marketplace.

3. Now, to finish up, about how much ice cream and sherbet do you use in your family in an average month during the summer?

Less than one quart	1
1–2 quarts (half gallon)	2
3–4 quarts (one gallon)	3
5–6 quarts (1½ gallons)	4
7–8 quarts (2 gallons)	5
9 quarts or more (more than 2 gallons)	6

4. When you buy a half-gallon of ice cream, what shape of package do you prefer— the square or the round?

Square	1
Round	2
No difference	3
Don't buy half-gallons	4

5. Denote sex.

Male	1
Female	2

Selected characteristics of the sample

	All interviews	Interviews conducted with questionnaire form	
		A	B
Total	270	135	135
Area			
Los Angeles	180	90	90
San Francisco	90	45	45
Sex of respondent			
Male	112	60	52
Female	158	75	83
Volume of use of ice cream			
Heavy user (9 quarts or more per month)*	81	25	56
Medium user (5 to 8 quarts per month)*	77	47	30
Light user (one gallon or less per month)*	112	63	49

* Average summer month.

EXHIBIT 2. Ice cream names ranked by percent of respondents who found them "especially appealing"[1]

Ice cream names[2]	For total sample[3]	By area		By sex		By user category[4]		
		S.F.	L.A.	Male	Female	Light	Medium	Heavy
Party Parfait	46%	27%	56%	40%	51%	43%	57%	32%
15	44	44	43	56	36	43	33	50
20	32	38	29	33	31	29	34	36
21	31	20	37	35	28	33	32	24
18	29	13	37	25	31	18	33	36
22	26	4	37	20	31	27	30	16
Pecan Dandy	24	9	32	18	29	22	30	20
3	24	31	21	17	29	18	20	32
1	21	18	23	19	23	20	30	18
13	19	16	21	21	18	22	27	12
6	18	18	18	21	16	10	37	14
19	17	13	19	21	14	18	13	18
23	17	9	21	15	19	19	17	12
24	16	9	20	15	17	21	15	8
25	16	16	17	10	21	13	21	16
26	16	11	19	13	19	16	21	8
4	16	13	18	12	19	16	27	11
11	16	18	14	13	17	16	20	12
16	16	16	17	12	19	18	20	12
7	15	4	20	23	10	22	13	9

10	14	13	14	17	11	12	10	18
5	14	18	12	15	13	12	13	16
27	13	13	13	10	16	11	13	20
28	13	4	14	10	15	13	13	12
29	13	4	17	13	12	8	17	18
8	12	9	13	12	11	12	13	11
30	11	11	11	10	12	11	11	12
31	10	11	9	10	9	8	11	12
32	10	13	8	7	12	8	11	12
12	10	9	10	10	10	6	10	12
9	8	9	8	8	8	8	13	5
14	8	9	8	6	10	4	7	12
17	7	9	7	8	7	10	10	4
2	7	7	7	6	7	8	3	7
33	4	2	4	3	4	2	2	12
34	4	7	2	3	4	3	2	8
35	4	—	6	2	5	3	4	4
36	3	4	2	5	1	3	—	8
Find none appealing	4	4	6	5	3	5	4	—

[1] An example of how to read the figures: Party Parfait was found especially appealing by 46 percent of 135 respondents; by 27 percent of San Francisco respondents; by 56 percent of Los Angeles respondents; by 40 percent of male respondents; by 51 percent of female respondents; by 43 percent of light users interviewed; by 57 percent of medium users; and by 32 percent of heavy users.

[2] Numbers refer to names tested which had not yet been used in the marketplace.

[3] Since each ice cream name was tested by one of the two samples of 135 respondents, the figures in this column represent a percentage of 135 persons.

[4] "Light user" uses one gallon of sherbet and ice cream or less in an average summer month; "medium user" uses five to eight quarts in an average summer month; "heavy user" uses nine quarts or more in an average summer month.

BASE: Two samples of 135 California ice cream users each.

EXHIBIT 3. Ice cream names ranked by percent of respondents who found them "unattractive" or "unappealing"[1]

Ice cream names[2]	For total sample[3]	By area		By sex		By user category[4]		
		S.F.	L.A.	Male	Female	Light	Medium	Heavy
35	50%	60%	46%	43%	56%	49%	57%	40%
34	38	49	32	37	39	38	43	28
36	37	29	41	26	45	41	34	32
30	36	22	42	38	35	43	26	36
17	36	51	28	37	35	16	43	48
8	31	47	23	29	33	24	33	36
9	31	53	20	29	33	22	33	38
2	30	49	20	27	31	14	43	36
33	28	27	29	20	35	36	30	4
32	24	22	26	18	29	24	26	24
14	23	27	21	35	16	22	23	23
31	23	16	27	13	31	25	23	16
28	21	16	23	25	17	21	19	24
11	20	20	20	19	20	14	23	23
23	20	20	20	13	23	14	17	32
24	16	13	18	15	17	14	23	8
27	16	9	19	17	15	17	19	4
29	16	16	16	10	20	14	15	20
25	14	13	14	15	13	16	13	12
13	13	13	12	12	13	16	13	9
7	13	27	6	6	17	2	23	16
20	13	9	16	12	15	13	18	12
4	12	27	4	12	12	8	7	18

Pecan Dandy	11	9	12	10	12	17	4	8
19	10	11	9	10	10	8	17	7
26	10	9	11	3	16	10	8	16
5	7	9	6	8	6	2	10	9
12	7	9	7	6	8	4	10	9
11	6	13	4	10	4	4	7	7
22	6		2	3	8	6	8	—
21	6	7	6	5	7.	6	4	8
Party Parfait	5	9	2	7	4	3	6	8
6	5	4	6	8	4	4	10	4
16	4	7	3	4	5	2	7	5
3	4	7	2	4	4	2	10	2
1	3	4	2	2	4	—	3	5
18	3	7	1	4	2	—	10	2
15	2	2	2	2	2	2	—	4
Find none appealing	10	6	12	12	8	13	6	7

¹ An example of how to read the figures: Name 35 was found unappealing by 50 percent of 135 respondents; by 60 percent of San Francisco respondents; by 46 percent of Los Angeles respondents; by 43 percent of male respondents; by 56 percent of female respondents; by 49 percent of light users interviewed; by 57 percent of medium users and by 40 percent of heavy users.

² Numbers refer to names tested which had not yet been used in the marketplace.

³ Since each ice cream name was tested by one of the two samples of 135 respondents, the figures in this column represent a percentage of 135 persons.

⁴ "Light user" uses one gallon of sherbet and ice cream or less in an average summer month; "medium user" uses five to eight quarts in an average summer month; "heavy user" uses nine quarts or more in an average summer month.

BASE: 270 California ice cream users divided into two samples of 135 each.

EXHIBIT 4

Market Facts, Inc., 100 S. Wacker Dr., Chicago 6, Ill.

Job No. 2-2702
Qu.No._____
Colo. 1-4

ICE CREAM QUESTIONNAIRE

Time Int.
Began:_____am/pm

Market Facts' Repr._____Date_____

City_____ Field Station _____

```
        5 ┌─┬─┬─┐ 7
        8 └─┴─┴─┘ 12
```

1. During the last three months or so, have you bought any ice cream for use at home?

    Yes   1 (CONTINUE INTERVIEW) No   2 (DISCONTINUE INTERVIEW)   13

2a. Have you bought any special flavors of ice cream in the last three months or so, that is, ice cream that contains fruit, or nuts, or a flavor besides the standard flavors, or some other ingredient?

    Yes   3 (GO TO QU. 2b)
    No   4 (SKIP TO QU. 3 PER QUOTA INSTRUCTIONS)   13

    2b. To whom do you serve special ice cream flavors?
        _____   14
        _____   15

        2c. (IF "FAMILY" MENTIONED) Which members of your family?
            _____   16

        2d. (IF "GUESTS" OR "COMPANY" MENTIONED) On what occasions
            do you serve special ice cream flavors to guests?   17
            _____
                                                                       18

3. Here are some special ice cream flavors that I'd like you to look at and read about. (SHOW ONE AT A TIME). Please look at this picture and read the description (GO THROUGH ALL 14 PICTURES, ONE AT A TIME).

4a. Now, I'll show you these pictures again. (PLACE ALL PICTURES BEFORE RESPONDENT AS DESCRIBED IN INSTRUCTIONS). Looking at all of these flavors here, imagine that you are in the ice cream section of a store and that these flavors are all in stock. Are there any flavors here that you would definitely consider buying? Which ones? (IF "NONE", INDICATE   19
    NONE AND ASK QU. 4b)
    _____
    _____   20

    4b. Which flavors would you be most likely to buy? (IF "NONE", INDICATE   21
        NONE AND ASK QU. 4c)
        _____
        _____   22

    4c. Are there any flavors here that you would definitely not consider buying?
        Which ones? (IF "NONE", INDICATE NONE AND ASK QU. 4d)   23
        _____
        _____   24

EXHIBIT 4 (*Continued*)

Job. No. 2-2782
Page Two

4d.   Which flavor would you be least likely to buy? (IF "NONE", INDICATE NONE AND ASK QU. 5)

[25]

[ ]

5.   Now, thinking back to special flavors of ice cream that have been sold in the past, are there any special flavors you or other members of your family especially like, but are not on sale anymore? Which ones? (IF "NONE", INDICATE NONE AND SKIP TO CLASSIFICATION DATA)

[26]

[27]

[ ]

[ ]

CLASSIFICATION DATA

[29]

Name & Initials of Resp. _____

[30]

Address _____ City & State _____

[ ]

Age: Under 24   1   25-34   2   35-44   3   45-54   4

55-64   5   65 & over   6   Refused   7   No answer   8   31

Which of the following groups includes your total annual family income -- would you say it is:

Under $2500   1 $2500-4,999   2 $5,000-7,499   3

$7,500-10,000   4   Over $10,000   5   Refused   6   32

How many people including yourself are living in this home?

1   2   3   4   5   6   7   8   9   10 or more   0   33

How many of these are children 19 years or under?

1   2   3   4   5   6   7   8   9   10 or more   0   34

If Children: What are their ages, that is, how many are (boys/girls)?

	Male	Female		
Under 5	_____	_____	35 [ ]	36
5 - 9	_____	_____	37 [ ]	38
10 - 14	_____	_____	39 [ ]	40
15 - 19	_____	_____	41 [ ]	42

Occupation of Chief Wage Earner: _____

[43]

Respondent employed outside of home   1   Respondent not employed outside home   2

Time Interview Ended: _____ am/pm

HRS/11 _

[80]

[1]

(FOR OFFICE USE ONLY)

1 2 3 4 5 6 7 8 9 10 11 12 13 14 15 16 17 18 19 20 21 22 23 24 25

[ ]

EXHIBIT 5. Rankings of names for ice cream (by percent of respondents who said they would)

Ice cream names[1]	Definitely consider buying (A)	Definitely not consider buying (B)	(A) − (B)[2]	Rank order
Pecan Dandy	48%	9%	39%	1
Chocolate Brazil	36	14	22	3
Cherry Cherie	36	12	24	2 (tie)
28	35	15	20	5
37	35	11	24	2 (tie)
Party Parfait	30	9	21	4
Wild Mountain Blackberry	27	15	12	6
15	27	20	7	7 (tie)
20	26	24	2	8
38	26	19	7	7 (tie)
36	21	23	− 2	9
7	16	33	−17	10
25	16	34	−18	11
18	13	35	−23	12

[1] Numbers refer to names tested which had not yet been used in the marketplace.
[2] Percentage differences between those who stated they would "definitely consider buying" and those who stated they would "definitely not consider buying."
BASE: 788 U.S. housewives who used ice cream.

EXHIBIT 6. Rankings of names for ice cream (by percentage of respondents who said they were)

Ice cream names[1]	Most likely to buy	Least likely to buy
Pecan Dandy	32%	5%
Chocolate Brazil	24	12
Cherry Cherie	23	10
28	18	10
37	26	8
Party Parfait	20	8
Wild Mountain Blackberry	14	11
15	16	15
20	14	19
38	13	15
36	11	16
7	11	26
25	7	21
18	7	27

[1] Numbers refer to names tested which had not yet been used in the marketplace.
BASE: 788 U.S. housewives who used ice cream.

EXHIBIT 7. Rank orders by region of names for ice creams housewives said they would definitely consider buying

Ice cream names[1]	East	South	South-west	West	Total[2]
Pecan Dandy	1	1	1	1	1st
Chocolate Brazil	2	3 (tie)	4	4	3rd
20	3 (tie)	9	11	7	8th (tie)
37	3 (tie)	6	3	3	4th (tie)
Cherry Cherie	3 (tie)	2	5	2	2nd
15	4	7 (tie)	9	8 (tie)	7th
28	5	3 (tie)	2	5	4th (tie)
Wild Mountain Blackberry	6	8	7	6	6th
Party Parfait	7	4	6	8 (tie)	5th
38	8 (tie)	5	8	9	8th (tie)
36	8 (tie)	7 (tie)	10	11	9th
7	9	11	13	10	10th
25	10	10	12 (tie)	12 (tie)	11th
18	11	12	12 (tie)	12 (tie)	12th
Number of respondents	198	197	198	195	788

[1] Numbers refer to names tested which had not yet been used in the marketplace.
[2] Total rank order based on average regional rank order scores.
BASE: 788 U.S. housewives who used ice cream.

EXHIBIT 8. Apparent effect of children on rank orders of names for ice cream (percent of housewives who said they would)

Ice cream names[1]	Definitely consider buying		Definitely not consider buying	
	With children	Without children	With children	Without children
Pecan Dandy	49%	45%	6%	13%
Chocolate Brazil	44	23	10	21
Cherry Cherie	38	34	11	13
37	38	32	8	16
28	37	31	14	18
Wild Mountain Blackberry	29	25	14	18
Party Parfait	28	32	9	9
15	28	26	18	24
38	27	24	18	20
20	24	27	25	22
36	22	18	22	26
7	16	16	34	33
25	16	16	32	34
18	14	10	31	41
Number of respondents	492	296	492	296

[1] Numbers refer to names tested which had not yet been used in the marketplace.
BASE: 788 U.S. housewives who used ice cream.

EXHIBIT 9. Rank orders by income group of names for ice creams housewives said they would definitely consider buying[1]

Ice cream names[2]	Under $2500	$2500–4999	$5000–7499	$7500–10,000	Over $10,000	All respondents
Pecan Dandy	38%	45%	52%	58%	45%	48%
Chocolate Brazil	33	35	40	38	36	36
Cherry Cherie	27	40	38	40	28	36
28	38	38	37	41	26	35
37	22	37	37	40	40	35
Party Parfait	38	36	32	30	22	30
Wild Mountain Blackberry	22	26	27	36	22	27
15	22	25	29	22	39	27
20	25	21	20	38	37	26
38	18	29	29	24	28	26
36	25	23	18	23	22	21
7	13	14	18	13	21	16
25	11	14	11	12	18	16
18	11	13	17	17	21	13
Percent of sample	7%	22%	34%	14%	11%	100%

[1] 12 percent of the total respondents refused to give their income in this study.
[2] Numbers refer to names tested which had not yet been used in the marketplace.
BASE: 788 U.S. housewives who used ice cream.

EXHIBIT 10. Percent of housewives by age group who purchased special flavor ice creams

Age Group	%
Under 25	52
25–34	51
35–44	49
45–54	52
55–64	46
65 and over	40
Refused to be interviewed or gave no answer	50
Number of respondents[1]	387

[1] Of the total sample of 788 respondents, 387 bought special flavor ice cream and 401 did not buy special flavor ice cream.
BASE: 788 U.S. housewives who used ice cream.

13

Research presentation, follow-up, and research process evaluation

N o MATTER WHAT the quality of the research on a project, much of the acceptance of the results depends on the way they are communicated to the relevant audiences. The researcher's standards are apt to be different from those of the executive to whom he wishes to communicate. The executive is not much interested in methodology—he wants the "results." While the written or oral presentation may be an anticlimax to the researcher, it is frequently all the executive hears or sees of the project. If the executive is to act on the basis of the results, he must be convinced of their value. The researcher finds that while he must make his presentation technically accurate, he must also make it understandable and useful.

Proper execution of the previous steps in the research process makes the research presentation easier to prepare. All steps, in one way or another, anticipate the presentation. If the overall problem is understood clearly, and if the information needed to achieve the objectives has been specified, then the framework of the presentation has been largely predetermined. Several parts of the presentation may be partially written during the conduct of the research, for example, it is customary to begin a presentation with a statement of the study objectives and to point out how the attainment of these will help "solve" the overall problem. This part of the presentation can be taken directly from earlier work.

Each project is different and, thus, the process of communicating the results is never automatic. Each requires originality. If the earlier steps in the research process have been well executed, however, it is more probable that a good presentation will eventuate. It is difficult to visualize a successful presentation originating from a study in which the objectives were not clearly defined.

Frequently a researcher will be required to make both an oral and a written presentation. In this section we will discuss both types.

WRITTEN RESEARCH REPORT

No two persons will prepare a written research report the same way. Differences in personality, imagination, and training will—and should—give each report a flavor all its own. But those who write convincing reports agree that the following principles should always be kept in mind.

Consider the audience

Many reports fail to achieve their objectives because the writer does not consider his "market"—the individuals who will read his report. Failure to understand the nature and capacity of these persons, their interest, or lack thereof, in the subject area, the circumstances under which they will read and evaluate the report, and the uses they will make of the report may doom the report before it is written.

Being a technical person himself, the researcher often tends to write a report as if it were intended for other technical persons. He tends to discuss the research problems involved in the project and to use the technical terms which are common to him but not to the reader. The result is often misunderstanding, suspicion, and even hostility.

Executives have individual preferences which must be considered. Some executives demand a minimum report; they want only the results—not a discussion of how the results were obtained. Others want considerable information on the research methods used in the study. Many executives place a premium on brevity, while others demand complete discussion. Some are interested only in the statistical results and not in the researcher's conclusions and recommendations.

Thus, the audience determines the type of report. The researcher must make every effort to acquaint himself with the specific preferences of his audience. He should not consider these preferences as unalterable, but any deviations from them should be made with reason and not from ignorance.

Different readers may present conflicting demands. For example, some persons may want more data on the technical aspects of the research process than others. These different interests are often hard to reconcile and may, in extreme cases, require the preparation of more than one report. In other cases, the basic report may include a minimum of detail but have appendices which cover the technical details for the benefit of those who are interested. Obviously, this problem of conflicting demands has no easy solution. The researcher has to be aware of such conflicts and use his ingenuity in reconciling them.

Keep the study objectives in mind

A good report is written with the goal of putting over certain points. These points should be the answers to the objectives of the particular inquiry. Merely to report the findings without reference to the objectives is to produce a sterile piece of writing. This requires the researcher to be on "intimate" terms with the problem. If the management group has not permitted the researcher to participate in formulating the problem and has either handed down the problem or, worse still, merely demanded certain information, then there can be no definite goal for the report and it will suffer. Under such conditions it will be difficult, if not impossible, for the report writer to draw conclusions and make recommendations.

Be selective

No report was ever written that contained all that was known on the given subject. If an attempt is made to include too much, there is always danger that the important points will be lost in the detail. Therefore, it is important to exclude anything that is not necessary. Since necessity in this sense is a matter of degree, the researcher must use his judgment in deciding what things can be omitted. Such judgments are particularly difficult in relation to explanatory material. The reasons for using certain techniques or the logic leading from findings to conclusions to recommendations for action often take a lot of space to explain. Such explanations can obscure what was actually done or the specific recommendations made. If explanations are not given, the researcher fears the reader will decide these things were not carefully thought through. The researcher must somehow reach a satisfactory compromise. He can mention that certain details have been omitted for the sake of brevity, and offer to supply them on request.

Be objective

The writer must at all times retain his objectivity. Often a researcher will become so enamored of a study that he overlooks his scientific role. This is a natural temptation since much marketing research is done within a sales environment. It is one thing to sell objective results and quite another to present results which have been "slanted" in such a way as to make them salable. The writer does neither himself nor his company any favors if he loses his objectivity.

All researchers have experienced situations in which specific studies were condemned by management because the results did not agree with the manager's judgment or, perhaps, a previous position he had taken on the subject. A few experiences of this type tend to cause the researcher to slant his results towards the answers that he believes management is hoping to find. The advertising manager will receive with enthusiasm a report that shows an expensive campaign has been successful, when he will be hostile to the same study if it indicates the advertising funds have been wasted. Obviously, the researcher must have enough courage to present and to defend his results if he is convinced they are sound. Occasional kudos may be obtained for providing what the manager wants to find, but it is hard to conceive of a solid research reputation being established on such a basis.

Have a purposeful organization

Mere recording of facts without purpose or organization inevitably results in confusion, and confusion leads to loss of interest. The objective of the report is to give the reader the overall "picture" in the shortest possible time. Therefore, each paragraph should be written with the thought of its position in the entire report in mind. The reader should be conscious of the organization so that at any one time he knows where he is in the report and where he is going. A working outline helps the reader comprehend the organization and helps the writer make certain that every point is covered without duplication.

Write clearly

It is easy to say "write clearly," but this is difficult for most people to accomplish. Clarity has many facets and is highly subjective. Despite this subjectivity, some basic principles can be itemized which, if followed, help to produce better reports.[1]

1. Use short, to-the-point sentences—avoid sentence structures which are too elaborate. Always prefer the simple to the complex.
2. Use words the reader will be familiar with but which will provide

---

[1] For a more comprehensive discussion of this subject, as well as report writing in general, see Sue R. Brandt, *How to Write a Report* (New York: Franklin Watts, 1968); William D. Smith, *Business Letters and Reports* (London: William Collins Sons & Co., Ltd., 1968); Walter Wells, *Communications in Business: A Guide to the Effective Writing of Letters, Reports, and Memoranda* (Belmont, Cal.: Wadsworth Publishing, 1968); Lionel D. Wyld, *Preparing Effective Reports* (New York: Odyssey Press, 1967); and Jessanon Dawe and W. J. Lord, *Functional Business Communication* (Englewood Cliffs, N.J.: Prentice-Hall, 1968).

variety and change in pace to the report. Avoid too many difficult words. The prime purpose of the report is to communicate the results of the study—not to impress the reader with the erudition of the writer. Avoid slang and clichés.

3. Make certain the words express *precisely* what the writer wants to say
4. Avoid mechanical flaws such as incorrect grammar. Too often a worthwhile report is discredited because of such flaws.
5. Be sure that the report has uniform style and format. It is usually desirable to write a first draft and then allow a day to elapse before rewriting it. It is wise to submit the revised draft to another researcher for review and comment before the final report is prepared.

The report format

There is no one *best* format for all reports. However, the physical format can be employed to create desirable emphasis and clarity. The use of widely spaced paragraphs, varied margins, separated headings, different type sizes and colors—all make it possible to emphasize major points and to clarify the sequence and relationship of ideas. A report must use the format that best fits the needs and wants of its readers. The following format is suggested as a basic outline which has sufficient flexibility to meet most situations. It should *not* be thought of as a rigid outline which must always be followed.

    I. Title page
   II. Table of contents
  III. Foreword (introduction)
  IV. Statement of objectives
   V. Methodology
      A. Research design
      B. Data collection method
      C. Sampling
      D. Field work
      E. Analysis and interpretation
  VI. Limitations
 VII. Findings
VIII. Conclusions and recommendations
  IX. Appendix
      A. Copies of forms used
      B. Details of sample with validation
      C. Tables not included in findings
      D. Bibliography, if pertinent

Each of these items is discussed briefly in the following paragraphs.

Title page. The title page should indicate the subject, date the report is prepared, for whom prepared, and by whom prepared. Sometimes it is not necessary to specify for whom the report is prepared, while at other times it is wise to indicate this precisely and to show who actually receives copies. Some research reports are confidential and for limited distribution; in such cases, it is particularly desirable to indicate on the title page who will receive a copy.

Table of contents.   If the report is lengthy or if it is divided into numerous parts, it is usually desirable to have a table of contents. If the report includes numerous charts, graphs, and tables, it is desirable to include a list of them immediately following the table of contents.

Foreword.   This section serves to introduce the reader to the research project. It should give the background of the problem (e.g., how and when it came into existence), the importance of the problem, the various dimensions of the problem, and whether any previous research was done which is pertinent to the specific project being reported.

Statement of objectives.   The specific objectives of the report need to be set forth clearly. The reader must know exactly what the report covers. If the particular project is part of a large problem, it is desirable to state the overall problem and the problem solution process. Sometimes it may even be wise to provide some background information as to how the problem arose and what previous research work, if any, has been carried out. If such information will help in understanding the report, it should be furnished, but it should be kept as brief as possible.

Methodology.   The purpose of the methodology section is to describe the research procedure. This includes the overall research design, the sampling procedures, the data collection method, the field methods, and analysis procedures. This section is difficult to write because it is hard to discuss methodology without using technical terms, yet much of the audience for the report will not understand technical language.

Research design.   A description of the research design should make it clear whether the study is exploratory, descriptive or experimental in nature and whether it is case, statistical, or experimental in character. In addition to describing the research design, the researcher must explain why the particular design was used—what its merits are for the project at hand.

Data collection methods.   Were data collected from secondary sources or from primary sources, by survey or observation? Again the researcher must explain why the method selected was appropriate for the project. A copy of the questionnaire or form for recording observational data may be included here. If the form is at all lengthy, however, it will probably be better in the appendix, where it will not break the continuity of the report.

Sampling.   In describing the sampling procedure, it is first necessary to indicate the nature of the universe studied. The exact sampling units, such as stores, housewives, or business executives, must be defined and the geographical limits specified. If there were any difficulties in identifying the sampling units in the field, the procedure used for overcoming such difficulties must be explained. If the sampling unit definition used differed from the commonly accepted one, this fact should be noted and the differences pointed out to avoid possible confusion.

Next, the researcher should describe the size of the overall sample and of each subsample and should explain the reasons for their size. In describing the sampling design employed, the writer must be careful not to use terms which will confuse the reader. Every effort must be made to describe the selection process adequately. Analogies may be useful. For example, if a probability sample were used, it might be best to describe it as a process "which is equivalent to putting the names and addresses of all women over twenty-one years of age, living in the state of Illinois, in a drum, stirring them around, and drawing out the names of two hundred. Such a process insures that every respondent has an equal chance of selection for the sample." Naturally, if complex designs have been used, the description will be more difficult. If the study covers a number of cities and counties, it is often desirable to include, as an exhibit, a map showing the distribution of the sample or a table indicating the sampling sites by regions, states, and counties.

Field work. In describing field work methods, the researcher needs to tell the reader enough to give some idea of the accuracy with which the work was done. This will usually include a description of the number and type of field workers used; how they were selected, trained, and supervised; and how their work was verified. A general summary of the degree of competence shown by the field workers is helpful to the reader. Copies of instructions or other forms used in the field operation can be included here or in the appendix.

Analysis. Relatively little can be said about the analysis and interpretation methods. The findings tend to show what has been done in this regard. If any special, statistical techniques have been used, they should be mentioned. If various executives have assisted in interpretation, this fact should be noted. This may help gain acceptance of the report, and, since interpretation is at least partially subjective, it helps the reader appraise the interpretation given.

Limitations. A good report "sells" the results of the study, but it should not "oversell." Every project has limitations. The competent researcher does not attempt to gloss over these points but instead calls them to the attention of the reader. This helps the reader form a more accurate interpretation of the results than he would otherwise do. It has the added advantage, from the researcher's standpoint, of giving confidence in the results presented. If the reader finds limitations which the report does not point out, he is apt to wonder how carefully the research was done.

Limitations may be of several types. One that should always be emphasized is the degree to which one may generalize from the results. If the universe studied is Cleveland, Ohio, the reader should be cautioned not to generalize about the United States at large. If the study is an exploratory one designed to find new hypotheses, the reader should be warned not to conclude that the results are an accurate measure of the phenomenon studied.

If particular questions in a survey seem to have confused respondents, the reader should be warned to use particular care in interpreting the results of these questions. If many not-at-homes were encountered in the field work and substitutions were made, the reader should be cautioned as to the effect this could have on the results. In short, the researcher should note any weaknesses in the research methods used.

In describing the limitations of the study, the researcher should point out the degree to which they could affect the results. If limitations are overemphasized and not put in their proper perspective, they may tend to destroy confidence in the valuable parts of the study instead of increasing confidence.

Findings. Findings are the results of the study. This section makes up the bulk of the report. It is not just an assortment of statistical tables and charts, but an organized narrative of the results. Summary tables and graphic methods of presentation should be used liberally. Highly detailed tables should be relegated to the appendix. The specific objectives of the study should be kept in mind and the findings presented with them in view. Too often, the writer feels he must present *all* the findings regardless of their bearing on the objectives of the study. The list of information needed to achieve the objectives, which was prepared in the problem formulation step, should limit the scope of the findings presented.

Conclusions and recommendations. Conclusions should be drawn with direct reference to the objectives of the study. The reader should be able to read the objectives, turn to the conclusions section, and find specific conclusions relative to each objective. If, as sometimes happens, the study does not obtain satisfactory data from which to draw a conclusion relative to an objective, this should be acknowledged rather than disguised.

While it is almost always necessary for the researcher to draw conclusions, it is not always possible or advisable for him to make recommendations. On occasion the researcher may be specifically asked not to make recommendations. In other situations where the researcher has worked on one problem but has limited knowledge of the company's background and general operating policies, he would be unwise to recommend definite courses of action even if asked to do so. Making recommendations assumes considerable knowledge of the total "picture," including the resources of the firm and all the alternative courses of action. Often the research worker does not have this knowledge.

Appendix.   The purpose of the appendix is to provide a place for those report items which do not fit in the research report proper because they are either too detailed or are too specialized. For example, the appendix may contain a detailed statement of the sample design, the formulas used to determine the sampling error, detailed statistical tables, and the various research forms used, such as the questionnaire and the written interviewer instructions. Nothing should be relegated to the appendix if its absence from the report proper will make it difficult for the reader to understand the results. If certain data are discussed in any detail, the tables containing such data should be included in the report at that point. In many cases the main ideas can be presented graphically in the findings section. In this case the tables on which the charts are based should be included in the appendix. This permits anyone who wishes to check the details to do so.

Summary report.   The report format suggested above does not contain any summary section. This exclusion is deliberate. The summary should not be prepared until the full report is written. Once the report is completed, a summary can be prepared quickly and efficiently. A summary, however, is usually prepared. Its objective is to present the highlights of the complete report so that executives can get the main ideas quickly. Some companies treat the summary as a separate report and send it to certain executives instead of the full report. In other instances, the summary is attached to the full report.

Report writers often place the summary at the beginning of the findings section, in which case the summary covers only the findings—it does not include any mention of the other sections in the report. If this is done the findings section is broken into two parts: (1) the summary, and (2) the detailed account of the findings. Other writers prefer to make the summary a separate section at the first of the report. This latter method makes it easy for the busy executive to read the summary and decide whether to go further. It also permits him to determine quickly who else in the organization should read the report. When the summary is made the first part of the report, the objectives, findings, conclusions, and recommendations are included in it.

Preparing the report

Textual material.   Before attempting to write a report, the researcher should prepare an outline. This outline will follow the general plan of the report as discussed above; however, it should be in considerably more detail. All tables and charts which will be presented should be planned.

Once an outline is completed, the writer prepares a first draft. This may go through several revisions. In the revisions the writer attempts to improve the clarity of expression and to make it briefer. He makes a final check of the conclusions and recommendations to be sure they are pertinent to the study objectives and are supported by the data collected. All mechanical details are also checked to be sure, for example, that no errors in arithmetic have been made.

Preparation of charts and tables.   In preparing the tables and charts, standard practices should be followed. These are described in most elementary books on statistics. Four of the more important rules for presenting data in tables or charts are as follows:

1. Each table and chart must be self-explanatory.
2. The title must describe fully the contents, including what the data represent, the geographical scope (for example, total United States), the unit of measurement (such as dollars, tons, pounds), the date, and the base for any percentages.
3. The source of the data should be given directly below the table heading or below the table. If the source is a more detailed table appearing in the appendix, this should be noted. For those tables which are based on the results of the current project, no source need be indicated.
4. The stub and column captions must tell exactly what is included in the line or column, but should not be so long as to hurt the conciseness of the table. Charts require special care in preparation. Since they are designed to facilitate an understanding of the results, the writer must make certain that they accomplish this objective. Obviously they should not be used if they are so complicated that they create confusion rather than prevent it.

ORAL PRESENTATIONS

Marketing researchers are often asked to present study findings orally to executives. This may involve informal discussion in an advertising manager's office, semiformal delivery in a marketing conference room, or fully-structured and formal presentation in a corporate auditorium or audiovisual communication center. The oral presentation may be intended to introduce or summarize a detailed written report, or it may be structured to interpret the findings of a general report for a special audience. Regardless of the setting or objectives, however, the oral presentation should be considered a prime opportunity to convey important research findings and to stimulate interest in specific research activities.

Thoughtful preparation can result in an oral presentation that "pays off" in three ways: (1) By bringing the research findings to the immediate attention of the people who count, the oral presentation can insure that the written report doesn't get lost or side-tracked in the corporate maze. (2) By giving the researcher an opportunity to put the report in full perspective, oral delivery can help busy executives realize quickly the significance and worth of the research findings. (3) By exposing the researcher to key management personnel, the speaking opportunity can bring increased recognition to the researcher and his team. Inadequate preparation, on the other hand, does injustice to the total research endeavor and reflects negatively on the researcher. Moreover, it is expensive. The direct expense can be measured in terms of the per-hour cost of bringing highly-paid executives together for an unproductive meeting. The indirect cost must be measured in terms of research findings that fail in implementation as the result of misunderstanding or misjudgment on the part of the listeners.

Many skills, particularly speaking skills, contribute to the success of an oral presentation, but given enough time to prepare for a presentation anyone can effectively convey technical information.

Planning, preparation, and organization

The first stage in the development of a successful oral presentation involves planning, preparation and organization. In this stage, the speaker plans the strategy of his presentation. He first answers a few essential questions: Who will be listening to the presentation? How much do they already know about the subject? What do they expect to learn from the presentation? How much should they know to respond competently to the presentation?

When you work up a speech, visualize the audience as they will be when you meet them. For example, if you are getting ready for a ticklish conference, think of the people who will be there. Consider the range of their information, interests, and prejudices. Which points are urgent? Which points need to be mentioned without laboring them? Which points have to be introduced gingerly, or dropped altogether? Keep the time limits in mind.[2]

The importance of careful audience analysis cannot be stressed too highly. The researcher should always remember that an oral presentation involves interaction between a speaker and an audience. It is not enough for the speaker to address the audience as though it were passive. Any time a speaker talks and an audience listens, there will be many interpretations of what the speaker is saying. Therefore, if the speaker wishes to communicate effectively to the audience as a whole, he must consider the range of unique perceptions of the people in the audience. In informal speech this is done with little conscious thought. The speaker can usually sense through the listener's expression, comments, or questions how well he is communicating. In speaking to a group, however, the feedback process is more subtle. Therefore it is important for the speaker to think of his presentation from the viewpoint of his listeners—not only while speaking, but while preparing the speech.

---

[2] James H. McBurney and Ernest J. Wrage, *Guide to Good Speech*, 3d ed. (Englewood Cliffs, N.J.: Prentice-Hall, Inc., 1965), p. 74.

The best way to communicate with an audience is to put the information that is to be conveyed in a context that is familiar to the audience. Suppose, for example, the researcher is talking about a consumer marketing survey. If he is talking to other market researchers, he may wish to use the semitechnical word "respondents" to refer to people interviewed in the survey. In talking with marketing executives, on the other hand, the words "consumers," "buyers," or "prospects" may be more meaningful. The more technical the subject matter of the presentation, the more important it is to relate key ideas or points to concepts or experiences that are familiar to the audience. This does not mean that the researcher should talk down to the audience. He should talk with it.

A script is perhaps the most essential aid to effective oral presentation. For an informal or semiformal presentation, a tightly organized topical outline on index cards is sufficient. But if the presentation involves a tight time limit, audiovisual aids, or is part of a rigidly structured program, the speaker should strongly consider writing a detailed script that reads just like he wants the talk to sound. The fully-detailed script offers many advantages. It can be accurately timed. Audio or visual aids can be cued for smooth continuity. The script eliminates the danger of the speaker's digressing from the topic or needlessly belaboring a particular point. Finally, a detailed script reassures the inexperienced speaker that he will not forget what he wants to say. The main disadvantage of the written script is obvious: uninspired reading of the script will result in a dull, monotonous presentation.

The main criterion of a good script is the clarity and impact with which it communicates the researcher's findings, interpretations, and recommendations. What is left out is as important as what is included. It is essential to find a central theme around which to organize the main points of the presentation. Any thought that does not directly contribute to the development of the presentation should be eliminated, although humor, illustrations, and anecdotal material all contribute to effective communication. The "trick" is to weave them into the presentation so they give meaning and significance to the points the speaker wishes to emphasize. When the speaker introduces statistics, for example, illustrations that give a sense of proportion or scale are often quite effective in helping the audience understand the meaning of the numbers. Of course, the makeup of the audience should be the decisive factor in the selection of the illustrations. A nontechnical audience may be grateful for an illustration of an abstract or technical concept that would be condescending to a more technically-inclined group.

There are several important differences between writing a report for publication and writing a script for oral presentation. In the first place, written and spoken language are quite different. In preparing a script the writer should say every phrase aloud several times, modifying it as necessary to capture on paper the easy and natural sounds of speech.

Further, the writer should avoid words that he would not use in conversation—particularly words that are difficult to pronounce. Complex sentence structure should also be avoided. Statistics should generally be rounded for convenient oral delivery. Rather than saying "1,378 men and 1,523 women responded to the questionnaire," it would be better to say "roughly 1,400 men and 1,500 women responded." It may seem that accuracy is being sacrificed. But when statistics are being cited, the price of slavish accuracy on paper may be totally muddled understanding by listeners who must try to keep track of all the digits in their minds.

A particularly important point to consider in writing a script is the value of developing main points from several perspectives. In a written report this would be redundant. But in listening to speech, many people miss as much as 50 percent of what the speaker is saying. So redundancy is not necessarily a sin in oral presentation. Such redundancy may take the form of a personal anecdote followed by an abstract generalization followed again by an illustration. In fact, it is not a bad idea for a speaker to have at hand real or convincing hypothetical examples of every important point in his talk. If he senses that he is leaving his audience behind, or if someone asks for an example, he is well equipped to clarify the point.

Pictures, graphs, or key words displayed on a screen are fine ways to strengthen a point. One authority lists the following items which may help a speaker get his point across:[3]

Graphs	Tabulations
Charts	Samples
Diagrams	Substances
Maps	Merchandise
Pictures	Demonstrations
Drawings	Processes
Photographs	Methods
	Exhibits, scale models

Visual aids do not take the place of good speaking, but for emphasizing many concepts they are indispensable. They are particularly good for dramatizing numerical information, illustrating physical or quantitative relationships or comparisons, highlighting key concepts or words, and showing dynamic change over time.

There are several points to consider in selecting appropriate visual aids:

1. The aid should enhance the idea being discussed by illustrating, demonstrating, simplifying, highlighting, or interrelating key concepts.
2. The information displayed should be accurate in representation and authenticity.

[3] Robert S. Casey, *Oral Communication of Technical Information* (New York: Reinhold Book Division, 1958), pp. 102–03. This is an excellent introduction to the topic. It contains extensive bibliographic references.

3. The simpler the visual aid the better. Avoid "busy" or unnecessarily detailed visuals. The viewer should be able to grasp the idea of the visual at a glance. This means keeping written copy to a minimum; making diagrams, drawings, or illustrations as straightforward as possible with a minimum of distracting elements; and editing tabular material to illustrate the point with a minimum of rows, columns, and numbers.[4]

4. Only one thought at a time should be displayed visually. If a visual is unavoidably complex, the speaker should help the audience read it by using a pointer to indicate significant features of the visual.

5. Display material or projected visuals should be clearly and easily visible from the most distant point in the meeting room.[5]

6. Physical factors also dictate the use of visual aids and associated display equipment. The speaker should consider the size of the audience and the meeting room, lighting and blackout provisions, and the availability of suitable equipment.

A brief discussion of some of the delivery equipment available for the display of visual aids follows.[6]

Display boards. These include chalk boards, magnetic boards, felt boards, and Velcro boards (one surface has tiny nylon hooks while the other surface has equally small nylon loops—pressed together, the surfaces stick together). Chalk boards are handy for writing out numbers, equations, charts, or diagrams as the talk develops. The other types of display boards, often called "slap boards," are less flexible but generally more colorful. Pictures, words, slogans, symbols are mounted on a backing material, cut into shapes, and slapped onto the board one by one to build up an idea. These devices are useful props for film or television talks.

Flip charts. In skilled hands the flip chart, which is essentially a very large pad of blank paper mounted on a metal or wooden easel, is an extremely useful aid. Key words or visuals can be sketched in advance on the successive pages of the pad. Various-colored felt-tip pens can be used for highlighting. Unobtrusive masking tape tabs can be placed on the bottoms of the pages to help the speaker turn the pages at the appropriate time. As the talk develops, the speaker simply reveals the page desired at any time. An even more refined technique involves writing a list of key words on one page. Each word is covered with a strip of opaque paper

---

[4] For an excellent basic introduction read Ed Minor, *Simplified Techniques for Preparing Visual Instructional Materials* (New York: McGraw-Hill Book Co., 1962). This book also contains an extensive bibliography. For a specialized discussion of slide and filmstrip production see *Producing Slides and Filmstrips,* Kodak Audio-Visual Data Book S-8 (Rochester, N.Y.: Eastman Kodak Co., undated).

[5] *Artwork Size Standards for Projected Visuals,* Kodak Pamphlet No. S-12 (Rochester, N.Y.: Eastman Kodak Co., undated).

[6] Casey, *op. cit.,* pp. 145–49.

attached with masking tape. As the speaker makes an important point he rips off a strip to reveal the appropriate key word. When he makes the next point, he rips off the succeeding strip. When all of the strips have been removed, the full list of words, which is often in outline form, is exposed.

Overhead projectors. Overhead projectors are becoming increasingly popular in conference rooms and classrooms. Opaque or transparent colored images are rendered on clear acetate sheets. A variety of processes are used to do this, ranging from crayon pencil sketching to more complex diazo processes. The acetate sheets are often mounted in die-cut cardboard frames. A projectable area of 7½ by 9½ inches is a popular size for these "projectuals," as they are called. Images of this size project quite clearly on a screen. More elaborate projectuals involving overlays (images added in succession to a base image to build up a complex visual), "reveals" (a similar technique for building complex images), and even moving images can be created. Since the projectual, or acetate sheet, is placed on a flat stage on the projector, the speaker can also write or draw on the acetate at the same time the image is being projected. The words or drawings appear on the screen as he writes. Special marking pens, available in a full range of colors, are used for this purpose. In this fashion, the overhead projector serves the same purpose as a blackboard —only the speaker need never turn his back to the audience. Overhead projectors are relatively portable. The projectuals, providing they are not too complex, are relatively inexpensive to create. Above all, the overhead's flexibility is limited only by the speaker's imagination.

Transparent slides. Transparent slides are probably the most widely used visual aid in formal and semiformal oral presentations. Slides are produced in several sizes. With the development of remote-control, magazine-loaded projectors, a speaker can operate the equipment himself and, thus, keep the presentation flowing smoothly. Anything that can be photographed provides suitable subject matter for this type of visual.

16 mm. film. Full-scale 16 mm. films are probably of little value in conveying the findings of marketing research. Short film clips, however, may definitely have a place. A speaker may wish to show candid reactions of consumers as they select test products from the shelf of an experimental supermarket, for example. Motion picture photography has many uses in laboratory and field situations. A researcher using motion picture photography for data collection may wish to use specific clips to illustrate sections of his oral report. Smaller, less expensive film formats are also available—8 mm. and super 8 mm., for example.

Video tape. The availability of low-cost video tape equipment opens many vistas for effective oral presentation of research findings. An oral report given at a headquarters office, for example, can be taped for distribution to branch offices. Video tape is also an excellent tool for improving oral delivery. The speaker can see himself in action and thereby discover unconscious bad habits. Still quite new in application, video tape will undoubtedly play an increasing role in data collection and data reporting.

Rehearsal

Careful rehearsal is the second major step in the development of an effective oral presentation. The speaker should read the script aloud several times to get the feel of it. He should rewrite any awkward-sounding phrases. There are several useful "tricks" to make the delivery of a script sound interesting, relaxed, and professional. One trick is to use marking pens to underline key phrases or words. Sometimes a word may be underlined to indicate proper emphasis to make the sentence sound natural. Some speakers develop fairly elaborate symbols that serve as road signs on the script to guide their pacing and delivery. A heavy black star may mean slow down here, or a red arrow may mean skip this section if time is running short. The best way to make a script sound natural is to learn it so well that a glance at the first words of a paragraph is sufficient to enable the speaker to ad lib the remaining content. When this level is reached, the speaker can benefit from the control provided by the script, yet avoid a stilted, mechanical delivery that comes from reading aloud.

When the speaker feels he knows the script fairly well, he may wish to deliver it into a tape recorder. This is a fine way to detect and correct poor enunciation or pronunciation. If the speaker feels that his voice sounds nervous and strained, he can also work on strategies to help him relax. If he is talking too fast or too slow, he can work on regulating his pacing.

EVALUATION OF THE RESEARCH PROCEDURE

Immediately following the writing of the report, the efficiency of the research project should be evaluated. Inevitably, certain research decisions have to be made with the benefit of little, if any, evidence. For example, the allocation of the sample between regions and city size groups may be based, in part, on some estimate of the homogeneity of the groups being studied. If the assumption is that people on the west coast are more homogeneous with regard to the characteristic being studied than, say, persons living in New England, then, all other factors being equal, more interviews would be scheduled in the latter region. An analysis of the findings would give some indication of the accuracy of this assumption. Such data on variance—even if only a rough approximation—will help in the planning of future studies and will enable the research worker to obtain greater efficiency.

Even though the questionnaire was thoroughly pretested before adoption, a "post-mortem" study will probably reveal certain ways in which it could have been improved. Closely tied with this is the possibility that the field work could have been improved through changes in the interviewer selection, training, and control procedures. Evaluation of the individual field workers is in order. What interviewers need to be dismissed?

The above discussion suggests only a few ways in which the evaluation process can be of benefit to the research department and the firm. Through such a process, better research work can be developed in the future.

Research work lends itself to experimentation, and the researcher usually has an opportunity to do some experimentation in each study he conducts. He can test a number of alternative decisions by designing experiments within the main project. Naturally, the experiments must not interfere with the main objectives of the study. For example, a test might be run to determine whether the use of an interviewer's quiz on field instructions resulted in better field work. On a random selection basis, half the interviewers could receive the quiz and half not. Each interviewer could then be graded on the basis of how well he followed the instructions, the number of completed interviews, cost per completed interview, and the number of unsatisfactory returns. The two groups of interviewers would then be compared to determine whether any significant differences resulted. Since the two groups were equated in advance by the use of a random selection method, any differences would be due to either the quiz or to random sampling fluctuations. Significance tests would then determine whether the differences could be explained entirely by sampling variations.

This is but one of many ways that the research worker can build into his research design tests which will help him to improve research technique.

SUMMARY

Excellent research is sometimes wasted because the research worker did not prepare a good research presentation. One common cause of this failure is that the writer did not consider the wants and needs of the relevant audience. Frequently the researcher uses technical terms and turns out a presentation which is scientific but over the heads of his audience. He should not hesitate to use honest salesmanship to put over the results of his work.

The previous research steps anticipate the report. If these steps were well planned and executed, the presentation should be relatively easy to prepare. In writing the report the analyst must keep the study objectives in mind, must find the proper balance what to include and what not to include, be objective in his thinking, have a purposeful organization, and write and speak with clarity.

There are many different research report formats. The choice of which to use depends on the characteristics of the persons who will read the report. The suggested format is one which contains: (1) an introductory section which includes a statement of the study objectives and the methodology used, (2) a presentation of the results, and (3) conclusions and recommendations. A summary report is prepared after the main report has been completed and can be used in a variety of ways, either as part of the main report or as a separate report.

An excellent oral report has substantial payouts. It is usually desirable to prepare a script for the presentation from the written research report. Audiovisual aids can be important in helping the researcher in his presentation, but none should be used unless they enhance the ideas under discussion through illustrating, demonstrating, simplifying, highlighting, or interrelating key concepts.

The research worker is frequently not in a position to see the effects of his work. In order to maximize the funds invested in research, it is desirable that the research group have some representation in top management circles. If such does not exist, it is usually difficult for a research worker to press for action based on his results. His best chance frequently lies in working through the individuals most directly affected.

The methodology used in a study should be evaluated immediately after completion to discover more efficient procedures. A careful review of the sample design, the questionnaire, and the field methods will almost always pay dividends. Research work lends itself to experimentation so most studies offer an opportunity to test new ideas.

PART **III**

Selected applications of
marketing research

Part III is devoted to a discussion of the application of marketing research in four specific areas—motivation, advertising, product, and sales control. In each of these areas specialized techniques have been adapted to the basic procedures discussed in Part II.

14

Motivation research

MOTIVATION includes ". . . all those inner striving conditions variously described as wishes, desires, needs, drives, and the like."[1] As such, motivation provides a bridge from ". . . the psychology of the individual to social processes and psychology of the group. Motives are one point at which an individual's own needs and resources converge with those of his group and of society as a whole. Without considering social processes, we cannot explain individual behavior in any but the simplest of situations."[2]

Motivation research attempts to determine the *why* of behavior. It is not limited to any specific type of behavior, but includes any area of consumer behavior which may relate to marketing problems. Consumer behavior is difficult to investigate for motivation is complex, usually involving a multiplicity of factors, about many of which the consumer may not be aware. While most individuals have a reason for their behavior, it may not always be logical.

Motivation research is used most extensively in marketing to determine why consumers buy one brand or type of product instead of competing alternatives. Such information helps in designing the product, its package, pricing, and advertising. The latter is especially important because most advertising seeks to explain why consumers should buy a given product. Therefore, it is necessary to have some understanding of what motivates different individuals. The following conclusions about why wallpaper had lost sales were arrived at from

---

[1] Bernard Berelson and Gary A. Steiner, *Human Behavior* (New York: Harcourt, Brace & World, Inc., 1964), p. 239.

[2] James H. Myers and William H. Reynolds, *Consumer Behavior and Marketing Management* (Boston: Houghton Mifflin Co., 1967), p. 79.

motivation research and illustrate the importance of such research in advertising:

People were afraid of choosing the wrong wallpaper, of not being able to rely on their own taste, and of then being "stuck" with the wallpaper after having spent a considerable amount of money. They felt that they could not afford to remove it if they did not like it. They would have to let it stay up long enough to repay their investment. Thus, the advertising appeal that wallpaper "lasts a lifetime" was exactly the opposite from the one needed to motivate purchase of the product.[3]

There are many different approaches to the study of motivation, although most researchers commonly assume that behavior *per se* can be explained using one or more psychological concepts. But consumer behavior is a complex subject and it should not be surprising to find disagreement about the validity of different research approaches. A substantial part of the problem of attempting to measure motivation is that so many variables are involved and that these operate differently under varying conditions even for the same person.

In many motivation research studies there is an implicit assumption, unacceptable for our purpose, that behavioral determinants—social and biological— generally operate in all subjects in roughly the same manner. This assumption is incorrect for the variables that originate socially: the heterogeneity of the environment and thus of socialization processes as well as its differential impact on people have been proven beyond doubt.[4]

Motivation research must take into account both conscious and unconscious motives. Indeed, any act of behavior usually involves more than one motive, and these need not only to be cited, but their relative importance measured as well. Most marketing researchers do not attempt to arrive at a complete understanding of all motivation factors involved. For example, the physiological motives, those which derive from the physical needs of the individual such as hunger and thirst, are very often ignored as being too obvious—too common to all individuals. The researcher will attempt to pick those motives which are most apt to have an effect on the demand for the product or service under investigation. This selection is not unlike the development of hypotheses which have to be tested to determine their applicability.

The measurement of motives is especially difficult in marketing because of the need to determine the motives of a number of individuals in order to aggregate behavior. Many of the techniques available for studying motivation have been developed for use on single individuals

---

[3] Ernest Dichter, *Handbook of Consumer Motivations* (New York: McGraw-Hill Book Co., 1964), p. 151.

[4] Francesco M. Nicosia, *Consumer Decision Processes* (Englewood Cliffs, N.J.: Prentice-Hall, Inc., 1966), p. 117.

over a relatively long period of time. A further ". . . note of caution needs to be stressed. . . . Since motives are both inferred from and taken into account for purposive behavior, there is always the danger of accepting circular reasoning—of taking a motive as an explanation of the very behavior from which it was inferred. When the conditions that produce or arouse a motive are known, or when there are independent measures of it, motives help to explain behavior. When such conditions are not met, motives may serve to describe behavior, but they do not explain it."[5]

Motivation research should not be defined as research using specific research methods; what is important is the purpose of explaining behavior, *not* the methods used. Too frequently motivation research is considered to be any research involving the application of techniques from clinical psychology to marketing studies. To some people the use of depth interviews and projective techniques constitutes motivation research, but *not* the use of such conventional methods as the direct question. This chapter takes the point of view that a variety of research methods can be used to study human behavior and its causes, and that they are all part of motivation research.

KINDS OF INFORMATION SOUGHT IN MOTIVATION RESEARCH

A variety of information is needed to do an effective job in diagnosing human behavior because of the need to ". . . focus attention on the *whole battery of inner conditions that play a dynamic part in a person's buying or not buying, responding favorably or unfavorably to some communication.*"[6] This battery of inner conditions includes ". . . cognitive factors such as information and misinformation people have, and perceptive factors such as the way they see a situation. These factors as well as the motivational forces such as attitudes, expectations, habits, and intentions—all influence the way the consumer behaves."[7]

It is difficult to describe what information is most applicable to studies dealing with motivation simply because literally *all* data having to do with the consumer are relevant. One rarely can have too much information about the "why" of consumer behavior. If one is not careful, however, one begins to cover the entire field of human behavior which covers such subjects as perception, learning, ethnic relations, culture and society, personality, and group influences. The problem is that any study

---

[5] Berelson and Steiner, *op. cit.*, pp. 240–41.

[6] George Horsley Smith, *Motivation Research in Advertising and Marketing* (New York: McGraw-Hill Book Co., Inc., 1954), p. 5.

[7] Rensis Likert, "Research on Consumer Motivation," *Boston Conference on Distribution* (1954), p. 55.

of motivation will, of necessity, impinge on several of these areas. Thus, there is no simple way of delimiting what subjects are, or are not, included in a motivational research study. The researcher must have enough insight to form hypotheses which focus on the factors most critical to the project at hand. The remainder of this section discusses, briefly, some of the more important types of information which are commonly sought in this type of research, namely, attitudes, assumptions, sensations, images, and motives.

Attitudes

Attitudes represent a predisposition to respond to given stimuli. They indicate the extent to which people accept or reject such marketing factors as advertising appeals, product features, and package designs. Essentially, attitudes are measured in order to establish what relationships exist between the stimuli and the extent of the response.

Attitudes are rarely all positive or all negative. Sellers find both positive and negative attitudes toward their products and advertising efforts among different consumers. No product and its advertising please all consumers, and thus it is necessary to select a particular segment of the market to please. The extent to which consumers accept or reject products and the characteristics of these various consumer groups are important in helping the seller decide to what market segments he should attempt to sell.

One must always determine what attitudes are silent. In a study for a savings and loan association respondents

. . . were asked to indicate on a four point scale how important they felt various benefits or claims were. Some of the benefits were "safety of money," attitude of window personnel," "interest rate earned," and "years in business." In the case of the last item—years in business—the survey showed that respondents felt that there were *big differences* among the various local institutions in terms of longevity, but that this was *relatively unimportant* to them in deciding where to save. Hence, years in business was not a salient factor in this situation.[8]

Since forces are constantly at work to alter consumer attitudes, no seller should assume that favorable attitudes toward his product or service will always remain favorable. Repeated "soundings" must be made to keep up with the trend of consumer attitudes.

Assumptions

Throughout life each person stores away items of information which are used constantly as references points for accepting and rejecting new

---

[8] Myers and Reynolds, *op. cit.*, p. 164.

ideas. Many of these reference points are subconscious because they are deeply imbedded in the subconscious mind. Many products are accepted or rejected because they "fit" or "don't fit" the assumptions and beliefs which act as the consumer's "frame of reference."

A knowledge of the assumptions and beliefs held by consumers is important. Many people tend to use price as an index of quality, and as a consequence a product which sells for substantially below what one considers the "normal" price runs the risk of being thought "cheap" or "inferior."

Consumers make a variety of assumptions—often without fact—about the products they buy. Beverages (such as beer) that come in pastel colored containers are thought to be "lighter" or "less strong" than those that come in darker colors; natural fabrics (such as wool) are considered better than synthetics; and products produced in one country are considered superior to similar products produced in another country.

Assumptions and beliefs are closely related to attitudes, but are typically thought to be more basic and more difficult to change. In many cases they are obtained from the previous generation and are implanted at an early age. Typically people hold certain assumptions and beliefs in common with their group affiliations, for example, with their social class.

Sensations

Sensations represent the reaction of the mind to either a mental or physical stimulus. Sensations are commonly produced by stimuli which affect a person's sight, smell, hearing, taste, and touch. The words sensation, feeling, and emotion are often used interchangeably. Technically a sensation has to do with a bodily response to a stimulus, while an emotion (such as love, hate, and fear) is the reaction of the mind resulting from the bodily response. The word "feeling" describes what is felt by both the body and mind. In this discussion, no attempt is made to distinguish carefully among these three words.

In a study on shaving it was found that men have contradictory feelings about this subject. Despite the time consumed, men find that:

Shaving, for one thing, permits much sensuous gratification, offering a range of stimulations. More of these are satisfied by the use of brush, lather, and safety-razor shaving, but they are still present with electric shaving. Sample quotations from more articulate men clearly point up the wealth of pleasure incident to hot and cold wettings, rough towels, creams and powders, and astringent pre- and after-shaves. This is virtually the only occasion when a normal man can indulge in toilet waters and scents. After all, the male is the decorative sex among both primitives and animals. Yet our particular society rigidly forbids him any other access to lotions and scents.[9]

[9] Pierre Martineau, *Motivation in Advertising* (New York: McGraw-Hill Book Co., Inc., 1957), pp. 61–62.

Images

Images are tied closely to sensations; they are the mental pictures that are formed as a result of stimuli. They are closely connected with symbols and associations. Consumers form certain images about products typically built around the product characteristics they believe are salient. The major influence of advertising appears to be felt in the areas of consumer perception of the brand. The brand image is the major organizing concept through which the consumer is guided toward perceiving unified patterns of stimulation. This imagery provides the emotional and sensual qualities which distinguish a brand from the general product class and help the consumer discriminate from brand to brand.

Image research is common in marketing because all aspects of marketing influence the image that a consumer has of the product. Frequently, one finds that consumers have a very precise image of a product even though they have never used it. In the early days of color TV a substantial percentage of the adult population had a negative image of the product and its performance even though only a small proportion had ever seen a television color program. Among those who had, the image was much more favorable.

The purchaser of a brand usually has the feeling that he has purchased a product which is distinctly different from another brand, even though he really cannot tell the difference in a "taste" test. This is typically the case with many packaged foods, beverages, and cigarettes. Product and brand images do change, although it is difficult to effect a change within a short period of time in the absence of a product change which is perceived by the consumer as being important.

Motives

All human behavior is caused or initiated through "needs"—it is not spontaneous. The term "motive" refers to one of the more compelling determinants of a person's action. Individuals act in ways which are designed to obtain certain goals. "Motivation arises out of tension-systems which create a state of disequilibrium for the individual. This triggers a sequence of psychological events directed toward the selection of a goal which the individual *anticipates* will bring about release from the tensions and the selection of patterns of action which he *anticipates* will bring him to the goal."[10]

Individuals have needs which are physiological (sex, thirst, hunger, etc.) and needs which are psychogenic (to protect our loved ones, to be accepted socially, to be approved of, etc.). Individuals are, of course,

---

[10] James A. Bayton, "Motivation Cognition, Learning—Basic Factors in Consumer Behavior," *Journal of Marketing* (January, 1958), p. 282.

motivated by a combination of these needs. One researcher believes " . . . that consumers are influenced at some time, to some degree, and for some products by at least 600 different motives. These include not only a host of *biological* and *social* motives, but a great variety of motives in other categories such as the *artistic, political, religious, intellectual,* and *economic* types of motives. To these should be added the *general* motives which cut across all of the other categories."[11]

In order to "trigger" effectively a particular want or need into a motivating force, it is necessary to have considerable knowledge of the attitudes, sensations, assumptions, and images which prevail about the particular brand and the product type as well. Take, for example, a food product. While eating is a biological necessity, the seller of a food product may decide not to use hunger as his basic appeal, but instead social approval, economy, taste, or even pride. His choice of which want to appeal to would be influenced by what he knew about the attitudes, sensations, assumptions, and images held by consumers. His knowledge of these factors would help him decide how to communicate the chosen appeal to consumers. With the food product example he would need to know, among other things, whether consumers thought his product to be fattening, inexpensive, good for children, and easy to prepare. Thus, while motives are distinct and separate factors, they are closely tied to the other factors discussed above.

Summary

Before turning to a discussion of the techniques which are available for obtaining information on "why" behavior, it is desirable to summarize the discussion thus far. This can be done by presenting parts of an actual study which was conducted to determine the meaning of shaving to American men. The report of the more pertinent findings of this study was not divided into attitudes, assumptions, motives, sensations, and imagery, yet all of these factors were involved even though they were not given the labels used in this chapter. Nevertheless, men are shown to have the *attitude* that shaving should be done leisurely even though it is also viewed as a waste of time. Shaving is *sensuous*, as witness the pleasure derived from hot and cold wettings and the use of astringents. Men *assume* that shaving is a symbol of masculinity, and the adult male *assumes* that regardless of how frequently he shaves he has a tough beard. A man is *motivated* to shave not only to "take off" his beard but to reorganize himself and reestablish his identity for his family and his job responsibilities for the coming day. Men have definite *images* of people who use a safety razor and brushless shaving cream. They are thought of

---
[11] C. Joseph Clawson, "The Coming Break-Throughs in Motivation Research," *Cost and Profit Outlook,* Vol. XI, Nos. 5 and 6 (May–June, 1958), p. 1.

as "plain" men who are probably lower-middle class. They are stereotyped as clerks, salesmen, policemen, foremen, and high school boys. In contrast, those who use electric shavers are thought to be more individualistic, more quick to adopt new devices, more urban and sophisticated, and more advanced socially (e.g., actors, company presidents, and college students).[12]

The reader will note that in the above example the various behavioral factors (assumptions, motives, attitudes, etc.) blended together to provide a total picture. The same should be true with any behavioral study. These factors were isolated for purposes of discussion, and, while the reader will find this classification helpful in conducting any motivational study, he must recognize that they all are interrelated and that they inevitably flow together, thereby lending concreteness to the final results.

The next section discusses some of the techniques which are available for conducting motivational inquiries. These techniques are classified and discussed under the following four headings: (1) nondisguised-structured, (2) nondisguised-nonstructured, (3) disguised-nonstructured, and (4) disguised-structured.

MOTIVATION RESEARCH TECHNIQUES

Nondisguised-structured techniques

This approach employs a standardized list of questions; thus, no attempt is made to disguise the purpose of the study. These questions are often used to obtain responses about beliefs, feelings, and attitudes and frequently to determine the intensity of feelings or attitudes. The discussion here will center mainly on the problem of intensity as it applies to attitudes.[13]

An attitude is an abstraction. Its existence has to be deduced either from overt or verbal behavior. By "opinion" is meant the verbal expression of an attitude. Probably it would be more realistic to say that an opinion is the verbal expression of a number of attitudes. While there is a technical difference between an opinion and an attitude, the two are often used interchangeably. The following discussion will not attempt to distinguish between them.

A variety of types of questions may be used to rate the attitudes of respondents. These range from the simple "yes" and "no" question to the use of elaborate scales.[14] Sometimes respondents are given a list of

---

[12] Martineau, *op. cit.*, pp. 61–65.

[13] A more detailed discussion on structured questions, including scaling, has been presented in Chapter 7.

[14] For an illustration of the use of four alternative scales and an evaluation of each see James Rothman, "Formulation of an Index of Propensity to Buy," *Journal of Marketing Research* (May, 1964), pp. 21–25. Also see G. David Hughes, "Selecting Scales to Measure Attitude Changes," *Journal of Marketing Research* (February, 1967), pp. 85–87.

alternative answers and asked to rank them relative to a given base. Regardless of the type of question, the answers are used to place the individual in some category (such as favorable or unfavorable) with regard to his attitudes or feelings about a particular subject.

Single-question technique. The simplest type of attitudinal study uses the single-question approach in which respondents are usually asked to select one answer from a number of alternatives,[15] For example, to find out consumer attitudes toward a given product the following question might be asked: "Which one of the following statements best describes your feelings about X product?"

1. I like it.
2. I dislike it.

Or more elaborate alternatives might be provided as follows:[16]

1. I think it is an *excellent* product.
2. I think it is a *very good* product.
3. I think it is a *good* product.
4. I think it is a *fair* product.
5. I think it is a *poor* product.
6. I think it is a *very poor* product.

The single-question technique has the advantage of being easy to administer and analyze. It does, however, possess serious disadvantages:

1. Unless the subject matter is specific, it is virtually impossible to construct meaningful categories. For example, the responses to .the general question, "How do you feel about X product?" would be difficult to interpret. When a person says it is a fair product, to what is he referring? What product attributes is he evaluating? Did he take into account the price of the product? Is he comparing the product with other products or against the job he thinks the product should do? Little information is provided about the context the respondent is using in replying to the question. Thus, in any study having to do with attitudes, the researcher must be sure that all respondents are rating exactly the same thing. Unless this is done, ambiguous results will be obtained.

2. Specified alternative answers may force the respondent to express an attitude he does not hold. Many individuals do not have a well-formulated attitude on a given subject. Indeed, they may never even have thought about the subject until they were asked a question about it. Thus, the study may be testing a nonexistent attitude on the part of some respon-

---

15 For an example of the use of what, in effect, is a single question approach to obtaining a measure of preference see Ralph L. Day, "Simulation of Consumer Preference," *Journal of Advertising Research* (September, 1965), pp. 6–10.

16 For an evaluation of the use of a ten point scale see William H. Reynolds, "Some Observations on a Ten Point Poor-to-Excellent Scale," *Journal of Marketing Research* (November, 1966), pp. 388–91.

dents. While this difficulty is no doubt true with any type of opinion question, it is more true with the single-question approach because the general tendency is to press for a response other than "don't know." Because respondents are "boxed-in" they are not likely to elaborate as to whether the alternative they select describes their true feelings.

3. Semantic difficulties are apt to be accentuated. When replies are limited to fixed alternatives, there is the maximum possibility for the respondent to misunderstand the meaning intended by the interviewer and vice versa, without the misunderstanding's coming to light.

4. Although respondents can be ranked relative to one another according to the category they choose, there is no way to determine how much one person differs in terms of "favorableness" or unfavorableness" from any other person. One might assign numbers to the various categories—say from 1 to 5 with 1 representing the least favorable category and 5 the most favorable category. However, such a scheme assumes that the numerical intervals mean the same thing to all respondents. If, using the scale 1 to 5, A is rated as 5, B as 3, and C as 1, it cannot be said with any certainty that A is five times as favorable as C or that B is three times as favorable as C, or that A's attitude is more favorable than B's by the same extent as B's over C's. It could, however, be said that A's attitude is more favorable than B's and that B's attitude is more favorable than C's.

Rather than assign numerical weights to the categories, respondents could be asked to indicate their degree of favorableness toward a given stimulus on a linear scale. For example, a scale running from 1 to 10 could be used with 10 representing the most favorable and 1 representing the least favorable categories. Such a scale may facilitate "answers" but does not solve the problem of measurement, since the units on the scale will have different meanings for different respondents.

Use of multiple questions. This technique uses a number of questions, and respondents are scored on the basis of their answers to all questions. The answers to individual questions are usually not important by themselves; what is important is the total score of all answers. It is generally thought that this approach makes it possible to distinguish in more detail between respondents as to the intensity of their feelings or attitudes. In other words, the scaling is more sensitive and can distinguish between individuals who differ only slightly in their attitudes.

The construction of these scales was discussed in Chapter 7 and is based on the same assumption as the single-question technique—namely, that individuals can be ranked with regard to their attitudes toward a given stimulus. These more complicated scales do *not* solve the problem of how *much more* favorable or how *much less* favorable one person's attitude is as contrasted to that of another individual.

Physiological tests. Because these testing devices are used extensively in advertising they are discussed in more detail in Chapter 15. The treatment here will be short. Over the years a variety of techniques employing special equipment have been developed to measure physiological responses to various stimuli. These include such techniques as the galvanic skin response, which measures change in perspiration; eye movement, which records the path followed by the eye in reading a message; and pupil dilation, which operates on the premise that a pleasant or interesting stimulus causes the pupil to dilate while an unpleasant or boring one causes contraction. The difference between before and after stimulus measures indicates "effect." All such tests have been developed because under certain conditions they are thought to be more accurate than verbal responses.

In summary, it is important to note that structured questions can provide considerable help in the study of human behavior. This is especially true for information about stereotypes of users of a given product. In recent years, projective techniques have been embraced by researchers without much real attempt to determine whether the structured type of question could be modified to obtain similar behavior information.[17] What has happened over the years is that the projective techniques used in marketing research have become more focused and the respondent is often asked to respond to structured questions dealing with the stimulus.

Nondisguised-nonstructured techniques

Nondisguised-nonstructured techniques have been derived largely from the work done by psychoanalysts. While this approach has a number of different variations, they all have one thing in common— neither the questions asked nor the answers given are predetermined. Such interviewing techniques are known by a variety of names, including depth interviews, qualitative interview, nonstructured interview, clinical interview, nondirective interview, focused interview, and camera-action interview. All are designed to provide more detailed information concerning the subtleties of human behavior, including the "why" component.

The flexibility of the unstructured or partially structured interview, if properly used, helps to bring out the effective and value-laden aspects of the subject's responses and to determine the personal significance of his attitudes. Not only does it permit the subject's definition of the interviewing situation to receive full and detailed expression; it should also elicit the personal and social context of beliefs and feelings. This type of interview achieves its purpose to the extent that the subject's responses

---

[17] See Ralph L. Westfall, Harper W. Boyd, Jr., and Donald T. Campbell, "The Use of Structured Techniques in Motivation Research," *Journal of Marketing* (October, 1957), pp. 134–39. Also see Darrell B. Lucas, "Can the Clinical Techniques be Validated?" in Robert Ferber and Hugh G. Wales, eds., *Motivation and Market Behavior* (Homewood, Ill.: Richard D. Irwin, Inc., 1958), p. 130.

are spontaneous rather than forced, are highly specific and concrete rather than diffused and general, are self-revealing and personal rather than superficial.[18]

The nondirective approach.   In the nondirective interview, the respondent is requested to talk about a given subject. The conversation is started with a broad initial question such as, "Tell me how you feel about————subject," and the respondent is encouraged to continue talking *without* receiving the stimulus of direct questions from the interviewer. The role of the latter is that of a recorder, although he is expected to be sufficiently sensitive and skilled to keep the respondent talking freely about the subject in a coherent fashion. This encouragement usually is in the form of such noncommittal statements as "tell me more," "why," and "that's interesting." The interviewer must create an environment in which the respondent feels absolutely free to discuss his feelings without any fear of disapproval or loss of status.

Regardless of the extent of interviewer skill present, the interpretation of the results is difficult because respondents are often not articulate in the way they express their feelings. Their replies are often ambiguous, since it is difficult to know the exact context in which the remarks were made. These are the very disadvantages which many researchers hope to overcome by using a more structured approach. Still, the nondirective interview is of considerable value in obtaining data which serve as sources of hypotheses.

Some interviews are more focused in that they concentrate more on a specific experience or set of experiences to which the respondent is known to have been exposed. Often the interest is to obtain information on the reactions of the respondent to these experiences and/or what factors prompted participation. The interviewer is typically provided with a list of topics (or suggested questions) which serve as her guide for conducting the interview. But the tone of the situation is one of permissiveness and, thus, the respondent is given considerable freedom in responding to the topical stimuli. Usually, the investigator has generated a set of hypotheses about the experience(s) under study and the object of the interviewing is to test their validity. Obviously, the more knowledgeable the interviewers are about the experiences to be discussed the more proficient they will be in their work.

Disguised-nonstructured techniques

Since many people are unwilling or unable to provide investigators with an insight into their conscious and unconscious motives, nondisguised techniques frequently do not get at real motives. Thus, more dis-

---

[18] Claire Selltiz, Marie Jahoda, Morton Deutsch, and Stuart W. Cook, *Research Methods in Social Relations* (New York: Henry Holt and Co., Inc., 1959), p. 263.

guised methods, typically referred to as projective methods, are often used. These were initially developed by clinical psychologists for the diagnosis and treatment of individuals who were suffering from emotional disorders. The use of projective tests requires specialized training, since considerable theory underlies their use and the ways of interpreting the data obtained. Despite this, such devices are helpful if only because they provide a way of overcoming the reluctance of some respondents to express their views on a taboo subject. Even where the respondent sees through the disguise of the test and knows the *real* purpose, projective methods are useful because respondents find it easier to express their feelings by transferring them to a fictitious character.

The stimuli (in projective tests) are capable of arousing many different kinds of reaction, for example, an ink blot, which can be perceived in different ways; a picture, which can elicit a variety of stories; a set of dolls, which can be made to behave in many ways. There are no "right" or "wrong" answers, nor is the respondent faced with a set of limited alternatives. The emphasis is on his perception of the material, the meaning he gives to it, the way in which he organizes or manipulates it. The nature of the stimuli and the way in which they are presented do not clearly indicate the purpose of the test nor the way in which the responses will be interpreted. The individual is not asked to talk directly about himself. The ostensible subject matter is the ink blot, the picture, the dolls, or whatever, not the individual's own experiences or feelings. However, the responses are interpreted as indicating the individual's own view of the world, his personality structure, his needs and feelings, his ways of interacting with people.[19]

There has long been considerable controversy over the validity of projective techniques among students of clinical psychology. To some extent this ambiguity about validity springs from clinicians expecting too much from the tests.[20] Some studies, however, have shown that such techniques provide more valid data than do direct questions.[21]

There are a variety of projective techniques, including word association, sentence completion, story completion, and pictorial tests. Each of these will be discussed briefly.[22]

---

[19] *Ibid.*, p. 281.

[20] Benjamin Z. Lebovits, "On Empty Bathtubs: A Reply to Meehl," *Journal of Projective Techniques and Personality Assessment* (September, 1964), pp. 307–13. For a discussion of the difficulties of developing valid projective measures see R. T. Green and B. G. Stacey, "A Flexible Projective Technique Applied to the Measurement of the Self Images of Voters," *Journal of Projective Techniques and Personality Assessment* (February, 1966), pp. 12–15.

[21] Howard L. Steck, "On the Validity of Projective Questions," *Journal of Marketing Research* (August, 1964), pp. 48–49.

[22] The most commonly used projectives, according to Mills, are the Rorschach, thematic tests, human figure drawings, and sentence completion. See David H. Mills, "The Research Use of Projective Techniques: A Seventeen Year Survey," *Journal of*

Word association.   Word association is one of the oldest and simplest projective techniques. The respondent is presented with a number of different words, one at a time. After each word he is asked to give the first word that comes to his mind. If the list of words presented is related to the subject of interest, the respondent may indicate some of his attitudes toward the subject with his responses. The underlying assumption is that by "free associating" with certain stimuli (words), the respondent will reveal his inner feelings about the subject being studied. Responses are timed so that those answers which the respondent "reasons out" are identified. The delay may indicate "blocks" and these must be taken into account in the analysis.

Word association tests are not difficult to administer, since to most respondents, taking the test is like playing a game. Nor is it difficult to construct a list of words. It does require, however, some skill and experience to interpret the results. The usual way of constructing such a test is for the researcher to prepare a list composed of a combination of "stimulating" and "neutral" words. What stimulating words to include depends on the purpose of the study. For example, if the purpose is to find responses to alternative advertising appeals, then the key words in these appeals will certainly be included in the list. On the other hand, if one is undertaking an exploratory study on, say, consumers' feelings about a particular food, then a great variety of words that might relate to food in general as well as that specific type of food would be used.

The words are usually read to the respondent one at a time and the interviewer records the first word "associated." Respondents should not be asked to write their answers because an additional variable is thereby added, namely the delay required for the respondent to put the association into written form.

There are several variations to the simple test situation described above. For example, respondents may be asked to give not only the first word that comes to mind, but the first three or four. Variations of this technique may be run as controlled tests, as contrasted to free association. For example, respondents may be asked, *What brand of cake mix comes to your mind first when I mention baking a cake?* or *What brand of detergent comes to your mind first when I mention soft and fluffy clothes?*

In analyzing the results of word association tests, the usual practice is to group responses along such lines as favorable-unfavorable and pleasant-unpleasant. Individual questionnaires should be checked for

---

Projective Techniques and Personality Assessment, 29 (4) (1965), pp. 513–15. For a more complete discussion of projectives see Joseph Zubin, Leonard D. Eron, and Florence Schumer, *An Experimental Approach to Projective Techniques* (New York: John Wiley & Sons, 1965).

consistency and for evidence of "blocks." The latter are usually indicated by a persons' inability to "associate" within a time limit such as five seconds. This is why interviewers should "time" respondents and then proceed to the next word if no answer is forthcoming.

Sentence completion. This technique is quite similar to word association. Respondents are presented with a number of incomplete sentences and asked to complete them. As with the word association test, respondents are asked to complete the sentence with the first "thought" that comes to mind. To insure that this is done, respondents are timed. Sentence completion tests may provide more information about the subject's feelings than word association, but they are not as disguised, and many respondents are able to diagnose the investigator's purpose.

Sentence completion can be used in a number of different ways in marketing research. Some examples taken from a magazine study are:

"A man who reads *Time* magazine is . . . ."

"A man who receives a gift certificate good for *Newsweek* magazine would be . . . ."

"*Business Week* magazine appeals to . . . ."

"*Life* magazine is most liked by . . . ."

Sentence completion questions can be worded in either the first or third person. No evidence exists to indicate one approach is better than the other.

Story completion. This technique provides the respondent with part of a story—enough to center attention upon a particular issue, but not enough to indicate the ending. The respondent is then asked to give the conclusion in his own words.

An example of the use of the story completion technique is as follows:

"A man purchased gasoline at his regular service station which sold a nationally advertised brand of gas. The station attendant, who knew the man, said, "Mr. Harris, your battery is now nearly two years old. We just got in a new product which when added to the water in your battery will prolong its life by about a year. It's a real good buy at $1.75."

"What is the customer's response?"

"Why?"

The story completion technique is quite versatile and has numerous applications to marketing problems, the most important of which is probably to provide the seller with data on the images and feelings that people have about a particular product. Obviously such findings are highly useful in determining advertising and promotional themes as well as reactions to the product itself.

Pictorial techniques. The pictorial techniques are similar to story telling except that pictures are used as the stimuli. The two main pictorial techniques are: (1) thematic apperception tests, and (2) cartoons.[23]

Thematic apperception tests. Thematic apperception tests, commonly referred to as T.A.T., have long been used by clinical psychologists. They have been described as consisting of:

> . . . a series of ambiguous pictures, about each of which the subject is asked to tell a story ("What's happening in the picture? How did it come about? What will happen next?"). It is assumed that in describing the characters depicted, in setting forth their actions and the influences which affect them, the subject indirectly tells something about himself. Any person in the story with whose actions the subject concerns himself, with whom the subject may be conceived as identifying, represents a medium through which the subject expresses his own inner tendencies. The thoughts, the feelings, the attitudes, the inhibitions, etc., expressed by the characters with whom he identifies provide clues to his own tendencies. This does not mean that basic tendencies are always directly revealed; unconscious defense mechanisms may transform their expression even in the T.A.T., but the T.A.T. will often provide indications of the operations of these mechanisms.[24]

An example of the pictorial technique is contained in Figure 14–1. The researcher found that the answers elicited through the use of this projective drawing were substantially different from those obtained through the use of direct questions and seemed to be better predictors of milk consumption. In commenting on the use of this technique, and projective techniques in general, the researcher states that "it can be particularly helpful in checking the veracity of responses to more direct questions, in obtaining information from consumers not easily obtained by more direct methods (i.e., where inhibitions are raised for one of several reasons), and in providing supplementary information."[25]

Some projective materials elicit more and better responses than others. This depends upon the ambiguity of the material, the extent to which the respondent is able to guess the conclusions, and the vagueness of the probe questions.

Cartoon tests. Cartoon tests are a version or modification of the T.A.T., but are simpler to administer and analyze. Cartoon characters are shown in a specific situation pertinent to the problem. One or more of the "balloons" indicating the conversation of the characters is left open and the respondent is asked to fill it in. In comparing the cartoon

---

[23] For a discussion of the scoring of such tests see M. Mike Nacuas, "Objective Scoring of the T.A.T.: Further Validation," *Journal of Projective Techniques and Personal Assessment,* 29 (4) (1965), pp. 456–60.

[24] Marie Jahoda, Morton Deutsch, and Stuart W. Cook, *Research Methods in Social Relations,* Part I (New York: Dryden Press, 1951), p. 215.

[25] Steck, *op. cit.,* p. 49.

FIGURE 14–1. Example of thematic apperception test

WOULD YOU THINK THAT MRS. A OR MRS. B DRANK MORE
MILK, OR POSSIBLY BOTH ABOUT THE SAME AMOUNT? (REASON
GIVEN?)

Mrs. A.   Mrs. B.

SOURCE: Howard L. Steck, "On the Validity of Projective Questions,"
Journal of Marketing Research (August, 1964), p. 46.

technique with the direct question in a study of the loyalty of buyers to
industrial suppliers, one researcher concluded that the indirect approach provided a better insight and measure of resistance to change
than did the direct method. He used a cartoon which showed a conference in progress. One of the participants (Pete) was saying:[26]

"Now this is our present supplier list. We've been with them for quite

---

[26] George M. Robertson, "Motives in Industrial Buying," in Robert S. Hancock
ed., *Dynamic Marketing for a Changing World* (Chicago: American Marketing Association, 1960), p. 394.

a while and they've been doing a good job. I see no reason for making any changes. The next subject is . . . ."

Tom, another man at the conference, interrupts to say: "Hold on Pete . . . loyalty is fine, but there are a lot of other considerations. I think we're due for a change."

The interviewer asked the respondent, "In this case, with which man would you be in most agreement? Why is that?"

In preparing cartoon tests, the researcher must be careful to use situations into which respondents can project themselves easily. That is, the picture must present a situation which is familiar to the respondent—one with which the respondent can identify. The test situation must be clear and unambiguous. The respondent must have no doubt as to what situation is portrayed.

Other techniques.   The techniques discussed thus far are those most commonly used in motivational studies. Psychologists have developed a great many other techniques, including the use of *play, psychodrama, puppetry, graphology,* and *finger painting.* All of these tests are based on the same concepts as the projective techniques discussed above. To date there appears to have been little use of these "other" techniques in marketing research.

Disguised-structured techniques

The attitudes which individuals hold can be determined by their beliefs, perceptions, judgments, and the amount and kind of information they possess on a given subject. In order to measure those attitudes which respondents might not readily and correctly express and to obtain the advantages resulting from the use of a structured questionnaire such as ease in administering and in coding, it is desirable to use disguised-structured techniques wherever ingenuity permits. Respondents usually perceive such tests as achievement-type tests for which there are right and wrong answers.

The basic premise underlying such tests is that respondents will reveal their attitudes by the extent to which their answers to objective questions vary from the correct answers. Respondents are provided with questions which they are not likely to be able to answer correctly. Thus, they are forced to "guess at" the answers. The direction and extent of these guessing errors is assumed to reveal their attitudes on the subject. For example, individuals tend to gather information which supports their attitudes and, therefore, the extent and kind of information an individual possesses on a given subject indicates something of his attitude.

Hammond has used a similar technique to measure attitudes toward management-labor relations. One part of his test consisted of giving the respondent two alternative answers to questions—each alternative was equally wrong, but in the opposite direction from the right answer. For example, one of his questions was, "Average weekly wage of the war worker in 1945 was (1) $37, (2) $57?" It was assumed that few people would know the correct answer, but that pro-labor respondents would guess the low figure and pro-management respondents the high figure. His results distinguished clearly between union and management members.[27]

In a hot cereal study, the disguised-structured technique was used by asking such questions as:[28] *How much do you think it costs for the hot cereal alone in an average bowl of cereal such as you'd serve at breakfast?* (¼¢ or less, ½¢, ¾¢, 1¢, 2¢, 3¢, 4¢, 5¢, 6¢, plus, don't know?) *Which of the following cereals do you think costs more per serving than a hot cereal, and which cost less? Do corn flakes cost more or less than hot cereal? Do Cheerios cost more or less than hot cereal?*

Questions similar to these were asked regarding vitamins, protein content, and the fattening qualities of hot cereals as contrasted to selected brands of cold cereal. Data from these questions revealed, for example, that dry cereal users exaggerated the cost of hot cereal. Considerable differences were evident between regions and city-size groups as to perceived vitamin content; the larger the city size, the better the vitamin rating for dry cereals.

Another variation of this technique is one which asks respondents to estimate the percentage of a group which possesses certain attitudes, beliefs, or feelings, or which behaves in a certain way. This test is based on the principle that individuals overstate the percentage of the group that agrees with their own attitudes.

In recent years researchers have been using a variety of psychological tests to classify respondents with regard to marketing variables. For example, the Pettigrew category width test has been used to classify respondents with respect to their willingness to accept risk. Subjects are asked to estimate maximum and minimum ranges for a variety of phenomena. A broad categorizer is one who ". . . tends to judge extreme instances of a category more distant from a central tendency value relative to judgments of the narrow categorizer."[29] Broad categorizers are those who strive to include maximum positive instances. The results correlated with a stated willingness to buy new products and showed that there was a relationship between willingness to buy and breadth of categorization as revealed by the test. Broad categorizers were more

[27] Kenneth R. Hammond, "Measuring Attitudes by Error-Choice," *Journal of Abnormal and Social Psychology*, 43 (January, 1948), pp. 38–47. The correct answer was $47.

[28] Westfall, Boyd, and Campbell, *op. cit.*, p. 138.

[29] Donald T. Popielarz, "An Exploration of Perceived Risk and Willingness to Try New Products," *Journal of Marketing Research* (November, 1967), p. 369.

willing to "risk" the purchase of such new products as cameras, dress shoes, auto tires, and so on.[30] Efforts to use the Edwards Personal Preference Schedule, however, to identify individuals who would buy Ford cars instead of Chevrolets, were without success.[31]

Such psychological tests are readily available and are easy to administer. Some researchers have thought a body of evidence might gradually develop that would enable one to predict consumer purchases by personality test, but at least one psychologist believes that personality variables are not as important in the buying process as has typically been thought.[32]

LIMITATIONS OF MOTIVATION RESEARCH

Caution in the use of motivation research techniques should be exercised not only because of the way these techniques are applied, but because the resultant data need to be analyzed in accordance with psychological theory. It must be remembered that these techniques were developed to obtain information from a single individual over a long period of time. It is another matter to obtain penetrating data from any sizable number of persons about their behavior when the contact time is usually less than an hour and when they appear as strangers to the interviewer.

It is worthwhile to note that many motivational studies are conducted by individuals who have little experience in dealing with the techniques involved. Too frequently the technique is borrowed with little understanding about why it was developed or how it must be used to be effective.

Small samples are a common weakness of motivational studies, but, while this limits the generalizations that can be drawn from them, it does not necessarily mean they are useless. Sometimes advertisers need a new idea or an insight more than they need measurement. The "fraud" of reporting a hypothesis as if it were an established fact applicable to a specified proportion of the population is, of course, unchallenged. But this observation in no way reduces the value of promising hypotheses provided they are reported candidly as hypotheses derived from limited data.[33]

---

[30] *Ibid.*, pp. 368–72.

[31] Franklin B. Evans, "Psychological and Objective Factors in the Prediction of Brand Choice: Ford versus Chevrolet," *Journal of Business* (October, 1959), pp. 300–69. For a discussion of personality variables and consumer behavior see Robert P. Brody and Scott Cunningham, "Personality Variables and the Consumer Decision Process," *Journal of Marketing Research* (February, 1968), pp. 50–57.

[32] J. Hunt, "Traditional Personality Theory in the Light of Recent Evidence," *American Scientist*, 53 (1965), pp. 80–96.

[33] G. D. Wiebe, "Is It True What Williams Says about Motivation Research?"

A further problem has to do with the way the various motivational techniques are used and the ways the results are analyzed and interpreted. Most motivational studies require highly skilled interviewers and analysts who have had training in psychology and sociology. Where a marketing researcher is confronted with the need for doing motivational research, it is usually advisable for him to enlist the efforts of a professionally trained social psychologist—one who has not only a good theoretical background, but one who has also a knowledge of survey methodology and some familiarity with marketing. Even when this is done, the problem of validation remains, since motivational data are usually subtle and need to be interpreted according to basic theory.

Despite these difficulties, there can be no question that motivational research is an important part of marketing research and that great strides have been made in its use. It is expected that even more progress will be made during the next decade in using this kind of research to help solve the time-old problem of why the consumer behaves as he does.

SUMMARY

The primary purpose of motivation research is to determine the "why" of consumer behavior. While there is nothing new about the study of motivation, it is only in recent years that marketing people have used the systematic techniques developed by the psychologists and sociologists. In order to do an effective job in diagnosing human behavior, it is necessary to obtain information about attitudes, assumptions, sensations, images, and motives.

A great variety of techniques is available for use in connection with motivation research. Those techniques were classified under the following four headings.

Nondisguised-structured techniques

These techniques center around the use of a standardized list of questions. Respondents are limited in their answers to a set of stated alternatives. No attempt is made to disguise from the respondent the purpose of the inquiry. Attitudinal information is frequently ascertained using such an approach. A variety of types of questions can be used to rate the attitudes of respondents. These range from simple "yes" and "no" questions to the use of elaborate scales. Regardless of the type of ques-

---

Journal of Marketing (April, 1958), p. 410. Also see Robert J. Williams, "Is It True What They Say about Motivation Research?" *Journal of Marketing* (October, 1957), pp. 125–33.

tions used, the answers are used to place the individual into some category—such as favorable or unfavorable.

Nondisguised-nonstructured techniques

These techniques have been derived largely from the work done by psychoanalysts. They are called by a variety of names, including the depth interview, qualitative interview, nonstructured interview, clinical interview, nondirective interview, focused interview, and camera-action interview. While there are differences among these types of interviewing, they all have in common the fact that neither the questions nor the answers are predetermined.

Disguised-nonstructured techniques

Since respondents frequently are unable or unwilling to provide the investigator with an insight into their inner feelings, it is often necessary to use projective techniques. These include word association, sentence completion, story completion, and pictorial tests.

Disguised-structured techniques

A person's attitudes can be determined by his beliefs, perceptions, judgments, and the amount and kind of information furnished on a given subject. Disguised-structured techniques take advantage of this fact and can be used to get at those attitudes which may not be correctly expressed in response to direct questioning. They cannot, however, provide deep insight into the "why" of a person's behavior.

Caution should be used in analyzing and interpreting findings from motivational studies. Most of these studies use small samples, thereby making it difficult to generalize the results to the universe. Results are hard to quantify since emotions, attitudes, and images have shades of meaning. Despite these and other limitations, there can be no question but that motivational research is an important tool of marketing research.

Case 14—1.   HYDE PARK PIANO COMPANY

The Ackerman Advertising Agency had as one of its accounts the Hyde Park Piano Company. The agency was trying to decide how to implement the copy platform which had been decided on for the fall and winter campaign. More specifically, the agency was attempting to determine whether a given picture of a child would be appropriate to use as the main illustration in the magazine advertising. The copy platform was that the advertising should stress the responsibility of parents to provide piano lessons for their children. The advertising was to point out that children need to learn to play the piano for future happiness; that piano playing will lead to a fuller, more content, and richer life.

The creative department felt that a large picture of an appealing little girl should dominate the ad in order to obtain attention as well as reinforce the copy. The copy writer said: "I want this child to be sensitive and somewhat introspective . . . one who will convey the impression that she loves music; that she can be deeply moved by the beauty and feeling of music. In other words, she must be identified by readers as a little girl who appreciates music and who, at the same time, can benefit from it."

After much effort the creative department obtained a picture of a little girl which met the requirements of the copy writer assigned to the account. The account executive, however, had certain reservations about the picture. He said, "I'll admit it has a lot of involvement, but I don't get the feeling that it's right for what we're trying to do. The little girl is just a bit too far removed from reality. I think we had better test this picture before we decide to use it." The problem of testing was turned over to the agency's research director. His findings appear below:

REPORT OF COPY TEST FOR HYDE PARK PIANOS

Purpose

The purpose of this study was to investigate the meaning of a proposed picture among a sample of mothers living in the local metropolitan area.

Method

The guiding principle of this study was the belief that people will reveal the meaning of visually perceived material through their associations with that material. For example, when encouraged to talk about the picture of the little girl, respondents bring forth significant associations evoked by the picture. These associations, insofar as they are common to a variety of people, may be considered to be representative of those associations evoked in similar people in the population at large.

A total of 56 women viewed the photograph and were questioned about their associations with it. The sample was divided as follows by socioeconomic groups:

Upper-middle	18
Middle-middle	19
Lower-middle	12
Lower	7
Total	56

Respondents were shown the picture and after being exposed to it for approximately 20 seconds were asked (with the picture still in their hands) what words they felt would best describe the little girl in the picture. Their replies were recorded verbatim. Respondents were then given a list of words and asked to indicate which of these words they thought applied to the little girl.

Findings

An analysis of the results shows that the little girl is described typically as being longing, yearning, fearful, forlorn, imaginative, wistful, and shy. She is seen as questioning, concerned with unsettled issues, an onlooker at others' play, unable to cope with social relations. Yet, she is also very appealing in her need for warmth and love. She tends to evoke a somewhat realistic childhood . . . one full of uneasiness, problems, and difficulties. A typical reaction was ". . . she seems to be introspective, perhaps even imaginative. I would guess that she's listening to music and that she's dreaming of the world around her. It's good photograph and shows a child who is sort of beautiful in a melancholy way."

Another typical remark on the negative side was ". . . she's deep in thought. Perhaps she's worried because she's all alone. I don't think a child of that age really ever looks so deep in thought. I know my daughter never does."

A tabulation of responses to the words offered to respondents to help them describe the little girl is shown below.

Word	Percentage of respondents selecting word
Longing	16%
Imaginative	14
Yearning	11
Wistful	10
Forlorn	9
Fearful	9
Shy	9
Secure	4
Graceful	6
Sweet	10
Musical	8
Artistic	19
Lonely	25
Practical	3
Wealthy	13

Our conclusion is that the picture reflects some anxiety but did, nevertheless, arouse a great deal of interest.

On the basis of the research findings, would you suggest any changes in the creative approach? If so, what do you recommend?

Case 14—2. CONLEY BOUGHTON AND ASSOCIATES

The Conley Boughton and Associates advertising agency was requested by its new beer account, the Riester Beer Company, to conduct a research investigation to determine what kind of an image men had of the Riester brand. The agency was anxious to obtain this information since work was soon to commence on the fall campaign. The spring and summer campaigns had been prepared by the client's former agency. Both the agency and the Riester Company had agreed that it would not be wise to attempt any advertising changes either in copy or media until the fall. Since the agency felt the proposed study would be especially helpful to the creative staff, it agreed to underwrite the entire cost of the study.

The agency's research director, Mr. Jacobsen, stated that the primary objective of the study would be "to find out what people think of the Riester brand of beer in contrast to other leading sellers. We must be able to analyze the findings by heavy versus light beer drinkers and by brand of beer most preferred." Because he did not feel that people could or would talk at great length about why they like a certain brand of beer, Jacobsen decided not to use a depth interview approach, but to rely on a sentence completion test and rating scale devices.

The Riester account supervisor, Mr. Smythe, advised Jacobsen to get some data on the current Riester advertising. Smythe said, "As you know, their present advertising relies heavily on a pretty gal to get the message across. They have used this girl now for several years and feel they have quite an investment in her. I'm sure they think she's a good symbol for their beer. Maybe we should keep her—I don't know."

The Riester brand was sold in only four states and received heavy competition from national, regional, and local brands. It was priced just below the national brands. The company was an old, established one which had successfully marketed its brand for over fifty years. In recent years sales had been declining, mainly because of the inroads made by the national brands.

Before putting the study into the field, Jacobsen decided to clear the questionnaire with Smythe and with the Riester Company's advertising manager. In presenting the questionnaire (shown as Exhibit 1), Jacobsen noted that Questions 7 and 8 would cover a number of different brands, for example, Question 7 would be asked for the Riester brand and four major competitors. This would mean, in essence, that Questions 7 and 8 would be repeated five times each for an equivalent of ten questions. He said that he felt the other four brands should be Hamm's, Budweiser, Falstaff, and Schlitz. He reported that the questionnaire had been pretested and that the average time per completed interview among those who drank beer was forty minutes. The study would be conducted only among men.

What changes, if any, should be made in the questionnaire?

EXHIBIT 1. Proposed Riester questionnaire

1. Do you drink beer?   ☐ Yes   ☐ No   (IF NO END INTERVIEW)
2. What brand of beer do you prefer above all others? _____
3. Which of the following brands of beer have you tried?
   ☐ Hamm's   ☐ Schlitz   ☐ Budweiser
   ☐ Riester   ☐ Falstaff
4. Do you ever drink draught beer?   ☐ Yes   ☐ No
   4a. (IF YES ASK) What brand of draught do you prefer? _____
5. About how many bottles or cans of beer do you think you drank last week?
   _____

6. I'm going to read off to you some sentences which I want you to finish. Say the first words that come into your mind.
   1) "Land of the Sky Blue Waters" means _____
   2) My friends say that Budweiser is _____
   3) I think the girl in the Riester beer commercial is the kind of girl who _____
   4) The kind of tavern that sells Budweiser is _____
   5) The last time I saw Schlitz in a store _____
   6) Riester beer is _____
   7) My wife thinks the Riester beer girl is _____
   8) Bartenders say Falstaff is _____
   9) The last time I saw Riester beer in a store I _____
   10) My friends say that Riester beer _____
   11) Hamm's beer is _____
   12) Bartenders say Riester beer is _____
   13) The kind of a tavern that sells Riester beer is _____

7. I'm going to read off a list of people. I want you to tell me whether you think they would, would probably, might not, probably wouldn't, or would not drink _____ brand of beer. (HAND RESPONDENT A SCALE CARD AND TELL HIM HE NEED ONLY GIVE YOU A NUMBER AS HIS ANSWER.)

EXHIBIT 1 (*Continued*)

Person	Would drink	Would probably drink	Might or might not drink	Probably wouldn't drink	Would not drink
Athlete	1	2	3	4	5
Factory worker	1	2	3	4	5
Young housewife	1	2	3	4	5
Intellectual	1	2	3	4	5
File clerk	1	2	3	4	5
Man with low income	1	2	3	4	5
Executive	1	2	3	4	5
Young man	1	2	3	4	5
Mature older man	1	2	3	4	5
Man who knows beer	1	2	3	4	5
Man who drinks beer with meals	1	2	3	4	5
Conservative man	1	2	3	4	5
Happy man	1	2	3	4	5
Man with high income	1	2	3	4	5
Modern man	1	2	3	4	5
Older woman	1	2	3	4	5
Truck driver	1	2	3	4	5
Foreman	1	2	3	4	5
Man who drinks beer only occasionally	1	2	3	4	5
Serious man	1	2	3	4	5
Farmer	1	2	3	4	5
College student	1	2	3	4	5
Accountant	1	2	3	4	5
Man who does not drink hard liquor	1	2	3	4	5
Professional man	1	2	3	4	5

8. I'm going to read off some words which some people use to describe a brand of beer. For the _____ brand of beer will you tell me whether the word applies, probably applies, might or might not apply, probably doesn't apply, or does not apply. (HAND RESPONDENT A CARD SHOWING THIS SCALE AND TELL HIM HE NEED ONLY GIVE YOU A NUMBER AS HIS ANSWER.)

Description	Applies	Probably applies	Might or might not apply	Probably does not apply	Does not apply
Carbonated	1	2	3	4	5
Strong	1	2	3	4	5
Fun	1	2	3	4	5
Dry	1	2	3	4	5
Good	1	2	3	4	5
Active	1	2	3	4	5
Light	1	2	3	4	5
Mild	1	2	3	4	5
Ordinary	1	2	3	4	5
Clear	1	2	3	4	5
Young	1	2	3	4	5
Relaxing	1	2	3	4	5
Sweet	1	2	3	4	5
Aged	1	2	3	4	5
Bitter	1	2	3	4	5

EXHIBIT 1 (*Concluded*)

Description	Applies	Probably applies	Might or might not apply	Probably does not apply	Does not apply
Expensive	1	2	3	4	5
Dark	1	2	3	4	5
Sharp	1	2	3	4	5
Regional beer	1	2	3	4	5
For everyday drinking	1	2	3	4	5
Nice aroma	1	2	3	4	5
Modern	1	2	3	4	5
Refreshing	1	2	3	4	5
Masculine	1	2	3	4	5
Tasty	1	2	3	4	5
Respected	1	2	3	4	5
Burning	1	2	3	4	5
Feminine	1	2	3	4	5
Old fashioned	1	2	3	4	5
Green	1	2	3	4	5

Classification data

RESPONDENT'S NAME _____

ADDRESS _____

MARITAL STATUS _____ AGE _____

ANNUAL INCOME   Under $5,000 ☐ $5,000–$9,999 ☐ $10,000 & over ☐

EDUCATION   Grammar school only ☐   Some high school ☐
High school ☐   Some college ☐   College ☐

OCCUPATION _____

- - - - - - - - -

INTERVIEWER'S NAME _____ DATE _____

Case 14—3. FLAHERTY AND ASSOCIATES

Flaherty and Associates, an advertising agency with annual billings in excess of $20 million, received an invitation to solicit, through presentation, the account of a large ball-point pen company. The prospective client requested each of the five agencies competing for its account to prepare in writing a suggested advertising plan for the next 12 months assuming a media budget of $750,000. The instructions regarding the suggested plan indicated that no specific advertising copy or art work was to be presented, but rather only the agency's "ideas" on copy platform (e.g., appeals and product claims). The agencies were told to do the same with media recommendations, that is, to present only their suggestions as to media types. The letter of instructions stated: "While we hope you will be reasonably specific in your recommendations, we do not expect—nor want—a final advertising plan for our coming fiscal year. Indeed, it would be impossible for you to accomplish such a mission, since you have not had the benefit of our thinking and experience. We are granting two interviews to each agency, and we know that the time here will be spent largely in getting a general background of the ball-point pen industry. The purpose of your presentation is solely to show us 'how you think about advertising problems.' "

The agency's new business committee, headed by the president, was comprised of the creative director, the media director, the research director, and two senior account supervisors. In discussing the agency's strategy in attempting to gain this new account, it was apparent that the agency possessed little research data upon which to make any concrete advertising appeals recommendations. The creative director asked about the desirability of having the research department do some copy appeals testing. He reported that he and one of the members of his department had worked up a number of different copy appeals. Before preparing these appeals, he and his associate had studied all print media ball-point pen advertising for the past several years, had visited drugstores and stationery stores and talked with retail sales clerks about how consumers bought these items, and had also talked with friends and neighbors about their experiences with these writing instruments. The creative director reported that he thought "we really have something in a couple of the appeals, but we don't want to bias you before research tells us how consumers react."

The research director said his department could, with little difficulty, quickly test these alternative appeals. He went on to say, however, that in his opinion this was not the right approach. He felt strongly that before any appeals were formulated the agency should attempt to gain an understanding of the social and personal meanings of writing and writing instruments. By undertaking a qualitative study of this type he thought that "all of us will have a frame of reference within which to conceptualize our approach to the problem."

The creative director said that "in a way I have arrived at these social and personal meanings through my own interviewing. After all, I have to think up the copy appeals, so I feel that I should personally talk to a lot of people who will give me their views on ball-point pens. In many ways we're talking about the same thing except that—at least in this case—I think I should do the interviewing, while I'm certain you think your department should. Am I right?"

In reply, the research director said: We're not talking about the same thing. It's excellent for you to have the interviewing experience you've described. But I'm suggesting we need to do some research in addition to what you've been doing. I have a professional social psychologist on my staff, and I know he can make quite a contribution to our thinking on this matter. I've already assigned him the job of obtaining information. He started last week and will be finished in another week or so." When asked what a study like this cost, the research director said: "About $500 out-of-pocket for the interviewing costs and another $500 to

$750 for the time spent by our analysts. If we farmed the job out it would cost $2,000 to $2,500."

After some discussion it was agreed that since the research work was under way the committee should do no further work until it received the research report. The creative director felt this decision was not right, since he wanted his copy appeals tested immediately. He was, however, overruled by the other members of the committee.

The highlights of the report prepared by the social psychologist appear as Exhibit 1. Prior to the next meeting of the new business committee the research director requested, in writing, that all members give careful thought to requiring similar studies for all new business solicitation.

1. How valid are the findings from the research study?

2. Critically assess the role assigned to the study by the research director.

3. Based on the report contained in Exhibit 1, what recommendations should be made to the agency's creative group?

EXHIBIT 1. Research report on social and personal meanings of writing and writing instruments

Writing is an intimate form of personal expression.

For centuries—probably since the advent of literacy—people have believed that handwriting reveals the writer; that it shows his character. Although for many years graphology remained a pseudoscience, much like phrenology and physiognomic psychology, in recent years the social sciences have come to accept the underlying premise of the folk-science—that handwriting does, indeed, reveal the personality. Most people are more or less aware of this, they reflect with some pride on their hasty—if illegible—scrawls, or their fine, full, generous handwriting.

The writing instrument is an extension of the self.

Out of this intimacy, each writing instrument, whether fountain pen, ball-point, or pencil, has a particular "feel" to the writer; it aids, inhibits, or in one way or another affects the flow of his thoughts. Many people have very well-defined notions as to the exact width of pen nib, softness or hardness of pencil lead, color of ink, etc., most comfortable to them. People develop quite distinct notions of the kind of writing instrument that will "best express" their personality, in terms of how the instrument "feels" as it moves across the paper, and looks thereafter.

In addition, people become fairly concerned with the appearance of the writing they produce, they feel that a fine-line pen with light blue ink will convey a different impression of themselves than will a thick stub pen with a glossy black ink. All in all, the instrument chosen to write with is an extension of the self—the writing it produces symbolizes the way one appears to oneself and the way one wants to appear to others.

Writing and the writing instrument have a social meaning.

The writing instrument used in correspondence and the care taken with penmanship symbolize the quality of a social relationship. The symbolic value of the writing instrument can be seen, for example, in the range of relationships from, at one end, the casual customer-salesman relationship expressed in the bill sent out by the local hardware store—which may even be scribbled in pencil—to the relationship implied

EXHIBIT 1 (*Continued*)

in the formal dinner invitation—which must be neatly written in ink with a fountain pen. Between these two extremes, there is a wide variety of behaviors. But in all cases where people write to each other, the instrument they use subtly communicates some feelings between the correspondents. The physical values of permanence and legibility, attributed in most cases to the fountain pen, are transmuted into social values of consideration and affection.

Fountain pens

Fountain pens are felt to be expensive, well-made objects with a definite set of social meanings. *

In general, when people think of "fountain pens," they tend to think of the more expensive brands. The "fountain pen" is fairly consistently thought of as an expensive and well-engineered product. Within this context, fountain pens have a consistent set of cultural meanings.

1. They are prestigeful; they represent a relatively high social status. People feel that the expensive brands of fountain pens carry a certain amount of prestige.

2. They represent conservatism and formality. The fountain pen, both in itself and in its writing performance, symbolizes an established and conservative person or occasion. The fountain pen is almost a traditional object by now; people feel that it is the expected good, reliable writing instrument, used by the person who prefers to avoid the experimental.

3. The major brands of fountain pens have full and sometimes historical images. People talk about the other major brands as though they implicitly assumed that "everybody knows what these brands are like." They talk about the way the brands used to be, the improvements that have been made—in short they act toward these major brands as they do toward other well-established cultural objects.

4. People develop attachments to a brand; the brand may have very meaningful and very personal associations. Since fountain pens are "traditionally" gift items— often given to commemorate an important event in the person's life like school graduation—an extra highly personal meaning often haloes out from the gift occasion to the brand of the fountain pen. Many of the respondents talk about the pen (specific) that they received on such an occasion, and go on automatically to talk about the general virtues of that brand.

The fact that the fountain pen may have been used throughout an important period of a person's life—to write high school and college exams, to write letters from the army overseas, as an important adjunct to a woman's office career—enhances the brand attachments. Both the importance of the gift occasion and the importance of the experiences through which the fountain pen is used combine to produce very powerful brand loyalties.

5. People also feel that a fountain pen is physically a more flexible instrument of self-expression than most other writing instruments. The fountain pen is felt to be one of the few writing instruments that can be adapted to personal needs; point size and ink color can be individualized to provide the maximum of self-expression. Everyone is familiar with the stereotyped figure, like the flirtatious woman who uses heliotrope ink on scented shocking pink paper, or the would-be virile man who uses a thick pen point and shiny black ink to gave the maximum strength to his signature. Of course, these are extremes, but in general people appreciate the extent to which a fountain pen can be made an instrument of personal expression.

With many people the fountain pen is such a personal object that it becomes very distasteful to the owner to permit strangers to write with the pen for fear of "ruining the point."

* Most of the subsequent discussion pertains primarily to lower-middle and upper-middle class groups, where the class culture places a high value on literacy and on etiquette—knowing how to do things right—and where the expensive fountain pen is a relatively common object. In the lower class groups, the expensive fountain pen is rather rare and remote, belonging to the world of "important businessmen," but not to the everyday world. Lower-class respondents showed much less familiarity with the major brands, and much less experience with them.

EXHIBIT 1 (*Continued*)

Ball-point pens

Most of the social qualities of the ball-point pen are negative.

By now, ball-point pens have acquired a rather negative cultural image. Many people remember the fanfare that greeted their arrival on the market; they refer to early promotional efforts with some amusement.

But by now, they are felt to be cheap, disposable, and rather poorly made.

Using a ball-point pen is to many people a symbol of lower status, not to be associated with important matters. People complain endlessly about their unsatisfactory writing qualities. Not only do they skip and smear, but they are felt to be socially inappropriate on many occasions.

The general negative social evaluation of the ball-point pen is well known; in brief, the ball-point is redolent of associations that most people feel are undesirable in a writing instrument—it simply doesn't "look good."

However, the ball-point is well established in highly informal, relatively nonsocial situations, especially in notes to oneself.

In situations where social evaluation is at a minimum, the qualities of the ball-point pen are highly appreciated. Whenever the appearance of the writing and the appearance of the pen itself are not important factors—for example, in note-taking, making out shopping lists, or for the first draft—people like the ball-point. In such contexts, people praise the pen as convenient, cheap, sturdy, and clean.

There is another factor, rather more subtle, that makes the ball-point pen particularly suitable for writing to oneself, rather than to others—that factor is the "feel" of the ball-point pen as it moves across the paper. The movement of the ball as it rotates gives the writer a feeling of freedom, or lack of restraint. It is difficult for people to verbalize a feeling like this, but it becomes clear when people are asked to contrast the ball-point and fountain pens on a series of qualitative continua.

The ball-point pen is seen as a free, fast instrument of self-expression. It can keep pace with the writer's thoughts; it does not impose either social or mechanical restraints on the writer. We have no way of testing this hypothesis, but it seems plausible that the ball-point lends itself to scribbling rather than penmanship, fast and impulsive writing rather than thoughtful socialized writing.

Within this context, the erratic writing qualities attributed to the ball-point pen become particularly irritating. People become highly irritated with the ball-point pen that skips or slides over the paper without depositing ink. It seems that the ball-point pen that occasionally skips while writing is far more annoying than the fountain pen that regularly runs dry. The ball-point is a far more personalized object than the fountain pen. People expect it to move fast and freely, and react with great irritation when it doesn't.

Currently, the ball-point pen is establishing itself as a writing instrument distinct from the pencil and the fountain pen. It occupies an intermediate position superior to the pencil where permanence is desirable, but inferior to the fountain pen where the writing quality or the pen itself is subject to more formal social evaluation. It is more durable than a pencil. Despite the irritation it evokes, people can become somewhat attached to a ball-point pen. Personal attachment is hampered by the fact that brand identification is almost entirely lacking. People have little opportunity to develop brand loyalty. Attachment to the specific fountain pen (as a "lifetime" pen) and to the fountain pen brand ["I'm a (brand) man myself"] are fairly common. They are almost entirely lacking in relation to the ball-point pen.

Except for a very small number of occupations, most Americans do not do much writing that is subject to social evaluation. The average housewife likes to keep a pen in her purse; the average man likes one in his jacket or shirt pocket, but these pens are bought to be "on hand" and may rarely be used. The ball-point, because of its sturdiness, cheapness, and convenience, meets the needs of the average person for a casual writing tool. It serves a need that a pencil cannot meet. It does not demand the financial and emotional investment that a fountain pen does. Within the limits of this intermediate position, the ball-point pen universe is becoming increasingly ramified. As our findings on brands show, people are coming to distinguish between

EXHIBIT 1 (*Concluded*)

the cheap, "give-away" unbranded pens, the "dollar" pens, and the pens produced by the major fountain pen manufacturers. The types of ball-point pens serve somewhat different functions—both as writing instruments and as pieces of personal property. Exhibit 2 illustrates the differences in profiles.

By and large, the brand images of ball-point pens are weak.

People feel that getting a good ball-point pen is more a matter of chance than of rational brand selection. Approximately 80 ball-point pens were owned by the people in our sample and by members of their families; but people could name the brands involved in only 50 cases. In other words, about 38 percent of the ball-point pens owned were, for all practical purposes, unbranded. In contrast, of the approximately 85 fountain pens owned, only four were of an unknown brand.

EXHIBIT 2. Profiles of fountain and ball-point pens

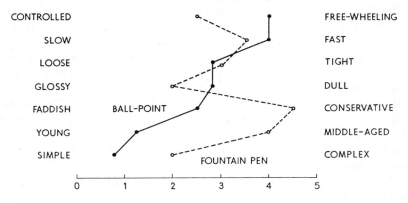

Case 14—4. SWIFT & COMPANY

The Product Manager for "Swift's Premium Turkeys," sold under the "Butterball" brand name, was reviewing the sales history of the company's prestuffed turkey line to determine what changes, if any, should be made in the marketing program. Prestuffed turkeys had been added to the regular line of Swift's Premium Butterball Turkeys in 1955 for the convenience of the consumer, who could now eliminate the time and labor which had been required to prepare the stuffing.

The product manager estimated that current total industry sales for prestuffed turkeys were 5 to 6 million pounds annually. This was less than 1 percent of total turkey consumption. He felt that this sales volume clearly indicated that prestuffed turkeys were not yet accepted by consumers in spite of the benefits which the product offered.

Sales of regular (unstuffed) Swift's Premium Butterball Turkeys had shown a marked increase since the turkeys were first distributed under the Butterball name. The product manager felt that this was due to the substantial improvements made in raising, preparing, and packaging turkeys which, when combined with the name Butterball, made a very favorable impression on consumers. These improvements were as follows: (1) the development of breeding and feeding methods which produced bigger, broader-breasted turkeys with a larger quantity of tender white meat; (2) the development of a method of dressing birds which eliminated pin-feathers, a source of irritation to housewives in preparing the turkey for roasting (pioneered by Swift); (3) the improved freezing of turkeys so that they acquired a brighter, more appealing color; (4) the introduction of a packaging method whereby the legs were tucked into the tail skin, thereby eliminating the sewing and trussing by the housewife after stuffing (another improvement pioneered by Swift); (5) the removal of the large leg tendons in each turkey to facilitate carving. Swift anticipated that many of these innovations would be industry-wide in a short period of time.

Retailer acceptance of the regular unstuffed Butterball turkeys had been exceptionally good. The product manager pointed out that although Swift had not allocated funds for cooperative advertising, expenditures on individual ads for Butterball turkeys placed in newspapers by retailers were substantial. Swift provided mats for these ads and other point-of-purchase materials for use by retailers.

It had been customary for retailers to feature turkeys as a "loss leader" to draw traffic to the store. Swift's marketing strategy was to convince retailers that Butterball turkeys were a premium product which could be sold at a good profit. The product manager felt that this strategy had been successful.

Upon introduction, the prestuffed turkey was added to the regular advertising program. They copy was, "Now *also* available already stuffed." Swift also added the phrase, "Martha Logan's old-fashioned bread stuffing" to the Butterball label on the plastic package. "Martha Logan" was the trade name of Swift's home economist. A substantial number of retailers included the prestuffed turkey in their local advertising of Swift's Butterball turkey.

At about the same time that Swift introduced its prestuffed turkey, a major competitor placed a similar product on the market containing Pepperidge Farms stuffing. The Pepperidge Farms organization baked specialty bread items which were distributed throughout the U.S. The competitor had been successful in obtaining good national retail distribution primarily due to advertising aimed at prestuffed turkey users along with 50-cent and $1.00 consumer refunds on each purchase.

A research report on prestuffed turkeys had been submitted to the product manager by Swift's Commercial Research Department. Part I of this report dealt with an investigation of unstuffed turkeys and prestuffed turkeys at the retail level among chain stores located in several northern metropolitan markets. Major findings were as follows:

1. Over two-thirds of the stores stocked prestuffed turkeys.

2. The price of Swift's prestuffed Butterball turkey was equivalent to that of its competitor.

3. About one-third of the meat market managers sampled felt that sales movement of prestuffed turkeys was slow. Another one-third thought sales movement was fair.

Part II of the report dealt with consumer attitudes and expectations regarding turkeys generally and prestuffed turkeys in particular. Major findings from a sample of 600 randomly selected consumers located in several northern metropolitan markets were as follows:

1. Most consumers (67 percent) mentioned buying frozen turkeys. (No reference to prestuffed turkeys.)

2. Turkey was served at Thanksgiving by 86 percent of the respondents and at Christmas by 68 percent. (No reference to prestuffed turkeys.)

3. Turkeys were served once by 21 percent of the sample customers, twice by 28 percent of them, and three times per year by 22 percent. (No reference to prestuffed turkeys.)

4. The brand name of the turkey purchased by 27 percent of the respondents was Swift's Butterball, but 31 percent of the consumers interviewed did not know the brand name. (No reference to prestuffed turkeys.)

5. Swift's Butterball turkey was mentioned by 53 percent of sample consumers as being "seen" or "heard of." (No reference to prestuffed turkeys.)

6. Seventy-four percent of the sample consumers had heard of prestuffed turkeys.

7. Unfavorable comments about prestuffed turkeys were made by 56 percent of the consumers sampled. These comments (in order of importance) included: (a) Prefer my own stuffing, (b) Fear spoilage—don't want to stuff too far in advance, (c) Probably wouldn't like the flavor of the stuffing, (d) Don't like the idea, (e) Question the ingredients of the stuffing, (f) Question how long the prestuffed turkey had been frozen, (g) Believe the stuffing may be soggy, and (h) Prefer to clean the turkey myself.

8. Eighty-nine percent of consumers sampled had not purchased a prestuffed turkey. Of the 11 percent who did purchase the product, Swift's Butterball was selected because: (a) It was a good brand—they were satisfied with the brand (37 percent of the 11 percent cited this reason); (b) This brand was carried by their store (19 percent); (c) They wanted to try it (19 percent). The major competitor's brand was selected because it was carried by their store (53 percent).

9. Of all prestuffed turkey users sampled, 33 percent didn't like the product at all, but 27 percent liked it very much and thought it was very

good. Of Swift users, 77 percent liked it very much and thought it was very good. Of all prestuffed turkey users, 45 percent stated they liked the convenience of the item. Swift users named juiciness, tenderness, flavor, convenience, and good meat as favorable factors.

10. Of all prestuffed turkey users sampled, 61 percent stated that they disliked the stuffing used in the turkeys. Of the Swift prestuffed turkey users, 49 percent had no complaints, but 35 percent disliked the stuffing primarily because of its flavor. Both Swift users and all prestuffed turkey users thought the right *amount* of stuffing was used.

11. Thirty percent of the prestuffed turkey users did not plan to buy another turkey because they did not like the stuffing, and 28 percent did not plan to buy because they disliked the product entirely. Most Swift users (87 percent) did plan to buy another prestuffed turkey. Sixty-two percent of this group cited convenience as their reason for another purchase.

12. Most consumers (69 percent) felt prestuffed turkeys were more expensive than other turkeys, but 51 percent felt they were worth more. Of the 51 percent, 23 percent cited the meat packer's added labor cost as a reason for the product's higher price and 15 percent mentioned the convenience factor.

13. Twenty-seven percent of the consumers sampled did not purchase a prestuffed turkey because they did not know about the product. Twenty-three percent had not purchased a prestuffed turkey because they preferred their own stuffing; and 20 percent did not buy because they questioned the taste and ingredients of the stuffing.

14. Forty-seven percent of the consumers sampled had not seen prestuffed turkeys in the store where they usually traded. Of the 47 percent, 27 percent stated they would not buy a prestuffed turkey if it were available.

15. Forty-eight percent of the consumers sampled said they did not intend to purchase their first prestuffed turkey. Of the 48 percent, 19 percent cited preference for their own dressing as their reason for not buying, and 12 percent questioned the ingredients of the dressing. Forty-one percent of the consumers sampled said they intended to purchase the turkey or were not sure. The primary reason for making the purchase was curiosity.

The product manager thought that Swift could afford to undertake an aggressive promotional program for prestuffed turkeys provided the potential could be verified and a plan to tap this market developed.

1. Evaluate the attitudes towards prestuffed turkeys in general and towards the Swift band in particular.

2. What marketing strategy should be adopted?

15

Advertising research

ADVERTISING is one of the more important decision areas facing the business executive. In 1969, it was estimated that American business spent over $19.5 billion on advertising.[1] Given such a large expenditure it is not surprising that a great deal of attention has been given to advertising research.[2] It is likely that more money has been spent on advertising research than on research in any other area of marketing. In recent years more and more applied research in communications has been done by behavioral scientists.

Advertising research is primarily of three types. One is concerned with the setting of advertising objectives. Ideally, one would want to see the "payout" in terms of sales and/or profits—but this is known to be a difficult measure to obtain except under unusual conditions. Since advertising interacts with other marketing inputs as well as with uncontrolled variables, it is not difficult to understand why a measurement of its effect is hard to come by.[3]

After deciding upon his objectives, the advertiser must next decide what his message should be. How should he present his message? What copy should he use? What headlines? what pictures? What situations? Many concepts have been developed by the behavioral scientist which are helpful in the construction of advertising copy. In the final analysis,

[1] Robert J. Coen, "Ad Volume Passes $19.5 Billion: 1970 Total Remains a Question," *Marketing Communications* (February, 1970), p. 54.

[2] For a penetrating discussion of research in advertising see Leo Bogart, *Strategy in Advertising* (New York: Harcourt, Brace & World, Inc., 1967), especially chapters 12 and 13.

[3] For a listing of the controllable and uncontrollable variables in advertising see Roy H. Campbell, "A Managerial Approach to Advertising Measurement," *Journal of Marketing* (October, 1965), p. 2.

however, it is the effect of the copy on the target segment(s) in the market which counts. Typically, such effect can only be determined via marketing research.

In addition to deciding what to say, the advertiser must also choose an appropriate vehicle(s). Should he use newspaper, radio, magazines, television, billboards—or some combination thereof? If he chooses radio or TV: What program? What day of the week? What time of day? The countless alternatives available to the advertiser make careful study necessary. Assumptions made relative to the number of people to be reached, the type of people forming the market, the desired frequency of message receipts by selected audiences, the periodicity with which the message should be received, and the context in which the message can best be presented will determine the media schedule—they can be usefully researched.

Basic marketing research techniques, as discussed in earlier chapters of this text, apply to advertising research, but many ingenious adaptations of these techniques have been made by advertising researchers. It is desirable, therefore, to study in detail some of the various types of advertising research. In addition, a number of specialized research agencies provide information on advertising. The student should be familiar with the more important of these.

This chapter is divided into three major parts which conform essentially to the advertising process. Part one covers advertising objectives and product appeals—what should be said about the product? Part two discusses copy testing—what is the best way to put the appeals into a message? Part three deals with media selection—what media types should be used; what vehicles within media types should be selected; what combinations should be used? The problem of how much to spend on advertising is not considered here because of space limitations.[4]

SETTING ADVERTISING OBJECTIVES

If the firm has specified its marketing target segment(s), refined its thinking about target segments in terms of geography, determined the relative importance of each segment, ascertained what product characteristics are important to each segment, developed the optimum product at a competitive price, set up the "ideal" channels strategy—then a big part of the advertising job is done. Essentially, advertising objectives consist of some measurable output which relates directly to sales and, hence, ultimately to profits. This is tantamount to saying that the advertising objective must relate to consumer behavior. But since consumer behavior is a function of a complex process, the advertiser must

---

[4] See Joel Dean, "Does Advertising Belong in the Capital Budget?" *Journal of Marketing* (October, 1966), pp. 15–21.

be careful to specify exactly what part of the process he seeks to influence. Thus, the first step ". . . is to acquire an understanding of the whys and hows and whens that lead a customer to purchase or not purchase a product. This amounts to an outline of the route a customer travels from a point of 'no need and/or no desire' for the product to actual purchase of the product."[5]

The end objective of communication is to ". . . suggest a way to meet those needs which are appropriate to the group situation in which the target finds himself at the time when he is moved to make the desired response."[6] This means that any communication must satisfy several requirements before it can "work"—including attracting attention, being understood, and being convincing.

Some writers see marketing communications as moving consumers through a hierarchy of steps comprised of unawareness, awareness, comprehension, conviction, and action. The end goal is to move prospects to "action," namely, the purchase of the product or service.[7] But this model, while helpful in organizing the testing of advertising, is not really very operational with regard to objectives. A focus on attitudes seems to offer a more useful way of operationalizing advertising goals.

Attitude research

Since considerable space was devoted to the technical problems of attitude measurement in Chapter 7, the discussion here will center on measuring the attitudes of target audiences towards products, and *then* attempting to determine the effect of advertising on these attitudes. Actually, more than a single measurement is needed; a marketer needs to measure attitudes towards his product's salient characteristics as well as towards those of competing brands. Such a set of measurements should give some indication of what *specific* attitudinal changes must be effected in order to obtain sales. Thus the goal of advertising can be stated in terms of changing attitudes bearing on selected product characteristics. This approach assumes that attitudes are predictors of behavior and that they can be measured with some reasonable degree of accuracy.

The average consumer is thought to have a reasonably stable set of attitudes towards those salient product characteristics pertaining to a

---

[5] James W. Taylor, "Two Requirements for Measuring the Effectiveness of Promotion," *Journal of Marketing* (April, 1965), p. 43.

[6] Wilbur Schramm, "How Communication Works," in Wilbur Schramm, ed., *The Process and Effects of Mass Communication* (Urbana, Ill.: University of Illinois Press, 1955), p. 13.

[7] Russell H. Colley, *Defining Advertising Goals for Measured Advertising Results* (New York: Association of National Advertisers, Inc., 1961), p. 60.

product class. With this as a "backdrop," he evaluates one brand against another. We would expect that consumers would differ with respect to what product characteristics were salient, as well as to how they perceived various brands, thereby giving rise to attitudinal segments. The goal of advertising often centers on attempting to alter the attitudinal set for the brand in question within a given segment in the direction of those product characteristics which were thought to be most salient. The messages hopefully generate over time a favorable "image." The acceptance of this brand would be based on how it fared versus the images of competing brands within the framework of what was thought to be salient for the product class.

One study showed that the salient product characteristics of dentifrices when translated into product appeals included "cleans teeth better," "makes mouth fresher," "better for children," and "removes bad breath better." Consumers who gave considerable weight to "getting teeth clean" and "makes mouth fresher" selected that brand which was rated highest on these two counts. The goal of advertising in such a case would be to reinforce these ratings among present users and to shift those attitudes of nonusers which pertain to these salient appeals.[8]

In addition, information is needed about the whole gestalt of behavior which surrounds the purchase and use of a product. This means that, among other things, one needs to know the role served by the product (i.e., the goals involved), the "system" which is employed by the users to obtain the desired goals, the events for which certain products are appropriate and others not appropriate, the standards employed by the consumer to ascertain whether the product is or is not performing satisfactorily, and how the product is perceived in terms of functional equivalents (substitutes).

The above types of information can be obtained using a variety of research techniques. One of the more common is the relatively unstructured interviewing approach used so commonly in motivation research. An illustration of this type of research and its value in helping the advertiser better understand his goals follows:

The study on shaving points to a very definite reservoir of masculine interest in toiletries, which is a potential sales aid if the appeals are skillfully handled. Sensuousness is an important source of both physical and psychological satisfaction, but it is a private pleasure. If it is made too outspoken, it signifies unmanly vanity. The advertising should capture some of the sensory aspects of shaving (the air of intimacy about the bathroom, the odors and smoothness of the lotions and the creams, the refreshed feeling afterward). But advertising cannot tackle these things head on. In one way or another, the basic reference of shaving is masculinity. A beard is vigorous, adult maleness, and removing

---

[8] Niels Vinding, "Awareness, Belief, and Choice as Effects on Tooth Paste Advertising," *Journal of Advertising Research* (March, 1964), pp. 19–21.

it is part of proclaiming it. Advertising should take account of this factor of masculinity somehow. Besides sports and men winning girls, there are many other possible angles for introducing masculinity on an implied, believable, and unobjectionable basis.

The assumption that now underlies most advertising related to shaving is that all men are alike, that they all have tough beards and tender skins, and that the advertising should only be concerned with these issues. There are many more meanings than these, and far more powerful motives.[9]

COPY TESTING[10]

Copy testing is research to evaluate alternative ways for the advertiser to present his message. The use of the word "copy" is perhaps unfortunate, since it seems only to refer to print media and, more specifically, to the headline and text of the advertising message. For this discussion, the word "copy" will refer to an entire advertisement, including the verbal message, pictures, colors, and dramatizations, whether the advertisement appears in print, or on radio, television, or some other medium.

This discussion of copy testing is divided into two major divisions, those tests which are made before the copy is released on a full-run basis, and those tests which are applied after the copy is run. The latter are sometimes considered tests of advertising effectiveness rather than copy tests. Actually, all advertising research represents an effort to improve the effectiveness of advertising, although it must be kept in mind that "there is no single criterion by which the effectiveness of all kinds of advertising can be measured precisely because advertising is not homogeneous with respect to its objectives, and the tasks that are assigned to it."[11] The basic distinction between "before" and "after" tests is the purpose of the test. If the objective is to make improvements in the advertising copy prior to the full-run release of the advertising, then the test is classified as a "before" test. The distinction is not always clear because some "before" copy testing methods call for the advertising copy to be run in one or several media. The results of such a test might be measured by the number of inquiries received after the test advertisements had appeared. Nevertheless, this would be considered a "be-

---

[9] Pierre Martineau, *Motivation in Advertising* (New York: McGraw-Hill Book Co., Inc., 1957), p. 65.

[10] We will not discuss research designed to test the effectiveness of different size message units (e.g., a 20-second TV commercial versus a 30-second one) or of repetition, despite the obvious importance of such subjects. For an up-to-date report on what is available see Leo Bogart, *Strategy in Advertising* (New York: Harcourt, Brace and World, 1967), pp. 174–92.

[11] Clarence E. Eldridge, "Advertising Effectiveness—How Can It Be Measured?" *Journal of Marketing* (January, 1958), p. 247.

fore" test since the purpose is to determine which copy to run eventually in all scheduled media.

Behind each of the various types of copy testing is an implicit assumption regarding how advertising accomplishes its effect.

If someone thinks that the ability of advertising to attract attention is directly related to its effectiveness, he will then, of course, measure the attention-getting ability and consider the results to be a measure of advertising effectiveness. If someone thinks the fact that an advertising phrase is remembered signifies effectiveness, he will use memory measurements as a criterion of performance. If someone believes that advertising has to give pleasure and be liked, he may then subject the pleasantries or the aesthetic values to measurement and will interpret a positive result as the proof of the effectiveness of advertising. In each case the researcher calls upon an implicit assumption about the mechanisms by which advertising achieves its effect.[12]

Most approaches to copy testing rely heavily on measuring recognition, recall, comprehension, believability, persuasion, and change in attude towards a brand or towards some product attribute. The research directors of the larger agencies give little value to measures involving recognition and persuasion. The latter is typically measured by asking consumers to indicate how persuasive an ad is to themselves. Research directors consider comprehension the best measure of effectiveness, and measures dealing with recall and attitudinal change only slightly less effective.[13] All of these measures involve assumptions on how advertis ing works, and all except the attitudinal change measure beg the question of how advertising works on predisposing people to behave in certain ways. Another basic problem is that pretesting cannot measure the long-term effectiveness of an ad, namely, its ability to precondition its reader or viewer towards purchasing the product or service at a later date.[14]

"Before" tests

Consumer jury. Consumer jury tests are based on the "rating" given an advertisement by a typical group of consumers. "Rating" implies the comparison of one advertisement with several others. This is what is usually done; however, respondents are sometimes asked to "rate" one advertisement on the basis of a given list of factors such as its attention-getting power and the believability of its claims.

[12] Alfred Politz, "How Advertising Affects Attitudes and Buying Decisions," *Evaluating Advertising Effectiveness* (New York: Association of National Advertisers, Inc., 1961), p. 2.

[13] Lee Adler, Allen Greenberg, and Darrell B. Lucas, "What Big Agency Men Think of Copy Testing Methods," *Journal of Marketing Research* (November, 1965), pp. 339–45.

[14] For a discussion of the cumulative effects of advertising see Donald Tull, "The Carry-Over Effect of Advertising," *Journal of Marketing* (April, 1965), pp. 48–52.

Although a consumer jury test may be made in a variety of ways, the usual procedure is to ask a relatively small group (say twenty-five to fifty) of consumers who represent potential buyers of the product to rate alternative pieces of copy. Different data collection methods may be used in implementing a consumer jury test. For example, personal interviews may be used or a group assembled and the members asked to vote on the alternative copy. The copy may be "dummied up" or the major theme placed on cards; respondents are then asked to rank the different alternatives in response to a request such as: "Here are a number of ads about X product. Please read each carefully and tell me which one you think would be most likely to cause you to buy the product."

The two common variations of the consumer jury test are order of merit and paired comparisons. The former consists of asking the respondents to decide which of a group of advertisements is best, which is next best, etc. The tabulation of responses is considered to show the order of merit of the alternative ads. These rankings, however, are given in response to a question, and, thus, the results must be evaluated in terms of the type of question asked. For example, any of the following questions might be used:

a. Which of these advertisements do you think is more interesting?
b. Which of these ads would influence you most to buy X brand?
c. Which of these ads do you think people will be most apt to read?

Order-of-merit rankings contain the implicit assumption that the respondent will like at least one advertisement, but this may not always be true, since the rating may be made on the basis of which ad the respondent dislikes the least. A further difficulty is that the respondent is often confronted with what appears to be two similar advertisements. Since he must rank them, he may make his choice on the basis of unimportant details.

The paired comparison method consists of requiring each respondent to state a preference for each advertisement relative to every other advertisement in the test. Some believe this series of individual comparisons leads to a more discriminating choice, but it probably leads to essentially the same results as the ranking method. Paired comparisons have the same weaknesses as ranking plus the difficulty that results from the number of individual choices that must be made. If ten ads are involved, for example, forty-five choices have to be made on each question.[15]

A variation of the consumer jury method is sometimes used to analyze

---

[15] The number of choices involved is equal to $n(n-1)/2$ where n represents the total number of ads included in the test. In the case cited above, this would be $10(9)/2$ or 45 choices.

TV programs and commercials. The procedure consists of exposing the audience to a program or commercial and having each member record on score sheets at specific intervals (indicated by signals) whether they liked, disliked, or were indifferent to what they had just heard or seen.

A similar way of measuring audience likes and dislikes for specific parts of a program or commercial is through the use of an electronic machine known as the Program Analyzer. This machine provides each member of the audience with two buttons. The respondent presses one button when he finds the program interesting, the other when he finds it uninteresting. When he wishes to show indifference, the respondent presses neither button. These buttons are hooked up to a recording machine which summarizes and makes a continuous chart of the reactions of the audience. While such machines are helpful in obtaining a measure of interest, they do not indicate the actual impression created.

The major advantage of the consumer jury method is that it tends to separate out the very weak ads from the very strong. Its use may prevent the advertiser from making a serious mistake. It is flexible and can be done quickly with a small dollar expenditure.

The major disadvantages are: (1) the assumption that respondents will like at least one advertisement, (2) ratings may be based on unimportant details, (3) only conscious ratings are obtained—not subconscious evaluations, and (4) respondents may attempt to assume the role of experts and, therefore, give a subjective rating based not on their own reactions, but on reactions which they think others will have.

Rating scales.   This method of copy testing requires the establishment of standards for effective copy and numerical weights for each standard. The weights or values indicate a standard's relative worth in the overall success of the copy. Ads are then "rated" in accordance with the scale values and a numerical score obtained. If the total weight for one item, for example, is 10, the analyst might give one ad 8 if he thought it was above average on that item. The total of the individual standard scores provides the numerical rating for an ad. Such ratings are not usually done by consumers, although there is no reason why they could not do so, but rather by advertising agency or advertising department personnel.

The Flesch readability formula is a rating scale, although it "rates" on only one factor. Dr. Flesch evolved his rating scale after research on readability. Ratings are based on the number of syllables in each word and the number of words in a sentence. Since people with different educational backgrounds vary in ability to read and understand written material, copy must be rated in terms of its audience. Therefore, an ad is rated, using the readability formula, and the score compared with the educational level of the audience the ad is attempting to reach. Flesch also developed a Human Interest Formula which measures the number of personal references. He argues that the more such references, the greater the probability of arousing interest on the part of the reader. While most rating scales have been developed for use with printed media, this method can be used for radio and TV copy.[16]

There are several other methods designed to measure readability.[17] The Dale-Chall formula is based on a list of 3,000 words which are easily understood, and on average sentence length. Another method is the ratio of main words to subsidiary words developed by C. R. Haas, which measures the economy of words. Haas also developed a ratio based on the relative number of verbs and nouns. He argued that advertising should be a heavy consumer of verbs which reflect action. Robert Gunning developed the Fog Index, which is similar to Flesch's in that it is based on the number of words using three or more syllables and average length of sentence. The Fog Index score can be related to the number of years of schooling required for easy understanding of the message.

The major advantage of a rating scale is that it provides a list against which to check an ad, and helps to single out the elements of an ad that are good and bad. The disadvantages are: (1) while the scale items may be well selected, it is difficult to set up relative weights regarding their contribution to the "ideal" ad; (2) different judges will rate the items differently, leaving the question of who is right; and (3) high scores may not be an indication of success, since the ad may have received high scores on most items but low scores on a few.

Language-difficulty measures are difficult to apply to titles, slogans, or brief statements.[18] And a high score does not necessarily mean that the message is effective in achieving its communication goal. This can only be determined through field research.

Rating scales have been used to measure the attitude change resulting from exposure to a particular ad. O'Neill used a relatively simple scale device to obtain a measurement of the differential effect on readers' attitudes of print ads, and concluded that ads could be evaluated prior to publication on the basis of impact on attitudes as contrasted to the recall of specific elements of the ad. O'Neill's "differential measurement" was obtained by asking respondents to rate a number of statements on the extent to which they applied to most companies in a given industry. A masked ad (the identity of the company was not revealed) was then shown to the respondents, who were asked to scale the degree to which the same statements used earlier applied to the

---

[16] Rudolph Flesch, *How to Test Readability* (New York: Harper and Brothers, 1951).

[17] Pompeo Abruzzini, "Measuring Language Difficulty in Advertising Copy," *Journal of Marketing* (April, 1967), pp. 22–26.

[18] *Ibid.*, p. 26.

company in the ad. The before-the-ad scores versus the after-the-ad-was-shown scores determined the impact.[19]

Mindak reports the use of the semantic differential (see Chapter 7) to test advertising copy. He used eight scales (sets of bipolarized words) to obtain a "before" measurement for eight concepts related to a new hand lotion (e.g., the ideal hand lotion, the hand lotion I buy, Soft Touch hand lotion, and products made by Toni), following which respondents were exposed to a commercial. The same eight scales were then applied to the same eight concepts to obtain the "after" measurement. Effectiveness of the commercial was obtained by comparing "before" and "after" scores. Such a study design suffers from the inherent disadvantages present in a before-after single group experimental design.[20]

Portfolio tests. These tests are named after the manner in which ads to be tested are "packaged." A group of ads, usually a mixture of ads to be tested and control ads, is placed in a portfolio. Sometimes the ads are actually placed in dummy copies of newspapers or magazines. Respondents who are thought to be representative of the target audience are given the folio and asked to go through it, reading whatever interests them and taking as much time as they want. After completing this task, the respondents are asked to recall (with the folio closed) the ads that they can remember. Such recall may be on a completely unaided basis, or the interviewer may aid recall by asking about specific ads or ads for specific products. For each recalled ad, the respondent is asked to "play back" as much of the ad as possible. This information is recorded verbatim. Additional questions may be asked about such things as the believability of the claims in the ad, the general reaction to the ad, and whether the respondent uses the product.

The value of this type of copy test is that it provides a measure of selective exposure, selective perception, and selective retention. The analyst can, it is argued, determine what filters through the consumer's predispositions and in what way it is altered in the process.

Frequently, the portfolio test is used to test the merits of two or more alternative ads. In such cases, an experimental design is used in which two or more sets of folios are prepared. The only difference between folios is that one set contains test ad A, another set contains test ad B, and so on. The nontest ads (control ads) are the same in all folios—and are positioned in the same order. By using small matched samples and

[19] Harry W. O'Neill, "Pretesting Advertising with the Differential Attitude Technique," *Journal of Marketing* (January, 1963), pp. 20–24.

[20] William A. Mindak, "A New Technique for Measuring Advertising Effectiveness," *Journal of Marketing* (April, 1956), pp. 367–78. Also see William A. Mindak, "Fitting the Semantic Differential to the Marketing Problem," *Journal of Marketing* (April, 1961), pp. 28–33.

comparing recall and playback scores among the various groups, a "winner" is obtained.

Maloney, after studying the results from a substantial number of portfolio tests, concluded that the ". . . recall scores derived from the vast majority of portfolio tests are of no practical value in spite of their noteworthy 'reliability.' The use of a folder or portfolio for presenting print ads to respondents for pretesting may offer some advantages. However, the author submits that the recall scores from portfolio tests— typically based on unaided recall of brand, product, or brand and product—are more subject to memory factors than are those recall measures based on aided recall or recognition. It is suggested that the observed shortcomings of portfolio test recall scores are largely due to the predominant influence of respondents' interest in, or awareness of, the brands and products advertised."[21] In brief, Maloney reasons that most portfolio tests are designed to aid in deciding whether to run ad A or ad B and that, in effect, product and brand are held constant. Thus, the only variables present (between the two sets of portfolios) are in the headline, copy, or graphic treatment of the ads. Because of the strong respondent interest in the product and the brand, only very large differences in the advertisements being tested will produce significant differences in recall. It must be noted that Maloney's criticism of portfolio tests is based on recall scores. He does not discuss the playback of copy details.[22]

Portfolio tests are not effective when the copy involves strongly negative and highly emotional appeals. Nor are they apt to elicit valid playbacks when personal matters such as hygiene are involved. If the ads tested are quite similar, the test will probably not distinguish between them. A further limitation is that respondents are queried immediately following their exposure to the folio. A test situation is created and does not indicate what respondents will say days later under "normal" conditions.

Folio-type tests can be run on either TV or radio commercials. Radio messages can easily be tested by inserting them into a taped "show" of say, fifteen minutes' duration. This can also be done with television, but although a rough story board can be filmed, the production expense is between $300 and $5,000. In the case of radio a portable unit can be taken into the home of respondents. This is difficult, however, to effect

---

[21] John C. Maloney, "Portfolio Tests—Are They Here to Stay?" *Journal of Marketing* (July, 1961), p. 32. Also see William D. Barclay, "Why Aren't Portfolio Tests Here to Stay?" *Journal of Marketing* (July, 1962), pp. 73–75; and John C. Maloney, "More 'Why' about Portfolio Tests," *Journal of Marketing* (July, 1962), pp. 76–77. Also see Dodds I. Buchanan, "How Interest in the Product Affects Recall: Print Ads versus Commercials," *Journal of Advertising Research* (March, 1964), pp. 9–14.

[22] Maloney, *op. cit.*

with television, and typically such interviewing is done on a group basis using a studio.

John M. Caffyn describes a method of testing TV commercials using "roughs." Participants view commercials via a TV set and answer questions in specially prepared booklets. Caffyn contends that attitude, image, and psychological questions can be accommodated in the interview format. He describes one situation in which the method was used as follows:

One advertiser did not know which of two actresses to use for a television commercial. In her role as a beauty editor, the actress would present the product to the viewer, and the effectiveness of the commercial would depend largely on her performance. Two Telpex roughs of the commercial were made: they were identical except that each featured a different actress in the main role. These were shown to a sample of 40 women at a test session, who were asked a range of questions such as, "If you had a personal beauty problem you wanted to discuss, which woman do you think you would prefer to talk it over with, the first or the second?" "Why did you choose that one?" Or, "Now, no matter what you said in the previous questions, which of the two women do you like best?" The study produced a clearcut finding in favor of one of the two actresses.[23]

Psychological tests.   These tests are somewhat related to the tests already discussed, but differ in the methods used. Effectiveness of an ad depends on the results which are achieved in the mind of the individual reached by the ad. Ideally, one could set up a list of the reactions which might result from a given ad, such as self-pity, security, fear, or nostalgia. Alternative ads could then be rated as to how readers responded with respect to these reactions. Dichter describes this as the establishment of a psychological profile and says:

Each form of reaction produced by an advertisement is represented by a vertical rank-order line. The degree of reaction is indicated on the line. By connecting all points a psychological profile of the effect produced by the advertisement is derived.

In an analysis of the effectiveness of an advertisement, one chart might read, for instance: This advertisement produces a high degree of identification, a strong feeling of pity, and only weak mental images—indicating that very little mental rehearsal of the use of the product is taking place.[24]

Psychological tests employ a variety of research techniques, including word association, sentence completion, depth interviewing, and story telling. Typically, a number of these techniques are employed on the

[23] John N. Caffyn, "Telpex Testing of TV Commercials," *Journal of Advertising Research* (June, 1965), p. 32.

[24] Ernest Dichter, "Psychological View of Advertising," *Journal of Marketing* (July, 1949), p. 61.

same study. The major objective is to find out what the respondent sees in various ads and what they mean to him.

Such studies can be undertaken either before or after the copy has run. As was pointed out in the chapter on motivation research, these are difficult studies to implement since only skilled interviewers can be used. Their content needs to be developed by a trained individual, and the results are difficult to interpret. The need for skilled interviewers leads to relatively small samples (sometimes as few as 10 to 15 respondents), so the results are hard to quantify and to project to large universes.

Laboratory testing. Pretest measures can be made using special laboratory measurements of the respondent's physiological responses to advertising. Through the years, considerable effort has gone into such testing because of its potential as an objective way of measuring responses to stimuli. Two of the older tests are the galvanic skin response and the eye movement. The former uses a device similar to a lie detector. This device measures electronically the emotional changes in a person by measuring changes in the amount of perspiration occurring on the hands. The effectiveness of an ad is judged on the basis of the "arousal" registered by the machine. To date, this method has played a negligible role in copy testing. Aside from the problem of sample size, there is the question of what is being measured, since arousal does not necessarily mean favorable reaction.

The eye camera is a device which records continuously the activity of the eye—both horizontal and vertical—as it reads printed material. By analyzing the route "taken," the researcher can determine what part of the ad produced the initial attention, what was interesting in the ad, and whether there was any part which appeared confusing. Interpretation of the results is difficult since it is impossible to correlate eye action with what the reader is thinking; for example, when the eye lingers at one point in the ad does this indicate interest or confusion?

One testing aid is a machine which measures pupil dilation. The basis of this test is that the pupil dilates when the respondent receives an interesting or pleasant stimulus. Conversely, the pupil contracts when the individual receives an uninteresting or unpleasant stimulus.[25] By comparing the changes induced by a message against a base line produced through the use of neutral stimuli a measure of effectiveness can be obtained. Of all physiological tests the pupil dilation one has the greatest potential in pretesting advertising copy, but much still needs to be learned about the relationship of reactions measured by the test and actual purchases in the market.

---

[25] Eckhard H. Hess and James M. Polt, "Pupil Size as Related to Interest Value of Usual Stimuli," *Science* (August, 1960), pp. 349–50.

Another device, the tachistoscope, permits the researcher to control the amount of time (in fractions of a second) that an advertisement (either in rough or finished form) is exposed to a group—or to an individual. This permits the researcher to study perception and comprehension under rigid time conditions. Thus, for example, the ability of outdoor billboard copy to impart a message can be tested under simulated exposure conditions.

Faison reports the use of a specially designed machine to pretest outdoor billboards. The test subject is seated with hands on a steering wheel. He is then asked to look through a viewer and through turns of the steering wheel keep a miniature car, which appears on a screen, on the road. Posters go by as he proceeds along the miniature highway. At the end of the "drive," the respondent is asked to recall what he saw.[26] This provides much the same type of information as the tachistoscope, but under more realistic conditions.

Inquiries.   Some advertisements are designed to produce direct results. When these results are inquiries or sales, a basis exists for accurately measuring the "worth" of the ad. In the case of inquiries, it is necessary to have previous data that provide a basis for estimating sales that will result from a given number of inquiries.

It must be remembered that a large number of inquiries does not necessarily mean that the advertising is successful—unless inquiries are the sole objective of the ad. If the objective of the advertising is to help in the long-term buildup of a general attitude, the number of inquiries may not necessarily be a sound basis for judging the ad's effectiveness. This would be particularly true with a single ad that was part of an advertising campaign.

An example of an inquiry test is one in which two headlines were compared through the use of a split run. The ad with the headline "New Jobs Are Offered in Television Station," returned six times as many inquiries as did the second ad with the headline "Television Courses for $11.60 per week."[27]

Inquiry tests may be handled in various ways as follows:

1. The same offer may be placed in different pieces of copy which are placed in different issues of the same media. The offers are "keyed" so that they can be traced to the specific advertising copy. Assuming that all other factors remain constant between issues—a difficult assumption to make—the difference in the number of inquiries received should indicate the "pulling power" of the different pieces of copy.

2. The same offer is placed in different advertising copy which ap-

[26] Edmund W. J. Faison, "Pre-testing Outdoor Advertising Designs," *Outdoor Advertising Association of America News* (November, 1960), p. 22.

[27] Alfred Politz, "The Dilemma of Creative Advertising," *Journal of Marketing* (October, 1960), p. 3.

pears in different magazines or newspapers. The assumption is that differences between media are either negligible or can be corrected for (say on the basis of circulation), and that the adjusted returns will indicate the best copy.

3. The same offer is placed in a medium which provides a split-run service. This is a procedure whereby half the copies of the magazine or newspaper contain one piece of copy and half another piece of copy. This is accomplished in a systematic way so that the two pieces of copy reach similar audiences.

A series of controlled experiments in seventy-two supermarkets in six cities tested the relative effectiveness of two promotional themes for apples, as well as the total effect of apple advertising and mechandising activities on the sale of apples and other selected fruits. The researchers used a double changeover experimental design ". . . in assigning treatments to the cities and time periods. This method of assigning treatments eliminated or equalized the influence of city and seasonal differences, thus increasing the accuracy of the experimental findings. The design used also permitted measurements of both direct and carry-over sales effects of each test theme or treatment."[28] The more pertinent study results were as follows:[29]

1. The apple use theme was more effective in promoting the sales of all apples than was the health theme.
2. Advertising of Washington State apples had only a small effect on the sales of oranges, grapefruit, and bananas.
3. Sales of each type of fruit were affected by the promotional and merchandising practices used with it.
4. Banana sales dropped slightly when both apple themes were used as contrasted to no promotion.
5. Price and display space devoted to each fruit had the greatest effect on sales.

Since sales tests do test ads under actual market conditions, they have definite advantages over the other tests which have been discussed. Nevertheless, they also have limitations:

1. Only immediate effects are measured. Long-term effects are ignored.
2. Only advertising copy which can be fitted to local media can be

[28] *Special Promotional Programs for Apples,* Marketing Research Report No. 446 (Washington, D.C.: Market Development Research Division, Agricultural Marketing Service, U.S. Department of Agriculture, January, 1961), p. 5. Also see James F. Merriman, "Evaluating Advertising Appeals through Sales Results," *Journal of Marketing* (October, 1958), pp. 164–67; and R. J. Jessen, "A Switch-over Experimental Design to Measure Advertising Effect," *Journal of Advertising Research* (March, 1961), pp. 15–22.

[29] *Special Promotional Programs for Apples, op. cit.,* p. 3.

tested. Technically this is not true, but the cost of each test in national media makes it a practical limitation.
3. The measuring instruments may not be sufficiently sensitive to detect small differences in sales. Therefore, such tests do not distinguish between ads that differ only slightly in effect.
4. Sales tests are time-consuming and so may not be useful where a decision is to be made quickly.
5. It is difficult to hold "all other" factors constant.

Simulated sales tests. Simulated sales tests are tests in which consumers are exposed to alternative pieces of copy through point-of-purchase displays or direct mail. For example, the copy to be tested can be made up in the form of store display material. Assume that two ads, A and B, are to be tested. Two groups of similar stores might be selected. Copy A point-of-purchase display is placed in the first group and copy B in the second group. Sales of the product are measured in each store before and after the introduction of the display pieces. The changes in sales between the two periods for the two groups of stores are compared and the group with the biggest sales increase is presumed to have the best copy. A similar type of study can be designed using direct mail or handbills. Results can be measured in sales made by mail or in coupons returned.

These simulated sales tests have the advantage of being simpler and less expensive to implement than actual sales tests. Otherwise they suffer essentially the same disadvantages plus the fact that they are artificial. The fact that an ad "pulls" better as a point-of-sale piece does not prove it will create more sales when run in a newspaper or magazine, although one is inclined to believe that it would.

"After" tests

Once an advertisement or a campaign has been "run" it is literally impossible to measure the effects of the message separately since the results are confounded by the frequency of the media schedule, the impact of the medium selected, and other market factors. Any "after" test is a test, therefore, of total advertising effectiveness, to a considerable extent.

"After" tests may be designed in a number of ways. All of them, with the exception of inquiry and sales tests, are based on the respondent's memory. The question arises as to the point in time after the ad has run at which the measurement should be made. Zielske reports that advertising tends to be forgotten at a rapid rate. His study shows that 63 percent of a sample of respondents could remember a given piece of advertising immediately after receiving thirteen successive weekly exposures. Within four weeks, the percentage who remembered had dropped to half, and after six weeks it had dropped by two thirds. Zielske also showed that the rate of forgetting decreased as the number of exposures increased. The study employed an experimental design; one group received the exposure (a food ad) for thirteen consecutive weeks, while the matched group received the identical exposure at thirteen four-week intervals (one whole year). Nearly a third more of the housewives who received them at weekly intervals remembered the ads at the end of the campaign, as compared to those who received them over a 52-week period. But the number remembering the ads at the end of the year was substantially higher (by 29 percentage points) for the group who received them at four-week intervals.[30]

Recall tests. This type of test is commonly used to measure the effectiveness of advertising messages. The procedure typically followed to obtain this measurement is as follows:

1. For testing an ad which has appeared in a magazine, respondents are "qualified" by determining if they are a reader of the magazine as shown by their ability to describe at least one editorial feature.
2. From "qualified" readers, a recall is obtained—using both aided and unaided techniques—of advertisers and products contained in the issue under study.
3. For those advertisers and products identified, respondents are asked to play back everything they can remember. All responses are recorded verbatim.

Recall scores ". . . reflect the advertiser's ability to register the sponsor's name, and to deliver a meaningful message to the consumer."[31] This assumes that the test measures selective exposure, selective perception, and selective retention by respondents. But the recall of factual information does not necessarily mean a change in behavior as it relates to sales.[32]

Recognition tests. These tests are commonly referred to as readership studies. In the print field such ratings are synonymous with "Starch scores." The procedure consists of taking "qualified" readers of a given issue of a magazine and asking them to point out what they saw and read. If an ad is reported as having been read, the interviewer asks the respondent to indicate what parts were read.

The validity of readership tests has been questioned by many re-

[30] Hubert A. Zielske, "The Remembering and Forgetting of Advertising," *Journal of Marketing* (January, 1959), pp. 239–43.

[31] William D. Wells, "Recognition, Recall, and Rating Scales," *Journal of Advertising Research* (September, 1964), p. 8.

[32] See Jack B. Haskins, "Factual Recall as a Measure of Advertising Effectiveness," *Journal of Advertising Research* (March, 1964), pp. 2–8.

searchers. W. R. Simmons, for example, found that readership claimed by nonreaders was about as great as that claimed by readers.[33]

The Advertising Research Foundation replicated the data collection methods of the Starch organization (described briefly above) using a single issue of *Life* with a probability sample of over 600 readers. The ARF study found that the recognition scores obtained were largely independent of the age, education, and socioeconomic levels of respondents; the amount of time which had elapsed since the issue was released; the amount of reading done in the issue; and the competency of the interviewer.[34] But since such findings do not "make sense," what does the recognition method really measure? It is not memory, as was typically thought by many. Lucas and Britt suggest that the scores really measure interest.[35]

The recognition method suffers from the fact that respondents may confuse specific ads with similar or identical ads seen elsewhere, may believe they saw the ad because of its being near familiar editorial material, may desire to please the interviewer, and may "cooperate" because of fatigue from the length of the interview.

MEDIA SELECTION

The goal of the advertiser is to select a media schedule from among the almost infinite number of alternatives which will maximize some combination of reach and frequency, meaning the number of people reached and the frequency with which they are reached. Such a decision presupposes that the advertiser has specified the market segment(s) which he wants to reach. He must then decide what frequency of message exposure is desired in order to effect a change in behavior which will affect the sales of his brand favorably and will try to reach the maximum number in the market segment with that frequency. The greater the frequency desired, the smaller the reach obtainable with a given budget.

The problem of media selection is complicated because not only is it necessary to choose among major media types, such as newspapers, billboards, magazines, radio, and television, but also specific selections must be made within each general type. If magazines are chosen, specific magazines and even issues must be selected. In radio and television

---

[33] W. R. Simmons, "Controlled Recognition in the Measurement of Advertising Perception," *Public Opinion Quarterly,* 25 (Fall, 1961), p. 470.

[34] See Darrell B. Lucas, "The ABC's of ARF's PARM," *Journal of Marketing* (July, 1960), pp. 9–20.

[35] Darrell Blaine Lucas and Steuart Henderson Britt, *Measuring Advertising Effectiveness* (New York: McGraw-Hill Book Co., Inc., 1963), p. 57.

there is not only the question of what networks or stations, but what programs, what day or days of the week, and what time of the day.

While the copy itself is thought to play the primary role in effecting a favorable impression, the media selected affect such things as the recall of the advertising message, the ratings of its sponsors, and coupon return.[36]

The number of readers, viewers, or listeners is basic in selecting a medium, but the characteristics of such persons must also be considered because not all persons are prospective buyers for a particular product. Some persons are better prospects than others because they consume greater quantities of the product type. Thus, a first step in making media comparisons is to distinguish between prospects and nonprospects in the audiences provided by the alternative media. The Advertising Research Foundation suggests that, following the elimination of non-prospects, the media analyst pay attention to the six levels at which the media vehicle operates to contribute to the effectiveness of the advertising message. These are as follows:[37]

1. *Vehicle distribution.*   This refers to the individual medium's circulation—the process by which it becomes available.
2. *Vehicle exposure.*   This deals with the exposure of people to the vehicle, e.g., reading a given issue of a magazine or watching a particular TV program.
3. *Advertising exposure.*   This is the same as level two above, but it involves the advertisement. It requires that the message physically come within the audience's attention range.
4. *Advertising perception.*   This requires that the audience have a conscious awareness of the advertisement.
5. *Advertising communication.*   The audience receives the message in context.
6. *Sales response.*

Levels one through three are concerned with the advertising medium and its ability to put the message before buying prospects. The cost per thousand consumers reached will vary substantially by level. There are no effective measures, however, for levels three, five, and six as they relate to media.

The problem of audience measure is difficult even at the definitional

---

[36] Charles Winick, "Three Measures of the Advertising Value of Media Content," *Journal of Advertising Research* (June, 1962), p. 32. Also see W. M. Weilbacher, "The Qualitative Values Advertising Media," *Journal of Advertising Research* (December, 1960), p. 12.

[37] *Toward Better Media Comparisons* (New York: Advertising Research Foundation, 1961).

level of what constitutes a reader, a viewer, a listener. In addition, there are other problems including:[38]

1. The variations in the composition and size of the audience of a given medium vehicle over time.
2. The variations due to geography, e.g., a TV show may get a high rating in one area because only two channels are available and a much lower rating in another where five channels are present.
3. The variations due to the rate at which different vehicles accumulate audiences, i.e., variations in how many are reached over a period of time as compared with one issue or program.
4. The difficulty of estimating the value of different sizes of message units within and between media—for example, the effectiveness of a 30-second TV commercial versus a 60-second TV commercial versus a full-page advertisement in a general interest magazine.
5. The actual geographical area covered. This is particularly difficult with electronic media.

Media audiences

With but a few exceptions, media research is concerned with measuring the size and composition of individual vehicle audiences. In the case of print media the audience is typically defined as being comprised of individuals who say they have seen one or more major editorial features. With TV and radio the audience can be defined in various ways such as sets tuned to a program or number of people listening or watching, depending upon the criteria used regarding time spent in or average number viewing or listening during a day. Since there are substantial differences in measuring print versus electronic media audiences, the discussion will deal with each one separately.

Print media. The first audience measures were the claims made by the media themselves. Since the size of the audience is a basic consideration in the selection of media, it is not surprising that many of these claims were exaggerated. To overcome this problem, publishers formed an independent organization, the Audit Bureau of Circulations (A.B.C.) to report circulation data through the use of certified audits.

A.B.C. audit reports show the paid circulation of a medium, the number of home subscriptions, and the number of newsstand sales. For newspapers, the circulation is broken by daily and Sunday editions. For magazines, A.B.C. shows data on the percentage of the audience in the major census regions and in several city size groups.

---

[38] For a conceptual discussion of the criteria to use in effecting media comparisons (e.g., persuasibility and impact) see Stewart A. Smith, "Criteria for Media Comparisons," *Journal of Marketing Research* (November, 1965), pp. 364–69.

Circulation is not the best measure of the audience, since it does not provide information about the number of readers. The media themselves are again the main source for such data, since readership is an important sales tool for soliciting advertising. Unfortunately, some reader reports are little more than sales promotion material, but many media provide reliable data.

Politz, largely as a result of work done for *Life* magazine, has developed a method for measuring the readership of an issue which has been widely accepted and used. The method, commonly referred to as the recognition method, defines a reader as an individual who is exposed to any of the editorial contents of a given issue. A person is counted as a reader only if, after examination of the editorial contents of the issue, he states that he is certain he has looked into the issue before. The audience is the sum of the readers.[39] This method is quite expensive because it requires long personal interviews using magazines from which the advertising has been eliminated. Stock has developed a simpler technique which he calls "recall" because it attempts to measure recent specific reading by the use of a relatively simple question: "When was the last time (if ever) you read (or looked into) a copy of ———— ?" In testing his method, Stock found that regardless of whether he used personal interviews, the telephone, or mail, the results were very nearly the same as obtained by the Politz method.[40]

Landis recommends another method which uses a probability-of-exposure index to determine audience size, accumulation, and duplication for specific media vehicles. His method is based on obtaining probability estimates that a given individual will be exposed to an average issue or TV show. The premise is that, if one can determine the distribution of exposure probabilities, the average audience size as well as accumulation and duplication can be determined. Landis validated his method by comparing his results with those obtained using other methods and found no substantial differences.[41]

The problem of providing an accurate estimate of the size of audience for a given publication is a difficult one. Just asking respondents to indicate whether they have looked at a particular copy produces unreliable data. The act of reading certain magazines has a status connotation and may inflate reported readership substantially. Conversely, the status of some magazines may produce negative findings. Belson reports that, where respondents are being asked this type of question for

---

[39] Alfred Politz Research, Inc., *The Readers of the Saturday Evening Post—Technical Appendix* (Philadelphia: The Curtis Publishing Co., 1957).

[40] J. Stevens Stock, "A Comparison of Eight Audience Estimates," *Journal of Advertising Research* (September, 1961), pp. 9–15.

[41] Jack B. Landis, "Exposure Probabilities as Measures of Media Audiences," *Journal of Advertising Research* (September, 1965), pp. 24–29.

a number of magazines, the order in which publications are presented to respondents will drastically affect the results. Thus, if respondents are asked first about monthly magazines, the readership figures are 35 percent higher than if they are asked about monthly magazines *after* they have been queried on weekly magazines and daily newspapers.[42] Belson also found that, in the case of monthly magazines, the figure (percent reading) obtained as a result of using a simple question on whether the respondent has looked at any copy within the past three months should have been about 60 percent higher.[43]

Media analysts need information on the duplication between magazines. Since consumer readership of three or more magazines is quite common, the problem of duplication is an important one, but rarely are data available showing the duplication among three or more magazines. An extensive study to determine duplication among all possible combinations of magazines is obviously an expensive, time-consuming activity. Agostini cites a study in France in which duplications were obtained for thirty magazines taken two by two, as well as for all the possible combinations of fifteen of the thirty magazines. This resulted in 32,767 possible combinations. He proposes (and validates) the use of a "shortcut" method to estimate the unduplicated audience of combinations of three, four, five, etc. magazines using total audience and duplication data of the magazines involved taken two by two.[44]

Wolfgang Schaefer points out that the main drawback to Agostini's method is the need for outside data, which requires periodical studies to be kept current. He recommends the use of a 13-point scale on which respondents are asked to indicate which scale number best describes their reading behavior of a particular vehicle.[45] This approach, in reality, obtains a set of reading probabilities similar to those obtained by Landis.[46]

A media buyer is also interested in the ability of a given medium to generate page traffic, that is, the number of persons who will see the advertisement. This actual usage is called exposure. It must not be confused with the perception of the advertisement. Measuring magazine advertising exposure by households has been done by Politz by sealing

---

[42] Harry Henry, "Belson's Studies in Readership," *Journal of Advertising Research* (June, 1962), p. 11.

[43] *Ibid*, p. 12.

[44] See J. M. Agostini, "How to Estimate Unduplicated Audiences," *Journal of Advertising Research* (March, 1961), pp. 11–14; J. M. Agostini, "Analysis of Magazine Accumulative Audience," *Journal of Advertising Research* (December, 1962), pp. 24–27; J. M. Agostini, "The Case for Direct Questions on Reading Habits," *Journal of Advertising Research* (June, 1964), pp. 28–33.

[45] Wolfgang Schaefer, "Scale Measures of Magazine Reading," *Journal of Advertising Research* (December, 1965), pp. 21–26.

[46] Landis, *op. cit.*

facing pages through the use of a small drop of glue which was easily broken by readers. "Glued" magazines were then substituted for regular copies in the subscription mailing and, at a later date, picked up from the subscription households and a count made of the number of glue seals which had been broken. This count showed the minimum number of individuals exposed to the pages.[47]

The Traffic Audit Bureau was formed to provide information for the buyers of outdoor advertising similar to the A.B.C. data for magazines and newspapers. This service provides estimates of the number of people who have a reasonable possibility of viewing a particular billboard.

Radio and television. Radio and television are very different from magazines and newspapers when it comes to measuring the size of their audiences. Such media leave no visible trace that they have been "received." The program and the advertising message are often mixed, and it is difficult to divorce the two. There are four basic ways to measure the size of the audience for any radio and television program. Each of these is discussed briefly below.

Coincidental method. This method is based on a sampling of telephone homes, using the telephone to solicit responses as to what radio and TV programs are being listened to or viewed. Typically, the respondent is called and asked whether anyone in the home is listening to the radio or viewing television and, if so, to what program and station he is tuned. The question is also asked, *What is the name of the sponsor, or product being advertised?* Ratings are based on the percentage of radio or television homes tuned to a particular program. This method measures average audience on the assumption that calls are spread evenly throughout the time of the program.

This system has the advantage of speed and economy; however, it has severe limitations. First, the results may not be valid since only telephone homes are included. Even where network shows are concerned, it is usually not economically feasible to obtain a sample of rural homes. For these reasons, the total size of audience cannot be estimated accurately.

A second difficulty is that such procedures do not produce any continuous information about the audience. One cannot tell how many homes are reached over a period of several programs, that is, what the cumulative audience is. Nor can one tell what the total audience is for a given program at any one time, since no measure of tuning in or out is obtained.

A third major limitation is that calls must be limited to certain hours

---

[47] *The Readers of the Saturday Evening Post* (Philadelphia: The Curtis Publishing Co., 1958). Also see *A Study of Advertising Penetration in LOOK Households* (New York: *Look*, 1959).

of the day and night, such as after 8:00 A.M. and before 10:30 P.M. Programs not included in this time span cannot usually be measured using the telephone coincidental method. There may also be a tendency on the part of some respondents to report that their radio or TV set is on when such is not the case.

Roster recall. This is a technique which consists of aided recall via personal interviews. The interviewing is done shortly after the particular time period (usually four hours) to be measured has been completed. A list or *roster* of programs by quarter hours is used to aid respondents in remembering what programs were listened to or viewed.

The ratings obtained by the use of the roster-recall method are dependent upon memory, and are subject to inflation or deflation as a result of the status, or lack of status, of certain programs. This is the method's biggest limitation, since the less popular shows tend to be discriminated against. Such a method does not provide any continuous information about the nature of the audience, nor does it permit measurement of the cumulative audience. Because respondents are queried about only a short time span, duplication analysis cannot be made. It is not possible to estimate the number of persons who view program A and also program B unless both programs fall within the time span on which the respondent is being interviewed.

The audimeter. This method receives its name from a machine of the same name used by the A. C. Nielsen Company. This machine is an electronic recorder which can be attached to a television set without interfering with its normal operation. It records on a tape when the set is turned on, and to what station it is tuned. All of this is keyed to time periods so that a continuous record of the use of the set can be obtained by decoding the tape.

Using the audimeter, the Nielsen Company provides a TV service which reports:

1. Total audience—number and percent of TV homes tuned to each network program for a minimum of six minutes.
2. Average audience—equivalent to the number of TV homes tuned to the full program (the average number of homes minute by minute).
3. Share of audience—percentage of TV homes viewing any program at that time period which is viewing a specific program.

Since the audimeter sample remains essentially the same from month to month, a measure of the cumulative audience can be obtained and, in addition, elaborate duplication data can be studied, since all programs over a long period of time are covered. Data can be broken down by such household characteristics as region, city size, age of male head, total family income, and presence of children. While this service provides more objective data than any of the other measurement methods in that it relies on mechanical observation, it must be remembered that because a set is "on" does not indicate it is being viewed, nor does it indicate who is viewing.

Diary method. This method obtains estimates of listening or viewing by having respondents record in a specially designed diary their radio listening and/or television viewing. Such an operation assumes that the panel members will cooperate by recording their listening or viewing at the time it occurs and, thus, will do it accurately. If this assumption is valid, then the diary method has an advantage—that of obtaining data on individuals viewing programs. Even so, the diary cannot provide a precise minute-by-minute audience flow as does the audimeter. A continous panel operation can provide much useful duplication data, not only between radio and TV programs, but also between such programs and other media to which the individual was exposed such as magazines and newspapers. The disadvantages of the diary method have been discussed in an earlier chapter.

Paul Keller points out that the audience turnover of the popular media vehicles is typically substantially less over a short period of time than with the less popular ones. If people like a vehicle, they tend to expose themselves to it repeatedly. In his studies of media audience accumulation he also found that:[48]

1. A close and predictable relationship exists between a program's one-time audience and its four-week accumulation.
2. The type of program does not seem to affect the accumulation pattern.
3. Daily daytime shows have a predictable accumulation pattern, except that those of a noncontinuous nature (e.g., quiz programs) accumulate audiences faster than continuous programs (e.g., serial dramas).

Information about the duplication of audiences *between* media types over time and by demographic and social groups is much needed. To date such data are almost never obtained because of the costs and reliability problems involved.

Media models.[49] Over the past several years a number of computerized media models have been developed. These models start by putting into the computer detailed information about the market for the product involved so as to be able to identify key segments. Such data as product behavior (e.g., brand shares, purchase rates, brand switching probabilities, and demographic characteristics) are inputted, as are data dealing with media behavior. Other information which is fed into the computer includes the audience characteristics over time of a set of media and

---

[48] Paul Keller, "Patterns of Media-Audience Accumulation," *Journal of Marketing* (April, 1966), pp. 32–37.

[49] For a relatively detailed discussion on this subject see *Evaluating Media* (New York: National Industrial Conference Board, 1966), pp. 107–33.

duplication and accumulation data. Values pertaining to different types of message units (e.g., size and color) are also included.

The Batten, Barton, Durstine & Osborn Advertising Agency's revised model stipulates that the advertiser state his objectives in terms of reach and frequency, and that relative values must be placed on each. More specifically, the output is tied to a frequency distribution of the number of times the desired audience is to be exposed to the advertising message per some time period, typically one year.[50] The model identifies and costs out that media schedule which comes closest to meeting the client's goals.

In its present form the model reports on a monthly basis the media being recommended, the number of units to be purchased, the composition and size of the audience reached, the total number of impressions, the distribution of exposure frequencies, the sources of frequencies by media type, the source of frequency by individual vehicles, and the cost. The latter takes into account the discounts granted by the media. A strong advantage to the model is that it can be used to determine what effect the use of media other than the ones being recommended would have on the output.

Although excellent progress has been made in developing media models, less has been accomplished in providing the models with more precise input data. Duplication and accumulation data involving a variety of media types are still missing, as are frequency of exposure data. The latter is particularly important since repetition is a primary determinant of the advertising budget. Good measures of target audiences on the basis of predispostition to buy the product type in question also are badly needed.

SUMMARY

Over the years the field of advertising has received considerable attention from research workers, but still there is no general agreement as to what are the best techniques to use to answer the questions: "What should be said about the product?" "What is the best way to put these appeals into words and pictures?" "What media should be selected?" It is doubtful if any single technique will be developed which will answer these questions satisfactorily.

For selecting advertising appeals, motivation research offers possibilities. Basic appeals should not be based on "guesses" as to what will motivate the consumer to buy the product. Motivational studies can furnish information as to the images of the product in consumers' minds

---

[50] This discussion is based on *ibid*.

and the relative intensity with which these images are held by various population groups.

Copy testing is designed to determine the best way of presenting the selected appeals. There are two major kinds of copy tests—"before" and "after." If the objective is to make improvements in the copy before it is released on a full-scale basis, then the test used is classified as a "before" test. The eight different kinds of "before" copy tests are as follows: (1) consumer jury, (2) rating scales, (3) advertising impact, (4) psychological tests, (5) "ad detector" and eye camera, (6) inquiries, (7) sales tests, and (8) simulated sales tests. Similar techniques are used in some of these tests so the differences are more a matter of degree than of kind. The three types of "after" tests are: (1) recall, (2) recognition, and (3) sales results.

In selecting media, the objective is to find the most efficient vehicle for carrying the message to potential buyers. This necessitates a determination of both the size of the audience delivered by alternative media and the characteristics of these audiences. Readership studies are used to obtain such information for printed media. For radio and television programs a number of methods are currently used, including the telephone coincidental, roster recall, audimeter, and diary. If an advertiser is using more than one medium, he is faced with the problem of duplication. While duplication studies are based primarily on quantitative data and fail to consider the value of repetition and the qualitative differences in media, they are still of value in helping to narrow down the alternatives in the media selection program.

Experimental studies offer considerable opportunities to determine the effectiveness of a single medium or of various combinations of media, but are expensive. Mathematical models to select the "best" media schedule (typically based on number of exposures) are being used more and more.

Case 15—1. SCOTT PAPER COMPANY

The Scott Paper Company was a leading producer of sanitary paper products including paper towels and napkins, toilet and facial tissues, and a wide assortment of other paper products for home and industrial use. Through aggressive merchandising and advertising, the company had built strong brand recognition and market acceptance of its products.

For a number of years the Scott Paper Company had been one of the pioneers in conducting studies to determine the effectiveness of its advertising in an endeavor to measure the contribution such promotional efforts made toward sales. By means of these studies, the company had developed sufficient information to enable it to judge, within reasonable limits, the level of advertising expenditures that were adequate for the promotion of consumer paper products, but had no reliable data whereby it was able to measure the effectiveness of its advertising efforts for the industrial paper business.

Scott's industrial marketing manager, Mr. Burt B. Roens, decided to plan and launch a study which would afford him and his associates some basis for evaluating the company's advertising program directed at the industrial market. "The broad objective of our study," said Mr. Roens, "was to determine the effectiveness of the three major expenditures in our industrial advertising budget: business magazine advertising, mail advertising, and distributor salesmen's incentives." The products selected for evaluation were Scott's "washroom line"—towels and toilet tissue sold to establishments such as manufacturing plants, hotels, restaurants, and public buildings. This line was chosen because of its universal usage in all types of business and industry.

This project actually consisted of five separate and distinct research studies: first, an industry awareness and attitude study; second, a magazine subscribers' awareness study made by two weekly publications; third, a study of mail advertising and business magazine advertising coupon returns and resultant follow-up personal sales calls; fourth, an analysis of the distributor salesmen's incentive program; and fifth, a comprehensive analysis of distributor sales and share of market. Each of these studies called for a different research technique, but all had one common objective—to measure the effectiveness of the overall advertising and promotion program. More specific research objectives as stated by Roens were:

1. To measure expenditures for business magazine advertising, mail advertising, and incentives against sales of Scott products.

2. To measure the registration of magazine and mail ads in the minds of readers.

3. To measure the immediate results of inquiries against historical averages of the pulling power of Scott ads, direct mail, and incentives individually and against various combinations of promotional elements in the test.

In designing the sample and methodology for these studies, Scott selected eleven test areas and eleven control areas, a total of twenty-two cities and surrounding counties. Company sales data for each of these markets were compiled for a period of three years prior to, during, and after the test, and a Scott share of market was determined. These test and control markets were matched in terms of employment, distribution, manpower, sales potential, and other factors. Each test city and its corresponding control city were separated geographically to prevent any overlapping of the promotional influence; for instance, test areas were not situated in the same states as control areas. Test areas were restricted primarily to the states of Ohio, Indiana, Kentucky, Alabama, and Louisiana, due to the limited availability of areas in which split runs could be employed. Metropolitan markets were selected as test areas within these states where Scott maintained a resident sales representative, and Scott had two or more active local distributors whose aggregate Scott sales exceeded a predetermined base amount.

The balance of the United States, with the exception of two or three states wherein special merchandising programs were in effect, was then available for selection as control markets on the basis that Scott had: (1) a resident representative; (2) two or more active local distributors; (3) a minimum sales volume comparable to a test city; (4) a share of market comparable to a test city; and (5) an S.I.C. profile comparable to a test city. Test markets were those which were to be subjected to advertising and promotion in various combinations and frequencies; in the control markets there was to be no advertising or promotion of any kind during the period of the study.

Procedures and methods employed for each research phase of the overall study are outlined in the following sections.

General program

A two year test program was laid out. During the first six months all business magazine advertising, mail advertising, and distributor salesmen's incentives were eliminated from the test areas. During the following 12 months business magazine advertising, mail advertising, and distributor salesmen's incentives were introduced in various amounts and combinations in the test areas. During the next six months, all forms of promotion were again stopped. Throughout the entire two-year period business magazine advertising, mail advertising, and distributor salesmen's incentives were eliminated from the control areas.

Eleven different input combinations were used. Advertising (business magazines) and direct mail were applied in "high level" and "low level" amounts; "high level" referred to a program with twice the frequency (hence dollar input) as the "low level." Only one level of distributor salesmen's incentive bonus was utilized.

1. Advertising, high level
2. Advertising, low level
3. Direct mail, high level
4. Direct mail, low level
5. Advertising, high level; plus direct mail, low level
6. Advertising, low level; plus direct mail, high level
7. Advertising, low level; plus direct mail, low level
8. Advertising, low level; plus distributor salesmen's incentive

9. Direct mail, low level; plus distributor salesmen's incentive
10. Advertising, low level; plus direct mail, low level; plus distributor salesmen's incentive
11. Distributor salesman incentive

Industry awareness and attitude study

This study was conducted in three stages and covered seven of the test areas and seven of the control areas (those test areas in which magazine advertising was an input factor, and their seven paired control areas). The study was conducted by personal interview, using a formal questionnaire and a sample representative of industry in each of the fourteen areas. All industrial establishments within the survey areas were stratified by size and type of industry. Only buyers of industrial washroom products who purchased for a plant with twenty or more employees were classified as eligible respondents, and a screening process was used to establish their eligibility.

The base, or precampaign, field work as conducted during the month before the magazine advertising, direct mail advertising, and incentive programs were introduced. This pretest survey disclosed that 97 percent of the buyers interviewed were familiar with Scott Paper Company, and 94 percent were able on an unaided basis to name one or more of the company's products. The second stage of this study was conducted five months later, after the first phase of the program was completed. The third stage was conducted just before the end of the 12-month advertising campaign.

Business magazine subscribers' awareness study

Scott determined that there were at least five primary buying influences in the sales of its towels and tissues: (1) plant engineering and maintenance; (2) top management; (3) building owners and managers; (4) owners of small businesses; and (5) purchasing agents and buyers.

Selection of the publications to participate in the test was based on three primary considerations:

1. The magazine had to reach the above primary buying influences for Scott washroom products.

2. The magazine had to be able to break out its circulation on a state or regional basis.

3. The magazine had to be able to carry ad inserts to this limited audience.

The company did not seek pretest copy. Instead, it was attempting to find out what happened to sales and awareness when a minimum of advertising and promotional dollars was spent versus the dollars needed for a high frequency, concentrated campaign. It was thus endeavoring to test two levels of expenditure—low level and high level, the latter being twice as much as the former.

First phase program. In the weekly publications in high level areas, ads were run every week for eight consecutive weeks, then every other week for five months. In the low level areas, ads were run in every other issue of these weekly publications for eight weeks, then once a month for five months. Ads in the monthly publications in the high level areas ran in every issue for seven months and in low level areas in every other issue for the same period.

Second phase program. In the weekly publications in the high level areas ads were run every week for eight consecutive weeks, then every other week for three months. In the low level areas ads were run in every other issue of the weekly publications for eight weeks, then once a month for three months. Ads in the monthly publications in the high level areas ran in every issue for five months, and in the low level areas in every other issue for the same period.

The objective in this advertising campaign study was to awaken prospects to the importance of top quality in terms of employee-patron benefits and satisfaction, and to stimulate requests to sample the company's top-of-the-line towel. The ads were limited to single page, two-sided inserts.

In addition, a coupon appeared in every ad offering a self-dispensing box of top-of-the-line towels so the reader could test the product at Scott's expense. This box was created specifically for the test and was unique in that it could be attached to any washroom wall without marring the wall surface.

Two weekly magazines participated in a subscriber-awareness study, field work for which was undertaken before, during, and after the two phases of the magazine advertising program were completed.

Direct mail and magazine advertising inquiry study

In each phase of the mail advertising campaign, a carefully selected list, totaling 40,000 names, was prepared by a professional organization to the following specifications: (1) two digit S.I.C.—manufacturing, construction, wholesale, retail, finance, public utility, services; (2) purchasing agent, owner, or manager specifically designated; (3) each test city receiving direct mail had its proportional share of the 40,000 names. This was not necessarily a complete census of each city, but came close to it with respect to establishments with twenty or more employees. Each of the individuals selected received reprints of the magazine ad inserts prepared as a direct mail piece, and each piece contained a tear-out, postpaid reply card offering the free sample box of towels.

First phase program.   In the high level areas one mailing was made every other week for three months, then no mailing for one month, then one mailing each week for six consecutive weeks. Low level areas received one mailing monthly for six consecutive months.

Second phase program.   In the high level area one mailing was made every other week for five months. In low level areas one mailing was made each month for five months.

A special follow-up system was developed for handling inquiries generated by both the business magazine and mail advertising. Each respondent received a sample box of towels and a letter from Scott's national sales manager citing product advantages and inviting the return of a tabulating card with four check-off boxes:

- ☐ Booklet "How to Appraise a Paper Towel"
- ☐ "Washroom Advisory Service" materials
- ☐ "Tell me where I can buy Scott towels locally"
- ☐ Write-in comments

If the tabulating card was not returned, the name of the respondent was sent to the nearest Scott district manager for suggested follow-up. If returned, data requested were sent to the respondent and the Scott district manager notified of this "red flag" sales lead for definite follow-up.

Analysis of distributor salesmen's incentive program

This promotional part of the test was an incentive program for distributor salesmen. The first phase program was called the "Scott Nest Egg Payoff," and it ran for ten weeks. Distributor salesmen were offered cash awards based on case sales of Scott washroom products to new customers.

The second phase was called "Vacation Bonus" and again ran for ten weeks. Cash awards were made on the same basis as in the first phase program.

Analysis of distributor sales and share of market

This final research project involved auditing sales activity for washroom products by each Scott distributor in the test and control areas. Distributors were to report the total number of cases sold, by brand, on a quarterly basis.

Through such analysis of sales the company expected to be able to relate the effectiveness of its advertising and promotional efforts to its sales performance.

In commenting on the findings of the experimental study Mr. Roens made the following points:

To measure the results of the experiment, we compared what we found in the field during the first survey, prior to our promotional efforts, to the findings in the field after the third survey of industry awareness and attitude and a year of promotional effort in the test cities. . . . These findings were converted into a simple index, the results of the pretest study being equivalent to 100.

Table 1 below shows a gain in each of the selected categories (direct mail, magazine advertising, and share of sample using Scott products) for the test markets and a marked drop in the control markets. . . . We could deduce from this that there is a strong relationship between awareness and market share . . . and also the fact that when advertising is withdrawn market share is adversely affected.

We next analyzed results of the various combinations of advertising and promotional effort. For this analysis, we compared a test city and its corre-

TABLE 1. Index of change in values—all cities (pretest survey = 100)

	Test cities	Control cities
Remembered direct mail	128	86
Remembered magazine advertising	102	63
Share of sample using Scott products	124	68

sponding control city. The results of this analysis were not quite as clear-cut in each individual case as the overall picture. Nevertheless, the trend was definitely in favor of the test cities, as Table 2 reveals. Moreover, it is interesting to note that by far the biggest gain in towel customers was made in the market where we threw in all three elements (magazine advertising, direct mail, incentive). . . . It shows again that, in the main, there was a definite drop in market share in those markets (control) where there was no advertising or promotion.

Explanation.   Test market A had a gain of 129 index points from the first to the third survey (12 months apart) in the number of companies surveyed using Scott towels. During this period, this particular city received a certain level of all three elements—magazine advertising, direct mail and distributor

TABLE 2. Index of change from first to third survey: Share of sample using Scott towels (pretest survey = 100)

Test market (activity assigned)	Markets	
	Test	Control
A. Magazine advertising (LL) + direct mail (LL) + incentive	229	47
B. Magazine advertising (LL)	167	117
C. Magazine advertising (LL) + direct mail (LL)	158	63
D. Magazine advertising (HL)	141	50
E. Magazine advertising (HL) + direct mail (LL)	127	24
F. Magazine advertising (LL) + direct mail (HL)	109	62
G. Magazine advertising (LL) + incentive	61	83

NOTE: HL indicates high level and LL low level.

incentive. In other words, this city had the biggest increase in the number of Scott towel customers for the 12-month period.

At the same time, its paired control market, which received no advertising, dropped 53 index points. In other words, the number of companies surveyed using Scott towels dropped markedly.

We have also kept track of the coupon returns from our direct mail program by date of mailing, test city, and by high and low levels of frequency. . . . As Table 3 shows, the high-level direct mail has generated the better rate of response. . . . In addition to coupon return information, we also recorded the results of personal calls made as a follow-up to returns from both magazine and direct mail advertising. To date, this shows that sales have been consummated at 25 percent of those establishments receiving a follow-up call; another 50 percent are indicated as being ready to buy in the near future.

TABLE 3. Direct mail campaign returns

	High level	Low level	Total
Total mailing list	9,790	30,000	37,790
Returns	2,863	5,924	8,787
Percent returns	29.2%	19.7%	22.1%

I might also add here that the results of the first phase distributor salesman's incentive plan show that considerable activity was generated here; final results have not yet been compiled.

Mr. Roens stated that at the time of his report the results of the distributor sales and market share analysis were still in process and not yet known. However, he went on to say:

We will not consider a particular (advertising) program successful unless it can generate profitable sales. We may find that sales increases are not big enough to cover the cost of generating them. On the other hand, we may find a certain combination which gives us our optimum return. At best, this can only give us an indication of the future direction we should take in our programming

Appraise and evaluate the general soundness of the advertising effectiveness research program.

Case 15—2. THE QUAKER OATS COMPANY

In the period following World War II, the pancake mix industry showed general weakness. The Quaker Oats Company, which had an important share of the market through its brand Aunt Jemima, was affected more than any other company and so was particularly concerned.

Quaker and its agency, the J. Walter Thompson Company, were aware that over a 20-year period the American diet had undergone substantial changes. Per capita consumption of wheat flour and potatoes had declined markedly, while meat and egg consumption rose sharply. Since these trends had a direct bearing on the use of pancake flour, the two companies decided to make a special study of the field before determining future advertising strategy. Accordingly, Quaker and J. Walter Thompson jointly asked Social Research, Inc., to examine the pancake mix field.

Social Research's study investigated such subjects as the general character of pancakes in the minds of housewives and their families, attitudes toward pancake mixes and their ingredients, the position of Aunt Jemima in the brand hierarchy, and the Aunt Jemima image. The findings of this research are summarized below:

SUMMARY OF SOCIAL RESEARCH, INC., PANCAKE STUDY

The general character of pancakes

1. Pancakes and waffles are thought of as a gift to the family. Housewives talk about them as something special they prepare for their families. Women do not deny that they themselves like pancakes, but they often stress that their husbands and children are the ones who really like them.
2. Housewives tend to feel "martyrish" when they prepare pancakes, even though they admit that with pancake mixes the preparation of the batter is not a problem. They complain about the length of time they have to stand at the stove, how difficult it is to get the family together in time to be served immediately, and the fact that they cannot sit down with the family and enjoy them.
3. Feeling guilty about not serving them more often, housewives may derogate pancakes as a food. The housewife does agree that pancakes are an economical, filling, satisfying kind of food, but she tends to think of them also as too heavy, too filling, and not especially suitable or valuable as a basic food in the family diet.
4. Pancakes have a complex, meaningful character. When respondents were asked to describe the kinds of people they thought would like pancakes most, the following emerged:
   . . . people who have a zest for living
   . . . healthy, growing youngsters
   . . . fat, jolly people, heavy eaters
   . . . hard-working men—laborers, farmers
   . . . poor people—stable, homey people with large families
   . . . gourmets

Attitudes toward pancake mixes and ingredients

1. Pancake mixes are very positively evaluated.
   a. They taste as good as home-made pancakes.

b. They are easy to prepare.

c. They are economical.

2. Despite individual preferences, the housewife usually feels that most mixes are probably made of much the same ingredients. Nevertheless, housewives have decided notions about what various foods can contribute to pancakes.

  a. Buttermilk—As a rule, respondents do not mention this ingredient spontaneously because it is something few housewives have readily available. While opinons vary widely as to what buttermilk can contribute to pancakes, they are usually positive.

  b. Soy—Most respondents claim little or no personal experience with soy flour, but it is evaluated as a highly nutritious health food, although one which tends to be strongly derogated as a flavorsome, appetizing ingredient.

  c. Buckwheat—Opinions about buckwheat tend to be either strongly positive or strongly negative. The minority who like it believe it has a distinctive flavor. Those who dislike it complain that buckwheat pancakes are heavy and coarse.

  d. Fresh Eggs—In general, fresh eggs are thought to be a decided asset in pancake making. They are seen as making pancakes light and fluffy, richer, tastier, more nutritious, and making them hold together.

Attitudes toward Aunt Jemima

1. Aunt Jemima is synonymous with pancakes and entertains strong loyalty.

2. Aunt Jemima is viewed as a good, old reliable brand.

3. Aunt Jemima is a likable figure—one who has a familiar face. She is warm, jolly, comfortable. She is a southern mammy who loves to cook. She is a symbol of quality. She is old-fashioned.

J. Walter Thompson studied the research findings and established the following advertising copy objectives as a result:

1. To project Aunt Jemima as a modern, up-to-date brand adapted to meet the needs and desires of today's housewife.

2. To make an especially forceful appeal to younger families where consumption of pancakes is greatest.

3. To make pancakes seem easier, more fun, more interesting to serve. To get pancakes served more often in more different meals.

4. To make consumers feel friendlier and closer to the Aunt Jemima brand. To utilize existing product advantages and new ones if they can

be developed. To teach that Aunt Jemima on its merits is a better product than competitive mixes.

Should the Quaker Oats Company approve the proposed advertising copy objectives?

Case 15—3. TOASTMASTER DIVISION

The Toastmaster Division of McGraw-Edison Company manufactured a line of electric toasters and other small electrical household appliances including blenders, coffee makers, fry pans, portable heaters, irons, hand mixers, can openers, and waffle grills. All these products were normally priced to sell at retail for less than $50 and were distributed nationally under the Toastmaster brand name, primarily through appliance and department stores.

The appliance industry, especially for small appliance items, was highly competitive, with more than thirty firms competing aggressively for the business in lines similar to those of Toastmaster. Moreover, most small appliance items had a high seasonal sales factor, with perhaps as much as 40 to 45 percent of all retail sales being made in the months of November and December. Toastmaster's products were competitive in design with those of other firms in the industry, although its prices were slightly higher. The company advertised its products extensively in magazines and newspapers.

In discussing print media campaigns with Toastmaster's advertising agency, the company's advertising manager made the following statement: "In essence, we want our consumer advertising to be exciting but completely believable. We want our advertising to startle, while delivering a potent, memorable sales message. In short, we want to gently jolt consumers into learning about Toastmaster as a manufacturer of a top line of automatic appliances, and remembering us for it."

With this advertising concept as a background, the Chicago office of Erwin Wasey, Ruthrauff and Ryan, Inc., the company's advertising agency, decided to conduct a copy test of four advertisements to see how well they carried out the objectives stated above. The agency's art and copy departments prepared four single product advertisements—one each for the toaster, fry pan, can opener, and coffee maker—and asked the marketing research department of the agency to pretest these ads.

The research department proposed to use the "portfolio" technique for the pretest and to conduct the study in two phases. The first phase would consist of providing four separate portfolios, each containing six "control" advertisements and one of the four Toastmaster ads. The same control ads were to be used in each portfolio and their positions would not be changed; one of the Toastmaster advertisements would be given the fourth position in each portfolio as follows:

Portfolio position	Advertisement
1	Bell Telephone Princess telephone
2	General Electric rotisserie
3	Staley spray starch
4	Toastmaster product (toaster, fry pan, can opener, or coffee maker)
5	Northern Tissue paper towels
6	New York Life Insurance
7	Gale Products outboard motors

Each portfolio would be shown to a separate sample of fifty women, or a total of two hundred respondents. Each respondent would be instructed to go through the portfolio just as she would a magazine. After she finished looking through the portfolio, it would be taken away and the respondent asked three "lead-in" questions that were unrelated to the ads she had seen, in order to take her mind off the portfolio. Next, the respondent would be asked to describe each ad she remembered seeing in the portfolio. If she did not recall the Toastmaster advertisement, she would be asked specifically if she remembered an advertisement for a toaster, fry pan, can opener, coffee maker. If such an advertisement were then recalled, the respondent would be asked to tell all she remembered about the ad and her verbatim answers would be recorded.

The second phase of the copy involved getting respondent reactions to the Toastmaster advertisements as a whole, that is, the headline, illustration, and copy. Here again the same four advertisements would be used, but the brand names would be blacked out so that respondents would be reacting to the advertisement and not to the brand. Twenty depth interviews would be made on each Toastmaster ad, each respondent being shown only one ad, thus providing a total of eighty depth interviews. These interviews, when analyzed, would shed additional light on the findings from the portfolio test.

1. Should the proposed research design be used to pretest the four ads? What changes, if any, should be made?

2. What kinds of tabulations can be made from the finding from the proposed study which will be useful to the copy department?

Case 15—4. VARIAN ASSOCIATES, INCORPORATED*

The marketing research director of the Tube Division of Varian Associates, Inc., was faced with the problem of responding to a request made by the manager of the operations research unit to specify exactly what

---

* Reprinted from Stanford Business Cases 1966, Volume II with the permission of the publishers, Stanford University Graduate School of Business. Copyright © 1966 by the Board of Trustees of the Leland Stanford Junior University.

types of decisions could and would be made using data obtained from the media survey then in the field. The media study had been initiated by the advertising manager of the tube division to obtain needed information on the readership of selected magazines and journals. At one time or another a variety of interested parties, including the division's advertising agency, the corporate public relations officer, the corporate director of research, and the division's marketing manager had participated in formulating the study design.

Varian Associates, with headquarters in Palo Alto, California, was one of the largest electronics companies in the world. Founded as an outgrowth of the pioneering work done before and during World War II on the klystron tube, the company grew from six people and $22,000 in sales to 6,400 employees and annual sales of $100 million. The company was organized into three major groups as follows:

Microwave tube group. Major products of the group consisted of klystron tubes, traveling wave tubes, magnetron tubes, gas switching tubes microwave components, solid state devices, crossed-field devices, backward wave oscillators, and klystron amplifiers. The basic applications for these products included early warning radar, radar astronomy, satellite communications, missile guidance, air traffic control, weather radar, UHF television, microwave relay stytems, beacons, microwave test equipment, navigation aids, and navigation.

Instrument group. The major products of the group included spectrometers, laboratory electromagnetics and superconducting magnets, recorders, frequency standards, and magnetometers. The basic applications for these products included quantitative and qualitative nondestructive analysis of chemical compounds, isotope identification, laboratory research, studies of the behavior of matter under the influence of precise magnetic fields, navigation, time keeping, communications, geophysical exploration, magnetic search, deep space probes, and oceanographic research.

Equipment group. This group produced such products as ultra-high vacuum pumps and systems, vacuum instrumentation, and linear accelerators. The basic applications of these products included appendage pumping, vacuum tube processing, mass spectrometers, physics experiments, evaporation and deposition, environmental testing, study of services, metallurgical studies, physical and biological studies, clinical radiation therapy, food irradiation, high energy physics studies, and radiation chemistry studies.

The tube group was the largest in sales of the three groups. It sold its products to both military and industrial companies typically on a contract-bid basis. The group employed a total of 40 salesmen and servicemen. In addition, a substantial number of men at the various headquarters offices assisted the field men when the occasion arose. The tube group spent several hundred thousands each year in advertising and promotion including media advertising, trade shows, workshops, publicity, direct mail, and catalogs.

The advertising manager of the tube group summed up his request for a media study by saying, "I want to know what magazines and journals are the most efficient to use to cover audiences that I specify as needing to receive certain messages." He also indicated that in preparation for a media study of some sort he was revising his master mailing list by omitting individuals who were not influential in the purchase of products produced by the tube group. This master list had been compiled over the years through sales reports, inquiries, trade shows, direct mail, and workshops. In order to bring it up to date all tube sales and service people were asked to indicate the names, titles, and addresses of all those people whom they thought were influential in deciding what supplier to use. The specific request read, "We would like to ask that you prepare a list of the ten most influential people in each of your major accounts; these should be people that you feel we should be reaching with our advertising."

After receiving the names from the field force and further culling, the master list contained approximately 3,500 names, of which 600 were indicated as being "prime influentials." It was decided to conduct the survey among all 3,500, but to identify the 600 separately so as to be able to follow up either by phone or mail on them where necessary.

The group's advertising agency was asked what information should be obtained in the media study. The agency's response is shown in Exhibit 1. After evaluating the agency's reply, as well as requests from other individuals, a final questionnaire was prepared (see Exhibit 2). Follow-ups were planned on the entire sample to obtain a high rate of returns. The questionnaire was mailed together with a stamped first-class return envelope.

At one of the several conferences held to implement the survey, the responsibility for analyzing the returns was given to the operations research unit. Since the same survey approach would very likely be used by other Varian groups, the OR unit was anxious to develop a standardized set of procedures for computerizing and analyzing the data. To do this they had to know *exactly* what decisions the advertising manager planned to make using the survey data, what additional information he wished to correlate with the survey data, and what "operational" measures he wanted to use. As an example of the latter the word "coverage" presented a problem. The term could be used in a variety of ways including the number of people reached by the average issue of a given magazine, or it could mean the cumulative audience reached by a given number of issues of a magazine.

The OR unit requested that the tube group marketing research manager get together with the division's advertising manager to respond to numerous suggestions pertaining to the development of a simple media model which could, it was thought, be made operational through the use of the survey data. The proposed model is described in Exhibit 3.

How should the marketing research manager and advertising manager of the tube group respond to the request from the OR unit?

EXHIBIT 1

HOEFER, DIETERICH & BROWN, INC.
ADVERTISING AND PUBLIC RELATIONS
414 JACKSON SQUARE, SAN FRANCISCO, CALIFORNIA 94111   YUKON 1-1811

Mr. Dick Barck
Marketing Department
Varian Associates
611 Hansen Way
Palo Alto, California

Dear Dick:

I enclose an outline of the kinds of information that we would find useful when the media preference survey is completed for the tube group.

Taking the groupings in order, we're interested in a breakdown of the company's primary areas of interest because different kinds of products should, obviously, be advertised to different kinds of systems manufacturers. You may be able to provide this information within Varian on most of the companies.

We want some sort of a breakdown on job function, because the new Business Publication Association (BPA) figures on circulation by member publication will be broken down in this manner. The functions that I have suggested are those used by *Microwaves* magazine in their own circulation analysis.

We would like to break the surveys into groupings by (1) specifying function and (2) approving function. In addition, if possible, we would like to have a "rating" as to degree of actual influence in the actual purchase.

As to the publications themselves, I have listed the magazines now under consideration for tube group promotion, plus two amateur-oriented publications being used by Eimac. The list should probably be checked with Bob Landon to make sure that we are covering his market adequately. I have consciously excluded questions dealing with the "most useful" editorial or "do you read the advertisements," because I frankly don't know what to do with this type of information after I have it. We don't care, in my opinion, whether he reads the magazine because it contains information pertinent to his job, or because it contributes interdisciplinary information in which he is interested, or because it provides general news about his industry. We do care whether or not he reads it regularly, and whether or not he considers it "must" reading. As to the advertising readership, it's our job to make the ads sufficiently interesting so that he *will* read them.

After the results are in, we will provide cost information which can be related to publication preferences and market coverage. It should be fairly simple to determine a "cost efficiency" rating by comparing the weighted percentage of regular readers to the absolute cost of a single advertising page.

Please call me if you have any questions.

Very truly yours,
HOEFER, DIETERICH & BROWN, INC.
/s/ Hal
Hal H. Marquis

EXHIBIT 1 (*Continued*)

Enclosure

cc: Mr. Paul Wagner
     Mr. Bill Engel
     Mr. Jim Kirby

1. Company's primary areas of interest:
   Communications systems manufacturers
   Telemetering & data systems manufacturers
   Electronic countermeasures systems manufacturers
   Navigation & guidance systems manufacturers
   Air traffic control & landing systems manufacturers
   Weapon control systems manufacturers
   Miscellaneous radar systems manufacturers
   Research & development laboratories
   U.S. government & military
   Microwave test equipment manufacturers
   Miscellaneous microwave components manufacturers
   General: materials, plasma, nuclear, magnetics, etc.
2. Job function of individual answering questionnaire:
   Application engineering
   Development engineering
   Design engineering
   Research
   Engineering management
   Purchasing
   Administrative management
   Production management
3. Individual's influence in buying decision:
   a. Specify components (rate 1 to 10)
   b. Review purchase decision (rate 1 to 10)
4. Readership of the following publications (rated "read occasionally," "read regularly," and "consider *must* reading"):
   Product: *Electronic Design, Electronics, EDN (Electrical Design News),
                E.E.E., Electro-Technology, Electronic Industries, Signal, Space Aeronautics, Solid State Design, IEEE Proceedings, IEEE Spectrum*
   Purchasing: *Electronic Procurement, Electronic Specifying and Procurement*
   Military: *Air Force & Space Digest, Armed Forces Management, Army, Ordnance, Data, Journal of the Armed Forces, Naval Institute Proceedings*
   Amateur: *CQ and QST*
   Horizontal: *Aviation Week, Astronautics & Aeronautics, Electronic News, Industrial Research, International Science & Technology, Missiles & Rockets, Research/Development, Scientific American*
5. Agency will provide information on circulation, cost-per-thousand-readers, and cost-per-page. Final figures should relate cost-per-page to weighted percentage of regular readers in Varian study.

EXHIBIT 2

VARIAN ASSOCIATES
EXECUTIVE OFFICES
PALO ALTO, CALIFORNIA

Robert T. Davis
Vice President, Marketing

Dear Sir:

Would you please help us in solving one of our marketing problems?
We're trying to improve our communications programs. During the next eighteen

months, we will, with your permission, be calling on you for your personal advice on the subject of magazine ads.

This survey is the first of the series and asks for your reading preference; the second will follow in about six months and will deal with the effectiveness of our ads; the third questionnaire, later in the year, will give you the opportunity to help us actually write our ads.

We hope you will take a few minutes to answer this questionnaire. Your response will be very meaningful and greatly appreciated.

Very truly yours,
Robert T. Davis

Inside are photographs of 28 magazines serving our industry. In the spaces provided, please check how often you read each of these magazines. If you do not read a magazine, simply leave the spaces blank.

EXHIBIT 3. Excerpts from the proposal by the OR unit to set up a media model

The proposed model (called MISER) has as its objective among selected audience groups the generation of a weighted readership scale *and* a readership distribution. The former provides a score based on reach and frequency of exposure within specified time periods while the latter consists of two distributions, the first of which yields the percentage of readers exposed once, twice, etc. The second distribution is cumulative. By comparing the weighted scores and the readership distribution of two or more alternative media schedules the user can decide which schedule best suits his objectives.

The media vehicle data which are being obtained by individuals from the survey will be collapsed into the following question—"What is the probability of prospect X being exposed to the *average* issue of each of a variety of print media vehicles?" No attempt will be made to measure the extent or degree of exposure. Thus, exposure is defined operationally as whether a respondent reports reading "something" within a particular vehicle.

The probability statement is used because of the problem of time. Assume a quarterly journal. If one knew that a prospect is exposed on the average to three out of four issues, then the probability of exposure to the *average* issue would be 0.75; if the exposure is two out of four it would be 0.50; and so on. Obviously, if the prospect is exposed to all four issues then it would be certain (1.0) that he read the average issue.

The problem of how to treat additional exposures (either within a specific vehicle through time or between media vehicles) is not easily solved. The problem is complex because of the need to ascertain at the margin the effect of each additional exposure given certain time intervals between exposures. Naturally the effect of repetition has to be evaluated differently for different products. In the case at hand it is proposed that the first exposure be rated at 0.9, the second at 1.0, the third at 0.9—all within a two months' interval on the assumption that your advertising will be centered on products which are relatively new and complex; therefore, the "reader" will need exposure to two ads in order to obtain "full" information. A special feature of the model calls for providing you with the opportunity of inserting the "current" media schedule to inoculate individual prospects, following which the schedule to be tested can be better evaluated through the weighting of additional exposures.

We estimate the total cost of building MISER at about $4,000, and that each schedule can be "tested" at a cost not to exceed $40.

16

Product research

THE SINGLE MOST IMPORTANT strategy of any firm is the development of a product line which meets the needs of certain groups of consumers. No other strategy has greater effect in the long run on the firm's profits and, hence, its survival. Thousands of new products are introduced to the market every year. A majority of the products on supermarket shelves were not in existence ten years ago. A study made in 1967 found that items added since 1957 by supermarkets accounted for 55 percent of the items handled, 52 percent of unit sales, 52 percent of dollar sales, and 57 percent of the dollar margin.[1]

The growth rate of many, if not most, U.S. corporations is tied closely to the success experienced in their new product work. As competition whittles away the profit margins on established products, companies must rely on new products to sustain their overall profit margins. Evidence of management's concern about and dedication to new products is found in the large amounts being spent on research and development. In 1960 American industry spent $9.4 billion on research and development.[2] In 1969 the figure reached some $19 billion.[3]

Only a small proportion of new products is successful. Just how small is not known precisely, but typical estimates indicate that about four out of every five new products are failures.[4] Even worse is the estimate

---

[1] Penelope Orth, "Tighter Test-Marketing Leads Rush to Pay-outs," *Printers' Ink* (August 25, 1967), pp. 7–9, 12, 14. The data were derived from a study sponsored by *Progressive Grocer* magazine and the A. C. Nielsen Company entitled "New Items in the Food Industry."

[2] "All Cranked Up for a New Round," *Business Week* (April 29, 1961), pp. 32–34.

[3] "Inflation Ups the R & D Ante," *Business Week* (May 17, 1969), pp. 78, 80.

[4] "How Many New Products Die," *Printers' Ink* (August 26, 1966), p. 19.

that seven out of every eight hours spent by research and development personnel is on products which turn out to be failures.[5]

The essence of any firm's new product policy is the identification of those product opportunities which will generate, over a stated time period, the greatest return on the funds invested in relation to the risk involved *and* which are in harmony with the firm's resources.

To operationalize the process by which the above objective is obtained requires that management take the following steps:

1. Develop an overall product strategy based on market needs, industry structure, and corporate resources.
2. Develop a flow of new product ideas from a variety of sources.
3. Develop procedures to screen on a preliminary basis the product ideas generated in step 2.
4. Develop procedures for final screening.
5. Develop product specifications with regard to optimum product attributes.
6. Product testing.
7. Test marketing.
8. Commercialization, including supervision of the product through its life cycle and its termination or phase out.

The contributions which can be made by marketing research in each of the above steps are significant. These will be discussed with respect to each step, but particular emphasis will be placed on the role of marketing research in steps five, six, and seven.

DEVELOPING A PRODUCT STRATEGY

If a firm identifies clearly its objectives in the marketplace, the development of a product strategy is made less difficult. This is particularly true if the firm conceptualizes its objectives around generic need or problem solving. It makes a great deal of difference whether a company, for example, visualizes itself as being in business to produce tennis racquets or to help solve the "problem" of recreation. Such a broad statement of goals provides all those concerned with product development with more latitude than would be the case if the objectives were articulated solely along product lines.

Consumption systems are a useful concept in helping to develop a meaningful product strategy. Products are used with other products, labor, and machines, and hence are part of a system. The parts of the system must, from the consumers' standpoint, be compatible. Knowledge

---

[5] *Management of New Products* (New York: Booz, Allen and Hamilton, Inc., 1960).

of consumption systems—which can only be obtained through time-consuming research—can help the manufacturer to

. . . better assess the possibility of effecting innovation. This is accomplished by an examination of the steps prior to and subsequent to the point at which the product in question enters the system. He can frequently estimate the vulnerability of his current product by evaluating the other products which enter the system before and after his own product or products which are used in direct conjunction with it.[6]

Innovation through integration of steps in the system is commonplace. The camera is a classic example of such integration since manufacturers have integrated into the product the range finder and the light meter. A Polaroid camera even develops the film.

Since products must be viewed as fulfilling needs, it should not be too surprising if opportunities arise for new products because of changes in the environment. In recent years products relating to pleasure and luxury have had a higher growth rate than average. Marketing research, by monitoring societal trends, can provide management with insights into opportunities provided by the shifting environment external to the firm.

CRITICAL FACTORS IN DECIDING NEW PRODUCT STRATEGY

The size of present and future markets for a product are critical. This information must be coupled with predictions about the gross margins which will be obtained and the marketing expenses which will be incurred. These are derived from information typically obtained by marketing research relating to such factors as basic trends, industry structure, and product life cycle.

Other factors influencing product strategy are those which have to do with the effect of the new product on the sales of present products (and, hence, on the profitability of the firm), the seasonality of sales, the probable reactions of channels of distribution, product modifications and their costs over the foreseeable future, financial requirements, and manufacturing implications. The information required regarding most of these critical considerations can only be derived through the use of marketing research.

Ultimately the firm's product strategy must be set forth in writing. One writer suggests that the strategy be stated in terms of sales volume, type and number of competitors, technical opportunity, patent opportunity, raw material, production load, value added, similarity to major

---

[6] Harper W. Boyd, Jr. and Sidney J. Levy, "New Dimension in Consumer Analysis," *Harvard Business Review* (November-December, 1963), p. 138.

business, and effect on present products.[7] But to these should be added limitations established by management regarding capital investment, payout periods, returns on capital invested, legal constraints, utilization of present manufacturing facilities, channel and sales force utilization, and relationship to present and planned technological and management skills.

DEVELOPING NEW PRODUCT IDEAS

An understanding of corporate goals and consumption systems, articulated in a manner similar to that described in the preceding section, should help in stimulating a flow of relevant new product ideas. The actual sources of product ideas are many and varied and the value of each will differ substantially from company to company. Suggestions and complaints from customers are a major source, but all of the following are potential sources of ideas:[8]

1. Company staff and company records (including research and development).
2. Channels of distribution, especially with respect to product modifications.
3. Competitors.
4. Government agencies, including the U.S. Patent Office.
5. Miscellaneous, including trade associations, advertising agencies, trade magazines, marketing research agencies, commercial laboratories, and consultants.

A steady flow of ideas is imperative, since it has been estimated that it takes, on the average, 40 ideas to yield one successful one.[9]

PRELIMINARY SCREENING OF NEW PRODUCT IDEAS

Because of the need to sort out worthwhile new ideas rather quickly, thereby preventing a jamming of the system, it is necessary to have a preliminary screening device which is fairly routine and low cost. The first step is usually to determine whether the product idea meets the criteria stated or implied in the company's strategy statement on new products. If it does not, it is eliminated, although provision is usually

---

[7] Charles H. Kline, "The Strategy of Product Policy," *Harvard Business Review* (July-August, 1955), pp. 91–100.

[8] Gustav E. Larson, "Locating Ideas for New Products," in *Developing and Selling New Products* (Washington, D.C.: U.S. Department of Commerce, Office of Domestic Commerce, 1950), pp. 3–12.

[9] *Management of New Products* (New York: Booz, Allen & Hamilton, 1960).

made to set aside for further screening any ideas that seem particularly powerful.

Most companies which employ a formalized preliminary screening routine do so by stating their criteria precisely and requiring that individual members of the review committee rate the new product idea on each criterion. Ratings may be on a category basis such as excellent, good, fair, or poor, or on a more detailed type of numerical scale (say from 1 to 10). The criteria may or may not be weighted.

In the process of rating a product idea, the committee will discuss the idea, usually at some length. They may seek help and advice from company specialists in manufacturing, marketing research and development, and finance. They may even ask marketing research to gather information about the potential market for the new product. The extent to which the committee seeks information is conditioned by its perception of the magnitude of the new product idea. Generally speaking, no idea survives a bad rating given by a majority of the committee, although new evidence may be submitted at a later date by a committee member or the sponsor of the idea which will cause the committee to reopen the case.

If the new product policy statement has been carefully detailed, it will contain the evaluation criteria. Such factors as sales volume, type and number of competitors, technical opportunity, investment requirements, payout period, and effect on present products usually are considered. Each of these can be set up as a criterion and "scaled."

FINAL SCREENING

Those products which survive the preliminary screening are ready for a final check. This screening will vary in its complexity and cost depending on how obvious the decision is. A new product idea may not go through the entire final screening process if it becomes quickly evident that the product could never produce the required return on investment. Thus, the new product process should not be conceived of as a mechanistic one through which all ideas are processed in a predetermined way.

The final screening centers around the marketplace and whether research and development can build a product which the market will prefer over available alternatives. This requires identification of the various market segments and estimates of the demands of the relevant segments in terms of product characteristics, reactions of competitors, and reactions of alternative channels of distribution. From these data, the researchers make a sales forecast for a period of years. Marketing activities must be included in forecasting sales and the resulting marketing costs calculated. These data, when coupled with cost information from the production department, permit estimates of potential profits and returns on investment.

For totally new products the analysis encompasses all the steps indicated in the preceding paragraph, *plus* that of developing budget and cash flow projections. Marketing research plays the key role in developing the sales forecast. For modified products the analysis required is less difficult because of company experience and the availability of existing market data.

DEVELOPING PRODUCT SPECIFICATIONS

That set of product attributes which are optimum for the market segment(s) to which the product will appeal must be determined. The "optimum" must take into account the characteristics of competitive products. Since the number of forms that a product can assume is almost unlimited, the determination of the best combination is a difficult undertaking.

As a result of the research conducted in connection with the earlier steps, much information should be available concerning those product attributes which consumers believe should be incorporated in the product. But it is one thing to have verbal expressions about product attributes and quite another to translate them into a specific physical entity. Consumers cannot give precise technical answers about how the product should be made, or even how it will be used. Many consumers provide conflicting views with respect to product attributes, for example, most consumers want high quality and low price.

The dimensions of the problem can be narrowed by defining as precisely as possible the particular market segment for which the product will be designed. The preferences of such consumers may be more homogeneous than for a wider group of consumers and, thus, more helpful. The products used by consumers become important standards for comparison. Working along these lines, marketing research can provide the research and development staff with important leads as to what will constitute a good product design. At the minimum, marketing research should provide a list of those features or attributes which *must* be included in the product as well as a list of those which *must not* be included. Any data on how consumers evaluate or test the product to determine its qualities are useful. It is very likely that consumers will test a product far differently from the technical staff.

What attributes are important

One *cannot* obtain a list of important product attributes by asking consumers: "What qualities should such a product have and what is the relative importance of each?" Such questions produce ambiguous answers which are difficult to interpret into product characteristics. In the case of consumer products, many respondents play back the advertising themes to which they have been exposed.

With new products, the researcher must find out what consumers want and *then* translate these desires into meaningful technical language. Consumers typically describe what they want in terms of product benefits, functions, and effects. These must be translated into ingredients, design characteristics, performance criteria, and even manufacturing procedures. Such communication problems indicate the necessity for the marketing researcher to work closely with the technical staff while trying to determine what is and what is not acceptable in terms of product attributes.

Motivational research techniques such as depth interviewing or the projective methods of word association, story telling, and sentence completion provide sound ways of obtaining from consumers their real feelings and thoughts about product factors. Using such techniques in a study dealing with detergents, one company found that when consumers said they "liked the suds" they had such different product attributes in mind as the amount of suds, the heaviness of suds, the time required to generate the suds, the permanency of suds, and the reactivating qualities of suds.

It was also found that people had reference to one of thirteen or more specific attributes when they talked about the way a detergent "cleans" such as "cleaning shirt collars" or "getting greasy dirt out." These same interviews also yielded information on how housewives evaluated different product attributes. It was found, for example, that while manufacturers use elaborate methods to test the strength of their detergents, an important segment of consumers test for strength by placing their hands in the water and noting how it feels.[10]

Relative importance of individual attributes

After the attributes that are considered important in a product have been determined, the next task is to determine their relative importance. Some idea has undoubtedly already been obtained in the process of specifying the attributes themselves. In determining attributes, however, the work is usually confined to a relatively small geographical area and the data are more qualitative than quantitative. It is important, therefore, to obtain more precise measurements of how many and what kinds of prospective users hold certain attitudes about the various product

---

[10] *Product Research Methodology* (Chicago: Market Facts, Inc., undated), pp. 11–12.

attributes since all the desired attributes cannot be included in one product.

Concept testing. In recent years increasing numbers of researchers have used concept testing as a way of determining whether potential customers understood the idea behind the product, and how they evaluated the product's attributes. It is possible to devise a concept test which describes alternative products and asks consumers to select the ones they prefer, and to indicate "why" they made their choices.

Concept testing is a highly flexible research technique, one which is relatively simple to make operational. It consists of showing to a sample of prospective consumers drawings or pictures of one or more products and then asking them to respond to a number of questions, some of which may involve rankings or scalings.[11] The drawings or pictures are the stimulus and are not unlike the idea behind a thematic apperception test. Structured rather than unstructured questions are typically used, however. Concept testing lends itself to the use of experimental designs.

The marketing research department in cooperation with the design department of the Elgin National Watch Company used concept testing as a way of determining whether consumers would accept such watch features as a thermometer, a barometer, and a fall-out indicator. Impressionistic drawings of nine watch styles were prepared and mounted in an exhibit which was then shown to several hundred respondents, who were asked to rank their choices and to indicate "why."[12] Figure 16–1 shows one of the drawings.

Preference distribution analysis. Useful data on consumer preferences can be obtained using paired comparison tests, the comparative monadic test, and rankings. In each case the objective is to obtain measures on the more important characteristics of the product over a range of values under conditions which focus choice on the innate features of the test product and which minimize the influence of such external factors as brand name, price, and packaging.

Of these three methods for preference distribution analysis, only the comparative monadic test needs further definition. This method uses two or more items which are evaluated independently using some form of rating scale. Matched samples are used to test and scale the test

---

[11] Concept tests can employ a variety of means to express the concept, although pictures or drawings are the most common. Concept tests employing cards which describe the product idea are often used to solicit evaluations. Some companies go so far as to use product models, samples, or prototypes as the stimulus in order to provide the consumer with a more complete view of what is being tested. For a more complete discussion of concept testing and how it is used by a variety of American companies see *Market Testing Consumer Products* (New York: The Conference Board, 1967).

[12] Taken from the Elgin National Watch Company (B) Case, copyright by the Board of Trustees of the Leland Stanford Junior University, Stanofrd, Cal., 1963.

FIGURE 16–1.

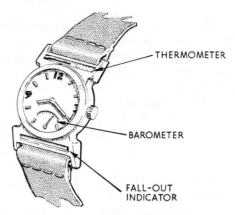

THERMOMETER

BAROMETER

FALL-OUT
INDICATOR

SOURCE: Elgin National Watch Company (B)
Case. Copyright by the Board of Trustees of the
Leland Stanford Junior University, Stanford, Calif.
1963.

items, with each group receiving one item. In a test designed to compare the paired comparison test versus the comparative monadic test, overall product preferences were the same, but nearly one-third of the testers preferred one brand on the first test and the second brand on the other test. The test did not reveal which type of test was more reliable—only that different results were obtained.[13]

The first step in a preference distribution analysis is to develop ". . . a scale of feasible values for each significant characteristic. The limits of the scale are the lowest value and the highest value preferred by any appreciable number of consumers. Between the extreme values, the scale is divided into a number of equal increments in ascending order. The width of the steps depends primarily on the consumer's ability to perceive differences."[14]

Following the construction of a product attribute scale, samples of the product are made up with each level of the particular characteristic and tested on a paired comparison basis using representative consumer samples. This amounts to testing products which incorporate each of the scale values against each other. From these tests the percentage of consumers who prefer each "level" of the characteristic (e.g., various quantities of chocolate in a candy bar) is estimated. And finally, the company's existing products and/or competing products can be analyzed to determine their level on the scale. Such an analysis should indicate

---

[13] Allen Greenberg, "Paired Comparisons vs. Monadic Tests," *Journal of Advertising Research* (December, 1963), pp. 44–47.

[14] Alfred A. Kuehn and Ralph L. Day, "Strategy of Product Quality," *Harvard Business Review* (November–December, 1962), p. 103.

the exent to which existing products match consumer preferences and will show any market segments which have not been served properly.

In a study to determine preferences for differing amounts of chocolate flavoring in ice cream, 928 respondents participated in ten coordinated paired comparison tests. The number of "chocolate levels" to be tested was set at five. Test batches were prepared with great care to make certain that all other product attributes were held constant.

Test items from each of the five batches were grouped with items from each of the other batches to form the ten possible unique pairs of the test items. Each pair was tested with a randomly selected unique subsample to avoid bias from learning or fatigue which might occur if the same individuals tested more than one pair . . . .

The results were something of a surprise, since they indicated that the level of chocolate thought to be the most preferred in the general population . . . was not the most popular level in the sampled population (Penn State students). Batch 2, with a substantially milder level of chocolate (80 percent of commercial normal) was preferred . . . and was not exceeded by any other level, which clearly establishes it as the most preferred level.[15]

The above procedure is both costly and time consuming because of the number of different characteristics typically involved, and because the product attributes are not mutually exclusive and must be viewed as being interrelated. The problem is to determine the "optimum compromise." When only one attribute is being scaled at a time and where independent samples are being used, it is not possible to determine how those consumers who vote for one value relative to one characteristic vote for other values of other characteristics.

It should be noted that the preference distribution concept cannot be universally applied. For example, some product attributes such as taste and appearance are so complex that it is doubtful if their effects can be summarized using a single scale. Further,

. . . the assumption that preferences for all scalable attributes are normally distributed should be avoided. Preferences for many items do not conform to a symmetrical unimodal distribution. Some products may be purchased by different groups of consumers with different uses and requirements for the product. Even if the preferences of those consumers who buy the product for each particular end use are normally distributed, the distribution of preferences over the entire market might be multimodal or skewed.[16]

Rating Scale Combined With Overall Preference Rating. A more complicated way of evaluating the more important product characteristics also uses rating scales, but in addition an overall preference rating

[15] Ralph L. Day, "Systematic Paired Comparisons in Preference Analysis," *Journal of Marketing Research* (November, 1965), pp. 406–12.

[16] *Ibid.*, p. 408.

is obtained for the company's existing or proposed product. Actually, this approach can be used where several product variations are being tested simultaneously, although the following example applies to a single product situation.[17]

Assume a cake mix manufacturer believes a product change might win greater consumer acceptance for his brand. He has determined from prior research that the main product characteristics are sweetness, spiciness, moistness, texture, and size of cake. A seven-point rating scale ranging from -3 to $+3$ is set up for each attribute; for example, a $+3$ rating means "too sweet," "too spicy," "too moist," "too fine in texture," or "too large a cake." A rating of 0 means acceptable sweetness, spiciness, etc. A -3 rating means "not sweet enough," "not spicy enough," "too dry," "too coarse," or "too small a cake." In addition, an overall preference rating is obtained for the product relative to a competitor or a test product. Such a study was made with the following results:[18]

		-3	-2	-1	0	$+1$	$+2$	$+3$	Average score
1.	Sweetness	4%	8%	20%	20%	22%	16%	10%	(0.36)
2.	Spiciness	—	—	15	75	10	—	—	(−0.05)
3.	Moistness	—	15	30	40	10	5	—	(−0.04)
4.	Texture	4	12	12	25	15	12	10	(0.21)
5.	Size of cake	5	5	20	35	20	10	5	(0.10)
6.	Prefer competitive product	2	8	20	30	15	15	10	(0.33)

It appears from the above data that the product tested is a bit too sweet, just right in spiciness, not moist enough, too fine in texture, and too large. But more precise information can be provided by relating the product characteristic scores to the overall acceptance. This can be accomplished by determining the relative overall preference for the product among those who rated it (-3) on sweetness as compared to those rating it (-2), (-1), etc. The overall preference is determined by the average of the ratings on this scale. Similar analyses will be made for each of the characteristics. With respect to sweetness, the following results found were those shown at the top of p. 707.

These data show that the average overall preference score for those consumers who said the product was not sweet enough (-3) was -0.20, while those who said the product was a bit too sweet $(+1)$ had an average overall preference for the product of 0.41. This relating of overall preference and sweetness suggests that a mix "a little too sweet"

---

[17] *Product Evaluation: An Examination of Research Procedures,* (Chicago: Market Facts, Inc., 1962),pp. 11–18.

[18] *Ibid.,* p. 14.

Consumers giving tested product indicated ratings on sweetness

	Not sweet enough						Too sweet
	−3	−2	−1	0	+1	+2	+3
Expressed this average degree of preference for product	−0.20	0.01	0.20	0.27	0.41	0.29	0.19

may be better than one "exactly right," because the highest average degree of preference for the product (0.41) was obtained from those consumers who gave the mix a (+1) on the sweetness rating.

This methodology leaves something to be desired, since it does not provide needed data regarding the optimum set (combination) of values. By dealing in averages, the values can be distorted as would happen in a polarized situation where heavy weights at the extreme produced an average value of approximately zero which would mean "acceptable."

It would be desirable to take those who had an overall preference for the product and to get a profile of their average scores for each characteristic and a measure of the dispersion, e.g., the interquartile range. This "profiling" for each of the overall preference groups (i.e., the +3's, the +2's, the +1's, the 0's, the −1's, etc.) would be helpful in determining what product attributes (e.g., moistness) should be changed to appeal to a larger market segment.

Factor analysis is helpful in determining what product attributes are critical to consumers. The advantage of this method of analysis is that it indicates which factors are most critical. One researcher asked respondents to rate a brand of coffee on fourteen attributes, after they had drunk a cup. The test subjects were not told which brand they were drinking. The study results indicated that individual differences regarding coffee could best be summarized in terms of four factors—those having to do with comforting taste, heartiness of flavor, genuineness of product, and freshness. Attributes like "alive taste" and "tastes like real coffee," were involved in defining the "genuineness" factor, and exhibited factorial patterns similar to the overall preference variable.[19]

Researcher Volney Stefflre uses a somewhat similar but more complex way of getting at consumer preferences. He asks small samples of consumers to indicate which brands in the marketplace are most similar to each other and then to "explain" why they are similar. From his measures

---

[19] See Bishwa Nath Mukherjee, "A Factor Analysis of Some Qualitative Attributes of Coffee," *Journal of Advertising Research*, 5 (March, 1965), pp. 35–38.

of "similarity" as well as the "why" data it is possible to determine what characteristics are critical. By concept testing a new product in much the same way, he can determine what items it is perceived as being similar to and, thus, what characteristics it must have to be accepted.[20]

PRODUCT TESTING

On the basis of the information developed from earlier steps the seller is now in a position to undertake research which will provide insights into whether he has been successful in developing the desired product. In many ways the types of testing described in the preceding section overlap with the types used to test the product under actual use conditions. Our discussion here will center on the research problems encountered when the objective is to test the product under "live use" conditions.

Paired comparison placement tests

Paired comparison placement tests are relatively simple in concept, but difficult to implement. Such tests typically involve two variations of the same product, variations which often differ in ways which consumers don't readily identify. Consumers are asked to use both products and then to choose the one they like most. If it is desired to test several different product variations, a number of paired comparison tests must be run. Each variation must be tested against each other variation. Respondents must have only two different products to compare at any one time, but may have different pairs at different times, or different groups of consumers may be used for different pairs. If respondents are asked to compare several different product designs at one time, the results obtained may be misleading. For example, assume that three product designs, A, B, and C are to be tested. Each respondent tests all three and is asked to pick the one preferred. The replies might be distributed as follows:

Product	Percent of respondents preferring
A	40%
B	30
C	30
Total	100%

---

[20] Volney Stefflre, "Market Structure Studies: New Products for Old Markets and New Markets (Foreign) for Old Products," University of California at Los Angeles (mimeographed, July, 1965), p. 5.

At first glance it would appear that design A should be the one selected for marketing. But is this conclusion valid? The 30 percent of respondents who voted for B might have preferred C over A if they could not have B. If this were true, 60 percent of the respondents would actually prefer design C over A. This "vote splitting" produces ambiguity which is not found if only paired comparisons are used. With paired comparison, three different tests would have to be run—A with B, A with C, and B with C.

The results of any paired comparison test are difficult to analyze. Assume that 80 percent of the respondents vote for product A and only 20 percent for product B. Does this mean that A should be chosen— that B should be rejected? This situation is similar to the problem of comparing three or more designs discussed earlier. Since the experiment does not reproduce the choices available in the market, it cannot be said with certainty that either A or B should be chosen. It may be that in an actual buying situation with other brands to select from, the persons voting for A would switch to some other product, while those voting for B would not do so. This is particularly possible if B has a unique feature which differentiates it from all other brands and if A is a composite product with no individually strong attributes.

The simplest type of paired comparison test is that in which the respondent is given the test product in an unidentified package and asked to try it and to compare it with the product she has been using. Such a test is not usually a satisfactory one, because respondents tend to vote in favor of the unknown brand. This may be a result of the respondent's desire to please the researcher or of the respondent's assumption that the new product must be better. In any case biased results are obtained.

A more common paired comparison test is to have respondents try two "masked" products under similar use conditions for a period of time. The interviewer then returns to get a preference rating and to find out what attributes were liked or disliked in each product.

Staggered comparison tests.   Such tests are similar to the "side-by-side" comparison tests discussed above, but differ in that respondents use one product first and then, either days or weeks later, try the second product. The identities of the two products are masked. One-half the respondents receive product A first and the other half receive product B first. Such a split is necessary to avoid a "tried last" bias.

Staggered comparison tests have many of the disadvantages of the paired comparison test, but in theory reproduce better the actual market, since customers usually buy one product at a time instead of two different brands of the same product at one time.

Both Pillsbury and Market Facts, Inc., have tested the staggered technique versus the regular paired comparison test. While the staggered test seems better in concept, it does not prove to differ in practice.

Both organizations found the staggered technique provided results equivalent to those obtained in the paired comparison study.[21]

Difficulties in conducting paired comparison tests. In appraising the paired comparison technique, it is important to keep in mind some basic weaknesses which reduce the confidence one can have in the results. For example, it is difficult to obtain and maintain the cooperation of members of a consumer use panel; to increase cooperation, incentives such as pay may be used. If the respondent is paid, she is more apt to feel some responsibility for completing the test. Even so, the sample may be biased because some people will not participate.

Another difficulty comes from the fact that the test can never simulate precisely the conditions in the marketplace under which buying decisions are made. For example, in a paired comparison test the respondent usually has no knowledge of price differentials and must, therefore, assume that no difference exists. It is doubtful if respondent statements as to how much more they would be willing to pay for a given product are very meaningful.

There is the further question of how valid the findings are relative to actual market behavior. The typical user of a product does not compare the merits of one product with those of others on a "side-by-side" basis. The participant in a consumer test realizes she is a test subject. She assumes that differences exist among the different products and that her job is to find them. In other words, in a test situation differences are apt to be magnified out of proportion to their importance in the "normal" market.

A test-retest study conducted by Pillsbury Mills, Inc., throws some light on the validity of findings obtained from paired comparison tests. Two tests were run using the same sample of respondents and the same disguished products. The package identifying marks were altered between tests, however, so the respondents did not realize they were testing the same products twice. Fifty percent of the respondents gave the same product preference in both tests, but 50 percent shifted their preference. These shifts of the latter 50 percent were almost entirely compensating, as only a 9 percent difference in preference was found between the two tests. The Commercial Research Department of Pillsbury, in commenting on these findings, stated:[22]

The fact that this large proportion of unreliable individual responses was largely compensatory suggests either that the qualitative distinctions between two cake mixes are of a liminal nature (i.e., exist on the very threshold of

---

[21] Commercial Research Department, Pillsbury Mills, Inc., *Product Testing* (Minneapolis: privately circulated, 1949) p. 10. Also see *Product Research Methodology, op. cit.*, p. 27.

[22] Pillsbury Mills, Inc., *op. cit.*

perception) to 50% of our population or that this unreliable 50% merely had no objective criteria for preferring one cake over another . . . .

The qualitative differences between form A and form B did exist, in spite of the low individual reliability, because the reliable persons (i.e., those who picked the same product both times) chose form A over form B by a ratio of more than 3 to 1. The unreliable respondents as a group chose neither form over the other and tended more to indicate "no preference." The reliable persons, therefore, either had more sensitive sensory perception or else they tended to have more objective and consistent criteria for judging preference than did the unreliable persons.[23] It is also possible that the stated preference for the same product on the second test was a matter of chance.

A technique called "paired in-sequence consistency" has been developed to measure random variations in reported preferences. This technique uses multiple blind paired comparison tests to identify those individuals who report a preference, but who do not have a real preference. This technique is illustrated below.

	1st test prefers	2nd test prefers	3rd test prefers	4th test prefers	5th test prefers
Subject 1	A	A	B	A	B
Subject 2	B	A	B	B	A
Subject 3	B	B	B	B	B
Subject 4	A	A	B	B	B

In this hypothetical test of two products (A versus B), ". . . subjects 1 and 2 appear to be inconsistent in five repeated comparisons of the same two products. Subject 3 expresses a consistent preference. Subject 4 is consistent except for a change at one point. Interpretation of these results will vary according to other data such as:

1. Subject 1 may be light-volume user.
2. Subject 3 may be a heavy-volume user.
3. Subject 4's tastes may be adapting to product B with repeated sampling.

"Interpretation must take into account the chance occurrence of each combination. Five straight preferences for A or B can be expected once in 16 times by chance from among customers who actually have no preference."[24]

Order in which products are tried also may bias results. In a paired-

---

[23] *Ibid.*, pp. 7–8.

[24] Allen Greenberg, "Paired Comparisons in Consumer-Product Tests," *Journal of Marketing*, 22 (April, 1958), p. 411.

comparison test of stockings, a bias in favor of the most recently tested product was discovered when respondents were asked to choose one or the other. But when the rating scale on various product qualities was completed after each product was tested, the bias was for the first product tested.[25]

Nondirective comparison method. This type of study attempts more nearly to duplicate actual market conditions in the test situation without going as far as a sales test. A specific example will illustrate the method.[26] Respondents were given a "pair" of products which were wrapped in exactly the same fashion. The respondents had no reason to believe any difference existed between the two. The housewife was asked to use the products, but was not told that any future interviewing would be done. She had no reason to think that she was participating in any kind of product test. Probably she thought of the products as free samples.

Approximately two weeks after the respondent received the free merchandise, an interviewer called and conducted a nondirective type of interview with the respondent about her experiences, if any, with the products. First, the interviewer ascertained whether both packages had been used. Following this the respondent was given several opportunities to indicate whether any differences had been noted. If no differences were volunteered, direct questions on differences were asked.

The results of the nondirective approach when compared to the paired comparison and the "staggered" techniques were as follows:

	Paired comparisons	Staggered	Nondirective
Not aware of any differences	21%	22%	93%
Aware of differences	79	78	7
Slightly aware of differences	62	60	2
Quite aware of differences	17	18	5

These findings suggest the possibility that the other two techniques provide an exaggerated picture of product differences. Whether this is due to imaginary differences or not is another matter. Some participants may have actually found differences after a careful search that they would not otherwise have noted. In any case the nondirective method points up the possibility that product differences, which may seem very important to management, are noticed by very few people. These minor differences, however, may become very real as advertising claims are made to the consumer or as the product is used over a

---

[25] *Ibid.*

[26] *Product Research Methodology, op. cit.*, pp. 24–32.

period of time. Thus, while variations of the paired comparison technique possess characteristics of value to researchers, their failure to reproduce fully the real world is still a significant limitation. More knowledge about these techniques and how they operate under varying conditions is needed.

Experimental design. In recent years, more use has been made of experiments in product research. Latin Square designs, in particular, offer great opportunities for increased sample efficiency. For example, assume that four product variations (A, B, C, and D) are being sales tested for four weeks through a sample of stores. The Latin Square design provides a technique which will largely eliminate the influence on sales of two important variables—time and store differences. This is accomplished by having each product variation offered in each store and in each time period as shown in the following 4 by 4 Latin Square design:

| Time period | | Stores | | |
(weeks)	1	2	3	4
1	A	B	C	D
2	B	C	D	A
3	C	D	A	B
4	D	A	B	C

Using analysis of variance, the researcher can separate the effects of the different stores, the different times, and the different products on the resulting sales.

Where desirable, a double changeover design can be used. This is a special arrangement of two or more Latin Square designs which makes it possible to measure the carryover effect of each product variation on the next variation in rotational experiments. This is done by reversing the application sequence in the second Latin Square. In the illustration below, note how square II reverses the sequence in which the product alternatives follow one another by time periods. Thus, the distribution of product alternatives within stores by time period one is the same in square I and square II. But in time period 2, B follows A in store 1, while C follows A in store 4; C follows B in store 2, but A follows B in store 5, etc.

		Stores				
		Square I			Square II	
Time period						
(weeks)	1	2	3	4	5	6
1	A	B	C	A	B	C
2	B	C	A	C	A	B
3	C	A	B	B	C	A

Factorial designs are another way of undertaking product experiments.[27] A study to determine the overall effect of color versus finish on consumer preferences and the preferred combination of color and finish of a household item tested twenty-five combinations of the product (five color variations in each of five finish variations).[28]

Supermarket customers were shown five product designs at a time and asked to select the most attractive in the following study arrangement of 25 product designs varying in color and finish (a = color 1 + finish A, etc.):

			Color		
Finish	*1*	*2*	*3*	*4*	*5*
A	a	b	c	d	e
B	f	g	h	i	j
C	k	l	m	s	o
D	p	q	r	n	t
E	u	v	w	x	y

Finish preferences: The first respondent saw designs a, f, k, p, u, all finishes across a single color (1), and picked the most preferred finish. She next saw designs b, g, l, q, v, all finishes across color (2), and so on through all five columns. She then ranked her five column choices by order of preference.

Color preference: The next respondent saw designs a, b, c, d, e, all colors across a single finish (A); then f, g, h, i, j, and so on, through all five rows and a final ranking of row choices.

A partial table of results follows:

Color		*Finish*	
1	26%	A	19%
2	17	B	13
3	18	C	37
4	24	D	17
5	15	E	15

Finish C appears to have a salient effect on preference. Colors 1 and 4 are the most preferred on the average, but not with the salience of the most preferred finish.

The five most preferred individual combinations of color and finish, determined by having respondents rank their five row choices (color) or their five column choices (finish), were as follows:

---

[27] For an illustration of the use of such a design, see Kenneth P. Uhl, "Factorial Design-Aid to Management," *Journal of Marketing* (January, 1962), p. 62.

[28] *Product Evaluation: An Examination of Research Procedures, op. cit.,* pp. 32–34.

Rank

1st	k(1C)
2nd	n(4C)
3rd	o(5C)
4th	p(1D)
5th	c(3A)

Finish C is salient in design preference. The most preferred colors (1 and 4) combine additively with finish C in designs that rate high in consumer preference. 1D and 3A rank high in preference but with smaller segments of the total sample than k, n, o.

TEST MARKETING

Test marketing is a procedure by which a company attempts to test a new product marketing plan by introducing it on a miniature basis before committing the product to the entire market. A basic assumption is that the test market results are projectable to the entire market. By determining the sales and expenses incurred with the new product in a selected group of test markets, the company hopes to be able to estimate accurately the profit possibilities in the entire market. This is a difficult research assignment because of the projection problems and because a large number of variables are involved in such a way as to make it difficult, if not impossible, to determine the causal relationships between any of them and profits.

It is important to note that test markets are seldom used to test whether a product is acceptable or not acceptable to the consumer. This can be determined more inexpensively through the use of the kinds of tests discussed earlier in this chapter. Companies put into test markets only those products for which there is strong evidence that they will be successful.

In discussing the role of test marketing one researcher notes that:

It is becoming the first phase of national distribution. It is increasingly viewed as an aid to capital budgeting and facility planning. How large a plant is needed for national sales? What is the optimum promotion spending level? How many dollars will produce how many sales? What is the return on investment? A company averaging 20% return may well reject a new product that produces only 8%. Another company might embrace the same product because its average return is 7%.[29]

Developing the test market plan

The heart of the test market plan is the company's intended national marketing plan for the new product. The nature and extent of the

---

[29] David K. Hardin, "A New Approach to Test Marketing," *Journal of Marketing* (October, 1966), p. 29.

research plan depends to a considerable extent upon how certain management is of its proposed national marketing strategies. Thus, if management is not secure regarding its national plan to use sampling instead of couponing as a way of introducing the new product, provisions for testing these alternatives should be built into the test marketing plan. Too frequently what happens is to plan the test market operation and then at a later date, based on the test market results, to plan the national operation.

More and more sellers are conceptualizing their test marketing efforts as controlled experiments during which certain selected marketing variables are tested to determine their effect on sales and profitability. Given an understanding of what management wants to test in order to finalize its national plan, the researcher can develop the proper test design and set up the necessary controls.[30]

Sample design

The selection of the appropriate test markets (usually cities or metropolitan areas) is a difficult one. Obviously the number selected is a function of the reliability desired in the projected results and the number of variables being tested. In studying the reliability of market tests based on the variation in share between the test markets and the control markets, one researcher found that the differences which occurred during the tests were no greater than those in evidence during periods when no testing was taking place. This raises doubt about the validity of test marketing operations.[31]

It is reasonable to assume that as the number of markets employed in the test increases the reliability of the projections increases if only by decreasing the chance of extreme errors. It is ". . . clear that employing a single test market is very risky. While a single market area may turn out representative of the country, the statistical odds indicate that there is a much greater chance of extreme error. In 1/5 of the cases, the projection error was in excess of +48 per cent or −36 per cent."[32]

One way to improve the sample design is to select from pairs of matched marketing areas using one set as the experimental group and the other as the control group. The matching can be accomplished on the basis of similarities in market shares of leading brands, media patterns, population, income, and so on. An increasing volume of data

---

[30] For information and illustrations on this subject see Benjamin Lapstein, "The Design of Test Marketing Experiments," *Journal of Advertising Research* (December, 1965), pp. 2–7.

[31] Frank Stanton, "What Is Wrong with Test Marketing?" *Journal of Marketing* (April, 1967), p. 44.

[32] Jack A. Gold, "Testing Test Market Predictions," *Journal of Marketing Research* (August, 1964), pp. 15–16.

is available for such purposes. The A. C. Nielsen Company provides store audit data on individual markets, thereby simplifying the task of matching on brand shares. In addition, Nielsen provides back data on the test markets selected. Somewhat similar data at the consumer level are provided by Market Research Corporation of America on a number of individual markets.[33]

But what about the situation where a totally new product is test marketed? Market share data cannot be used to match test markets. In such cases the selection of test markets is no easy undertaking. The following criteria are suggested:[34]

1. The markets should not be "over-tested."
2. The markets should be "normal" regarding the historical development of the product class involved.
3. The markets should be typical regarding the competitive advertising situation.
4. No single industry should dominate the markets.
5. The markets should represent different geographical regions (where different conditions might affect sales) so that results can be projected.
6. Markets which contain groups not normal to the product's target should be avoided.
7. The markets should have a media pattern similar to the proposed national media plan.
8. The markets should not be too small to provide meaningful results or so large that the testing becomes unusually expensive.
9. The markets should be relatively self-contained, that is, not too much "waste" circulation going outside the market and no strong outside media present.

The problem of how to project the test market results to the national level is also difficult. One test used three different projection methods —buying income, sales ratio, and share of market. The formulas were as follows:

1. $\text{National sales estimate} = \dfrac{\text{total U.S. income}}{\text{test area income}} \times \text{test market sales.}$

2. $\text{National sales estimate} = \dfrac{\text{national sales of a related product}}{\text{test area sales of same product}} \times \text{test area sales.}$

---

[33] An experiment to determine the efficiency of using matched samples of markets found substantial benefits. See Stanton, *op. cit.*

[34] Frank Ladek, Leonard Kent, Perham C. Nahl, "Test Marketing of New Consumer Product," *Journal of Marketing* (April, 1960), pp. 29–33.

3. National sales = share of market ratio in the test area × national
   estimate   sales of the product class.

The share of market method provided the most accurate national projection of sales, but this method possesses limitations in that it requires accurate estimates of national sales of the product category involved, it assumes that the test product will not expand the sales of the product class, and it is more expensive to apply because it requires information that necessitates auditing the total product class.[35]

Test Market Data

Many different kinds of marketing information can be obtained from sales tests, such as:

1. Sales in units.
2. Market share.
3. Characteristics of consumers who buy the product.
4. Characteristics of consumers who sample the product, but who do not buy it again.
5. Frequency of purchase by different groups of consumers.
6. Ways in which the product is used.
7. Maximum profitability as a result of varying the quantity of such marketing inputs as advertising and couponing.
8. Effectiveness of various coupon and cents-off introductory offers.
9. Effectiveness of the advertising copy in getting certain points about the product across to selected groups.
10. Effectiveness of overall marketing program in obtaining trial and usage at the consumer level.
11. Effectiveness of the overall marketing program in obtaining support from the trade.

Total unit sales and market share are usually the first items looked for in test market results. Factory shipments will not suffice for either the sales or market share data. A substantial part of such shipments goes into dealer stocks and, of course, information about sales of other brands cannot be obtained in this way. It is, therefore, necessary to set up either a consumer panel or a store audit, usually the latter. It may be possible to obtain data from regular services such as A. C. Nielsen Company or Market Research Corporation of America. Both of these organizations maintain services which provide data on certain test cities.

---

[35] See Gold, *op. cit.* For further discussions of Gold's methods see Edwin M. Berdy, "Testing Test Market Predictions," *Journal of Marketing Research* (May 1965), pp. 196–98, and Gold's reply, *Journal of Marketing Research* (May, 1965), pp. 198–200.

Some local media maintain store audits and consumer panels that can be used.

Brand loyalty. A measurement of brand loyalty is probably the single most important item of information to obtain in a test market, since without it total consumer sales can be misleading. During the introductory period, the advertising and the introductory price offer may succeed in getting people to sample the product. The important question, however, is whether a substantial portion of the people who try once will become loyal customers. A continuous consumer panel is useful for measuring repeat purchases. With such a panel the purchasing activities of the sampling units can be studied over a continuous period of time, and the extent of brand loyalty or brand switching can be determined.

Current efforts to maximize the value of test market data are centering on the development of models for predicting the long-term sales level of a product from early sales in test markets. Percentages of those who make an initial purchase and of those who make a repeat purchase are determined from consumer panel data. As soon as such figures are obtained for a few periods of time, estimates of the long-term sales level can be made by projecting probabilities of repeat purchasing over a sufficient period to estimate a long-term sales stability level.[36] Variations of this model are numerous; one of the more simple ones assumes that ". . . the probability that a consumer buys a particular brand during a unit time period depends only on whether she bought that brand during the immediately preceding period."[37]

Consumer reactions. Those customers who sample the item, but who do not try it a second time should be interviewed to find out why. This type of information can help to determine what probabilities exist for changing these consumers to repeat buyers. In analyzing the results it must be kept in mind that no product can satisfy all people and that the very reasons why some people reject the product may be the same reasons why other people prefer it.

Some researchers are optimistic about the probability of building computer models which can be used in lieu of the kind of test procedures discussed earlier. Since test marketing does disclose the product to competition, costs substantial sums, takes considerable time, and poses severe projection problems, a reliable predictive model would be warmly welcomed. Such models, however, require considerable data which can only be obtained by the use of marketing research. For ex-

---

[36] Louis A. Fourt and Joseph W. Woodlock, "Early Prediction of Market Success for New Grocery Products," *Journal of Marketing* (October, 1960), pp. 31–38.

[37] William D. Barclay, "A Probability Model for Early Prediction of New Product Market Success," *Journal of Marketing* (January, 1963), p. 63.

ample, it is necessary to have information about consumers with respect to their demographic characteristics, media exposure habits, product usage, and attitudes towards salient product characteristics. In addition, information is needed which establishes input-output relationships between various marketing variables and sales. Despite the enormity and complexity of building models which will reliably predict the acceptance of new products, several have been built and more will be made operational over the next decade.[38]

PRODUCT LIFE CYCLE

Many, if not most, products pass through a life cycle comprised of an introductory period, a growth stage, maturity, and decline. Each of these stages requires a different set of strategies and tactics if the firm is to cope successfully with the problems unique to the particular stage.[39]

Because it is difficult to predict with precision the movement of a product from one stage in the cycle to the next, and because of the need to vary marketing inputs according to the stage in the cycle, continuous market information is critical. Clues can be obtained via marketing research which are helpful in predicting the movement of a product from one stage to the next. Rates of change in sales, trial and repeat buying measures, the impact of price changes, the effect of a product modification by a competitor, or a shift in channel strategy by a competitor are other illustrations of information a continuous reporting system can provide which helps management follow the product life cycle.

During the introductory and growth stages of a product, emphasis is placed on product acceptance, product image, and distribution. In all three of these areas marketing research can play an important and critical role in obtaining information which management must have if it is to make "good" decisions. A firm, wherever possible, will try to extend the growth period of the product. This can best be done by adopting strategies which accomplish one or more of the following: creating new users, finding new uses, generating more varied uses among present users, and obtaining more frequent usage of the product among present users.[40] Clearly marketing research is indispensable to the development of strategies designed to accomplish these goals.

---

[38] See Donald A. Wells, "Testing Marketing and the Computers," *Printers' Ink* (August 26, 1966), p. 37; and "Simulation Sharpens Product Testing," *Printers' Ink* (August 25, 1967), pp. 15–16.

[39] For a discussion of the product life cycle concept see Theodore Levitt, "Exploit the Product Life Cycle," *Harvard Business Review* (November–December, 1965), p. 93; and Arch Patton, "Top Management's Stake in the Product Life Cycle," *Management Review* (June, 1959), p. 9.

[40] Levitt, *op. cit.*, pp. 87–93.

The decline stage for a product sees volume for the product class as a whole trending down, profits disappearing, and heavy pressure forcing prices down because of a surplus of supply facilities. Retailers and distributors lose interest in the product class and some discontinue it or reduce the number of brands carried. Little selling effort is provided. At some point the company must decide whether the product should be dropped or the conditions under which it will be continued as part of the product line. Substantial profits can often be derived by eliminating weak items in the line. One company eliminated 592 items out of a total of 875, with the result that sales increased, marketing costs decreased, and profits increased by 24 percent.[41] Marketing research obviously has an important role to play in helping management evaluate the effect of keeping or eliminating weaker products.

PACKAGE TESTING

Technical experts can provide excellent data on the durability and cost of alternative packages, but generally cannot indicate what shape, colors, and symbols should be used. Packages have become increasingly important as a result of the increase in self-service. Thus, the package is, in reality, a part of the advertising program. These conditions demand a unique package which will help to sell the product.

Conditions of sale will affect the package design. For example, a product being sold in one section of a food store will have different packaging requirements than a product which is sold in other places within the same store. This is true because the package will be in competition with different products and therefore needs to be different to attract attention.

In many ways, the testing of packages is similar to the testing of advertising copy. Most packages contain advertising copy in some form or another. This should be tested in a manner similar to that used in testing copy themes.

The symbols used can be tested to determine whether they are usually associated with the kind of product which the package contains. Such tests are similar to word association tests and are executed in much the same fashion. Colors can be tested in a similar way, although psychologists have made sufficient studies to provide much basic information on the emotional reactions of people to various colors.[42]

It is important to keep in mind that any tests which are made on

[41] Charles H. Sevin, *Marketing Productory Analysis* (New York: McGraw-Hill Book Co., 1965), pp. 62–63.

[42] For informative discussions concerning packaging see "The Process of Mass Acceptance," *Modern Packaging* (February, 1959), p. 75; and Ernest Dichter, *The Man in the Package* (New York: The Paraffined Carton Research Council, 1957).

color, design, shape, and advertising copy must take into account the display conditions under which the product is sold. For example, one color might be desirable *if* the product is placed among competing products which have other colors. The distance of the display from the eye of the consumer also needs to be considered. For example, cereal products are usually placed on a fairly high shelf because of their bulky nature. This fact needs to be considered in designing the size and form of the advertising appearing on the package.

Paired comparison tests should not be used to test alternative package designs. Such tests are subject to all the limitations noted earlier plus the fact that the consumer is affected by what she considers to be the most artistic design, regardless of its association with the product or its ability to attract attention on a shelf. Sales tests can be run, but they are artificial; the new package suffers against the old one because the latter has been on the market for a period of time. If the sales tests are run on competing new designs, the results are apt to be more valid, but this assumes that both are superior to the existing package. Probably the best approach to the problem of package design is the use of a number of different research techniques, including symbol association, color association, and those techniques used to test advertising copy.

SUMMARY

Marketing research can provide much help in the design of products. Too often, individual firms fail to provide the proper balance between technical and marketing research. In developing a new product six steps are involved: (1) selecting the product field, (2) selecting the specific product, (3) designing the specific product, (4) pilot-testing the new product, (5) sales-testing the new product, and (6) continuous checking on the new product after it is introduced to the market.

In determining the attributes of the optimum product, the research must determine what attributes are important and the relative importance of each. The use of conventional questions such as, "What features do you want in this product?" are not likely to uncover a complete listing of important attributes. Research must develop a consumer's language and translate this into a producer's technical language for action. The use of clinical interviewing techniques is preferred. Scaling devices can be used to obtain an approximate rank of the various product attributes.

The three major types of consumer use tests are (1) paired comparisons, (2) staggered comparisons, and (3) nondirective. All three have serious shortcomings in that they fail to duplicate actual market conditions. Evidence indicates that the results obtained by paired comparison and staggered comparison tests vary little. In both situations, the fact that the respondent knows she is participating in a test and that she is expected to find differences can easily lead to the reporting of exaggerated differences. Test-retest studies reveal considerable instability among respondents as to just what products they prefer, but are helpful in identifying those individuals who have no real preference.

The nondirective method duplicates actual market conditions better than the other two types of tests. It does not produce as many reported differences as either the paired or staggered comparison tests.

In recent years, more use has been made of experimentation and product acceptance scaling in product research. These techniques, while possessing obvious limitations, are conceptually sound and offer considerable promise. Certainly the experimentation offers a more analytical way of approaching the problem of product testing than the more conventional methods.

Test marketing is a method of testing a company's marketing plan for a new product before going national. It is not a test of whether the product is acceptable to the consumer, but rather of the extent of the consumer's response given certain marketing inputs. Marketing research is critical since data on sales, market share, brand loyalty, and consumer reactions must be obtained and evaluated.

The life cycle concept, despite certain limitations, is a valuable planning aid. Marketing research can often indicate with considerable precision what stage of the life cycle the product class is in and how quickly it will pass into the next stage. Given such information, marketing management can predict what marketing strategies and tactics will be required to exploit the market opportunities to the maximum degree.

Package testing is complex and in many ways is similar to the testing of advertising copy. Prospective package designs must be considered in relation to the packages of competitive products. Paired comparisons and sales tests generally are not suitable methods for testing new packages against old ones. They may be useful, however, in testing a number of alternative new designs. Color and symbol association tests are helpful.

Case 16—1. LOCKE COMPANY

The Locke Company produced a line of quality power lawn mowers. Company engineers were successful in developing a mower which was substantially quieter than any machine then on the market. The sales manager knew from experience that many buyers judged the power of a motor by its sound; therefore, he was concerned about whether the new sound might give the impression that the new mower was not as powerful as the earlier model. In discussing his fears with his advertising manager, he found the latter, as well as the Locke Company's advertising agency, to be concerned primarily with how to describe this "new sound" in the company's advertising. After considerable discussion, the two men hired a local marketing research firm to obtain information which might be helpful on both subjects.

A total of 61 homeowners participated in the tests which ensued. They were divided into four groups, each of which was brought together specifically for this study. None of the men was aware of the details of the study until each group was assembled—all they knew was that the group was to talk about lawn mowers.

Each group of men was told that they were going to hear tape recordings of two types of power mowers. The mowers, they were informed, were essentially the same type, but one had some features that were different from the other mower. The tape recordings used for the test included the following sequence:

1. Man's voice announcing the experimental model.
2. Thirty seconds of the sound of the experimental mower.
3. Man's voice announcing the standard mower.
4. Thirty seconds of the sound of the standard mower.
5. Eight minutes of the sound of the experimental mower.
6. Eight minutes of the sound of the standard mower.

Before these tapes were played, each respondent completed the first six questions in the questionnaire shown as Exhibit 1. The rating scales following question #6 were then explained. Respondents were to complete both the "user description" and "mower description" scales for each of the two mowers. (Two sets of scales were provided although only one is reproduced in Exhibit 1.) If the statement at the left applied to the mower under consideration, a check was to be placed in the left-hand column; if the statement seemed to apply only partially, a check would be placed in one of the other columns depending on how closely it seemed to apply.

The groups of men listened to the introduction of the tape consisting of the announcements and the thirty-second demonstrations. The recorder volume was set so that the voice was at a natural speaking level in the room. Once set, it remained at that level for both eight-minute demonstrations.

The respondents then rated each mower independently while the recording was being played. Eight minutes provided sufficient time for every person to complete the mower descriptions and the user descriptions. In two of the groups the tape of the experimental mower was played first, and in two groups the standard mower was first. This was done to cancel out any bias that might arise because one of the two sounds was heard before the other.

No brand names were used during the testing so that the respondents had no way of identifying these mowers.

As a last step in the test, the respondents were interviewed in a group concerning their reactions to the sounds of the mowers and their attitudes toward power mowers in general.

The findings from the study are summarized in Exhibit 2.

1. Should the company introduce the new, quieter mower?

2. What should be the creative strategy for the advertising campaign, whichever model is marketed?

EXHIBIT 1. Power mower study questionnaire

1. What make of lawn mower do you own? _____
2. Is it manual or powered?   ☐ Manual ☐ Powered
3. (IF POWERED) Is it self-propelled?   ☐ Yes ☐ No
4. How long have you owned it? _____
5. Did you own a power mower before you got the present one?   ☐ Yes ☐ No
6. (IF YES) What make? _____

Rating scales

User descriptions	*Applies*					*Does not apply*
For strong men	—	—	—	—	—	—
For average guy	—	—	—	—	—	—
For small, light man	—	—	—	—	—	—
For man with high income	—	—	—	—	—	—
For man who doesn't like lawn care	—	—	—	—	—	—
For women	—	—	—	—	—	—
For person who wants the best	—	—	—	—	—	—
For a perfectionist	—	—	—	—	—	—
For a man on a budget	—	—	—	—	—	—
For quiet, thoughtful men	—	—	—	—	—	—
For the man who is proud of his lawn	—	—	—	—	—	—
For factory worker	—	—	—	—	—	—
For the professional man	—	—	—	—	—	—
For man to whom cost is no object	—	—	—	—	—	—
For children	—	—	—	—	—	—

Mower descriptions

Efficient	—	—	—	—	—	—
Rugged	—	—	—	—	—	—
Dangerous	—	—	—	—	—	—
Gentle	—	—	—	—	—	—
Vibrating	—	—	—	—	—	—

EXHIBIT 1 (*Continued*)

Mower descriptions	Applies					Does not apply
Old fashioned	—	—	—	—	—	—
Trouble free	—	—	—	—	—	—
Powerful	—	—	—	—	—	—
Easy to handle	—	—	—	—	—	—
Rough cutting	—	—	—	—	—	—
Fun to use	—	—	—	—	—	—
Noisy	—	—	—	—	—	—
Hard to control	—	—	—	—	—	—
Fragile	—	—	—	—	—	—
Smooth cutting	—	—	—	—	—	—
Durable	—	—	—	—	—	—
Satisfying to use	—	—	—	—	—	—
Smooth running	—	—	—	—	—	—
Sluggish	—	—	—	—	—	—
Modern	—	—	—	—	—	—
Close cutting	—	—	—	—	—	—
Strong	—	—	—	—	—	—
Safe	—	—	—	—	—	—
Luxurious	—	—	—	—	—	—
Throws stones	—	—	—	—	—	—
Good weed cutter	—	—	—	—	—	—
Good mulcher	—	—	—	—	—	—
Solid	—	—	—	—	—	—

EXHIBIT 2. Summary of findings

As we expected, the recorded sounds of the experimental and standard mowers provided listeners with sufficient stimuli to visualize the mowers not only in terms of the noise output but in terms of a wide list of characteristics, plus profiles of the types of people for whom this new mower would be most appropriate.

The sound of the experimental mower gave listeners a definite impression of a *smooth, gentle,* and *nonvibrating* machine that is *easy to control* and *safer* than the standard model. It is thought to be much more appropriate for *women* and *smaller men* than the regular mower, yet it is seen as *capable of doing a better job.* There is no feeling that efficiency has been sacrificed for quietness.

Following are detailed comparisons between the mowers:

The mower descriptions (Table 1)

Respondents rated each of the mower sounds independently, yet these ratings are *meaningful only when the two sets of ratings are compared.* In this way the sound of the standard mower provides a base against which the sound of the experimental mower can be compared.

In comparison with the sound of the standard mower, the experimental model was visualized as *much more:*

Smooth running
Gentle
Luxurious
Modern

EXHIBIT 2 (*Continued*)

Satisfying to use
Smooth cutting
Fun to use

It was seen as much less:

Noisy
Vibrating
Old fashioned

The experimental "quiet" mower was thought to be *considerably better* as far as being:

Easy to handle
Safe
Trouble free
Close cutting

The standard mower was thought to be *considerably more:*

Rough cutting
Hard to control

The new mower was believed to be *somewhat more:*

Durable
Efficient
Solid

Moreover, the standard model was seen as *somewhat more:*

Dangerous
Sluggish

In only one area did the standard mower rate higher than the experimental model: it was thought probably to be a good weed cutter. There were a number of variables on the basis of which people were not able to make significant distinctions between the two mowers:

Powerful
Strong
Throws stones
Rugged
Good mulcher
Fragile

These latter variables serve as a check on the validity of the ratings. One would not expect that people could rate the mowers from sound as far as mulching ability is concerned, or in terms of the mower's tendency to throw stones. However, in addition, these nondiscriminatory items indicate that the impressions derived from the sounds are not in terms of the *strength* of the machines. The sound of the experimental mower does not suggest that it is more *solidly constructed* and therefore more *durable.*

Group interviews on the mower sounds substantiate these ratings. Men fear that the more noise a mower makes, the greater the vibration—the greater the vibration, the more likely the mower is to fly apart. It also follows that the quieter the mower, the safer it is since the vibration will be much smaller.

In a sense, these verbalizations, however, are rationalizations of impressions received from the sounds of the mowers. The *ratings* were made too quickly for much thinking to be done concerning a rationale for each particular rating. The ratings are therefore the result of a spontaneous reaction to the sound without methodical thought.

EXHIBIT 2 (*Continued*)

TABLE 1. Mower descriptions

Description	Experimental mower rating (a)	Standard mower rating (b)	Difference (a − b)
Smooth running	86%	30%	56%
Gentle	77	30	47
Luxurious	71	25	46
Modern	83	42	41
Satisfying to use	79	39	40
Noisy	44	83	−39
Smooth cutting	77	38	39
Fun to use	66	28	38
Vibrating	48	84	−36
Old fashioned	32	68	−36
Rough cutting	37	70	−33
Easy to handle	71	40	31
Safe	67	39	28
Hard to control	27	55	−28
Trouble free	65	42	23
Close cutting	73	51	22
Durable	75	55	20
Efficient	76	58	18
Dangerous	47	65	−18
Solid	75	58	17
Sluggish	24	41	−17
Good weed cutter	54	70	−16
Powerful	65	74	− 9
Strong	74	68	6
Throws stones	70	65	5
Rugged	70	74	− 4
Good mulcher	63	60	3
Fragile	32	32	0

° Almost all ratings were checked in either the far left or far right columns. It was decided, therefore, to tabulate the results by counting the percentage that checked the "applies" column or one of the columns on that side of the center of the scale.

The user descriptions (Table 2)

The experimental mower was rated higher than the standard mower for almost all user categories. These ratings strongly indicate a preference for the quieter mower as well as emphasizing that the experimental mower seems to suggest more ease of control.

The following descriptions were applied with *much greater strength* to the new mowers for:

Women
Small, light man
Quiet, thoughtful man
Person who wants the best
Man who is proud of his lawn
Man to whom cost is no object
Perfectionist
Professional man

The experimental mower was thought to be *considerably more* appropriate for:

Man with high income
Children

EXHIBIT 2 (*Continued*)

In addition, the quiet mower was believed to be somewhat *more appropriate* for the "average guy." The standard mower was visualized as *more appropriate* for only "strong men." Respondents were *not* willing to discriminate significantly between the mowers on the following variables:

Man who doesn't like lawn care
Man on a budget
Factory worker

TABLE 2. User descriptions

Description	Experimental mower rating (a)	Standard mower rating (b)	Difference (a − b)
For women	74%	22%	52%
For small, light man	80	30	50
For quiet, thoughtful man	63	16	47
For person who wants the best	64	19	45
For a man who is proud of lawn	68	25	43
For a man to whom cost is no object	57	14	43
For a perfectionist	63	22	41
For professional man	69	33	36
For man with high income	55	31	24
For children	33	10	23
For strong men	45	63	−23
For average guy	74	59	15
For man who doesn't like lawn care	43	46	− 3
For a man on a budget	53	54	− 1
For factory worker	53	54	− 1

° Almost all ratings were checked in either the far left or far right columns. It was decided, therefore, to tabulate the results by counting the percentage that checked the "applies" column or one of the columns on that side of the center of the scale.

The qualifying tape recorded interviews

Following each rating session, discussions were opened to allow the groups to talk about the sounds of the mowers as well as to give some of their ideas about power mowers in general.

One of the first reasons given for preferring a "quieter" mower, the men said, was that they often feel they are annoying the neighbors when they go out to mow the grass. One man described this as feeling as if he would like to sink into the ground the minute the motor begins. Others felt that the neighbors were all watching and annoyed. These impressions are multiplied for neighborhoods where men like to cut the grass on Sunday morning.

In addition, the loud mower noise automatically makes the man using the mower pretty conspicuous. Most men do not like the chore of cutting the grass, and the fact that the mower motor announces their work to the entire neighborhood is rather hard to take.

Aside from possible effects on neighbors, one of the greatest assets of the quieter mower is that it implies less vibration. Many men said that they dislike vibration even more than the noise. Excessive vibration implies that the mower is not constructed solidly enough, but more important it suggests the mower is dangerous and hard to control.

Some men felt that the "quiet" mower is probably a 4-cycle unit, since they

EXHIBIT 2 (*Concluded*)

believe that 4-cycle engines are quieter and smoother running than 2-cycle engines. These same men firmly believe that a 4-cycle motor is inherently better than a 2-cycle.

Conclusion

The only finding concerning the sound of the new model that might be considered negative is the association with the term "luxurious," and the fact that men regard it as highly appropriate for "men to whom cost is no object" as well as for "men with high income." Expectations, therefore, are that this new mower will be in the higher price range. This is not necessarily serious, however, since almost any really important improvement in a mower will probably be expected to increase the cost, or at least it will be expected to be installed primarily in the top price lines.

Case 16—2.   GENERAL FOODS—MAXIM COFFEE*

The Maxwell House Division of General Foods was the leading company in both the regular and soluble coffee markets. This dominant position was traceable to the company's historic strength in the regular coffee market, and the early development and introduction of high quality soluble (instant) coffees in the early 1950's. As a result of flavor improvement, soluble coffee sales grew dramatically during the middle and the late 1950's and were the leading growth factor in the total coffee market of that period.

Not content with this success, General Foods was aggressively developing another new coffee, produced by a process called freeze drying. This coffee was markedly different (in appearance and flavor) from either regular or "traditional" soluble coffees. The overriding problem during the initial development period was the high per unit production cost, but the research group assigned to the problem expressed confidence that a freeze-dried coffee could be produced at a "reasonable" cost. Their recommendation to proceed was followed shortly by the assignment of a new product marketing group to the task of compiling appropriate consumer research and developing the most effective marketing strategy for the new brand—Maxim. This new product group, headed by Mr. Ken Carter,[1] who served as the product manager, worked towards the goal of preparing a fully defined national marketing plan.

Top management approved Carter's recommendation that the Maxwell House Division test market Maxim to determine its market performance and to evaluate his national marketing plan. Carter based his recommendation for test marketing Maxim on the following considerations:

---

* Reprinted from Stanford Business Cases 1968 with the permission of the publishers, Stanford University Graduate School of Business. © 1968 by the Board of Trustees of the Leland Stanford Junior University.

[1] A disguised name used here to represent the several product executives who eventually worked on the project.

1. The impossibility of achieving even regional roll-out without increasing production capacity (a course of action which would involve constructing at least one $10 million plant).
2. The need to determine Maxim's effect on sales of other company brands.
3. The wish to ascertain Maxim's ability to sell at its required premium price in the face of the coffee market's high price elasticity.
4. The chance to test promotional techniques and advertising copy.

Choice of test market

As the test market area in the east where soluble coffee sales were high, Carter chose the Albany-Plattsburgh marketing· area, which included both the Albany/Schenectady and Burlington/Plattsburgh urban areas. He based this choice on several factors: the Albany urban area, with 351,800 TV homes, was close to the average high-soluble-market size (361,500 TV homes); Albany-Plattsburgh soluble coffee sales were 39.8 percent of the market, close to the overall eastern average of 42.9 percent; a test conducted earlier, using a sample of 700 from Albany, showed that the area followed a typical eastern usage pattern by coffee type— 30 percent exclusive ground, 50 percent both types, 20 percent exclusive instant (versus eastern averages of 24 percent, 57 percent, and 19 percent); and Maxwell House Division commanded a 53 percent share of the Albany-Plattsburgh soluble coffee market (39.5 percent Instant Maxwell House, 5.5 percent Yuban, 8.0 percent Sanka), a share which approached closely the Division's 50.7 percent high soluble average market share.

Test market advertising & media plan

When Maxim entered the Albany-Plattsburgh test market, Mr. Carter translated the national marketing plan into a scaled model for the individual market sizes involved. The overall test market media budget faithfully represented the national media budget, attaining an almost identical allocation of media dollars per television home—$0.278 versus $0.234.

The Albany/Schnectady and Burlington/Plattsburgh urban areas were sufficiently distant to be treated as separate media areas. The former was representative of areas with 250,000 to 1,000,000 TV homes, while the latter corresponded to smaller areas with 75,000 to 250,000 TV homes. Television "weight" was directed at these two urban areas roughly in proportion to their size. Thus, Albany (which had 80.5 percent of the test market television population) received 77.7 percent of the television expenditures, while Plattsburgh's 19.5 percent got 22.3 percent. Carter distributed this television advertising over the year in almost identical proportion to the national high soluble plan; for example, in the 250,000–1,000,000 area he placed 1.6 percent of the TV budget during the first week, 42.5 percent during the next thirteen weeks, 24.2 percent during the next thirteen, and 31.5 percent during the last twenty weeks, as compared with a national structure of 1.6/42/22.6/31.9 percent.

Carter departed from the national media plan by using network television as well as spots. After running the originally selected "freeze-dried announcement" for almost a year, he departed from the original copy strategy by introducing two new commercials "to attract attention and renew interest": a 20-second version of the "freeze-dried announcement" and a key 60-second "cracking-ice" message (see Exhibit 1).

The division's marketing research department performed studies immediately after each campaign to determine the relative effectiveness of these three copy platforms (see Exhibit 2). The original 60-second "freeze-dried announcement" produced favorable results—49 percent of the respondents who had watched the TV vehicle (The Ozzie and Harriet Show) recalled the Maxim name, while 70 percent of those who recalled the ad considered Maxim different from other coffee, and 65 percent felt that its flavor would compare favorably to ground coffee.

A similar study of the 60-second "cracking-ice" and 20-second "freeze-dried" commercials showed that they met predetermined standards satisfactorily as follows:

	Predetermined standards for total recall	Actual total recall levels
Cracking-ice (60 sec.)	35%	37%
Freeze-dried announcement (20-sec.)	17–18%	30%

The increased emphasis on product concentration in the "cracking-ice" commercial registered the idea more effectively than had the original 60-second "freeze-dried announcement" (11 percent versus 3 percent). Both the new commercials topped the original "announcement" with respect to the percentage who felt that Maxim would taste better than ground coffee (29 percent and 37 percent versus 17 percent). Researchers felt that the higher flavor mentions from the original commercial resulted from a particular sequence showing a line of perking coffee pots and that the modification of this sequence in the "cracking-ice" commercial adequately explained its poorer record for references to flavor.

Test market promotional plan

Carter also translated the national promotional plan to test market proportions. Of the total homes in the Albany area, 50 percent received free 2-ounce jars and 25¢ repurchase coupons, while in the smaller areas 50 percent got free-jar coupons. These promotional activities required an expenditure of $196,000.

Meanwhile, the market research department performed five studies to compare these promotion techniques with a 6-serving packet gift. To accomplish this it set up four consumer panels, subjecting each panel to one of the following promotional alternatives: (1) free-jar coupon, (2) 2-ounce sample jar and 25¢ coupon, (3) a kit with a 6-serving package and a 25¢ coupon, and (4) a control group which received no promotion.

The 6-serving package proved the most effective and efficient means of gaining immediate product trial (76 percent versus 68 and 29 percent) and remembrance (88 percent versus 81 and 62 percent). However, quite surprisingly, all panels developed comparable levels of Maxim purchasing, the control group actually taking the lead in this respect with 34 percent versus an overall average of 31 percent (see Exhibit 3). On the surface, these results pointed to the possibility of abandoning sampling and couponing, or at least employing the least costly technique (i.e., the 6-serving package); however, the marketing research director noted that the spatial proximity of the four panels to each other and to neighbors who also received samples had in all likelihood distorted the test results by facilitating interaction between members of the four panels and other triers, a process which may have blurred the distinctions between them.

Pricing in the test market

During the test, Maxim maintained a price relationship to Instant Maxwell House just slightly lower than that eventually favored by Carter. When Instant Maxwell House adjusted its price downward, reflecting the general drop in instant coffee prices, Maxim followed suit, so that the premium structure was altered only slightly.

Maxim test market performance

On the whole, Maxim's performance in Albany satisfied Carter, as the new brand bettered almost all standards set for it. Maxim quickly became the area's most popular instant coffee, as measured by consumer panel data which traced its use to better than 3 out of 10 households. It rapidly exceeded its 7.8 percent test market share goal, moving to a 12 percent Nielsen store audit share in the third month and finally settling at a firm 13–14 percent.

Panel data showed rates of cumulative purchase and repeat purchase which, at seven months, compared favorably with two other successful General Foods products, Alpha-bits and Minute Rice. After six months, 45 percent of the panel had tried Maxim and 49 percent of those had repurchased.

As Exhibit 4 indicates, Maxim increased the division's market share in Albany about 53 percent prior to the test to over 62 percent eight months later. Carter estimated that Maxim had taken its business from other brands roughly in proportion to their previously held share, a validation of his brand-switching model and an assurance that Maxim would not cannibalize other General Foods coffee brands. Panel data also showed that Maxim had fulfilled another goal by increasing the soluble ratio to total coffee sales by as much as 2 percent. However, Nielsen data (which many considered more reliable) contradicted these consumer panel results by reporting an actual decline in the soluble ratio from 41.7 to 35.0 (see Exhibit 4).

As a result of Maxim's consumer acceptance, its unit shipments exceeded the first year objectives by 87 percent. Usage by jar size also followed an acceptable pattern; more and more consumers took up the 4- and 8-ounce sizes as they passed the trial stage. Soon the two larger sizes accounted for over 80 percent of Maxim's Nielsen volume.

Maxim achieved good distribution, quickly moving into food stores that commanded 90 percent of the area's food sales and climbing slowly to 95 percent by the end of five months. A shelf space study showed that Maxim had gained an average 9.2 percent of the grocer's soluble coffee shelf space within three months.

Finally, two waves of attitude data—one taken in the second month, the other in the fifth month, indicated a generally favorable attitude toward Maxim, the proportion of the sample with a favorable reaction dropped slightly by the second wave (from 83 to 72 percent), a fact which the marketing research director attributed to attitudinal polarization (see Exhibits 5 and 6). By the end of the fifth month, awareness of Maxim's name and advertising had reached high levels: 95 percent of the coffee users had heard the name and 42 percent recalled it without aid. The attitude study (see Exhibit 5) found a high level of advertising awareness among both triers (79 percent) and nontriers (76 percent).

Performance problems

In spite of these encouraging results, two usage problems did emerge in the Albany test market. Several studies showed that Maxim triers, apparently unaware of its greater concentration, sometimes judged it too strong and consequently adopted unfavorable attitudes. A few even considered the premeasured 6-serving packages too potent. In the second month attitude study, 13 percent of those who had tried Maxim considered it too strong—a fact which Carter attributed to improper preparation on their part.

A second problem was that Maxim attained a lower rate of purchase by volume than other brands. One report showed that Maxim averaged only 4.2 ounces per purchase, while Nescafe averaged 8.8 ounces, Instant Maxwell House 6.6, and Yuban 5.8. Carter isolated at least three factors influencing this situation. First, Maxim's 4- and 8-ounce sizes were simply smaller than competitive medium- and large-sized offerings (generally 6- and 10-ounces, respectively). Secondly, the conversion of ground coffee users most likely worked against high volume purchases, since these buyers did not often convert to exclusive Maxim use as a soluble user might have. Thirdly, the newness of Maxim still prompted trial-buying of the 2-ounce size, an influence which further dragged down its average volume per purchase. Finally, Maxim's greater cup yield per ounce was thought to explain further these smaller purchases.

1. What conclusions should General Foods draw with regards to adding Maxim to its line?

2. What further information, if any, should it seek before making a decision?

3. Appraise the testing procedure which has been used up to this point.

EXHIBIT 1.

20-second freeze-dried announcement

Announcer. "Look at a new form of coffee. Freeze-dried coffee. Maxim. Concentrated crystals of real percolated coffee, with the power to turn every cup in your house into a percolator. Try new Maxim."

(Accompanied by *sound effects*: crystals dropping into cup, pouring of water, and perking. *Visual effects*: close-up of spoon and crystals, close-up of label with spoon in foreground, cup changing into percolator, close-up of jar.)

60-second cracking-ice

Announcer. "Discovered: an entirely new form of coffee. Freeze-dried coffee. New freeze-dried Maxim! With the power to turn every cup in your house into a percolator! Maxim's secret? Pots and pots of freshly brewed coffee are frozen. The ice is drawn off in a vacuum and you have freeze-dried coffee. Real percolated coffee in the form of crystals. And because so much coffee is concentrated in Maxim crystals, you need less per cup than with any other form of coffee. Let Maxim turn every cup in your house into a percolator. Maxim, from Maxwell House.

(Accompanied by *sound effects*: crackling of ice as mold separates and loud, final crackle, sound of vacuum, perking coffee, more crackling ice, another vacuum effect. *Visual effects*: vacuumized ice turning into coffee crystals, coffee cup turning into percolator, coffee pots being poured into mold and frozen ice again turned into coffee crystals, two ladies making Maxim, their coffee cups turning into percolators, close-up of label.)

EXHIBIT 2. Comparison of Maxim TV advertising by recall tests

	60-second "cracking-ice"	20-second version of "announce-ment"	Original 60-second "announce-ment"
Recalled brand name (% program audience)	37%	30%	49%
Correct recall of product	29	13	NA
Specific recall (% total recallers)	63	38	68
Process (net)			
Flavor	32	12	47
Concentrated, need less (total)	11	4	3
From Maxwell House (net)	4	3	12
Visual recall			
Process	55	12	43
Cup of coffee being made (crystals in spoon)	17	12	13
Percolators, pots	15	5	26
Comparison of Maxim flavor vs. ground			
Maxim tastes better than ground	29	37	17
Maxim tastes same as ground	37	37	48
Maxim does not taste as good as ground	26	19	14
Comparison of Maxim flavor vs. other instants			
Maxim tastes better than other instants	67	71	63
Maxim tastes same as others	20	19	21
Maxim does not taste as good	7	4	1
Sample size	(432)	(432)	(342)

EXHIBIT 3. Comparative trial and recall by promotional method (period: 2 months after delivery of sample and/or coupon)

	Coupon	Kit	Jar
Trial			
Used coupon/sample	29%	76%	68%
Used repurchase coupon	—	13	14
Tasted Maxim past 2 months	40	77	71
Consider Maxim regular brand*	8	11	16
Have Maxim on hand†	35	39	48
Remembrance			
Remembered sample/coupon	62	88	81
Remembered repurchase coupon	—	53	50
Base: total receiving each promotion	(310)	(205)	(297)

* BASE: Instant users (214/144/221).
† BASE: Respondents who had instant on hand (205/138/217).

Levels of purchase

	(Base)	November Maxim share of purchasers	November Maxim share of volume
Kit sample	(112)	27%	14%
Jar sample	(159)	33	18
Free-jar coupon	(137)	30	16
Control (no promotion)	(160)	34	22
Total	(568)	31	18

EXHIBIT 4. Nielsen data on share of soluble coffee volume (Albany test market)

Brand	Mar.	Apr.	May	June	July	Aug.	Sept.	Oct.	Nov.	Dec.	Jan.	Feb.
Maxim	—	—	0.3%	8.5%	12.0%	13.4%	14.4%	13.3%	16.0%	15.6%	14.2%	13.1%
IMH	39.5%	35.8%	38.6	35.7	36.0	34.0	32.1	34.2	33.1	34.9	36.0	34.9
Yuban	5.5	6.0	6.2	5.3	4.4	4.4	5.3	4.5	4.8	4.4	4.4	4.7
Sanka	8.0	8.5	8.1	8.1	8.0	7.3	7.9	6.7	7.6	7.4	7.9	7.7
Nescafe	13.0	14.2	10.1	10.2	10.4	9.3	11.4	12.1	9.9	9.8	10.7	12.4
C & S	11.4	11.9	10.5	10.0	8.8	7.0	8.7	7.1	9.2	9.2	9.1	8.3
Bordens	3.9	4.5	4.2	4.0	3.5	3.1	3.1	3.1	3.1	3.2	3.1	3.4
COB	10.5	0.8	10.8	8.4	7.0	13.0	8.2	10.4	8.5	8.0	7.1	7.8
A.O.	4.4	4.5	6.8	6.2	5.9	4.1	4.1	4.3	3.6	4.0	3.9	3.5
Total market (000 48-oz. units)	53.1	49.5	50.7	46.5	44.7	45.3	43.1	49.1	47.6	52.6	49.5	42.7
Soluble Ratio	41.7	40.6	37.2	36.6	38.6	35.8	38.8	36.0	36.9	37.1	36.2	35.0
Maxwell House total share	53.0	50.3	53.2	57.6	60.4	59.1	59.7	58.7	61.5	62.3	62.5	60.4

Nielsen vs. consumer panel data on Maxim share of Albany market

	June	July	Aug.	Sept.	Oct.*	Nov.*	Dec.*	Jan.	Feb.
Nielsen store audit data	8.5%	12.0%	13.4%	14.4%	13.3%	16.0%	15.6%	14.2%	13.1%
Consumer panel data	14.5	14.0	14.0	14.0	17.0	17.0	17.0	14.5	15.0

* Newspaper coupon ran October 16, mailed coupon December 1. Effect was felt in all three months.

EXHIBIT 5. Maxim product attitude and awareness studies in Albany

	Second month (sample 231)	Fifth month (sample 217)
Favorable reaction	83%	72%
Tastes better/like percolated	43	53
Convenience	3	3
Use less	3	4
Other	36	21
Unfavorable	15%	27%
Too strong	11	6
Expensive	1	5
Other	5	19
Brand awareness		
Unaided	36%	42%
Aided	57	53
Total	93%	95%
Consumer trial		
Sample/coupon	49%	49%
Other	13	20
Total trial	62%	69%
Base (respondents who tried Maxim)	(143)	(147)

	Among triers	Among non-triers
Percent aware of advertising (fifth month)	79%	76%
Major points recalled		
Freeze-dry process	38	23
Tastes better/like percolated	22	14
Concentrated/use less	3	5

EXHIBIT 6. The significance of polarization

The concept of polarization refers to the difficulty of maintaining a neutral attitude in the face of either intense feeling (ego-involvement) or increasing certainty (learning). If ranked along a scale, a person's attitude, by definition, must have some positive or negative value or it becomes no attitude at all. But though an individual may adopt an initial attitude near the zero point, as his knowledge on the subject grows or as he assumes a stronger emotional attachment to his view, he will concurrently move toward a more extreme positive or negative position on the attitude scale. This conceptualization or attitudinal formation defines the zero point as the point of least "intensity-certainty" along a u-shaped curve that represents the tendency for intensity, certainty, and attitudinal valence to rise together.

The Maxim research director implicitly drew upon this concept to explain Maxim's declining favorableness score. At the start of its introductory period the thoroughly ill-informed subject might well have adopted an attitude at or near the zero point. At this stage he might have responded charitably to questionnaires to hide a slightly negative attitude, simply to avoid giving the unsociable impression that our society attaches to negativism. However, if this same subject, whose initial viewpoint has seemed too puny to express or defend, had continued to learn more about Maxim and had further experienced the ego-involvement that might have accompanied spending

EXHIBIT 6 (*Continued*)

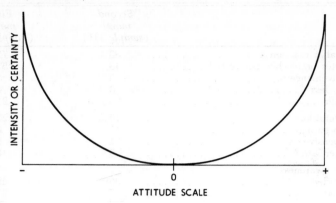

his hard-earned cash on the product, he would soon have abandoned his shyness and would have expressed his derogatory opinion with gusto. Obviously, if many such individuals had existed, such behavior would have damaged Maxim's rating during the stages of introduction.

Case 16—3.   BOOK PRESS, INC.

Book Press, Incorporated, with headquarters in a large middle western city, published an encyclopedia with it sold to the consumer household market, as well as to schools and libraries. Known as a medium-size firm in the industry, Book Press had sales of $32 million. Its product line consisted of an adult encyclopedia, a junior encyclopedia, and a variety of related books, such as dictionaries, atlases, cook books, and specialized reference books (medical, legal, business, etc.). The adult encyclopedia which retailed at $175 accounted for approximately 70 percent of the company's total dollar sales. Because the company's operations were of a highly seasonal nature, with the peak production period occurring in November, December, and January, the executives were considering entering the high school and college yearbook market which would extend their peak production time through May.

The company was a fully integrated activity with the exception of the actual printing and binding, which were contracted out. It employed editorial, art, proofreading, and layout specialists and had a manufacturing department which supervised all printing and binding. This staff on a continuous basis conducted revision work of the company's encyclopedia line and, in addition, was responsible for the introduction of new "companion" items which were typically single units. Revision work was of a continuous nature; the printing of an "annual supplement" caused the full-time staff to be employed at peak efficiency from September to December.

Book Press followed accepted industry practices in marketing its products. It employed a sales staff of between 16,000 and 18,000 which consisted almost exclusively of part-time workers, operating locally, who were paid on a straight commission basis. These individuals were selected, trained, and supervised by district managers who worked full time on a commission basis. District managers received 15 percent on all sales made in their districts, while salemen received approximately 35 percent.

In addition to the above sales staff, the company had a school and library sales division which consisted of approximately 250 individuals (both men and women) who solicited schools and libraries. These salesmen typically worked full time and were given a $50 weekly draw which was deducted from their commissions. Each was given an exclusive territory with respect to libraries and schools. The size of this territory varied by population density; for example, the company had three salesmen in the Chicago metropolitan area, but only one for the entire state of North Dakota. These salesmen were carefully trained and supervised because of the nature of the market and because the company considered librarians and educators opinion leaders who could influence heavily the sales of their books.

Such salesmen received a 50 percent commission on all school and library sales. Almost without exception, library and school salesmen also sold to the household market where they received a 35 percent commission. Company executives estimated that the average library and school salesman received 70 percent of his income from the household market and 30 percent from libraries and schools. The average income in this group was $10,200, from which the individual paid his own expenses which amounted to about $2,000 annually. Many library and school salesmen were former school teachers who had started such selling work on a part-time basis.

The company spent about $150,000 annually in media advertising. Advertisements were run regularly in such magazines as *The Instructor,* *Grade School Teacher,* and the *Journal of the National Education Association.* No consumer advertising was run by the company. In addition to trade advertising the company did contact libraries and schools by mail— especially with regard to announcements of its new books and the annual updating changes made in its encyclopedia.

The high school and college yearbook was chiefly a memory book—a family album of the school. An examination of yearbook sales indicated that the number of copies purchased depended upon the number of people whose pictures appeared in the book. The yearbook publishing industry was thought to represent a $45 to $50 million market. About 15,000 different yearbooks were published annually, with the number of volumes of each averaging between 700 and 800. Most yearbooks were distributed in June.

A study made by the company with regard to this market yielded the following main points:

1. There were about 30,000 schools in the U.S. that were of the type to issue yearbooks. Of these, only 15,000 issued books on a regular basis. This 50 percent included a disproportionate number of smaller schools.

2. Yearbooks were being produced on either a guaranteed sale or unguaranteed basis. The former usually involved the compulsory payment of an annual fee which entitled the student to receive a yearbook among other things. Unguaranteed sale meant simply that the yearbook was produced on the hope that a sufficient number of books would be sold to cover the expenses incurred. In colleges and universities, the guaranteed sales plan was used more frequently than it was in high schools.

3. Sales of yearbooks were correlated with the size of the student body. The larger the school, the lower the percentage of students buying.

4. The average dollar sale per school was estimated at $4,200, with an average book selling price of $5.50.

5. It was estimated that by 1975 total high school and college enrollment would be 21 million and would necessitate an additional 10,000 schools, the vast majority of which would be high schools.

6. Most yearbook staffs followed what was done in previous books. Only rarely were distinct innovations in subject copy attempted.

7. Preliminary planning for yearbooks usually started about a year before the proposed delivery date. Where faculty advisors or sponsors were reappointed from year to year, the scheduling and production were simplified. Because the yearbook was a student project, each new staff had to be reeducated to the needs of the job.

8. Despite the acceptance of a schedule by the student staff it was frequently upset because students wanted to make last-minute changes.

9. Many printers who were selling to this market supplied the student staffs with various aids and devices that reduced the process of decision making to a minimum. One printer provided a supply kit which included material needed for production, copy sheets on how to sell advertising, and a program for selling the book to students. In addition, the following were included: photo stickers for picture identification; samples of type styles and sizes and headline styles and sizes; envelopes for mailing copy; suggestions for selecting covers; paper and binding material swatches; and applied color swatches.

10. All budget work had to be cleared by the faculty advisor and all negotiations had to be stated in writing.

11. The industry was comprised on numerous small printers plus three large integrated "manufacturers."

Book Press executives believed that their present operations involved processes highly similar to the steps involved in the publication of high school and college yearbooks. Further, its staff was considered to be more specialized and skilled than any of the three large integrated manufacturing companies then servicing this market. But the factor that encouraged the possibility of entry was the possibility of using the company's library and school sales staff. This staff over the past 20 years had concentrated on establishing contacts with library and school administrators throughout the United States. Virtually every college and university, and perhaps as high as 50 percent of all high schools, had been contacted. The contacts had been kept reasonably fresh because of the need to make periodic calls with revised editions and annual supplements to the encyclopedia.

Book Press believed that it would be at a cost advantage in dealing with its potential competitors. This advantage lay primarily in the use of its existing staff since costs of printing and binding were fairly standardized.

How could Book Press, Inc. use marketing research effectively in arriving at a decision relative to entering the yearbook market?

Case 16—4. FOREST APPLIANCE COMPANY

The Forest Company, a leading large appliance firm, sold a line of major appliances including automatic and wringer washers, dryers, refrigerators, stoves, home freezers, and air conditioners. The company's research and development department recommended that the spin speed of the automatic washer be increased substantially. This increased speed would permit clothes to be dried more quickly and thoroughly since more of the water would be eliminated from the fabrics and would also permit a reduction in the time of the spin cycle. The change would add approximately $10.00 to the cost of each unit at retail.

Several years before, a major competitor had produced a machine on which the spin speed had been increased. This particular feature had been the subject of a national advertising campaign and dealers had promoted it aggressively. At that time the Forest Company had investigated the new feature by conducting a survey among buyers of the new washer. The study revealed that many housewives were having difficulty with their machines which blew a fuse when they went into the spin cycle. The machine also had a tendency to "walk" because of the vibration set up as a result of the fast spin. The following year the competitor reduced the spin speed to what it had been before the change.

The Forest research and development department asked for advice from the marketing department as to whether this additional feature would prove a good sales argument and whether it would be worth the additional $10.00 to consumers. The sales manager viewed the possible change with mixed feelings. He recognized that a faster spin did have certain advantages, but he was afraid that the average housewife might be fearful of buying a machine which spun clothes at approximately 1,050 times a minute. He was also concerned that the bad impression created by the competitor's product several years earlier had caused many housewives to feel that a higher spin speed would necessitate fastening the machine to the floor to prevent "walking," and also to have extra duty wiring to prevent fuse blowouts. The development department assured him that this would not be true with the new model. In testing the product under simulated use conditions, however, it was found that there was some tendency for clothes to be more matted and tangled as a result of the high spin speed than was true with a lower speed.

As a result of these conflicting views, the sales manager believed it was necessary to determine how consumers might react to this new feature before a decision was made. In discussing this problem with the firm's marketing research director, the sales manager indicated that a study should be made to determine whether consumers were aware of the number of revolutions per minute of their present machine when it was in the spin part of the cycle, and what a substantial increase in spin speed would mean to them. Would they, for example, think it an important feature—an aid to their laundry problems—or would they be afraid that the increased speed would blow fuses, cause the machine to "walk," or mat the clothes?

The research and development department indicated that it had to have an answer from the marketing department within the next thirty days since production plans for the new model had to be finalized by that date. The marketing research director and one of his analysts immediately went to work to draw up a questionnaire for a telephone study to be made in the nearby Chicago metropolitan area. The research director thought that because of the time deadline he had no alternative but to conduct the questionnaire by phone. In explaining his selection of the Chicago metropolitan area, he said, "I feel this will provide an adequate sampling universe because most metropolitan area housewives will have similar attitudes and feelings about this proposed new product feature. Metropolitan areas represent the major potential for the sale of automatic washing machines. I'm not too concerned about the reactions of small city dwellers or farm dwellers."

After several pretests, a final questionnaire was prepared. This questionnaire appears as Exhibit 1. At about the same time, the analyst finished preparing the sample design to be used on this particular study. A write-up of this design appears as Exhibit 2.

In view of the objectives of this study, should the research director proceed with the questionnaire and sample design as indicated in Exhibits 1 and 2?

EXHIBIT 1. Washing machine telephone questionnaire

1. Do you own a washing machine?   Yes ☐   No ☐
    (IF NO, SKIP TO CLASSIFICATION SECTION AND TERMINATE INTERVIEW)
2a. Is your washing machine a wringer type or an automatic? (IF WRINGER, ASK
    Q. 2b, IF AUTOMATIC, SKIP TO QUESTION 3).   Wringer ☐   Automatic ☐
2b. What is the brand name of your wringer type machine? (SKIP TO CLASSIFICATION SECTION AND TERMINATE INTERVIEW) _____
3a. What is the make or brand name of your automatic washer? _____
3b. When this washer was installed was it necessary to have any special wiring work
    done for it to take care of the extra voltage?   Yes ☐   No ☐
3c. Since this washer was installed in your home have you had any electrical problems while it is in operation such as dimming of lights, or a lot of fuses blowing
    out?   Yes ☐   No ☐
4. About how old is your automatic washer? _____ (years)
5a. Does it have any special features which permit you to wash delicate fabrics
    differently than other wash loads?   Yes ☐   No ☐   (SKIP TO Q. 6).
5b. What are these special features? _____
    _____
    _____

6. Where in your home is your automatic washer located? _____
7a. Is it bolted or fastened in any way to the floor?   Fastened ☐   Not fastened ☐
    Comments: _____
    _____

7b. (IF FASTENED, ASK) Why did you have it fastened down? _____
    _____

7c. (IF NOT FASTENED, ASK) Does your machine ever move about or change position
    while you're using it?   Yes ☐   No ☐   (SKIP TO Q. 8)
7d. (IF YES TO Q. 7, ASK) Does it move every time you use it or just sometimes?
    Every time ☐   Sometimes ☐
7e. What would you say causes it to move like that? _____
    _____
    _____

7f. Would you say that all brands or makes of automatic washers move like yours
    or that some brands move around more than others?
            Some move more ☐   All the same ☐   (SKIP TO Q. 8)
7g. (IF ANSWER TO Q. 7f IS SOME MOVE MORE THAN OTHERS, ASK) Which brands
    do you think move around more than others?
    _____   _____
7h. (FOR EACH BRAND MENTIONED IN Q. 7g, ASK) Why would you say that _____
    _____ washer moves more than some of the others?

7g. Brand	7h. Reasons
_____	_____
	_____
_____	_____
	_____
_____	_____
	_____

EXHIBIT 1 (*Continued*)

8a. Some housewives I've talked to tell me that some makes or brands of automatic washers spin faster than others when they are in the spin cycle: Is this right— do some brands spin faster than others or do they all spin at about the same rate?

    1. Some spin faster   2. All spin about the same
       (ASK Q. 8b–8e)   (ASK Q. 8f–8h)

8b. What brands do you think spin the fastest? _____

8f. What advantages do you think would result from a faster spin? _____

8c. What advantages do you think result from this faster spin? _____

8g. What disadvantages do you think result from a faster spin? _____

8d. What disadvantages do you think result from a faster spin? _____

8h. Do you think a high speed spin would have any effect on the appearance of the clothes when you take them out of the washer?
        Yes ☐   No ☐

8e. Does a high speed spin have any effect on the appearance of the clothes when you take them out of the washer?
        Yes ☐   No ☐

9. How many revolutions or turns a minute do you think your automatic spins in a minute? Make a guess! _____ revolutions per minute.

10. Do you wash each time you accumulate a load or do you have a regular washday? Each time accumulate load ☐   Have a regular washday ☐

Classification data

Do you live in a house or apartment?   House ☐   Apartment ☐
How many children under twelve years of age are in your family? _____
Comments: _____

_____
_____
_____
_____

INTERVIEWER _____ DATE _____

EXHIBIT 2. Recommended sampling procedure on telephone survey on automatic washers

Respondents (housewives) will be sampled on a systematic random basis from the Chicago and suburban alphabetic telephone directory. The sampling universe will be broken down into two groups: (1) the Chicago group, consisting of 180 respondents who use automatic washers, and (2) the Chicago suburban group, consisting of 120 respondents who use automatic washers, for a total sample of 300 respondents. The Chicago group will be interviewed on a basis of every 17th name (a number chosen at random) off every 12th page (there are 2,155 pages in the Chicago alphabetical directory; 2155 ÷ 12 = 180). If that 17th name is a business listing, then the next name on the page will be called.

EXHIBIT 2 (*Continued*)

If an interview is not completed at that name, the 34th name will be called; if an interview is not obtained there, the 51st name will be called; etc. Once a call is completed, the next page selected will be used.

To obtain the suburban sample, data from *Sales Management's* Survey of Buying Power, which contains population and income estimates as of January 1, were used. The total population of the 26 Chicago area suburbs listed in *Sales Management* was broken down into five annual income groups, defined as follows:

		Percent of total population (suburbs)
Group E	$ 0–$2,499	3.8
Group D	$ 2,500–$3,999	9.5
Group C	$ 4,000–$6,999	29.1
Group B	$ 7,000–$9,999	19.1
Group A	$10,000–and over	38.5

Five suburbs have been selected on the basis of the similarity of the distribution of their population within income groups to the overall distribution. The five suburbs have been added together and their income distribution compared to that of the total for all suburbs. The results are shown in the table below. A quota of 24 (1/5 of 120) interviews will be selected from the phone books for these five suburbs in a manner similar to that used in Chicago.

Suburb	*Quota*	*Income groups*				
		E	*D*	*C*	*B*	*A*
Chicago Heights	24	4.2	12.3	35.2	18.5	29.8
Harvey	24	3.2	10.0	37.9	20.3	28.6
Blue Island	24	3.2	9.0	33.2	21.6	33.0
River Forest	24	3.9	3.8	10.3	10.5	71.5
Forest Park	24	3.1	8.2	34.4	23.2	31.1
Average percent		3.5	8.7	30.2	18.8	38.8
Total suburban percent		3.8	9.5	29.1	19.1	38.5
Range of error		−0.3	−0.8	+1.1	−0.3	+0.3

17

Sales control research

MARKETING MANAGEMENT relies heavily on sales control research in setting marketing policies, in planning marketing operations, and in controlling marketing operations, including the functioning of the sales unit. In its broadest meaning, sales control research covers the *identification* and *measurement* of all those variables which individually and in combination have an effect on sales. Thus, such activities as sales forecasting, sales territory evaluation, inventory control, and salesman's performance are included.

Any marketing expenditure (input) assumes some kind of a result (payout). The marketing director must have enough knowledge of the market and his organization's performance to estimate the impact of his organization's efforts on the market. Sales control research

. . . contributes at every stage to the development of the company's annual sales plan, which details assignments of the sales organization in the years ahead. For example, it offers realistic historical benchmarks for the purposes of forecasting the coming year's sales, establishing sales goals for units and individuals in the sales organization, and setting guiding norms of activity or efficiency (such as for salesmen's frequency of calls on customers or prospects, allocation of salesmen's time, size of orders, etc.). The analysis of sales is also invaluable to sales management in pointing up the need for changes in the design of sales territories, the size and dispersion of the field sales force, salesmen's compensation, and sales training methods. Other important applications in the area of sales planning are policy determination (for example, setting minimum order size) and preparation of sales expense budgets.[1]

---

[1] *Sales Analysis,* Studies in Business Policy, No. 113 (New York: National Industrial Conference Board, Inc., 1965), p. 4.

Sales control research makes up a major portion of the activity of most marketing research departments. Research studies dealing with the development of market potentials, market share analysis, determination of market characteristics, and sales analysis are the four most common activities undertaken by a marketing research unit. Short-range forecasting, long-range forecasting, and establishment of sales quotas and sales territories are also standard activities.[2]

The interrelationship of activities in sales control research has led to much confusion in terminology. Since this chapter will discuss primarily sales forecasting, market analysis, and sales analysis, it is desirable to give specific meaning to each. *Sales forecasting* will be used to mean the prediction of sales of a particular product, company, branch office, or other unit for a given period of time. *Market analysis* will apply to those studies of individual markets which seek to determine the sales potential(s) within them. Several potentials may be of interest, such as industry sales potential and company sales potential. *Sales analysis* will include the analysis of a company's sales to ascertain such things as distribution of sales by territories, by type and size of customer, by order size, by product, and by combinations of these classifications.

SALES FORECASTING[3]

The sales forecast is the factor around which most business planning centers. Such important areas of decision making as production and inventory scheduling, planning of plant and equipment investments, manpower requirements, raw material purchases, advertising outlays, sales force expenditures, and cash flow needs are dependent on the sales forecast. It follows that any significant error in the forecast will have far-reaching and serious consequences. The increasing availability of economic data, the continual improvement of technique, and the expanded computational ability provided by the computer have made it possible for firms to forecast their sales with considerable accuracy.

The ability of the computer to process large quantities of data and to test a variety of relationships has contributed greatly to the generation of improved forecasts. The computer is especially important to those firms which produce and sell thousands of diverse items and need to establish a sales forecast for either each product or a large number of

---

[2] Dik W. Twedt, ed., *A Survey of Marketing Research: Organization, Functions, Budget, Compensation* (Chicago: American Marketing Association, 1963), p. 41.

[3] For more detailed discussions of forecasting techniques, see Robert Ferber and P. J. Verdoorn, *Research Methods in Economics and Business* (New York: The Macmillan Co., 1962); Robert G. Murdick and Arthur E. Schaefer, *Sales Forecasting for Lower Costs and Higher Profits* (Englewood Cliffs, N.J.: Prentice-Hall, Inc., 1967); and Robert S. Reichard, *Practical Techniques of Sales Forecasting* (New York: McGraw-Hill, Inc., 1966).

product groups. The vast capacity of large computers makes it possible to store and process quickly large quantities of detailed data, such as orders received, units produced, and dealer inventories. As a result, firms can use more variables in their forecasting efforts including general economic indicators, industry data, plans for new products, anticipated action and reaction by competitors, and price and promotion plans, and can use statistical techniques, such as multiple correlation, that would otherwise not be feasible because of the tremendous volume of calculations required.[4]

Sales forecasting is a complex subject which uses a variety of concepts and techniques, some of which are highly sophisticated. A detailed treatment is not feasible here, but the following discussion describes the more typical approaches to the problem.

Jury of executive opinion

One of the simplest methods of forecasting sales is by a jury of executive opinion. Each of a number of executives makes an independent forecast of sales for the next period, usually a year. These forecasts are more than just opinion. Each executive has considerable factual data available to him, and presumably possesses mature judgment.

Once the various executives have made their estimates, some method of reconciling the differences or averaging them must be determined. The chief executive of the company may consider the various estimates and make a final decision. A better procedure is to bring the group of executives together to discuss their estimates. Discussion may bring out new ideas and lead some individuals to modify their previous estimates. If the group cannot come to general agreement, the chief executive will have to make the decision.

Some firms combine this method with a more objective statistical approach whereby the marketing research department first indicates the range within which sales will probably fall. Probabilities may even be used to indicate the likelihood of sales falling within certain ranges.

The jury method has the advantage of simplicity and the fact that a number of different, specialized viewpoints are represented. Its chief disadvantage is that it is based on opinions. The opinions are all apt to be influenced in a similar direction by general business conditions and conditions in the specific company, i.e., the executives are apt to become overly optimistic or overly pessimistic together.

---

[4] For a more complete discussion of the use of the computer in sales forecasting see Murdick and Schaefer, *op. cit.*, pp. 243–62.

Sales force composite method

This forecasting method is similar to the previous method. Instead of having the men at the top of the organization estimate sales, however, the men actually making the sales make the estimates. Each salesman estimates his next year's sales, usually by product and possibly even by customer. These estimates are cumulated to arrive at a company forecast.

Branch managers may go over each salesman's estimates, compare them with the previous year, and discuss changes or lack of changes with the salesman. Similarly, the central office may study the summary for each branch and discuss any points of question with the branch manager.

Salesmen may be able to state probabilities of selling various amounts of each product or product group to each present customer and to each prospective customer. As new developments occur after the original forecast, salesmen may be able to revise these probabilities, thereby providing current data on which to base changes in the firm's overall sales forecast. If a salesman has knowledge of what the trend is in the firm's share of each customer's business, and if he knows what changes in the company's marketing activities will occur during the coming year in his territory, it is possible that he can do a good job of sales forecasting.

This method has the advantage of letting each salesman have a part in developing his sales goal for the next year, instead of receiving a quota, about the development of which he knows nothing. This tends to make each salesman feel more a part of a team and gives him a greater sense of responsibility for accomplishment of the forecasted volume.

A second advantage of the method is that estimates are made by the individuals most intimately in touch with local situations. Such a forecast takes into account problems and opportunities existing in each small segment of the market in a way no home office forecast can ever do.

Salesmen's estimates also have several limitations. As a group, salesmen will tend to be overly optimistic or pessimistic as conditions change. If their forecasts are used as quotas, salesmen tend to understate their probable volume so as to be on the "safe" side. One company has found salesmen's estimates run 30 to 40 percent below results, but others regularly come within 5 percent of performance using the same method. Salesmen are also unlikely to have much knowledge of basic economic trends that may influence the company. An additional disadvantage is that forecasting is not the salesmen's speciality. Time they spend in forecasting might better be spent in selling.

Statistical methods

Statistical methods range in complexity from relatively simple trend extrapolations to the use of sophisticated mathematical models. More and more companies are tending toward the use of advanced methods in which the computer correlates a host of relationships.

Trend analysis via extrapolation.   In its simplest form, the assumption is made that sales for the coming time period will be equal to the current level *or* that sales will change to the same degree that sales changed from the prior period to the current period. Such simple predictive models are more reliable than might at first be thought—especially for very short periods of time (a month or a quarter) under stable conditions.

Extrapolation techniques assume that ". . . some past tendency or trend in the variable being forecasted reflects what is going to happen. Accordingly, an attempt is made to quantify this tendency or trend and to derive a forecast by extrapolating the relation into the future. No consideration is given to possible determinants of past or future fluctuations in the variable except for the use of time as an explanatory factor."[5] Extrapolations can be accomplished via moving averages and other mathematical techniques. In undertaking any kind of a trend analysis, the researcher must keep in mind that any time series is made up of four factors: long-term trend, cyclical variations, seasonal variations, and irregular variations. If the pattern of these factors is at all well developed, each of them can be separated from the others. The first three (trend, cyclical, and seasonal) can then be projected to determine the sales pattern for the future.

Correlation analysis.   Correlation analysis is a method of measuring the relationship between two or more factors. It is used in sales forecasting to measure the relationship between a company's sales and other economic series. For example, an automobile manufacturer may find his sales are related to personal income—when income goes up his car sales go up and when income goes down his sales drop. To use this relationship in forecasting car sales, the manufacturer must determine the degree of relationship. If income rises 10 percent, do car sales rise 10 percent, 30 percent, 2 percent, or what? Correlation techniques enable the producer to determine the average degree of relationship.

One may wonder how the discovery of a relationship between sales and one or several other factors helps to forecast sales. The problem is shifted to forecasting the other factors. However, this indirect approach has two advantages. First, such general economic series as personal income are forecast by many people. A particular company then has the

---

[5] Ferber and Verdoorn, *op. cit.*, p. 442.

advantage of the thinking of a number of experts on such forecasts. On the average, this should enable the company to make a better forecast of the related series than it could of sales. Second, in some cases a lead-lag relationship may be found between a series and the company's sales. Income changes might precede changes in auto sales by three months. Where such a relationship exists, the correlation with the related series has a direct advantage. A building supply company, for example, has found a high correlation between the sales of its products and building contracts awarded; however, sales seem to lag five months behind building contracts.

Correlation analysis has the advantage of being more objective than the previous methods discussed. If sales are related to a widely used series, the forecaster has the advantage of many opinions to aid him in forecasting the other series. A third advantage of the method is that it can be done by an office staff or a consultant, thus leaving the executives and sales organization free to carry on their regular operations.

Survey methods

This approach to forecasting is the least used because of its expense, the time required (particularly when done by mail), and its problems of reliability. Surveys at the consumer level dealing with intentions to buy have not, as yet, contributed significantly to forecasting reliability. More success has been obtained with the prediction of capital expenditures by business firms through surveys conducted by the U.S. Department of Commerce. Surveys can, however, be quite useful in getting information which will be useful in making the forecast; for example, the number of households owning and the number not owning a color television set may be useful to a TV manufacturer. A survey of customers to determine their buying intentions relative to the vender's product is similar to having company salesmen get information from customers on which to base their sales estimates.

More advanced techniques

In recent years, many companies have turned to more sophisticated techniques of sales forecasting than those described above. Step regression is one of these techniques. It ". . . is essentially a multiple-correlation problem, with one important addition: the approach considers all possible influences on sales, automatically accepting those that play a significant role and automatically rejecting those that do not. Looking at all this another way, in addition to considering the relationship between each independent variable and sales, step regression also considers the interrelationship between the independent variables."[6]

Computerized models have been set up and operated by a number of companies in an effort to improve the accuracy of their sales forecasts. For example, the Scovill Manufacturing Company uses a complex time series model which takes into account seasonal, cyclical, and irregular factors.[7] The speed in calculation provided by the computer enables the analyst to include many variables in sophisticated models and, in addition, to calculate estimates of accuracy such as standard errors and confidence limits.

Combination of methods

If all or several of the methods of forecasting are used simultaneously, the resulting forecasts will probably be more reliable than the forecasts obtained from the use of any one of the methods. If executive opinion, salesmen's composite, and statistical methods all give approximately the same result, one has a good deal of confidence in that forecast. If widely different results are obtained, however, analysis of the differences will tend to lead to a better conclusion.

MARKET ANALYSIS

The marketing decision maker, for a variety of reasons which will be discussed later, is interested in obtaining a set of geographical sales potentials which can be defined as ". . . relative measures of total possible sales of a commodity or a group of commodities under specific marketing conditions at a stated time, in a specified geographical area relative to the total area under consideration. The measure is concerned with the relative level of possible sales. Possible sales enter into the consideration of geographical sales potentials merely as a concept and no dollar values need to be attached to it."[8]

Since most products are similar to a number of others, consumers often engage in considerable substitution; therefore, the degree of substitution as well as the conditions under which it takes place must be considered in the development of potentials. The decision as to whether to include or exclude closely related substitutes will often have a pro-

---

[6] Reichard, *op. cit.*, p. 168.

[7] For an example of the use of the computer and time series analysis see Robert L. McLaughlin, "The Breakthrough in Sales Forecasting," *Journal of Marketing* (April, 1963), pp. 46–54.

[8] Fritz Kafka and Benjamin Lipstein, *A New Approach to Geographic Sales Potentials,* paper presented at a meeting of the Northern New Jersey Chapter of the American Marketing Association (May, 1959), p. 1.

nounced effect on estimated sales potentials. For example, in considering the relative sales potential for canned peas one would have to consider the possible sales of frozen peas, since the latter can be viewed as a close substitute.

Market potentials and sales forecasts are not necessarily the same thing, although the two are often used interchangeably. When ". . . this is done, it usually is the term 'potential' which is misused. The dictionary defines 'potential' as 'existing in possibility: capable of development into actuality.' "[9] Thus, market potentials typically refer to total sales possibilities. Several different potentials may be considered, depending on what conditions are stated. One potential could have to do with the conditions of use, for example, the amount of toothpaste which would be used if all persons using toothpaste brushed after every meal. Another potential could be one based on brushing only once a day, and so on. Thus, the word "potential" is meaningless unless one knows the conditions under which the term is used.

In this chapter we are mostly concerned with the potential which exists for sales of a given product by the entire industry. Such potential estimates are usually needed by small geographical units. If total industry sales for a given product were known at the national level and by small geographical units, they would provide an accurate measure of one type of potential. But in the case of most products such data are not available, and alternative data have to be used.

Uses of market potentials

Defining sales territories. The design of sales territories is usually based on some estimate of potentials. For a given firm, there is an optimum potential that is sought for each salesman's territory. If the potential is below this level, the salesman cannot use all of his time to advantage. If his territory has too much potential, the salesman cannot handle it all, and sales are lost.

Of course, the optimum potential will be influenced by travel distances and average size of order. With experience, however, a company can develop a good measure of the optimum potential. Certainly, the firm can eliminate extreme cases where one salesman has more potential than he can exploit properly while another salesman has a territory with so little potential that he can barely cover his expenses. In such a case, reallocation of territories to make potentials approximately equal will almost assuredly lead to greater sales results. The elimination of some areas entirely and concentration on the markets with high potential may increase sales while simultaneously reducing expenses.

---

[9] D. Maynard Phelps and J. Howard Westing, *Marketing Management* (Homewood, Ill.: Richard D. Irwin, Inc., 1968), p. 474.

Allocation of sales efforts.   Allocation of sales effort is closely related to the design of sales territories. For example, assume a product is sold nationwide. Should 10 percent of the selling effort be allocated to the New York City market and 5 percent to Chicago? Or should New York have several times as much sales push as Chicago? Should both of them be increased or decreased relative to the United States? Decisions on these questions should be based on comparisons of the potentials in the various markets.

All selling effort, sales force, advertising, and nonadvertising promotion, should be allocated only after a consideration of potentials. In the case of national advertising, this can be done by comparing circulation data (readership, viewing, listening) for media with market potentials. If a product has high potential in the south, media with heavy concentration in the south can be used. With local advertising, expenditures can be matched even more closely with potentials. Advertising can be allocated to each city in proportion to potential. For example, one firm which sold throughout the country used national advertising, but backed this up with local advertising in key markets. New York City had 16 percent of the potential in these key markets and was given 16 percent of the local advertising budget.

Potential not sole criterion for allocating sales effort.   The primary usefulness of market potentials is to focus attention on the relative worth of individual markets. No firm should, however, rely completely on such rankings as a basis for allocating sales resources. Potentials do *not* reveal the competitive structure of the market and the firm's ability to exploit that market. For example, Chicago may represent a high potential to a given firm, but competition may be so strongly entrenched that the expenditures needed to gain a satisfactory brand share would be too great.

Ideally, the firm needs to augment its potential data with information about the competitive structure of the individual markets. One firm, for example, ascertains the following information about each of its markets:

1. The number of brands in the market and the brand share of each.
2. The trend of each major brand's market share over the past several years.
3. The amount of money spent by the major brands in advertising currently and over the past several years.
4. The price structure.
5. The distribution structure with particular reference to the leading retail outlets and exclusive distributor franchises.
6. The availability of evening local-station television time.

These data are then used in connection with the company's experience in the market plus the data on market potential. These three factors from the basis for this firm's allocation of its sales resources to the various markets.

Assuming that both potential and competitive structure data are available, the firm must still make some estimate of the responsiveness of each market to given inputs of advertising and sales effort. Further, the firm's position in the market must be considered. Theoretically, the firm will allocate funds to a given market up to the point where the funds can be used as profitably elsewhere. For example, funds would be allocated to market area A until the point where the next increment of funds would produce the same or greater results in, say, market B. Past performance and experiments are the two major ways of determining this effect of sales expenditures in different markets.

Actually, market responsiveness is a function of the potential, the competitive structure, and the firm's input into the market. The latter includes managerial ability as well as adequate finances. Thus, the firm must appraise realistically its own abilities—both qualitatively and quantitatively.

The ultimate objective is to make an optimum allocation of the sales resources among the alternative markets. This cannot be done precisely since it would require exact measurements, both short and long run, of the effect of a given increment of sales effort. However, a careful study of the potential and competitive structure should permit the firm to array the markets in order of their likelihood of response to sales efforts. By matching the available sales resources against the requirements of these markets, it is possible to arrive at a satisfactory distribution of funds. One firm in following this procedure found it best to spend its money in the smaller markets because the competitive structure was more con-ducive to relatively good sales results despite the lower potentials.

Setting sales quotas

Sales quotas should be set after market potentials have been derived and sales territories established. The potential for each territory is then known, but sales quotas must also consider past sales performance, changes to be made in the amount of supporting sales effort during the coming year, and anticipated activities of competitors. Quotas are usually set for each sales territory and for each salesman. They are ordinarily not the same as potentials, or even of the same relative size. One market may have twice the potential of another, but may have local competitors that take a large share, so that a given firm's quota may be smaller there than in an area with less potential.

Sales quotas set in light of sales potentials furnish a much better basis for measuring the efficiency of salesmen than do quotas set by the old rule of thumb—last year's sales plus 5 percent. If two salesmen turn in the same annual sales volume, they are usually paid about the same and are held in equal esteem by the sales manager. If market analysis shows salesman A to have a territory with far less potential than salesman B, the sales manager may wonder if salesman A may not actually be superior. A shift of the two might lead to an improvement in total sales. The following table illustrates.

	Salesman A	Salesman B
Sales last year	500,000	635,000
Territory potential	2,000,000	4,000,000
Percent of potential	25.0%	15.9%

The difference in the percentage of potential obtained may be because of different abilities, concentration on different types of customers, different use of advertising, different frequency of call, etc. Further study should result in better results in territory B. If, in fact, salesman A is superior, total firm sales may be increased by putting him in the territory with the greater potential.

Methods for developing market potential

Two major methods are available for estimating market potentials. One of these involves the use of direct data, i.e., data on the actual product for which one wishes to estimate potentials. The other method involves the use of corollary data—data related to, but different from, the product at hand. Corollary data methods can use single or multiple factors, and the latter can be combined in a variety of ways. The more important variations are discussed in the following pages.

Direct data method. Total sales of a particular commodity can be used as the basis for estimating market potentials for one brand of that product. Such data give the composite experience of the entire industry and take into account not only the characteristics of the individual markets (population, income, buying habits, etc.), but the past sales efforts of the firms comprising the industry.

The usual procedure in using such data is to break down total industry sales by the firm's sales territories, and then to express these territorial totals as percentages of the industry sales for the entire area covered by the firm. This percentage distribution is used as a measure of the relative potential existing in each market. These percentages can then be applied to the firm's estimate of total sales to arrive at a potential figure for each market.

Table 17–1 illustrates this procedure for a company which sells throughout the United States.

TABLE 17–1. Illustration of use of direct data method

Company sales territory	Total industry sales Volume* (000)	Total industry sales Percent of U.S.	Company potential*	Actual company sales*
1	$ 104	3.13%	$ 30,300	$ 24,140
2	208	6.25	60,500	56,110
3	156	4.69	45,400	47,300
4	312	9.38	90,800	71,040
5	52	1.56	15,100	19,870
	etc.	etc.	etc.	etc.
Total	$3,328	100.00%	$968,000	$1,023,660

* Volume can be expressed in either dollars or units.

Comparison of potential sales with actual sales indicates that this company is weak in sales territories 1, 2, and 4 and strong in territories 3 and 5. It might be concluded that management should exert itself in the weak areas where the firm has not been able to obtain its "proper" sales. Such a conclusion, however, does not take into account the cost of exploiting these deficit areas. Therefore, it cannot be stated categorically that it will be profitable to attempt to reach potentials in such territories. Local competition may be unusually stiff in some areas. There is disagreement as to whether a company should concentrate its sales effort in its weak or strong territories. An analysis such as the above, however, will highlight those areas which need to be investigated to determine why the company is not obtaining its share of the market. This is the first step in deciding what action, if any, should be taken.

Total industry sales data may be obtained in some cases as a result of licensing or the imposition of taxes. For example, all states impose taxes on liquor and gasoline, and these receipts can be used to estimate the total gasoline and liquor consumption by states. Many states make these available by counties. Trade associations frequently compile total industry data by having their members report shipments. Where the members of the association represent a substantial majority of the industry, these data are adequate—assuming that they are reported accurately. Only a few associations collect and distribute total sales data. An outstanding example is the National Electrical Manufacturers' Association, which reports the shipments of various appliances to retailers by trading areas. Thus, the total number of electric refrigerators shipped to retailers in a trading area during a given period of time is available to all association members.

In the absence of data on the total sales of individual commodities, these may be approximated through the use of data for somewhat broader categories. For example, *Sales Management* furnishes annual estimates of sales by classes such as food stores and drugstores. These data are available by counties and even cities of over 10,000 population.

Other sources of total sales data are the A. C. Nielsen Company and Market Research Corporation of America. As previously discussed, these companies obtain and report consumer purchases by various market divisions. They have specialized, to date, in packaged food and drug items. These companies report total sales and the sales of the major brands. Their services are available on a subscription basis.

The principal advantage of using total industry sales to measure market potential is that actual results (sales) are being used. The method is straightforward and does not require as much clerical work as do some of the other methods.

Several limitations prevent this method from being used by more firms. First, there are very few commodities on which total sales data are available. Even where data are available, they are usually available only at the state level, thereby precluding a breakdown by sales territories that do not follow state lines. Sometimes the data are ambiguous in that they cover several variations of the commodity. For example, a manufacturer selling a high-priced item would probably be in error if he used total unit sales as a guide, since the distribution of the higher-priced units may not be the same as for the other units.

The most important limitation to this method is that past sales are used to indicate market potentials, that is, no attention is given to the potentials except as they are revealed through past experience. Past sales were made with the help of certain advertising and sales methods. Changes in these activities, as well as changes in price and product, may shift demand and redistribute total sales.

The standard industrial classification system

The analyst is always concerned about the need for breaking down the total market into reasonably homogeneous parts so that each can be studied separately. Unless this is done, it is difficult to collect and analyze quantitative marketing data and to relate such work to published statistics. Because the Standard Industrial Classification system (S.I.C.) as developed by the federal government is by far the most widely used system of industrial classification, it is described here in some detail.

The S.I.C. system is intended to cover the entire field of economic activity, that is, agriculture; forestry and fisheries; mining; construction; manufacturing; transportation; communication; electricity; gas, and sanitary services; wholesale and retail trade; finance, insurance, and real estate; services; and government. Reporting units are establishments, *not* legal entities or companies. Each establishment is classified according to its major activity. The S.I.C. distinguishes two board classes of establishments—operating establishments or economic units which produce goods or services *and* central administrative offices and auxilliary units which manage or provide services for other establishments of the same company. The latter type is only partly measured by the S.I.C. system.[10]

All manufacturing industries are combined into about 20 major groups, 150 subgroups, and 450 groups. The following is an illustration:[11]

Group No. 358—Service industry machines.
Industry No. 3501—Automatic merchandising machines. Includes establishments primarily engaged in manufacturing automatic merchandise units, also referred to as vending machines (excluding music, amusement, or gaming machines) and coin operated mechanisms for such machines.

Firms which are grouped together in the S.I.C. system have a considerable amount in common. The advantage of using this system is that the government publishes a wide variety of data by such groupings (e.g., the Census of Manufactures) and the classification has been kept reasonably current to reflect changes in the American manufacturing scene. But the system is not without its drawbacks.[12]

1. When an establishment produces two or more products, the S.I.C. is based on the *principal* product which is so determined on the basis of sales. Thus, the data on the primary product are "inflated."
2. When an establishment is integrated (produces a component part), it is not shown as part of the group which produces that product.
3. When an establishment is part of a company complex which engages in centralized buying, the fact is not taken into account in the S.I.C. data.
4. When a firm makes a specialized product, it may be grouped with producers of other unrelated types of products in a miscellaneous category (for example, furniture casters are classified in S.I.C. 3429, "Hardware, not otherwise classified").

The need to relate S.I.C. groups to geographical areas can be met through the use of the federal government publication entitled *County Business Patterns*, which contains statistics based on information re-

---

[10] For a detailed presentation of the S.I.C. system, see the *Standard Industrial Classification Manual* (Washington, D.C.: Superintendent of Documents, U.S. Printing Office, 1957), and *Standard Industrial Classification Manual, 1967* (Washington, D.C.: Office of Statistical Standards).

[11] *Standard Industrial Classification Manual, 1967, op. cit.*

[12] Francis E. Hummel, *Market and Sales Potentials* (New York: The Ronald Press Co., 1961), pp. 74–76.

ported under the Federal Old Age and Survivors Insurance Program. Data are presented by S.I.C. within counties on the number of employees, payrolls, total number of establishments, and number of establishments by employment size. Only for the large counties is the information given for the 150 industry subgroups—otherwise the data are limited to the 20 major industry groups.[13]

Corollary data. The corollary data method is based on the idea that if a given series is related to another or to a group, the second series may be used as a measurement of the distribution of the first.

Single factor indexes. Single factor indexes are the most simple of the corollary data methods of market analysis. A typical example is the use of the sales of one product to indicate the market potential of another. This is most apt to be satisfactory if the two items have a closely related demand—that is, the demand for one is derived from the other or is a complementary demand. Automotive replacement parts offer a good illustration of a derived demand. The demand in any area is closely related to the number of cars of that type in the area. Therefore, the number of cars of a given make can be used as an index of the potential for spare parts for that car (see Table 17–2).

TABLE 17–2. Hypothetical illustration of use of corollary data—single factor method

Company sales territory	*Chevrolet cars registered*		*Potential for Chevrolet parts (000)*
	Number (000)	*Percent*	
1	331	2.91%	$ 58.2
2	873	7.68	153.6
3	741	6.52	130.4
4	529	4.66	93.2
5		5.17	103.4
etc.	etc.	etc.	etc.
Total U.S.	11,359	100.00%	$2,000

The reader will note that this procedure is essentially the same as for direct data. In using corollary data of this type, the researcher must be cautious to see that the two series are actually related.

Factors other than sales of related products are also used in the corollary data, single factor method. For example, population and household data are frequently used to indicate market potentials. The reasoning back of this use of population data is that where people are, sales can be made and, therefore, if one area has twice as many people as another, it has twice the sales opportunity. Total retail sales are often

---

[13] For a more detailed discussion see Richard M. Hill, "Techniques of Measuring Market Potential for Wholesalers," *University of Illinois Bulletin,* 59 (1962), pp. 15–19.

used as an index, since it is reasoned that such data indicate actual consumer purchases. Sales of specific store types, such as food stores or drugstores, may be better in many cases.

Ability to buy is an important indication of potential. *Sales Management* publishes each June its market data book which includes estimated disposable income, population, and retail sales. Disposable income is shown for four income groups for the metropolitan areas.

The availability of data by income groups is an important improvement over total income. For example, if a product is one which will be purchased by only the higher-income groups, then only these groups need be considered in preparing the index.

Many analysts in developing industrial market potentials use only the number of production workers to weight the relative value of the various S.I.C. groups and/or to determine the relative worth of individual counties. Thus, a county employing one thousand workers in a given S.I.C. group would be rated as being twice as important as one employing only five hundred.

Of course there are many series which can be used as indexes in given cases. All have one general weakness—it is hard to establish the relationship between the index series and the product at hand. To be sure the two have a relationship, it is usually necessary to compare the two series over a period of time. But, if total industry sales are available for this comparison, it would be wise to use the direct data method.

In some cases, this difficulty is overcome by comparing the particular company's sales with possible index series. The index series most closely resembling the company sales pattern is used. The obvious weakness of this approach is that the net result is to tend to establish sales potentials for various markets in the same relative amounts that company sales have existed in the past—not in proportion to actual potential. This is not entirely true, since a series that matches the sales pattern in general may still point up specific areas that do not match.

If a close relationship does not exist between the index series and the company's sales, then the index series may give a mistaken impression of the relative potentials in various markets. Population, for example, fails to account for differences in buying power and, therefore, may not be a good index for many consumer goods. Retail sales tend to be concentrated in cities and to understate the buying power in rural areas. Sales by store types do not account for sales of "nontype" products, for example, many drug products are sold in grocery stores.

Multiple factor indexes. All market potential indexes are not developed from a single series; some are combinations of several factors, occasionally as many as twenty. Many of these indexes are developed by particular companies or industries to measure market potentials for their products. Others are developed by independent organizations, frequently publishers, as indexes of market potential for consumer products in general.

Special multiple factor indexes are designed to measure the relative potentials of different markets for a particular product. Such indexes have the advantage of taking into account several factors which influence the sales of the given product. When such indexes are constructed for specific products, it seems logical that they should measure potential relatively accurately. They have some pitfalls, however, which make them much less foolproof than they appear. The individual preparing the index usually uses his judgment in selecting the factors to combine. Whether this judgment is sound or not cannot be proven. Furthermore, who is to say how many factors should be used, or, once the factors to use have been determined, how to combine them?

As indicated above, many subjective decisions tend to be made in using the multiple factor procedure. Many such judgments are based on estimates of how close the indexes obtained correspond to actual sales results. If this comparison is used to select an index, one can argue that sales themselves might as well be used as a direct index, that is, if sales data are available for purposes of comparison, they are available for use as a direct index. They would be superior to the other index if the sign of accuracy in the other index is its similarity to actual sales. A multiple factor index, however, may correspond in general with the sales pattern, but may still show specific areas that do not correspond.

Multiple regression analysis is frequently used to eliminate some of the subjective aspects of the multiple factor method such as determining the relative importance of alternative factors and the weights to be assigned each factor.[14] But since the dependent variable (the geographical sales potential) is not known, it is not possible to obtain an estimate of the regression equation. To overcome this problem analysts frequently resort to company sales as a substitute for sales potentials. Kafka and Lipstein suggest that the dilemma can be at least partially resolved through the use of principal component analysis which is similar to factor analysis. The objective of this method is to isolate those elements which measure the potential. As an illustration, they cite the problem of estimating the geographic sales potentials for pharmaceuticals using the four variables of population, per capita retail sales, number of physicians per 10,000 population, and number of pharmacists per 10,000 population. Using a sample of counties, all possible coefficients of correlation of each variable with the other three were computed and used to determine the relative importance or weight of each variable. Indexes for

---

[14] Through the use of regression equations such as $Y = a + bX_1 + cX_2$ where Y = geographical sales potential; X_1 and X_2 are the correlated variables; and a, b, c, are the partial regression coefficients which are used to weight the variables.

each county were then computed through a weighting of the relative deviation of each variable from its overall average via the coefficients (weights) derived.[15]

General multiple factor indexes have been developed by a number of organizations. They usually are constructed as indexes of consumer purchasing power and are presumed to be indexes of market potential for consumer goods in general.

The best-known general index of this type is the *Sales Management Buying Power Index*. This index is constructed from three factors— income, retail sales, and population. Income is weighted 5, sales 3, and population 2.[16] For each county in the United States income, retail sales, and population are reduced to percentages of the U.S. total. These percentages are weighted as indicated above, the products summed, and the total divided by 10 (the sum of the weights). This gives an index for each county as a percent of the U.S. total. General indexes of this type differ from special indexes only in the fact that they are designed for use with many products rather than with one specific product. Presumably, this makes these general indexes more a measure of real market potential instead of merely a measure of a particular firm's past sales distribution.

Comparisons of different general indexes, however, show many significant variations in the potentials for the same markets. How does one pick the index to use in this dilemma? One solution is to compare the indexes with actual sales and to select the one which most closely approximates sales. But in this situation, one is again partially measuring sales potential by past sales.

A major weakness of the general index is that it is general, i.e., is not designed to measure the potential for a specific product. This assumes that the relative market potential in a given area is the same for all consumer products. This, of course, is not true. Air conditioners have a larger potential in hot climates, overcoats in cold; automobiles sell best where income is high, potatoes do not. Thus, while general indexes are available for quick and easy use, they have little else to recommend them over special indexes.

Use of surveys to determine potentials. This procedure consists of projecting sample survey results to the total market through the use of published market data. With industrial products, the S.I.C. system provides a unique and effective way of projecting survey data. The problem is to obtain reasonably accurate information on purchases from firms included in the sample. Data may be gathered either by mail or personal interview.

---

[15] Kafka and Lipstein, *op. cit.*, p. 1.
[16] "Survey of Buying Power," *Sales Management* (June 10, 1968).

The following steps illustrate the use of the survey method to determine potentials for an industrial product using the S.I.C. system:

1. Determine the specific purchases of a specific product from a sample of industrial companies within each industry class. In addition to information about the product, it is imperative to obtain data on the number of employees so that the survey results can be projected.
2. From the sample data for each S.I.C. group, compute the average dollar purchases of the product in question per worker.
3. Multiply the average purchases per worker by the total U.S. number of workers for the applicable S.I.C. group. This will provide an estimate of the national market potential for the specific S.I.C. group.
4. Use the number of workers for the S.I.C. group within a county as a way of distributing the total market potential to the various geographical areas. Thus, if Los Angeles County employs 10 percent of all the workers in a given S.I.C. group, then Los Angeles will have a potential of 10 percent times the estimated national potential.
5. Where more than one S.I.C. group is involved, the individual group figures are totaled by county and a U.S. total obtained by adding the county data. The individual county's relative worth is then calculated by dividing its total by the national total.

An illustration of the above procedure is provided in Tables 17–3 and 17–4. The former table shows how a national market potential was obtained, while Table 17–4 indicates how the market potential for the Chicago trading area was determined. The market potential for Chicago of $589,000 represents 11.6 percent of the national market.

As might be expected, it is more difficult to use the survey approach to determine market potentials for consumer goods than for industrial goods. Buying intention studies are typically limited to major purchase items for obvious reasons. Even so, their reliability can be questioned because of the assumptions made regarding future conditions under which the purchase will or will not be made. These contingencies have to do with the external environment, changes involving the individual and the family unit, and the interaction of the two.

Some companies have worked out procedures for using warranty cards as a way of estimating potential despite the relatively low level of returns involved. Others use data from various studies which show ownership and use of their product by various income, age, and geographical groups.

The procedure for estimating market potentials for consumer goods using the survey method is essentially the same as for industrial goods. Purchase data for the specific item are obtained via a sample and correlated with family characteristics information; for example, it may be determined that families with incomes of less than $5,000 a year buy

TABLE 17–3. Example of market potential calculation for product "Y" using market survey approach for national area, P. A. Whitman Manufacturing Co.

S.I.C. (1)	Effective industries (2)	Market survey results			Product purchases (3)	National market number of workers (6)	Estimated national market potential (7)
		Product purchases (3)	Number of workers (4)	Average purchases per worker (5)			
3611	Electric measuring	$ 1,600	3,200	$ 0.50		34,913	$ 17,456
3612	Power transformers	50,150	4,616	10.86		42,587	462,494
3621	Motors, generators	28,400	10,896	2.61		119,330	311,451
3622	El. industrial controls	40,100	4,678	8.57		46,805	401,118
3631	Household cooking equip.	2,600	2,104	1.24		23,502	29,142
3632	Home refrigerators	149,600	5,215	28.69		47,981	1,376,574
3633	Home laundry machines	35,200	3,497	10.07		35,493	357,414
3634	Minor el. appliances	1,200	3,208	0.37		31,218	11,550
3635	Vacuum cleaners	1,875	402	4.66		4,572	21,305
3636	Sewing machines	600	912	0.66		8,182	5,400
3639	Appliances NEC	225	1,100	0.20		9,029	1,805
3661	Tel. and Tel. equipment	65,500	6,451	10.15		62,345	632,801
3662	Radio and TV equipment	132,100	6,889	19.18		67,137	1,287,687
3693	X-ray	14,000	491	28.51		5,725	163,219
	Total	$523,150					$5,079,416

Column
(1), (2) Four-digit S.I.C. industries making up the industrial market for the product.
(3) Dollar value, classified by industries, of purchases of product "Y" as reported by those plants included in the survey.
(4) Number of production workers as reported by those plants included in the survey.
(5) Average dollar value of product "Y" purchases per production worker for each effective S.I.C. industry. Computed by dividing column 3 by column 4.
(6) Number of production workers for the entire U.S. industrial market for the given S.I.C. industries. "Basic Marketing Data on Metal-working," Iron Age (1957), p. 31.
(7) The resultant estimated national market potential for the total market. Computed by multiplying column 6 by column 5.

Source: Francis E. Hummel, Market and Sales Potentials (New York: The Ronald Press Co., 1961), p. 110.

TABLE 17–4. Example of market potential calculation for product "Y" using market survey approach for Chicago, Illinois area, P. A. Whitman Manufacturing Co.

S.I.C. (1)	Effective industries (2)	Market survey national average purchases per worker (3)	Chicago market number of workers (4)	Estimated Chicago market potential (5)
3611	Electric measuring	$ 0.50	1,168	$ 584
3612	Power transformers	10.86	2,464	26,759
3621	Motors, generators	2.61	3,293	8,594
3622	El. industrial controls	8.57	6,084	52,139
3631	Household cooking equip.	1.24	2,055	2,548
3632	Home refrigerators	28.69	5,400	154,926
3633	Home laundry machines	10.07	495	4,984
3634	Minor el. appliances	0.37	8,454	3,127
3635	Vacuum cleaners	4.66	760	3,541
3636	Sewing machines	0.66	850	561
3639	Appliances, NEC	0.20	1,639	327
3661	Tel. and Tel. equipment	10.15	27,681	280,962
3662	Radio & TV equipment	19.18	1,894	36,326
3693	X-ray	28.51	466	13,285
Total	....			$588,663

Column

(1), (2) Four-digit S.I.C. industries making up the industrial market for the product.

(3)   Average dollar value of product "Y" purchases per production worker for each effective S.I.C. industry as determined from market survey.

(4)   Number of production workers for Chicago trading area for the given S.I.C. industries. "Basic Marketing Data on Metalworking," *Iron Age* (1957), pp. 58–59.

(5)   The resultant estimated Chicago area market potential. Computed by multiplying column 3 by column 4.

SOURCE: Francis E. Hummel, *Market and Sales Potentials* (New York: The Ronald Press Co., 1961), p. 112.

$112 of the product, families with incomes of between $5,000 and $7,500 buy $128, families with incomes of over $7,500 buy $142 of the product. Since family income data can be obtained at the county level, the sample results can be easily projected to a national level and, in so doing, the relative worth of each county and major city are also determined.

SALES ANALYSIS[17]

Sales analysis is a term which is used with a variety of connotations. In many instances it is used to describe the entire area discussed in this

[17] See *Sales Analysis,* Studies in Business Policy No. 113 (New York: National Industrial Conference Board, 1965).

chapter. This seems too broad a definition for precision of meaning since market potential studies often involve little in the way of sales analysis. Here the term sales analysis will be used to mean actual analysis of sales results.

Sales analyses usually are made on one or more of four bases—territory, product, customer, and order size. The objective of these analyses is to find the areas of strength and weakness, the products which are producing the greatest and the least volume, the customers who furnish the most productive sales results, and the size of order which accounts for the majority of the firm's business. Such information enables a company to concentrate its sales efforts where they will bring the greatest return.

Each of the four bases for analysis will be considered in turn. The general approach is the same in each case.

Sales analysis by territory

The invoice is usually the basic sales record. It contains the following data which are essential to sales analysis: (1) customer's name, (2) customer's location, (3) products sold, (4) quantity of each item sold, (5) price per unit, (6) total dollar sales per product, and (7) total dollar amount of order. In some cases it may be desirable to add further information about the customer such as size, type of business, user or middleman, chain or independent, etc.

A first step in analysis is to decide what geographical control unit to use. The county is the typical choice, since counties can usually be combined to form larger units such as sales territories. The county has another advantage in that market potentials are usually developed on a county basis because that is the smallest unit for which many items of data are available. Comparisons between potentials and results are simpler when both are in the same units.

Sales are then tabulated by territorial units. The results may be compared with sales potentials previously developed. Those territories in which sales fall below potential can then be given special attention. Is competition unusually strong in these areas? Has less selling effort been put there? Is the sales force weak? Studies of these points will help the company bolster its weak areas. Sales effort can be concentrated where it will do the most good.

Sales analysis by product[18]

Frequently a company's product line grows over a period of time with relatively little overall planning. The result is a line which includes some products which produce large sales and others which contribute little to

[18] For a more detailed discussion see Charles H. Sevin, *Marketing Productivity Analysis* (New York: McGraw-Hill Book Co., 1965), pp. 53–71.

total volume. If sales are analyzed by product, it is possible to identify those products that contribute the most to sales and should be exploited to the fullest extent. The limelight is also thrown on those products which are contributing little to sales and possibly should be dropped.

As in analysis of geographical areas, deciding what product units to use in product analysis is a problem. At one extreme a firm might classify products only by such general groupings as industrial and consumer. At the other extreme a firm might classify separately each product variation by color, size, etc. The general classes have the advantage of ease of handling, but by combining several items they may hide important variations. Analysis by detailed breakdowns is more expensive but is more apt to show the weak and strong spots in a way that will permit constructive action.

Product analysis may be particularly effective when combined with area analysis. Such a study may show that while area A is above quota in total sales, it is very weak in sales of product 2. Analysis of this type makes it much easier to spot the places where action should be taken.

Sales analysis by customer

Similar procedures to those described above may be used to analyze sales by customers. Such analyses typically show that a relatively small percentage of customers accounts for a large percentage of sales. Distribution cost accounting should then be applied to determine the smallest customer it is profitable to keep on the books. Those smaller than this size may be dropped with profit. In many cases, analysis of this sort combined with a study of sales calls will show that as much time is spent on the small accounts as on the large. Greater concentration of sales effort on the larger accounts may well increase sales.

Analysis by customer combined with analysis by area and product may be particularly helpful in "pin-pointing" weak spots in the sales program. Some areas may not be developing sales with a particular type of customer that has proven profitable in other areas. This may be particularly true for individual products. When this is discovered, remedial action can be taken because the precise point of weakness is known.

Sales analysis by size of order

Sales analysis by size of order may be helpful in finding points of good sales volume but low profit. Sales are classified by the size of the order on which they originated. If cost accounting data are available which will indicate the cost of securing and handling an order, it is possible to determine the sales which are being made at a loss. This analysis may be pushed to find areas, products, and customers where small orders are prevalent. This may lead to action in setting a minimum order size, to training salesmen to develop larger orders, or to dropping certain products, areas, or customers.

Distribution cost analysis

This type of analysis synthesizes the various pieces or parts of the sales analysis program as discussed above. It is ". . . a technique used by individual business concerns for the determination of the costs of performing specific marketing activities and for the determination of costs and profits for various segments of the business such as products or product groups, customer classes, or units of sale—and a study of possible alternatives."[19] The use of this technique can produce dramatic results. In one case profits were increased 300 percent, and in another marketing expenses were cut from 22.8 to 11.5 percent of sales and a net loss of 2.9 percent was turned into a profit of 15 percent. The latter was accomplished by shifting some marketing effort from the 68 percent of the company's accounts that had been unprofitable.[20]

Any distribution cost analysis should start with an attempt to prepare a detailed statement of the marketing activities carried on by the firm. Next, costs (both direct and indirect) must be itemized by the functional expense accounts. A problem arises here with joint costs and how they should be allocated. This can be done by a variety of methods, including time studies, invoice line counts, and space measurements.

Next, costs must be determined for the various business segments such as customers and sales territories. It is essential that costs by function be related to the various segments and done in such a way as to indicate the effect of scale on costs and gross margin. Once again, the problem of allocation becomes important. Many analysts argue that a cost should not be charged to any product or customer unless it can be shown to have a clear and unambiguous relationship. Rather, they hold, all questionable "noncausative" costs should be treated as overhead. While overhead must eventually be absorbed, the latter method makes more clear what will be lost or gained by dropping or adding a product or a customer.

Sales analysis and potentials

Ultimately, the objective of any distribution cost analysis and the computations of potentials is to help the marketing manager make better

---

[19] American Marketing Association Committee on Distribution Costs and Efficiency, "The Values and Uses of Distribution Cost Analysis," *Journal of Marketing* (April 1957), pp. 395–96.

[20] Charles H. Sevin, "A Rational Approach to Marketing Cost Reduction," *Indiana Business Review* (June, 1958), pp. 5–6.

decisions regarding how to allocate the firm's marketing resources. Since the potential in any area is a function of the number and worth of prospective customers, and since the cost analysis relates costs and scale of buying, the logical next step is to undertake a marginal analysis to determine which accounts within which areas represent the most likely units on which to exert additional pressure.

Since the return will vary by customer and by product, the marketing manager must decide precisely where to make his allocation. Thus, knowledge of each major account, including its potential by product, is essential, as is knowing the trend of share of account potential and the trend of expenditures to obtain this share. Through *ex post facto* types of analyses—or through experiments—it can frequently be determined what results are likely to be obtained with accounts of certain sizes (given the present "share") with additional inputs. For example, one company determined that with accounts representing $100,000 and over annual potential, it was literally impossible to obtain better than a 30 percent share regardless of the nature and magnitude of the inputs.

The decision maker should *always* be searching for causal factors. Since potentials are typically structured by geography, the variations may well be a function of different kinds of customers. This is more difficult to ascertain and cope with for consumer goods than for industrial products.

It must also be recognized that typically the firm is concerned not just with making additional inputs into certain markets. It is also concerned with "the other side of the coin," namely, reducing inputs into certain areas. The information required is the same.

SUMMARY

Quantitative sales control includes forecasting, market analysis, and sales analysis. Sales forecasting is an especially difficult and technical function. The sales forecast is the basic guide for planning within a company. The responsibility for preparing the forecasts may or may not fall to the marketing researcher. Methods of forecasting vary from estimates made by the sales force or executives to complex statistical procedures involving correlation and trend analysis.

Market analysis involves the development of sales potentials for individual geographic markets. Knowledge of potentials helps a company to allocate its selling effort most efficiently among markets. More specifically, market potentials are used in establishing sales territories, allocating the sales force and advertising expenditures, and in setting sales quotas. Potentials may be developed in two major ways: (1) through direct sales data, or (2) through corollary data surveys. The corollary data method is used to develop both specific and general market indexes. The direct data method has the advantage of being based directly on actual sales results. At the same time this is a disadvantage since it indicates potentials only in terms of what has been done before. Corollary data methods use factors related to the given product as guides to market potentials. Sometimes a number of such factors are combined. Special indexes developed in this manner may be satisfactory guides to potential sales, but they are highly subjective and, hence, open to question. The multiple correlation method eliminates some of the subjective aspects, but tends to measure potential in terms of past sales again. General indexes presumably get away from this direct relationship to past sales, but the choice of a general index is usually based on comparisons with past sales.

Surveys have the advantage of adaptability to the specific product of interest and, theoretically, should be more accurate. They are also a more expensive method.

Analyses of sales results are useful in connection with sales potential estimates and in themselves as indicators of strong and weak points in the sales program. Sales analyses on the basis of territories, products, customers, and order size are common. Analyses of sales by territory can be compared with market potential figures to indicate spots which need special attention. Analyses by product, customer, and order may suggest changes in product line, customers called on, and size of order accepted. These analyses are particularly useful when combined and when used with distribution cost analysis.

Case 17—1. TALCOTT AND COMPANY*

Talcott and Company manufactured and sold a wide variety of paper products for both industrial and household use. One of its product lines, multiwall bags, was used for packaging cement, fertilizer, chemicals, animal feeds, sugar, charcoal briquets, and other consumer and industrial products. Sales of multiwall bags were concentrated in the eastern provinces; however, company executives wished to expand into the western Canadian market. With that thought in mind a new multiwall bag factory was built in Vancouver, British Columbia. As the plant neared completion, the marketing manager began to plan how to enter this new market. One problem was to decide how many salesmen were needed, where they should be located, and what territories they should have.

Talcott and Company owned and operated timber lands, sawmills, wood pulp and paper mills, and manufacturing plants for making paper

---

* Case is a revised version of a case originally published by Graduate School of Business, Northwestern University. Revised by M. D. Beckman and R. H. Evans. Reprinted from "Cases in Marketing: A Canadian Perspective," by M. D. Beckman and R. H. Evans, Prentice-Hall of Canada Ltd. 1972, by permission of the authors and publisher.

into a variety of products. The latter included newsprint and other printing papers, wrapping and packaging paper products (such as kraft paper, multiwall paper bags, waxed papers, and flexible packaging materials), paperboard products (such as corrugated and solid fiber shipping containers), and tissue and sanitary papers (such as facial and bathroom tissue and paper towels). The "Jay" and "Silfen" brand names were used on consumer items. The company also sold part of its timber in the form of lumber, plywood, and shingles. Sales were heavily concentrated on the west coast, and totaled $461 million, more than twice the figure of ten years earlier. Multiwall bag sales accounted for less than 10 percent of the total.

Talcott and Company acquired through a merger the Northwoods Corporation. The Northwoods Corporation had, among other plants, a pulp and kraft paper mill at Vancouver, British Columbia. The acquisition of this mill gave Talcott the raw material source it needed for making multiwall bags west of the Rocky Mountains. Accordingly a bag manufacturing plant was built adjacent to the mill.

Since Talcott had no previous sales experience in the area, considerable information was needed before sales plans and sales territories could be established. Consequently, the company conducted a survey of bag users in four western provinces[1] to determine who used multiwall bags, and the users' size, location, and other characteristics. Instead of hiring a commercial research firm to make the survey, the marketing manager used four new salesmen who were to take over the four-province area when sales efforts actually began. None of these men had had any previous sales experience selling multiwall bags, but they all had attended the company's three-month sales training school. The purpose of the school was to familiarize new salesmen with the company, the paper industry in general, and specific Talcott products, such as multiwall bags. The survey cost less than $50,000, the principal part of which was salaries and expenses of the four men for the eight-month period.

The salesmen spent a month familiarizing themselves with the techniques and problems of interviewing. They "acted out" interviews among themselves, and tape recorded these practice interviews so that each man could hear himself and others, and thereby recognize the weak points of each presentation. At the end of the month, the manager assigned each salesman to a section of a state; as soon as the man completed the section, he moved on to the next area. Each salesman called on all the possible users of multiwall bags in his section, as shown on a list supplied by the company's market research department. To prepare the list, the

---

[1] The provinces were Manitoba, Saskatchewan, Alberta, and British Columbia.

market research department had assembled names and addresses of firms listed in trade magazines and trade association directories of the cement, fertilizer, and other industries making products that could be packaged in multiwall bags. However, the salesmen discovered that not all the firms listed were actual bag users. For example, a fertilizer manufacturer might make either solid or liquid fertilizer, or both, yet Talcott could consider him a potential customer only if he made solid fertilizer, and only if he sold some of his output in bags as contrasted with selling it in bulk. In addition, it was necessary to determine whether the manufacturer used paper or textile (burlap) bags. As a result, some of the survey calls were unproductive from the standpoint of reaching potential customers. It was discovered, however, that there were potential customers who had not been listed; the salesmen believed they learned about most of these firms from bag users whom they visited.

The salesman's responsibility was to meet each potential customer personally and to learn what he could about the types and approximate quantities of bags each used annually, the number and types of packaging machines used (the latter affected the types and sizes of bags needed), the number of bag suppliers from whom the customer bought, his delivery requirements (i.e., did he order frequently and in small quantities, or did he order in large lots and carry a considerable inventory), whether he received shipments by truck or rail, and the relative importance to him of price, service, and reciprocity as buying motives. The salesman also attempted to judge the customer's receptiveness to Talcott as a new supplier. Following the salesman's visit, Talcott mailed a letter to each firm on which the salesman had called, thanking the firm's officials for their cooperation.

The salesmen's estimates of bag purchases by each firm, and the resulting province-wide totals, were compared with available industry data on bag shipments to each province, and the estimates adjusted proportionately so that the total estimate for each province agreed with the industry figure. The data on shipments were tabulated by an industry trade association, the Paper Shipping Sack Manufacturers' Association, from its members' reports of monthly bag shipments. Though individual buyers or sellers were not identified in the reports, an association member could determine his own market share by comparing his shipments with the industry total. Discrepancies between the company estimates by provinces and the industry shipment figures could occur because of inaccurate estimates by the salesmen, because of inaccurate industry figures resulting from incorrect reports by member firms, or because of the purchasing policies of the bag users. For example, a manufacturing plant located in Alberta might have a headquarters office in Montreal where purchasing was done, yet shipments would be made to the Alberta plant. From the estimates of bag consumption thus obtained,[2] the marketing manager divided the four province areas among the four available salesmen as shown in Exhibit 1.

The marketing manager realized that the territories were too large for the salesmen, both in geographical size and in relation to the time the salesmen should spend with each potential customer. The latter was directly related to the volume of the firm's bag purchases, i.e., the greater the bag consumption, the more frequent should be the salesmen's calls. Talcott had found that a salesman could make an average of 4 calls a day, or 1,000 calls a year, based on a 5-day week, 50-week year. The marketing manager estimated the number of calls needed ranged from a minimum of 12 calls per year to a maximum of 52. On the average, salesmen were expected to call at least 12 times a year on firms buying between 100,000 and 1 million bags annually, 24 times a year on those buying between 1 million and 2 million bags, and 36 or more times a year on buyers using more than 2 million bags. Some of the largest bag users were manufacturers of cement, flour, chemicals, and animal feeds; the largest of these firms used as many as 25 million bags annually.

The marketing manager knew that he would need more salesmen to cover the four provinces adequately, but he could not justify to Talcott management the hiring of additional salesmen until the existing men were making enough sales to cover their cost to the company. The company had found this point was reached when a man brought in approximately $200,000 a year in sales. The marketing manager also realized that, if it later became necessary to divide the present territories, the salesmen might be upset at losing part of the territories they had worked to develop. To overcome this problem, the marketing manager planned to offer the present salesmen their choice of any new territories that might be carved from the existing areas.

The decision to locate an office in Red Deer, Alberta illustrates the factors considered by the marketing manager in establishing the territories.

The Alberta territory included all of Alberta. The marketing manager established the office in Red Deer because of its central location. He reasoned that a salesman would be more likely to call on Edmonton and Calgary bag users if he were based somewhat centrally rather than at any one of them. The salesman also would be less likely to have to be away from home on weekends, because of the shorter travel distances involved (i.e., the shorter distance from Red Deer to any of the other cities than from Calgary, for example, to Edmonton). The company believed it was important to the salesman's family life, and consequently

---

[2] Of all the information the salesmen obtained, only the bag consumption figures were used in establishing sales territories. The salesmen used the rest of the information in subsequent sales calls.

EXHIBIT 1. Sales territories for multiwall bags in four western provinces, with estimated bag consumption, number of firms buying bags, and number of sales calls needed

Office	Salesman	Territory covered	No. of firms buying bags	Estimated annual bag purchases	No. of sales calls needed per year
Vancouver, British Columbia	Howard	Southern BC	135	111,507,000	1,888
		Northern BC	32	37,818,000	502
		Total	167	149,325,000	2,390
Red Deer, Alberta	Albright	North. Alta.	93	71,675,000	1,480
		South. Alta.	45	17,886,000	488
		Total	138	89,561,000	1,968
Regina, Saskatchewan	Orland	South. Sask.	68	81,928,000	976
		North. Sask.	35	18,051,000	436
		Total	103	99,979,000	1,412
Winnipeg, Manitoba	Roberts	South. Man.	103	75,044,000	1,241
		North. Man.	31	35,904,000	541
		Total	134	110,948,000	1,782

his job satisfaction for him to be at home on weekends. The marketing manager felt, however, that the Edmonton area eventually would warrant a sales office because of the large bag consumption in Edmonton.

Company executives did not establish sales quotas from the data on estimated purchases. The executives realized that many of the firms that were buying bags probably were well satisfied with their present suppliers and would be unlikely to switch suddenly to Talcott. As a result, the estimated bag consumption data for a territory were considered only a very rough guide to the actual sales the company could expect to make. This was especially true of bag users whose purchasing offices were located in other parts of the country.

1. In determining the number of salesmen, what factors should be considered? What would be the optimum number for Talcott and Co.?

2. Appraise the research program that was undertaken by Talcott and Co.

Case 17—2.   BELONDE OFFICE MACHINE COMPANY*

In September of 1968 the market research director of the Belonde Office Machine Company was ready to issue the 1969 sales forecast of $50,000,000, as well as the separate sales quotas for each salesman and branch. The sales forecast was made each year with the assistance of a consulting economist retained by the company. It included considerations of the company's productive capacity, past experience, and economic projections. The total was then broken down by counties and assigned to salesmen and branches on this basis.

Until 1965 the sales manager had made all forecasts and had used ten-year moving sales averages for each branch and sales territory. Any changes in total anticipated sales were taken into account by applying a correction factor to the moving averages.

In the fall of 1965 the marketing vice president decided that due to the increasingly competitive nature of the market, a market research department should be established. The forecasting job was turned over to this group which, by 1966, had established a new system for determining quotas. Instead of using simple ten-year moving averages, a number of "measures of potential" were introduced initially for each of the counties in the United States. The new program involved the collection and analysis of the following data for each county:

---

* Reprinted from Stanford Business Cases 1961–2, Volume II with the permission of the publishers, Stanford University Graduate School of Business. © 1962 by the Board of Trustees of the Leland Stanford Junior University.

a. Belonde's sales for the past year expressed as a percent of total company sales.
b. Total industry sales for the past year expressed as a percent of nationwide industry sales.
c. Ten-year moving sales averages for Belonde.
d. Personal income and total population percentages.
e. The following government statistics expressed as percentages of national totals:
 1. Total employment.
 2. Taxable payroll.
 3. Number of business enterprises.

In determining the quota, these items were not weighted equally. This can best be illustrated by summarizing the procedure for estimating the 1969 figures (see Exhibits 1 and 2):

a. A weight of 15 applied to the average of the percent of industry sales in each county and the percent of Belonde's sales in each county.
b. A weight of 15 was further applied to the ten-year moving average of Belonde's sales.
c. A weight of 30 was assigned to the average population and personal income.
d. A weight of 40 was applied to the average of the three government statistics (employment, taxable payroll and number of business enterprises).[1]

Soon after receiving the new quotas, Phil Winters, the sales manager, became concerned with the heavy emphasis placed upon population, personal income, and government statistics. His group had had little or no participation during the past two years in helping to set the quotas and had become worried increasingly by the changes made in determining them. Finally, Winters arranged a meeting with Ted Sloan, director of market research. The gist of their conversation ran as follows:

SLOAN: "Good morning, Phil, what can I do for you?"

WINTERS: "Well, Ted, I've been looking over your new quotes for my branches, and I just don't understand some of the changes you've made, as the old system seemed to be working pretty well. You know, every time a change is made it makes it hard for me."

SLOAN: "I'm afraid I don't follow you. Why is that, Phil?"

WINTERS: "Well, Ted, you know my boys just get to understanding how these things are set up, then bang! they are all different. This not

[1] Experience during 1968 indicated that the government statistics had a closer correlation to actual sales than the income and population figures. So in preparing the 1969 quotas the government weights were increased from 30 to 40 while the income and population weights were reduced from 40 to 30.

EXHIBIT 1. Quota determination

Salesman: Harry Evers	ADAMS COUNTY % of U.S.	Weights	%'x Wt.	PULASKI COUNTY % of U.S.	Weights	% of Wt.	Salesman: Bill Downs
Industry Sales Last Year in County	.49	15	6.60	.51	15	8.325	
Belonde's Sales Last Year in County	.39			.60			
10 Year Average of Belonde's Sales in County	.42	15	6.3	.56	15	8.4	
Population	.50	30	16.50	.77	30	25.2	
Personal Income	.60			.91			
Employment	.04			.07			
Taxable Payroll	.20	40	9.88	.31	40	16.68	
Number of Business Enterprises	.50			.77			
Weighted Average			.3928			.5861	
Company's 1969 Sales Estimate -- $50 million							
Dollar Quota Adams County - (50 x 0.3928) = 196,400				Pulaski County = 293,050			
Percent of Quota Obtained Last Year: 73%				120%			

EXHIBIT 2. Sales performance, 1959–1967

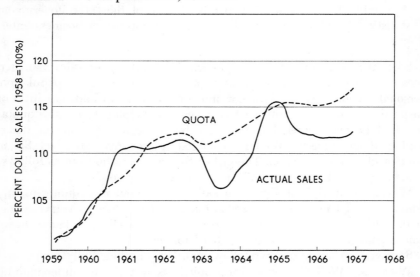

only confuses them, but sometimes they think the change is a reflection on their efforts. This affects their morale!"

SLOAN: "I'm sorry to hear that, Phil, but in order to get more accurate quotas established there must be some changes."

WINTERS: "Yes, Ted, but that's another thing. Some of the changes you made here just don't make sense to me."

SLOAN: "What are you referring to?"

WINTERS: "Well, look at the weights you apply to the percent of industry and Belonde sales in each county. Also the ten-year moving average in the 1969 quota setup. Combined, they only have a total weight of 30, and you know, Ted, those are the only things we used to use for the entire quota."

SLOAN: "Explaining that one is easy, Phil. Today you must have a more scientific approach to these things. For example, we found out in just one year that government statistics such as employment, taxable payroll, and number of business enterprises have a close correlation to office machine sales."

WINTERS: "Ted, if that's the case, then why the hell didn't our total sales figures and your quota estimates jibe better for 1967 and 1968? But there is one other way that your system falls down. For example, take Harry Evers in Adams County. There is a guy who has only been selling for two years, yet under your system he is up against guys like Bill Downs, who has been selling for fifteen years."

SLOAN: "I see what you are up against with Evers, but your idea of experience just doesn't hold water to that extent. Whether a man has been on for one year or ten years shouldn't have too great an effect on his results providing the quotas are properly set up and the right parameters are used in developing them."

WINTERS: "Ted, some of your stuff is O.K., as I said, but *you* don't work with these boys like I do, right down on the firing line, and believe me, experience *is* important in selling anything."

Upon returning to his own office, Phil Winters ran into several salesmen, one of whom was Harry Evers. Harry's opening remark to Phil was, "Gosh, Phil, I never seem to be able to catch up with my quota. I sure hope I get a better break next year. How do they put these things together, anyway?"

Should Winters continue to oppose the sales quotas established by the research department?

Case 17—3. THE IRESON CHEMICAL COMPANY

"A substantial growth in sales and a shift in market strength from the northeast to the south and southwest have knocked our sales territories completely out of line," said Bill King, sales manager of the Ireson Chemical Company. "The morale of the sales force is low," he continued, "because some of the men feel that the present territories don't afford an equal opportunity to earn commissions."

Ireson Chemical was a wholesale chemical house supplying specialized chemicals to paper processors in 24 states. The several thousand
potential users of the company's products ranged in size from small operators to giants such as International Paper and Crown Zellerbach. Competition was intense, with sales going to the firms offering the best
combination of quality, service, and price.

The company's sales increased significantly between the years 1960
and 1970. A continuation of this trend was expected. Although the company started in the east, it extended operations westward after World
War II.

The typical Ireson customer purchased $7,000 in chemicals yearly,
although the range was from $20 to over $50,000. Some sales were contracted, but most were solicited directly by the company's ten-man sales
force. About 70 percent of the Ireson line consisted of standard items
for which purchasing agents made the final buying decision. The remaining items were specialized "brand" products and required the approval of production personnel. The chemical companies faced a buyers'
market; thus the demands for service were heavy. A purchasing agent
from one of the larger paper firms said to an Ireson salesman, "We might
as well get one thing straight. You know as well as I do that your competitors can meet you in price and quality, so if you want our business
we had better see some real service."

Salesmen, during their calls, checked the performance of products
sold previously, followed up delivery promises, and sought to introduce
the customers to new uses for existing products, as well as to new products. Ireson salesmen were expected to have a chemical engineering
background because of the technical orientation of their customers.

Salesmen averaged five calls daily in metropolitan centers, and four
in nonmetropolitan areas. Typically, the men spent four days of each
week on metropolitan calls. Accounts were classified by purchases as
A, B, or C—the limits for A accounts being "over $25,000," for B ac-
counts "between $5,000 and $25,000," and for C accounts "below $5,000."
A accounts were called on weekly, B accounts monthly, and C accounts
quarterly. About 10 percent of a man's time was devoted to "service callbacks."

The Ireson Company employed ten salesmen ranging in experience
from 6 months to 25 years. Mr. King was generally satisfied with his sales
force and thought them technically qualified to sell the full line.

Each salesman had a monthly drawing account of between $400 and
$500. "This," said Mr. King, "is justification for the missionary work that
they are required to do." Above the draw, compensation was by straight
commission. Commission rates varied with the profitability of products
and, according to the sales manager, there was no apparent tendency
for salesmen to overlook the full line in favor of higher-margin items.
"The nature of our selling is such," said Mr. King, "that the salesman

first has to establish himself with the account. Once this is done, full-line selling is no problem."

Mr. King was convinced that differences in compensation (see Exhibit 1) arose from the distribution of territories rather than from differences in the individual abilities of the salesmen. He said, "I would expect some variations in commissions earned, but not to the extent we've experienced. I don't see that much difference among our salesmen."

Mr. King gave the following appraisal of his ten salesmen:

"Phil Haney is our 'old' timer," having been with us since 1935. He is one year from our mandatory retirement age of 65 and he likes to remind people of his many years of seniority. He hasn't been partiticularly easy for me to work with. Phil has strong personal ideas about selling, many of which are 'academically' outdated, but are apparently accepted by his customers. He has what you might call an old-time personality and has been tremendously successful over the years. I often wonder what kind of volume could be generated by combining Phil's personality with some of our new merchandising techniques. Phil has always worked Manhattan, although initially he also sold to all of New York City.

"Gary Whalen is in his sixth year with the company and sells to accounts in the New Jersey-Pennsylvania area. Whalen is an excellent salesman who is obviously aware of the 'smoothness' of his sales approach. He carries this self-assurance to the extent that he often becomes very indifferent whenever I offer a few suggestions for improvement in his sales techniques.

"Norman Ives is probably the most ambitious, aggressive, and argumentative salesman we have. He has been with the company since 1946, following his discharge from the Army. He reached the rank of Lt. Colonel at the age of 30, but had no interest in a military career. Norman really stormed into his present territory in 1949, and in the first year doubled its volume. He's extremely independent, but will work hard to implement any sales program that he agrees with. If he doesn't agree, though, I get absolutely no cooperation. Last year, Norman's territory began to slip, I think primarily because of a shift in market strength. His compensation fell from $13,000 to $10,500 in one year.

"Bob Ericson has been with the company three years now and I still get the feeling that he is unsure of himself. He seems somewhat confused and overworked, probably because he's trying to serve too many accounts in too large an area. Surprisingly enough, though, the general growth in the territory has given Bob a significant increase in sales this year.

"Dick Richards is the 'mystery man' of the sales force. Neither the other salesmen nor myself know very much about Dick's personal life. He's quiet and unassuming and knows our line amazingly well. I've often wondered why Dick chose sales over research work. Sales in his territory have continued to grow, which is unusual, considering an opposite trend in neighboring territories.

"Warren Sharp is the guy on the sales force who keeps the rest of us going. Warren is slightly rotund and always good-natured. His accounts seem genuinely happy to see him when he makes a call. He worked the New York state territory for his first two years, and then moved to the west coast when we took on Joe Gordon. At first, I worried about Warren's ability to get serious enough to make a sale. However, this has not proved to be a problem.

"Gus Billings joined the company in 1953 after four years with a competitor. Gus is easy-going, even-tempered, and very popular with his customers. Despite his even temperament, Gus was somewhat upset the last time I saw him. We plan to activate five more states in his territory, which would make Gus responsible for a geographical area covering roughly one fourth of the United States. He is already calling on 81 accounts in six states, and this keeps him away from home much of the time.

"Ben Owens joined us in 1954 after receiving an M.S. degree in chemistry from the University of Pennsylvania. After the normal three-month training program, during which time Ben travelled with Gary Whalen, he stepped into his territory and was immediately successful. Ben is earnest and conscientious and has increased his sales volume each year. He's not what you would call the 'salesman type,' but he is always exceedingly successful in using the merchandising techniques that I try to implement.

"Joe Gordon is the youngster of our sales force at 27. He has New York state. The territory is relatively inactive, and we usually try to assign it to new salesmen. Sales have dropped from the time that Joe took over, and he is very apologetic about the situation. I've told him that he would have to expect some tough moments, and I think his determination 'to make a go of it' will be realized because of his conscientiousness. He's always receptive to any help that is offered and tries hard to put suggestions to use. That territory has always been a 'dog.'

"Jim Davey is in his third year and I'd say he's a good salesman. Jim always dresses impeccably in Ivy League fashion and he has good bearing. He responds well to any suggestion that I make to him. It's a funny thing, but whenever I travel with Jim the sales in the territory increase for the next several months. After that, right back to the previous level. Accounts within the territory are scattered, which keeps Jim on the road most of the time."

Aside from the morale problem, Bill King had other reasons for wanting to change the territories. "We expect continued growth," he said, "and at least for the time being I plan to add no new people. I'm positive that by redistributing the sales territories we can get more sales effort from the sales force as a group and thus handle our growth."

Exhibit 1 presents a detailed breakdown of performance by salesmen

EXHIBIT 1. Performance by salesmen, 1970–1971*

Salesman	Territory	Terr. #	Sales Record 1970	Sales Record 1971*	Accounts Metro	Accounts Non-Metro	Accounts Total	1971* Compensation	Selling cost % to Sales 1971*	Planned Sales* 1972	Planned Accounts 1972	Est. Share 1971	Est. Share 1972	Selling Cost % to Planned Sales
IVES	Maine, N. Hamp., Vert.	1	NOT COVERED UNDER PRESENT TERRITORIAL ARRANGEMENT							$37	7	—	26.0	
	Mass.		$405	$340	54	13	67			270	54	24.0	18.6	
	R.I.		100	67	13	–	13			34	7	39.7	49.6	
	Conn.		100	100	13	7	20			67	13	21.2	19.9	
	Total Territory		405	507	90	20	100	10,500	2.1	405	81	23.2	19.9	2.6
GORDON	New York State	2	203	170	27	7	34	5,500	3.2	135	27	50.3	50.3	4.1
HANEY	New York City (Manhattan)	3	1490	1620	162	–	162	15,500	.96	1420	142	18.7	18.6	.3
RICHARDS	New York City (other Boroughs and Long Island)	4	605	670	61	7	67	12,000	1.8	743	74	25.3	25.2	1.6
WHALEN	New Jersey	5	135	169	27	7	34			203	40	10.6	16.5	
	Pennsylvania		1080	1010	88	13	101			880	88	18.2	17.0	
	Total Territory		1215	1179	115	20	135	12,500	1.1	1083	128	14.9	17.0	1.2
ERICSON	Del., Md., Wash. D.C.	6	NOT COVERED UNDER PRESENT TERRITORIAL ARRANGEMENT							67	13		20.0	
	Virginia, W. Virginia		100	135	13	13	26			135	27	19.9	16.2	
	North Carolina		100	135	20	7	27			170	34	16.5	16.3	
	South Carolina		34	67	7	7	14			135	27	11.0	16.5	
	Georgia		100	100	7	13	20			100	20	16.5	14.9	
	Florida		67	135	27	0	27			170	34	20.2	16.1	
	Total Territory		401	572	74	40	114	8,500	1.5	777	155	16.3	16.4	1.1
DAVEY	Mississippi	7	34	67	7	7	14			67	13	16.7	16.6	
	Alabama		100	135	13	13	26			135	27	16.3	16.3	
	Kentucky & Tenn.		–	34	7	–	7			34	7	16.5	16.5	
	Total Territory		134	236	27	20	47	7,000	3.0	236	47	17.4	17.4	3.0
OWENS	Ohio & Indiana	8	NOT COVERED UNDER PRESENT TERRITORIAL ARRANGEMENT							67	13		17.1	
	Illinois		639	511	51	7	58			506	57	16.2	16.2	
	Michigan		235	235	40	7	47			200	40	15.1	15.1	
	Wisconsin		NOT COVERED UNDER PRESENT TERRITORIAL ARRANGEMENT							34	7		16.6	
	Total Territory		874	906	91	14	105	11,500	1.4	807	111	15.1	15.7	1.4
BILLINGS	Minn., Iowa, N. Dak., S. Dak., Nebraska	9	NOT COVERED UNDER PRESENT TERRITORIAL ARRANGEMENT							100	20	—	19.6	
	Missouri		67	235	40	7	47			304	61	11.4	15.1	
	Kansas		–	34	7	–	7			67	13	8.3	16.6	
	Ark., La., Okla.		NOT COVERED UNDER PRESENT TERRITORIAL ARRANGEMENT							67	13	—	14.7	
	Texas		67	135	20	7	27			340	67	6.6	14.6	
	Total Territory		134	404	67	14	81	7,500	1.9	878	174	7.9	15.5	1.4
SHARP	Mont., Wyo., Idaho	10	NOT COVERED UNDER PRESENT TERRITORIAL ARRANGEMENT							100	20	—	18.7	
	Utah, Colo., Ariz., N.M.		"	"						135	27	18.9	16.6	
	Wash., Oregon		67	100	7	13	20						16.7	
	Calif.		235	270	39	7	45			340	67	11.3	14.3	
	Nevada		NOT COVERED UNDER PRESENT TERRITORIAL ARRANGEMENT											
	Total Territory		302	370	45	20	65	7,500	2.0	575	114	15.2	15.4	1.3
	GRAND TOTAL, UNITED STATES		$4,103	$6,534	749	162	910	$98,000	1.5	$7,059	$1,053	14.6	17.8	1.4

* Projected.
† 000's omitted.

EXHIBIT 2. Number of customers by dollar volume by salesman, 1971

Salesman	0/$999	$1,000 /$2,499	$2,500 /$4,999	$5,000 /$9,999	$10,000 /$14,999	$15,000 /$24,999	$25,000 /$49,999	$50,000 /$99,999	Total
Ives	32	30	15	10	5	5	2	1	100
Gordon	10	5	4	12	1	2	—	—	134
Haney	26	30	20	34	22	20	10	3	162
Richards	9	3	13	15	15	8	4	—	67
Whalen	16	40	30	10	10	21	6	2	135
Ericson	34	32	21	8	8	7	4	—	114
Davey	14	10	6	7	9	—	2	—	47
Owens	33	11	19	13	15	9	3	2	105
Billings	30	6	13	14	16	2	—	—	81
Sharp	10	12	24	8	10	—	—	1	65
Total	214	179	165	128	111	74	30	9	910
$ Volume totals (000)	107	304	619	960	1,387	1,480	1,125	675	6,657
Cumulative $ total (000)		411	1,030	1,990	3,377	4,857	5,982	6,657	
Cumulative % volume	1.6	6.2	15.5	29.9	50.7	73.0	89.8	100	
Cumulative % accounts	23.5	43.2	61.3	75.4	87.6	95.7	99.0	100	

for the years 1970 and 1971. Exhibit 2 lists the number of customers for each salesman by dollar volume.

1. What research, if any, should Ireson do to improve its design of sales territories?

2. What conclusions can be drawn from the data at hand relative to Ireson's sales territories?

Case 17—4. FARGO INSTRUMENT COMPANY

In January, 1970, the Fargo Instrument Company was created as a wholly owned subsidiary of the Burbank Corporation, a large west coast electronics company. At the time of its inception, the Fargo Company had the worldwide marketing rights to a specialized line of sophisticated scientific instruments which ranged in price from $5,000 to $75,000. Three markets were believed to hold most of the potential for these products, as follows: (1) governmental agencies; (2) universities; and (3) industrial research laboratories.

Fargo would compete with some six other U.S. companies for these markets. Although Fargo's product line was considered to be high in quality, its products displayed little uniqueness, so that Fargo competed primarily on the basis of price, delivery, and service. The typical buying process for such instruments was a lengthy affair (6 months or longer) and involved several buying influentials. Fargo planned to use a domestic sales force of 18 men, of whom 8 were already operational. Most of these men had engineering or scientific backgrounds. They were paid a salary plus a commission. The sales organization had a backup technical staff to provide a fast and efficient warranty service.

In January, 1970, the marketing director and the sales manager met to discuss ways in which they could prepare a reliable forecast of their first year's sales. Inventory costs and intense competition made the reliability of this forecast extremely important. The sales manager felt strongly that any initial forecast would need to be updated at regular intervals, and proposed that his salesmen be utilized to effect this updating. He argued that the sales force would eventually know more about what was going on in the marketplace than any one else and that such data, if properly codified, could serve as the basis for monthly revisions in the forecast. He believed that this should be done by salesman for each product and then aggregated to generate the new or revised forecast.

After considerable discussion with the marketing manager, the sales manager proposed the following system for linking the individual salesman with the monthly forecast.

1. For each prospect contacted, each salesman would fill out a call report which would indicate: the particular product (model) of interest;

the probability that the prospect would buy any brand of such a model during the remainder of the calendar year and another probability that such a purchase would be made within the next 90 days; if a probability of purchase was indicated, then the probability of the prospect's buying the Fargo product would be indicated.

2. Upon receipt of the call report in the office, the sales manager would correct each of the probability estimates, since he expected salesmen to be consistently optimistic about their ability to make a sale. Initially, he would use a correction factor of one, but as he accumulated data on actual and expected sales by each salesman, he would compute new probability estimates based on exponential smoothing.

3. He further would estimate the expected value for the calendar year and for the next 90 days by multiplying the probabilities against the value (list price) of the product(s) in which he was interested. Thus, for example, if the probability of purchasing in the next 90 days was 0.50 and the probability of buying Fargo was 0.50, then the conditional probability was 0.25. If the purchase value was listed at $50,000, then the expected value for this prospect was $12,500.

4. By aggregating the expected values of all accounts at any point in time, a 90-day as well as a remainder of the calendar year sales forecast could be generated. In addition, the probabilities for each product could be graphed to determine the variance around the mean expected value.

The marketing manager was impressed by the proposed system, but felt that in addition to helping provide better forecasting data it could be useful as a way of directing the activities of the entire marketing group, including, of course, the sales force. In particular, he raised the question of what action could be taken to improve the probability that a given prospect with a high probability of buying an analytical instrument would select the Fargo brand. He further wanted to know how information pertaining to such activities could be built into the system so that his group could make better marketing decisions in the future. He turned this problem over to his assistant with instructions to develop both the conceptual and operational framework for determining what marketing inputs should be made (and when), with respect to individual prospects and how such inputs affected the conditional probabilities assigned to the prospect.

What framework should be developed? How should it be validated? What effect will the codification of inputs have on the reporting system and the forecasting system already proposed?

Indexes

Index of Cases

Index

This book has been set in 9 and 10 point Caledonia, leaded 2 points. Part numbers are in 12 and 30 point Craw Clarendon Book; chapter numbers are in 30 point Craw Clarendon Book. Part titles and chapter titles are in 18 point Craw Clarendon Book. The size of the type page is 27 × 45½ picas.